Like many others I have eagerly anticipated this f Henebury's, *The Words of the Covenant.* And the wait for Volume 2, which we now have before us, has been worth it. Henebury applies his keen and thorough analytical skills to the New Testament. The result is another outstanding work of biblical theology. This book not only explains the story of the New Testament, it shows how the latter Testament is in accord with the intended meaning of the Old Testament prophets. In doing so he demonstrates great continuity between Old Testament expectations and New Testament fulfillments in Jesus. Henebury's discussion of the biblical covenants and how these relate to God's kingdom program is magnificent.

This book (along with Volume 1) would be helpful no matter what era in which it was written. But because of current theological trends it is even more needed today. We have entered an era in which reliance upon the assumptions of theological systems, with little scriptural support, is winning out over inductive study of Scripture based on sound hermeneutics. This makes Henebury's contributions even more helpful for the student who wants to know what "the Bible says." And while Henebury's findings are often contrary to the current supersessionist and over-spiritualized findings that are rampant today, his conclusions are thoroughly orthodox and consistent with what many fine scholars in church history have also stated. As with Volume 1, I highly recommend this book.

Michael J. Vlach, PhD, Professor of Theology,
Shepherds Theological Seminary.

With this volume, Dr. Henebury has completed the important work he began in *The Words of the Covenant: OT Expectation*, demonstrating that God means what He says and that those who would seek to please Him are not at liberty to reinterpret or morph the plain meaning of what God has said. In that work, he established the importance of the biblical covenants as the only sound framework within which the big picture of the Bible must anchor its interpretation. He also brought an understanding of the natural expectations readers of the Old Testament would have had when Jesus arrived on the scene—an understanding that Jesus did not overthrow, contrary to much teaching today. In this second volume, the work is extended to show that New Testament revelation is consistent with a natural reading of the covenants. It serves as a powerful corrective to the notion that the New Testament is required in order to make sense of the Old. Together, the two volumes ground our reading of the Bible as a unit and establish boundaries beyond which the meaning of the text may not be coaxed. As with everything Dr. Henebury writes, there are important ideas and thought-provoking discussions enriching the journey along the way—even if the reader may not always agree. Highly recommended.

Tony Garland, ThD, Author, *A Testimony of Jesus Christ: A Commentary on the Book of Revelation*, Founder, SpiritandTruth.org.

It has been said that Dispensationalism is more driven by a proper understanding of God's covenants than any other biblical truth. Thus, new generations of Bible readers are always in need of a fresh exposition of God's covenant structure. This reality is particularly true concerning the controversies surrounding a proper interpretation of the New Covenant. Here, Dr. Paul Henebury has provided a helpful exegetical and philosophical explanation and apologetic for the outworking of the New Covenant in biblical history. Dr. Henebury's readers will certainly benefit from his labors as expressed in the present volume.

Andy Woods, PhD, President, Chafer Theological Seminary,
Author, *The Coming Kingdom.*

Having established in Volume 1 the significance of the much-neglected biblical covenants, Henebury's second offering convincingly demonstrates covenantal continuity in the New Testament. What the covenants set out in plain terms in the Hebrew Scriptures can be seen to form a major presupposition for the apostolic writers. Along the way, the author gently places a knife to the throat of one or two sacred theological cows.

Unsurprisingly, most of the theological heat that Henebury's work may generate comes down to the issue of Israel and her promised restoration. Henebury believes words mean things, and when those words are God's, and are formalized in covenants that are "gracious amplifications of plain speech about matters of great importance," theologian and Bible reader alike should take note. Henebury's work is important, and I am very grateful that he has committed his insights to two substantial volumes.

Perry Trotter, Author, *Israel in the Biblical Worldview.*

Paul Henebury is doing something so obvious that you have to marvel that no one has done it before, let alone done it so well. He is avoiding the Scylla of creating extra-textual theological covenants and imposing them on Scripture; and he is avoiding the Charybdis of creating textually-inferred dispensations and imposing them on Scripture. Instead, Paul starts with the directly-textually-identified Biblical covenants, and lets Scripture structure itself accordingly. This is likely the best and most productive path forward, because it relies most directly on the explicit statements of Scripture.

Daniel J. Phillips, Author, *God's Wisdom in Proverbs.*

This is the anticipated second volume to Paul Henebury's magisterial study in the biblical covenants. He continues with the New Testament, introducing us to our covenant Messiah, Jesus Christ, and the ministry He completed in the Four Gospels. He then explores the unfolding of Christ's covenant ministry in the theology of Paul, the general epistles, and the capstone of the Apocalypse. Dr. Henebury's work covers the important passages and themes relating to God's covenant purposes with humanity and specifically His chosen people. I believe the reader will be truly enriched as I was as his book steers our hearts and minds through the New Covenant that our majestic Savior fulfilled bringing mankind eternal salvation.

Fred Butler, Volunteer Coordinator,
Grace To You Radio Ministries.

Paul Henebury's *The Words of the Covenant, Volume 2* is a thought-provoking and rigorous work that will challenge readers to reconsider how the biblical covenants are essential to understanding the entire biblical narrative. Henebury masterfully uncovers the profound continuity between Old and New Testament revelations, demonstrating that God's promises are steadfast and foundational to His redemptive plan. His deep engagement with Scripture and incisive analysis push beyond surface-level interpretations, offering fresh insights into God's covenantal framework. I have thoroughly enjoyed this book, and highly recommend it to anyone seeking a clearer understanding of the Bible's overarching storyline and the covenants that shape it.

Peter Goeman, PhD, Associate Professor of Old Testament,
Shepherds Theological Seminary.

THE WORDS OF THE COVENANT
A BIBLICAL THEOLOGY

Volume Two, New Testament Continuation

Paul Martin Henebury

THE WORDS OF THE COVENANT: A BIBLICAL THEOLOGY

Volume Two, New Testament Continuation

Paul Martin Henebury

And I will give the men who have transgressed My covenant, who have not performed the words of the covenant which they made before Me, when they cut the calf in two and passed between the parts of it… I will give them into the hand of their enemies and into the hand of those who seek their life.
– Jeremiah 34:18, 20.

Likewise He also took the cup after supper, saying, "This cup is the new covenant in My blood, which is shed for you."
– Luke 22:20.

SOJOURNER
PRESS

Cover design by Michael Miller and Hunter Hays

Editing by Peter Goeman

For bulk, special sales, or ministry purchases, please contact us at sales@sojournerpress.org

The Words of the Covenant: A Biblical Theology
Volume 2: New Testament Continuation

Published by Sojourner Press
Raleigh, NC, 27603
sojournerpress.org

ISBN 978-1-960255-16-7 (Paperback)

ISBN 978-1-960255-18-1 (Hardback)

ISBN 978-1-960255-17-4 (Epub)

Dedicated to Dr Karl Scheffrahn, DDS.

Whose support during hard times will never be forgotten, and in whose Bible Studies the first form of my Biblical Covenantalism was presented.

Acknowledgments

I will keep my thanks brief. I have greatly benefitted from the works of many scholars, both those who would affirm many of my observations and those who would think that my "literal" approach to God's covenants is overly simplistic and unacademic. One does not have to agree with an author in order to gain insight from them. Iron sharpens iron.

I want to thank all those readers of Volume One who have asked and kept asking me, "When will volume two be published?" Your kind proddings kept me going. I truly appreciate your enthusiasm, which lifted me when life took a difficult turn.

Ian Alexander Hicks, Tony Garland, and Perry Trotter read various drafts of the work as it was in production and offered valuable feedback. Peter Goeman has been a joy to work with as my editor. His encouragement joined with his professional eye was just what this project needed.

Many thanks to Tony Garland, Andy Woods, Perry Trotter, Michael Vlach, Peter Goeman, Dan Phillips, and Fred Butler for your "blurbs." It is easy to fool oneself about the merit of one's work, but you all surprised me with the generosity of your words. Speaking of generosity, I owe a debt of gratitude to Shawn and Cindy Sauers for helping to get this project over the line.

Finally, a little story. This book is dedicated to my friend Dr. Karl Scheffrahn ThM, DDS. I first encountered Karl when he attended a weekend seminar held at Tyndale Seminary in 2006. After I finished my lecture, Karl asked me if I would be willing to speak at the forthcoming opening of his dental clinic in East Texas. I agreed, we parted, and I forgot about it. Things became "complicated" at the seminary, and I left to do a bit of wilderness wandering—a circumstance that saw almost miraculous provision from former students and freedom for me to explore God's covenants and to ask new questions about their purpose. It was then that, out of the blue, Karl called me and reminded me of my promise. I drove out to Minneola from Granbury and spoke at the opening as arranged. Karl then invited me to teach a Bible Study every month in Minneola. It was there that I began presenting the first fruits of my studies in "Biblical Covenantalism." Karl's kindness, not only in the warmth of his friendship, but in his gifts to cover expenses, and him even providing free dental care for my family, can scarcely be sufficiently acknowledged. God used Karl to bless my family and to greatly encourage me when my world was imploding. It is only right that this work be dedicated to him. Thank you, Karl!

Acknowledgments

Contents

Preface

It has been three years since the appearance of the first volume of this biblical theology was published. *The Words of the Covenant: A Biblical Theology, Volume One, Old Testament Expectation* made a case for paying closer attention to the covenants Yahweh has made, tracking them through OT history from Genesis to Malachi, concluding that our Creator made those covenants as a gracious way of telling us what He intends to do with this world. The covenants are never morphed, reconfigured, or expanded, and they never undergo typological reconstruction. God means what He says, especially when He takes a solemn oath to do it!

During the intervening time, I have continued to grow in my understanding of the subject, and that is in no small way due to my interaction with a host of scholars with whom I disagree quite a lot of the time. But I am a great believer in the dictum that you often learn more from those with whom you disagree than those with whom you agree. I am grateful to these interlocutors.

One thing is for sure. Satan has certainly upped the ante while I have been writing volume two! There has been a significant uptick in spiritual warfare while writing this book, more particularly in the year before it was completed.[1] These attacks have been painful and have left their scars, but the Lord is faithful. This is not to say that this is a book that had to be written or anything like that. Just that there has been a strong sense of being in the battle during its production. I trust that in producing this work, I am obeying the Spirit's prompting and not my own vanity!

I now offer this second volume and truly hope it will bless you, the reader, and stimulate you to study the limitless wonder that is the Bible. I expect disagreement, but hope to foster exploration. Only the Word of God is infallible. This book is far from that, though it is my humble attempt to understand God's book in light of the oaths God Himself took. Trust in the Lord (Prov. 3:5-6) and believe passionately that God means what He says!

Paul Martin Henebury, September 2024.

---

1 One small example is that three separate individuals had to decline to assess my work for health reasons.

INTRODUCTION

Sovereign LORD, you are God! Your covenant is trustworthy... - 2 Samuel 7:28

Why I Call Myself a Biblical Covenantalist

If you are anything like me, you may be tempted to skip this part of the book and go to the first main chapter. But let me try to persuade you to stay with me. This introduction ought to be given at least a quick read, if for no other reason than it gives you, the reader, an opportunity to discover what I, the author, want to communicate in the rest of this big book.

The Words of the Covenant: A Biblical Theology, Volume Two, New Testament Continuation picks up where the first volume left off—on the note of expectation left by Yahweh when He gave the covenants and repeated them over many centuries during the OT era. The expectation derives from the multiplied promises of restitution for the people of Israel in their own covenanted land in a Kingdom of peace and safety ruled over by Messiah.

"Biblical Covenantalism" is my name for a biblical theology of the divine covenants. It results from when the central oaths of God's covenants are tracked throughout the Bible. It might be understood as a derivation of what is usually called Dispensationalism. Although having said that, it is important to acknowledge how focusing on the covenants of God causes the emphasis to shift onto what I believe is sturdier ground methodologically. This change in emphasis can be seen in several ways:

1. Because the covenants are hermeneutical, the hermeneutics of Biblical Covenantalism are more biblically established.

2. Because the covenants of Scripture are teleological and eschatological, more stress is placed upon history as a continuing project of which we are a part.

3. Because of the strong Christological implications of several Davidic and New covenant texts, the system itself is more Christocentric.

In my opinion, these elements of Biblical Covenantalism make it more robust and more prescriptive than the standard dispensational models.

Emphasizing God's covenants with man does entail a reconsideration of parts of the dispensational model. Two examples spring to mind: (1) the central place for Christ in this approach, and (2) the emphasis on the New covenant and its relevance to the Church and its intimate connection to Christ Himself.

Years ago, I wrote a dissertation on the dispensational theological method. At first, I thought that I could help provide this approach with a sturdier platform. But I gradually saw that Dispensationalism has been built upon the wrong foundation. "Dispensations" or "administrations" do not feature prominently in the writings of the inspired authors. They are barely mentioned. It is hard to pin them down and define them well, and what often ends up being asserted is not all that convincing. One example of this would be the oft-repeated dictum that every dispensation ends in failure. The problem with this is that the Tribulation does not end in failure, either for the saints (Rev. 14:13) or for Christ. But of course, the Tribulation is usually not included as a dispensation, not even by pretribulationists (for some reason that escapes me). And why is the Millennial Kingdom sometimes not considered a dispensation? Isn't it a stewardship given to a Man (Isa. 11:1-5; 42:1-4)? It does not end in failure either.

The covenants God made with Noah, Abraham, Moses, and David, however, are hugely important. And they are programmatic. Then the forgotten covenant Yahweh made with Phinehas is also more influential than is often stated. And then there is the New covenant in Christ's blood, which tops them all because it is through it (through Him) that those other covenants are eventually fulfilled. They are fulfilled not via typology or spiritualization, but literally. Because the change in method involved a de-emphasis on dispensations and a stronger emphasis on God's covenants, I decided to call the approach what it is instead of what it isn't.

In short, the divine covenants, I believe, are the foundation upon which "Dispensationalism" ought to be built. It is no great sacrifice to relegate dispensations and promote God's covenants. We must then listen carefully to the covenants, and we must permit them full authority to shape our biblical theology. That is, we should be Biblical Covenantalists.

Finally, in the intramural conversations with our brothers who are covenant theologians or progressive covenantalists, we will not be talking about dispensations while they are talking about covenants. We will not be comparing apples and oranges. Instead, we too will be joining the discussion about covenants, but in our case, I believe we will have the upper hand in that our covenants will be those of the Bible itself.

Definition of a Divine Covenant

As this is a book concerning itself with God's covenants with man, we'll start with reminding ourselves of what a covenant is and why it is such a vital biblical theme. Here is my definition:

> A biblical covenant between God and man is a solemnly sealed and explicit declaration of intent and obligation, about a matter of great importance. It binds one or both parties to fulfill the words of the covenant oath. The parties to the covenant cannot be changed out.

I appended to this definition a note about the function of a biblical covenant: "The function of a covenant is to amplify or reinforce the plain terms of the oath between the parties in order to clarify their relationship and clear away ambiguity or misinterpretation, thereby ensuring a unified understanding of the terms." I have also referred to a divine covenant as "an amplification of plain speech." It is God getting on the megaphone to try to call our attention to something of great importance.

In the first volume, I attempted to demonstrate how the covenants repeat over the centuries without significant alteration. I also showed how they mix with one another in the prophetic writings and how they become associated with the figure of the coming Ruler. Hence, by the time the OT is over, a considerable amount of information has been gathered, which in turn produces a large body of expectations among the faithful. These expectations, as we shall see, are not rerouted in the NT.

This brings us to the present volume. As the subtitle suggests, the continuation of the covenant program begun in the OT is the hallmark of the NT, but with the inclusion now of the Church, the Body of Christ, wherein there is neither Jew nor Gentile (Eph. 3:4-6). The pressing concern for the interpreter of the NT is whether the Church is now the center of the whole redemptive program of God or a stage in its development. Supersessionism, in its various forms, believes that the Church fulfills the promises to Israel (and the nations) that are found in the OT. I, along with many others, do not. The covenants forbid such a conclusion. I refer to NT "Continuation" and not NT "Continuity," because while the evident "discontinuity" of the "new man" (Eph. 2:15), the Jew-Gentile Church must be investigated, the covenant oaths of the OT remain prophetically and hermeneutically intact. The Church fits within that larger covenant program.

The Plan of the Book

As you can see from the table of contents, this book is divided into eight parts, with several appendices bringing up the rear. The first chapter, with the rather boring title, "Covenants First: Some Methodological Issues," addresses many issues that the crossover from the OT to the NT raises. This includes matters such as the use of the OT in the NT, the close proximity of the dates for the NT books as compared to the OT, and so on. Chapter 2, "God's Covenants in the Old Testament," goes over the main theses of the first volume to orient the reader to where I'm coming from. Then

I turn in Chapter 3 to what might be called the elephant in the room of NT studies, the New covenant in Christ. At first, this was going to be an appendix at the end of the book, but it seemed more honest to place it up front where readers could chew on the subject before being immersed in it when we get to the epistles of Paul. Hence, "The Terms of the New Covenant and Its Parties" sets out the stall, as it were, and provides a description of my thinking on the New covenant. I urge readers not to be put off by the relatively few express mentions of the New covenant. What one needs to be on the lookout for are assertions and contrasts that fit the New covenant as it is expounded in Luke 22, 1 Corinthians 11, 2 Corinthians 3, and Hebrews 7–12. You are going to see many references to 2 Corinthians 3:6 because the apostle Paul nonchalantly calls himself and his co-workers "ministers of the new covenant," thereby indicating, among other things, that the "new covenant" stands for the good news of Jesus Christ. This New covenant message is a recurring theme in the book.

Chapter 4 is devoted to the Person of Jesus Christ and His immense importance to the theology and worldview of the Bible. Many themes found throughout the book are covered in "The Unparalleled Significance of the Son of God." But since Jesus is so crucial to Biblical Covenantalism, I wanted a place where He was given the spotlight. The Messiah has come—Jesus, the Son of God. The reality of Jesus and His words and works nearly two millennia ago must be appreciated if we're to grasp adequately the prophetic teaching of both Testaments. It is true that Jesus changes everything, but it is just as true that He has not changed everything yet. How He will change things in the future depends upon the covenants of God. They must be heard, or we will get the Bible's eschatology and teleology wrong.

Part Three has chapters that concern "The Annunciation Passages in Matthew and Luke" (Chapter 5), "Covenant and Kingdom in John the Baptist" Chapter 6), and "The Beginning of the Ministry of Jesus the Christ" (Chapter 7). In these chapters, it is very clear that no redirecting of the OT expectation is forthcoming. Not even the notes on the inclusion of the Gentiles are foreign to OT teaching.

After all of this, we come to the meat of the Gospels in chapters 8 through 12. Part Four comprises two long chapters on Luke and Matthew. I chose to place Luke before Matthew not because I was being ornery, but because I wanted to disorient the reader slightly so as to gain more attention to what these Gospels are saying with regard to God's covenants. In these chapters, I recognize that we must, for instance, walk carefully through Jesus' Kingdom teaching in Luke, and likewise, we must recognize Matthew's two main uses of the word "Kingdom," especially in the Parables.

In chapter 10, we examine Mark, followed by John in chapter 11. Most people would not think of covenant in connection to John's Gospel, but as a matter of fact, it is implicit in John's thinking. Here I also survey John's Epistles. I follow this up with a review of "The Covenantal Backdrop of the Gospels" in chapter 12 to underline the fact that covernance permeates these books.

Part Six kicks off with chapter 13, "Covenant and Kingdom in Acts." I wondered where I should put this chapter, but since half of Acts concerns the apostle Paul, I grouped it in with his writings. Then comes three chapters on Paul, bearing the unimaginative title, "Paul: Apostle of the New Covenant" (Parts 1–3). Having such a title might be looked upon by some dispensationalists as going too far. Some dispensationalists do not believe that Gentiles in the Church have any connection to the New covenant, while many others believe the Church bears a strange sort of hybrid relation to it because of its connection with Jesus. I investigate these positions both in chapter 3 and again in chapter 14. However, I find both basic positions to be kicking "against the goads" (Acts 9:3). The grammatical-historical hermeneutic is not driving these interpretations. Not only do 1 Corinthians 11:25 and 2 Corinthians 3:6 explicitly state that Christians are in the New covenant, but the whole theological trajectory initiated in Jesus Christ makes it essential. Whatever hangups some dispensationalists have with the New covenant and the Church are, in my humble opinion, methodological and theological in origin, not exegetical. You cannot appeal to Jeremiah 31:31-34 to prove that the New covenant is only made with Israel and ignore 2 Corinthians 3, where nearly every NT scholar you pick up says that Paul is alluding to the Jeremiah passage when addressing Christians. As the colorful saying goes, "That dog won't hunt."

The three chapters on the epistles of Paul address many issues relating to the covenants, especially the Abrahamic, Davidic, and the New. In these chapters, I explore the vital connection between the Church and Christ's resurrection, teleology and eschatology in Paul's writings, the return of Christ, Israel, the Church, and more.

The book of Hebrews receives a thorough treatment in this work. Chapter 17 is an exposition of its teaching from a deliberately premillennial perspective. For many years I have thought that Hebrews reads more like an OT prophetic book than anything else in the NT. As far as context is concerned, it would not be out of place nestled in the Olivet Discourse (Matt. 24/Mk. 13). In terms of the New covenant, which is a major theme in the book, there is an air of expectation created by the author; an expectation of the coming Kingdom of Messiah. I try to analyze this in chapter 17.

After Hebrews I delve into the epistles of James, Peter, and Jude, where covenant strands can be found, and certain questions arise. Then in Part Eight, I give my understanding of the book of Revelation in chapter 19 ("Converging Themes in the Apocalypse"). I indulge in a little polemical writing in this chapter, as it is important that the plain-sense approach adopted here be distinguished from the non-literal approach prevalent in so many commentaries and taught in the majority of seminaries.

The chapter which follows the study of Revelation concentrates on the question raised by John's vision of the New Jerusalem with its inhabitants in and around it ("The People(s) of God"). The book proper is closed with chapter 21, "The Christocentrism of the Bible," which tries to pull together the main strands of this biblical theology, giving due credit to the One through whom and for whom we exist—the Lord Jesus Christ.

A group of appendices tackles matters which might be of additional interest to most readers. The book is finished off with bibliography, author, and Scripture indices. I have annotated the bibliography in an effort to help students who are building a library.

The introduction is the last thing one usually writes for a book. By the time it is typed out, the author has rearranged his content, scratched his head over sentences he must have been responsible for but now can't fathom what they mean, and realized that what he thought was good argumentation contained rather large gaps in logic, invented spellings for words which never existed (and shouldn't exist), and been humbled by errors that ought to have been caught. I have tried with the aid of several helpers to ferret out my mistakes, but I'm sure lots of them remain to be discovered.

My prayer is that this book and its predecessor will help the reader know God's Word better and appreciate and trust our God more. May He guard you from any of my inadvertent errors and impress upon you any of His Truth that I have reproduced.

PART ONE:
FIRST THINGS FIRST

1

COVENANTS FIRST: SOME METHODOLOGICAL ISSUES

Indeed I have spoken it;
I will also bring it to pass.
I have purposed it;
I will also do it. - Isaiah 46:11b

Before we launch into the main parts of the book it is necessary to say a few preparatory things which will help orient the reader.

The Divine Covenants and the New Covenant

I have been studying the divine covenants in Scripture in detail for about 16 years, and I have noticed that of late the covenant concept has received a little more attention than it has in a very long time. The importance of realizing that the covenants of God outlined and repeated in the OT are essential to a correct reading of the whole Bible has often been overlooked by evangelical interpreters. Still, today much work in biblical theology pays only lip-service to the unconditional Noahic, Abrahamic, Priestly, Davidic, and New covenants and their impact on the inspired writers. For sure, covenant theology has been a major interpretive system since just after the Reformation, and it is still an active theological view today. But covenant theology errs greatly in not basing its position on the actual covenants God made and instead overlays those covenants (or most of them) with a man-made set of theological covenants, chief of which is the covenant of grace, which then becomes the all-determiner of meaning for their system.[1] Pious minds may have created it, but it takes a certain kind of overconfidence and complacency to subordinate the covenants of God so plainly

1 Here is an example: "The covenant of grace tells us that the whole Bible is about one thing: God redeeming a people for himself through Jesus Christ" (Michael G. Brown and Zach Keele,

revealed in Scripture with a "covenant of grace" that is nowhere declared in Holy Writ.

As one covenant theologian has said, "Many evangelical Christians today find it difficult to believe that everything in Scripture after Genesis 3:15 concerns God's kingdom administered through the unfolding of one covenant of grace."[2] To which we answer, "Yes, we find it very difficult to believe that position." Yet I respectfully acknowledge the truth that covenant theology does at least find a central place for the idea of "covenant" in its approach.

Another newer approach which emphasizes covenants is Progressive Covenantalism—a Baptist view that tends to minimizes the theological covenants of covenant theology, but which is also determinedly and admirably covenantal. Unfortunately, this view too does not treat the covenants of the OT as they ought to be treated. God's covenants become putty in their hands, and so it all ends up very close to where covenant theology ends up; by treating the Church as the "New" or "True Israel" and with amillennial eschatology.[3] Here again though credit must be given to a position which strives to interpret God's Word covenantally.[4]

Sadly, most dispensationalists have not permitted the covenants of Scripture to direct their system either. As I showed in Volume One of this biblical theology,[5] dispensationalists have, by-and-large, subsumed God's covenant oaths beneath the mesh of "dispensations" and stewardships which I believe ill define what is being described in Holy Writ.[6] Scripture highlights covenants *not* dispensations.[7]

On a related note, covenant theologians rightly refer to their system as a hermeneutic.[8] Their theological covenants play a large role in their redemptive-historical

Sacred Bond: Covenant Theology Explored [Grandville, MI: Reformed Fellowship Inc, 2012], 69).

2 Richard Pratt Jr., "Reformed Theology is Covenant Theology," *Ligioner Ministries*, Jun 1 2010, https://www.ligonier.org/learn/articles/reformed-theology-covenant-theology.

3 I shall insert my observations about these two systems here and there in the book but will deal more fully with them in the Appendices. Progressive Covenantalism is closely associated with New Covenant Theology.

4 See Michael G. VanLaningham, "A Response to the Progressive Covenantalists' (and Others') View of the Land Promises for Israel," in *The Future Restoration of Israel: A Response to Supersessionism*, ed. Stanley E. Porter and Alan E. Kurschner (Eugene, OR: Pickwick, 2024), 2-23, 71-85.

5 Paul Martin Henebury, *The Words of the Covenant: A Biblical Theology, Volume One, Old Testament Expectation* (Maitland, FL: Xulon, 2021), 24-28.

6 There are some encouraging signs that this is beginning to change. E.g., *Forsaking Israel: How It Happened and Why it Matters*, ed. Larry D. Pettegrew (The Woodlands, TX: Kress, 2021), 210. However, there is a long way to go. Progressive Dispensationalism does better in this department, yet they too make the covenants somewhat pliable, especially in the NT. See Craig A. Blaising and Darrell L. Bock, *Progressive Dispensationalism* (Grand Rapids: Baker, 2000), 128-211.

7 In saying this I do not want to give the impression that dispensationalists do not acknowledge God's covenants. But they do generally give them a subordinate place to "dispensations" so that dispensations drive their approach. This can readily be seen in their works. For an excellent work that addresses this better than most see Paul N. Benware, *Understanding End Times Prophecy: A Comprehensive Approach* (Chicago: Moody, 2006), 35-78, 86-89.

8 See, e.g., J. I. Packer's Introduction to Herman Witsius, *The Economy of the Covenant Between God and Man: Comprehending A Complete System of Divinity*, Volume One (Escondido, CA: den Dulk Christian Foundation, 1990).

interpretation of Scripture. Dispensationalists refer to their system as a hermeneutic as well, but whereas the covenants of covenant theology dictate much of the hermeneutical approach of that view, the same cannot be said about the dispensations of dispensational theology. The various dispensations are *not* hermeneutical, nor indeed are they all clearly derived *via* the grammatical-historical hermeneutics lauded (legitimately)[9] by dispensationalists.

Biblical Covenantalism is different in that the divine covenants are seen as hermeneutically fixed. They are also generated from within the Bible itself, and therefore productive of an interpretive way forward.. The work before you is a biblical theology of the NT which highlights the major role that God's covenants play in the NT. I do not claim that "covenant" is the central idea of either Testament. I only say that God's covenants are far more influential and decisive than they are usually thought to be. This book and its predecessor attempt to show the great significance of covenant in God's Word and what that ought to lead to.

One proposal in this volume is that we see ourselves as transformed and being transformed by the New covenant in Christ's precious blood. As I shall demonstrate, on the basis of Isaiah 42:6; 49:8; John 1:29; 1 Corinthians 11:25; Hebrews 9:16-17, etc., I believe that Jesus Himself is the New covenant incarnate. As saints we are now found "in Christ." Part of what that means is that Jesus' death was the sacrifice that ratified the New covenant, and Jesus' resurrection incorporates the saints into New covenant life. Once Israel is brought to right relation with God, it will be through the transformation—instantaneous this time—wrought by the encounter of the Jewish remnant with the once dead but now living New covenant Messiah.

As I have stated previously, the New covenant facilitates the literal fulfillment of the other divine covenants. *In sum, because Christ has come, the New covenant must be given pride of place in our reading of the theology of the NT. This involves reading the great work of Jesus Christ in both His first and second comings in that light.*

Two Testaments, But One Bible

> The covenants constitute the framework of the larger story. They are the backbone of the biblical narrative.[10]

When we cross over from the OT into the NT, we might think that we ought to expect clear continuity. After all, the covenants and the Prophets of the OT have led us to expect a great future for the nation of Israel in a great Kingdom presided over by the coming Ruler, Messiah. Even though God's special people (Israel) had gone and done their own thing, we would still think that God would stick with His covenants and promises to that nation and bring them to Himself. We would also expect to see the arrival of the Messiah, the One whom Israel was anticipating. Israel would

9 Rightly, that is, as long as grammatical-historical hermeneutics is properly defined. See Robert L. Thomas, *Evangelical Hermeneutics: The New Versus the Old* (Grand Rapids: Kregel, 2003).

10 Peter J Gentry and Stephen J. Wellum, *Kingdom through Covenant: A Biblical-Theological Understanding of the Covenants* (Wheaton, IL: Crossway, 2012), 138.

finally have peace and prosperity under the protection of their Christ. They would be able to trust in Him to reign over them, and they could look to Him for blessing and guidance.

As we enter the NT through the doors of the Synoptic Gospels this picture doesn't seem to be upset. This indeed is the track that we were on when we left the OT. Matthew, of course, starts off with a genealogy of the King,[11] and includes a number of announcements in the early chapters of his biographical narrative that encourage the reader to believe that with the coming into the world of Jesus, the promised Kingdom was "at hand." Likewise, in Luke's Gospel the early chapters emphasize the theme of the King.

Yet when we get to the end of these Gospels, the ground seems to have shifted under our feet. No longer are we primed to think that the Kingdom is just around the corner. Jesus is rejected and murdered, and after He is resurrected in glory and ascends to Heaven, God seems to work in a new way through a fairly innocuous yet strong band of Jesus' former disciples and the descent of the Holy Spirit at Pentecost in Acts chapter 2.[12]

We then move into the time of the Church and the formation of the Body of Christ. The Pauline literature focuses mainly on the "new man" the Church, which is composed of both Jew and Gentile, although the further away we move from the time of Christ, the more Gentile-dominated the Church becomes. By the end of the NT (and the first century A.D.) the complexion of the people of God looks very different than what one would have assumed after studying the Law and the Prophets.

The focus of the NT after the first chapters of the Acts of the Apostles onwards moves away from the nation of Israel and shifts onto the Church. For many interpreters, this means that the expectations created by the covenants and promises in the OT must take on new meanings.[13] No more, we might be tempted to believe, is the focus of God where it was in the OT covenants. No more are the writers of the new Scripture concerned with promises of land and a throne in Jerusalem and national prosperity, all of which were distinguishing marks of Israel's covenants. Instead the emphasis swings toward a multiethnic group of Jews and Gentiles—the *Ekklesia* or Church.

What has happened? The answer to that question depends upon who you read or choose to listen to. The reply comes back from one quarter that God may have moved unexpectedly from what He said in the OT covenants, but He still moved in continuity with those covenants, or at least not in contradiction of them when "properly understood." They tell us God has now realized what He predicted in the OT, but He has realized it in an unforeseen way in Jesus Christ and through the Church. The OT

11 Matthew divides his genealogy into three distinct periods: Abraham to David, David to the Exile, and the Exile to Jesus. The reason this is worth mentioning is because here an inspired writer sets out several epochs, none of which comport with the traditional dispensations of dispensationalists. We must go carefully, therefore, when delineating dispensations.

12 The sense of expectation lingers until at least Acts 2 and 3.

13 This is a constant refrain in G. K. Beale, *A New Testament Biblical Theology* (Grand Rapids: Baker, 2011), 195, 202, 431, 570.

expectations of land, throne, and temple were evidently not the actual concrete things that Yahweh had in mind when He made those covenants. They were types and shadows of the realities uncovered for us in the latter NT. These are seen as greater realities than what was described in the OT.

Another set of experts will say that the Church has always existed, first as believers within OT Israel, and now in this Gentile/Jew people group. In other words, the Church has always been here, but only after Calvary has it been expanded beyond Israel. Both of these outlooks take the position that the Church is now the "true Israel" because it is "in Christ," and Jesus Christ is the real Israel. For them, there is no future for Israel as an administrative structure.

We shall look occasionally at the proposals of these schools of interpretation. They deserve a respectful hearing. But I think it will become clear that not only do they not take the covenant agenda of the OT seriously, but they also fail to understand what is going on in the NT, at least as far as the big picture is concerned.[14]

A larger problem with these approaches is a little more sensitive to explain and may savor of unintended impoliteness. However, I see no way around the issue other than to face it head-on. The problem that looms in front of us is that the covenant-making God of the OT, the God who hates oath-breaking (Jer. 34:15-19; Ezek. 17:15-18), is seen as a God who simply does not mean what He says even when He puts Himself under oath to do something. You see, the trouble is not that the God who repeatedly raises particular expectations in His covenants is *not* believed when He initially states something. It is that a God who supposedly fulfills these oaths in totally *unforeseeable* and *non-literal* ways in the NT *is telling us to believe Him now*!

But what exactly are the pious *to* believe? This introduces a matter that is essential to grasp, even if grasping it is not easy. When reading the two Testaments we naturally want to see what is promised in the OT being brought to fulfillment in the NT: we look for the correspondences. *But what if many of those correspondences do not yet exist?* What if fulfillment for many lies not in the past but in the future? And what if our misunderstanding of where we are in our historical positioning in the Creation Project tempts us into making connections with covenant fulfillment that are not really there?

We may further ask which expectations, raised by the wording of the NT, are *fixed* as to their meaning, and what expectations may undergo radical unforeseeable transformation in the eschaton? How are these experts going to assure us that they have it right when they employ spiritualization, typology, recapitulation, echo, and such to reinterpret the OT covenants, and seem happy to use the same tools on any unyielding prophecy in the NT?

14 The big picture is, of course, creation. We are all prone to overlook the obvious, and the most obvious fact about us is that we live within God's created order. It is impossible for us to think without reference to it. The Lord is at work in creation and every other concept in the Bible pays its dues to it. This grand theme of creation is what, in Volume One, I called "The Creation Project."

I spent much time in the previous book trying to prove that God's covenants do not and cannot change; a plain fact that the NT itself is at pains to underscore (see Gal. 3:15; Heb. 6:13-18; cf. 2 Sam. 7:28).

It is worth it here to remind ourselves of Yahweh's own final presentation of Himself in the OT. After the prediction of the coming of the "Messenger of the covenant" (Mal. 3:1-2), who comes to "purify the sons of Levi" (Mal. 3:3), so that they offer righteous offerings to God on behalf of Israel (Mal. 3:3-4), when God comes in judgment (Mal. 3:2, 5), what do we read on the back of these promises?

> For I *am* the LORD, I do not change;
> Therefore you are not consumed, O sons of Jacob (Mal. 3:6).

The hope of the realization of these prophecies is squarely based upon the character of God. Because He does not change, and He it is who speaks thus to Israel, the nation has survived and will continue to survive. The "change" in God is not possible, ergo a change in His covenant promises is not possible. There can be no un-prespecified "transformation" of the oaths of Yahweh.

But we have a problem. For many good men insist that the NT writers *do* transform the promises. This is a major bone of contention, especially between dispensationalists on the one hand and covenant theologians and Progressive Covenantalists on the other.[15] My advocacy of Biblical Covenantalism may be seen as a ramping-up of the dispute, owing to the fact that God's unilateral covenants are the focus of the system.

Keeping Our Eye on the Ball

There is no doubt that the problem of the NT's use of the OT is one of the most hotly contested issues in biblical studies. What is one to make, for example, of Matthew's application of Hosea 11:1 to Christ (Matt. 2:15)? Or, continuing with Hosea, why does Paul quote Hosea 2:23 and 1:10 in Romans 9:25-26? And what was James thinking when he cited Amos 9:11-12 in the Jerusalem assembly (Acts 15:16-17)? To top it all, what on earth was passing through Peter's mind when he claimed Joel 2:28-32 was occurring right in front of his eyes at Pentecost (Acts 2:14-21)? Finally, Peter is at it again later in Acts 2:30. Is he saying that the resurrected and ascended Jesus is presently sitting upon David's throne in heaven?

If we are to arrange this material in the right order it seems that we will have our work cut out for us. Taking Peter's use of Joel 2 as an example, despite some scholars being prepared to say that Joel's prophecy really happened at Pentecost, many are left wondering what to do with all the specific details in Joel which patently *didn't* occur at the birth of the Church.

15 Progressive Covenantalism presents itself as a *via media*, but in truth it is just a revised approach to Baptist covenant theology with a reworking of the theological covenants and more emphasis on typological interpretation.

We are going to have to be patient. We are going to have to read very closely. We will need to use our imaginations to try to place ourselves within the milieu of excitement and expectation of the times. We will be open to hearing what others have said, and we will have to on occasion admit that we don't know all the answers.

Will our understanding of the divine covenants help us, and if so, how? The answer is varied, but here are some of the ideas that we will be exploring in this work:

1. Whether one takes 2 Chronicles 36 or Malachi 4 as the last chapter, the OT ends with a wave of covenant expectations as yet unfulfilled. These covenants cannot be simply off-loaded prior to reading the NT. To do so is to mis-prepare to understand the NT. And indeed, as we peruse the first chapters of the Gospels, what do we find but clear references to the divine covenants. For instance, Matthew 1:1 declares, "The book of the genealogy of Jesus Christ, the Son of David, the Son of Abraham." Here Matthew is directing us to two principal players in the OT narrative, and their chief importance to the biblical story is their connection to the covenants that God made with them. Then in verses 20 and 21 we see that emphasis is given to David,[16] followed by a mention of Jesus and His saving significance, which I will argue is intimately connected with the New covenant. In the next chapter, we see the Magi asking, "Where is He who has been born King of the Jews? For we have seen His star in the East and have come to worship Him." (Matt. 2:2). It is noteworthy that they come to worship this Davidic King, who therefore must be divine.[17]

2. There has been some interesting work done on the covenantal structure of John 13-17 and 20-21,[18] but the covenant concept makes its presence felt throughout John's work.

3. Although the words "covenant," "oath," "swore," and such-like crop up fairly infrequently in the NT,[19] the main themes of the NT are vitally related to covenantal concerns.[20] Think of Paul's stress on God's covenants in Romans 9 to 11, or indeed his use of the central chapter of the Abrahamic covenant, particularly Genesis 15:6 in Romans and Galatians. In Galatians he also takes pains to prove that Christians are "children of Abraham." Then there is the characterization of his ministry as a New covenant ministry, and the

16 Already in Matt. 1:6 David is referred to as "David the king" twice.

17 Exactly as was indicated in Matt. 1:23.

18 Notably by Rekha Chennattu, *Johannine Discipleship as a Covenant Relationship* (Grand Rapids: Baker, 2005).

19 The book of Hebrews is an exception to this rule.

20 Newman suggests reasons for why there is a relative paucity of "covenant" terminology in the NT. He believes the Christological focus of the NT writers took precedence over covenants *expliciter*. He also comments that "The identification of Jesus with the new covenant could have operated at such a deep level of shared Christian conviction that it...did not receive far reaching elaboration in Christian writings" (Carey C. Newman, "Covenant, New Covenant," in *Dictionary of the Later New Testament and Its Development*, ed. Ralph P. Martin & Peter H. Davids [Downers, IL: InterVarsity, 1997], 246).

Lord's Supper is a New covenant ordinance. In Hebrews, Christ presides as High Priest of the New covenant.

4. The huge question of the New covenant and its connection with the Person and Work of Christ, along with the Church's relationship to the New covenant is central to the present book. In the previous volume I argued on the basis of passages like Isaiah 42:6 and 49:8 that Jesus Christ is Himself the New covenant embodied. Pursuing that line in this volume will mean attaching that teaching to the Gospel, and hence its exposition in the Apostolic record. When one recalls Paul referring to himself and his colleagues as "ministers of the New covenant" in 2 Corinthians 3:6, the importance of the new covenant surfaces all the more. That is how the great Apostle saw himself and his calling. The sole occurrence of this phrase should not blind us to its very real importance. Of course, its existence as a Pauline doctrine does not prove its preeminence either, but I hope to demonstrate that it is the key to a better understanding of Paul.

5. The prophetic direction in which God's other covenants (esp. the Abrahamic and Davidic[21]) are treated, even if sometimes in a more oblique manner, demonstrate that the Apostolic authors were still very much concerned with them and influenced by them. Covenant was an important cognitive category for these first theologians.

6. It must be remembered that Jesus Christ Himself was intimately associated with God's covenants. As one writer put it, "From the immediate aftermath of Jesus' public ministry he was proclaimed to Jews in Israel and the diaspora as the Messiah/Christ, in fulfillment of the covenantal promises of Yahweh."[22]

7. The culmination of all things in the Kingdom of God and the New Heavens and New Earth validates the theses that propelled the first volume.

The Problem of the Use of the Old Testament[23] in the New

This is an area of study where questions abound. Is the NT a fulfillment of the Old, or is it a continuation of the Old? Which is to say, do the covenants "jump the tracks" in the NT, assigning fulfillment to the Church what was promised to Israel? Do the

21 The "Priestly covenant" of Numbers 25 is not treated in the NT because of its preoccupation with the Church. However, it would be a mistake to believe that this covenant of peace will not come to full fruition in the Kingdom.

22 Paul Barnett, *Jesus and the Rise of Early Christianity* (Downers Grove, IL: IVP, 1999), 34.

23 It should be understood that to speak of the NT's use of the "Old" Testament is itself an anachronism, since there was no NT during the time it was being written and compiled. See Richard B. Hays and Joel B. Green, "The Use of the Old Testament by New Testament Writers," in *Hearing the New Testament*, ed. Joel B. Green (Grand Rapids: Eerdmans, 1995), 223.

apostolic authors take liberties with the OT texts they cite? If the NT fulfills many of the OT prophecies, but only once they undergo "transformation" can we really say fulfillment has occurred? Would we permit excuse of a non-inspired prediction? Are there different senses of the word "fulfillment"? Just what is going on when the NT writers quote or allude to the OT? I refer to it as a problem in the heading, but that is true for the most part if we wish to have all of our questions answered. Most of the time the issues are clear to see, but there are some texts that pose difficulties for everyone concerned with reconciling the two Testaments.

Very often the difference between premillennialists and amillennialists is in the latter's willingness to rework covenant passages in the OT so that they fit first advent scenarios. I shall give my opinion about how the apostolic writers employ the OT when necessary, although this book is not the place for a detailed investigation of the subject. The main operating assumption that I will employ will be to ask how the OT quotation (often lifted from the LXX), comports with the covenantal plan of the Creation Project, and of Jesus' role within it.

Typology

One of the topics separating the present approach from many biblical theologies is the matter of typology. I believe that there is a type/antitype relation between the Testaments. However, I am extremely wary of using typology to establish a biblical teaching. This is because typology is in the nasty habit of promoting confirmation bias. It tends to speak sweet nothings into the ears of the person employing it. Typology should *never* be used to teach doctrine, and it ought to be submissive to plain statements of Scripture, especially if they are sworn oaths. And most certainly typological interpretation should never be permitted to decide what the words of God mean. For this reason, a person who believes *prima facie* God's covenants cannot subscribe to the following: "Biblical theology is a way of analyzing and synthesizing the Bible that makes organic, salvation-historical connections with the whole canon on its own terms, especially regarding how the Old and New Testaments progress, integrate, and climax in Christ."[24]

The underlined words are crucial to grasp. These writers hold that Christ's first coming is the antitype, towards which all of the OT types point.[25]

The climax they are speaking of is at the first coming.[26] Now if you take the first coming as the "climax" of most of the Bible's storyline you are going to have to find

24 Jason S. DeRouchie, Oren R. Martin, and Andrew David Naselli, *40 Questions about Biblical Theology* (Grand Rapids: Kregel, 2020), 20 (my emphasis).

25 The most influential writer on the subject of typology based upon his work on the OT in the NT is G. K. Beale. Beale has influenced scholars both within his covenant theology camp, and also those outside it like Progressive Covenantalists. See e.g., G. K. Beale, *Handbook on the New Testament Use of the Old Testament: Exegesis and Interpretation* (Grand Rapids: Baker, 2012), 13-27. Although I cannot discuss it here, I see numerous problems with Beale's approach. I reviewed Beale's *A New Testament Biblical Theology* at my blog, paulmhenebury.com.

26 Jason S. DeRouchie, et al., *40 Questions about Biblical Theology*, 29, 51, 52, 59, 67, 68 n. 14, 225, etc. "The age of eschatological fulfillment has come in Christ" (Ibid., 96, my emphasis).

ways of packing an awful lot of pesky OT covenant prophecy into the first half of the first century A.D. A good way to do that is to convert lots of things into types (even if they are included in covenants). When you have done that, you are free to declare things like, "Every significant whole-Bible theme climaxes in the person and work of Jesus the Messiah,"[27] and, "God designed some types to repeat and develop through the progressive covenants before they climaxed in Jesus."[28] Hence, "if God gives you eyes to see"[29] this first coming fulfillment, you will agree with the authors. If you don't think most of the OT covenants are fulfilled at the first advent, then you have "missed the point" and are not interpreting Scripture like Jesus did.[30] They assert: "How the NT fulfills the OT promises strongly influences the progressive covenantal understanding of typology, which sees Christ [in His first coming] as the ultimate antitype of all previous types."[31]

So, when it comes to God's own covenants with Israel (e.g., Abrahamic, Priestly, Davidic) they can be fulfilled in Christ and the Church. This, of course, is clear supersessionism, but today this is denied, and we are given statements such as this: "Progressive covenantalism does not see the church as directly extending or fulfilling Israel. Rather, Christ is the antitype of Israel, who fulfills Israel's identity, purpose, and mission such that in Christ the church inherits all the covenant blessings."[32]

This rather double-dealing pronouncement has to be picked through, but what it ends up asserting is that the Church indirectly inherits all of Israel's covenant blessings through Christ.[33] Hence, via their typology the covenant oaths do not include the specific substance of what God is swearing to perform, but only a transitive shadow. Since "The type is but the shadow; the antitype is the substance,"[34] one is left with a God whose oath cannot be believed until and unless one fully comprehends the antitype He had in mind. The "Israel" to whom the covenants were made "is but the shadow." If that is true, what was the point, one may well ask, of making a covenant at all? In Progressive Covenantalism, even more than in covenant theology, typology provides the big guns to blast away the plain sense of covenant promise.[35]

27 Ibid., 59.
28 Ibid., 85.
29 Ibid., 86.
30 Ibid., 53.
31 Ibid., 192.
32 Ibid., 68.
33 An example of this comes from Hamilton: "Having celebrated the ways that the church experiences the typological fulfillment of the promises God made to Israel in Ephesians 1:3-14 and prayed for the church in Ephesus in 1:15-20a, Paul describes the way Christ has been enthroned as king in 1:20b-23" (James M. Hamilton, Jr., *Typology*, 171). The problem with these assertions is that only one of them, Paul's prayer, can be corroborated from the text. There is no hint of apostolic typological interpretation in Eph. 1:3-14, and Eph. 1:20-23 makes Christ Head of the Church at God's right hand, not ruling as a King from the throne. But typology is brought to bear on the text and lo and behold it yields the desired conclusions. Hamilton is a historic premillennialist, but his typology produces replacement theology.
34 Ibid., 85.
35 For a relatively brief but thorough refutation of the typological assumptions of Progressive Covenantalism as found in its most influential work, Gentry and Wellum's, *Kingdom through Covenant*, see Michael Grisanti, "A Critique of Gentry and Wellum's, *Kingdom Through Covenant*: An Old Testament Perspective," *MSJ* 26 (Spring 2015), 129-137.

Let us take a look at a different scenario, the rapture. Personally, I believe in the pretribulation rapture position, but it is folly to try to prove it via types. For instance, Enoch and Noah are offered as types of the pre-trib rapture, but Enoch had to live for 365 years in a very evil world; Noah had to live there for even longer, and then he had to endure a far from luxury cruise during the most terrifying cataclysm that has ever occurred. Looked at that way they become types of a post-trib rapture. Yet those of a pretribulational disposition could, with very little effort, turn all this on its head and present a viable pre-trib typology, with these men being rescued before God's wrath is visited on humanity.

Although typology should not be dismissed, we should recognize that where there is an institution, or a story, or a historical event, there is a type in it for someone. In his classic *Progress of Dogma*, James Orr objected to the "artificial system of typology and allegorizing interpretation" of covenant theology, whereby it "sought to read back practically the whole of the New Testament into the Old."[36] But how many covenant theologians would agree with his opinion? In Gerhard Maier's work, typology is permissible on the basis of a double meaning of Scripture and within prescribed limits.[37] His second rule for typological understanding bears repeating:

> Second, we observe in Scripture itself that typological understanding never creates new revelatory data. It only underscores, illustrates, and amplifies what has already been stated clearly. In other words: typological understanding enriches but does not replace a previous understanding of revelation. It is checked by philological-grammatical understanding.[38]

This is most important to recognize because much modern typological interpretation *does* claim to create new revelatory data unknown to those who received the initial revelation, and it does change and replace previous understanding of God's words.

But the most important thing to say about typology is where it is all said to lead. Typology is viewed as at least a corroborative, but all too often as a constructive hermeneutical approach by systems such as covenant theology and Progressive Covenantalism.[39] Without it, these systems have considerably less persuasive force. But since these systems are all committed to a first coming hermeneutic that seeks the majority of fulfillments at the cross and resurrection of Jesus (and the Church in Him), they employ typology to ensure that the covenant promises to the nation of Israel (the remnant) find their fulfillment in the first century A.D.

---

36 James Orr, *The Progress of Dogma (*New York: A. C. Armstrong and son, 1907), 303.

37 Gerhard Maier, *Biblical Hermeneutics*, trans. Robert W. Yarbrough (Wheaton, IL: Crossway, 1994), 85-87.

38 Ibid., 87.

39 After reading most of the main publications by progressive covenantalists I have to say that it is an extremely ill-named position. It relies so heavily upon its own typological assumptions that it deserves to be called "Typologism." Typology, not the covenants, is definitely in the driving seat in this system.

Typological theories are also tethered to evaluations of biblical history, so that a salvation-historical method will yield different types than a Kingdom-oriented method.[40] This being so, I would strongly advocate for *not* making typology a part of one's hermeneutics. If the reading of Scripture one is proposing relies upon a particular brand of typology for establishing itself, that is a huge red flag. Types ought only to be used to validate what God has said, not to dictate His meaning. Typology is post-theological but very often (and regrettably) not post-exegetical in nature. Baker states our attitude well:

> The essential meaning of a biblical text is its literal meaning, which was generally clear to the original reader and may be clarified for us by means of grammatical-historical study. This meaning might include reference to the typical significance of an event, person or institution, and in this case is likely to be clear in the text. So sound exegesis is a prerequisite for typology, but typology is not itself exegesis or interpretation of a text. Rather, it is theological reflection on relationships between events, persons and institutions recorded in biblical texts.[41]

In this biblical theology there will be no accent on typology. There is more than enough material in the covenants and promises to explore without getting bogged down in uncertain and question-begging types and shadows and their interpretation. Others can major on those things (and they certainly do). You will not find them here.[42]

Is the Church a Parenthesis in the Plan of God?

Dispensational thinkers have often sought to explain the rise of the Church in the biblical narrative as a parenthesis, but I am uncomfortable with this position. In my view, the Creation Project includes separate but somewhat overlapping plans for the nations, for Israel, and for the Church. These plans have different historical starting points and different historical conclusions. In the case of the nations and Israel the beginning and ending points of their separate plans are interrupted by the introduction of another plan, with the culmination of their respective plans being placed in

40 An older but still helpful introduction to this field is W. Edward Glenny, "Typology: A Summary of the Present Evangelical Discussion," *JETS* 40:4 (Dec 1997), 627-638.

41 David L. Baker, *Two Testaments, One Bible: The Theological Relationship Between the Old and New Testaments*, 3rd ed. (Downers Grove, IL: IVP, 2010), 181. Baker's whole discussion of Typology is worth reading.

42 Because I define "faith" as dependence upon God (as opposed to my native independent setting) I react to any notion that God's words need passing through "the agreed upon findings of contemporary scholarship." This is particularly so when the prophetic utterances of God are at issue (most will take God's declarations in the Gospel at face value). Though these men may be very devout and godlier than myself, I cannot stand with these brethren when they make God's oaths mean something different than the precise words God swore. Put simply, why stress types when God has made covenants (Heb. 6:16-17)?

abeyance until the great event of the second advent of Jesus Christ and the inauguration of the promised Kingdom of God.

I think it is wrong to talk about the discontinuity between Israel and the Church until we have appreciated the roles that both play within the wider covenantal program of God. For example, both "peoples" have a place within the Abrahamic covenant: Israel in terms of natural descendants and land (e.g., Gen. 12:2, 7), the Church in terms of the blessing upon the nations both through Abraham's Seed Jesus Christ and our faith-participation in Him (Gal. 3:16-29). And if we are paying attention, we can see that both the Church right now and the remnant of Israel in the future are parties to the New covenant in Christ (cf. 1 Cor. 11:25; Rom. 11:25-29). Furthermore, we must not forget that both entities play an implicit and strategic role in the Creation Project itself as it unfurls in history. It is therefore a mistake to refer to the Church as a "parenthesis" because the word leaves the impression that a new thought has been interjected into a sentence or program which could stand alone without it. It is better to think of God's Creation Project as containing *several strands* or plans which go into operation *at different times* in the history of the fallen world.

The plan for Israel begins after the confusion of languages and the separation of nations (Gen. 10–11). The plan for the Church begins after Israel's rejection of Jesus' ministry (Acts 2).[43] Since God has unfinished business with Israel, the plan to save the nation is taken up after the Church is completed (Rom. 11:25-29). I believe that it is better to think in terms of these plans within the one Project that God has for Creation. The Church is not in any sense "Plan B." It is Plan 1b. There's a big difference![44]

The Close Proximity of Dates of the New Testament Books

An interesting phenomenon in regard to the reading of the OT and the New is the respective chronologies of the authorship of the books within each. Whereas the OT was written over a period of approximately 1,300 years—taking Job as the earliest book (c. 1750 B.C.) and Malachi as the last book (c. 450 B.C.) —the NT was written within one average human lifespan. This represents a vast difference that ought to be given more consideration than it has been.

The Writing of the Old Testament

If we consider the span of years for the writing of the OT, we get something like this (citing representative examples):

43 This rejection is implied in the narrative of Matt. 12.

44 Some writers have used the idea of "intercalation" instead of "parenthesis." Lewis Sperry Chafer famously advocated for this term. See his *Systematic Theology*, Volume IV (Dallas: Dallas Seminary Press, 1978), 41. The word is not a pretty one and even scholars prefer to employ the more straight-forward word "sandwiching" which puts across the basic idea well. The concept of intercalation or sandwiching one episode between the beginning and the end of another episode is not foreign to the Bible itself. Most notably Mark's Gospel is known for this phenomenon. Having said this I would want to emphasize the fact that the Church is just as much in the plan of God as was Israel.

Job (18th Century B.C.)
The Pentateuch (Mid 15th Century B.C.)
Many Psalms, Proverbs, Ecclesiastes, Canticles (10th Century B.C.)
Jonah, Amos, Hosea, Micah (8th Century B.C.)
Isaiah, Nahum, Zephaniah, Habakkuk (8th to 7th Century B.C.)
Jeremiah, Ezekiel, Daniel, 1 & 2 Kings (6th Century B.C.)
Zechariah, Ezra/Nehemiah, Malachi (5th Century B.C.)

During that time history witnessed the beginning of the nation of Israel under Moses, the dominance and eventual waning of Egyptian and Babylonian dynasties, the Hittite, Assyrian, Persian empires, and the onset of the Greek Empire. Israel rose to become a powerful state in the days of David and Solomon, then split into two kingdoms until some centuries later both kingdoms went into captivity.

The story of Israel dominates the OT, yet that book also includes the account of Creation and Fall. It speaks of the world before the great flood—a world that is buried beneath the rocks and stones and seas. The flood came some 2,500 years before the call of Abraham, which itself was around 500 years prior to the Exodus and the writing of the books of the Pentateuch. That is to say that the OT was not only written over a very long time period, but the history it records covers a far greater expanse of time than that. Accordingly, there is a great mass of data that must be collocated and explained, and that is without introducing all of the prophetic content within the Hebrew Bible.

What this amounts to for progressive revelation is that if a person is going to truly track the development of God's word chronologically, he must situate himself within the various biblical milieus which pass before his eyes. He will have to try to match the voice of the protagonist being described (e.g., Adam, Noah, Abraham, Joseph, Moses, Joshua, Samuel, David, Elijah, Jeremiah, Daniel, etc.) with what is being revealed about them and their times at the time they lived. Moreover, since prophecy is such a significant part of that revelation, any study of the progress of revelation will need to incorporate the cumulative impact of the prophetic word as it makes its transit through the different eras.

The Writing of the New Testament

But when we arrive in the NT, we are up against a far different phenomenon: a decidedly condensed timeframe in which God discloses His Apostolic word. For my part, I believe that the Gospel of Matthew is very early, written in the 40's A.D. That was the view of the early Church. I am not going to mount a defense of the date of Matthew here, but I believe John Wenham made a brilliant defense of Matthean priority in his book *Redating Matthew, Mark and Luke,* which I strongly recommend.[45] That aside, the point that must never be lost sight of is the fact that the books comprising our

45 John Wenham, *Redating Matthew, Mark and Luke: A Fresh Assault on the Synoptic Problem* (Leicester: IVP, 1992).

NT were written very closely together in time. So closely, there was scarcely any time for what T. D. Bernard called "The Progress of Doctrine."[46] Here are the approximate dates of the NT books:

Matthew (40-45 A.D.)
James/Jude (45-47 A.D.)
Galatians (48-50 A.D.)
1 & 2 Thessalonians (49-52 A.D.)
Mark (50-53 A.D.)
1 & 2 Corinthians (54–57 A.D.)
Romans (56-57 A.D.)
Luke/Acts, Ephesians, Philippians, Colossians (60-62 A.D.)
Pastoral Epistles (62-64 A.D.)
Hebrews, 1 & 2 Peter (65-67 A.D.)
John/Epistles of John (80-90 A.D.)
Revelation (94-96 A.D.)

If we start with a date of circa 40-41 A.D. for Matthew[47] and end with the writing of John's Revelation circa 94-96 A.D., we get about a 55-year timespan. A short 55-year timespan is in itself is worth remembering. But a closer look reveals that most of the NT books are written inside a 25-year window, from Matthew (c. 41 A.D.) to 2 Timothy (c. 65-67 A.D.). When this 55-year timespan is brought alongside the 1,300-year gap between the first and last books of the OT, the contrast is indeed striking. There was plenty of time for the gradual unveiling of God's revelation in the Hebrew Bible, but nothing comparable for the NT.

That there *is* doctrinal development from the Gospels and Acts to the Revelation is indisputable, and Bernard shows that the order of the NT books was not accidental. But for the most part, the progress is muted compared to the OT. And just as the time covered by the OT is longer than the time in which it was written (circa 3,500 years at least), so it is with the NT. But the variance in time span is not nearly so pronounced. The birth of Jesus was around 6 B.C. and John wrote Revelation in 95 or 96 A.D. This means that the total duration covered in the NT narrative is a mere century. When progressive revelation is thought about within a window of 100 years, as opposed to 3,500 years, we again see the huge disparity. Whereas the OT period allows for a prolonged progression, this is not the case with the NT.

Progressive revelation is either accelerated in the NT, or else it continues at about the same pace, or is slower than in the OT. As it turns out, I think a case can be made for all three options, although an accelerated pace seems preferable. If one looks at

46 Thomas Delaney Bernard, *The Progress of Doctrine in the New Testament,* numerous editions.

47 John Wenham, *Redating Matthew, Mark and Luke: A Fresh Assault on the Synoptic Problem,* xxv.

doctrines such as the deity of Christ, miracles, the birth, identity, and makeup of the Christian Church, and the coming of Christ again in power; all these things are crammed together in a relatively few pages and compounded in a brief span of time.

To sharpen the focus, a perusal of even the earlier writings of the NT—the Thessalonian Epistles (c. 49-52 A.D.), the Corinthian Letters (c. 54 & 56 A.D.), Romans (c. 56 A.D.), Ephesians and Colossians (c. 60-62 A.D.)—speak to many of these things in a mature and profound way. And this is all packed into a mere 15 years! Is it not surprising that Paul's Thessalonian correspondence carries with it implications of a developed Christology and eschatology taught even to a young church?[48]

Yet consideration of another matter lessens the surprise. The inspiration of all Scripture by the Holy Spirit of God does not demand an evolutionary growth of knowledge from early naiveté to robust comprehension, at least not in the Apostolic authors! Such a state of affairs would necessitate a teaching similar to the doctrine of abrogation in Islam where the later Medina suras of the Koran correct and supplant the early Meccan suras. But we do not see anything like this in the Bible. The Holy Spirit gave the incontrovertible Truth to the authors from the outset. I am persuaded that the canonical selection and arrangement of the books was superintended by the same Spirit so that it is most unwise to imagine much, if any, growth in Apostolic understanding of the essential doctrines. Certainly, we must not be so ignorant as to suppose that the relative brevity of First Thessalonians (c. 49-50 A.D.) in comparison with Romans (c. 56 A.D.) constitutes any proof that the Apostle Paul has matured in knowledge. There is a meager 6 or 7 years between the production of the two Pauline books!

What this leads to is the realization that if one is seeking to locate and trace a development in Paul's thought or John's thought, he is going to be up against it.

Diachronic or Synthetic?

A further consideration flowing from this realization of the chronological proximity of the NT books is that the choice between a diachronic or a synthetic presentation of NT theology cannot be made on the basis of such an ephemeral development of doctrine.[49] While no one disagrees that the various "samples" of inspired apostolic writing the Holy Spirit has left us with are characterized by different styles, genres, and emphases, the stubborn fact that they were all penned within a relatively short period makes the choice of method worth careful reflection. In this work it will be seen that I am not impressed by atomizing the theologies within the NT. Yes, I do believe there is an important place for analyses of Pauline, Petrine, and Johannine theologies, but I thoroughly reject the notion that they can be pitted against each other.[50] It is import-

48 See below in my comments on the Thessalonian Epistles.

49 Marshall only delineates two phases of development: 1. The recorded life of Jesus (the Gospels), and 2. The Apostolic period (I. Howard Marshall, *New Testament Theology: Many Witnesses, One Gospel* [Downers Grove, IL: InterVarsity, 2004], 22-23).

50 I add an important proviso. Not everything written in the NT is directed at the Church, even if the Church can glean much benefit from it.

ant to notice that, for example, when Peter uses the term "salvation" he includes the idea of resurrection. In contrast, Paul usually speaks of the moment and state of being saved. These preferences are reconcilable whether we adopt a systematic approach or an analytical, authorial approach. One thing the systematic approach has going for it is that it neutralizes the temptation to splinter NT theology into NT theologies.[51]

In Volume One, I used a chronological, author-driven approach that best suited my view of progressive revelation and covenantal development. For reasons I have already given, I see no need to retain a chronological scheme for the NT. I do, however, intend to treat the inspired authors individually before attempting an overall synthesis. This will mean, for example, that while discussing Paul's theology, especially as it pertains to God's covenants (and in particular the New covenant), I will not restrain myself from reaching over from one epistle to another to fill in a point I am trying to make. This procedure is common enough but worth mentioning to the reader.

51 See Donald Guthrie, *New Testament Theology* (Downers Grove, IL: InterVarsity, 1981), 72. Guthrie opted for a systematic methodology.

2

GOD'S COVENANTS IN THE OLD TESTAMENT

As it is written in the Prophets. - Mark 1:2a

In the first volume of this work, I attempted to lay out the Bible's picture of God's Creation Project in the OT. I focused my attention on the covenants of God and tried to present a cogent argument for their hermeneutical priority and theological importance. I want to briefly remind the reader of what was said there in this present work.[1]

The "God Words–God's Actions" Motif

We saw that God performs what He has said He will perform. There is no need to second guess what God will do after He has told us what He is going to do. God means what He says.[2]

Although it is one of the most recognizable chapters in the Bible, a significant truth about Genesis 1 is very often overlooked (as it was by me for many years). There is a correlation between God's intentions, what God says He is going to do, and what He does.[3] The reader can check this for themselves as they read through the books of the Bible. In and of itself this correlation does not raise an eyebrow. However, the fact that this correlation exists ought to alert the student of the Scriptures that Yahweh works this way: He does *not* say one thing and then do something different. His *modus operandi* is found in Isaiah 46:11b: "Indeed I have spoken it; I will also bring it to pass. I have purposed it; I will also do it."

1 Readers are invited to read the fuller discussions of these points in Volume One.
2 I realize that this places me in opposition to most biblical scholars, but they are not my judges.
3 For example, "And God said, Let there be light: and there was light. And God saw the light..." (Gen. 1:3-4a); "And God said, Let us make man in our image, after our likeness: and let them have dominion... So God created man in his own image... And God blessed them, and God said unto them... and have dominion..." (Gen. 1:26-28).

Another way of putting it is that as far as God's own activity is concerned, when compared with what Yahweh declares He is going to do, there is no room for spiritualizing, expansion, or transformation. When His words and His actions are correlated, Yahweh is utterly predictable. This provides solid grounds for faith!

God Has Laid Out His Plan of History Covenantally

It is a plain fact that there is no good exegetical evidence for a covenant before the flood. Divine covenants are post-flood devices and were not made in "the world that then was" (2 Pet. 3:6 KJV). The very first covenant known to history is the one made with Noah and his family and with the rest of creation (Gen. 9:11). Covenants are a major talking point in evangelicalism at the present time, but a lot of what is said about them fails to get to ground level, as it were. Biblical covenants are often insufficiently defined, and their function barely considered. My definition is as follows:

> A biblical covenant between God and man is a solemnly sealed and explicit declaration of intent and obligation, about a matter of great importance. It binds one or both parties to fulfill the words of the covenant oath. The parties to the covenant cannot be changed out. The function of a covenant is to amplify or reinforce the plain terms of the oath between the parties in order to clarify their relationship and clear away ambiguity or misinterpretation, thereby ensuring a unified understanding of the terms.[4]

What covenants do is to underscore the word of God to men who tend to interpret things independently of what God says.[5] They are amplifications of plain speech about something of importance.[6] That means they are hermeneutical just as much as they are promissory. The hermeneutical fixity of God's covenants is what lends them their importance as determiners of biblical history, and hence biblical theology.[7]

What the Divine Covenants are About

There are six divine covenants in the Bible:[8]

---

4 *The Words of the Covenant*, Volume One, 42.

5 My position on human beings in relation to their Creator is that whether saved or lost we are all "preset" by the Fall to be independent of our Maker. Hence, faith is when we willingly depend upon what God tells us in His Word.

6 Speaking of the covenant of Nehemiah 9:38 Schreiner declares, "The substance of the covenant was a pledge to be faithful to covenant obligations" (Thomas R. Schreiner, *The King in His Beauty: A Biblical Theology of the Old and New Testaments* [Grand Rapids: Baker, 2013], 217).

7 See the fine remarks of Thomas R. Schreiner in *Covenant and God's Purpose for the World* (Wheaton, IL: Crossway, 2017), 13-18. Unfortunately, Schreiner allows for equivocation of the terms of the covenants.

8 Richard Averbeck counts "five major covenants" but also notices the Priestly covenant of Num. 25:10-13. See Richard E. Averbeck, "Israel, the Jewish People and God's Covenants," in *Israel, the Church, and the Middle East: A Biblical Response to the Current Conflict*, ed. Darrell L. Bock and Mitch Glaser (Grand Rapids: Kregel, 2018), 22.

1. The Noahic covenant was concerned with one thing: that God would never again bring a cataclysmic global flood upon the earth (Gen. 9:11). However, its effect is more profound. This covenant preserves the present creation conditions so that nature exhibits a uniformity that will not be upset until the New Heavens and New Earth. Since it is the first recorded covenant, it prescribes the plain-sense hermeneutical orientation of future covenants, especially divine covenants.

2. The Abrahamic covenant is about three things (not one thing, as covenant theology believes). It concerns Abraham's descendants through Isaac, the child of promise, and the nation (Israel) that comes from them. It is about a designated land gifted to them by Yahweh, and it is about the blessing upon the peoples of the earth through the Abrahamic line (Gen. 12:1-3, 7) and the greatest son of Abraham (Gal. 3:16).

3. The Mosaic covenant is a bilateral Law covenant that in the end could only condemn the sinner. But it did have the great benefit of keeping Israel distinct from its neighbors enough to preserve the Jews as a distinct people.

4. The "Priestly" covenant is the forgotten covenant of Scripture. It is a unilateral covenant that promises the offspring of Phinehas, the Zadokites, a continual priestly ministry before Yahweh.

5. The Davidic covenant is of course the covenant of kingship and dynasty. The heir of David will one day sit upon the throne of Israel in Jerusalem, and His reign will encompass the whole world (Isa. 11:1-10; Jer. 23:5).

6. Finally, the New covenant is the great covenant of salvation and restoration. Promised both to Israel (Jer. 31:31-34; Isa. 59:20-21) and to the nations (Isa. 49:8; 1 Cor. 11:25).

The unilateral covenants (i.e., Noahic, Abrahamic, Priestly, Davidic, and New) are incontrovertible and inviolate.

The Covenants Interlink with Each Other, Particularly in the Prophets

There are several passages in the OT where we see the various divine covenants drawn together in a group. The clearest passages where this phenomenon is found are in Jeremiah 33:14-33 and Ezekiel 37:21-28. It makes sense that covenants integrate since God's program is coherent. The key covenant that makes this system come together is the New covenant. Ezekiel is a good example. We see the New covenant introduced in Ezekiel 36:25-27, which is universally acknowledged as a New covenant text. Chapter 37 begins with the vision of the valley of dry bones (Ezek. 37:1-14), followed by the illustration of the two sticks (Ezek. 37:15-20).

Then comes the prophecy about Israel in the future Kingdom (Ezek. 37:21-28). The land aspect of the Abrahamic covenant is mentioned in Ezekiel 37:21c, the Davidic covenant is in Ezekiel 37:22, 26. The cleansing of the New covenant comes in at Ezekiel 37:23 (cf. Ezek. 36:25), and finally, the Priestly covenant is to be inferred from Ezekiel 37:26-28. But the covenant that brings it all together is the New covenant.

The Covenants with Noah, Abraham, Phinehas, and David do not Contain the Means of Their Own Fulfillment

I want to redouble your attention to this startling fact: *As they stand,* not one of these divine covenants—especially the Abrahamic, Priestly, and Davidic—can be fulfilled entirely![9] The reason the New covenant is the one that brings the other unconditional covenants[10] together is that it is the covenant of reconciliation. As I have stated repeatedly, the Noahic, Abrahamic, Priestly, and Davidic covenants do not contain promises of reconciliation with Yahweh in them. While it is true to say that, for example, Genesis 22:18 hints at the coming Christ through whom blessing would come upon the nations, the how (redemption and substitution) was never addressed. The same is true for the Davidic covenant, which, like the Abrahamic covenant, is often featured in the NT. Each of them must link up with the New covenant so that the element of salvation is provided to them, leading to their literal fulfillment. Even though Christ has obvious associations with the Abrahamic and Davidic covenants, He does so in the predictive sense but not in the deeper sense of instigator.

The New Covenant is very closely connected to the Person and Redemptive Work of Messiah

As the person of the Coming Ruler is gradually revealed in the OT, it becomes clear that not only will He reign over Israel and the nations, but as Yahweh's Servant, He will also sacrifice Himself for them. In doing this the Messiah will be made "a covenant for the people" (Isa. 42:6; 49:8). This work of the Servant (Isa. 52:13-53:12) identifies Him with the New covenant. The New covenant deals with the sin problem, and the sacrificial blood of Jesus Christ is the blood of the New covenant. There is no other New covenant sacrifice.

9 Not even the Noahic covenant, which comprehends the created sphere, is immune from "non-fulfillment" in the sense that the world is fallen and cursed.

10 Let us remind ourselves that a- post- and historic premillennial interpreters all argue against the terms "unconditional" and "unilateral." In relation to the way these interpreters treat the divine covenants this is understandable because all of them believe these covenants are amenable to hermeneutical and prophetic transformation; what earlier proponents would simply call spiritualization. They make this claim because they say the covenants have both conditional and unconditional elements to them. That is true. And it is also largely irrelevant. This is because these scholars neglect to isolate and study the specific *oaths* of these covenants. Once that is done, it becomes evident that the covenants involving Noah, Abraham, Phinehas, and David are unconditional, as is the New covenant.

The Combined Witness of the Law and the Prophets Creates an Inescapable Expectation Grounded in the Oaths of God

Crucial for an accurate understanding of the Creation Project and for the biblical theology of the OT is that we take seriously the powerful note of expectation that the oaths of God produced in the faithful. A godly Israelite in, say, the 6th century B.C. would place his faith in the promises of Yahweh as gradually revealed in the Scriptures of Israel up until his time. There is zero evidence that he would indulge in typology and spiritualization. He would believe what God said. That is what biblical faith is at its core. As David L. Baker observes:

The predominant emphasis of the promises in the prophetic books is the renewal of the people of God. The people will be brought back from exile to live again in the Promised Land (Jer. 16:14-15; 29:10; 32:42-44; Ezek. 20:42; 36; Amos 9:11-15), where they will experience peace and abundance (Jer. 31:10-14; Ezek. 34:25-31) and a renewed relationship with God (Jer. 31:31-34; Ezek. 16:62-63; 37:26-28; Hos. 2:16-23). God will pour his Spirit upon them (Isa. 32:15; 59:21; Ezek. 39:29; Hag. 2:4-5) and they will have a new heart and a new spirit (Jer. 24:7; Ezek. 36:25-27). The promise of descendants is barely mentioned in the prophetic books, except that the continuance of the Davidic dynasty is reinterpreted in terms of the coming messianic king (Jer. 23:5-6; 33:14-26; Ezek. 34:23-24; Mic. 5:2-4) who will bring about a new age of righteousness and justice (cf. Isa. 32:1; 42:1-3; Hos. 2:19).[11]

One thing a 6th century Israelite would not do is to take all the covenant oaths of Yahweh, reinterpret them, and redirect them to the Church. He would not do this because He would rationally believe that the expectations created by God's own oaths were unchangeable and immune from the tinkerings of typological interpretation.[12] It would be a completely irrational move for him to believe otherwise.

But he would not "expand" God's covenant oaths and redirect them away from national Israel and onto the mostly Gentile Church because he would know absolutely nothing about the Church. The Church is a post-Pentecost reality that he would be entirely ignorant about.

Biblical Covenantalism in Five Sentences

At this point it may help if I jot down what I believe to be the essence of my approach.

1. Covenants must be understood primarily by the oaths which bind those who make them.

11 David L. Baker, *Two Testaments, One Bible*, 207. See also G. R. Beasley-Murray, *Jesus and the Kingdom of God* (Grand Rapids: Eerdmans, 1986), 22.

12 Commenting on Hebrews 6:14 Block declares, "the author highlights the irrevocability of the promise by characterizing YHWH's purpose/determination (*boule*) as unchangeable (*ametathenos*, 6:17) and sealing the promise with an unchangeable oath" (Daniel I. Block, *Covenant: The Framework of God's Grand Plan of Redemption* (Grand Rapids: Baker, 2021), 454).

2. The covenants of God bind Him to His oaths, which means that if they are unilaterally sworn, they must come to pass precisely in accordance with the words that were used.

3. Since God only made covenants about major aspects of His Creation Project, nothing else in the Scriptures can circumscribe, resignify, or contradict the fixed oaths that He made.

4. Covenants are primarily hermeneutical in nature, which means a close study of them will yield a better understanding of the whole Story of the Bible and the future.

5. The Noahic, Abrahamic, Priestly, and Davidic covenants are unconditional as to their promises, and they are to be implemented on the basis of Jesus Christ's mission as the New covenant "Lamb of God" who acts as "a covenant to the people" to ensure the full realization of God's purposes.

I hasten to add that there is quite a bit more to it, but I would be satisfied if anyone studying my work were to start the dialogue with those five points. Biblical Covenantalism in this mode is, I believe, a more easily articulated and persuasive outlook when dealing with other theologies than is dispensationalism. This is because *the attention of everyone is turned toward covenant* and the correct biblical expression of God's covenant project.

3

THE TERMS OF THE NEW COVENANT AND ITS PARTIES

But now He has obtained a more excellent ministry, inasmuch as He is also Mediator of a better covenant, which was established on better promises. – Hebrews 8:6[1]

New Covenant Texts

It may be surprising to learn that in the many discussions of the New covenant it is not easy to come across a description of what it is the New covenant does! In some ways this is understandable because only Jeremiah 31:31 mentions "a new covenant." But the idea behind the New covenant is found in many OT passages. The main New covenant passages in the OT which I would identify are these: Deuteronomy 30:1-6; Hosea 2:14-23; Isaiah 32:15; 42:6; 49:8; 54:5, 10; 55:3; 66:19; Ezekiel 11:19-25; 16:60; 36:26-27; 37:24-26; Zechariah 8:7-8, 20-23; and Malachi 3:12.

In addition to these the New covenant is implied in places like Isaiah 2:2-4; 11:10; 27:9; 43:25; 52:13-53:12; 55:7; 59:21; 61:8; Jeremiah 24:7; 32:38-40; 33:8; 50:5, 20; Ezekiel 34:25; Amos 9:15; Micah 4:2; 7:18-20; Joel 2:28–3:8; Zephaniah 3:11-13; Zechariah 8:8; 12:6-14, and Malachi 1:11.

Isaiah 42:6 and 49:8 are of great importance because they directly concern Jesus Christ. He it is who will be made "as a covenant" of salvation for both Israel and the Gentiles.

The texts above all have in common themes of heart (or land) transformation. It is Yahweh Himself (through the Spirit) who will cause this renewal. The passages

1 Notice it says Christ "is" (*esti* - present indicative) the Mediator, not "will be" (*esomai* - future tense) the Mediator.

envisage a complete restoration of sinful humanity (usually but not always Israel) to God. Hence, at its core the New covenant is the salvation covenant.[2]

There are other texts in the OT that might be identified with the New covenant, particularly in the Psalms (e.g., Psa. 96:11-13), but these are sufficient. In an excellent presentation, Dave Fredrickson cites many of the same texts, though sometimes expanding the contexts, including Deuteronomy 30:1-6; Isaiah 32:9-20; 59:15b-21; Jeremiah 32:36-44; Ezekiel 16:53-63; 36:22-38; 37:21-28; Joel 2:28–3:8; and Zechariah 8:1-17; 12:6-14.[3]

I think there are more passages that Fredricksen should have included (are we ready to say that Isaiah 53 does not pertain to the New covenant?). But what his selection highlights is the aspect of spiritual renewal and cleansing, with the Spirit's role prominent in several places.[4] If, as Fredrickson and most other scholars agree, Isaiah 42 and 49 are New covenant passages, then we find there are clear statements that Christ's redemptive work includes the Gentiles (Isa. 42:1, 6; 49:6-8; 52:15).

J. Dwight Pentecost agrees with the above passages (minus Deut. 30, which he links to the "Palestinian" or Land covenant) and adds Isaiah 55:3; 61:8; Hosea 2:18-20; Micah 7:18-20; and Zechariah 9:10.[5] Three of those passages allude to Christ. Let's just take a quick look at some of the passages.

The end of Ezekiel 16, particularly verses 60-63, is identified by Fredrickson and Pentecost as a New covenant passage. The prophet says: "And I will establish My covenant with you. Then you shall know that I am the LORD, that you may remember and be ashamed, and never open your mouth anymore because of your shame, when I provide you an atonement for all you have done, says the Lord GOD" (Ezek. 16:62-63).

The central promise in this prophecy of a future regathering of Israel is the promise of atonement.[6] None of the other covenants of God promise atonement. But this does match the New covenant promise in Jeremiah 31:34.

If we next look at Isaiah 32, what do we find? It begins with a messianic prediction: "Behold, a king will reign in righteousness, And princes will rule with justice" (Isa. 32:1).

---

2 Pettegrew groups the provisions of the New covenant into 1. Transformation through a new heart, 2. God's consummation of His relationship with Israel, 3. Physical and material blessings on Israel, 4. The permanent indwelling of the Spirit, and 5. The law inside the believer. (Larry D. Pettegrew, *The New Covenant Ministry of the Holy Spirit* [The Woodlands, TX: Kress, 2013], 29-31). When Romans 8:18-23 is considered alongside of point 3 above we see that the restoration of creation (e.g., Amos 9:11-15; Isa. 11:6-9) depends upon the completed salvation of God's people.

3 Dave Fredrickson, "Which Are the New Covenant Passages in the Old Testament?" in *Dispensational Understanding of the New Covenant*, ed. Mike Stallard (Schaumburg, IL: Regular Baptist Books, 2012), 63. Note, I will be interacting below with two longer essays by Beacham and Decker. These were edited for inclusion in Stallard's book.

4 The abundant physical blessings often associated with the New covenant are the outcome of God's redemption.

5 J. Dwight Pentecost, *Thy Kingdom Come: Tracing God's Kingdom Program and Covenant Promises Throughout History* (Grand Rapids: Kregel, 1995), 164-172.

6 In the context the regathering occurs prior to the covenant.

The final verses of the chapter speak of the coming of the Holy Spirit affecting men and nature, emphasizing the ubiquity of righteousness (Isa. 32:15f. Cf. Hos. 2:18-20). There is no mention of "covenant" in Isaiah 32 (and I'll throw Zech. 12 in here as well), so what marks it out as a New covenant chapter? The answer is the work of righteousness wrought by the Holy Spirit.

These elements (viz. the Spirit and salvific righteousness) are even more clearly displayed in Isaiah 59:16-21, whose final verse reads:

> "As for Me," says the LORD, "this is My covenant with them: My Spirit who is upon you, and My words which I have put in your mouth, shall not depart from your mouth, nor from the mouth of your descendants, nor from the mouth of your descendants' descendants," says the LORD, "from this time and forevermore" (Isa. 59:21).

There will come a time when the elect of Israel will be given a "Spirit-covenant" which will enable them to think and speak (and act) God's words. This covenant brings radical change of heart and mind[7] leading to complete transformation of body and soul. It brings, in other words, full salvation.

The New Covenant is all about Salvation

The New covenant is all about salvation and righteous standing with God through the renewing work of the Spirit. The Spirit is not always mentioned, but it is clear from several passages that He is the Agent of transformation. Think about the author of Hebrews' argument about Christ's New covenant work: "Not with the blood of goats and calves, but with His own blood He entered the Most Holy Place once for all, having obtained eternal redemption" (Heb. 9:12; cf. Heb. 10:15-18).

Then tie this in with what is said in Hebrews 10:29 about the one who counts "the blood of the [New] covenant...a common thing" and has thereby "insulted the Spirit of grace"! The blood and the Spirit are the essential aspects of the New covenant.

Redemption in all its aspects—salvation, the provision of righteousness by the imparting of a new nature by the Spirit, and the fruitful consequences of it all—that is what the New covenant is about.[8] Therefore, it seems to me that one cannot simply restrict one's understanding of this covenant to the salvation of Israel without introducing some preformed theology into the interpretation. This seems especially true for several important reasons which will need exploring. If there are passages that refer to God's salvation reaching out to the Gentiles, and the New covenant is all about salvation, are we prepared to teach that the Gentiles will be saved by another means than the one God used for Israel? Consider Isaiah 56:6-8:

---

7 Both the Hebrew term (*leb*) and the Greek word (*kardia*) describe the inner man, not just the emotional aspects.

8 See Bruce A. Ware, "The New Covenant and the People(s) of God," in *Dispensationalism, Israel and the Church: A Search for Definition*, ed. Craig A. Blaising and Darrell L. Bock (Grand Rapids: Zondervan, 1992), esp., 73-83.

Also the sons of the foreigner
Who join themselves to the LORD, to serve Him,
And to love the name of the LORD, to be His servants—
Everyone who keeps from defiling the Sabbath,
And holds fast My covenant—Even them I will bring to My holy mountain,
And make them joyful in My house of prayer.
Their burnt offerings and their sacrifices
Will be accepted on My altar;
For My house shall be called a house of prayer for all nations.
The Lord GOD, who gathers the outcasts of Israel, says,
"Yet I will gather to him
Others besides those who are gathered to him."

These words seem to me to prove the inclusion of the Gentile nations in the New covenant.[9] If Israel is God's chosen vessel to witness to the nations (e.g., Zech. 8:13, 22-23; Mic. 4:2; cf. Gen. 12:3) it seems logical that in testifying about Messiah they will speak of His New covenant work in them. If there are passages designated by all parties within dispensationalism as New covenant passages which refer to the Gentiles, how can some claim the Gentiles not be included in the New covenant? Ponder these prophecies:

The LORD has made bare His holy arm
In the eyes of all the nations;
And all the ends of the earth shall see
The salvation of our God.
So shall He sprinkle many nations.

Kings shall shut their mouths at Him;
For what had not been told them they shall see,
And what they had not heard they shall consider.

These come from Isaiah 52:10 and 15. Verse 15 comes within the great prophecy about the Suffering Servant that we usually locate in Isaiah 53, but which actually starts in Isaiah 52:13. This appears to bring this famous passage within the list of New covenant texts. If a person is going to restrict the New covenant to Israel on the basis of Jeremiah 31 and Ezekiel 36, he is going to have to untangle these kinds of verses. I am persuaded that a plain-sense hermeneutic matched with a right understanding of progressive revelation leads inevitably to affirming full participation of saved Gentiles in the New covenant.[10]

9 I do not believe the Bible indicates what Pettegrew calls "trickle down blessings" for the Gentiles, but rather full-on participation (Pettegrew, *The New Covenant Ministry of the Holy Spirit*, 32).

10 Let me make it clear that this does not mean Israel's national promises are shared with the Gentiles. The New covenant only ensures fulfillment of God's other unilateral covenants on those designated by God in those covenants.

God set the world in motion, permitting the Fall and the devastation that it has brought in its wake. He made covenants with man (post-Flood). These covenants are signposts and promises to the better world that He still intends to bring about. Again, the first five of those covenants are:

> 1. The Noahic covenant establishes this post-flood world in perpetuity until the New Heavens and New Earth are made.
>
> 2. The Abrahamic covenant ensures that the descendants of Abraham, Isaac, and Jacob[11] will always be a people before God, and that they will inherit a land (I tend to include the "Land covenant" here). It also makes provision for God's blessing to be spread among the other nations of the world through Israel.
>
> 3. The Priestly covenant promises the descendants of Phinehas (who would be the Zadokites) that they would be granted an everlasting priesthood.
>
> 4. The Davidic covenant promises that an heir of David will always sit upon his throne in Jerusalem.
>
> 5. The bilateral Mosaic covenant binds Israel to God in a theocratic relationship based on obedience. Its ties to the Abrahamic covenant mean that even when Israel reneges on their oath, Yahweh can bless them eschatologically.

We may grant that each of these covenants has elements that can be explored further, but for my purpose the descriptions above will do.

As they stand, their full realization is impossible. Granted, blessing has come to the nations in the Person of Christ, an Israelite, through the Abrahamic covenant, but it has not come to them *as nations*. Furthermore, Israel is not in right relationship to God. The dynasty of David in Israel is absent a king, and nobody can claim that the pledge to Phinehas (however difficult it may be to comprehend) is being fulfilled, or ever has been fulfilled. Yes, there will be no more global floods upon the earth. But when all is said and done, if these five covenants are all God makes, there can be no transition to the New Creation from this sin-cursed old one.

Within all these great covenants and their gracious promises there is nothing that can bring them to completion. They have no provision for salvation built into them. They stand as impotent in themselves as any prognostication from any false prophet in history. Why so? What is the problem? The problem is and always has been "Sin!" Sin gets in the way. Sin prevents the realization of God's program for Creation. "Every man at his best state is altogether vanity" (Psa. 39:5 KJV), which cashes out as "every sinner admitted into God's Kingdom would poison it." Let me be blunt. God simply cannot fulfill His wonderful promises on a bunch of rebellious reprobates like us!

11 When the Bible groups Abraham, Isaac and Jacob together it is talking about ethnic Israel, not the Church.

So how does God deal with sin? The answer is through His beloved Son, Jesus Christ, and faith in Him. Good! Redemption is only through Christ. Jesus Christ is the means of salvation for sinners whereby sinners become saints. I might add here that the salvation of those saints who died before Christ is also wrought by or through Him, even if the content of their faith was not in the crucified Nazarene.[12]

The New Covenant Deals with Sin

But there is a snag here. The New covenant is particularly concerned with the question of sin and salvation. God can't write his instruction on any mind and heart that has not first been changed (cf. Jer. 31:33; Ezek. 36:26-27; 2 Cor. 3:3-6). Left to ourselves we will not believe (Isa. 53:1). God will have to save men if He is to sanctify them (cf. Jer. 31:34). If the reader will study the New covenant texts provided at the beginning of this chapter, he will see that sin is almost always the problem that the covenant addresses. This is where Christ comes in. We must ask what connection Christ's sacrifice has to the covenants above. Is Calvary connected at all to a divine covenant? And since Christ has come and made the way of salvation plain, what is the hold-up? Why aren't the unilateral covenants of God playing out now just as Yahweh promised? I believe the answer is that the New covenant still awaits its fulfillment regarding the nation of Israel. In a future day the sins of the remnant of Israel will be cleansed through the New covenant.

Think upon these verses which are usually identified with the New covenant:

> "The Redeemer will come to Zion,
> And to those who turn from transgression in Jacob,"
> Says the LORD.
>
> "As for Me," says the LORD, "this is My covenant with them: My Spirit who is upon you, and My words which I have put in your mouth, shall not depart from your mouth, nor from the mouth of your descendants, nor from the mouth of your descendants' descendants," says the LORD, "from this time and forevermore" (Isa. 59:20-21).

They are aimed at Israel, just as Jeremiah 31. And the covenant mentioned in Isaiah 59:21 has close affinities with Jeremiah 31:31-34. The wording is different, but the sentiment is the same. In Isaiah, the Spirit is promised exactly as He is in the accepted New covenant passages of Isaiah 32:15, Ezekiel 36:26-28, Joel 2:28ff., and Zechariah 12:10. Notice again that the covenant relates humans to God's Spirit, which also coincides with the arrival of the Redeemer to turn away transgression in Jacob. According to Paul, this passage awaits fulfillment (Isa. 59:20-21 is quoted in Rom. 11:26), so it

12 In John 8:56 the Lord says, "Your father Abraham rejoiced to see My day, and he saw it and was glad." But Abraham did not know about the Romans, nor about crucifixion. He knew that the Promised One would one day come. For more on this issue, see John S. Feinberg, "Salvation in the Old Testament," in *Tradition and Testament: Essays in Honor of Charles Lee Feinberg* (Chicago: Moody Press, 1981), 39-77.

cannot be fulfilled at the first advent. The great promises of the other covenants are being held up, as it were, until the second advent. They depend upon it. The other covenants will be triggered when Israel receives the New covenant and mourns for its rejection of their Messiah (Zech. 12:10).

An Initial Compilation

Sticking with Isaiah 59, if we gather together the various elements of this passage and the work of Christ that I have been discussing, this is what we get:

1. Israel as a nation needs to be saved.
2. Without Israel's salvation the other divine covenants cannot go into full effect.
3. Salvation is wrought by Jesus Christ alone.
4. In order to receive Christ's salvation, one must believe in Him.
5. Believers receive the Holy Spirit.
6. When Israel's sins are redeemed, they receive the Spirit and are changed.
7. Christ's salvation is connected with a covenant (e.g. Isa. 59:20-21).
8. The salvation of Israel is connected to the New covenant (Jer. 31:31-34).

Whatever the connection between Jesus Christ and the New covenant is, there is a great deal of overlap. Christ's work is covenantal. But aren't these passages for Israel? Yes, but we are not finished.

Isaiah 42 and Matthew 12

We need to remind ourselves of what Isaiah has said in chapters 42 and 49, both of which concern Christ as "the Servant" of Yahweh. Matthew applies Isaiah 42:1-3 to Jesus.

> That it might be fulfilled which was spoken by Isaiah the prophet, saying:
>
> "Behold! My Servant whom I have chosen,
> My Beloved in whom My soul is well pleased!
> I will put My Spirit upon Him,
> And He will declare justice to the Gentiles,
>
> A bruised reed He will not break,
> And smoking flax He will not quench,
> Till He sends forth justice to victory;
> And in His name Gentiles will trust" (Matt. 12:17-18, 20-21).

Matthew adds, "And in His name Gentiles will trust," which is not in the passage, at least directly. Yet it is what Isaiah is teaching. If we continue with Isaiah for a few more verses this becomes clear:

> "He will not fail nor be discouraged,
> Till He has established justice in the earth;
> And the coastlands shall wait for His law."
>
> Thus says God the LORD,
> Who created the heavens and stretched them out,
> Who spread forth the earth and that which comes from it,
> Who gives breath to the people on it,
> And spirit to those who walk on it:
>
> "I, the LORD, have called You in righteousness,
> And will hold Your hand;
> I will keep You and give You as a covenant to the people,
> As a light to the Gentiles" (Isa. 42:4-6).

The "coastlands" of verse 4 is almost certainly not the coast of Israel. The term refers to habitable land, to islands and land masses. The "earth" (*'eretz*) can and does refer to Israel, but not here. Its repetition in verse 5, where it is set in opposition to the heavens, together with the mention of the "peoples" (*'am*), means that the context demands that the whole earth is being spoken of; and this provides the way for the explicit promise to the Gentiles in Isaiah 42:6. Matthew sees this and summarizes it with "And in His name Gentiles will trust."

The verses are about Jesus Christ. And they are about salvation being brought to the Gentiles. Furthermore, they are about Christ being trusted by the Gentiles. And they are about Christ being called "a covenant."[13]

Which covenant could Christ be?

The Terms of the New Covenant Are About Christ

I am saying that the content of what is to be believed in order to be included in the New covenant is Jesus Christ Himself! His Person and work form the faith-content of the oath.

But can a person be a covenant? Some scholars object to the idea. But why not, so long as faith in that *person* is the essential faith-ingredient of covenant? We are to believe in Jesus, not in a set of propositions separate from Him.

This is why Paul can refer to his calling as being one of "ministers of the new covenant, not of the letter but of the Spirit" (2 Cor. 3:6). If we examine 2 Corinthians 3,[14]

13 When Isaiah 42:6 (49:8) says "I will give You as a covenant to the people" it is not saying that Christ will be like a covenant; it is not a simile. It is better to read it as an identification. It is like saying, "This knife can be used as a can-opener" or "I will give my van as a moving truck." The knife is the can-opener, and the van is the moving vehicle. The NET Bible (1st ed., www.bible.org, 2005) renders the place in question "I protect you and make you a covenant mediator for the people." The word for "mediator" does not appear in the text. The reason the NET Bible gives for this is that "A person cannot literally be a covenant" (n. 15). We know of course that Jesus is "the Mediator of the New Covenant" (Heb. 9:15).

14 I shall have a lot to say about 2 Corinthians 3 in this book.

we come across language remarkably close to the New covenant language of Deuteronomy 30:4-5 and Isaiah 59:21, and especially Jeremiah 31:33 and Ezekiel 36:26-27. Paul writes to the believers at Corinth without missing a beat: "Clearly you are an epistle of Christ, ministered by us, written not with ink but by the Spirit of the living God, not on tablets of stone but on tablets of flesh, that is, of the heart" (2 Cor. 3:3).

Then the Apostle anticipates the argument of Hebrews when he contrasts the difference in access to God between the Mosaic covenant and the New covenant ministry of the Spirit, which he is commissioned to preach! (2 Cor. 3:7-18).

In Deuteronomy 30:4-5, we get the earliest example of a promise of inner transformation of a sinful people resulting in divine acceptance and blessing. This involves a change of heart and an obedient walk; indeed a "circumcision of the heart." We are reminded of Paul's words in Colossians 2:11-14, especially verse 11, "In Him you were also circumcised with the circumcision made without hands, by putting off the body of the sins of the flesh, by the circumcision of Christ." Perhaps this is also what Paul is referring to in Philippians 3:3 when he declares, "We are the circumcision, who worship God in the Spirit"? He isn't claiming (contra N. T. Wright[15]) that the Church is now Israel in Christ, but that inclusion in the New covenant is necessary for all, Jew or Gentile, to be God's covenant people.[16]

Isn't this precisely what we see in Jeremiah 31:33, Isaiah 59:21 and Ezekiel 36:26-27? Deuteronomy 30 is a New covenant passage and is accepted as such by the majority of authorities.

Then there are many scriptures that portray the Gentiles as seeking the Lord and being saved. Isaiah 11:10 declares, "The Gentiles shall seek Him." Isaiah 60:3 says, "The Gentiles shall come to your light, and kings to the brightness of your rising" (cf. Jer. 16:19). Malachi 1:11 speaks of the same thing:

> For from the rising of the sun, even to its going down,
> My name shall be great among the Gentiles;
> In every place incense shall be offered to My name,
> And a pure offering;
> For My name shall be great among the nations,"
> Says the LORD of host.

When we recall the blessing of the Abrahamic covenant in Genesis 22:18, we should not be surprised by this. But wouldn't it be odd for these blessings to be part of one covenant (the Abrahamic), yet not be brought about through Jesus Christ, who is to be made another covenant (Isa. 42:6)? If "the iniquity of us all" was laid upon Him (Isa. 53:6), what kind of theological alchemy is it that claims that some of the blood

15 N. T. Wright, *The Climax of the Covenant: Christ and the Law in Pauline Theology* (Minneapolis: Fortress, 1993), 14. Wright is the foremost modern representative of those who assume that Christ is Israel "in person" and the Church is therefore Israel in Him. See Idem, *Paul and the Faithfulness of God* (Minneapolis: Fortress, 2013), 828-834.

16 This does not of course mean that God's covenant promises to Israel as a nation are null and void. His covenants cannot *be* null and void.

was New covenant blood only when it was applied to Israel, while the rest of it was just blood that wrought salvation for the rest of us?

I realize that my reasoning is open to proper interrogation, but it is sound. If God is Yahweh, the covenant God, and He is a God who makes covenants and steers history according to their course, and if He has designated His Son "a covenant to the people...a light to the Gentiles" (Isa. 42:6), why is it surprising to discover that the blood that redeems us is covenant blood?

It is through the blood of Jesus that everything is reconciled to God (i.e., atoned for). That is why I have taught that the New covenant provides the means for the other divine covenants to be fulfilled to the letter—those covenants dictate God's program for this world.

Psalm 2:8 tells us that the nations will be given to Christ as an "inheritance." We can hardly think that the majority will remain in defiance and unbelief. In fact, Psalm 22:27 distinctly says that:

> All the ends of the world
> Shall remember and turn to the LORD,
> And all the families of the nations
> Shall worship before You.

Jeremiah foretells a time when:

> And you shall swear, "The LORD lives,"
> In truth, in judgment, and in righteousness;
> The nations shall bless themselves in Him,
> And in Him they shall glory (Jer. 4:2).

The nations will turn to "Yahweh is Salvation"—to Jesus. They will glory in King Jesus. They will be bought by His blood.

Citing Isaiah 19, Michael Vlach demonstrates how, "The people of God concept expands to include Gentiles alongside Israel who also exists as the people of God."[17] Vlach takes care to distinguish the national identities of Israel and the other nations, but he has no hesitation in calling Christians "New Covenant Christians" later in his book.[18] And no wonder, since we are also numbered as God's people (cf. Acts 15:14).

In summary, I believe it is proper to claim that Christ is a covenant. There is a stream of connections flowing out of this claim:

1. Christ's blood is the blood of the New covenant.

2. The New covenant is the only covenant that addresses salvation.

3. Paul uses salvation terminology derived from OT New covenant passages and applies them to the Church.

---

17 Michael J. Vlach, *He Will Reign Forever: A biblical Theology of the Kingdom of God* (Silverton, OR: Lampion, 2017), 164.
18 Ibid., 461.

4. He claims to be doing New covenant ministry while reminding the Church that the Lord's Supper celebrates Christ's "blood of the New covenant."

The arguments, some quite explicit, some circumstantial, are stacking up to show that Christians are indeed made parties to the New covenant. This could never have been revealed in the OT if what most dispensationalists (rightly) affirm to be the case is true: that the Church is not mentioned there. But there is provision for the blessing to enter through the Abrahamic promise to the nations. That provision allows for a progressive revelation of the New covenant through the Gospel by the Apostolic proclamation of the death and resurrection of Jesus Christ, "the Lamb of God who takes away the sin of the world" (Jn. 1:29).

Gentiles and Their Connection to the New Covenant

The relation of the Church/Gentiles to the New covenant has proven to be a thorny issue for dispensationalists. Since the only explicit New covenant text (in Jeremiah 31:31-34 and repeated in Hebrews 8) identifies Israel and Judah as parties to the New covenant with God, the contention is that the Church is associated with the New covenant in a less direct way, or perhaps not connected at all! We are confronted with a list of possibilities. Michael Vlach listed "Six Views on New Covenant Fulfillment" which I shall employ:[19]

1. The New covenant will be fulfilled in the future with national Israel; the Church has no relationship to the New covenant (some classical dispensationalists).

2. There are two New covenants—one with Israel and another for the Church (some traditional dispensationalists including John Walvoord).

3. The New covenant is completely fulfilled with the Church; there is no future fulfillment with national Israel (covenant theology and some non-dispensational systems).

4. The New covenant will be fulfilled with Israel but the spiritual blessings of the covenant are applied to the Church today (some traditional and revised dispensationalists).

5. The New covenant will be fulfilled with Israel but the Church is an added referent to the New covenant promises so there is a sense in which the New covenant is being fulfilled with the Church. The New covenant has two referents—Israel and the Church (some revised dispensationalists; Paul Feinberg).

19 https://mikevlach.blogspot.com/2019/07/six-views-on-new-covenant-fulfillment.html. Accessed 8/15/23.

6. Since the New covenant was given to Israel for the purpose of also blessing Gentiles there is literal fulfillment of the spiritual blessings of the New Covenant to all believing Jews and Gentiles in this present age, while the physical/national promises await fulfillment with Jesus' second coming when national Israel is incorporated into the New covenant (some revised and most progressive dispensationalists).

I am not going to comment on Option 2 (two New covenants) other than to say it is not held by anyone today and always was a stretch. Neither am I going to say much about Option 3 (the New covenant is fulfilled in the Church) because being held by non-dispensationalists, it is irrelevant to my current objective, and this whole work is an argument against it.

Looking now at Option 4 (the Church gets the "spiritual blessings" of the New covenant), I have to ask, "What are these spiritual blessings?" Is the answer salvation? And does stating this mean the New covenant is mainly about physical blessings upon Israel? But those "physical" matters are taken up in the other covenants with Israel.[20] Let us remind ourselves of what Jeremiah 31 promises:

> But this is the covenant that I will make with the house of Israel after those days, says the LORD: I will put My law in their minds, and write it on their hearts; and I will be their God, and they shall be My people.
>
> No more shall every man teach his neighbor, and every man his brother, saying, "Know the LORD," for they all shall know Me, from the least of them to the greatest of them, says the LORD. For I will forgive their iniquity, and their sin I will remember no more (Jer. 31:33-34).

This is not a promise of land or throne or great productivity. It is the promise of redemption. The New covenant is about redemption! When redemption is mixed with the other covenants what you get is the coming Kingdom of God on earth—literally fulfilled in line with those covenants. I will come back to Option 4.

Is the New Covenant Made Strictly with Future Israel?

Focusing on Option 1 (the Church has no part in the New covenant), I want to interact with a piece by Roy Beacham, who wrote a paper entitled "The Church Has No Legal Relationship to or Participation in the New Covenant," which he presented under a different title at the Council for Dispensational Hermeneutics (CDH) conference in 2009.[21] I think there are several problems with his thesis as well as its central concern.

---

20 Blessings such as are recorded in Hosea 2:18, 21-22 and Amos 9:13 come about strictly speaking as a result of Christ's presence in the earth and may be seen as the earth's response to the coming of its King and the resurrection of the saints. The "covenant" of Hosea 2:18 may be seen as the New covenant's beneficial influence on the Noahic covenant, since that covenant was also made with the earth and its creatures.

21 This was published with changes as Roy E. Beacham, "The Church Has No Legal Relationship to or Participation in the New Covenant," in *Dispensational Understanding of the New*

Biblical Covenants Were Not "Legal Contracts"

Beacham seeks first to correct what he thinks are two misconceptions. First, that the New covenant should be studied as a contract or treaty, not primarily as a promise. He thinks the New covenant must be understood against the Ancient Near Eastern (ANE) background. Secondly, he believes the New covenant should not be understood as being primarily soteriological (spiritual) but as physical in its coverage.[22]

In the first place, it is simply incongruous to parallel ANE covenants with those in the Bible, particularly those that God made.[23] This is what Beacham does. We must also remember that covenants between God and men were metaphorical, although certainly not unreal.[24] Further, it is wrong to claim that biblical covenants were contracts and that, therefore, they were primarily legal in nature. They were not. As for the first point, several scholars have warned about equating the covenants of Scripture with those of the ANE.[25] To be fair, Beacham himself does note that John Walton is (surprisingly) against his view that covenants in the Bible are to be understood against the background of the legal practices of the ANE.[26]

As for the second assertion, the trouble is that even the Land or Royal Grant and Suzerain-Vassal Treaties of *certain parts* of the ANE were not like our contracts.[27] Referring to the New covenant, Jakob Jocz observed:

> It is easy to misunderstand the situation if we take the concept of covenant in the legal sense to mean a juridical contract whereby God binds Himself constitutionally... The covenant is not a legal document by which God finds Himself committed... The covenant is the highest expression of His determination to be our God.[28]

Covenant, ed. Mike Stallard (Schaumburg, IL: Regular Baptist Books, 2012), 107-144. I shall be interacting with his lengthier article of the same name at the CDH website: https://dispensationalcouncil.org/wp-content/uploads/2018/07/09_Roy_Beacham_ANE-Covenants-and-NC.pdf. I shall refer to it as "Website article" below.

22 Beacham, Website article, 1-2.

23 The very first covenant we know about is the Noahic covenant in Genesis 9. Yahweh did not follow the conventions of the day, and His covenants (which are unique Divine-human covenants) should be interpreted within the confines of scriptural revelation.

24 See Richard Averbeck's chapter in *Israel, the Church, and the Middle East: A Biblical Response to the Current Conflict*, ed. Darrell L. Bock and Mitch Glaser (Grand Rapids: Kregel, 2018), esp. 24-25. Cf. George E. Mendenhall and Gary A. Herion, "Covenant," in *The Anchor Bible Dictionary*, ed. David Noel Freedman, Volume 1 (New York: Doubleday, 1992), 1201.

25 For example, Charles H. H. Scobie, *The Ways of Our God: An Approach to Biblical Theology* (Grand Rapids: Eerdmans, 2003), 475.

26 Beacham, Website article, 6 n. 6.

27 See also Ralph Smith, "The Covenantal Structure of the Bible," 7, https://www.berith.org/pdf/The-Covenantal-Structure-of-the-Bible.pdf. Smith points out that "A contact is a limited commitment, continuing only so long as the mutual benefit continues. The covenant is not a contractual type of relationship, limited by the mutual benefit of the parties involved." This is not to endorse Smith's reading of the covenants.

28 Jakob Jocz, *The Covenant: A Theology of Human Destiny* (Grand Rapids: Eerdmans, 1968), 240-241.

Covenants were not legally binding in the sense that there was some high court that could be appealed to.[29] They are not to be subsumed under the category of law.[30] Rather, they were sworn oaths, sometimes to a deity and sometimes to one another. Furthermore, they were often (not always) *imposed* by the more powerful party. In more garden-variety situations, they were solemn oaths made between friends, or even enemies, with no judicial aspect at all. More tellingly, divine covenants between Yahweh and men could not be judicial. God cannot be held to a standard outside of Himself.[31] Hence, the covenants of God are grace-based rather than legal-based.[32] There is no contradiction here. Although the Law of Moses includes commandments (as does "the law of Christ," Gal. 6:2), this does not equate to a legal code.

This puts Beacham's thesis in trouble. If one looks at the covenant between Abraham and Abimelech in Genesis 21, it is clear that it is based upon the culture of honor and shame. Jonathan's covenant with David in 1 Samuel 20:11-16 is in private before the Lord. It cannot be said to be a legal procedure. In neither instance was there a written document![33]

The New Covenant is Not Grounded in Any "Legal" Text of Scripture

Beacham claims that "A better understanding of ANE covenants effects [sp] a better understanding of biblical covenants. Ignorance of the one leads to misunderstanding of the other."[34] I have shown, albeit briefly, that this is not the case. Further on in the document he has an important footnote[35] where he argues (against Rod Decker) that:

> The New Covenant is not just a promise or prophecy which might find broad, unspecified application or fulfillment; it is a legal instrument. Every covenant, as a legal instrument, specifically includes the name of all contracting parties and any incidental participants in the instrument. By specifically including

29 It is permissible to claim the "Book of the covenant" in Exodus 20–24 as reflecting certain legal customs of the day. See Daniel I. Block, *Covenant*, 161-164. Even so, Block states that "this is not law in the in the modern Western sense of legislation but a document composed to create a worldview and to serve a pedagogical purpose" (Ibid., 164).

30 This is even true of the Mosaic covenant. E.g., "Nothing could be more basic to a proper understanding of the Mosaic era. It is not law that is preeminent, but covenant. Whatever concept of law may be advanced, it must remain at all times subservient to the broader concept of the covenant" (O. Palmer Robertson, *The Christ of the Covenants* [Phillipsburg, NJ: P&R, 1980], 171). Hence, covenant *may* include law, but covenant does not equate to law. See also, Thomas Edward McComiskey, *The Covenants of Promise: A Theology of the Old Testament Covenants* (Grand Rapids: Baker, 1985), 72.

31 When one comes to God's covenants it is impossible to bind God legally. To attempt to do so would be to place a law above God. God's covenants are based solely on God's own character.

32 John Murray, *The Covenant of Grace* (Phillipsburg: NJ, P&R, 1953), 31. Law and grace are opposed to each other.

33 Something more akin to a legal agreement is found in Ruth 4:1-14 where Boaz becomes the kinsman-redeemer before witnesses. But no covenant was sworn.

34 Beacham, Website article, 16.

35 Ibid., 16 n. 56.

> the names of all parties and participants in the instrument, all others are excluded.[36]

He goes on to assert (in response to Decker) that the legal status of the New covenant necessitates that it only be with the named party, viz., "the house of Israel and with the house of Judah" (Jer. 31:31/Heb. 8:8). But this requires him in this instance to treat Jeremiah 31 (and Ezek. 36) as formally solidified covenants, which they are not. Neither are they once-for-all contracts. They are prophecies of a *future* covenant which Yahweh will make! The fact that Israel and Judah are named in an OT context does not prevent God from naming other parties, especially since the covenant has not yet been made.

I have shown above that Gentiles are included in New covenant texts like Isaiah 42:6 (which commentators generally note stresses the nations and which Matthew 12 emphasizes). Furthermore, Paul uses the same language of spiritual heart transformation and circumcision for the Church as is found in New Covenant passages in the OT (cf. Deut. 30:4-5; Ezek. 36:26-27 with 2 Cor. 3:3 and Col. 2:11).

Confusing the Function of the Separate Divine Covenants

Beacham refers to Ezekiel 36:22-39 as a New covenant passage and picks out the provisions of the New covenant as he understands them.[37] But I believe that much of Beacham's argument relies on investing the provisions of the New covenant with more than they actually contain. He separates many items that are essentially wrapped up in redemption but adds a few material blessings. This is common enough among dispensationalists, and I believe it is a harmful error. For example, he includes the land promise and restored abundance among the New covenant terms. But the land promise is part of the Abrahamic covenant, and the restoration of blessings stems from the theocratic promises in the Mosaic covenant, which is brought over into the New covenant because of Israel's obedience. Further, since mankind is connected with the ground from which he was created, theologically speaking, it ought to go without saying that a righteous humanity will see its reflection as it were, in the renewal of the ground (Gen. 2:7; 3:9). Great productivity is a blessing of the original creation.[38] In saying this, I want to make it clear that I do not hold that the New covenant supersedes the other unconditional covenants![39]

Many dispensationalists fail to see that the route to literal fulfillment of the covenants with Abraham, Phinehas, and David is through the inner spiritual transformation of the New covenant. There would be no reason to include the physical and political blessings in those covenants within the provisions of the New covenant itself.

---

36 Ibid., 18.

37 Ibid., 20-21.

38 Basically, all the other 'provisions' which Beacham sees in Ezek. 36 are a result of the inner work of the Spirit!

39 "The New Covenant is never thus set over against the Abrahamic and Davidic covenants, as if they needed to be replaced by something better" (Alva J. McClain, *The Greatness of the Kingdom* [Grand Rapids: Zondervan, 1959], 157).

In fact, what that would do is make the other covenants of God essentially void. God's covenants run in an orderly stream and are realized by their eventual connection with the New covenant; who is, as we have shown and will show again, Christ Himself.

Let me continue with two more quotes from Beacham. He states:

> The soteriological benefits that Israel experiences at the ratification of the New Covenant are not exclusive either to Israel or to the New Covenant. Many people, throughout human history, have experienced spiritual blessings like those promised to Israel under the New Covenant. Their spiritual experience, however, neither originates in the New Covenant, nor places them under the New Covenant. Salvation is trans-historical and offered to all who believe. The New Covenant is eschatological and offered to Israel alone.[40]

Every system has to account for the salvation of sinners before Christ, and who would disagree with the sentiment that "Salvation is trans-historical and offered to all who believe"? The issue is concentrated on the form that salvation takes. Beacham holds that "The New Covenant is eschatological and offered to Israel alone." He states:

> God's promise that all Israel will be saved at the ratification of the New Covenant does not make the New Covenant God's eternal covenant of salvation with the church or with all of mankind, the elect, or anyone else. *Salvation is judicially grounded in the person and work of Christ, not the New Covenant.*[41]

Salvation certainly is judicially grounded[42] in Christ, but on what basis?[43] The usual answer is "the blood of Christ." But according to Christ Himself, His blood is "My blood of the new covenant" (Matt. 26:28). You cannot separate the blood of Christ from the New covenant.

Beacham avers that "Salvation is judicially grounded in the person and work of Christ, not the New Covenant." We see here that he distinguishes Christ *from* the New covenant, in his case because he believes that covenants (including the New covenant), are legal agreements. But such a separation between Christ and the New covenant does not exist (cf. Isa. 42:6; 49:8).

Reading 1 Corinthians 11

Before moving on to Options 4, 5 and 6, which are developed along a continuum, I want to notice how Beacham deals with the "New covenant" passages in 1 Corinthians 11. In short, he claims that Paul thinks that when Jesus spoke the words about the New covenant in His blood He made a distinction between Israel and the Gentiles/

40 Ibid., 22.
41 Ibid., n. 66 (my emphasis).
42 Please note that the words "legal" and "judicial" are not synonyms.
43 Salvation is "judicial" in the sense that it depends upon the judgment of God, not an external standard.

Church.[44] But the normal way to understand Paul would be to view these texts as new revelation about the New covenant. Beacham writes:

To assert that participation in the blood of the New Covenant must, of necessity, mean participation in the New Covenant itself is fallacious. The assertion is a fallacy of identification because the—blood of the covenant is not the covenant itself. At best, the blood (as associated with the cup) only represents the covenant; it does not constitute the covenant.[45]

The blood is not the covenant itself, but the blood *is* all New covenant blood. There is none available for another purpose. When Moses doused the people with the blood of the Sinai covenant in Exodus 24 that made them parties to the covenant. Similarly, when sinners of any age are saved through the shed blood of Christ by being "sprinkled" with it, they become participants in the covenant that the blood represents.[46]

Beacham believes that the New covenant has not been ratified,[47] and that it is even now purely eschatological. Therefore, he believes that in 1 Corinthians 11:25, although referring to the New covenant, the apostle *is not actually concerned with it*, but rather with the Lord's Supper as a memorial. At best this makes Paul look sloppy. If the New covenant is only for future Israel, why would he refer to it when teaching Gentiles? And why would he not qualify his meaning? To my mind, those who hold that the New covenant is not made with the Church are far less clear on these questions than the apostle to the Gentiles appears to be.[48] When one takes the OT texts, which include Gentiles in the New covenant, and combines them with the NT texts, it begins to look like those men who deny the New covenant to all but Israel have a theological agenda playing in the background.

Participants But Not Parties?

Option 4 says that the Church benefits from the application of the spiritual blessings of the New covenant. It participates in it but is not a legal party to it. This position allows for a more generous, inclusive interpretation of Luke 22, 1 Corinthians 11, and 2 Corinthians 3. Further, it can deal with the central passage in Hebrews 7–10, although perhaps without pressing its implications far enough. In this view, Jesus instigates the New covenant at the Lord's Supper with His disciples. Being Jews, the disciples must be included as parties to the New covenant.

---

44 Roy Beacham, Website Article, 42.

45 Ibid.

46 There is no obstacle to those who were under the old covenant being brought under the New covenant. The Mosaic covenant was not everlasting and so those who died under it would have to be brought into relation to Christ in the New covenant. Otherwise, millions of Jewish saints would not be under any covenant! In my opinion, every saint from whatever period and whatever nation will participate as New covenant parties in the coming Kingdom of God. In short, no New covenant participation, no Christ, and if we don't have Christ we don't enter eternity.

47 Roy Beacham, Website Article, 43-44.

48 I could have missed it, but I could not find an interpretation of 2 Corinthians 3 in Beacham's article.

Problems start to arise, however, because the disciples become the foundation of the Church, with Christ as the cornerstone (Eph. 2:20; 1 Cor. 3:11). Yet Option 4 does not allow the Church to be a party to the New covenant. Hence, in this view we still have the "schizophrenic" intention behind Calvary. We also have dissonance in the ministry of Paul and his teaching. Consider the words of institution of the Lord's Supper, which Paul quotes and which seem unequivocal:

> For I received from the Lord that which I also delivered to you: that the Lord Jesus on the same night in which He was betrayed took bread; and when He had given thanks, He broke it and said, "Take, eat; this is My body which is broken for you; do this in remembrance of Me." In the same manner He also took the cup after supper, saying, "This cup is the new covenant in My blood. This do, as often as you drink it, in remembrance of Me." For as often as you eat this bread and drink this cup, you proclaim the Lord's death till He comes (1 Cor. 11:23-26).

By saying "as often as you drink it" (i.e., "this cup"), Paul is referring the Corinthian Christians to "the New covenant in My blood" that was mentioned immediately before. I cannot comprehend how an apostle claiming to be a minister of the New covenant, and who teaches Gentile Christians to partake of the token of the New covenant, could consistently hold that those same Christians were not parties to that covenant.

When discussing the argument of the Epistle to the Hebrews, Rodney Decker, in a brilliantly argued paper, summarizes with these words::

> It is not, in my opinion, possible to postulate two new covenants without doing violence to the unified, four-chapter argument of Heb 7–10. Nor is it possible to divorce Christians from some relationship to the new covenant so described. Perhaps there is more than one way to explain this relationship, but related we must be if the evidence of Hebrews 7–10 is given due weight. We are not only related to Jesus as our high priest, but the text seems to demand that we are directly related to the new covenant itself for it is on this basis that we draw near to God. To conclude otherwise, if I may say so, is to intrude a predetermined system into the text before we allow the text to speak for itself.[49]

Decker subscribes broadly to Option 4. But his own premises indicate that he has not come to the most accurate conclusion. I think this is because, like Beacham, he held to the essentially legal nature of the New covenant. One wonders how Jesus could be our High Priest if we are not parties to the covenant He mediates.

There is always more to say, but that sets me up for what, to my mind, are the two most plausible options.

49 Rodney J. Decker, "The Law, the New Covenant, and the Christian: Studies in Hebrews 7–10," 29. https://dispensationalcouncil.org/wp-content/uploads/2019/03/09_Rod_Decker_The-Law_The_New_Covenant_and_the_Christian_Studies-in-Hebrews-7-10.pdf.

The Church is Included in the New Covenant

So we turn to the last two options in Vlach's list:

> 5. The New covenant will be fulfilled with Israel but the Church is an added referent to the New covenant promises so there is a sense in which the New covenant is being fulfilled with the Church. The New covenant has two referents—Israel and the Church (some revised dispensationalists; Paul Feinberg).
>
> 6. Since the New covenant was given to Israel for the purpose of also blessing Gentiles there is literal fulfillment of the spiritual blessings of the New Covenant to all believing Jews and Gentiles in this present age, while the physical/national promises await fulfillment with Jesus' second coming when national Israel is incorporated into the New covenant (some revised and most progressive dispensationalists).

I have stated that, in my opinion, it is a mistake to view the New covenant as entailing physical promises.[50] Those are contained in the other covenants, but they require "releasing," especially at the mass conversion of Israel at the second advent (e.g., Isa. 66:8). The New covenant, therefore, is the salvific conduit through which the other covenants mix as they pass through it to their literal fulfillment. Hence, I agree with Option 6, apart from the inclusion of the word "physical."

Having taken out the physical element, I think one can argue that the difference between Option 5 and Option 6 is semantic. Asked to phrase Option 6 another way, it is easy to imagine someone coming up with something that sounds like Option 5. In summary, the New covenant is given to Israel (although they will not enter into its provisions as a nation until Christ returns), but since "salvation is of the Jews" (Jn. 4:22), the Church becomes an added referent to the New covenant in Christ's blood.

The Apostle Paul as a Minister of Confusion or Clarity?

I have already said that to understand Paul's mention of "the new covenant in My blood" in 1 Corinthians 11:25 as anything less than a clear indication that the Gentile Christians were seen by him as parties to the New covenant when they took "the cup," makes him a pretty shabby communicator. The same can be said about 2 Corinthians 3:6: "Who also made us sufficient as ministers of the new covenant, not of the letter but of the Spirit; for the letter kills, but the Spirit gives life."

The word rendered "ministers" (*diakonos*) is used in verse 3 (and throughout the chapter). For example: "Clearly you are an epistle of Christ, ministered by us, written not with ink but by the Spirit of the living God, not on tablets of stone but on tablets of flesh, that is, of the heart" (2 Cor. 3:3).

50 Although I don't much care to split hairs about this. If others see physical elements in the New covenant, that is fine by me. I only insist that all these are associated with the redemptive and restorative work of Christ.

Some have argued that all Paul is doing in 2 Corinthians 3:6 is drawing a rough parallel. The argument is that "ministers of the new covenant" (*diakonous kainēs diathēkēs*) does not mean that Paul and his companions are *actually* ministering the New covenant, only that their ministry *resembles* the future New covenant dispensation. I struggle a bit here. For the New covenant work of the Spirit at the second advent is a complete work resulting in complete obedience (e.g., Deut. 30:6; Ezek. 36:25-27; Zeph. 3:13), which is quite unlike what we experience today. Still, if Paul is drawing a parallel, one has to ask in interrogative tones, "Why even mention such a thing?" How is the argument helped by dropping a "by the way, our ministry is sort of like what the New covenant ministry will be like" in verse 6? Why make a comparison of covenants here at all? The apostle could just have talked about the old covenant and had done with it.

It surely looks like Paul views "the ministry of the Spirit" (2 Cor. 3:8) as synonymous with his present work "as [a] minister of the new covenant, not of the letter but of the Spirit" two verses earlier. And even if the definite article is missing, so that it reads "a new covenant" instead of "the new covenant" in verse 6, how far does that take us? The contrast is between the Mosaic covenant and *some* covenant—a covenant involving the Spirit's gift of new life. Which covenant could that be? The Abrahamic, Priestly, and Davidic covenants do not include the Spirit's saving action in their terms. The answer that is staring us in the face is the New covenant![51] Then consider this text:

> That at that time you were without Christ, being aliens from the commonwealth of Israel and strangers from the covenants of promise, having no hope and without God in the world. But now in Christ Jesus you who once were far off have been brought near by the blood of Christ (Eph. 2:12-13).

The Gentiles in Corinth were "without God in the world." The blood of Jesus Christ brought them (and us) near to God. The text also includes us in the strand of the Abrahamic covenant reserved for Gentiles: "in you all the families of the earth shall be blessed" (Gen. 12:3; cf. Gal. 3:13-16).

But wait, Paul here speaks of "covenants" plural. Does he mean we are included in the Priestly Covenant with Phinehas (Num. 25)? Assuredly not. What about the covenant with David? Again no. The Abrahamic then? Yes, Gentiles receive blessing through the third aspect of that, but that is one covenant out of three. We need another covenant. And we have one: "This cup is the new covenant in My blood. This do, as often as you drink it, in remembrance of Me" (1 Cor. 11:25).

Salvation Prior to the New Covenant

Someone once put to me the following argument, which deserves an answer:

---

51 Scott J. Hafemann, "The Covenant Relationship," in *Central Themes in Biblical Theology: Mapping Unity and Diversity*, ed. Scott J. Hafemann and Paul R. House (Grand Rapids: Baker, 2007), 56.

> Both Noah and Abraham received the imputed righteousness of God *before* the promise of the New covenant was made, so their being redeemed was not dependent on the New covenant. And I see no reason to believe that the redemption of the believers in the Body of Christ is dependent on the New covenant since their redemption is also based on the imputed righteousness of God.

First, since no one merits salvation, righteousness must be imputed. If it is imputed, it must have its source somewhere in someone. That source is not in another person in Adam's lineage (cf. Psa. 49:7), but through the incarnate Son of God (Gal. 4:4-5; 1 Tim. 1:15). The only way for a sinner to be saved is by the merits of "the man Christ Jesus" (1 Tim. 2:5). Yes, Noah built a boat and Abraham believed what God said about his seed; but God reckoned their faith as righteousness *in view of the coming sacrifice of His Son* for mankind. Jesus is the Source of the sinner's righteousness.[52]

Now if sinners of every age are saved on the basis of Calvary, they must perforce be redeemed by the blood of Christ. Therefore, we must ascertain the relationship of the blood of Christ to the New covenant. We know Jesus said that His blood was the blood of the New covenant. So did Paul. The author of Hebrews spends more time talking about blood than anyone else in the NT. For example, he asks:

> For if the blood of bulls and goats and the ashes of a heifer, sprinkling the unclean, sanctifies for the purifying of the flesh, how much more shall the blood of Christ, who through the eternal Spirit offered Himself without spot to God, cleanse your conscience from dead works to serve the living God (Heb. 9:13-14)?

In Hebrews there is no doubt at all about what "the blood of Christ" signifies. Jesus "is also Mediator of a better covenant, which was established on better promises" (Heb. 8:6). And the "better covenant" that He mediates is the New covenant (Heb. 9:15)!

> Jesus the Mediator of the new covenant, and to the blood of sprinkling that speaks better things than that of Abel...Therefore Jesus also, that He might sanctify the people with His own blood, suffered outside the gate. Now may the God of peace who brought up our Lord Jesus from the dead, that great Shepherd of the sheep, through the blood of the everlasting covenant... (Heb. 12:24; 13:12, 20).

That being so, the assertion is that because Jesus Christ saves every saved person in any age, they are necessarily saved eschatologically through the New covenant. If that sounds anachronistic, it is perhaps because the New covenant is seen as an external thing rather than embodied in a Person. This understanding impacts the whole Christocentric orientation of the Scriptures. In this view, none are finally saved unless the blood of Christ is applied to them. And the Kingdom that they enter in the next age is a New covenant Kingdom.

---

52 This is how Job's testimony in Job 19:25, for example, is to be understood.

The Major Pillars of My Position on the New Covenant

After this survey of the questions about the terms of the New covenant and those who are party to it, I want to summarize my understanding briefly in twelve points. I humbly ask the reader to ponder each assertion:

1. Jeremiah 31 is not to be thought about as the definitive statement on the New covenant. There are many other passages which, although they don't name the covenant as the New covenant, are rightly considered as important OT New covenant passages (e.g. Deut. 30:1-6; Isa. 32:9-20; 42:1-7; 49:1-13; 52:10-53:12; 55:3; 59:15b-21; 61:8; Jer. 32:36-44; Ezek. 16:53-63; 36:22-38; 37:21-28; Hos. 2:18-20; Joel 2:28–3:8; Mic. 7:18-20; Zech. 9:10; 12:6-14).

2. None of the great theistic covenants of the Bible (i.e., the Noahic, Abrahamic, Mosaic, Priestly, Davidic covenants) have a provision of redemption set within them. That means they can never be fulfilled! Sin bars the way.

3. However, the problem of unfulfillment is overcome by Jesus Christ in the New covenant.[53]

4. Since it deals with sin and salvation to eternal life, the New covenant deals with the promise of the Holy Spirit.

5. Two key New covenant passages, Isaiah 42:1-6 and 49:1-8, speak both to Israel and to the nations. Isaiah 42:1-3 is quoted by Matthew 12:17-21 and is applied especially to "the Gentiles." Matthew might also have quoted Isaiah 11:10, 42:15, 60:3, Jeremiah 16:19, and Malachi 1:11.

6. Further, Isaiah 42 and 49 identify a person as a covenant who will bring salvation to both Israel and the Gentile nations. The New covenant is the "salvation covenant."

7. The Apostle Paul uses New covenant terminology and applies it to Christian redemption in Colossians 2:11-14 and Philippians 3:3.

8. Not only that, but Paul explicitly says that Christians taking the Lord's Supper are celebrating "the blood of the New Covenant" (1 Cor. 11:25). Paul also declares that his ministry is a ministry of the New Covenant in 2 Corinthians 3.

9. Jesus said that His blood was New covenant blood (e.g., Lk. 22). His disciples partook of the symbolism of it, and they formed the foundation of the Church (Eph. 2:20).

53 This does not mean that the New covenant supersedes the other covenants as is taught by O. Palmer Robertson, *The Christ of the Covenants*, 272.

10. Hebrews 7–10 names Jesus as our High Priest, which He can only be on the basis of the New covenant, since that is the only covenant He mediates as High Priest.

11. Jesus Christ and the New covenant are one. He is the covenant mentioned by Isaiah 42:6 and 49:8. As the Lamb of God (Jn. 1:29), He is the covenant "animal" that makes the New covenant with His own body and blood (Heb. 9:16-17). There is (and never was) any salvation outside of Him. Therefore, the New covenant should not be viewed as an agreement external to Him who made it.

12. We must beware of impeding our own understanding of God's Word by wandering away from Scripture to fragmentary pagan notions of treaty and covenant. We will be in poor shape to "hear" the Scripture if we fail to listen with both ears and to read with both eyes. This is all the more important when the matter under consideration is the oaths of God!

Summary of Part One

• When Yahweh binds Himself with an oath He must stick precisely to "the words of the covenant" that He swore to perform.

• The covenant oaths Yahweh made, which are clearly set out in Scripture, are not permitted to dictate the meaning and flow of the Bible's storyline in Covenant Theology, Progressive Covenantalism, Dispensationalism, and Progressive Dispensationalism. These systems often either overlay alternative covenants on top of God's covenants, reinterpret God's covenants, or downplay the status these covenants deserve.

• Since the first advent of Christ, the New covenant must be given pride of place as we read the NT. This is because Christ embodies the New covenant, and also because it is through Christ that the other unconditional covenants (viz., Abrahamic, Priestly, Davidic) will be fulfilled, and that literally.

• The first halves of the Four Gospels (the Synoptics particularly) form a stream of continuity with the expectations raised by the Hebrew Bible. Even as they progress, these Gospels do not abandon these covenantal connections. When we read Scripture, we must be aware of the prevailing and ongoing influence of God's covenants upon the Apostolic authors.

• Typology is the interpretative haunt of all approaches to biblical theology that emphasize "first-coming hermeneutics." From this mistaken impulse, typological interpretation takes center stage, not the grammatical meaning of God's words.

• Christians would do well to recall that God's actions follow His words in both Testaments. This would help them gain assurance from God's promises to them, and it would guide them in their reading of the Scriptures.

• Although He is closely associated with the Abrahamic and Davidic covenants through lineage, the Lord Jesus is in Himself the New covenant.

• Even though differences of opinion about the application of the New covenant exist, those positions which do not see the New covenant made with the Church fail to adequately account for the strong connection of the New covenant with the Person and the blood of Christ. These positions also must indulge in questionable exegesis of clear texts to avoid what the texts are declaring. This undermines the claim to be employing pain-sense or literal hermeneutics.

PART TWO: THE COMING OF THE COVENANT MESSIAH

4

THE UNPARALLELED SIGNIFICANCE OF THE SON OF GOD

That in all things God may be glorified through Jesus Christ,
to whom belong the glory and the dominion forever and ever.
Amen. – 1 Peter 4:11

The OT is replete with messianic prophecies. A sampling of the better-known messianic passages would include Genesis 49:8-10; Deuteronomy 18:15-19; Psalm 2:6-9; 110:1-4; Isaiah 9:6-7; 11:1-10; 52:13-53:12; 61:1-2; Jeremiah 23:5-6; Daniel 2:44-45; 7:13-14; 9:25-26; Micah 5:2; Zechariah 9:9-10; 11:12-13; and 12:10. There are many others, but from those listed above the student of Scripture can gain a good understanding of the coming King, God's Messiah.

Among the data concerning Messiah in these references is the stunning fact that He comes both to reign irresistibly and to suffer vicariously. This then involves not one coming but two. The crucial matter for theology is separating the prophetic teaching correctly between the two advents. If this is not done correctly, it will skew the interpretation not only of the two comings but also of the eschatological picture which the Bible presents.

The NT provides details of Messiah's first advent while filling out the picture of His second advent. Because He came two millennia ago, the temptation for us will be to focus more on the greater detail of the first advent and not so much on the second. While this is understandable, it is not always advisable. If due attention is not paid to the covenantal teaching of the OT, Christ will be seen as not only dying on a Roman cross, rising from the dead and ascending to His Father, but He will be seen as presently reigning over this wicked and fragmented world from heaven in such a hands-off way as to be a virtual no-show.[1] Our present evil world bears all the marks, not

1 This while the Bible directly tells us that Satan is "the god of this age" (1 Cor. 4:4).

of Christ's rule, but of the rule of the prince of the power of the air (Eph. 2:2). Good men may preach Jesus as King in the face of a world of evidence to the contrary. That will not be done here. It is no unbelieving impiety to declare the obvious! If we want to see the effects of Jesus' rule, we shall have to wait until He returns "in His own glory, and in His Father's, and of the holy angels" (Lk. 9:26).

The Absolute Uniqueness of Jesus Christ

The person of Jesus of Nazareth is unique and inimitable in all of human history. He is the Son of God. He is the Messiah, the great long-expected Figure of whom the whole OT speaks. Jesus is *the* human being among all other human beings; the One among the billions. He is peerless, above all comparison, too great in His humility, wisdom, and character to have any rival. His full significance in time has been apprehended by few men, if any, and it grows and will grow until finally the world will realize what God has achieved through Him. The story of stories is and will be about Jesus the Christ (Heb. 1:2)![2]

Now that the Messiah has come, and people have seen and heard Him and have been forever changed by Him and have written about Him, there is no going back to before His Incarnation and ministry. The bits and pieces that can be put together from the OT Scriptures have been filled out in the appearance of Christ on the world stage. We have the Four Gospels and Paul's epistles—those wonderful theological expositions of the meaning of His coming.

The world has been changed, although quite imperceptibly when compared with what the prophets spoke about. The first advent of the Son of God left in its wake our NT and a lot of unanswered questions. Where is the reign of justice and peace that was promised? Where is the Great King in Jerusalem? When will the untold and untellable number of sufferings and tragedies come to an end? When will the meek inherit the earth? When will the wolf lie down with the lamb? If we are not careful, we may be tempted to ask whether God has forgotten His covenant oaths.

As alluded to above, one answer that has always been popular among many believers is that the promises, at least the greater part, have been fulfilled already, but in quite unexpected ways. We must, we are told, all look to the cross and interpret the OT (and the NT) from there. We must see the spiritual implications of Calvary and understand what fulfillments were unleashed. Here, for instance, is how a recent work puts the matter:

2 We are not to think of "Christ" as being a surname. It signifies His messiahship. See, Greg Lanier, *Old Made New: A Guide to the New Testament Use of the Old Testament* (Wheaton, IL: Crossway, 2022), 83-99, also Eckhard J. Schnabel, *New Testament Theology* (Grand Rapids: Baker, 2024), 425. The standard work on this subject is Matthew Novenson, *Christ Among the Messiahs: Christ Language in Paul and Messiah Language in Ancient Judaism* (Oxford: Oxford University Press, 2012). Although I believe Novenson is quite right to stress "Christ" being an honorific, its root meaning "anointed" remains important. Cf. Larry W. Hurtado, *Lord Jesus Christ: Devotion to Jesus in Earliest Christianity* (Grand Rapids: Eerdmans, 2003), 98-101.

> The various components of the covenants reach their goal and end in Christ... As a result, the church of Jesus Christ—composed of both Jews and Gentiles—receives every spiritual blessing in the heavenly places through the Holy Spirit... Christ is the antitype of Israel, who fulfills Israel's identity, purpose, and mission such that in Christ the church inherits all the covenant blessings.[3]

That is how so-called progressive covenantalists perceive fulfillment. Many godly men from other camps agree with these words and have expressed similar sentiments. And yet, to the watching world (and to some within the Church), these "spiritual" answers look lame. This does not help Christianity's cause. The Church has often failed to convince the world that it really possesses anything of God. The spiritual and typological "fulfillment" of God's oaths and promises looks very human and hardly constitutes a ringing endorsement of the Christian claim for the inspiration of the Bible. Spiritualization and "unexpected fulfillments," which bear little or no verbal relation to the prophecies they supposedly fulfill, do not shout "God-breathed." The correspondence between God's words and God's actions, as demonstrated in the first volume, falls flat on its face if God does not mean what He says.[4] Many proclaim that the kingdom has come, but where is the Kingdom?

We are grateful for the retrievals of the Reformation, but the Reformation contained dross too (everything we do does). What the Reformers kept was the Augustinian supersessionist approach to biblical prophecy.

Jesus' words, "if it were not so I would have told you" (Jn. 14:2), set the standard, and the world needs to see that standard—God's standard—imposed upon God's creation. The covenants pointed to that. Spiritualization, transformation, extension, expansion, typologizing, or whatever else one wants to call it points away from it. That is why hermeneutics that contravene the plain sense of God's covenants has to be rejected, however worthy of our esteem its promoters are.[5] They interpret, as it were, from the inside, from within fallen and failing history. The covenants of God allow us to look from the outside, from the perspective of the larger Creation Project.

The approach I advocate takes the glorious reality of the Christ event, and lines it up with the covenantal expectation of the OT. One of the first things that must be done is to remember that the mission of Jesus is *one work in two phases*. We might call them the Isaiah 53 phase and the Isaiah 54 phase. The first concerns (mainly) the first coming; the second concerns the second coming. But it is one Christ with one object, the reconciliation of all things to God (cf. Col. 1:20). The road map is in the

3 Jason S. DeRouchie, Oren R. Martin, and Andrew David Naselli, *40 Questions about Biblical Theology* (Grand Rapids: Kregel, 2020), 67-68.

4 E.g., *The Words of the Covenant*, Vol. 1, 83-84. Examples are all over Scripture.

5 Despite their welcome focus on the covenants of Scripture, Peter J. Gentry and Stephen J. Wellum's *Kingdom through Covenant,* propagates the same old supersessionist revisions of those covenants based upon a first coming hermeneutic (e.g., 34, 40, 54, 86, 89, 92, 94, 95, 99, 100-101, 103-105, 107, 541, 553-554 etc.), forcing the covenants to "transform" (see 598, 608), with Israel's promises being fulfilled by the Church (e.g. 228, 243, 247, etc.). This is assuredly not an approach to the divine covenants that we can endorse.

covenants, and they must be followed, even when we think that they are in need of a little imaginative reinterpretation.

The Error of Holding Our Hermeneutic at the Cross

This introduces one of the most difficult matters, for because Christ has come and lived and spoken and died and left such an impression, it is hard not to keep our eyes there. It is difficult not to hold our hermeneutics at the cross and remain there doggedly, even perhaps when the voice of the OT is lost as a result. All this is compounded by the undeniable fact that our salvation hinges on what Jesus accomplished at His first coming. We are grounded in it and we must proclaim it. But our understanding of the Creation Project cannot be rooted at the cross and resurrection seeing it is but one half of Christ's mission.[6]

We must have the power of recall. There is a whole "Bible" written prior to the cross. It was the Bible of Jesus and of the Apostles. It yet speaks! It speaks covenantally. Those covenants are unchangeable and non-negotiable. They are as solid as the achievement of Calvary. In fact, they depend upon it! What an error it is then to undermine the work of the second coming with an incorrect and mislabeled "fulfillment theology" of the first coming. No, the Son of God will be given this world to rule over, not in some anemic spiritualized way that leaves creation in the chaotic thrall of "spiritual wickedness in high places" (Eph. 6:12 KJV), but in the fully realized sense of Psalm 2:8-9 and Isaiah 11:1-10.

Christ is at the Center of the Story[7]

As we contemplate the greatness of Jesus Christ, I want to situate Him right at the center of the Creation Project and God's covenant plan. To do that, a good place to begin is in Colossians 1:13-20:

> He has delivered us from the power of darkness and conveyed us into the kingdom of the Son of His love, in whom we have redemption through His blood, the forgiveness of sins. He is the image of the invisible God, the firstborn over all creation. For by Him all things were created that are in heaven and that are on earth, visible and invisible, whether thrones or dominions or principalities or powers. All things were created through Him and for Him. And He is before all things, and in Him all things consist. And He is the head of the body, the church, who is the beginning, the firstborn from the dead,

6 The cross and the resurrection provide the essential preconditions for the coming Kingdom of God and the glory that God will receive in that Kingdom. Before His crucifixion Jesus took the only oath that He ever swore at His first coming, and it concerned His second coming in power (Matt. 26:63-64). That is where we should look for the setting up of the Kingdom. Cf. Erich Sauer, *From Eternity to Eternity: An Outline of the Divine Purposes* (Grand Rapids, Eerdmans, 1954), 130.

7 For a superb treatment of the greatness of Jesus Christ with which I mostly agree see Richard C. Gamble, *The Whole Counsel of God: Volume 2, The Full Revelation of God* (Phillipsburg, NJ: P&R, 2018), 384-422.

> that in all things He may have the preeminence. For it pleased the Father that in Him all the fullness should dwell, and by Him to reconcile all things to Himself, by Him, whether things on earth or things in heaven, having made peace through the blood of His cross.

This passage does not feature the word "covenant," but its subject matter is distinctly covenantal. In the thirteenth verse, we are told that God, the Father, has "delivered us." The Father is the Deliverer and can be properly called the Savior (as in 1 Tim. 1:1; 4:10).[8] Notice next where the Father has "conveyed" us. It is "into" the Son's Kingdom. This Kingdom is viewed by Paul in the context as being both in some sense with us but also ahead of us.[9] It is, as they say, both "already" but "not yet."[10] The "already" part is our status as Spirit-indwelt "resident aliens" in this world. The "not yet" makes us look up and gain perspective from our futures instead of the present (as in Col. 3:1-2). Both parts are expressed well by John when he says: "Beloved, now we are children of God; and it has not yet been revealed what we shall be, but we know that when He is revealed, we shall be like Him, for we shall see Him as He is" (1 Jn. 3:2).

This is what makes us "strangers and pilgrims" (Heb. 11:13). We are "citizens of heaven" (Phil. 3:20), but not dwellers in heaven. I think this is the sense the apostle has in mind when he says we are conveyed into the Kingdom of the Son (Col. 1:13).

It is a mistake to conclude from Paul's words that we are presently *participating* in the Kingdom of God. We are in "this present evil world" (Gal. 1:4 cf. Phil. 2:15). The Kingdom of God does not impinge upon the kingdom of Satan like bleach in dirty water. Call us "pessimillennialists" all you want, but Church History will not validate claims that we are in God's Kingdom today. Nor will it validate such claims until Jesus returns (cf. Jn. 16:33; 1 Cor. 7:31; 2 Tim. 3:12-13; Tit. 2:11-13; Jam. 4:4; 1 Jn. 2:16).

In a similar way, we are said to have become "partakers of the inheritance of the saints in the light" (Col. 1:12), but we have not yet *received* the inheritance (Col. 3:24), which is the Kingdom (1 Cor. 15:50; 1 Thess. 2:12). For instance, when Paul says that Christians have been "delivered...from the power of darkness" (Col. 1:15), we must remember that the same apostle elsewhere encourages us to actively "cast off the works of darkness, and... put on the armor of light" (Rom. 13:15 cf. Eph. 5:8), and to "have no fellowship with the unfruitful works of darkness" (Eph. 5:11). At the same time, we are still subject to assault from the powers of darkness (Eph. 6:12). Paul is not saying we have entirely broken away from "darkness," but that we have changed sides, and are called to walk in the light (Eph. 5:8; Rom. 13:12; 1 Jn. 1:5-7). We have switched allegiance to God's Son and, in so doing, have become

8 Notice also that just as a human father requires a son or daughter in order to be a father, so God the Father requires a Son to be who He is. Therefore, we should understand that the doctrine of the eternal Sonship of Christ supports the doctrine of the eternal Fatherhood of God. God's "paternity" is part of his eternal function within the Trinity, so Christ's Sonship must be viewed as eternal in consequence. I don't say that is all one can point to in support of the eternal Sonship of Christ, just that this text assumes the doctrine.

9 Cf. the "inheritance" language of Col. 1:12 and the "reconciliation" language of Col. 1:19.

10 There is a lot of unhelpful talk about "already/not yet" interpretation. For some, it is a method of hermeneutics or a way of reinterpreting second coming prophecy to make it conform to the first coming. One is tempted to use synonyms, like "now" and "later."

eschatological people—hoping for the King and His Kingdom. The Spirit has come in the New covenant for believers,[11] so that we are represented in heaven while we are here on earth (Eph. 2:6), but the promised Kingdom has not arrived in any tangible form.[12]

Whether or not one accepts the reading "through His blood" in Colossians 1:14, it is plain enough in the context that the blood of Jesus secures our pardon and freedom (see Col. 1:20). By the preposition "*en*" ("*in* whom") Paul has in mind the "sphere" of Christ. Thus, to be "in Christ" is not only to be out of Adam (1 Cor. 15:22), but to be placed spiritually, not just in the Church, but also in union with Christ and placed among those objects that will comprise the culminating Kingdom. This "Kingdom" (Col. 1:13) makes up part of the whole reconciled reality, which the apostle goes on to speak about in Colossians 1:20. The Kingdom in this setting is the finally restored Cosmos when the reconciling of all things is achieved by and through the Son after the Millennium when the Son delivers up the world to the Father (cf. 1 Cor. 15:20-26; Psa. 2).

Even though Paul then enters into a description of the preeminence of Christ, it is important to tie Colossians 1:15 in with the previous two verses. We who are redeemed are a vital part of the ongoing work that the preeminent One is doing. Indeed, this fact, when understood in tandem with what comes next, is at the heart of Biblical Covenantalism. We are to see ourselves within the continuing Creation Project.

As "the image of the invisible God" (Col. 1:15), Jesus represents God in the physical universe in a unique way. We are "made in the image and likeness of God" (Gen. 1:26), but He is the Image! Hebrews 1:3 calls Him "the radiance of His [God's] glory and the exact representation of His nature or substance." Thus, we come to the miracle of the Incarnation. Not just with the event of it but with the significance of it. God became man (cf. 1 Tim. 3:16)[13] in the world He made for man (Jn. 1:10)! Marvelous!

Jesus Christ is the incarnate Son of God as King, Redeemer, Brother, and even Image *for us*! The entrance of God as man into the material realm—to walk in it, eat in it, suffer and die in it; and one day to reign in it—places a value upon the "natural world" and especially upon human beings, which lifts the biblical worldview head and shoulders above the failing systems of man. As Karl Barth never tired of pointing out, the humiliation of Christ is the exaltation of mankind.[14] Not in the corporate-universalistic terms envisaged by Barth, but in the representative sense of the Exalter of those who have faith.

A great deal might be said about the term "firstborn" in Colossians 1:15. Primarily it concerns the right of inheritance and prominence among brethren. As the examples of Isaac and Jacob and Judah and Solomon show, the first to be born is not the

11 No other covenant includes the gift of the Spirit. See the fuller discussion of this when we turn to Paul's theology.

12 I am not convinced that verses like Rom. 14:17 and 1 Cor. 4:20 prove we are in the Kingdom in a spiritual sense now.

13 This is the reading of the majority Byzantine text, present in the NKJV but not present in more recent translations. Older manuscripts read the relative pronoun "who" (*hos*) instead of "God" (*theos*).

14 This is not an endorsement of Barth, but he did see some truths clearer than others at times.

main idea in "firstborn."The primary idea involves status, not physical birth. Notice how this is true in Psalm 89:27, "I also shall make him My first-born, The highest of the kings of the earth." The verb translated "make" in the verse carries the idea of placing or constituting, but not generating. The psalm also portrays the promise to the firstborn as earning the very highest status among the "kings of the earth," further underlining this understanding of the word.

So it is here in Colossians. Some primordial creation of the Son, as per the Arian heresy, is not at all in the Apostle's mind. There is a time in Paul's thoughts, though not the time of the original creation, but rather that of the second creation heralded by the resurrection.[15] Colossians 1:13-15 also states that Christ the Son is "over all creation." We turn now to discuss the significance of this insight.

The World Depends on Christ for its Being Created and its Continued Existence

Importantly, all creation was made through Him (Col. 1:16). Jesus is the ever-living Word through Whom the Father spoke the world into being (Jn. 1:3; Heb. 1:2). All creation was also made *for* Him (Col. 1:16). Jesus is the One for Whom the Father made the world. This staggering fact calls us all to prayerful meditation. He made it "for Him." This world. You and I. Creation is a Gift from the Father to the Son. And while we may despise God's gifts, the Son does not. The created realm is valuable to Jesus first of all because it is His from God the Father! And it is for that reason He redeems it. Yes, and for that reason He will beautify it (cf. Rom. 8:20). This world will not be discarded like an old car when He comes, like some teach. It will be regenerated by the One who saved it. Jesus will be enthroned within it (Matt. 19:28). That is the only fit place for Him to be within it (cf. Lk. 1:33; Zech. 14:6; Rev. 19:16). As James Fergusson put it so quaintly, "The setting forth of his glory is a rent due by all creatures."[16] And there will come a day when it will be paid before Him in person in His creation.

All creation is held together by Him (Col. 1:17). Christ's Lordship over the elements of bread and water and life and death is a logical outcome of what Paul speaks of in this verse. Everything that is—that possesses being—whether it be visible or invisible (v. 16), exists providentially under His hand. The writer of Hebrews expresses a similar thought, "And He is the radiance of His [God's] glory and the exact representation of His nature, and upholds all things by the word of His power" (Heb. 1:3a).

Among the many similarities of thought between the two passages is that of the whole disposing of the history of the Cosmos devolves upon Christ. John Owen, in his magisterial exposition of Hebrews, writes:

15 Compare "the firstborn from [among] the dead" in Col. 1:18, where this is made clearer.

16 James Fergusson, *The Epistles of Paul to the Galatians, Ephesians, Philippians, Colossians and Thessalonians, & David Dickson, The Epistle to the Hebrews* (Edinburgh: The Banner of Truth, 1978), 337.

> And from these last words we learn:
>
> I. Our Lord Jesus Christ, as the Son of God, hath the weight of the whole creation upon his hand, and disposeth of it by his power and wisdom.
>
> II. Such is the nature and condition of the universe, that it could not subsist a moment, nor could anything in it act regularly unto its appointed end, without the continual supportment, guidance, influence, and disposal of the Son of God.[17]

It is this "by Him, for Him, subsisting because of Him" teaching that situates the Son unquestionably at the center of the unfolding revelation of God to men. It may be explored in several promising ways. We will briefly discuss three.

First, we can confidently study the earliest chapters of the Bible "Christologically," knowing that He will be found there. This is not the same as saying that Christ is in every verse, or that He is hidden behind every possibility of a "type." He can be "seen" without having to be placed here and there by over-eager theologians. The OT itself must determine how exactly Christ is there in the text. All that this NT teaching does is alert us to His necessary presence as God.

Second, the divine interest and investment in history as revealed in Scripture must be seen as purposive, and therefore, the redemption of the world accords with that larger purpose. As Owen reminds us, passages like these remind us that we must be reconciled to God through Jesus Christ.[18] There can be no other way!

But just here, we can, if we are not careful, become somewhat trite. We can slap our huge "Glory" poster over everything and step back and think we have said something profound, when, as a matter of fact, we have simply relabeled God's purpose without defining it. This can be seen in the many unsatisfactory treatments of God's glory, where it is made the decisive goal of everything that happens as if He depended on the outcome of history. But God is maximally glorious and needs nothing. His aseity means that He is independent. He displays His glory, but He does not need to seek it. If He did, He would become contingent upon the responses of His creatures. Therefore, I think it preferable to include the glory of God within the broader category of His Name. But more of this another time.

In the third place, we should not be surprised that this a "communicative" world (Psa. 19:1-4). It was formed by and for the Word! As I proceed, I shall have cause to return to this vital aspect of reality. I shall only say now that due to the Fall, our tendency, even as believers, is to reinterpret what God has communicated to us whenever it crosses our pious expectations.

17 John Owen, *Exposition of the Epistle to the Hebrews*, Vol. 3 (Edinburgh: Banner of Truth, 1991), 105.

18 Ibid., 99.

The World is Led into its Future Regeneration by Christ

As the providential upholder of the world that was given to Him, God's Son Jesus is ushering it to the desired end. One may be forgiven for not seeing this from our perspective, but that is what He tells us. And when we believe it, we start to see life differently. Hope enters in. "Even already a hidden tie connects this future resurrection-body with the resurrection life of the Redeemer."[19]

As N. T. Wright observes, "The worldview questions, when posed to the early Christians, elicit a set of resurrection-shaped answers."[20] The hope of "all creation" is entwined around the person and work of its Creator and Redeemer— more especially in connection with the resurrected Redeemer and His second coming. The basis of this hope is wrapped up in the sacrificial work at the cross which was accomplished at His first coming. However, as we shall see, the sacrifice and the hope—the first and second comings—are pulled together in conjunction with the New covenant in Christ. And the "trigger" for the New covenant is the resurrection and its astonishing declaration— "JUSTIFIED!"

The Total Dependence of the Created Order on Christ

Let us finish off the exposition of Colossians 1:13-20, which leads into a preamble involving the New covenant.

> And He is the head of the body, the church, who is the beginning, the firstborn from the dead, that in all things He may have the preeminence. For it pleased the Father that in Him all the fullness should dwell, and by Him to reconcile all things to Himself, by Him, whether things on earth or things in heaven, having made peace through the blood of His cross (Col. 1:18-20).

Paul uses the phrase "all things" repeatedly in this section (Col. 1:16, 17, 18, 19, 20), to illustrate the total dependence of the created order on Christ. The "fullness" (Col. 1:19) is understood by the translators of the NKJV as the fullness of God, and I agree. But in light of the immediate context, I would suggest that God as Creator of "all things" is especially in view. Thus, the Source of everything is its Sustainer and Owner and Redeemer (Col. 1:20a). Here is an enigma: that the One who was "despised and rejected" sustained the despisers and rejectors! What is more, the materiality of Christ—His becoming human so that His blood could be shed for humans (v. 20b), and His remaining human in resurrection so that man's original eminence among the creatures could persist—is seen as central to God's good pleasure. The passage proclaims a fabulous truth, the truth of a Christological World.[21]

Because Paul is writing to the Church, he naturally relates this stunning truth to the doctrine of the Church. Christ the preeminent One is "the head of the body." He

19 James Orr, *The Resurrection of Jesus* (London: Hodder and Stoughton, 1908), 287-288.
20 N. T. Wright, *The Resurrection of the Son of God* (Minneapolis: Fortress, 2003), 581.
21 See on this Carl F. H. Henry, *God, Revelation and Authority*, Vol. 3 (Wheaton: Crossway, 1999), 167.

relates to the Church analogous to how the head relates to the body. He is more than this. He saves, forms, and sanctifies the Church. He is foremost in the Church. He has "first-place" (Col. 1:18c) in it while not yet enjoying preeminence in the hearts of people outside the Church.

Although I have begun with Colossians, it would be a mistake to reduce Christ's glory to the Church. He bears a special relationship to the Church as its Bridegroom, but He bears a relationship to everything as its Creator. Hence, I am just now using this passage mainly to demonstrate the centrality of Christ to my understanding of the biblical story. That story cannot come to its desired close without "the blood of His cross." And mention of the blood leads us to "the New covenant *in [His] Blood*" (Lk. 22:20; 1 Cor. 11:25). Its function, its timing, and its fulfillment dictate how it all comes together.

Messiah, the Priest-King

It is clear enough that the priestly office of Christ was inaugurated at the cross (Heb. 9:11-12) and continues with His intercessory work on behalf of the saints (Heb. 4:14-16; 7:25). But Messiah is a King-Priest (cf. Zech. 6:12-13), just like His precursor (Heb. 7:1). These two functions can be seen in Psalm 110:1, 4. It is important to pay attention to the occasion when these two roles will be assumed. The NT makes it quite clear that Jesus is now functioning as our High Priest. As He is, like Melchizedek, a Priest-King who combines both roles, we must ask whether the two functions are coterminous.

> Thus says the LORD, "In a favorable time I have answered You, and in a day of salvation I have helped You; and I will keep You and give You for a covenant of the people, to restore the land, to make them inherit the desolate heritages" (Isa. 49:8).

This is a New covenant passage. But notice how Christ's covenant function includes restoration of the land.[22] This is not something that Christ has yet done. Even though it is clear that He is our great High Priest right now, I do not believe that Jesus is presently functioning in His kingly role. Please take note of these verses from the psalm which confers both roles on Messiah. Psalm 110:2-3 notes that, "The LORD will stretch forth Thy strong (a) scepter (b) from Zion, saying, (c) 'Rule in the midst of Thine enemies.' (d) Thy people will volunteer freely in (e) the day of Thy power..."

Let us link these phrases up with some of their appropriate textual cousins:

> (a) "scepter" (Gen. 49:10; Num. 24:17). Both references refer to a time on earth when Messiah wields the scepter of power.
>
> (b) "from Zion" (Psa. 2:6; Isa. 2:3; 51:1, 11; 52:6-7; 61:2-3; Mic. 4:7; Zeph. 3:14ff.; Zech. 8:3). Zion has a special place in Israel (Psa. 87:2). These and other passages connect the reign in Zion with the second advent.

22 This will be through the Abrahamic covenant coming into contact with the New covenant.

(c) "rule in the midst of your enemies" (Gen. 49:8; Zech. 14:16-19). Even after Christ has set up his earthly reign, there will be people who chafe under His rule. It is from these that Satan will gather an army after his release from the pit (Rev. 20:7-9).

(d) "Your people will volunteer freely" (lit. "will be freewill offerings," Jer. 32:40-41; Ezek. 36:24-28; Matt. 23:39). The "people" here is Israel (David would only be thinking in those terms), and their willingness relates to their being brought under the New covenant after accepting Jesus their Messiah (Zech. 12:10).

(e) "the day of Your power" (Matt. 24:30; 2 Thess. 1:9). When tied to the previous phrase, this indicates that the timing of the start of the reign of verses 2-3 is not the first but the second advent.

In addition to the above connections, Hebrews 10 explicitly has Jesus still "waiting" to fulfill Psalm 110:1: "But this Man, after He had offered one sacrifice for sins forever, sat down at the right hand of God, from that time <u>waiting till His enemies are made His footstool</u>" (Heb. 10:12-13).

In the context of Psalm 110, God's people (Israel) will offer themselves to the Lord when they know Him for Who He is—the King Messiah who comes from heaven (Dan. 7:13-14). He will rule from Jerusalem (Isa. 2:1-5; 11:1-10). He does not do that until He comes again (Heb. 9:28). I say, therefore, that although Jesus is now the High Priest after the order of Melchizedek, He is *not* yet reigning as a King.

I know Progressive Dispensationalists use Peter's words in Acts 2:30-36 to try to prove that Jesus assumed the throne of David right after the resurrection.[23] But in view of the above (plus Acts 3:19-21), it seems apparent that the second advent was in Peter's thoughts, thereby avoiding any requirement for spiritualizing the throne. Christ is not now sitting upon David's throne (Rev. 3:21), but He shall after He returns (Matt. 19:28). Jesus Christ is the only High Priest that there will ever be from the resurrection onward. All God's elect, be they within remnant Israel, the Church, or the redeemed nations, have (or will have) Christ as their High Priest. They will also have Christ as their King (cf. Dan. 2:35).

Barth saw the coming of Jesus from heaven to die on earth as His journey into a far country.[24] He wrung many high and noble thoughts out of the picture, but he got the picture wrong. Jesus went into a far country from earth back into heaven. It is crucial that we see things this way round. Our hope rests in His current intercession and imminent return to reign.. Jesus takes up His scepter upon His arrival back on earth, having received the Kingdom from the Father (cf. Lk. 19:11-27). And He brings with Him the restorative influence of His own resurrection.

23 See my exposition of that passage in the chapter on Acts below.
24 See particularly his *Church Dogmatics* IV!

Jesus and the Restitution of All Things[25]

Jesus is supremely an eschatological Figure. By "eschatological" I have in mind a broad definition, including God's plan in Christ, not just a message about end times. Eschatology is bound to teleology and should therefore be studied progressively.

Although the resurrection occurred in our space/time, it does not really "belong" in our history, but in our future history. It is the prefigurement of glory. It points to the future. The glorified body of the man Christ Jesus awaits the time of His return to bring to pass the "regeneration." This regeneration will see the twelve apostles seated on twelve thrones judging the twelve tribes of Israel (Matt. 19:28; Lk. 22:30). The need for judgment in the regenerated Kingdom is seen in many OT texts, like Isaiah 11 and Micah 4. The "regeneration" cannot be the New Heavens and Earth because no judging is required in that perfect Kingdom.[26] Scripture tells us that the earth is the locus of God's Kingdom work (Psa. 115:16), both in the Millennium (Psa. 2:6-10; Isa. 2:1-4; Matt. 19:28; Acts 3:19-21; Rev. 20:4-6), and in the New Heavens and New Earth (Rev. 21:1-22:5). The future is this-worldly. To put it in the words of Mark Saucy:

> Like Eden, the prophets' vision for human flourishing is fully resourced by God's own gracious provision in a new covenant relationship and a Spirit-anointed servant leader. For humanity under the new covenant, a new heart dominated by God's own spirit grants the spiritual platform necessary to both follow the Servant and together prosecute the task of culture-making that converts the nations into a worldwide theocracy displaying the perfections of the living God.[27]

The Logic of Resurrection

As I said above, the resurrection of Jesus Christ does not really "belong" in this age. It is out of place, an anachronism. When the atheist assures us that people do not rise from the dead, we have to agree with him. They don't. At least in general. Of course, if they assert it as some scientific law, we will beg to differ because one Man did rise from the dead (Acts 17:3; 26:23). Jesus is risen (1 Cor. 15:20)! But what a strange

25 This section homes in on the subject of worldview and might be seen as something of a digression. But I wanted to include it because of its ties to the consummation of the covenants.

26 For an excellent treatment of the this-world implications of the Kingdom, see Michael J. Vlach, *The New Creation Model: A Paradigm for Discovering God's Restoration Purposes from Creation to New Creation* (Cary, NC, Theological Studies Press, 2023), 71-112. This book marks an advancement in dispensational biblical theology. See also Steven L. James, *New Creation Eschatology and the Land: A Survey of Contemporary Approaches* (Eugene, OR: Wipf & Stock, 2017).

27 Mark R. Saucy, "One Nation under God: Does the World Need an Israelite Theocracy?" in *The Future Restoration of Israel: A Response to Supercessionism*, eds. Stanley E. Porter and Alan E. Kurschner (Eugene, OR: Pickwick, 2023), 133-134. In a footnote, Saucy writes, "A new enablement for the source of life, the heart, is where most scholars place the locus of the new covenant's novum" (Ibid., n. 40). This is a top-notch essay about the important theme of nationhood and "landedness" in the Bible.

declaration! Amid the countless human beings who have come and gone upon the stage of history, only One has had His physical body resurrected. This singular event, which occurred very many years before we were born, is the anchor of our Christian hope. Without it, as Paul says, "we are of all people the most pitiable" (1 Cor. 15:19).

Contrary to some points of view, the uniqueness of an event does not invalidate its credibility. In the strictest sense, every event, or at the very least many events, are unique because they often include elements that are not repeated in similar events. Just so, as there is only one Savior of the world, and all restoration hope is tied to Him, one would not expect another to be resurrected independently of His resurrection or, indeed, independently of God's timetable. The Christian story is predicated upon such a simple logic.

But the resurrection does not merely fit nicely inside the Christian story as a necessary article of faith. It actually fits within a necessary world and life view. I might say it is pivotal to any accurate world and life view. This is not to say that the resurrection is recognized for what it is in the world, any more than Christ Himself is accorded the recognition that is His due. It is to say that the explanatory value of the empty tomb, at the level of the big questions of life, is immense. Indeed, it is essential.

This earth is cursed and will stay cursed (Gen. 3:17). God's curse on the material realm cannot be ameliorated. Notwithstanding, the resurrection of Christ does counter its affects. Resurrection is from death. And since it is Christ's resurrection, it is a New covenant reality, activated by His blood.

It follows from this that the resurrection of Jesus only makes sense in a cursed world. Its necessity and powerful counterinfluence are only needed in *this* world, a world where covenants guide the way forward. No resurrection is necessary in the New Creation. While it is true that the resurrected body must go into the New Creation, the New Heavens and Earth are maximally physical, as well as maximally spiritual. Thus, God does not need a reason to create another pure physical realm to replace the present cursed one other than the fact that He has to do away with what He had cursed. In continuity with that, no covenants are required in a curse-less world.

Could God make a new material realm by fiat and create glorified bodies for the saved souls of the saints in conjunction with that new realm without the requirement of resurrection? Conceivably yes, but then there could be no place for the resurrection. The logic of resurrection requires a state of physical imperfection, which is renovated or restored by its *connection* to resurrection and the resurrection's connection with the New Creation.

It could also be shown that any proper acknowledgement of Jesus as Lord and Christ brings with it a corresponding acceptance of His bodily exaltation to heavenly glory. And it is just this fact that makes the resurrection a sort of glorious anachronism, since, in this world, our bodies return to dust.

Because He is Risen

Jesus is the only Savior of sinners because He Himself is without sin (Heb. 4:15). Moreover, to no other man could divine attributes be predicated. It is these attributes of full deity that qualified Jesus to bring sinful mankind to God (1 Tim. 2:5; Rom. 9:5). But bringing mankind to God must include God's original intention for man and woman. Nothing can be left out. Human beings were created to combine spiritual and physical qualities in a unique way and, in so doing, to reflect the spiritual and material realms of creation within the image they had been given. But the material was cursed, and death has wrought its dismal effects upon our physical frames.

As I write this I look out at a great many various changing shades of green in the leaves, the grass, and the surrounding hills. But for all its splendor, I look at bearers of the curse with which God struck the ground for Adam's sake. Created from that earth, his body was doomed to fall back into it until the time the material creation was ready to be restored. That event will itself be triggered by the physical glorification of the Church (Rom. 8:18-23), when the Savior comes for it at or near the end of this "present evil age" (Gal. 1:4). But the transformation of believing humanity and the re-pristination of our environment in the Millennium does not have its source in a mere decision to act from the Throne of Glory. It finds its source in the historical fact of the empty tomb and the declaration: "He is not here but is risen" (Lk. 24:6)! And because He is risen, we shall rise (1 Cor. 15:52), and this earth shall be lavished with peace (Isa. 55:12). And its languishing beauty, so rarely glimpsed as its Creator wanted it to be seen, shall show through under the hand of the covenant King who reigns from Jerusalem (Psa. 50:2; 90:17).

Is this an Easter meditation? Not a bit of it. It is a thought to fill every waking hour. The solitariness of the third day points to this future and fills the present with a strong expectation of eventual change.

Finally, think also of the unusualness of Christ's resurrection. A glorious person with no defilement and unlimited authority walked for a short time in our cruel world, and His eating, drinking, teaching, and coming and going are part and parcel of *our* history. We all sense that this world is not what it should be.[28] Perhaps the force of this "should" is what makes it hard sometimes to think of a benevolent Creator over it all? The tension between how the earth ought to be and what it all too often is a tension sometimes portrayed in art (e.g., Brueghel; Watteau) and music (e.g., Mahler) —where the spoiler is always lurking and can get in the way of our sight of God.[29] In this world the Lord of the future world rose in all His essential glory. Nothing of this age enters the age to come unchanged or untouched by the New covenant, because nothing fits into the age to come unless it is associated with the covenants and the Resurrected One who was made "as a covenant" (Isa. 49:8) —the One who in His present state goes into that age unchanged, yet changes all else.

The Movement from Israel to the Church in the Life of Jesus

One area where the emergence of doctrine must be carefully observed is in the life of Jesus, recorded in the Gospels and the overspill of that life in the earliest chapters of the book of Acts.

28 No one sounded this note better than C. S. Lewis in numerous works.

29 It does not get in the way of God's sight of us.

In the Gospels, the Synoptics especially, the onus is on Israel and its Messiah. The annunciation chapters in Matthew and Luke are borne out of the cumulative expectations created by the Prophets. The fact that a messenger from heaven reinforces that expectation must not be glossed over by a hasty reading of the early chapters from the perspective of the Church.[30] This is true also of places such as the kingdom parables in Matthew 13, the Olivet Discourse in Matthew 24 (Mark 13), and the teaching in Luke 19, 21, and Acts 1 through 3. Even though it heavily depends upon Christ's cross-work, the book of Hebrews might also be profitably interpreted within the same general atmosphere as these important chapters in the Gospels.

The doctrines of the Church are compressed within a very small timeframe. It should not be assumed, therefore, that the last book of the Bible deals with only that short timeframe and the revelation it contains. Since Revelation alludes to the OT more than the other NT book (although Hebrews quotes the OT more), it seems reasonable to think that it falls into line with those OT books and the expectations raised in them.

The upshot of this is that when considering things like the covenantal outlook highlighted in the OT and bringing it alongside the chronological compression of data in the NT,[31] one should not carelessly use the latter to snuff out the expectations that were accumulated over many centuries by the various writers of the OT. Because the Jews were always going to reject their Messiah and the Church was always going to come into being does not mean that the one is replaced by the other. It just means that the dynamic involved in the separating of the two advents must always be kept in mind as the NT is read.

Christ Representing but not Displacing Israel

Those believers who insist upon saying that the covenants of God as represented in Genesis 15 (Psa. 105:6-11), Numbers 25 (Psa. 106:28-31), and 2 Samuel 7 (Psa. 89) have been fulfilled in Jesus Christ do so because they have been operating under the thrall of a powerful deductive system constructed out of theological covenants that have been tethered to the cross. One of their guiding assumptions is that Jesus is the "true Israel,"[32] and Israel's covenants are fulfilled in Him through the Church.[33] As

30 While it is true that the four Gospels were written in the early Church era, this does not mean that they should be seen as attempts to fashion a Jesus story for a particular congregation. No, they are historical accounts first and foremost, and their theology is the theology of Jesus as He taught it.

31 By putting things this way, I am assuming the Gospels to be deliberately planned and executed portraits of Jesus and not the remains of oral transmission, contra James D. G. Dunn, *Jesus Remembered*, 172-173.

32 Nick Batzig writes, "In the Old Testament, everything that seems to be for the nation of Israel had to be passed down to Jesus, who then fulfilled the realities of the promises for us in His own person and work" (Batzig, "Who is the True Israel of God," https://tabletalkmagazine.com/posts/who-is-the-true-israel-of-god/). This kind of assertion is commonly found in Reformed writers.

33 E.g., Kim Riddlebarger, *A Case for Amillennialism: Understanding the End Times* (Grand Rapids, Baker, 2003), 69.

often happens in these matters, a little truth is blown up into a dominating principle, eliminating crucial facets of biblical truth.

It is true that, in some sense, Christ does represent Israel. This may be hinted at in the interplay of the Servant Songs of Isaiah, where sometimes Israel is the Servant, and other times the Servant is Messiah. Similarly, Matthew 2:15 cites Hosea 11:1 in a way that merges Israel with Christ.[34] Other writers throw in passages such as 2 Corinthians 1:20[35] and 1 Corinthians 10:11,[36] which are misused as if they give carte blanche to anyone who wishes to apply covenant promises to themselves without the inconvenience of being a named party to the covenant. Nobody really believes all God's promises in the OT are theirs today, but they need the room to cherry-pick.

That said, it ought to be manifestly clear, not only from the covenants of the OT but from the plain statements of the NT, that Jesus, as a representative of Israel, does not become the "true Israel" leaving no room for redeemed national Israel in the future. Matthew 19:28, Acts 26:7, Romans 11:1-29, and many more passages spell out a future for ethnic Israel in line with their covenants, which dispels amillennial deductions but are in total accord with the New covenant expectations of the redemption of Israel through Messiah's New covenant work. Christ represents Israel to secure its national identity and the exact fulfillment of God's oaths to the nation (Isa. 54:5-10; Jer. 31:31-37; 33:14-21; Zech. 2:8).

The Phenomenon of One Messianic Work in Two Phases

It ought not to come as a great surprise that Christ's mission of redeeming and regenerating the Creation is divided up between His first and His second coming. Every orthodox believer understands this. They may prefer to speak of it as two separate works to bring about one conclusion, but all would agree that the second coming is necessary to complete the work of the first.

Very well then, what of it? The significance of this fact is often not given its proper weight. I believe the reason for this is our predilection to look back at the first advent, for which we have more information, rather than to look forward to the second advent. The combining of the two advents in texts like Micah 5:2; Isaiah 9:6-7; 61:1-2; Zechariah 9:9-10; Malachi 3:1-3; Matthew 3:11-12; Luke 22:17-20; and 1 Corinthians 11:23-26 proves that God sees the work of His Son as one work. But the rejection motif found in, for example, Psalm 22:1-21; 118:22; Isaiah 53:1-9; and Daniel 9:26 shows that this one work would be interrupted. Jesus Himself predicted this by cutting off Isaiah 61:1-2 in mid-sentence (Lk. 4:16-21), as well as in His private words to His disciples (e.g., Mk. 8:31; 9:22; 17:25), His more guarded words to His enemies (Jn. 2:19; cf. Mk. 14:58; Matt. 12:39-41), and in speeches such as the Parable of the Minas (Lk. 19:11ff).

34 These passages in particular are used as proof-texts by supersessionists.

35 "For all the promises of God in Him are Yes, and in Him Amen, to the glory of God through us" (2 Cor. 1:20).

36 "Now all these things happened to them as examples, and they were written for our admonition, upon whom the ends of the ages have come" (1 Cor. 10:11).

This division of Christ's Servant-work into two stages highlights the provision within the predetermined Creation Project for a right response from humans to Christ. Sinners are not forced to think and act as they do towards Jesus by any power of God. To do such a thing would both undermine God's own image in man, as well as obviate the God-endowed potential of men to act responsibly towards their Creator, sin notwithstanding. When God offers salvation to a person it is not offered half-heartedly, nor in contradiction to God's will. As both Creator and Sustainer of the world, God is actively ushering history to a predetermined goal. But that goal includes the free choices (however one defines "freewill") of His creatures, which are integrated into the whole scheme, thus making it possible for the gospel to be sincerely offered while being accepted or rejected. In precisely the same way, Jesus and the disciples offer the Kingdom of God to Israel (Matt. 4:17; Mk. 1:14-15; Matt. 10:5-7) even though the Lord knows it will be rejected and will be scheduled in the events of Christ's second coming (Matt. 19:28; 25:31).

On this basis we can say that although God knew the inevitability of separating the mission of Christ into two parts, and the necessity of the Messiah going to the cross, that did not remove responsibility for rejecting the Kingdom away from the Jews, nor indeed did it mean that the offer of the Kingdom of God was not genuine. For anyone who asks, "What would have happened if they had accepted Jesus before the crucifixion?" The answer is that the questioner has not sufficiently understood these truths.

The New Covenant and Jesus Christ

Scripture places the person of Christ in the middle of everything. Not only did God create through His Son (as the Word or *Logos*), but everything was made *for* Christ (Col. 1:16). We may, therefore, view creation as a gift of the Father to the Son.[37]

Seeing it this way drives home to us the fact that this world is not just a convenient stage for our fallen history, a vehicle to be abandoned when Christ returns. Some eschatological systems treat this material realm as a mere transportation system for the bodies of the elect. Or more pointedly still, it is treated as a stage for the outplaying of history with no primary importance to God other than to deliver the elect into heaven. After that, it is to be cast off and destroyed. Hence, in amillennialism particularly, the planet is viewed in a reductionist sense as merely a carrier, which affects the Christian worldview regarding God's overall purpose for this present earth. Though blighted by evil, this world is important in its own right and will be restored to bring God glory.

How is this to be achieved? *My contention is that Christ will accomplish it through the New covenant.* In other words, I contend that God "reconciles all things to Himself" by Jesus Christ through the New covenant.

I am aware that some may want to jump in and subsume the details of the other biblical covenants into the New covenant and declare them all "fulfilled" in and by

37 This is suggestive for the interpretation of 1 Cor. 15:25-28.

the person of Christ at the first coming. This is the conclusion often assumed by those who employ what is called a "redemptive-historical hermeneutic," which is a circular method of reading a prepackaged theology into every passage of Scripture. This is not what I am doing.

What is required for all God's restorative purposes to be consummated is universal righteousness—the reflection of God in creation. And this reconciliation of all things to its Owner is accomplished *by* the Owner, Christ Himself. I submit that at the heart of this great work are the covenants of the Bible.

The promises appended to the biblical covenants are not supplemented with a means of fulfillment within those same covenants. The fulfillment lies outside of those covenants, within the New covenant, as it supplies the Noahic, Abrahamic, Priestly, and Davidic covenants with the means of their realization. And the New covenant must be "enabled" by Christ, the "Man from Heaven" (1 Cor. 15:47). Hence, *the plan of God outlined in the biblical covenants converges on the crucified Jesus and emerges from the resurrected Jesus*!

In referring to my approach as Biblical Covenantalism, instead of retaining the moniker Dispensationalism, I may be rowing against an impossible tide. I reluctantly agree. But because I have become convinced that there are real methodological problems with Dispensationalism (not its eschatology note),[38] and the divine covenants are emphasized more by the inspired authors, I have immersed myself in the latter. The OT may not refer directly to the New covenant until Jeremiah 31:31, but the concept was known before and after Jeremiah put a name to it.[39] Although I have chosen not to give the subject the same prominence as I give to the unifying New covenant, I continue to press the point I made in Volume One, that since Isaiah 42:6 and 49:8 identify the Servant "as a covenant to the people,"[40] and it is Jesus as the Lamb of God whose blood is "the blood of the New covenant," it is proper to assert that Jesus is the New covenant in His person.[41] This correlation can be found in many authors. While

38 These issues include defining oneself by dispensations instead of covenants, the descriptive nature of Dispensationalism as over against a more prescriptive alternative, the failure to grasp that the phrase "Dispensationalism is a hermeneutic" does not correspond to the practice of that hermeneutic, which ought to direct attention to the covenants and away from dispensations, which often are not easily arrived at via said hermeneutic; the lack of a place for Jesus Christ as the fulcrum of the Bible Story, and the vacillation over the participation of Christians in the New covenant. See the Appendix, "Contrasting Dispensationalism and Biblical Covenantalism."

39 See Walter Kaiser, *The Promise-Plan of God*, 200.

40 I recognize that there are both covenant scholars from different spectrums who think that Isaiah is referring to Israel in these verses, but I argue that a people in need of saving cannot be made as a covenant of salvation. The majority view is that these passages are messianic in purpose.

41 Unger held that Jesus was the "covenant for the people" (1279), but strangely equated the covenant with the Abrahamic covenant. See Merrill F. Unger, *Unger's Commentary on the Old Testament, Volume 2, Isaiah–Malachi* (Chicago: Moody, 1981), 1256. In his comments on the Davidic covenant, Richard C. Gamble notes that it is a messianic covenant and references Isaiah 42:6-7 and 49:8-10 in his proofs. See *The Whole Counsel of God: Volume 1, God's Mighty Acts in the Old Testament* (Phillipsburg: NJ, P&R, 2009), 494 n. 66 & n. 67. Strangely, neither author connects the Servant's redemptive role with the New covenant.

stopping short of equating the Servant as the embodiment of the New covenant itself, Duane Lindsey wrote:

> In comparison with the next phrase ("and a light for the Gentiles"), it appears that the servant is not literally either "a covenant" or "a light" but one who in someway is a cause, source, mediator, or dispenser of covenant realities or illuminating benefits. The figure of speech is probably metonymy of effect (the covenant) for the cause (the covenant mediator). The servant is the messianic "messenger of the covenant" of Malachi 3:1. In short, He is the mediator of the New covenant with Israel, elaborated in Jeremiah 31:31-34 and referred to in numerous other prophetic texts (cf. Isa 54:10; 55:3; 59:20-21; 61:8; Ezek 16:60-63).[42]

Lindsey is expounding Isaiah 42:6, and he has a point. But I believe on the basis of Isaiah 49:8, plus Luke 22:20; 2 Corinthians 3:6; and Hebrews 9:16-17 that restricting it to a figure of speech fails to do justice to both the language and the theology.[43] Commendably, Lindsey himself notes that Franz Delitzsch[44] believed that the Servant is the covenant itself.[45] And as Larry Pettegrew observes:

> The personification of the covenant by the Servant is also remarkable. Up to this point one might have thought that the Servant was only a mediator like Moses was for the Old Covenant... But in the Servant songs one learns that the Messiah would be more than a mediator. As Odendaal points out, "He is the impersonated, incarnated covenant. We may regard him, in other words, to be the one who is able so fully to represent the *'ām* in the covenant, that he himself can be considered to be the incorporated covenant."[46]

Covenant theologians can be found who agree with this identification. In his foreword to a book of essays by Reformed theologian Cornelis Venema, Sinclair Ferguson declares outright that Christ is the covenant:

> Ultimately God's covenant with his people is not *found in* Jesus Christ; it is Jesus Christ. The new covenant, the final covenant, the covenant in which is

---

42 F. Duane Lindsey, "Isaiah's Songs of the Servant Part 1: The Call of the Servant in Isaiah 42:1-9," *BSAC* 139 (Jan 1982), 25.

43 Another source that takes "a covenant for the people" as a metonymy is Michael Rydelnik and James Spencer, "Isaiah," in *The Moody Bible Commentary*, eds. Michael Rydelnik and Michael Vanlaningham (Chicago: Moody, 2014), 1082. The authors specifically relate Isaiah 49:8 to the New covenant.

44 Franz Delitzsch, *Commentary on the Old Testament by C. F. Keil and F. Delitzsch*, Vol. 7 (Grand Rapids: Eerdmans, 1969), 180, who equates the Servant here with "the Messenger of the covenant" in Mal. 3:1.

45 See also Thomas Edward McComiskey, *The Covenants of Promise: A Theology of the Old Testament Covenants* (Grand Rapids: Baker, 1985), 90-91.

46 Larry D. Pettegrew, "The New Covenant," *MSJ* 10 (Fall 1999), 262-263.

> experienced the fullness of God's promise "I will be your God and you will be my people" is made in him.[47]

I readily acknowledge that Ferguson and Venema would say that the New covenant is the covenant of grace in its last iteration, but the main point is the same. In a similar vein, Michael McKelvey notes:

> God states that he gives the servant himself as a "covenant"... This means that the servant is the embodiment of all that the new covenant reveals. All God's saving, life-giving, restorative, covenantal purposes are found in him and brought about through him.[48]

Likewise, O. Palmer Robertson states, "The anticipation of the future focuses on a single individual who shall embody in himself the essence of the covenant..."[49]

This identification of the Servant in Isaiah 42:6 and 49:8 as "a covenant to the people" cannot be stressed too much. It is far too significant to be left out in the cold as an OT vestige. Something substantial must be made of it. I cannot put this too strongly, *the coming of Jesus Christ into the world and the institution of the New covenant in His blood brings that covenant to the fore. The other covenants, the Abrahamic and Davidic covenants mainly, have to be understood in the light of their connection with the New covenant.*

Since Jesus Christ shed the blood of the New covenant (1 Cor. 11:25), the covenants with Abraham and David, as expounded in the NT, have to be interpreted with the New covenant in mind. To repeat what has been said before, something to look out for is the way the Noahic, Abrahamic, Priestly, and Davidic covenants connect with the New covenant. What the New covenant does is provide the atonement that is necessary to make the oaths of the other unilateral covenants attainable.

The Correct Emphasis Upon the Two Comings

There is a world of difference that results from the decision about whether a particular prophetic passage is interpreted as being fulfilled at the first coming of Christ in humility or His second coming in glory. The resultant impact upon one's thinking about the Bible can scarcely be exaggerated. One recent scholar puts the matter bluntly:

---

47 Cornelis P. Venema, *Christ and Covenant Theology: Essays on Election, Republication, and the Covenants* (Phillipsburg: NJ: P&R, 2017), ix.

48 Michael G. McKelvey, "The New Covenant as Promised in the Major Prophets," *Covenant Theology: Biblical, Theological, and Historical Perspectives*, eds. Guy Prentiss Waters, et al. (Wheaton, IL: Crossway, 2020) 206. This identification is also found in Barnabas and Justin Martyr. "For Barnabas, however, Jesus is the covenant; for Justin he is the *new* covenant" (Ligon Duncan, "Covenant in the Early Church," 297).

49 O. Palmer Robertson, *The Christ of the Covenants*, 51. By the "covenant," he means the covenant of grace of which the New covenant is the last installment.

> With respect to Abraham and the covenant named after him, we recall and reaffirm that Jesus fulfilled on the cross Yahweh's covenant cutting with the patriarch... With regard to David and the covenant named after him, Jesus fulfilled that royal covenant proleptically on Palm Sunday and penultimately on his ascension and acceptance of all authority from his father in heaven..., and he will fulfill it ultimately when he returns among his people as King of kings and Lord of lords.[50]

But interpreting the covenants as being primarily fulfilled at the first coming inevitably forces the interpreter to claim that OT covenants, such as the Abrahamic and Davidic, would be fulfilled in ways that no one could have anticipated.[51] When one considers all the messianic passages in the OT, a considerable number of them highlight the second coming (as we now know it to be), but the majority of biblical scholars view these prophetic texts as being largely fulfilled at Christ's first coming. I believe this to be a grave mistake that will adversely affect one's comprehension of God's Creation Project.

I passionately believe that the inclusion of the one work of Christ in two phases (first and second advents) ought to be a *key factor* in how we read our Bibles and see ourselves within the Creation Project.[52] We ought to parse first coming truths from second coming truths, with the hermeneutical aids offered to us in the divine covenants.

This, if I may say so, would be an important step forward in "dispensational" reflection, as it would encourage more focus upon the centrality of Christ in Biblical Theology from the standpoint of plain-sense interpretation. This, in turn, would, I believe, inspire young scholars to develop a biblical covenantal theology that is unafraid to explore how the covenants of God and the person of Jesus Christ interact in the progress of revelation, in the Church, and in the coming Kingdom. We need to dispense with "dispensations" as primary structural markers and focus our attention on the covenants and the phenomena of the two comings of the Son of God. Without meaning any disrespect to anyone, "Dispensationalism" should really be "Biblical Covenantalism."

The Covenantal Mindset of the New Testament Writers

The NT does not contain as many blatant covenant indicators as the OT. A simple word search for "covenant" or "oath" will not produce a daunting list to sift through. If a search is made for "new covenant," again, one is not going to be inundated with

50 Jeffrey J. Niehaus, *Biblical Theology: The Special Grace Covenants*, Vol. 3 (Wooster, OH: Weaver Book Company, 2017), 8.

51 Ibid., 18. Niehaus is there speaking of the Mosaic and Davidic covenants, but the same is applied to the Abrahamic.

52 Of course, sharing this point of view is no guarantee that the relevant texts will be correctly assigned. For an amillennialist who also believes the first and second comings are "two parts... of the same event," see Richard B. Gaffin Jr., *In the Fullness of Time: An Introduction to the Biblical Theology of Acts and Paul* (Wheaton, IL: Crossway, 2022), 279.

references. You will come up with nine NT passages. What, then, is one to do whose whole project is to ground biblical theology in the covenants of God? Should one give up?

The answer is a very decided no! As a matter of fact, when we dig deeper into the overall message of the NT, we uncover very many covenantal connections. There appears an atmosphere of what Daniel Block aptly calls "covenance" throughout the Gospels and the Epistles.[53] We find the same thing in OT books that do not speak overtly about covenant, such as Micah, Joel, Habakkuk, and Zephaniah. Modern NT scholars are now calling attention to the important role of covenant in the NT writings. In particular, the epistles of Paul are shot through with New covenant overtones.[54] Köstenberger and Goswell write:

> The significance of covenant for the New Testament cannot be gauged simply by the frequency with which the word "covenant" appears on its pages, namely 33 times, mostly in Paul (9 times) and Hebrews (17 times)...the theme of covenant is explicitly touched on by Paul only in Romans 11, 1 Corinthians 11, 2 Corinthians 3, and Galatians 4, but it can be said to underlie his teachings as a significant subtext.[55]

Another way of detecting the effects of covenant on the NT writers is to search for names like "Abraham," "Isaac," "Jacob," "Moses," and "David." Not every mention of these names is for covenant purposes, but many are. And, of course, we cannot ignore the way the Lord Jesus Christ is spoken about in every NT book and the covenant ramifications of His mission. As Jeffrey Niehaus has stated, "Jesus, born under the law, functioned at several points as the last and greatest covenant lawsuit prophet of the old covenant before he ushered in the new covenant in his blood."[56]

The apostle Paul, writing to a Gentile congregation, referred to himself and his co-workers as "ministers of the New Covenant" in 2 Corinthians 3:6ff.[57] Paul labels his evangelical ministry, and the tag he chooses is the New covenant in Jesus Christ![58] It would seem, then, that no matter how infrequently he uses the term, we ought to view the letters of Paul, which are extensions of his ministry, as New covenant letters!

There is no need to argue for the value of covenant to the writer of Hebrews. That book is not understandable without the covenant theme. Even the General Epistles and John's Revelation presuppose the covenants of the OT, or so I will argue. I propose

53 Daniel I. Block, *Covenant*, 1-10.

54 I devote three chapters to Paul later in which I show how the apostle wrote as "a New covenant Christian." See e.g., Brant Pitre, Michael P. Barber and John A. Kincaid, Paul, *A New Covenant Jew: Rethinking Pauline Theology* (Grand Rapids: Eerdmans, 2019); James P. Ware, *Paul's Theology in Context: Creation, Incarnation, Covenant & Kingdom* (Grand Rapids: Eerdmans, 2019).

55 Andreas J. Köstenberger and Gregory Goswell, Biblical *Theology: A Canonical, Thematic & Ethical Approach* (Wheaton, IL: Crossway, 2023), 695.

56 Jeffrey J. Niehaus, *Biblical Theology: Volume 3, The Special Grace Covenants*, 22.

57 See Ibid., 161-163. See also my exegesis of the passage below.

58 "It is not freedom from the law as such that is the subject in 2 Cor. 3:7 - 4:6, but rather the ministry of the new covenant" (Victor Paul Furnish, *II Corinthians: A New Translation with Introduction and Commentary* [Garden City, NY: Doubleday & Company], 237).

that, rather than leaving the OT covenants of Yahweh in a typological hinterland with their oaths neglected, all the Apostolic writers presuppose these covenants—especially the Abrahamic, Davidic, and New covenants—in all their writings.[59]

The Kingdom of God as a Covenant Kingdom

The Kingdom of God in Scripture is bound closely to the notion of covenant.[60] Covenants are sworn to guarantee a promise to perform something of importance and always involve a solemn binding oath (Heb. 6:16-17). As such, they are *hermeneutical in nature*. God has graciously bound Himself to perform "the words of the covenant" oaths He has sworn:

> God gave *an oath* for the faithful (Micah 7:20) performance of Covenant promises (Gen. 22:16, and 26:3), thus condescending to present the strongest possible assurance. Now God would not swear to an equivocal covenant, to a covenant which in *its plain grammatical sense* conveys promises we have referred to, and yet means something very different.[61]

On this basis, the combination of the oaths of the Abrahamic and Davidic covenants, especially once they have "passed through" the New covenant, are as secure as anything can be. In this important sense, the coming Kingdom of God is a New covenant Kingdom.[62] The OT texts are decidedly eschatological (e.g., Jer. 31:31-34; Ezek. 36:33-36; Psa. 96:11-13; Isa. 26:1-9). In the NT, we encounter the phrase "the Kingdom of God" many times (especially in Luke-Acts).[63] I will be devoting a lot of space to the subject of the Kingdom of God, but just here I will say something about how the NT phrase "the Kingdom of God" relates to the covenants. There are two basic ways the term is employed. The first is the general rule of God over His creation. In this sense, the OT calls Yahweh a King.[64] The other use of the term refers to the coming Davidic-New covenant aeon (e.g., Matt. 6:10; Lk. 14:15; 19:11).

Readers of the NT should notice that the inspired writers use the phrase "Kingdom of God" quite naturally, as if everyone is expected to know what is being talked about. This is in spite of the fact that it is not an OT term. As will be demonstrated, especially in the early parts of the Synoptics, the term "Kingdom of God/Heaven"

59 "When coming to the New Testament, Scripture assumes all the biblical covenants are fully understood" (David E. Olander, "The Importance of the Davidic Covenant," *JODT* 10 [Dec 2006], 54).

60 Peters refers to the Kingdom as "expressly covenanted." See George N. H. Peters, *The Theocratic Kingdom*, Vol. 3, 371.

61 George N. H. Peters, *The Theocratic Kingdom*, Vol. 1, 300.

62 Alva J. McClain, *The Greatness of the Kingdom* (Grand Rapids: Zondervan, 1959), 157. Cf. J. Dwight Pentecost, *Thy Kingdom Come: Tracing God's Program and Covenant Promises Throughout History* (Grand Rapids, Kregel, 1995), 190-191; Robert L. Saucy, *The Case for Progressive Dispensationalism: The Interface Between Dispensational & Non-Dispensational Theology* (Grand Rapids: Zondervan, 1993), 112-113.

63 Not forgetting the Gospel of Matthew's use of the synonymous phrase, "the Kingdom of Heaven."

64 Yahweh is also called the King of Israel prior to the time of Saul.

refers to the expected Kingdom promised in the OT covenants. In my comments on the different Gospels, I will be trying to distinguish such references from the way the term is used, for example, in Matthew's parables of the kingdom, where it often takes on a different hue.[65]

Long ago, McClain noted that a kingdom included three things: a ruler, a realm, and rulership (i.e., the ruler ruling over the realm).[66] This is true, although certain aspects of the Kingdom of God may be in place prior to its full realization.[67] For instance, when John the Baptist and then Jesus Himself preached the words, "Repent, for the kingdom of heaven is at hand" (Matt. 3:1-2; 4:17), they clearly were not proclaiming a kingdom in process. John's and Jesus' Kingdom was one to be entered (Matt. 5:20; 7:21; Mk. 10:15, 23-25). Jesus' own teaching shows that He viewed the Kingdom as future (Lk. 11:2; 13:29; 19:11; 22:16, 18, 30; Mk. 15:43; Matt. 19:28; 25:31 cf. Acts 1:8). In that future, Jesus will sit upon a throne of glory on this earth. Matthew 19:28 says, "Assuredly I say to you, that in the regeneration, when the Son of Man sits on the throne of His glory, you who have followed Me will also sit on twelve thrones, judging the twelve tribes of Israel."

The Lord says "amen" to the veracity of this prediction. That "amen" guarantees there will be a "regeneration" of this earth and Jesus Christ will rule over it. This regeneration is what is referred to in Isaiah 11:1-10, Amos 9:13, and Micah 4:1-5. Isaiah says:

> The wolf also shall dwell with the lamb,
> The leopard shall lie down with the young goat,
> The calf and the young lion and the fatling together;
> And a little child shall lead them (Isa. 11:6; cf. 65:25).

The inclusion of David's father Jesse in Isaiah 11:1 and 10 links this prophecy with the Davidic covenant. This King will "judge the earth" (Isa. 11:4 cf. Psa. 2:6-9), but that does not entail the voiding of Jerusalem's promises:

> Behold, the days are coming,' says the LORD, 'that I will perform that good thing which I have promised to the house of Israel and to the house of Judah:
> In those days and at that time
> I will cause to grow up to David
> A Branch of righteousness;
> He shall execute judgment and righteousness in the earth.

65 Erich Sauer speaks of four ways the "kingdom" is used in Scripture (OT kingdom, present spiritual kingdom, visible future kingdom, and eternal kingdom), and advises close attention to the context to determine the meaning in each case. See his *From Eternity to Eternity*, 176. I do not like the word "spiritual" as applied to the kingdom because I prefer to think of the parables of the kingdom (Matt. 13) as presenting a kingdom-in-the-making. However, all the main premillennial writers on the subject warn about delimiting the kingdom to a single meaning.

66 Alva J. McClain, *The Greatness of the Kingdom*, 17.

67 An obvious example is the gift of the Holy Spirit (2 Cor. 3:3-6).

> In those days Judah will be saved,
> And Jerusalem will dwell safely.
> And this *is the name* by which she will be called:
> THE LORD OUR RIGHTEOUSNESS (Jer. 33:14-16; cf. 23:5-6).

Here the Davidic King is identified as reigning from Jerusalem (cf. Isa. 2:3; Rom. 11:26). The context certainly does not fit this present world. Jeremiah is referring to Jesus' coming reign on the regenerated earth. This is the Kingdom of God envisaged in the OT Prophets and predicted in the sampling of passages from the Synoptic Gospels given above.

Another important passage on this topic is the institution of the Lord's Supper in Luke 22 and Matthew 26:28-29 (cf. Mark 14:24-25). While eating the Passover with His disciples, Jesus told them that He would not eat it "until it is fulfilled in the kingdom of God" (Lk. 22:16); likewise with the cup (Lk. 22:18). This was performed at the same time as Jesus' utterance about "the new covenant in My blood" (Luke 22:20), thus indicating that the Kingdom of God is intimately related to the New covenant. It is perhaps even more clear from the Matthean and Markan renderings where Jesus speaks of "My blood of the covenant" (Matt. 26:28/Mk. 14:24 NASB).[68] Block remarks:

> Their wording links this observation directly to the Israelite covenant-ratification ritual in Exodus 24:8, where the Hebrew version of this expression (*dam habberit*) refers to the blood sprinkled on the people, binding them by covenant to YHWH. The expression also occurs in Zechariah 9:11, where "the blood of your covenant" provides the grounds for YHWH's ultimate restoration of Israel after its judgment.[69]

I think this correlation is correct. Christ's new covenant blood relates God's people to God in a new way, making possible their restoration in the Kingdom of God.[70]

The epistle to the Hebrews does not use the term "Kingdom of God," but it does strongly indicate that the New covenant era which it foresees is one and the same with it. The long quotation of Jeremiah 31:31-34 in Hebrews 8:8-12 is associated with Jesus as "the Mediator of the new covenant" in Hebrews 8:6 (cf. Heb. 12:24) and the future "kingdom which cannot be shaken" (Heb. 12:28).

Another thing to note is the presence of the Holy Spirit in believers after Christ's ascension. This is inextricably linked with the New covenant, and, therefore, with the Kingdom of God in some initial but real sense. Just as the Spirit is given as a pledge of our coming glorification (2 Cor. 1:22; 5:5; Rom. 8:11), He is also a pledge of our place in the coming Kingdom. When Paul declares, "For the kingdom of God is not eating and drinking, but righteousness and peace and joy in the Holy Spirit" (Rom. 14:17), it is possible to understand him to be talking about the future Kingdom in which food

68 The Byzantine Text of the KJV and NKJV includes *kainos* (new) within the phrase.

69 Daniel I. Block, *Covenant*, 521-522.

70 Notice the next verse: "But I say to you, I will not drink of this fruit of the vine from now on until that day when I drink it new with you in My Father's kingdom" (Matt. 26:29).

and drink are of little relevance.[71] What matters is "the redemption of our body" in the Kingdom, which is achieved through the Spirit (Rom. 8:23).

Covenants in the Gospels

When we study the four Gospels the reader may wonder where the covenant thread has gone. But just a little deeper look will reveal the Gospel writers' reliance on ideas within the covenants.[72] The Infancy narratives of Matthew and Luke are replete with covenant associations.[73] Matthew 22:32, where Jesus rebukes the Sadducees by informing them that God's covenant words to Moses[74] mean that the patriarchs are alive rely upon God's covenant (Exod. 2:24). The coming Kingdom (Matt. 16:28), when Christ will sit upon His glorious throne (Matt. 19:28), is a Davidic throne (Lk. 1:68-69), which itself is grounded in the covenant with Abraham (Lk. 1:72-73).

Then, of course, there is the high point in the Synoptic narratives where Jesus institutes the long-awaited New covenant, as "the Lamb of God" (Jn. 1:29, 36) through His own blood (Lk. 22:20).[75] Moreover, Jesus' claim to be the Messiah was a declaration that He is the One prophesied by the covenants.[76] It is not an exaggeration to say that the whole warp and woof of the Gospels is covenantal.

Summary of Part Two

- The Bible interpreter will always be tempted to seek for second coming fulfillments at the first coming. If the texts are not parsed correctly, typological interpretation and spiritualization will inevitably be employed to handle the discrepancy.

- The fact that Messiah has indeed come to earth must be included within our evaluation of eschatological texts. Yet we must perceive His rejection and, hence, His second coming in our assessments.

- Because of His exalted status as co-Creator and rightful Owner of all creation, the Lord Jesus Christ is the fulcrum upon which the entire Creation Project hinges. The staggering truth that He has entered the world as a man, allowed Himself to be mistreated and murdered in it, and has brought redemption and life to sinful humanity, even as He upheld creation for them is the wonder of wonders. Jesus guarantees God's covenant plan to be fulfilled to the letter. However, maintaining that the Bible can be viewed Christologically in this way does mean that He can be "seen" in every verse of Scripture.

71 See George N. H. Peters, *The Theocratic Kingdom*, Vol. 2, 34-35. Also, Alva J. McClain, *The Greatness of the Kingdom*, 434.

72 One example is Cleon L. Rogers, Jr., "The Davidic Covenant in the Gospels," *BSAC* 150 (Oct 1993), 458-78.

73 See Matt. 1:20; 2:2; Lk. 1:26-33; 55, 69; 2:4, 11, etc.

74 "I am the God of Abraham, the God of Isaac, and the God of Jacob" (Exod. 3:6, 15-16).

75 Paul R. Williamson, *Sealed with an Oath*, 184.

76 George N. H. Peters, *The Theocratic Kingdom*, Vol. 3, 349-360.

- We must also consider the fact the Servant work of Jesus is one work split into two phases. An overreliance on the first or second phase leads one into error.

- While the other unilateral covenants of Yahweh are external covenants depending on the victory of Christ, the New covenant is in many ways identical with Christ. He is the Lamb of God, and His blood is the blood of the New covenant. Hence, when He mediates life through the New covenant, He mediates Himself!

- Although the term "covenant" is not mentioned with great frequency in the NT, the writers of the NT were imbued with the spirit of the covenants. They thought in covenantal terms and assumed their validity.

- The doctrine of the Kingdom of God is a covenant idea. Although the coming of Christ into this world and the commencement of the New covenant make the Kingdom less straightforward, the same covenant expectations we meet with in the OT and the early Synoptics still prevail because the Gospels are covenantal writings.

PART THREE:
THE COVENANTS IN THE EARLY CHAPTERS OF THE GOSPELS

5

THE ANNUNCIATION PASSAGES IN LUKE AND MATTHEW

Let it be to me according to your word. – Luke 1:38

Turning now to the Gospels themselves, the annunciation passages in Matthew and Luke are our first introduction to the way the Holy Spirit will pick up the threads of the OT and join them with the new revelation that came with the advent of Jesus Christ. We start with those passages where angels announce the birth of the Savior. I am going to begin with Luke's account because Luke stresses the two-comings of Jesus. By presenting Luke's material first and then moving on to Matthew, I hope the reader will see some of these texts in a new light.

Elizabeth and Zacharias

In Luke 1:5 we discover that Elizabeth, the wife of Zacharias the priest, is advanced in years. Zacharias is burning incense to God in the Temple (Lk. 1:9). Luke tells us that the announcing angel was standing to the right of the altar of incense (Lk. 1:11). This little detail is an indication of the kind of accuracy that was sought by the best ancient historians. If at all possible, they would seek out eyewitnesses to the things they were writing about.[1]

The announcement begins in verse 13, which is God's answer to the prayers of Zacharias and Elizabeth about a child. God is going to answer their prayers. Their child will be great (hence the angel-messenger), and he will "be filled with the Holy

1 See Richard Bauckham, *Jesus and the Eyewitnesses: The Gospels as Eyewitness Testimony* (Grand Rapids: Eerdmans, 2006), 5-10, 24-36; Paul Rhodes Eddy and Gregory L. Boyd, *The Jesus Legend: A Case for the Historical Reliability of the Jesus Tradition* (Grand Rapids: Baker, 2007), 269-406; Craig S. Keener, *The Historical Jesus of the Gospels* (Grand Rapids: Eerdmans, 2009), 89-94.

Spirit" from infancy (Lk. 1:15).[2] This statement about the Holy Spirit should not be missed, for it certainly would not have been missed by Zacharias, being as it was, firmly associated with special divine empowerment for a God-appointed task (e.g. Exod. 31:3; 35:31; Judg. 14:6; Neh. 9:30). This son, John, as he is to be named, will turn many of the children of Israel to their Lord, going in the spirit and power of Elijah (Lk. 1:17). We get a quotation from an OT text, which is a prophecy of the latter-day ministry of Elijah. The announcement does not say that John is Elijah, but that he comes in "the spirit and power of Elijah."[3] He comes "to turn the hearts of the fathers to the children" (Lk. 1:17), which, not coincidentally, is taken from the very last verse of our OT (Mal. 4:6).

Because Zacharias doubts the angel's words, he is stricken dumb for a time. The angel introduces himself as none other than Gabriel (meaning "man of God"). Gabriel is one of only two angels named in the Scriptures, the other being Michael. It was Gabriel who had spoken to Daniel centuries earlier (Dan. 8:16; 9:21). Notice that Zacharias needed to take Gabriel's words on faith at face value. He was not to spiritualize the words. He was to believe what was said. Because he doubted, he became a sign—a sign of disbelief.

The Annunciation of Jesus' Birth in Luke

Luke 1

Mary

In the next pericope we are told of the angel Gabriel's visit to Nazareth[4] "in the sixth month" to appear at Joseph's house (Lk. 1:26) to speak to Mary, his betrothed. There is a lot of continuity with OT expectation in Gabriel's words to Mary. The first point of continuity has been debated (although not by believers), is that when Isaiah 7:14 uses the Hebrew term *almah*, he meant a virgin. Although there is some debate about the meaning of the Hebrew term, there is no doubt that the Greek word used by the NT authors, *parthenos*, does indeed mean "virgin." Since the Holy Spirit used this term twice (Lk. 1:27; Matt. 1:23), and Matthew's usage expressly links the announcement to Isaiah's prophecy in Isaiah 7:14, we know that the *almah* of Isaiah should be translated "virgin" not "maiden." But further, we know that the one whom Isaiah was predicting was coming into the world.

The declaration that a virgin will conceive is followed by another point of continuity with the OT. Gabriel loaded his announcement with Davidic covenantal terminology: "The Lord God will give Him the throne of His father David. And He will reign over the house of Jacob forever, and of His kingdom there will be no end" (Lk. 1:32-33).

2 Notice the difference between this text and what is said in Isa. 11:2 where Messiah utilizes the endowment of the Spirit to rule the Kingdom.

3 In the Gospel of John, the Baptist explicitly says he is *not* Elijah (Jn. 1:21).

4 Many critics of the NT have tried to assert that Nazareth did not exist at this time, but any good Bible dictionary will refute this error.

Joseph would have shared his Davidic lineage with Mary and later to her Son, whom he would call his own.[5] These words of the angel would only have been understood in one way. Familiar covenant themes like the Davidic throne and the promised everlasting Kingdom would have immediately crossed Joseph's mind.

Hence, the Davidic covenant is introduced right at the commencement of Luke's account. Whatever form of "reinterpretation" one thinks happens after the resurrection of Joseph's Son, *nobody at the birth of Jesus is taking God's words in any way other than literally*. Joseph was a physical descendant of King David. If Luke intended to persuade his readers that these nationalistic promises were to be "expanded" or that they were to be fulfilled differently than expected, he surely would have made the transition clear somewhere. From a close study of the evidence, it is my contention that he never, in fact, does anything to disabuse the reader that the promises were literally intact. What he does do, as we shall see, is "double-down" on these covenant issues. While it is true that the Gentiles will be included in God's blessings, a product of the Abrahamic covenant, we will see nothing in Luke–Acts that throws doubt upon Israel's national hopes in the first two parts of the Abrahamic covenant[6] and the Davidic covenant.[7] Whatever the scholars say happens afterwards, we will let unfold as it is revealed.

Luke 1:38 records Mary's words, "Behold the maidservant of the Lord! Let it be to me according to your word." Did she really have in mind fulfillment via a set of thematic and typological structures supposedly scattered among the OT texts and *not* the covenant pledges as they would have been delivered to her? It does not appear to be so from Luke's presentation.[8]

Elizabeth

Next, we read of Mary's visit to Elizabeth (Lk. 1:39-45) and Elizabeth's words: "Blessed *is* she who believed, for there will be a fulfillment of those things which were told her from the Lord" (Lk. 1:45).

"She who believed" is Mary. *What* Mary believed were the Davidic promises that were conveyed to her, which she shared with Elizabeth. They were words Elizabeth apparently thought would be fulfilled to the letter. Now we come to the 'Magnificat.'

> And Mary said: "My soul magnifies the Lord,
> And my spirit has rejoiced in God my Savior.
> For He has regarded the lowly state of His maidservant; for behold, henceforth all generations will call me blessed.
> For He who is mighty has done great things for me, and holy *is* His name.

5 Paul Barnett, *Jesus and the Rise of Early Christianity*, 101.

6 Ethnic descendants and land.

7 A king reigning from Jerusalem.

8 Kaiser comments that God "fortified her and gave her deep contentment in the promised work of her heavenly Father" (Walter C. Kaiser, Jr., *The Promise-Plan of God*, 243). The song gave Mary assurance not only that she would not be disgraced but that she would have a prominent part in the realization of Israel's covenant destiny.

> And His mercy *is* on those who fear Him From generation to generation.
> He has shown strength with His arm; He has scattered *the* proud in the imagination of their hearts.
> He has put down the mighty from *their* thrones, and exalted *the* lowly.
> He has filled *the* hungry with good things, and *the* rich He has sent away empty.
> *He has helped His servant Israel,* In remembrance of *His* mercy,
> *as He spoke to our fathers, to Abraham and to his seed forever*" (Lk. 1:46-55, my italics).

Again, from Mary's response, it is quite clear that she is thinking in covenantal terms. She mentions her nation Israel (Lk. 1:54), while alluding to the Servant Songs of Isaiah.[9] She also recalls the covenant with Abraham and his physical descendants (Lk. 1:55). According to her words, the promises of the Abrahamic covenant to Israel are "forever." Commentators have noted a possible connection between Mary's song and Hannah's prayer in 1 Samuel 2:1-10.[10] There certainly are similarities, but for my purposes, it is sufficient to note that Hannah ends on a messianic note grounded in the Abrahamic promises of kings, which anticipates the Davidic covenant (1 Sam. 2:10). Mary ends by calling to remembrance the Abrahamic covenant (Lk. 1:55). The minds of both women were informed by covenantal understanding.

Zacharias

We are not yet out of the first chapter of Luke's Gospel and are right smack in the middle of covenant expectation. The next witness to God's oaths is Zacharias. Upon agreeing with his wife that his son would be named John, which demonstrated his belief in what Gabriel had said, his tongue was loosed, and he began to extol God. What he said echoed the words of Mary. Zacharias spoke of both the Davidic (Lk. 1:69) and the Abrahamic covenants (Lk. 1:72-73). Zacharias said that God "has raised up a horn of salvation for us in the house of His servant David, as He spoke by the mouth of His holy prophets, who *have been* since the world began" (Lk. 1:69-70).

The reference to "a horn of salvation" was a way of speaking about the brute strength of the Deliverer. Marshall says, "It suggests the strength of a fighting animal."[11] It is plainly messianic. The great one who is coming will rout His enemies and claim His throne. This has been predicted by God's prophets "since the world began,"

9 The Servant Songs refer to Israel as a nation in Isaiah 42:19; 43:10; 44:1-2, 21; 45:4; 48:20. Some writers see portions of Isaiah 49 as referring to the nation of Israel (cf. Isa. 49:3). My view is that Messiah the Servant is called "Israel" in verse 3 because He is the representative and surety of the nation before Yahweh. For a different analysis and refutation of the identification of the Servant as national Israel see Gary V. Smith, *Isaiah 40–66: An Exegetical and Theological Exposition of Holy Scripture*, NAC (Nashville: B & H Publishing Group, 2009), 344-346. The context does not sustain the view that the Servant is the nation in this chapter since it is the nation ("the tribes of Jacob," Isa. 49:6) which is in need of rescuing.

10 Richard B. Hays, *Echoes of Scripture in the Gospels*, 197-198.

11 I. Howard Marshall, *Commentary on Luke*, NIGTC (Grand Rapids: Eerdmans, 1989), 91.

which would include Moses' record of the first messianic prophecy of Genesis 3:15.[12] Zacharias believes what the prophets said and attaches it to God's covenants, specifically the covenant with Abraham:

> That we should be saved from our enemies and from the hand of all who hate us, to perform the mercy *promised* to our fathers and to remember His holy covenant, the oath which He swore to our father Abraham: to grant us that we, being delivered from the hand of our enemies, might serve Him without fear, in holiness and righteousness before Him all the days of our life (Lk. 1:72-75).

The words of Zacharias recall several OT themes: deliverance, peace, safety, and also consecration to Yahweh. These are all covenant themes. He too is strongly influenced by the covenants of God and what they say about his people Israel. The oath of God to which Zacharias is alluding in verse 73 is not a word-for-word quotation of anything in Genesis, but rather a valid inference from the Abrahamic covenant. The "we" who he has in mind here is not the Church, which Zacharias would know nothing about. The "we" is connected with a genealogical and religious relationship to "our father Abraham" (Lk. 1:73).

Zacharias began his inspired paean with, "Blessed *is* the Lord God of Israel, for He has visited and redeemed His people, and has raised up a horn of salvation for us in the house of His servant David" (Lk. 1:68-69, my emphasis). He is indicating the nation of Israel. He, like Mary, connects the covenants with Abraham *and* David.

Luke 2

As we begin Luke's second chapter, the census is mentioned, mainly because it furnishes the reason for Joseph and his family to go south to Bethlehem, the town of David's birth (Lk. 2:4-5),[13] while also giving the location for the extraordinary vision of the shepherds in Luke 2:8-20. It is to them we must go next.

The Shepherds

That event outside of Bethlehem, like everything in the infancy narratives, is also filled with covenant expectation. Notable is that the angel announced, "Good tidings of great joy which will be to all people. For there is born to you this day in the city of David a Savior, who is Christ the Lord" (Lk. 2:10-11).

12 For the record, I believe that the doom of the serpent by the hand of the woman's seed must indicate an Avenger from God who is also human. Whether it also means that Genesis 3:15 indicates that He is a savior is another thing. I am open to the possibility. See e.g., James M. Hamilton, Jr., "The Skull Crushing Seed of the Woman: Inner-Biblical Interpretation of Genesis 3:15," *Southern Baptist Journal of Theology* 10 (Summer 2006), 30-54.

13 Twice Luke draws our attention to this detail. In Luke 2:5 it could be said that the mention of "the city of David" (meaning the city of his birth) fits what is noted about Joseph's lineage, but in Luke 2:11 the announcement of the angels is pointedly messianic. In Matthew 2:6 the chief priests and scribes cite Micah 5:2 to prove that the promised Ruler of Israel would come from Bethlehem.

The star (Matt. 2:7-10) and the chorus of angels (Lk. 2:8-14) are of great emblematic significance, but this is practically obscured because of our familiarity with the stories. No OT personage is given these tokens as a sign of their birth. The celestial and the heavenly celebrate the Child who would be King—yes, over Israel, but also over "all peoples" (Lk. 2:10). The reference to David in Luke 2:11, and especially the linking of the titles "Savior" and "Christ" tie together the Abrahamic, Davidic, and the New covenants. The name "Christ the Lord" signifies the divine identity of the Child (cf. Psa. 110:1; Isa. 7:14; Mic. 5:2; Zech. 11:12-13), something that many first-century Jews missed.

The promise of the Savior was not only for Israel but was for the Gentiles too, just as the Abrahamic covenant (Gen. 12:3) and the New covenant (Isa. 49:6; 52:15) predicted. Luke is sensitive to the fact that the divine-human encounter, the intent of which is described in Luke 2:14, is understood from the shepherds' vantage point. Luke may have tracked down some of these men some sixty years later. Whether that occurred or not, the evangelist wants his readers to know that "the shepherds returned, glorifying and praising God for all the things that they had heard and seen, <u>as it was told them</u>" (Lk. 2:20). What the angel told them they would find in "the city of David" was exactly what they *did* find, because God means what He says. Shepherds were very low on the social scale, being considered unworthy to testify before the court.[14] But they were not too lowly for the God of creation to honor them with the most spectacular birth announcement ever witnessed in history!

Simeon

In the next story, Luke tells us that Simeon was "waiting for the Consolation of Israel, and the Holy Spirit was upon him" (Lk. 2:25). As far as Simeon was concerned, Jesus was to have a dual salvific role to the Gentiles and also to Israel: "For my eyes have seen Your salvation which You have prepared before the face of all peoples, <u>a light to *bring* revelation to the Gentiles</u>, and the glory of Your people Israel" (Lk. 2:30-32).

This dual role differentiated Israel from the Gentiles but spoke of salvation to both groups. By speaking about salvation, Simeon was alluding to the New covenant, which is the only biblical covenant that is about salvation.[15] One is reminded of Isaiah 42:6b, "I will keep You and give You as a covenant to the people, as a light to the Gentiles." Not so coincidentally, it recalls Isaiah 49:6:

> Indeed He says, "It is too small a thing that You should be My Servant to raise up the tribes of Jacob, and to restore the preserved ones of Israel; I will also give You <u>as a light to the Gentiles</u>, that You should be My salvation to the ends of the earth."

14 Walter C. Kaiser, *The Promise-Plan of God*, 330.
15 This fact cannot be emphasized enough.

As I have shown previously, Isaiah 42 and 49 both assert the fact that the Servant (Messiah) will be made "as a covenant to the people" (Isa. 42:6; 49:8).[16] This is New covenant territory. I am not saying that Simeon is citing these two texts. He may have had them in mind, but they do convey his meaning in Luke 2:32. His private words to Mary were undoubtedly troubling to hear, "Behold, this *Child* is destined for the fall and rising of many in Israel, and for a sign which will be spoken against" (Lk. 2:34).

Such words may have come across as confusing in light of everything that had been said to her before. How could her Son, the future King, heir to the everlasting throne of David (cf. Lk. 1:32-33), become "a sign which will be spoken against" (Lk. 2:34)? That He would be the cause of "the fall and rising of many in Israel" would not have been very surprising, but surely most people would see Him for who He was? That, at least, is what Jesus' mother could be forgiven for thinking. Recall the cryptic response to the news that the shepherds were spreading after their visit. Luke 2:19 records, "Mary kept all these things and pondered *them* in her heart." Matthew Henry has a wise comment on the passage. He says that just as Mary had trusted God with her reputation when carrying the child, she now quietly trusted God for what would happen in the future.[17] Notwithstanding, there is an air of foreboding in Simeon's remark.

Anna

After the meeting with Simeon, another elderly saint, Anna, was moved to speak (Lk. 2:36-38). Luke does not give us her exact words, but they appear to have been centered on Jerusalem and its deliverance (cf. Isa. 62:11-12). Mark Kinzer notices, "Since the hope for Jerusalem's redemption resounds at the beginning of the Gospel but is not in fact attained in the course of the events recounted in Luke's two volumes, attentive readers recognize that Luke's story is incomplete."[18]

This perception of incompleteness in Luke's eschatology is seen again in Luke 13:34-35 and Acts 1:6. Still, there is no doubt that Luke has set us upon a clear path, which aligns with OT eschatological expectations.[19]

---

16 Some evangelicals seemingly deny that these passages refer to the Messiah. It suits their theology better to believe that the "servant" is Israel. See e.g., James M. Hamilton, *Typology: How Old Testament Expectations are Fulfilled in Christ* (Grand Rapids: Zondervan, 2022), 71. For arguments affirming a messianic interpretation see Paul R. Williamson, *Sealed with an Oath*, 158-160; Richard B. Hays, *Echoes of Scripture in the Gospels*, 217-218; and my *The Words of the Covenant*, Vol. 1, 254, 256.

17 Matthew Henry, *Matthew Henry's Commentary In One Volume*, ed. Rev. Leslie F. Church (Grand Rapids: Zondervan, 1961), 1417.

18 Mark S. Kinzer, "Zionism in Luke–Acts," in *The New Christian Zionism: Fresh Perspectives on Israel and the Land*, ed. Gerald R. McDermott (Downers Grove, IL: InterVarsity Press, 2016), 151.

19 "These songs testify to the expectation of ordinary Jews, that in sending a saviour God would deliver his people from the fear of their enemies, and set them up to serve him in righteousness and holiness in accordance with the many promises he had made through his prophets" (David Seccombe, *The King of God's Kingdom: A Solution to the Puzzle of Jesus* [Carlisle: Paternoster Press, 2002], 189).

When crossing over from the Prophets to the opening chapters of Luke's Gospel, there is barely a bump in the road. These examples confirm to us that the expectations raised by the OT prophets of a literal Davidic Kingdom ruled over by the Messiah. George N. H. Peters wrote long ago that:

> The Kingdom being identified with the elect Jewish nation, it cannot be established without the restoration of that nation...If the Kingdom is the Theocratic-Davidic, then embracing the throne, Kingdom, and land of David, it must also include the nation to whom it was alone specifically covenanted; that is, the Jewish people, one branch of Abraham's natural seed...[20]

The description certainly fits the infancy narrative of Luke. But what about the other birth narrative in Matthew?

The Annunciation of Jesus' Birth in Matthew

Matthew 1

The Gospel of Matthew is just as covenantal as Luke. Matthew famously begins his Gospel with a genealogy. Placing a genealogy upfront like that bespeaks a narrative rooted in the Jewish heritage. Starting your book off with a genealogy hardly seems to be a great attention-grabber, but Matthew's Gospel certainly did not suffer on account of it (by all accounts, Matthew was the most popular Gospel in the early Church).[21] This way of beginning a narrative about a person would have been more eye-catching for a first-century Jewish reader than for today's reader.

The genealogy is, as everyone knows, stylized. The selectivity and pointedness of the structure of these verses would have been noticed immediately by any Israelite, although this would doubtless have been lost on many Gentile readers. "Jesus Christ, the Son of David, the Son of Abraham" (Matt. 1:1) at once connects not only the historical personages of Abraham and David (two of the most illustrious figures in Israel's history), but it also links Jesus with the covenants that God made with them. As the list continues, some of the kings from Judah are named. After the Babylonian captivity, we see some of their descendants (from the line of kings) until we arrive at Jesus' stepfather, Joseph, in verse 16. Then Matthew draws a conclusion based on the shape of the genealogy he has constructed.[22]

Matthew has written a Gospel for his people, the Jews,[23] a work that would have suited both curious non-Christian and Christian Jews. However, such a remark must

---

20 George N. H. Peters, *The Theocratic Kingdom*, Vol. 2, 48.

21 For an outstanding defense of Matthean priority, see John W. Wenham, *Redating Matthew, Mark and Luke: A Fresh Assault on the Synoptic Problem* (Downers Grove, IL: InterVarsity, 1992). Though it is not the last word on the subject, I cannot recommend this work too highly.

22 By saying this, I am not claiming that the descendants of Joseph listed here are fictitious; only that Matthew has deliberately omitted certain names while including those of four women.

23 Hagner says, "There is...little in the Gospel that is effectively explained as finding its raison d'etre in a supposed gentile readership" (Donald A. Hagner, *Matthew 1–13*, WBC [Dallas: Word Books, 1993], lxv).

be followed up with a recognition of the fact that one of the principal matters he is communicating to his people is God's open hand to the Gentiles. Matthew "clearly intends the theme of the good news for Gentiles to bracket the whole Gospel."[24] That the "fourteen generations" mentioned by author are somewhat artificially arrived at, revealing something about how Matthew is going to use the OT (he quotes a form of the LXX).[25] Here he employs it to call attention to the Davidic ancestors of Jesus, drawing an apparent connection with the Hebrew name "David," which has a numerical value of fourteen.[26]

Is Matthew being deceptive? Jewish readers of his book would certainly know of the omissions and would also be aware of the unconventional inclusion of proselyte women into a genealogy. They would easily detect Matthew's stylizations; and there is no doubt that he wanted them to. Matthew 1:17 is there to confirm those very suspicions. But it is there too to draw the readers' attention to the Davidic ancestry of Jesus, and, therefore to His claim to the throne. This emphasis is especially brought out in the two episodes recorded in chapter 2:1-12, but also in the angel's declaration that "He will save His people from their sins" (Matt. 1:21). "His people[27]" is a way of speaking which Luke's Gospel employs three times to refer to Israel (Lk. 1:68, 77; 7:16). That the David/Jesus link was at the forefront of the author's mind seems clear also from the lack of any interest in the Maccabean period.[28] Hence, Jesus' lineage through Joseph made Him the rightful heir to the covenant promises to David.

The first "fulfillment formula" in this Gospel has to do with the virgin conception: "So all this was done that it might be fulfilled which was spoken by the Lord through the prophet, saying: '*Behold, the virgin shall be with child, and bear a Son, and they shall call His name Immanuel*,' which is translated, 'God with us'" (Matt. 1:22-23).

What Mathew does with this quotation from Isaiah 7:14 is to show first that Isaiah was referring to a virgin birth. But he also employs the birth of Jesus as a literal fulfillment of the prophet. As we shall see, this is not the only sense of fulfillment that Matthew uses.

The second chapter opens with the visit of the Magi, "wise men from the East," who followed a star to Bethlehem and somehow knew that the King of the Jews had been born. Significantly, they also knew that this King was divine, for on no other accounting could their "worship" of Him be explained (Matt. 2:1-2). The Holy Spirit leaves us with tantalizingly little information about these men, who would have been accompanied by a notable retinue. The whole story is told in the most concise way

24 J. D. G. Dunn, *Jesus Remembered*, 341.

25 "Of the twenty formal quotations peculiar to Mt, seven are Septuagintal. Seven are non-Septuagintal. In six there is a mixture of Septuagintal and non-Septuagintal" (Robert H. Gundry, *The Use of the Old Testament in St. Matthew's Gospel* [Leiden: E. J. Brill, 1967], 149).

26 Herbert W. Bateman IV, Darrell L. Bock, Gordon H. Johnston, *Jesus the Messiah: Tracing the Promises, Expectations, and Coming of Israel's King* (Grand Rapids: Kregel, 2012), 425.

27 Recall that this is spoken to Joseph, whom the angel addressed as "son of David" (Matt. 1:20). In Matthew, all nine occasions the phrase is used (twice in Matt. 20:30-31) the focus is upon Jesus' lineage. This is even true of Matt. 1:20, where the angel is speaking to Joseph, since the message is about Jesus.

28 John Nolland, *The Gospel of Matthew*, NIGTC (Grand Rapids: Eerdmans, 2005), 85

possible, as if to signify that for all this fanfare, the Messiah was to be rejected by His people. In my opinion, the sanest understanding of the star is that it was supernatural and probably angelic (cf. Rev. 1:20; 9:1). Stars in nature do not move and stand over buildings (Matt. 2:9). Therefore, it is futile trying to associate this star with a celestial body.[29]

One thing is for sure: the Magi's arrival in Jerusalem caused a big stir. Enough of a stir that King Herod himself was disturbed by the commotion. So much so that he "gathered all the chief priests and scribes" and had them tell him "Where the Christ was to be born" (Matt. 2:4). These were the "upper echelon of the priestly order,"[30] showing perhaps the perturbation of Herod. One interesting thing about this enquiry is that, aside from the genealogy in Matthew 1:1-18, Herod's question is the first mention of the "Christ" in the Gospel. But the visitors did not refer to Him as the Christ, only as the king. Hence, here we have Herod, an Idumean, learned in Jewish religion, tying together the titles of Christ and King (or at least Matthew does so). This again shows how alive the expectation of prophetic truth was at this time, and it is even more heightened by the quotation of Micah 5:2 by the religious leaders (Matt. 2:6). The use of the verse as a proof text is straightforward enough, and it gave the impatient Herod the information he wanted—Christ was to be born in Bethlehem, Judah.[31]

The Flight to Egypt

Joseph is told to leave for Egypt before Herod finds and tries to kill the child. He and Mary take Jesus away that night "until the death of Herod." What Matthew does next looks interpretively strained. He claims that Hosea 11:1 is fulfilled in this incident (Matt. 2:13-15), or at least in the return from Egypt. But Hosea 11:1, in its original setting, speaks about Israel, not its Messiah. What is Matthew thinking? John Sailhamer offers a convincing argument that the evangelist is connecting Hosea with Numbers 24:8. I believe he is right, but why didn't Matthew simply cite the book of Numbers? After calling upon Isaiah 7:14 (Matt. 1:22-23) and Micah 5:2 (Matt. 2:6) to give plain-sense fulfillments of OT prophecy concerning Jesus, what is he doing here? Surely, we cannot believe that he is suddenly changing tack and dispensing with literal fulfillment?

It has been suggested that Matthew is here employing a special Judaic form of interpretation.[32] But such things are easier to say than to prove.

What Sailhamer and others[33] have to offer is a recognition that Hosea 11 is forward-leaning in its intention. Sailhamer calls attention to Brevard Childs' canonical interpretation, wherein the prophetic thrust of the book's later composition furnishes

---

29 David Hill, *The Gospel of Matthew*, NCBC (Grand Rapids: Eerdmans, 1982), 83

30 John Nolland, *The Gospel of Matthew*, 112.

31 As the Magi were "divinely warned" after seeing the child (Matt. 2:12), it may not be a stretch to surmise that they were likewise supernaturally informed about the birth of Christ.

32 E.g., Arnold G. Fruchtenbaum, *Yeshua: The Life of Messiah from A Messianic Jewish Perspective*, Vol. 1 (San Antonio, TX: Ariel, 2020), 20-21.

33 For example, Abner Chou, *The Hermeneutics of the Biblical Writers* (Grand Rapids: Kregel, 2018), 134-135.

a messianic expectation rooted in the declaration of Hosea 3:5: "Afterward the children of Israel shall return and seek the LORD their God and David their king. They shall fear the LORD and His goodness in the latter days."

Sailhamer believes that Hosea himself did intend the arrangement which Childs attributes to later compilers. He reminds us of his oft-repeated dictum, that the historical event recorded in Scripture is not the same as its significance to the writer(s). It is the significance of the exodus within the theology of the Pentateuch that has been missed, says Sailhamer.[34] But not by Hosea! The prophet is exegeting the "messianic meaning" of the Torah in a way similar to Matthew. Three of the four Pentateuchal poems (Gen. 49; Num. 24, Deut. 32) combine to point towards the coming of the Messiah.[35] Numbers 24:8-9 and Genesis 49:9b are especially salient here.[36] Hence:

> When Matthew quoted Hosea 11:1 as fulfilled in the life of Christ, he was not resorting to typological interpretation of OT events. He was, rather, drawing the *sensus literalis* of the OT description of the exodus from the book of Hosea, and it in turn was drawn from Hosea's exegesis of the *sensus literalis* of the Pentateuch.[37]

This appears to me to be a very plausible and satisfactory explanation of the whole problem. Abner Chou has come to similar, though not identical, conclusions about an eschatological "new exodus" and "new David" through studying the Psalms (e.g., Psalm 18) and the "second exodus" motif in the Prophets.[38] What Chou, and especially Sailhamer, have done is to obviate any resort to typological interpretation in Matthew 2:15.[39] Matthew (and Hosea) were exegeting a theme or messianic thread.[40]

Two More "Fulfillment" Issues

We have not left Matthew 2, and we must confront two more "fulfillment issues." After Herod hears about Jesus being from Bethlehem and discovers that the Magi have left, he sends soldiers there to kill all the young males under two years of age (Matt. 2:16-18). This odious act was fully in line with Herod's character, particularly in his old age. In this incident the desperate unfairness of the world is compressed. Innocent mothers are deprived of their children because Jesus was born in Bethlehem. God

34 John H. Sailhamer, *The Meaning of the Pentateuch*, 514-515. His whole argument (510-521) needs to be appreciated.

35 Ibid, 518.

36 Ibid, 520.

37 Ibid, 515, cf. 521.

38 See, in addition to the above, Abner Chou, *The Hermeneutics of the Biblical Writers*, 107-110.

39 Some recent typological explanations of the use of Hosea 11:1 run confusingly to Hosea 11:10-11 in an attempt to show that "Matthew is showing that the greatest significance of Hosea 11 is not the old exodus but the new exodus" (Mitchell L. Chase, *40 Questions About Typology and Allegory* [Grand Rapids: Kregel, 2020], 61). See also, James M. Hamilton Jr., *Typology*, 271. However, Hosea 11:10-11 and its context shows Israel returning "trembling like a bird from Egypt" which better suits their return in, e.g., Ezra 8:21-23, not a spiritual second exodus wrapped up in the life, death, and resurrection of Jesus. See Hamilton, *Typology*, 272-276.

40 This matter may also be viewed in terms of corporate solidarity. See, for example, Michael Vlach, *The Old in the New*, 137-141.

could have prevented the atrocity, but He is not obliged to intervene in the evils perpetrated upon the earth—only to judge them.

The killing of the infants is interpreted by Matthew through a reference to Jeremiah 31:15. In its original context that verse nestles within a promise of future comfort for Israel (Jer. 31:7-26), although not too comfortably. Ramah was the town north of Jerusalem where the people were gathered before being sent into exile (Jer. 40:1). Rachel died near Bethlehem (Gen. 35:19), which is south of Jerusalem. Again, we have to ask, what is Matthew doing? The answer probably is to be found in the two locations involving Rachel: one near Bethlehem and one near Ramah (her tomb, 1 Sam. 10:2). Rachel's tears are the tears of the mother of Israel (see Ruth 4:11), and therefore, she represents the grieving women of her land. More tribes of Israel came from Leah than Rachel, but Leah was buried to the north (near Hebron) along with Abraham, Sarah, Isaac, Rebekah, and Jacob (Gen. 49:29-32). So, Rachel stands for the grieving mothers, both in Jeremiah and in Matthew. Matthew's use of the word "fulfilled" (*eplerothe*) is not in the sense of a particular fulfillment of an OT prediction, but a general fulfillment of a metaphor employed by Jeremiah and applicable in the offence of Herod.

Matthew is not finished yet. In the final two verses of chapter 2, he notes that God warns Joseph to avoid the reign of Archelaus in Judah, and so settles north in the Galilean town of Nazareth (Matt. 2:22-23). Matthew claims that the saying of the prophets was fulfilled, that "He shall be called a Nazarene". Notice that Matthew is gathering this from "the prophets" and not a single source. No OT prophet contains such a passage.

The evangelist is not being as cryptic as he might first appear. The root of "Nazareth"[41] and "Nazarene" is *netser* in Hebrew, which is translated "Branch" in Isaiah's great prophecy of the coming King in Isaiah 11:1. He is making use of the wordplay.[42]

Matthew's "Fulfillment" Formulas: A Summary

To summarize, Matthew has employed four fulfillment quotations in his infancy narrative: 1:22-23; 2:15; 2:17-18, and 2:23. Only in the first is a straightforward correspondence found (from Isa. 7:14).[43] The other three fulfillments involve themes, analogies, and metaphors. This fits the Jewish readership for whom Matthew first wrote his Gospel, although Gentile readers might scratch their heads. But in each case, there is some affinity between the OT passage and the fulfillment that Matthew says it points to.

---

41 Matthew spells the name three different ways in his account, thereby lending it a somewhat elastic form by which he might more easily refer it to the Hebrew *neser* and thus relate it to the "Branch" of Isaiah 11:1.

42 Donald A. Hagner, *Matthew 1–13*, 40-42 has an excellent discussion of the passage. See also Nolland, *Matthew*, 128-131.

43 Matthew also records the chief priests and scribes' citation of Mic. 5:2 (Matt. 2:4-6). Since it is not his own interpretation, he does not include a fulfilment formula.

In an excellent essay on the meaning of "fulfillment," Charles Dyer concludes that one should not try to determine if an OT prophecy is actually fulfilled just because of word *pleroo* is used. He states:

> The only safe approach to determining the fulfillment of prophecy is first to understand the prophecy in its original context. Then one must examine the New Testament to see if the prophecy corresponds to the later events that actually happened. Biblical fulfillment occurs when the meaning of a specific Old Testament prophecy finds its exact correspondence in a New Testament person, activity, or event.[44]

The Preexistence of Christ in John's Prologue

Although it is not an annunciation story, it is proper to include here a note about how John begins his narrative. John self-consciously invokes the creation story, but he introduces the *Logos*, or "Word,"[45] as the Principal in the making of the world: "In the beginning was the Word, and the Word was with God, and the Word was God. He was in the beginning with God. All things were made through Him, and without Him nothing was made that was made" (Jn. 1:1-3).

Here the *Logos* is no incidental actor in the Creation Project. He, for it is a "He," is there at the very beginning of everything. Before Adam, before angels, the Word was present, and He was together "with God." John 1:14 and 18 make it clear that "God" in the Prologue is God the Father, with the exception of the last part of John 1:1; "and the Word was God." In that place this *Logos* is Himself designated as deity.

This either means there are two "Gods," or it means that God is a plurality, one Being but with more than one "expression." That is, the apostle declares at the start of his Gospel that the God of the OT is at least a plurality of "Persons" in a single essence.[46] And this Word, who John will go on to identify as Jesus prior to His being born into the world (Jn. 1:17), is the one through whom God (the Father) made everything.

This introduction forms a stark contrast to the infancy narratives in Matthew and Luke, although it must be said that both of those writers do include a reference to Jesus' deity (Lk. 1:32, 35; Matt. 1:23). The one who is born into lowly circumstances

44 Charles H. Dyer, "The Biblical Meaning of 'Fulfillment,'" in *Issues in Dispensationalism*, eds. Wesley R. Willis and John R. Master (Chicago: Moody, 1994), 70. The whole chapter is a must read.

45 I will use the terms *Logos* and Word interchangeably in this chapter because John's use of *Logos* requires some explanation. For a fuller examination, see Paul Martin Henebury, "Jesus Christ, The Logos of God: An Inquiry into the Johannine Prologue and Its Significance," *Conservative Theological Journal*, 8 (March 2004), 87-105.

46 I do not intend to drift into systematic theology here. The Christian doctrine of the Trinity has been ably defended and expounded multiple times. My purpose here is to come at John's words in a way that demonstrates the several glories of Jesus in the biblical worldview, and therefore show how He is central to how we ought to think about the world. For excellent delineations of the triunity of God, see Millard J. Erickson, *God in Three Persons: A Contemporary Interpretation of the Trinity* (Grand Rapids: Baker, 1995); and Robert Letham, *The Holy Trinity: In Scripture, History, Theology, and Worship* (Phillipsburg, NJ: P&R, 2019).

in Bethlehem, and who grows up in obscure Nazareth in Galilee is the Creator of the land, the sea, the plants, the animals, and of human beings. The Word is the Creator, which means He is the definer. What He thinks and says about His creatures is what they are. I think it is fair to state that the very Being of the *Logos* who will be Messiah is that His words and actions correspond to each other.

The prologue continues: "In Him was life, and the life was the light of men" (Jn. 1:4). This verse makes the claim that the *Logos* of God is the source of the life of men. This would be natural enough to infer since the varied concepts represented by the Greek term Logos—word, reason, world-constituting intelligence, etc.—presuppose life in its highest possible expression. We must not, however, allow ourselves to associate John's use of *Logos* with the purely Greek philosophical idea. In saying that the *Logos* is divine and personal, John knows he is going beyond Greek philosophy. In fact, it seems far more likely that he had something else in mind.

Stuhlmacher leans toward the influence of OT wisdom (*hokmah*) but does not convince.[47] Some writers believe the Aramaic concept of *memra* is present in John's prologue,[48] but there is good reason to question this view. Lindars claims there is little in common between the idea of *memra* (e.g., in the 2nd century A.D. Targum Onkelos) and John's *Logos* because *memra* "is a stylistic device to soften anthropomorphisms of the OT, so that 'the word of the Lord' is simply a synonym for 'the Lord.'"[49] In other words, because *memra* is used in the context of paraphrasing and functions as a "stand-in," it ought not to be pressed beyond that function. It has been shown (especially by Jacob Neusner)[50] that one must tread very carefully when using the Targums to interpret early Judaism (actually Judaisms), never mind the NT. Each citation must be "demonstrated on a case-by-case basis."[51] Simply collecting long quotes from these Aramaic paraphrases is unconvincing because it just accumulates unsifted material with large question-marks still hanging over it.

It seems far more likely that John had in mind the *dabar Yahweh* or Word of God.[52] The Hebrew term *dabar* could function similarly to the Greek *logos*.[53] It would, therefore, not be a stretch for John to equate the two and fashion it to apply it to God's Son, who became incarnate.

So, John presents the *Logos* as the divine, eternal Creator, through whom everything was made and in whom the life of every human is based. He is the one through

47 Peter Stuhlmacher, *Biblical Theology of the New Testament*, 683-684.

48 This position is argued for with many citations by Arnold G. Fruchtenbaum, *Yeshua*, Vol. 1, 206-257. Unfortunately, the author does not provide plausible evidence for reading post-first century (and often much later) Targums into early first century inspired writings. He does not consider the *dabar Yahweh* (Ibid, 199), nor OT wisdom as options, although both have been widely discussed.

49 Barnabas Lindars, *The Gospel of John*, NCBC (Grand Rapids: Eerdmans, 1982), 83.

50 Jacob Neusner, *Judaism When Christianity Began: A Survey of Belief and Practice* (Louisville: Westminster John Knox Press, 2002), 9-10.

51 C. A. Evans, "Judaism, Post-A.D. 70," in *Dictionary of the Later New Testament & Its Development*, eds. Ralph P. Martin and Peter H. Davids (Downers Grove, IL: InterVarsity, 1997), 607.

52 Ibid. See also D. H. Johnson, "Logos," in *Dictionary of Jesus and the Gospels*, eds. Joel B. Green, Scot McKnight, and I. Howard Marshall (Downers Grove, IL: IVP, 1992), 484.

53 See George R. Beasley-Murray, *John*, WBC (Waco, TX: Word, 1987), 6-10.

whom God can be approached. Not only that, but upon belief "in his name" (Jn. 1:12), a person may attain the inestimable honor of becoming a child of God. A transaction occurs whereby a believer is "born... of God" (Jn. 1:13).

Matthew and Luke tell us that the child who is to be born will be divine. Matthew, in his citation of Isaiah 7:14, goes on to translate "Immanuel" for us. Jesus will be "God with us" (Matt. 1:23). This contrast of roles, from creating the fabric of the world to becoming a helpless creature of the world, is stunning in its commitment to creation. Luke's presentation of this aspect of Jesus' nature is perhaps best seen in these words of Gabriel: "He will be great and will be called the Son of the Highest; and the Lord God will give Him the throne of His father David. And He will reign over the house of Jacob forever, and of His kingdom there will be no end" (Lk. 1:32-33). We see that there is no discontinuity in Matthew, Luke, and John in the characterization of Jesus as divine. Indeed, His name, "Yahweh is salvation," contextualizes all three perspectives. Jesus will be God with mankind dwelling with us as a man (Matthew). He is the Son of God who will one day reign on David's throne (Luke). And His place of origin is before creation and intimately involved in its purpose and goal (John). John too has Him entering the world (Jn. 1:14), but he places special emphasis on His unpopularity with many and His rejection by most men (Jn. 1:10-11). It is not possible to take the position where all this is new, but there is an interesting mix of wonder and disapproval developing. "This child," Simeon remarks, "is destined for the fall and rising of many in Israel, and for a sign which will be spoken against... that the thoughts of many hearts may be revealed" (Lk. 2:34-35).

6

COVENANT AND KINGDOM IN JOHN THE BAPTIST

He was not that Light, but was sent to bear witness of that Light.
– John 1:8

Once we move away from the annunciation chapters in Matthew and Luke, it does not take long until we run into the proclamation of the Kingdom of God (usually called "the kingdom of Heaven" in Matthew). If we are talking about the Kingdom of God in these early chapters, then we are talking about the covenant with David and his line. Jesus is David's Son and heir. The question to be asked is whether the kingdom concept in the NT has Israel as a geopolitical nation in view. We must proceed chronologically, being careful not to read the rest of the NT into the history of the life of Jesus in the Gospels. John does not major on the theme of the Kingdom, mentioning it only three times (Jn. 3:3, 5; 18:36), and I will include his sparse statements as we go.

The so-called Synoptic Gospels, Matthew, Mark, and Luke, all have a good deal to say about the Kingdom. It must be stressed that Jesus' teaching on the Kingdom should be understood *as it is reported*, and not overlaid with assumed adjustments in Paul. Whether or not one believes that Paul's letters precede the writing of the Gospels, who would dare to say that the words of Jesus have been twisted into conformity to the great apostle? Who but a denier of inerrancy and inspiration would claim that we do not actually have what Jesus preached but a reconstruction and redaction of His teaching?

John the Baptist Preaches the Kingdom

After Matthew has completed his narration of Jesus' birth, ending with His family's relocation in Nazareth, he plunges straight into John the Baptist's preaching of the Kingdom of heaven (Matt. 3:1-2). Before examining in detail the preaching of Jesus concerning the Kingdom—a process that will span several chapters—we need to look at His forerunner.

The Gospels and Josephus[1] accord John the Baptist a place of honor as a highly respected (at least among the general populace) and powerful influence in Judea and Galilee in the twenties A.D.. From Luke 3:7, 15, 21, Matthew 3:5, and Mark 1:5 it is clear that he drew a lot of attention and that his impact was significant. He even had a band of followers (Lk. 7:19; Jn. 3:25), and some of these men continued to be identified as his disciples for years after his demise. The Apostle Paul encountered some as far afield as Ephesus in Acts 19:1-7. John's job was not to grant certain initiates private access to Messiah's identity. No, John introduced Jesus with the ancient equivalent of a loud bang!

John the Baptist's preaching is chock full of OT references. Walter Kaiser notes over fifty allusions or quotations of the OT, mainly from Isaiah, Malachi, and Jeremiah.[2] John is a new prophet of God who has appeared on the scene after more than four centuries of silence, but he is an OT prophet in character and substance. His ministry is announced suddenly, Elijah-like, by Matthew: "In those days John the Baptist came preaching in the wilderness of Judea, and saying, 'Repent, for the kingdom of heaven is at hand!'" (Matt. 3:1-2).

In contrast to Jesus, who will begin His ministry in the north, John preaches in the southern part of Israel, but in the wilderness, baptizing in the river Jordan (Matt. 3:5-6; Lk. 3:3; Jn. 1:28). His message includes moral reformation and repentance (Matt. 3:8; Lk. 3:3, 10-14), so he, like the OT prophets before him, was concerned with justice and righteousness. This is not surprising as the Kingdom of God on earth requires these things. The reason John gives for preaching repentance is the coming Kingdom of heaven (or God), and the preparation for "He who is coming."

> I indeed baptize you with water unto repentance, but He who is coming after me is mightier than I, whose sandals I am not worthy to carry. He will baptize you with the Holy Spirit and fire. "His winnowing fan *is* in His hand, and He will thoroughly clean out His threshing floor, and gather His wheat into the barn; but He will burn up the chaff with unquenchable fire (Matt. 3:11-12).

What is striking about John the Baptist's message is that it conjures imagery more associated with the Hebrew prophecies that concern what we know as the *second* advent. In the OT this phenomenon arises continually. It is a constant theme that does not go away.[3] In the NT, although it is only to be expected that a great deal of importance is attached to Christ's first coming, the emphasis upon the second coming is just as strong as it is in the OT.[4]

---

1 See Flavius Josephus, *Antiquities of the Jews*, 18.116-119.

2 Walter C. Kaiser, Jr., *The Promise-Plan of God: A Biblical Theology of the Old and New Testaments* (Grand Rapids: Zondervan, 2008), 234. Kaiser is relying on a work, *John the Baptist, Forerunner and Martyr* by J. Elder Cumming.

3 E.g., Isa. 9:6-7; 11:1-10; 26:15; Jer. 3:14-18; 23:1-8; Ezek. 34:25-30; 37:15-28; Zech. 14:16-21.

4 See *The Words of the Covenant*, Vol. 1, 59-62.

This opinion about Matthew 3:11-12 is not accepted universally, however. There are many who believe that because the baptism with the Holy Spirit occurred as a consequence of the first coming, the baptism[5] of fire and the separation of wheat from chaff must also be sought for there.[6] This does not follow, however, because the Bible many times forges the first and second comings of Messiah into one passage, with hindsight helping us to distinguish what happens when.[7] Matthew's language is reminiscent of the Parable of the Wheat and Tares that he records in chapter 13. Jesus is reported as saying this:

> The field is the world, the good seeds are the sons of the kingdom, but the tares are the sons of the wicked *one*. The enemy who sowed them is the devil, the harvest is the end of the age, and the reapers are the angels Therefore as the tares are gathered and burned in the fire, so it will be at the end of this age... Then the righteous will shine forth as the sun in the kingdom of their Father. He who has ears to hear, let him hear! (Matt. 13:39-40, 43).

There was nothing in Jesus' ministry that matches the "fire" and the separation—a term of eschatological judgment.[8] The language of Matthew calls to remembrance such passages as this one:

> "For behold, the day is coming, burning like an oven, and all the proud, yes, all who do wickedly will be stubble. And the day which is coming shall burn them up," Says the LORD of hosts, "That will leave them neither root nor branch. But to you who fear My name The Sun of Righteousness shall arise with healing in His wings; And you shall go out and grow fat like stall-fed calves. You shall trample the wicked, for they shall be ashes under the soles of your feet on the day that I do *this*," says the LORD of hosts (Mal. 4:1-3).

This prophecy pertains to the second advent, as indeed do parts of Isaiah 40, which is used by Matthew, Mark, and Luke to portray John the Baptist (Matt. 3:3; Mk. 1:1-4; Lk. 3:4-6). Jesus applied this Scripture to John in Luke 7:27. The Gospel of John records this passage as being upon the lips of John the Baptist himself when he was asked to identify himself (Jn. 1:23).[9] Isaiah foresees a time when Jerusalem's "warfare is ended" and "her iniquity is pardoned" (Isa. 40:2), and when "The glory of the LORD shall be revealed, and all flesh shall see *it* together" (Isa. 40:5).[10] So Isaiah 40:5 matches the second advent, not the first. We are within a mystery here, one that must merge contingency with predetermination. John's call to repentance was bona fide, but the rejection of it was certain. We see a similar thing in Acts 3, where Peter tells

5 Actually, it is "baptize," not "baptism." I think this is exegetically important since to baptize in the context implies a widespread effect.
6 For example, Charles L. Quarles, *Matthew*, EBTC (Bellingham, WA: Lexham, 2022), 142-143, who sees it as punishment in hell upon death.
7 See e.g., Mic. 5:2; Isa. 9:6-7; Zech. 9:9-10; Mal. 3:1-4; 1 Cor. 11:23-26.
8 E.g., George Eldon Ladd, *The Presence of the Future*, 184-185.
9 Luke uses more of the prophecy than do the other evangelists.
10 See also Isa. 35:2.

the Jews that Christ will return, but only if they repent (Acts 3:19-20). Of course, due to their hatred of Jesus, this is not really in the cards. This means that the Church era will intervene between the first and second comings even though the offer of repentance is a real one.

John the Baptist and Elijah

Saying that Isaiah 40 refers to the second advent does not mean that some part of it cannot be concerned with the first advent. John the Baptist is the forerunner of the Lord. Therefore, when Jesus later spoke in reference to John the Baptist, saying "Elijah has come already" (Matt. 17:12-13), He is saying that John is a true Elijah figure, even when John had himself told the people that he was *not* Elijah (Jn. 1:21). Because Christ was rejected for who He was, John's Elijah-like role was also rejected. Jesus testified of John the Baptist that "if you are willing to receive *it*, he is Elijah who is to come" (Matt. 11:14). The vast majority of the Jews were not willing.

But there is a fascinating double entendre in Jesus' witness to John, as can best be seen if we reexamine what is said in Matthew 17:

> And His disciples asked Him, saying, "Why then do the scribes say that Elijah must come first?" Jesus answered and said to them, "Indeed, Elijah is coming first and will restore all things. But I say to you that Elijah has come already, and they did not know him but did to him whatever they wished" (Matt. 17:10-12).

What is interesting about the Lord's testimony here is that He seems to both give the impression that John the Baptist's ministry ended with his martyrdom (Matt. 14:1-11), but He also said that "Elijah is coming first and will restore all things" (Matt. 17:11). Many scholars have argued that the fulfillment of the Elijah prophecy (Mal. 4:5) is to be confined to John the Baptist.[11] But their explanations of Jesus' use of the future indicative *apokathistemi* ("will restore") in reference to *John's* coming, not Elijah's, is suspect. That Elijah had just been seen alongside Moses on the Mount of Transfiguration (Matt. 17:1-8) no doubt caused the disciples to ask their question about Elijah's coming first (for they saw Jesus before they saw Elijah). John's ministry does not force us to conclude that there is no future work for *Elijah* to do. Malachi refers to Elijah coming "before the coming of the great and dreadful day of the LORD" (Mal. 4:5). That is certainly not a reference to Christ's first coming![12]

11 E.g., Leon Morris, *The Gospel According to Matthew* (Grand Rapids: Eerdmans, 1992), 443; Robert H. Mounce, *Matthew* (Peabody, MA: Hendricksen, 1991), 169; Donald A. Hagner, *Matthew 14–28* (Dallas: Word Books, 1995), 499. Cf. William L. Lane, *The Gospel of Mark*, NICNT (Grand Rapids: Eerdmans, 1974), 326-327.

12 It is to be noted that Malachi refers to "the Law of Moses, My servant" immediately before mentioning Elijah (Mal. 4:4). The last three persons spoken of by the prophet (and, therefore, the Prophets) are Moses, Elijah, and Yahweh (Mal. 4:3-5). This may well have triggered the question of the disciples after seeing them together on the mount.

The puzzlement enters because interpreters neglect the separation of first and second coming prophecies and proceed to stuff second coming texts into first coming settings. This "first coming hermeneutic," when applied to prophecies about the second coming, always distorts the OT. It gives "impressionistic" interpretations of the prophets, excluding important details, ignoring discontinuities,[13] often concerning the land, Jerusalem, or the temple. But there need not be any confusion for the modern reader.[14] John the Baptist was described as going before Jesus "in the spirit and power of Elijah" (Lk. 1:17). In 2 Kings 2:9-10 Elisha asks Elijah for a double portion of his spirit. Just what that entailed is hard to know for sure (although Elisha is recorded as performing twice the miracles that Elijah did). But if Elijah's "spirit" was transferable to Elisha, why would it not also be transferable to John the Baptist? And if so, it could be said that Elijah did come through John the Baptist (although not in the sense of possessing him!).[15] It would also mean that, at the very least, it would remain an open question whether Elijah is to return prior to Jesus' second coming.[16]

One's understanding of the eschatological ministry of Elijah in relation to the ministry of John the Baptist seems to depend upon one's view of eschatology generally and the interpretation of the book of Revelation in particular.[17] Although it enjoys less than majority support, the fact remains that, despite John being the fulfillment of Elijah "if you will receive it," this does not solve the problem of the second coming emphasis in Malachi 4, nor does it address John's own denial that he was Elijah: "And they asked him, 'What then? Are you Elijah?' He said, 'I am not' (Jn. 1:21).

There is a straightforward way to reconcile the problem. What if John's coming "in the spirit and power of Elijah" would have sufficed if Jesus had been received for who He was? I recognize that this option is unpopular because it requires that a genuine offer of the Kingdom was preached, which creates tension with the necessity of Calvary. The suffering Servant must precede that glorified Servant.

However, this is only an apparent paradox. There exists a parallel tension in some expressions of soteriology where the offer of the Gospel is said to be genuine for all to whom it comes, yet only the elect will believe. If one asks how an individual can be offered salvation if they are not elected to receive it, the answer that is usually given is no external influence is applied to the will so that a genuine offer is genuinely refused.

13 When comparing passages, it is important to note both similarities and dissimilarities, but it is the dissimilarities that are the most crucial to ponder.

14 In his book on *Typology*, 135-139, James Hamilton says that Elijah and Elisha prefigure Jesus and John. But since John is said to be Elijah-like this would make Elijah typify both Jesus and John. This is hard to swallow.

15 I am certainly not suggesting that Elijah somehow dwelt within John. But Elijah's spirit (however it is understood) may have had an influence on John's appearance and ministry. Of course, this is just speculation.

16 Craig L. Blomberg, *Matthew* (Nashville, TN: Broadman Press, 1992), 266. See also Stanley D. Toussaint, *Behold the King: A Study of Matthew* (Grand Rapids: Kregel, 1980), 211; and the insightful treatment of Ed Glasscock, *Matthew*, 357-359. Mark also refers to this incident (Mk. 9:11-13), but employs the present tense (*apokathistanei*), which focuses attention on John's sufferings. See e.g., Louis Barbieri, *Mark* (Chicago: Moody, 1995), 199-200.

17 I am referring to one of the two witnesses in Revelation 11. If, as I believe, one of these witnesses is Elijah, then John the Baptist cannot be conceived as the fulfillment of Malachi 4's Elijah prophecy. See comments in that place.

I have little interest in this book to engage in the debate between Calvinist and Arminian views on salvation. I only mention it because many evangelical scholars believe in the tension and because it is analogous to the problem presently before us. Perhaps the tension between the offer of the Kingdom and the rejection and suffering of the Messiah is deliberate. In fact, upon reflection, how else could one claim that Israel's rejection of their promised Liberator was a real rejection? The scenario, as I understand it, must look something like this:

1. Messiah/Christ is prophesied as both coming to reign and to suffer vicariously.

2. Logically He will suffer before He reigns.

3. His suffering is said to include rejection and death.

4. Therefore, the OT leaves us with a Savior who dies before He becomes King.

5. From an OT perspective, this means that either Messiah will rise from the dead immediately after He is killed and assume the role of King of the Earth, or that there is a time gap between His resurrection and His glorious reign.

6. If the latter, there must of necessity be two comings of Messiah; one to suffer and die, and one to conquer and rule.

7. An alternative might be that Messiah's reign would be spiritual and invisible rather than (or prior to) being physical, but from an OT vantage point this is not even hinted at.

8. If there are two comings of Messiah, then Elijah would have to be a precursor to both.

This is where John the Baptist coming "in the spirit and power of Elijah" enters in. John is the forerunner of the first coming of Christ, and according to Matthew 17:12, he was destined to suffer (his death being alluded to). A resurrected John could be the forerunner of the second coming, but to what point? Elijah himself was transported up to heaven, seemingly without seeing death.[18] He therefore would be in a good position to return in line with the expectation raised by Malachi 4. Revelation 11:5-7 describes an Elijah-type figure who will prophesy for three and a half years before being killed by the Beast of the Abyss.

Leaving aside the interpretation of the book of Revelation for the present—although a futurist interpretation certainly lends credence to Christ's statement that "Elijah is coming first and will restore all things" (Matt. 17:11)—it would seem reasonable to assume that since Malachi so emphasizes the ministry of Elijah in connection with the *conquering* Messiah (viz. at the second coming), Elijah himself will

18 It is unnecessary to press this point.

indeed return to prepare the way for the future coming of King Jesus. We therefore extend the list of above points to include the following assertions:

> 9. At the first coming of Messiah as the suffering Servant John the Baptist is "Elijah" coming in Elijah's "spirit and power."
>
> 10. At the second coming of Messiah as Conqueror and King, Elijah himself returns to prepare the way.[19]

There is little difficulty then in accepting John the Baptist's first coming ministry as "Elijah" who prepared the way for Messiah, preached the coming of the Kingdom of God, and was rejected. However, there are *two* comings of Messiah, and although this is hardly discerned in the OT and was not perceived until after the resurrection in the NT, it is necessary that Elijah come to prepare the way of the victorious Davidic King Messiah in the future.

John the Baptist's Kingdom Message

There is no doubt that John's chief function was to announce the arrival of the Coming One of OT expectation. Yet by his own admission, he did not know the Messiah as such until Jesus' baptism (Jn. 1:33). Hence, for some time prior to pointing to Jesus as "the Lamb of God who takes away the sin of the world" (Jn. 1:29), John preached less specifically of the imminent arrival of Israel's Messiah. He testified that when he baptized Jesus, he saw the Holy Spirit descend upon Him in the form of a dove (Mk. 1:9-10). He already knew that he was not worthy to loosen Messiah's sandal strap (Mk. 1:7),[20] because the Coming One was mightier than he (Mk. 1:7). By the time of Jesus' baptism, John understood Jesus to be the mighty one he was preparing Israel to meet (Matt. 3:13-15). He knew Jesus was the Christ (Jn. 3:28). Nevertheless, it appears that it was not until after baptizing Jesus that he understood that Jesus was also the Son of God (Jn. 1:33-34; cf. Matt. 3:16-17).[21]

The times in which the Baptist preached were often difficult for the general populace of Israel, with the lavish lifestyles of the rich and powerful being paid for by taxation of the lower classes. This, amid the uncertainties of the agrarian way of life, would have made John's radical call to faith and repentance difficult to hear. What about overthrowing the oppressor? Why must the common people repent? These questions may have run through the minds of many as they listened to John.

---

19 Add to this the prophecy about "the Messenger of the Covenant" in Mal. 3:1-3 (especially vv. 2-3) and you're back in a second coming scenario.

20 "In Judaism this was such a degrading act that a Hebrew slave was not to undertake it" (Darrell, L. Bock, *Luke 1:1–9:50*, BECNT [Grand Rapids: Baker, 1994], 320-321).

21 Because the Gospels report all these facts, it is ridiculous to think that Jesus was at one time a disciple of John, as for example, James D. G. Dunn, *Jesus Remembered*, 350-352. Compare the suggestion by Webb that, "Through his baptism by John, Jesus was... effectively joining John's movement and becoming a follower of John" (Robert L. Webb, "Jesus' Baptism by John: Its Historicity and Significance," in *Key Events in the Life of the Historical Jesus: A Collaborative Exploration of Context and Coherence*, by Darrell L Bock and Robert L. Webb [Grand Rapids: Eerdmans, 2009], 135).

Judea was under direct Roman governance. While in Galilee, Herod Antipas ruled capably but always attempted to extend the Hellenist influences that he had imbibed during his many years in Rome.[22] John's call for "fruits worthy of repentance" (Lk. 3:8) would have struck a powerful counter note to the encroaching Hellenism, as well as the lifestyles of those who promoted it. It would also have added fuel to the fire of messianic expectation that nearly all NT scholars comment on.[23]

When we piece together the message of John the Baptist in the Four Gospels it is clear that he is presaging a new age. It has been well said, "For John the Baptist the kingdom corresponded to everything that the name 'Israel' represented."[24] He demands repentance (conversion) in view of the coming Kingdom, yet He does not refer to Jesus as King but as "the Lamb of God"—a name that speaks of sacrifice. This is intriguing. John is filled with the Holy Spirit and preaches God's words, yet those words present a tension between preparing for the Kingdom of God and the fate of the Lamb of God. This seeming paradox is intensified with the understanding that Jesus is God's Son. Obviously, righteous living is needed in the face of the Kingdom's arrival, but *why does John point to Jesus as God's Lamb and not God's King?* Few writers have posed this question, but it seems to be worth asking.

The only adequate answer to the question would appear to be that John comprehended enough of his calling and mission to know that Christ would have to first die and then be presented again to Israel (cf. Psa. 118:22-23). That would explain the ambiguity in his identification with Elijah and his denial of the name since his ministry concerned Jesus as Lamb of God, not King of kings. But that would also mean that he knew that his call to repentance in light of the Kingdom would fail since the Lamb of God to whom he pointed would be handed over to the Romans for execution.

When we look at Matthew 11:18-19 we get a hint of this: "For John came neither eating nor drinking, and they say, 'He has a demon.' The Son of Man came eating and drinking, and they say, 'Look, a glutton and a winebibber, a friend of tax collectors and sinners!' But wisdom is justified by her children."

Jesus' rebuke was aimed at "this generation" (Matt. 16:16), the generation who heard and saw both John the Baptist and Jesus. If John was aware that many were calling him demon-possessed (Lk. 7:33, probably in part on account of his uncouth manner and appearance), he would have known that his message was being rejected along with his person by many, and that, as a consequence of that, the Lamb of God whom he pointed out would likewise be rejected.

Another possibility that needs to be considered is that John the Baptist's idea of the coming Kingdom was spiritual. Specifically, it would not be the expected geopolitical kingdom but rather a kingdom of saints in this evil world ruled by God from

22 Paul Barnett, *Jesus and the Rise of Early Christianity*, 114-121.

23 See here Herbert Bateman's thorough review of the evidence in Herbert W. Bateman IV, et al., *Jesus the Messiah*, 303-325. The realist eschatological expectation of a future Davidic Kingdom is sometimes diluted by amillennial interpreters. See e.g., Herman Ridderbos, *The Coming of the Kingdom* (Phillipsburg, NJ: P&R, 1962), 8-15. Ridderbos highlights the soteriological aspects of the Kingdom.

24 Ronald E. Diprose, "A Theology of the New Covenant: The Foundations of New Testament Theology," *Emmaus Journal* 16 (Winter 2007), 165.

heaven. This is by far the most accepted view. But it suffers on account of its idiosyncrasy. Modern scholars may not find much wrong with the "secret spiritual meaning" of such a Kingdom proclamation, but there is no doubt at all that such powerful preaching, and in such a manner, would only foment the expectations of the covenants of God in the hearts of the people. If John wanted to point people to a spiritual kingdom, he certainly went about it in an odd way!

More than this though is the fact that John said of the Coming One, "His winnowing fan *is* in His hand, and He will thoroughly clean out His threshing floor, and gather His wheat into the barn; but He will burn up the chaff with unquenchable fire" (Matt. 3:12).

What should be noticed here is that the threat of clearing the threshing floor and burning up the chaff—with "unquenchable fire" no less—does not refer to the first coming but must refer to the second (cf. Matt. 13:30, 39). Despite this, it is connected by John with the first coming, which the previous verse demonstrates: "I indeed baptize you with water unto repentance, but He who is coming after me is mightier than I, whose sandals I am not worthy to carry. He will baptize you with the Holy Spirit and fire" (Matt. 3:11).

The baptism with the Holy Spirit is, as we all know, a gift that comes as a result of Jesus' passion and resurrection (e.g., Jn. 7:37-39; Acts 11:16-17). But what is the "fire"? Is it a figurative way of referring to the endowment of power that comes from the Holy Spirit? Or perhaps the refining of one's heart, or of the people of Israel? There are diverse opinions.[25] I take the reference to "fire" as divine judgment, as verse 12 (and Lk. 3:17) appears to indicate, although it probably does not refer to hellfire. It might refer to God as "a consuming fire" (Deut. 4:23), who spoke out of the fire (Deut. 4:12). In the imagery of the coming of Yahweh, He is described as having "devouring fire from His mouth" (Psa. 18:8; Isa. 30:27, 30; cf. Zeph. 3:8). According to Malachi, the coming of "the Messenger of the covenant"[26] will be "like a refiner's fire" (Mal. 3:1-2). Since only one baptism is mentioned, many take the word "fire" as an image of rejection.[27] But it is rejection by God that logically leads to literal judgment.[28] Theologian Graham Cole supports the traditional view that the fire in Matthew 3:11 refers to coming judgment.[29] If there is any connection between Matthew 3:11-12/ Luke 3:16-17 with the OT verses given above, then there is a link to the second

25 The 19th Century NT scholar, Frederic Godet, thought that the "fire" did not signify judgment, but instead denotes the purging of the old nature. See F. Godet, *A Commentary on the Gospel of Luke*, trans. E. W. Shalders, Vol. 1 (Edinburgh: T & T Clark, 1881), 180. See also David Hill, *The Gospel of Matthew*, 94.

26 See *The Words of the Covenant*, Vol. 1, 350-351. My understanding of Mal. 3:1 is that "My messenger" is John the Baptist, and "the Messenger of the covenant" is Christ.

27 E.g., Darrell, L. Bock, *Luke 1:1–9:50*, 322-324.

28 Craig L. Blomberg, *Matthew*, 80. Schnabel notes that the term "Lord of the harvest" is a reference to final judgment in Matthew 3:12; 13:30, 39 (Eckhard J. Schnabel, *Early Christian Mission: Jesus and the Twelve*, Vol. 1 [Downers Grove, IL: InterVarsity, 2004], 312).

29 Graham A. Cole, *He Who Gives Life: The Doctrine of the Holy Spirit* (Wheaton, IL: Crossway, 2007), 181-182. This view is associated with Origen, who knew the Greek very well. See also A. T. Robertson, *Word Pictures in the New Testament*, Vol. 1 (Nashville: Broadman Press, 1930), 28.

coming. So, without wishing to press the matter more than it can bear, I think there is a distinct possibility that in Matthew 3:11-12/Luke 3:16-17 we have another instance where the two comings are perceived as one event.[30]

John the Baptist is a commanding figure in the early part of the Gospel accounts. He did no miracle, but his presence and mission made him "more than a prophet" (Matt. 11:9). He made sure that Jesus got a fitting introduction, even if he came to understand that the majority in Israel would reject his message. His message was a covenant message. The Kingdom he proclaimed was in continuity with the Kingdom anticipated in the Hebrew Bible. He was in the line of OT prophets, but he introduced the One who would, through His death on the cross, bring about the promised New covenant—at least for the Church, if not for national Israel.[31] The "kingdom" he preached would be recognized as the Davidic kingdom with a throne in Jerusalem, not a spiritualized one.

30 I called attention to this phenomenon in the first volume.

31 John himself would not have recognized the transition to God dealing with the new *ekklesia* since he was put to death before it was revealed.

7

THE BEGINNING OF THE MINISTRY OF JESUS CHRIST

And the devil said to Him, "All this authority I will give You, and their glory; for this has been delivered to me, and I give it to whomever I wish." – Luke 4:6

The beginning of the ministry of Jesus was His baptism by John in the River Jordan (Lk. 3:21-23). John the Baptist not only prepared the way for Jesus, but he also inaugurated Him to go forth from the waters as the Messiah (or Christ). Here then is Jesus, "the Messenger of the covenant."[1] The covenant He brings with Him is the New covenant. He brings Himself, the New covenant offering.

As a point of interest, William Dumbrell points out that John was holding out the possibility of covenant renewal or recommitment to the people at the very place (the Jordan Valley) where a covenant renewal had taken place prior to entering into Canaan (Deut. 29-32).[2] In my opinion, there is a covenant connection between the place of Jesus' becoming "Christ" and Deuteronomy 29-32, but it is not one of covenant renewal. Rather, the significance lies in the fact that the Messenger of the New covenant has arrived. Malachi's prophecy (Mal. 3:1a) is referenced by Mark as being fulfilled (Mk. 1:2). However, the prediction of the "Messenger of the covenant" (Mal. 3:1b), while fitting Jesus to a tee, may not have been completely fulfilled at His first coming. Like so many other OT prophecies, the first and second comings are fused together in Malachi 3. The eye of faith must follow Him from beyond the Jordan (Jn. 1:28) and seek to understand His mission, which ultimately is a more involved New Covenant mission.

1 The Baptist's message did not include the call to return to the [Mosaic] covenant. He cannot therefore be rightly described as a "messenger of the covenant." For a thorough presentation of the position taken in this book, see E. Ray Clendenen, "'Messenger of the Covenant' In Malachi 3:1 Once Again," *JETS* 62 (Mar. 2019), 81-102.

2 William J. Dumbrell, *The Search for Order: Biblical Eschatology in Focus* (Grand Rapids: Baker, 1994), 161.

Here at long last is the Hope of the ages! The promised Conqueror, Redeemer, Servant, Messiah, and King! The instrumental Character in the Creation Project. He accomplishes it through covenant. And He does it in continuity with covenant expectation.

The Baptism of Jesus

The vocal introduction that John the Baptist gave Jesus would surely have made a lot of people take notice of Him.[3] John was famous throughout the land, so the honor he gave to the polarizing figure of Jesus would have made both his friends and foes pay attention.

But Jesus was not like John. He was not a fiery ascetic like His forerunner, nor did He have the charismatic lure of the man in the wilderness. But Jesus was unique. This uniqueness started, of course, with His virgin conception and birth, and was later exemplified in Luke's fascinating story of the twelve-year old who astonished the teachers in Jerusalem (Lk. 2:41-50). But when, as a grown man, John baptized Him, something unusual happened. Here is Luke's abbreviated report:

> When all the people were baptized, it came to pass that Jesus also was baptized; and while He prayed, the heaven was opened. And the Holy Spirit descended in bodily form like a dove upon Him, and a voice came from heaven which said, "You are My beloved Son; in You I am well pleased" (Lk. 4:21-22).

If we had read of the Spirit of God's descent upon Moses, Elijah, or Jeremiah it would surely be remembered as the high point of their lives. We do read about Moses' face shining after he met with God in Exodus 34:29-30, and about the Spirit carrying Elijah away in 1 Kings 18:12. We also read about Elisha's request for a double-portion of Elijah's spirit in 2 Kings 2:9, and about the Spirit of God filling Bezalel to enable him to make the furniture and fixtures of the Tabernacle (Exod. 35:30-33). But there is nothing in the Hebrew Bible like the descent of the Spirit upon Jesus of Nazareth. John the Baptist testified that he saw "the Spirit descending from heaven like a dove, and He remained upon Him" (Jn. 1:32), and later Peter related this to Jesus' anointing by God:

> The word which *God* sent to the children of Israel, preaching peace through Jesus Christ—He is Lord of all—that word you know, which was proclaimed throughout all Judea, and began from Galilee after the baptism which John preached: "how God anointed Jesus of Nazareth with the Holy Spirit and with power, who went about doing good and healing all who were oppressed by the devil, for God was with Him (Acts 10:36-38).

This event marked Jesus out as the most significant character in the Bible, and this was at the outset of His ministry. Not only did He receive the Spirit, but He was also

3 N. T. Wright, *Jesus and the Victory of God*, 160-162.

declared to be God's "beloved Son" by the voice of the Almighty Himself (Lk. 3:21-22; cf. Jn. 1:32-34). The combination of His Sonship and His anointing by the Spirit at His baptism makes Jesus the only candidate to bring about the realization of God's covenants with men. It was early days, but the die was cast. No wonder then that John the Baptist declared, "He must increase, but I *must* decrease" (Jn. 1:30).

The "power" that Jesus received at His anointing was immediately put to the ultimate test. There is no greater foe in creation than Satan. Again, our sensibilities are dulled by the retelling, but no OT hero goes up against the devil in the way that Jesus does in Matthew 4 and Luke 4. The very fact that Satan comes to tempt Jesus, the newly proclaimed Messiah, should elicit our rapt attention. Here indeed is One greater than Jonah and Solomon (Matt. 12:41-42).

Satan Tempts the Christ

There are so many amazing stories about Jesus in the Gospels that they can vie for precedence and obscure somewhat from our minds their individual greatness. This problem of over familiarity certainly applies to the Temptation of Jesus. Here I shall follow Matthew's report:[4] "Now when the tempter came to Him, he said, 'If You are the Son of God, command that these stones become bread.' But He answered and said, 'It is written, "*Man shall not live by bread alone, but by every word that proceeds from the mouth of God*"'" (Matt. 4:3-4).

Jesus Christ may have been the anointed of God, but He was still human. His humanity was no façade for the full power of God behind it. To be what He came to be for us, He had to be "the man Christ Jesus" (1 Tim. 2:15), who laid aside His divine prerogatives (Phil. 2:5-7) that we might be saved (1 Tim. 1:15). Therefore, when it is said that He spent forty days fasting in the wilderness and was hungry, we may fairly deduce that He was famished, and not at His best physically or mentally. We must insist on this if we are to take His humanity seriously, and, indeed, if He is to be any sort of example for us (Heb. 4:15; 1 Pet. 2:21). For just as we grow faint and weary and our brains get fogged over if we do not eat, we must not for false piety's sake pretend that Jesus' flesh was above such ordinary things. His temptation by Satan came not when He was in tip-top mental and physical condition, but when He was vulnerable and weak—which is to say, at the most inconvenient time.

The first temptation takes advantage of Jesus' great hunger: "If You are the Son of God, command that these stones become bread" (Matt. 4:3). We must not think that all there was to this temptation was the satisfaction of breaking a self-imposed fast. Clearly, the fast was in view of this imminent confrontation and Jesus knew that Satan would take this tack. If there had been any witnesses, they probably would have seen a more involved interaction than what we have here. Scripture is a true record of what took place, but not necessarily a full record. We have been given what the Holy Spirit

4 For good arguments for Matthew giving the original order, see I. Howard Marshall, *Commentary on Luke*, 166-167. This is the generally accepted view. See also G. H. Twelftree, "Temptation of Jesus," in *Dictionary of Jesus and the Gospels*, eds. Joel B. Green, Scot McKnight, and I. Howard Marshall (Downers Grove, IL: IVP, 1992), 823.

wanted us to have. It is enough for His purposes, and therefore, for ours. The doubt-filled "ifs" of Satan in these temptations add more frustration to the scenario. Jesus is being tempted to provide His credentials.

Notice what Satan does not ask. He does not ask "If you are the Messiah." Messiah may or may not have the authority to deal with "the god of this age" (2 Cor. 4:4), but the Son of God definitely would. The heart of Satan's strategy is to get Jesus to rely upon His divinity instead of upon the Spirit of God with whom He has recently been anointed. Recall that it was at His baptism that Jesus heard God's voice declaring, "This is My beloved Son" (Matt. 3:17). Now the Tempter baits his hook by casting suspicion on this truth. It is a little matter to clear up. Just turn these stones into bread, and all doubts will be answered.

But Jesus is not under any obligation to anything but the Father's providence, and that has thus far not given Him bread. "In his hunger he saw occasion to believe in God rather than to act on his own. The one from whom he receives his life is God."[5] The Lord knows this, and so He blocks the temptation by turning the attention to the words of God: "He answered and said, 'It is written, "Man shall not live by bread alone, but by every word that proceeds from the mouth of God"'" (Matt. 4:4).

The point of this response is that Jesus' outlook is positioned under the authority of the Word of God. This is in contrast to Eve in Genesis 3, where Satan got her to remove herself from the umbrella of the Word and to locate herself beyond its authority. Eve allowed herself to become independent of God's Word, and so lent herself a permission she was never meant to have, namely a permission to make up her mind without necessarily having to remain within the limits of what God had said. This state of autonomy is the default stance of every sinner ever born, and hence, of every Bible interpreter ever born, saved or lost. The only way for the saint of God to avoid lapsing into this default of independence is to follow Jesus' example and take God at His Word! I am persuaded this means that we must not spiritualize Scripture, nor ought we to rely on any hermeneutic where the plain sense of the words is obscured, redirected, typologized, or otherwise changed. Faith in Scripture that has been spiritualized is faith in that spiritualization (or transformation etc.). It is not faith in what God actually said.[6]

Furthermore, notice how Jesus' answer shows His complete reliance upon God's Word. He will not act independently of it. Boiled down to its essentials, all temptation is a lure away from dependence upon God's words. This was what Satan succeeded in getting Eve and then Adam to do in the garden, and it is now the default setting of every sinner, even the saved sinner.[7]

---

5 Adolf Schlatter, *Do We Know Jesus?* (Grand Rapids: Kregel, 2005), 98.

6 This is a major problem with Reformed theology (Covenant & New Covenant Theology) because it insists in understanding the Bible through "covenants" not found in Scripture and in employing spiritualization and typological hermeneutics on vast areas of the Bible. Often the reinterpretations of God's words, even covenant words, are believed and not the words themselves. For this reason, such books as Kevin DeYoung's *Taking God At His Word: Why the Bible Is Knowable, Necessary, and Enough, and What That Means for You and Me* (Wheaton, IL: Crossway, 2016), come across as shallow exhortations to take *some* of God's Word seriously.

7 See my *The Words of the Covenant*, Vol. 1, 101-104.

Jesus knew that His mission as the God-man was not to access His divine nature when things got hard for His humanity. Hence, there is but one safe path for Him and us: to believe that God means what He says even when one is tempted by opinions and circumstances to make the words mean something other than what they actually say.

Jesus' answer to the Tempter comes from Deuteronomy 8:3, where Yahweh mentions how He tested Israel:

> Every commandment which I command you today you must be careful to observe, that you may live and multiply, and go in and possess the land of which the LORD swore to your fathers. And you shall remember that the LORD your God led you all the way these forty years in the wilderness, to humble you *and* test you, to know what *was* in your heart, whether you would keep His commandments or not. So He humbled you, allowed you to hunger, and fed you with manna which you did not know nor did your fathers know, that He might make you know that man shall not live by bread alone; but man lives by every *word* that proceeds from the mouth of the LORD (Deut. 8:1-3).

There is no doubt that this passage is grounded in the covenant at Sinai (cf. Deut. 7:9, 12). As Peter Craigie states, "The act of *remembering* prompts obedience to the covenant law."[8] In Deuteronomy 8:18 we read about Yahweh establishing "His covenant which He swore to your fathers." Since Moses and his generation were still very much alive when it was spoken, this covenant can only be that which was sworn to Abraham, Isaac, and Jacob. Therefore, Jesus' words to Satan were not only well chosen, because they informed the Adversary that Jesus would rely upon God for food, but because they were rooted in the covenants. God's covenants, despite a slew of scholars to the contrary, are hermeneutically fixed. Jesus is saying that the words of God, especially the covenanted words, must be believed. They constitute His foundation when He stands against Satan.

Notice also that the Lord is not pitting physical needs against God's words. If the Father has not provided food, it is not for Jesus to resort to His supernatural powers to make food appear in front of Him. He is telling Satan that "every word that proceeds from the mouth of God" is more important than food for the body, however essential that is (Job 23:12). In His extremity, Jesus still held up the absoluteness of the Word of God. This is the pedestal He put it upon! Therefore, the devil could not find a way through.

The second temptation in Matthew concerns the protection of God:

> Then the devil took Him up into the holy city, set Him on the pinnacle of the temple, and said to Him, "If You are the Son of God, throw Yourself down. For it is written: 'He shall give His angels charge over you,' and, 'In *their* hands they shall bear you up, Lest you dash your foot against a stone'" (Matt. 4:5-6).

8 Peter C. Craigie, *The Book of Deuteronomy* (Grand Rapids: Eerdmans, 1976), 185.

The "pinnacle"[9] of the temple was one of the highest points in Jerusalem. Perhaps Satan imagined that this place, even though it was absent the Shekinah glory, would spice up the temptation. In any event, the baiting refrain, "If you are the Son of God," is more prominent this time, backed by a "proof-text" from Psalm 91:11-12. In this well-known psalm the promise of help is to those who abide "in the shadow of the Almighty" (Psa. 91:1). It promises they will be protected from outside evil, *not* from their own impetuosity. What Satan was doing was misapplying the Scripture. He took it at face value; he did not spiritualize it, but he did try to utilize it for a frivolous end. This reminds us why context is so important for proper interpretation. Otherwise even some "literal" interpretations can lead us astray. In these cases, there will always be a better literal option available.

"Jesus said to him, 'It is written again, "You shall not tempt the LORD your God"'" (Matt. 4:7). The Lord did not allow Himself to get pulled into an argument about context. He showed that the devil was wrong by citing a passage that nullified the temptation. If it is sinful to try to tempt God, then it is clear that Psalm 91 is being misused. But note again that the plain sense of the passage is never at issue.

When we come to the third temptation (as Matthew has it), we need not be long delayed by trying to ask how Christ could be shown all the world's kingdoms from one location. On a globe this would be impossible,[10] but if Satan produced a kind of screen where the kingdoms were depicted, that would work.[11] Perhaps Mt. Hermon[12] or Mt. Pisgah was used to add to the overall impression.[13] However it was done, this is the record of the event: "Again, the devil took Him up on an exceedingly high mountain, and showed Him all the kingdoms of the world and their glory. And he said to Him, 'All these things I will give You if You will fall down and worship me'" (Matt. 4:8-9).

This was an extremely presumptuous enticement, and it ended in a rebuke. There is no "if" placed at the start of it. There is no more beating around the bush. Rather than misapplying Scripture or trying to lure Jesus into acting independently from God, this temptation has Satan trying to draw Jesus into bypassing His necessary humiliation.[14] He could receive the "Kingdom" without having to endure the misery and pain. If one recalls that the Creation Project culminates with the reign of the Messiah upon the earth God made "through Him and for Him" (Col. 1:16), we can see that this tempts Jesus to gain something that He is legitimately entitled to, but to gain it

9 This may refer to the flat porch overlooking the Kidron Valley over 400 feet below.

10 Incidentally, it would also be impossible on an ancient flat earth model because of refraction and perspective.

11 I reject the idea that Satan could put the images in Jesus' mind.

12 Since there was some *supra*-natural power behind this temptation the mountain might have been located anywhere.

13 I see little problem in Satan (under God's authority as in Job 1) being permitted to whisk Jesus to a suitable location for the temptation before returning Him. But the fact is, we simply do not know how this was carried out.

14 Incidentally, I do not take 1 Corinthians 2:8 as referring to Satan. The Tempter wanted Jesus to avoid the crucifixion.

by illegitimate means. What Satan is trying to do is to offer the Davidic rule independently of God and without Jesus first redeeming the world.[15]

Mention of the Davidic rule reminds us that the concept of covenant was in the minds of both Satan and the Lord. Not a transformation of the covenant either, for if Jesus knew that the Davidic covenant, not to mention the New covenant, were to undergo transformation (e.g., via a certain typology) this would have been no temptation at all. Furthermore, it would have been a pure waste of time from the devil's point of view. If the Kingdom was not to be geopolitical and earthly, Satan's domain would remain untouched.

It is just here that we must introduce Luke's account, because he includes some added information: "And the devil said to Him, 'All this authority I will give You, and their glory; for *this* has been delivered to me, and I give it to whomever I wish. Therefore, if You will worship before me, all will be Yours'" (Lk. 4:6-7).

What this text reveals is extremely telling. There is no reason to deny that it was within the Accuser's power to give the kingdoms of this world to whomever he chose.[16] He is elsewhere called "the god of this age" (2 Cor. 4:4) and "the ruler of this world" (Jn. 12:31; 14:40; 16:11). John tells us that "the whole world lies under the sway of the wicked one" (1 Jn. 5:19). In Revelation 13:2 we read that "The dragon [Satan] gave him [the beast] his power, <u>his throne</u>, and great authority," while "all who dwell on the earth" will worship the beast, who will be under the authority of Satan (Rev. 13:4, 8; cf. Rev. 12:9). One writer who examined this text gives the following opinion:

> Though created for dominion, in acceding to the serpent's suggestions [Adam and Eve] surrendered true dominion to Satan. From that moment on they and their descendants will struggle to maintain what is left to them of their dominion over the earth...It makes sense, therefore, to say that the kingdoms of the world have been delivered up to him—not by God, but by the human race to whom they were originally entrusted.[17]

I would not go so far as to say that God has had no hand in temporarily giving over the earth to Satan while mankind has. That is possible, but it does not fully fit the passages above. Besides this, we should recall that in order for it to be a real temptation, Jesus would have had to have known that what was offered was a real possibility (we cannot entertain the notion that He was ignorant of Satan's power and authority). If He knew that Satan was lying about having such power, then the whole edge of the temptation would have been blunted. Moreover, Jesus does not question the devil's assertion of authority over the earth any more than He questioned his interpretation of the Kingdom. Satan's ability to grant authority over the earth was the lure here. However, *the test did not lie in that direction.* Rather, the rub was in the final clause,

15 D. A. Carson, "Matthew," in *EBC*, ed. Frank E. Gaebelein, Vol. 8 (Grand Rapids: Zondervan, 1984), 114.

16 Contra I. Howard Marshall, *Commentary on Luke*, 172.

17 David Seccombe, *The King of God's Kingdom*, 119.

"If you will fall down and worship me" (Matt. 4:9).[18] There must have been enough truth in the offer of rule over the nations for the audacity of the deal (to worship Satan) to have had even a little purchase. And that is what makes this last temptation so significant for Bible interpretation. If Satan made a bona fide offer, then what was presented to our Lord was actual dominion over the earth on the qualification that He worship Satan.

The ramifications of Jesus succumbing to this are another matter. For one thing, the entire covenantal structure of the Creation Project would be in ruins. That said, the whole reason for this temptation is that the Tempter was clearly aware of the reality of the two-part mission of Christ and the corresponding truth of the coming earthly Kingdom. Since modern amillennialism has largely abandoned the spiritual interpretation of the Kingdom (i.e., equating it with Heaven)[19] this does not present as much of a problem for the system as it once did.[20] But the fact that amillennialism still teaches that the Kingdom began with the Church is brought into question by this event. If Jesus grabbed the Kingdom back after His resurrection, the only sense in which it could be done is if the Kingdom was spiritualized into the pilgrim Church. Postmillennialism, which teaches that the Kingdom will be brought about by the Spirit of God working through the Church, is also called into question here. If Jesus already has the Kingdom, then why delay in making it what it should be? It is not as if the saints are in any better shape now than they were two millennia ago. Only premillennialism answers the questions that the third temptation brings up. The other two main positions do not give persuasive answers.

We must take notice of the continuity with OT covenant expectations that is implicit in this interchange. Amillennialism and postmillennialism do not really do this. This is an important hermeneutical passage that has often been evaded. Jesus does not accuse Satan of an empty promise. In order for this to have been a temptation the "carrot" had to be real—world rule was the "carrot." It was available. And since that is precisely what Jesus has been promised, any eschatology that calls it into question is to be rejected.

Summary of Part Three

- At the announcement of the birth of John the Baptist to Zacharias, it was necessary that the angel's words were taken at face value and not "transformed" or spiritualized. Hence, we have an implicit warning not to disbelieve or alter the surface meaning of the revelation as given. Zacharias' speech shows he understood the Abrahamic and Davidic covenants literally.

18 Most interpreters are clear about this. E.g., Donald A. Hagner, *Matthew 1–13*, 68; D. A. Carson, "Matthew," 114; Ed Glasscock, *Matthew*, 88.

19 This is in no small part due to the arguments of Anthony A. Hoekema's book *The Bible and the Future* (Grand Rapids: Eerdmans, 1994).

20 But see on this Michael J. Vlach, *The New Creation Model: A Paradigm for Discovering God's Restoration Purposes from Creation to New Creation* (Cary, NC: Theological Studies Press, 2023).

- Mary received the angel Gabriel's declaration at face value and in conformity with the covenant expectations generated by the Prophets. The same can be said of the testimonies of the shepherds, of Simeon, and of Anna.

- Matthew begins his account by connecting Christ to the Abrahamic and Davidic covenants. He highlights earthly kingship in his genealogy, which prepares the reader for the meaning of Christ's kingship. The Magi enquire about a King of the Jews, based upon OT prophetic expectation.

- The doctrine of the preeminence of Christ is an important theological property of God's covenant program. This can be seen by matching up the covenant-loaded angelic messages and their human interpretations (e.g., through Mary and Zacharias) with their central concern, Jesus. Even the third temptation of Satan in Matthew 4 may be seen as an attempt to bypass the New covenant.

- John the Baptist's preaching contains nothing of a heavenly-spiritual Kingdom. His call to repentance is in view of the Kingdom's imminence. What can be said about John's preaching goes equally for the early preaching ministry of Jesus.

- Satan's temptations of Christ prove that he sees the Kingdom as earthly and physical. Satan offered Jesus an earthly Kingdom that is (presently) under Satan's control. If that is not the case, and it was never God's intention (despite His oaths) to have Jesus reign upon the earth, then the temptation loses its force.

PART FOUR:
COVENANT AND KINGDOM IN THE REST OF LUKE AND MATTHEW

8

COVENANT AND KINGDOM IN LUKE

Now as they heard these things, He spoke another parable, because He was near Jerusalem and because they thought the kingdom of God would appear immediately.
- Luke 19:11

The Kingdom of God is Covenantal

The whole subject of the Kingdom of God in the teaching of Jesus, not to mention its use by the Apostle Paul, is crucial for an accurate portrayal of NT theology. Unsurprisingly, it is vital for a correct understanding of the covenant program of God also. When the Bible speaks about the Kingdom, it does so on the basis of covenant! God's oaths to Abraham and David in particular are presupposed in the teaching of Jesus about the Kingdom of God. Simply put, Kingdom promises are covenant promises![1]

The fact that this is often overlooked is, as I have said before, because either the covenants of God are relegated to a second tier, or because the covenants are reinterpreted to fit into a first advent ecclesial paradigm.

As a reminder, *my method in this book is to try to let the biblical text explain itself as it is pondered, without bringing an idea to the passage that is alien to its context, and without assuming fulfillment in the Church.* As we shall see, just permitting the text to say what it says steers us away from having to convert God's covenants with Abraham, Phinehas, and David, as well as the New covenant, into being "fulfilled" in ways utterly at variance with the words that God used to make them.[2] One may claim that because the inspired writers had a theological point of view when they wrote, we too

1 Robert L. Saucy, *The Case for Progressive Dispensationalism*, 60ff.
2 See e.g., J. Dwight Pentecost, *Thy Kingdom Come*, 142-143.

must follow suit. That may be so, but we must ascertain what that theology is. That can only be done if we let the text unfold gradually.

Before proceeding I want to repeat that in exploring the subject of the Kingdom of God as portrayed in each of the Gospels, the ground upon which the discussion can even take place is covenantal. What must be stressed is that Jesus' teaching on the Kingdom must be understood as it is reported, and not overlaid with adjustments we may think we find in Paul. Whether or not one believes that Paul's letters precede the writing of the Gospels, who would dare to say that the words of Jesus have been reshaped to make them conform with what the great apostle would go on to write? Who but a denier of inerrancy and inspiration would claim that we don't actually have *what Jesus preached* but a reconstruction and theological redaction of His teaching? No, the words of our Lord will be read as being spoken circa A.D. 26 to 30. In that setting they ought to be understood. Naturally, our main focus will have to be on Matthew and Luke since Mark and John deal less with the teaching of Christ on the Kingdom, but all the Evangelists will be considered. In this chapter, I am going to look at the Gospel of Luke.[3]

The Kingdom of God in Luke

According to Richard Hays, "The overall design of Luke's two-volume work... highlights God's purpose in fulfilling the promise of redemption for his people Israel."[4] There is little doubt that this purpose is concentrated on the Kingdom of God, for more than half of the NT's uses of the term are found in Luke/Acts.[5] Luke never uses the term incidentally; he is always strategic in his placement of it. Therefore, it must be considered as central to his purpose. But what is the Kingdom of God?

It seems that the majority opinion is that the "kingdom of God" is the promised Kingdom of the Davidic covenant, yet not what everyone expected. Somehow the covenant with David and his line has changed from a Jewish/Israelite-based covenant into a Church-based covenant. Oftentimes there is a presumption that since Luke/Acts is a two-volume work, and Acts deals with the Church, Luke's concern in his Gospel is with ecclesiological matters all the way through. The result of this position is that the theme of the Kingdom of God in Luke's Gospel is read in light of the Church, not in its original Israelite covenantal context.[6]

---

3 One of the notable things about Luke that is often missed is his eschatology which is firmly rooted in OT ideas. See e.g., Isaac Oliver, *Luke's Jewish Eschatology: The National Restoration of Israel in Luke-Acts* (Oxford: Oxford University Press, 2021).

4 Richard B. Hays, *Echoes of Scripture in the Gospels* (Waco, TX: Baylor University Press, 2016), 191.

5 In Luke's Gospel, "kingdom of God" occurs 32 times, with a further 7 times in Acts.

6 A good example of this is the book *Reading Luke: Interpretation, Reflection, Formation*, Scripture and Hermeneutics, ed. Craig G. Bartholomew, Vol. 6 (Grand Rapids: Zondervan, 2005). While this volume is insightful, its essays on theological interpretation all presuppose that the "kingdom of God" in the Gospel is fulfilled in the Church. The approach of the present book is to let the text "play out" and see what it says.

It would help to begin with a basic definition of the Kingdom. The Kingdom of God may be defined as "the rule of God through Jesus Christ as it unfurls towards its consummation along with the consummation itself."[7] This rule will one day involve the actual reign of Christ over the world. I shall bring these aspects out as we go through. Let's begin with Luke 4:14-21:

> Then Jesus returned in the power of the Spirit to Galilee, and news of Him went out through all the surrounding region. And He taught in their synagogues, being glorified by all. So He came to Nazareth, where He had been brought up. And as His custom was, He went into the synagogue on the Sabbath day, and stood up to read. And He was handed the book of the prophet Isaiah. And when He had opened the book, He found the place where it was written:
>
> "The Spirit of the LORD is upon Me,
> Because He has anointed Me
> To preach the gospel to the poor;
> He has sent Me to heal the brokenhearted,
> To proclaim liberty to the captives
> And recovery of sight to the blind,
> To set at liberty those who are oppressed;
> To proclaim the acceptable year of the LORD."
>
> Then He closed the book, and gave *it* back to the attendant and sat down. And the eyes of all who were in the synagogue were fixed on Him. And He began to say to them, "Today this Scripture is fulfilled in your hearing."

Providence supplies the right reading from Isaiah into the hands of Jesus. The text is Isaiah 61:1-2a, and in keeping with Luke's emphasis upon the work of the Spirit after Christ's baptism and temptation, we get a quotation that speaks about "the Spirit of the Lord." In Isaiah the "vengeance" of which the prophet spoke in Isaiah 61:2b is fused together with the message and ministry of the anointed one that comes before it. However, at the beginning of Jesus' public ministry we find Him deliberately stopping the reading, closing the book (scroll) and announcing that what has just been read is being fulfilled. If He had continued to read on, He could *not* have claimed fulfillment. Everything that was read out at the synagogue at Nazareth was indeed being fulfilled or was about to be. But Jesus is aware of a division in Isaiah's prophecy. The twin events of vengeance upon God's enemies and comfort for those who mourn appear at the second coming, not the first. By omitting the second part of the quotation of Isaiah 61:2, not only was Jesus adverting to the division of the passage, so was Luke. This has to be kept in mind when reading the book. Clearly there is more work for Christ to do in this world, and it is covenant related.

---

7 McClain defines it as "the rule of God over His creation" (Alva J. McClain, *The Greatness of the Kingdom*, 19).

We must also pay attention to the fact that the plain sense of Isaiah 61:1-2a is appealed to for the fulfillment of God's words. In the original setting it is clear that there is much still to do. Look, for example, at Isaiah 61:3, which develops the comfort side of the second advent prediction:

> To console those who mourn in Zion,
> To give them beauty for ashes,
> The oil of joy for mourning,
> The garment of praise for the spirit of heaviness;
> That they may be called trees of righteousness,
> The planting of the LORD, that He may be glorified.

In the first instance, the consolation being spoken of refers to "Zion," which indicates Jerusalem. The mention of "beauty for ashes" and "righteousness" calls to mind God's New covenant with Israel (e.g., Isa. 32:16-18; 59:20-21). At the end of Luke 4 we find Jesus being mobbed by admirers, to whom He retorted, "I must preach the kingdom of God to the other cities also, because for this purpose I have been sent" (Lk. 4:43).

It can hardly be the case that what was preached by Jesus in Nazareth was much different than what He taught in Galilee's other towns (Lk. 4:44). He depicts the Kingdom as just ahead and approaching. Hence, from Luke 4:14-21 we see that the preaching of the Kingdom of God at the commencement of Jesus' public ministry, as Luke presents it, included a separation of the fulfillment of covenant expectation in terms of the first and second coming of Messiah. But the literal meaning of the Kingdom does not change (otherwise there would exist an equivocation in Isaiah and also an implied equivocation in Jesus' teaching). The second coming prophecies pertain to the Kingdom of God, and this has to be kept in mind when we study the Gospels.

In Luke 5:17-20 we find Jesus forgiving the sins of the paralytic man who was lowered through the roof. Owing to the fact that God's covenants have been prominent in Luke's narrative until this episode, we might ask on what covenantal basis could Jesus forgive this man's sins? It might be objected that I have begged the question putting it this way. But when one recalls that Jesus' name does not just mean "Savior," but it *designates* Him as Savior, I do not think we are taken off course by the question. Actually, I think we are kept on course. The previous miracle of the healing of the leper (Lk. 5:12-16) recalls to our minds Isaiah 53:4a—a New covenant Servant Song. It is by the blood of Jesus that sinners are saved (in both Testaments), and Jesus will specifically refer to His blood as "the blood of the New covenant" in Luke 22:20. So in forgiving the sins of the paralytic, therefore, Jesus is simply acting in His Servant role as the One who will bring not just the words of salvation but the means of that salvation. To lean on John's Gospel for a second, *as the Lamb of God* (Jn. 1:29), a decidedly covenant moniker, Jesus will establish the way, the truth, and the life (Jn. 14:6). It seems obvious that Jesus sees His entire mission in covenant terms. And so does Luke! Therefore, the forgiveness of the paralytic in Luke 5 should be understood as taking place under the auspices of the New covenant.

In Luke 12:31 Jesus issues the proclamation, "Seek the kingdom of God." The Kingdom of God here can be interpreted as future. If it were present, clearly there would be no need to seek for it. In any case, as the closest associates to Jesus, they knew that He would need to bring the Kingdom in and that they would be included (Lk. 12:32).[8] It is fair to assume then that the Kingdom Jesus was commending was the future Davidic Kingdom, the New covenant Kingdom. In the Parable of the Mustard seed in Luke 13:18-19, the Lord says: "Then He said, 'What is the kingdom of God like? And to what shall I compare it? It is like a mustard seed, which a man took and put in his garden; and it grew and became a large tree, and the birds of the air nested in its branches.'"

I shall be exploring the parables in Matthew 13 (mirrored here) in more detail, but I just include this to show that Luke is very concerned with the Kingdom. Further, I wanted to notice the obvious fact that a mustard seed will grow into a mustard tree or plant. That will always be the expected outcome.[9] It will not develop into some unexpected plant. Thus, the note of expectation being in line with fulfillment is illustrated again for us. There will only be a natural transformation, as expected. In like manner, the OT expectation and the NT fulfillment will be predictable. Just so, the eschatological Kingdom is in view in Jesus' description of Jewish people being excluded from the company of the pious saints, "When you see Abraham and Isaac and Jacob and all the prophets in the kingdom of God, and yourselves thrust out" (Lk. 13:28). The Kingdom to which Abraham, Isaac, Jacob, and the Prophets aspired was geographical, Jerusalem-centered, and covenantal.

But the question, "What is the kingdom of God like?" is worthy of a little consideration. As Jesus continues in the passage, it becomes clear that He is asking about the growth of the Kingdom and a particular aspect of that growth. In Luke, the picture is of a fully grown tree that, like all trees, attracts the birds that perch on its branches. The idea seems to be that when the Kingdom of God comes to its own, it will be ready to be occupied by those who were meant to occupy it—the saints.

But Jesus goes on to speak about the godly from beyond Israel: "They will come from the east and the west, from the north and the south, and sit down in the kingdom of God" (Lk. 13:29). This future, wherein those from all corners of the world will be included in the Kingdom, shows that saints will come from all the points of the compass. The context does not give us enough information to decide whether these are Jews or Gentiles, but it would not be a stretch to count Gentiles among their number.[10] This is exactly in line with the covenantal expectation grounded in the Abrahamic and New covenants (Gen. 12:3; Isa. 49:6-8). I confess to having one or two questions about this depiction of the Kingdom. For instance, how does it gel with Daniel's picture of the smiting stone in Daniel 2? That stone destroyed the worldly kingdoms and grew steadily until it covered the whole earth. Is our Lord alluding to

8 The futurity of the Kingdom comes out better in the comparative text in Matt. 6:33. See Michael J. Vlach, *He Will Reign Forever*, 299, 303.

9 Recall what was said about leopard tracks leading to a leopard and not a bear in *The Words of the Covenant*, Vol. 1, 20-22.

10 Alva J. McClain, *The Greatness of the Kingdom*, 330.

the same thing here? Does this mean that Jesus' reign over the earth will begin in one place (Jerusalem) and gradually branch out over the earth, say over several years? Or is this growth the spread of the truth about Jesus and His salvation over the course of Church History until it climaxes in the new aeon itself? I don't think the second option is a live option because Christ's first coming could not be construed as wiping out the kingdoms of man as Daniel describes it. I am not sure about how exactly it will all pan out. One thing I am sure about is that what comes next anchors the context firmly in Israeli ground.

The Lament Over Jerusalem

> O Jerusalem, Jerusalem, the one who kills the prophets and stones those who are sent to her! How often I wanted to gather your children together, as a hen *gathers* her brood under *her* wings, but you were not willing! See! Your house is left to you desolate; and assuredly, I say to you, you shall not see Me <u>until *the time* comes when you say</u>, "*Blessed is He who comes in the name of the LORD!*" (Lk. 13:34-35).

I have underlined the key phrase "until the time comes when you say" because it shows that the reception of Jesus as Messiah, and therefore the reception of the coming Kingdom of God, refers not to a heavenly Jerusalem but to an earthly Jerusalem. Many Covenant theologians and New Covenant theologians miss this and connect the future Kingdom to the New Jerusalem of Revelation 21–22. But Jesus speaks of *this world's* Jerusalem! The words "Blessed is He who comes in the name of the LORD!" are from Psalm 118:26a and are connected by Luke to the second advent (Lk. 13:35).[11] The Psalm follows this with a blessing upon Messiah from the temple.[12] Just a few verses earlier there is the prophecy of Jerusalem's rejection of Messiah:

> The stone *which* the builders rejected
> Has become the chief cornerstone.
> This was the LORD's doing;
> It *is* marvelous in our eyes (Psa. 118:22-23).

Again, we can see here that prophecy about the first coming is integrated with prophecy about the second coming, even in the same passage (Psa. 118:22-26). When reading the Bible, it is important to be on the lookout for this phenomenon. Otherwise, one is liable to ascribe second coming passages to the first coming and so skew the interpretation.

---

11 Some more liberal leaning scholars have suggested that Jesus was trying to bring about the prophesied Kingdom by his actions. See J. D. G. Dunn, *Jesus Remembered*, 793. This at least has the merit of taking His words and actions as being in line with OT prophecy. Wright cites the verse to prove that the temple was abandoned and left vulnerable to attack (N. T. Wright, *Jesus and the Victory of God* [Minneapolis: Fortress Press, 1996], 166, 184-185, 334). In one place does he stress the final decisive clause (Ibid., 642). There he observes that "Jesus was announcing, and embodying, the return of YHWH to Zion."

12 "We have blessed you from the house of the LORD" (Psa. 118:26b).

What we can see so far is that Luke's conception of the Kingdom is future and fully in step with the expectations raised by the OT covenants, particularly those with Abraham and with David. But an objector might say that this is about to change with Jesus' pronouncement in Luke 17.

The Kingdom in Your Midst

> Now when He was asked by the Pharisees when the kingdom of God would come, He answered them and said, "The kingdom of God does not come with observation; nor will they say, 'See here!' or 'See there!' For indeed, the kingdom of God is within you" (Lk. 17:20-21).

Considerable study has been applied to these verses, and an array of interpretations put forth. Perhaps most common is the view that Jesus is claiming that the Kingdom is inside of people; that is, of those who will open their hearts to accept it. In this outlook, the Kingdom is an internal spiritual thing; hence, the phrases "does not come with observation" and "within you" would mean that the Kingdom is internal and spiritual, not external and physical.

Such an interpretation is favored by some whose theology already requires such a spiritual kingdom. However, Jesus' words about "outward observation" were not intended to imply that there would be nothing to see. All the Gospel writers record that He performed many signs and miracles whose purpose was to call attention to the manifestation of God's recuperative power at work in the ministry of Jesus. But the question of the Pharisees about when the Kingdom would come had within it a misunderstanding that it would *only* come abruptly with apocalyptic force. Jesus has arrived with the fanfare provided by John the Baptist, and He has preached a Kingdom to come. Yet He is Messiah! He is the promised One. To look for signs beyond what He was *already* doing proved that the attention, and thus the thinking, was all in the wrong place.

It would be better to translate *entos hymon* as "in your midst" (e.g., NASB, NET, CSB, cf. ESV) or "among you,"[13] rather than "within you" (NKJV). Another meaning that has been proposed is "within your grasp,"[14] which lends more urgency to the expression. These alternative renderings throw light back on Christ and provide another more plausible option. Marshall, for example, believes that "Jesus is speaking of the presence of the kingdom of God among men, possibly as something within their grasp if they will only take hold of it."[15] He notes the possibility that the kingdom is present only when Jesus Himself is present.[16] This is a good interpretation and is favored by some. A variation of this view suggests that it is preferable to see the Kingdom as present in the Person of Jesus,,[17] even when it is not outwardly manifested

---

13 James D. G. Dunn, *Jesus Remembered*, 444.
14 N. T. Wright, *Jesus and the Victory of God*, 469.
15 I. Howard Marshall, *Commentary on Luke*, 655.
16 Ibid., 655-656.
17 Leon Morris, *The Gospel According to St. Luke*, TNTC (Grand Rapids: Eerdmans, 1975), 259.

fully.[18] The King is right in front of the religious leaders. The people had asked Jesus for a sign already, and He had reprimanded them (Lk. 11:29). The Pharisees believed they would be first in line for the Kingdom. But they are looking right through the One who personified it.[19] Hence, Jesus warned them "nor will they say, 'See here!' or 'See there!'" (Lk. 17:21), as if there was someone or something *apart* from Him that would enlighten them. Marshall's point about the presence of the Kingdom coinciding with Jesus' presence, in my opinion, ought to be retained, although the Bible's fusion of the first and second advents should always be recalled.

This text is especially helpful when coming to grips with the two basic ideas of the Kingdom as presented in the Gospels. That Jesus is the Christ and was, therefore, the King "among" the Jews in the first century is hard to deny.[20] But He was rejected, as predicted by the Prophets, and He will return "a second time" (Heb. 9:28) as the King of kings (1 Tim. 6:13-15; Rev. 19:19-20). The view that the Kingdom is present only when the King is present is also consonant with the OT and will help us when we encounter the NT Church.[21]

Jesus then, is the "kingdom in your midst" whom the Pharisees ought to believe in order to gain entrance to the impending Kingdom of God. Jesus had been preaching an imminent yet future Kingdom, and the Pharisees also held to a future Kingdom. But they could never get into the Kingdom while they steadfastly ignored the King.[22]

In Luke 17 Jesus clarifies His meaning with the disciples in this important passage:

> Then He said to the disciples, "The days will come when you will desire to see one of the days of the Son of Man, and you will not see *it*. And they will say to you, 'Look here!' or 'Look there!' Do not go after *them* or follow *them*. For as the lightning that flashes out of one *part* under heaven shines to the

18 Some hold to an eschatological interpretation of Jesus' words. Toussaint believes, "The best way to take the words of the Lord Jesus in Luke 17:21 is to say that His return with His kingdom would not be gradual so that it can be observed in a slow metamorphosis, but it will be so sudden that it will be said of the kingdom, "Lo, it is in your midst." This interpretation is vindicated by a number of factors" (Stanley D. Toussaint, "The Church and Israel," *CTJ* 2 [Dec 1998], 358).

19 See Alan J. Thompson, *The Acts of the Risen Lord Jesus: Luke's Account of God's Unfolding Plan* (Downers Grove, IL: IVP, 2011), 40. Thompson holds that Jesus is reigning now, which for several reasons I deny.

20 It should be recalled that John's Gospel addresses this issue directly: "Pilate therefore said to Him, 'Are You a king then?' Jesus answered, '<u>You say *rightly* that I am a king</u>. For this cause I was born, and for this cause I have come into the world, that I should bear witness to the truth. Everyone who is of the truth hears My voice'" (Jn. 18:37, emphasis mine). I shall return to this verse further on in the book.

21 I personally have no real complaint about envisaging the kingdom of God as being expressed in two modes. The first being "established" by the reality of the historical events of Jesus' incarnation and resurrection and the irreversible theological changes which were released in consequence of them. But employing the word "kingdom" in such a limited way leaves a hole that is very hard to fill with enough suitable content. Therefore, I much prefer to understand the kingdom in more tangible terms.

22 This helps us to understand similar passages in Luke (Lk. 10:9, 11; 11:20).

> other *part* under heaven, so also the Son of Man will be in His day.[23] But first He must suffer many things and be rejected by this generation" (Lk. 17:22-25).

Although Jesus does not refer to the Kingdom in this passage, He does focus attention on Himself and His future coming, which confirms the link between the Kingdom and Jesus as the King. His ancestor, King David, experienced the friction between being anointed King (1 Sam. 16:11-13) but not reigning as King for a protracted period. Similarly, Jesus was the King, but He would not receive the Kingdom when He came the first time. What is striking is that Jesus inserts a teaching about His rejection at the hands of "this generation," which will necessitate His coming again to rule. The Pharisaic expectation contained truth insofar as it taught "apocalyptic" externals, sights and sounds, but since it failed to include the details about the Suffering Servant (Isa. 53) and the dying Messiah (Dan. 9:26), their understanding went awry. The reality was no Jesus, no Kingdom. The physical presence of Jesus, even if He was to undergo suffering, introduced the Danielic "Son of Man" and hence His kingly rights.

"The Days of the Son of Man"

Luke 17:22-25 reveals that "the days of the Son of Man" correspond to the second coming ("as the lighting that flashes," etc., cf. Matt. 24:26-27, 29-31, 37). So again, we can see that Jesus' self-understanding of His mission was that it involved two phases. I might call the first phase "the New covenant phase" because, as we are soon to discover, Jesus initiated the New covenant (Lk. 22). It might be helpful to think of phase two as "the covenant consummation phase," meaning that the full complement of God's unilateral covenants will be realized after Christ returns.

Luke 17:26-37 is challenging as it appears to be specific and non-specific at the same time. The examples of the day that Noah entered the Ark (Lk. 17:26-27), and the day that Lot left Sodom (Lk. 17:28-29) indicate that a particular doom in a twenty-four-hour period is in view. This is followed by the words, "Even so will it be in the day when the Son of Man is revealed" (Lk. 17:30). The most natural reading of this is that Jesus is referring to the actual day of His return. If this is correct, then there is no clear mention in these verses of the Tribulation like we find in Matthew 24 and Mark 13. The note of great haste continues in verses 31-33 with the warnings not to turn back to grab anything (Lk. 17:31), and to remember Lot's wife, who simply looked back (she probably stopped in order to do so) and was destroyed (Lk. 17:32; cf. Gen. 19:26). There is little doubt in my mind that the actual day of Jesus' second coming is in view here: "Even so will it be in the day when the Son of Man is revealed" (Lk. 17:30). But what is one to do with the verses that follow?

> Whoever seeks to save his life will lose it, and whoever loses his life will preserve it. I tell you, in that night there will be two *men* in one bed: the one will be taken and the other will be left. Two *women* will be grinding together: the

23 When Jesus refers to Himself as "the Son of Man… in His day" (Lk. 17:24), this ought to recall Dan. 7:13-14.

> one will be taken and the other left. Two *men* will be in the field: the one will be taken and the other left (Lk. 17:33-36).

Verse 33 seems to require longer than a mere day to occur. It rather looks like it pertains to a period of many days, perhaps even years. Luke utilizes this saying (or something similar) in two other places; Luke 9:24 and 14:26, and it appears in a discipleship setting in Matthew 10:39 and after Jesus rebuked Peter in Matthew 16:25 (cf. Mk. 8:35). It is also found in John 12:25. Clearly, Jesus used this contrast many times. One might say that it is quintessential to His teaching. In Luke 17 the context demands that it is not hyperbolic, so it could be a veiled reference to the Tribulation (cf. Dan. 12:1). The remaining verses fit a scenario of judgment, but it is not easy to decide whether the ones taken or those left are being judged. In the examples of Noah and Lot, those who were left were judged.[24] This tilts the odds in favor of the "taken" being saved and the "left" being judged.[25]

Luke 18 brings the focus back from the eschaton to Jesus' day.[26] But there are one or two verses that are pertinent. After illustrating the importance of persistence in prayer, Jesus adds, "Nevertheless, when the Son of Man comes, will He really find faith on the earth?" (Lk. 18:8).

This reference to His coming is preceded by words about judgment: "I tell you that He will avenge them speedily" (Lk. 18:8). "Them" refers to those who pray to God for justice. Christ's return will be that swift judgment. This assures the saints that, although they may have to wait until Christ's appearing, their pleas are heard.[27] His Kingdom will be just.

Eschatological references to the Kingdom continue in Luke 18, first with the warning that one must receive it "like a little child" to enter (Lk. 18:16-17). This assumes that the entrance to the Kingdom lies ahead of them. This is followed by the story of the Rich [Young] Ruler (Luke does not give his age) who is promised "treasure in heaven" (Lk. 18:22) if he forsakes all and follows Jesus. The promised reward is future, but is the "treasure in heaven" the same as the Kingdom? That is to say, is the Kingdom of God a heavenly and not an earthly reality? In watching the man walk away,[28] Jesus tells His disciples how difficult it is for a rich man to enter the Kingdom of God (Lk. 18:24-25). The future of the Kingdom is again clear, but what of its location?

---

24 Even with Lk. 17:33 those who lose their lives are "taken" and those who save their lives are "left."

25 Bock calls this "the most natural reading" (Darrell L. Bock, *Luke 9:51–24:53*), 1437.

26 We see the same thing in Luke 20 and 22, after the eschatological teachings of Luke 19 and 21. Since Christ's passion has to be recorded, this is inevitable, but it does show how much weight Luke placed upon eschatology and the Kingdom of God.

27 An illustration of this is the gathering of the prayers of the saints and the actions of the angel in Revelation 8:3-5. The answer to the prayers waited until the right time.

28 Luke does not record the man leaving.

The Location of the Kingdom in Luke

The answer to this question can be partly constructed from the surrounding verses. The young man's question was about inheriting eternal life, which he no doubt equated with the future Kingdom.[29] Luke had already referred to treasure in heaven in Luke 12:31-33, where it is something to be stored up. The evangelist does not say much about the location of the Kingdom, but I think it is possible to gather his allusions together to demonstrate that an *earthly location* is assumed.

Before this pivotal event, the Lord had told His disciples, "I tell you the truth, there are some standing here who shall not taste death till they see the kingdom of God" (Lk. 9:27). What Peter, James, and John saw was the Lord's transfigured glory in an earthly setting with Moses and Elijah; the latter was predicted to return to earth to herald the Lord's coming (Mal. 4:5). Peter himself would later seem to understand this event as an adumbration of the Lord's second advent (2 Pet. 1:16). If the intention was to create an impression of a heavenly kingdom as opposed to an earthly one, it would have made more sense for Jesus to have been lifted up from the earth.

In the middle chapters of Luke's Gospel, we encounter Jesus employing the phrase "the kingdom of God has come near you" (Lk. 10:9, 11; 11:20[30]; cf. 17:21). These have a this-world feel akin to the "among you" passage in Luke 17:21.[31] The ministry and miracles of Jesus introduce the Kingdom as it is present in the person of Christ.[32]

At this point I want to go back to Luke 13:28-29 since they are important here: "There will be weeping and gnashing of teeth, when you see Abraham and Isaac and Jacob and all the prophets in the kingdom of God, and yourselves thrust out. They will come from the east and the west, from the north and the south, and sit down in the kingdom of God."

There would be no reason for anyone to travel from any point of the compass if they could not find the Kingdom of God here on Earth. Moreover, this earthbound Kingdom is the one connected to the covenant with Abraham, Isaac, and Jacob. Once more then, Luke's emphasis falls upon the future Kingdom.

The Rewards of the Kingdom and the Prediction of the Passion

After the departure of the Rich Ruler, Peter comments that the disciples have left everything to follow Jesus (Lk. 18:28), to which he receives the reply that whatever sacrifices they have made for His sake, they "shall receive many times more in this present time, and in the age to come eternal life" (Lk. 18:30). This is not an easy reply to digest, for what does Jesus mean by rewards "in this present time"? I believe the answer is to be sought in the idea of storing up treasure, which we have just read about in the previous pericope (Lk. 18:18-27, esp. v. 22). The sacrifices in this life are reckoned to our account and magnified "many times... in the age to come" (Lk. 18:30).

29 Craig A. Evans, *Luke* (Peabody, MA: Hendricksen, 1990), 275.
30 "The kingdom of God has come upon you."
31 If we think of them as such, they do not teach anything other than that the Kingdom was present when Jesus was present.
32 Although the Kingdom was rejected. When Jesus returns it will be imposed.

These gifts come to the saints in addition to the gift of eternal life. We shall have to relate eternal life with the Kingdom further on in this book, but it is clear from this that the differences in rewards point to a layered society in the eschaton.

What comes straight after the teaching of rewards is Jesus' prediction of His own ensuing sacrifice, a concept that the disciples could not understand (Lk. 18:34). As we have seen, the necessity of His sacrifice was foreknown by Jesus, and He will state it plainly in the next chapter. Luke comments that despite Jesus wording the news in the most unambiguous fashion, the meaning "was hidden from them, and they did not know the things which were spoken" (Lk. 18:34).

Luke 18 finishes with the author inserting the tale of the healing of the blind man (Lk. 18:35-43). The one who is blind proclaims the true identity of Jesus as "Son of David" to those who see. Without trying to read into the text, Luke, who is so interested in the Kingdom, might be alluding to this idea through the context of this blind man who connects Jesus' healings with His messiahship.

The Key Lukan Passage on the Two Comings

It is a bold and somewhat subjective statement to make, but the Parable of the Pounds (or Ten Minas[33]) in Luke 19:11-27 is perhaps the key passage in this Gospel, if not in all the Gospels, on the theology of the two comings of Messiah.[34] Since I believe it to be so crucial, I will give it special attention. The parable is introduced as follows: "Now as they heard these things, He spoke another parable, because He was near Jerusalem and because they thought the kingdom of God would appear immediately" (Lk. 19:11).[35]

The "things" to which verse 11 refers is the story of Zacchaeus, specifically Christ's announcement that salvation had come to the home of the tax collector and that even though he had sinned against his own people, "he also is a son of Abraham." This is to say, although Zacchaeus's complicity with the ruling class put him beyond the pale as far as the Jewish religious leaders were concerned, through faith in Jesus he became an inheritor of the Abrahamic promise and so became a true Jew.

The new parable of Luke 19:11 is given a certain prominence by its introduction. Luke supplies two reasons for it. Firstly, they were nearing Jerusalem, the city of the Great King (Psa. 48:2; Matt. 5:35). Jerusalem was where Christ would soon meet His death (Lk. 18:31-33).

The second reason for the parable is crucial to grasp if one is going to "rightly divide the word of truth" (2 Tim. 2:15). The parable is, in part, given to disabuse disciples of any notion of an *immediate arrival of the Kingdom of God.*[36] This clear fact

33 One mina was equivalent to about four month's wages.

34 Surprisingly, this parable is given a relatively slight treatment by Darrell Bock in his classic commentary on Luke.

35 It is telling that some biblical theologies from amillennialists omit mentioning verse 11. E.g., Benjamin L. Gladd, *From the Manger to the Throne: A Theology of Luke* (Wheaton, IL: Crossway, 2022).

36 "The immediate establishment of the Kingdom on earth was contingent upon the attitude of Israel toward her Messianic King, for to that nation pertained the divine promises and

does not deter those who insist that Christ set up the (mostly spiritual) Kingdom of God at His first coming, which He rules over from heaven.[37]

Several matters rise to the surface here. First, one should notice that the meaning of the Kingdom of God is best understood as *the earthly covenanted realm* over which the Messiah would reign. It is not a heavenly kingdom (as the parable itself will dispel). Second, this covenanted Kingdom upon the earth will appear, but not in the disciples' near future. Third, Jesus was going to Jerusalem *to die*, not to bring in the Kingdom. Finally, for these reasons, those biblical interpreters who assert that Jesus became King in the first century A.D. and, therefore, that some form of the Kingdom of God was inaugurated at the first advent, must do so in the face of Jesus' own teaching here *at the end of His ministry.*[38] This fourth point will need to be reemphasized once we leave the study of the Four Gospels and delve into the Acts and the Epistles.

The first three verses of the parable are as follows:

> Therefore He said: "A certain nobleman went into a far country to receive for himself a kingdom and to return. So he called ten of his servants, delivered to them ten minas, and said to them, 'Do business till I come. But his citizens hated him, and sent a delegation after him, saying, 'We will not have this *man* to reign over us'" (Lk. 19:12-14).

The "citizens" who reject Christ are, of course, the Jews, the "faithless and perverse generation" of Luke 9:41. They do this because they hate Him. The Greek word is *miseo*, and refers here to the loathing and hostility towards the whole person not just his actions.[39] This may seem a little strong since, if many of these people had been asked about their opinion of Jesus, they may not have considered themselves as haters of Him. But the deep recesses of the heart are prone to be covered by self-deception. Such was the unequivocal impact of Jesus' words and works. Only a sustained dislike of Him would explain the attitude of the general populace to Him. It is true that often the Jewish leaders are characterized as holding enmity against Jesus, but the people, in all probability due to the influence of their leaders, did not want Jesus either.[40]

---

covenants (Rom. 9:4)" (Alva J. McClain, *The Greatness of the Kingdom*, 319). The reason for God dealing with Israel *en bloc*, so to speak, was because they were under covenant to Him.

37 Benjamin L. Gladd, *From the Manger to the Throne*, 184-186.

38 The similarity of this parable with the Parable of the Talents in Matthew 24:14-30 has been the subject of much discussion. Three points should be made. (1) Jesus was an itinerant teacher, and it is unthinkable that He would only utter one parable at only one time. As N. T. Wright has said, "Is there a storyteller on record who told stories only once, and then in the least elaborate form possible?" (*Jesus and the Victory of God*, 633-634, n. 83). (2) Matthew's Parable of the Talents is not about the person of the rejected and returning king. (3) The fact that Jesus used similar parables to convey different teachings should alert us to the danger of too quickly equating comparable sayings of Jesus reported elsewhere.

39 H. Seebass, "*miseo*," *New International Dictionary of New Testament Theology*, ed. Colin Brown, Vol. 1. (Grand Rapids: Zondervan, 1975), 555.

40 The mention of a delegation sent after the nobleman recalls the Jewish delegation sent to Rome in A.D. 6 to implore Caesar not to allow the despised Archelaus to continue as ethnarch over Judea. See Craig A. Evans, *Luke*, 287.

It is important to pay attention to the words that Jesus places into the mouths of those who reject Him: "We will not have this man to reign over us" (Lk. 19:14). The nobleman in the story had not yet assumed the crown. Translating this image into the chronology of Jesus' mission, this means that Jesus (again) was well aware that He was not going to rule when He came the first time. It is not that He did not have the right to rule (Luke 1 through 4 makes that clear), but that even though He was Messiah the King, He was also the Messiah who would be cut off on behalf of others (Dan. 9:26; Isa. 53:5-6).

The promised Davidic Kingdom could not be set up to flourish over the kind of recalcitrant opposition it would always encounter in the unyielding hearts of sinners. Sin and its effects must first be dealt with. That is the job of the New covenant. And as we shall see, the New covenant requires Christ's blood to inaugurate it. The parable does not contain an offer of the Kingdom via acceptance of the King because the hour is now late. The scene is set. Notwithstanding the triumphant entrance into Jerusalem, which is shortly to come, Jesus is journeying to His death, and death will take Him, at least for a brief time. This parable predicts Jesus going to heaven (the "far country" in the parable) to receive a kingdom and then return.[41] He has not returned yet! Therefore, He is not *ruling* yet. We must recall that the Kingdom is Davidic, which is to say it is covenantal. The significance of it being covenantal is that its broad character is already hermeneutically defined. It cannot be what it wasn't previously specified to be.

The Parable of the Pounds continues in verses 15-26 with a description of the three stewardships given by the nobleman to his servants and their reckoning "when he returned, having received the kingdom" (Lk. 19:15). It takes me away from my purpose in this book to expound this part of the parable, but notice that the nobleman is now returned as a king who rules.

Having now dealt with his servants, the king turns to those who rejected him: "But bring here those enemies of mine, who did not want me to reign over them, and slay *them* before me" (Lk. 19:27).

Remembering that in a parable one thing can stand for another, the severity of the treatment of those who insisted they would not have the new king to reign over them should not be minimized. The OT depicts Yahweh coming in wrath upon His enemies (e.g., Isa. 2:19-21; 61:2; 63:1-6), and the NT will follow suit (e.g., 2 Thess. 1:7-10; Rev. 19:11-16). None of the king's enemies enter his kingdom.

---

41 See Paul Barnett, *Jesus and the Rise of Early Christianity*, 72-73, 113. The hearers of this parable were familiar with the concept of someone going away to receive a kingdom because the Caesars were known to dispense rule that way (e.g., Herod the Great and Herod Antipas). However, when one comprehends John's prologue, it is a bit odd that the exalted Son of God should have to leave the earth He had been given to receive the Kingdom. The strangeness of this is, of course, explained in the fact that He must first secure the victory over sin and death as the obedient Servant, even if that meant being despised, rejected, and crucified (cf. Heb. 12:1-2).

The King Enters Jerusalem (and Weeps)

After the Parable of the Pounds, Luke records three related episodes: The Triumphal Entry (Lk. 19:28-40), Jesus Weeping over Jerusalem (Lk. 19:41-44), and the Temple Cleansing (Lk. 19:45-48). Jesus sends some disciples to get a colt for Him to ride upon (Matthew 21:7 notes that a donkey was brought too). In this fascinating little story, Jesus knows beforehand what they will find and how to answer those who question them. It is the answer that interests us: "If anyone asks you, 'Why are you loosing *it?*' thus you shall say to him, 'Because the Lord has need of it'" (Lk. 19:31).

Jesus specifically refers to Himself as *ho kyrios* ("the Lord"). Without going to the lengths of demonstrating it, I feel secure in the belief that He was not using the term in the sense of "Master" but as a self-reference to His rights as the God-man.[42] This both suits Luke's employment of the term,[43] the kingly setting of the pericope, and the circumstantial setting of the event. Then Luke notes that a multitude of disciples proclaimed His entrance into the city. Matthew has "a very great multitude" (Matt. 21:8). This may mean that, along with the many followers of Jesus, others got caught up in the excitement. What is certain is the very clear cries of the crowd: "'Blessed is the King who comes in the name of the LORD!' Peace in heaven and glory in the highest!" (Lk. 19:38).

The disciples of Jesus were shouting out a familiar line from Psalm 118:26, only instead of saying, "Blessed is he," they proclaim, "Blessed is the king." Luke alone records this, which fits his emphases (although he does not include the reference to the "King" of Zechariah 9:9). He also adds the refrain about "peace in heaven and glory in the highest" that instantly takes the reader back to the angelic choir at the announcement of the birth of Jesus in Luke 2:14. Hence, though the other evangelists highlight the Davidic connection of the scene,[44] Luke chooses to return to what was heralded by the angels on high. This creates a somber preface to his unique recording of Jesus weeping over the city that should have welcomed Him.

The emotion that must have welled-up inside Jesus must have been overwhelming.[45] The term for weeping (*klaio*) here means "strong crying."[46] God has chosen Jerusalem to put His name there (see 1 Kings 11:13, 32, 36; Psa. 132:13-14), but Jerusalem has chosen to refuse God! It is hard to face rejection. It is crushing to know the reason for your rejection is enmity against you. Added to this in Jesus' case is the Lord's knowledge of what the cost of that rejection will be to the people (Lk.

---

42 See Walter L. Liefeld, "Luke," in *EBC*, ed. Frank E. Gaebelein, Vol 8. (Grand Rapids: Zondervan, 1984), 1011.

43 Luke uses the word "Lord" 77 times in his Gospel and always to refer to God or Jesus.

44 Matthew stresses David (Matt. 21:9), Mark the kingdom (Mk. 11:10), and John simply the King (Jn. 12:13).

45 There is a mix of emotions in this event. The people are yelling His praise, Jesus Himself is overcome, and the Pharisees, who only see Him as a "teacher," confirm their rejection of Jesus by calling upon Him to stop what they see as blasphemy.

46 J. J. Van Oosterzee, *The Gospel According to Luke*, Lange's Commentary, Vol. 8 (Grand Rapids: Zondervan, 1980), 297; and A. T. Robertson, *Word Pictures in the New Testament*, Vol. 2 (Nashville: Broadman Press, 1933), 246.

19:43-44). Christ arrives as the true Son of David, as the rightful heir, but He is discarded—at least for now.

What is meant by the words "this your day" in verse 42? I think it unlikely that Luke is referring to the specific day of Messiah's arrival as corresponding to Daniel's sixty-ninth week (Dan. 9:25).[47] The book of Daniel is not pinpointing a specific day, although the prophecy is about Jesus. I believe Marshall is right to interpret the force of the saying as, "If only you knew now," etc.).[48] It has, therefore, the same meaning as "the time of your visitation" (Lk. 19:44).

When Jesus goes into the temple, He enters as "Messiah the Prince" (Dan. 9:25), and as the "Branch" who will be both King and Priest (cf. Zech. 6:12-13), but not in Herod's temple. This temple has forgotten how to worship God. But God has not overlooked how He ought to be worshipped. Jesus' overthrowing of the tables serves as a graphic reminder of the Creator and Savior's opinion of sullied worship.[49] God's Creation Project will never be successful if left to human devices. Even the best of us manage to turn something good and innocent into something mired by compromise and ambition.

The Parable of the Vineyard

Bock refers to this as "one of Luke's most comprehensive parables—and an extremely significant one."[50] The waves of servants who are sent by the owner of the vineyard (God the Father)[51] stand for the prophets (Lk. 20:10-12). The reason for sending the servants is that "they [the tenants] might give him some of the fruit of the vineyard" (Lk. 20:10). Nothing should be read into this motive[52] as the Lord simply uses it to get to the point, which is the knowing rejection of the Son. Verse 14 is where this is brought out: "But when the vinedressers saw him, they reasoned among themselves, saying, 'This is the heir. Come, let us kill him, that the inheritance may be ours'" (Lk. 20:14).

The truly astonishing words and works of Jesus, combined with His impeccable character and John the Baptist's testimony, gave more than sufficient proof of his true identity to anyone with a grasp of the Hebrew Scriptures. The fact that Jesus referred

47 This was the position of Sir Robert Anderson, *The Coming Prince or The Seventy Weeks of Daniel* (London: Hodder and Stoughton, 1865), 119-129.

48 I. Howard Marshall, *Commentary on Luke*, 718.

49 "Never could there be more plausible colours cast upon any act; the convenience, the necessity of provisions for the sacrifice: yet through all these do the fiery eyes of our Saviour see the foul covetousness of the priests, the fraud of the money-changers, the intolerable abuse of the temple. Common eyes may be cheated with easy pretexts; but he that looks through the heart at the face, justly answers our apologies with scourges" (Joseph Hall, *Contemplations on the Historical Passages of the Old and New Testaments* [London: T. Nelson and Sons, 1868], IV.XXV, 563).

50 Darrell L. Bock, *Luke 9:51–24:53*, 1591.

51 In the Parable of the Pounds, it is the nobleman (Jesus) who takes a journey into a far country. In this parable it is the owner of the vineyard (God) who takes the journey. In the former, the lesson is centered around the fact that Jesus actually does go away, whereas in this context the God the Father does not leave; His journeying is only for the sake of illustrating the coming of the son and His treatment.

52 The prophets were not "fruit-inspectors."

to Himself as "the Son of Man" (especially in the latter half of this Gospel) only adds to the guilt of those who refused Him.[53] This guilt is further intensified by the fact that the Jewish leaders were indeed plotting to kill Jesus exactly as the parable indicates (Lk. 20:14 with 19:47). The administering of justice upon the evil tenants in the parable only aggravated the hatred of the "chief priests and scribes" because they already knew that Jesus had told the parable against them (Lk. 20:19). Hence, the quotation of Psalm 118:22 in Luke 20:17 indicates not only that the Christ was rejected because He didn't match up to the religious leaders' faulty idea of a messianic Conqueror, but because they *knew* that Jesus was the Christ yet sought to kill Him anyway. But the quotation is interesting in that light: "The stone which the builders rejected Has become the chief cornerstone" (Lk. 20:17).

The image is of builders looking at and then discarding a stone in their plan to build something (i.e., a kingdom).[54] Their attempt fails since another [God] chooses the discarded stone not only to place in the new structure, but to use it as the very cornerstone of His project (another Kingdom). We may infer here that Jesus means that the messianic Kingdom and rule will come, but not before His own rejection by those who ought to have acknowledged Him as the Owner's "son."

This chapter includes another OT quotation that delves deeper into His identity. In Luke 20:41-44 Jesus asks the religious leaders about king David:

> And He said to them, "How can they say that the Christ is the Son of David?
> Now David himself said in the Book of Psalms:
> 'The LORD said to my Lord,
> Sit at My right hand,
> Till I make Your enemies Your footstool.'
>
> Therefore David calls Him 'Lord'; how is He then his Son?"

The quotation is from Psalm 110:1, a psalm that combines priesthood and crown (Psa. 110:1, 4). The crown is, of course, the crown of David. The priesthood is not the Levitical High Priest's function under the Law, but is another non-Judaic office, related to Melchizedek (Gen. 14). There is a covenant with David that includes a "Son" who is higher than the founder of the dynasty, a greater descendant of David (Psa. 132:17-18), whom these teachers ought to have anticipated. Jesus was a great miracle worker and moral teacher who was being hailed in front of them as "the Son of David" (Lk. 18:38-39) and "the King who comes in the name of the LORD" (Lk. 19:38). This exchange is similar to the earlier one concerning the ministry of John the Baptist (see Lk. 20:1-8). It fixes the guilt of the religious leaders by forcing them to take sides. And they choose the wrong side.

---

53 See also the stunning passage in Lk. 22:70.

54 It is not unusual to find scholars failing to reconcile the various strands of God's Word, instead putting cleverly devised but erroneous interpretations in their place.

Luke's Great Eschatological Discourse

Most of chapter 21 is given over to what might be called Luke's version of the Olivet Discourse (cf. Mk. 13 and Matt. 24). He has already recorded Jesus' teachings in Luke 17:20-37 along with some eschatological remarks in Luke 19, but here is where a fuller development of Jesus' eschatology takes place. In keeping with my goal to present Jesus' teachings on the covenants within their proper context, I will first comment on Luke 21 as if it were our sole example of this discourse. In another chapter I shall attempt to briefly pull the combined witness of the Synoptics together.

The prelude to the discourse is the disciple's observation in Luke 21:5 about the grandeur of the temple complex and Jesus' retort that it would all be cast down (a prediction of the Roman conflict that ended in A.D. 70). This elicits a question from the disciples: "Teacher, but when will these things be? And what sign *will there be* when these things are about to take place?" (Lk. 21:7).[55] What follows in reply goes well beyond A.D. 70. The Lord refers to "the end" (Lk. 21:9), and most of what He will say appears to concern the time of the eschaton. We see, for instance, the mention of those who come in Jesus' name, posing as Christ (Lk. 21:8). Accompanying these false christs will be "fearful sights and great signs from heaven" (Lk. 21:11), which are quite beyond the purview of the first century, although commentators have tried to link Jesus' words with apocalyptic language to make it fit A.D. 70.[56] This looks like an attempt to burden the discourse with a genre that will make it relate to the Fall of Jerusalem, but the cosmic signs, if taken as real, surely point to the events preceding the second coming.

When one analyzes the verses, I think it is important to put oneself into the disciples' situation, and not into some imagined scenario wherein the Gospel writers are assuming a fulfillment in the tragic events that occurred forty years after these words were uttered.

Let us begin with verse 11: "And there will be great earthquakes in various places, and famines and pestilences; and there will be fearful sights and great signs from heaven" (Lk. 21:11). What sort of "fearful sights and great signs from heaven" are being referred to? The preposition indicates that the signs (plural) are not mere atmospheric anomalies, but rather that they are heaven-sent.[57] If this is so, then "great earthquakes…famines and pestilences" as well as the "fearful sights" (or "things that strike terror," *phobētron*), call to mind other prophetic oracles.[58] One obvious passage is in Revelation 6, where all of these phenomena are reported (Rev. 6:8, 12-14). That

55 See Robert H. Stein, "Jesus, The Destruction of Jerusalem, and the Coming of the Son of Man In Luke 21:5-38," *Southern Baptist Journal of Theology*, 16 (Fall 2012), 19. Stein has said that the whole understanding of the passage depends on how this verse is interpreted. I understand, but respectfully disagree. The key verse is Lk. 21:22. Stein does not explain how the cosmic signs of verse 11 concern the fate of Jerusalem in A.D. 66–70.

56 Marshall, *Commentary on Luke*, 765.

57 Think of the judgments from heaven in Rev. 6, 8, and 9.

58 Many have tied Lk. 21 with Jeremiah's temple sermon in Jer. 4, but aside from the uncreation narrative in Jer. 4:23-24 there is not much from the prophet to interpret Luke.

chapter was written long after A.D. 70 and concerns things to come. Another passage that Luke 21:11 calls to mind is Joel 2:30-31:

> And I will show wonders in the heavens and in the earth:
> Blood and fire and pillars of smoke.
> The sun shall be turned into darkness,
> And the moon into blood,
> Before the coming of the great and awesome day of the LORD.

Luke cites Peter using this passage in Acts 2, and I shall have more to say on that when we arrive there. But as they stand, Joel's words are predictive of what we call the second advent of Christ, complete with manifestations reminiscent of Luke 21:11. I agree with Vlach that what we have in Luke 21:8-11 comes after the events of Luke 21:12-19. Hence, "But before all these things" (Lk. 21:12) refers to 21:8-11.[59] The "signs" ought to be understood as signs of the end (21:9), not "apocalyptic" descriptions of the destruction of Titus's armies.

The Days of Vengeance

Luke 21:12-19 can be fitted into the first century. But what about the prediction of Jerusalem being surrounded by armies? Is it correct to conclude that this is a reference to A.D. 70? I am not so sure. We must give the passage room to breathe, as it were. We should recall that the desolation of Jerusalem was written about by the Prophets.

Zechariah 12:2 says, "Behold, I will make Jerusalem a cup of drunkenness to all the surrounding peoples, when they lay siege against Judah and Jerusalem." Yahweh has promised to protect Jerusalem when this occurs (Zech. 12:7-9), although it will be far from unscathed (Zech. 14:2-3). The thing about Luke 21:20 is that it is set within a context that turns the thoughts in a certain direction. Here are the verses:

> Then let those who are in Judea flee to the mountains, let those who are in the midst of her depart, and let not those who are in the country enter her. For these are the days of vengeance, that all things which are written may be fulfilled. But woe to those who are pregnant and to those who are nursing babies in those days! For there will be great distress in the land and wrath upon this people. And they will fall by the edge of the sword, and be led away captive into all nations. And Jerusalem will be trampled by Gentiles until the times of the Gentiles are fulfilled (Lk. 21:21-24).

Apart from the resemblance of verses 21 and 23 to Matthew 24:16-19 and Mark 13:14-18, which shall be explored in their place, what Luke has left us is a deliberate route back to Isaiah and his prophecies of God's vengeance in Isaiah 34:8, 61:2, and 63:4. Those prophecies do not concern the first century. They are decisive, describing God's judgment upon the nations of the world and their armies "in recompense for the cause of Zion" (Isa. 34:8). The Isaianic context is worth reproducing:

---

59 Michael J. Vlach, *He Will Reign Forever*, 389.

> Come near, you nations, to hear; and heed, you people!
>
> Let the earth hear, and all that is in it, the world and all things that come forth from it.
>
> For the indignation of the LORD *is* against all nations, and *His* fury against all their armies; He has utterly destroyed them, He has given them over to the slaughter.
>
> Also their slain shall be thrown out; their stench shall rise from their corpses, and the mountains shall be melted with their blood.
>
> All the host of heaven shall be dissolved, and the heavens shall be rolled up like a scroll; all their host shall fall down as the leaf falls from the vine, and as *fruit* falling from a fig tree.
>
> "For My sword shall be bathed in heaven; indeed, it shall come down on Edom, and on the people of My curse, for judgment. The sword of the LORD is filled with blood, it is made overflowing with fatness, with the blood of lambs and goats, with the fat of the kidneys of rams. For the LORD has a sacrifice in Bozrah, and a great slaughter in the land of Edom. The wild oxen shall come down with them, and the young bulls with the mighty bulls; their land shall be soaked with blood, and their dust saturated with fatness."
>
> For *it is* the day of the LORD's vengeance, the year of recompense for the cause of Zion.
>
> Its streams shall be turned into pitch, and its dust into brimstone; its land shall become burning pitch. It shall not be quenched night or day; its smoke shall ascend forever. From generation to generation it shall lie waste; no one shall pass through it forever and ever (Isa. 34:1-10).

The call is for all the earth to hear the doom of Yahweh; in fact, "the world and all things that come from it" (Isa. 34:1). It's as if God's revulsion with everything that despoils the earth has finally reached a boiling point. This is the decisive "day of Yahweh's vengeance" (Isa. 34:8). It is concentrated upon Edom and Bozrah, which comprises modern day Jordan. This, in turn, reminds us of another "vengeance passage" in Isaiah 63:

> Who is this who comes from Edom, with dyed garments from Bozrah, this One who is glorious in His apparel, traveling in the greatness of His strength —"I who speak in righteousness, mighty to save."
>
> Why is Your apparel red, and Your garments like one who treads in the winepress?

> "I have trodden the winepress alone, and from the peoples no one was with Me. For I have trodden them in My anger, and trampled them in My fury; their blood is sprinkled upon My garments, and I have stained all My robes. For the day of vengeance is in My heart, and the year of My redeemed has come.
>
> I looked, but there was no one to help, and I wondered That there was no one to uphold; therefore My own arm brought salvation for Me; and My own fury, it sustained Me.
>
> I have trodden down the peoples in My anger, made them drunk in My fury, and brought down their strength to the earth" (Isa. 63:1-6).

Here again we find Edom and Bozrah mentioned. Now the Avenger is depicted as traveling from there to help His people ("My redeemed" in verse 4). We ought to note too, the unmistakable similarity with Revelation 14:19-20 and 19:15. The challenge is to interpret the Isaianic passages rightly. From what has been assembled so far, it looks like these "vengeance passages" to which Luke is calling our attention fit the second coming, not the first. There is one more passage to look at:

> "The Spirit of the Lord GOD is upon Me, because the LORD has anointed Me to preach good tidings to the poor; He has sent Me to heal the broken-hearted, to proclaim liberty to the captives, and the opening of the prison to those who are bound; to proclaim the acceptable year of the LORD, and the day of vengeance of our God; to comfort all who mourn, to console those who mourn in Zion, to give them beauty for ashes, the oil of joy for mourning, the garment of praise for the spirit of heaviness; that they may be called trees of righteousness, the planting of the LORD, that He may be glorified" (Isa. 61:1-3).

If you think some of this looks familiar, you are right. The first part of this oracle was read out by Jesus in the Nazareth synagogue (Lk. 4:17-21). Everyone notices that the Lord suddenly cuts off the quotation at Isaiah 61:2a after the words "to proclaim the acceptable year of the Lord" (Lk. 4:19). The Lord does not proceed to the next phrase which is, "And the day of vengeance of our God" (Isa. 61:2b). The reason He stops the reading where He does is quite obvious That part of the prophecy was not fulfilled at Christ's first coming—it is a second coming prediction. One should notice the consolation of Zion in the context (Isa. 61:3a), which matches Isaiah 34:8 and 63:7 ("the great goodness toward the house of Israel"). The case is strong. Jesus in Luke 21:22 is referring to His second advent, not to A.D. 70! There is a lot going on in Isaiah 34, 61, and 63. The passages Luke alludes to speak of Yahweh's decisive act of vengeance. But each passage also refers to salvation and comfort, which are New covenant themes. The latter part of Isaiah 61 and 63 is about future Israel being blessed among the nations (Isa. 61:6-11; 63:7-19).

The "Times of the Gentiles"

A great deal has been written about "the Times of the Gentiles," especially by dispensational writers. But before we can know what it refers to, we must situate it in the discourse in which it stands. I have given reasons why Luke 21:20-23 concerns the end of days. Jesus speaks of Jerusalem being surrounded by armies (Lk. 21:20) and of the city being trampled down by the Gentiles (Lk. 21:24b). It seems natural to think of Zechariah 12:1-3 and Revelation 11:2. The context of "the Times of the Gentiles" in Luke therefore points to the end time siege of Jerusalem by the armies of the Gentile nations. But could Jesus mean something more than that? For that to be so, the phrase would have to resonate with nuances of prophetic significance.

EXCURSUS: The Fuller Meaning of "Times of the Gentiles"

The phrase "the Times of the Gentiles" is found only once in the Scriptures in Luke 21:24. It sits in the middle of Jesus' eschatological discourse after He enters Jerusalem just prior to His passion. The term is of interest because it is such an unusual turn of phrase. Why did Jesus not simply state, "Jerusalem will be trampled by Gentiles until God comes to wreak vengeance on Israel's enemies," or some such words of woe that would fit the context well? He didn't. He said, "Jerusalem will be trampled by Gentiles until the times of the Gentiles are fulfilled" (my emphasis). There is a period of time that is given over to the Gentiles.[60] A period which, it appears, required little or no explanation among the Jews who heard about it.

Dispensational interpreters have generally designated "the Times of the Gentiles" as a long period of time stretching over many centuries. John Walvoord, for instance, writes, "For the Gentiles, the tribulation marks the close of the extended period of the 'times of the Gentiles' (Luke 21:24), that period marked by Gentile control of Jerusalem since 600 B. C."[61]

His fellow Dallas Seminary professor J. Dwight Pentecost says:

> The "times of the Gentiles" has been defined as that period of time in which Jerusalem was under the dominion of Gentile authority (Luke 21:24). This period began with the Babylonian captivity when Jerusalem fell into the hands of Gentiles. It has continued unto the present time and will continue through the tribulation period, in which era the Gentile powers will be judged.[62]

In a later work Pentecost provides this more reflective definition:

60 "The period is one of gentile domination of the city, but a limit is set to it, namely the fulfilment of an allotted time" (I. Howard Marshall, *Commentary on Luke*, 773).

61 John F. Walvoord, *The Millennial Kingdom* (Grand Rapids: Zondervan, 1981), 257.

62 J. Dwight Pentecost, *Things to Come: A Study in Biblical Eschatology* (Grand Rapids: Zondervan, 1976), 315. Pentecost goes on to adduce Dan. 2 and 7, which describe "the...prophetic outline of the course of the period" (Ibid., 316-317).

> The times of the Gentiles is that extended period of discipline on God's covenant people during which time no Davidic descendant sits on David's throne ruling over David's kingdom. It extends from the destruction of Jerusalem and the emptying of the throne of David by Nebuchadnezzar until the ultimate repentance.[63]

While these understandings of the term may be correct (particularly the last one), it should be noted that they are not based upon exegesis of Luke 21:24 in its context. Darrell Bock, who is a Progressive Dispensationalist, has written one of the most comprehensive commentaries on Luke's Gospel. He disagrees with Walvoord and Pentecost. He thinks the verse indicates "a short- and long-term view."[64] Bock claims, "More likely, the 'times of the Gentiles' is a general way to describe the current period in God's plan, when the Gentiles are prominent but will culminate in judgment on those nations."[65] Bock does read his already-not yet views into the text at times,[66] but his more guarded opinion is worth pondering.[67]

From the premillennial but not dispensational side comes Craig Blomberg, who believes "that some interval of time must separate the destruction of Jerusalem from the complete fulfillment of all of God's plans for Israel and the nations."[68] This somewhat vague answer may be the best we can muster under the circumstances. Still, there are a number of important cross-references that are due consideration. Nearly everyone who comments on this verse relates it to Romans 11:25b: "Blindness in part has happened to Israel until the fullness of the Gentiles has come in."

As with "the Times of the Gentiles" in Luke, the Apostle Paul's terminology appears without explanation but presupposes an agreed upon understanding. In Paul's case, "the fullness of the Gentiles" is set in opposition to the restoration of Israel. It assumes it in fact.

It ought, therefore, to be possible to deduce a plausible meaning for both terms. Again, it is not necessary to over-complicate matters. The "fullness" (the normal Greek word is *pleroma*) of the Gentiles is clearly a terminal point, after which ("until") the blindness of Israel will presumably be lifted. In this view, the "fullness of the Gentiles" signifies the completion of God's present way of dealing with the Gentile powers in His Creation program. And if there is to be a "completing" of this interaction with the Gentiles, it is surely not pushing the envelope to surmise that the period in which God is "filling" the Gentiles might be known as "the Times of the Gentiles." Of course, we still have to try to discover just what that period covers, but the supposition looks to be relatively safe.

63 J. Dwight Pentecost, *Thy Kingdom Come: Tracing God's Kingdom Program and Covenant Promises Throughout History* (Grand Rapids: Kregel, 1995), 115. Similar to this is Andrew M. Woods, *The Coming Kingdom*, 36-37.

64 Darrell L. Bock, *Luke 9:51–24:53*, 1680.

65 Ibid., 1681.

66 Ibid., 1680, 1696 n. 51.

67 See also Mark S. Kinzer, "Zionism in Luke-Acts," 150-151. Kinzer relates it to Acts 3:17-21.

68 Craig L. Blomberg, *A New Testament Theology* (Waco, TX: Baylor University Press, 2018), 587.

John Murray has argued that the verb *eiserchomai* ("has come in") indicates entering the Kingdom of God and eternal life,[69] and so he confidently asserts that "the fullness of the Gentiles" means that the Gentiles enter the Kingdom. But the word *erchomai* usually means "enter" where it is used. It does not suddenly take on a technical sense when its object is the Kingdom. Murray forces a theological interpretation onto the text. The basic meaning is plain. In Romans 11:25, "the fullness of the Gentiles" concerns the completion of a program, after which Israel is restored. Paul does not indicate whether this "completion" ends in joy or despair. That is not where his thoughts are tending.

It seems reasonable to conclude that the "fullness of the Gentiles" of Romans 11:25 is *the last part* of "the Times of the Gentiles" of Luke 21:24. On that basis, the "Times of the Gentiles" probably signifies the period between the subsuming of Israel under foreign Gentile powers (Babylonian, Persian, Greek, Roman, Turkish, British) together with the loss of its kingly line. Hence, Pentecost's second definition in *Thy Kingdom Come* looks to be an accurate understanding of the phrase.[70]

The Coming of the Son of Man

> And there will be signs in the sun, in the moon, and in the stars; and on the earth distress of nations, with perplexity, the sea and the waves roaring; men's hearts failing them from fear and the expectation of those things which are coming on the earth, for the powers of the heavens will be shaken. Then they will see the Son of Man coming in a cloud with power and great glory (Lk. 21:25-27).

These remarkably powerful words refer to the return of the Messiah to earth after He has been to "a far country" to receive His Kingdom. Jesus comes back in such irresistible power that the earth's inhabitants are shaken with fear and perplexity. The fear is not hard to understand. The creation all around them is in upheaval at the return of its Maker. The perplexity of verse 25 is brought about because the normal course of events has ceased. The usual way of the world is interrupted (one might say intercepted). History is to be radically diverted towards God and His *original* purposes for creation. Man is confronted with his creatureliness, his lowliness, his inferiority, his stupidity. The coming of Christ brings to an end "the Times of the Gentiles."[71] According to the covenants with Israel, that nation is to be preeminent (e.g., Deut. 28:13; Zeph. 3:20). All eyes will look to Jerusalem, where the promised Ruler sits and reigns (Jer. 3:17).

---

69 John Murray, *The Epistle to the Romans*, NICNT, Vol. 2 (Grand Rapids: Eerdmans, 1982), 93.

70 See also the article by Tony Garland, "Daniel and the Times of the Gentiles," available at https://www.spiritandtruth.org/teaching/documents/articles/125/125.pdf?x=x

71 The very mention of "the Gentiles" shows that Jesus has Jerusalem and Israel's fortunes in mind. Therefore, the "redemption" mentioned in Lk. 21:28 is the redemption of the remnant of Israel.

> So you also, when you see these things happening, know that the kingdom of God is near... Heaven and earth will pass away, but My words will by no means pass away (Lk. 21:31, 33).

The particular "words" that "will by no means pass away" are the words of prophecy Jesus has just uttered. They refer to the Kingdom of God, and that is founded upon the divine covenants. The Kingdom is not something that arises after the ascension of Christ. It comes when He comes.[72] And since He has gone, the Kingdom is therefore yet to come. Luke 21:31 tells us that the Kingdom of God will be near after the second coming of Christ. That Kingdom includes, I am persuaded, the "recompense for the cause of Zion" (Isa. 34:8), the giving of "beauty for ashes," and the exchange of "the garment of praise for the spirit of heaviness" (Isa. 61:3). These occur in the aftermath of the coming of the Great King—the beginning of the Kingdom of God.

The Institution of the Lord's Supper

I firmly hold that the words of the institution of the Lord's Supper (Lk. 22:14-20) are some of the most important words in the NT, if not the entire Bible. From the standpoint of Biblical Covenantalism, it is here that the covenant of covenants, the New covenant, comes into being, at least partially, bringing with it the combining of the other unilateral covenants in the Lord Jesus Christ but without dissolving any of them or altering them. The Abrahamic and Davidic covenants remain intact and unaltered within (or under the auspices of) the New covenant, as do the Priestly and Noahic covenants, even though their full realization is held in abeyance till Christ returns. What Jesus does by shedding His own blood for sinners generates the prospect of each covenant being ultimately fulfilled precisely as written.

This is essential to understand. The NT does not record a lot of covenant language in comparison with the OT, *but it is just as covenantal.* The "covernance" of the NT must be unlocked with a New covenant key.

The occasion for this world-changing event was the annual celebration of the Passover Seder, although Jesus may have had to celebrate it prematurely because, by the time the real Passover was eaten, He would be dead.[73] The links between the Passover meal and the Lord's Supper are clear in Luke 22:15 and underlined by Paul's referring to Jesus as "Christ our Passover" in 1 Corinthians 5:7. The Passover is connected to the Mosaic covenant, which is to be replaced by the New covenant. Jesus' role in this is critical.

If I may comment here about the importance of the Pauline designation with reference to the Gospel accounts (particularly in Luke 22:19, where the words "do this in remembrance of me" are present), the fact that Paul has used the term "Christ our

72 This does not contradict what was said about Luke 19:12ff. Jesus should have been accepted for who He was. But the reality is that Jesus must officially "receive" the kingdom from God as the God-man and then justly bring it to saved humanity after vanquishing His enemies.

73 See Robert H. Stein, "Last Supper," in *Dictionary of Jesus and the Gospels*, eds. Joel B. Green, Scot McKnight, and I. Howard Marshall (Downers Grove, IL: InterVarsity, 1992), 446.

Passover" points to the replacement of the traditional Passover lamb of the Mosaic covenant with the "Lamb of God" of the New covenant.[74] If this surmise is accurate then we have a strong indicator of the fact that Christ's once for all sacrifice not only superseded the OT Passover ritual, but that in doing so a continuity of the Passover *in* Jesus was created.[75] Since the old Mosaic covenant does not have a provision for a change in the Passover sacrifice, we are left to conclude that the only way that Jesus, the Lamb of God, can be linked to the Passover (by Paul[76]) in a more than incidental way is if *another* covenant has taken over the Passover,[77] amplifying its significance in the Person of the Messiah. As Bock puts it, "He has become the lamb who launches a new age."[78]

> Then He said to them, "With *fervent* desire I have desired to eat this Passover with you before I suffer; for I say to you, I will no longer eat of it until it is fulfilled in the kingdom of God" (Lk. 22:15-16).

Jesus' anticipation of this Passover is explained when He uses it to institute the "New covenant in my blood" in verse 20. This is prophetic, as the words "until it is fulfilled" clearly show. The gap between His partaking of the Passover and the appointed time when He again eats it (Lk. 22:15-18), forms another link between the Passover and the New covenant; re-situating it in the Kingdom of God, which once more is a future reality to be manifested upon His return.

> And He took bread, gave thanks and broke *it*, and gave *it* to them, saying, "This is My body which is given for you; do this in remembrance of Me" (Lk. 22:19).

As pointed out above, the words "do this in remembrance of Me" are unique to Luke's account, and they throw an interesting light upon the event. The Lord is emphasizing Himself, which, when He speaks about His blood in the next verse, joins the New covenant to His Person! He was doubtless told about this wish of the Lord by one who was present (Paul also includes the words in 1 Corinthians 11:24-25). The command to remember relates to both parts of the institution, as Paul shows. The remembrance is not a mawkish sentiment driven by a realization of approaching doom, understandable though that would have been. None of the evangelists say that Jesus

---

74 It is worth noting that the Lord's Supper bears a double reference to both the sacrificial offering of "the Lamb of God" for sin and as the covenant sacrifice for the New covenant. See James D. G. Dunn, *Jesus Remembered*, 816. Also, Peter Stuhlmacher, *Biblical Theology of the New Testament,* 152-161.

75 Joel B. Green, *The Gospel of Luke*, NICNT (Grand Rapids: Eerdmans, 1997), 763, who makes a link between Christ's atonement and the New covenant.

76 In 1 Corinthians 10:16 the apostle asks, "The cup of blessing which we bless, is it not the communion of the blood of Christ?" Stein says the term "cup of blessing" is taken from the third cup of the Passover (Stein, "Last Supper," 447), but there is no biblical warrant for the assertion.

77 "It signifies, not a temporal repetition but a new, eschatological beginning" (I. Howard Marshall, *Commentary on Luke*, 806).

78 Darrell L. Bock, *Luke 9:51–24:53*, 1727.

was sad or distressed as He reclined in the Upper Room. That trial was to come in Gethsemane (Lk. 22:39-44). The reason for remembering Jesus is plainly centered around His death for us, but we should also consider His humble earthly ministry among sinners. The chance to live human life as God the Creator intended is predicated on what Jesus achieved.

> Likewise He also *took* the cup after supper, saying, "This cup *is* the new covenant in My blood, which is shed for you" (Lk. 22:20).

Matthew and Mark have "this is My blood of the new covenant" (Matt. 26:28/Mk. 14:24). I see no reason at all why Jesus could not have said both Luke's version and Matthew and Mark's version.[79] What is very significant is that this is the first recorded instance of the term "New covenant" since its sole mention in Jeremiah 31:31. Although it is given sparse utterance, the notion of the coming New covenant reverberates through the OT and is the source of hope for Israel (and the Gentiles). Jeremiah was simply giving a name to a concept that occurs throughout the Hebrew Bible (e.g., Deut. 30:1-6; Isa. 32:9-20; 42:1-7; 49:1-13; 52:10–53:12; 55:3; 59:15b-21; 61:8; Jer. 32:36-44; Ezek. 16:53-63; 36:22-38; 37:21-28; Hos. 2:18-20; Joel 2:28–3:8; Mic. 7:18-20; Zech. 9:10; 12:6-14). Now the Lord reintroduces this saving covenant at this decisive moment. The solemnity surely deepened as He spoke the phrase and brought it into the closest relation to Himself and His impending death.

The words "New covenant" would stir powerful thoughts in the disciples' minds of Israel's restoration and glory. The prophetic expectation would have been heightened. It is little wonder that forty days later they asked the resurrected Jesus, "Lord will You at this time restore the kingdom to Israel?" (Acts 1:6).

Such a question would have been fostered also by these words: "But you are those who have continued with Me in My trials. And I bestow upon you a kingdom, just as My Father bestowed *one* upon Me, that you may eat and drink at My table in My kingdom, and sit on thrones judging the twelve tribes of Israel" (Lk. 22:28-30). Was this proffered kingdom something new and unexpected? Nothing indicates that it was. What may well have been surprising was the promise of the disciples' position *in* the Kingdom. There were twelve tribes in Israel and twelve main disciples (although Judas Iscariot would be replaced). But is it tenable to believe that the disciples hailed from all of those tribes? Actually, the question is moot, because the special duty of the twelve will be that of judging the tribes, not leading them. Jesus will be upon David's throne as Gabriel had said (Lk. 1:32). It would be naturally assumed the twelve tribes would mean the twelve tribes of Israel.[80] The name "Israel" would mean nothing else to the disciples, but those Jews directly descended from Abraham, Isaac, and Jacob. Whatever is or is not to become of the meaning of that term later in the NT is not my concern right now. My concern is to read what is in Luke, not to impose presumed Pauline reconstructions into the time before the cross. There is no room in the

79 In Matthew's version, Jesus makes a direct reference to the forgiveness of sins (Matt. 26:27-28).

80 I shall discuss the complexion of the twelve tribes further on.

context for swapping out the expected messianic New covenant Kingdom for a multinational spiritual one.[81] Luke 22 will not suffer it.

The Kingdom of God and the New Covenant

Before moving on, I must insist a little more that we carefully consider the relationship of the Kingdom of God and the New covenant. The Kingdom of God is the New covenant Kingdom. The New covenant *Kingdom* is the covenanted Kingdom spoken of so often by the OT Prophets. It arrives, to use the metaphor in Daniel 2, once the "stone cut out without hands" strikes down the kingdoms of man and the messianic Kingdom of righteousness replaces it.

But how can this be true when the Lord instituted the New covenant in Luke 22 in anticipation of its coming into effect after His passion? This important question may be answered briefly by considering the following two points:

> 1. The fusion of the first and second comings of Christ in the OT are not always apparent. But here at the Lord's Supper, and in consideration of Luke 19:11 etc., we can clearly see a two-phase work. The first phase is centered on the cross and resurrection of Christ and the New covenant benefits that were unleashed from them, presently enjoyed by the Church (1 Cor. 11:25-26). Thus, the salvific benefits of being in the New covenant (and hence not under the Law) are present in "this present evil age" (Gal. 1:4), while the storied Kingdom of God still waits in the wings for the return of the King.
>
> 2. Any attempt to introduce the Kingdom of God right after the cross and resurrection, however noble, constitutes a misunderstanding of the term as it is used in the Gospels, and a direct contradiction of our Lord's declaration immediately prior to Calvary and Mt. Olivet (Lk. 19:11ff). That the book of Acts in particular employs the term will have to be explained, but it is my contention that although one may validly speak of aspects of the Kingdom of God in the preaching ministry of the Apostles, the focus is not on the "already" but rather on the "not yet."[82]

---

81 Any theological interpretation which converts this expectation into an ecclesial one has gone the wrong way. E.g., "The Institution Narrative...is a key transitional text for linking the royal Davidic identity and mission of Christ with the early apostolic church as the restored Davidic kingdom" (Scott W. Hahn, "Kingdom and Church in Luke-Acts," in *Reading Luke: Interpretation, Reflection, Formation*, Scripture and Hermeneutics, ed. Craig G. Bartholomew, Vol. 6 [Grand Rapids: Zondervan, 2005], 306, cf. 318, 320). The expectation of a restored and beatified New covenant Kingdom where all God's covenants are fulfilled cannot be diverted or altered even by God. In fact, especially by God, since He has placed Himself under oath to fulfill those covenants.

82 I realize, of course, that this position must be argued for, not merely asserted.

Christ the Son of Man and the Son of God

After His arrest, Jesus stood before the chief priests and scribes and was asked two pointed questions. The first was issued in this form: "If You are the Christ, tell us" (Lk. 22:67). Jesus' reply to this was as straightforward as a scholar of the Tanakh could wish for: "Hereafter the Son of Man will sit on the right hand of the power of God" (Lk. 22:69). This answer confirms the connection between the two titles from the OT. "Son of Man"[83] was Jesus' favorite term for Himself. Here He is calling attention to His exalted status at the hand of judgment, even though He is here *being* judged for His life. The Christ is so high that He sits at the right hand of God in heaven as well as upon the vacant throne of David.

The second question and reply is even more startling: "Then they all said, 'Are You then the Son of God?' So He said to them, 'You say that I am'" (Lk. 22:70).[84] The forthrightness of Jesus' response must have shocked the assembled judges. From their blinkered perspective, the condemnation of the prisoner was fully justified, even though it was they who insinuated Jesus' meaning (and Jesus does not contradict them). From a biblical perspective the implication in Jesus' answer is hugely impressive. It combines the three greatest identifications of the OT coming King in one and thrusts them into the forefront before an audience of OT scholars, removing any doubt from the reader's mind about the identity of the Speaker. In Daniel the "Son of Man" figure "was given dominion and glory and a kingdom, that all peoples, nations, and languages should serve Him" (Dan. 7:14). The Kingdom of the Son of Man will be everlasting. In Daniel 9:26 the Christ is "cut off" on behalf of others, and in Psalm 110:1 the Pharisees and scribes had agreed to the identification of Christ with the Son of David and heard Jesus relate Him to the Son of God (Matt. 22:42; Lk. 20:39-44, 46).[85] Several other passages in the Hebrew Bible make the connection between the Messiah and deity (e.g., Psa. 2:2-12; Mic. 5:2). As we shall see, Matthew's record of the same event explicitly mentions the coming of Christ and the setting up of the Kingdom (Matt. 26:64).

When the chief priests and scribes were done with Him, they sent Jesus to Pilate with the accusation: "We found this *fellow* perverting the nation, and forbidding to pay taxes to Caesar, saying that He Himself is Christ, a King" (Lk. 23:2). No doubt they were hoping that Jesus making Himself a king would alert the temperamental governor enough to execute Him speedily, but they were wrong. However, we should remember the incriminating evidence Luke has already left us.[86]

83 The literature on the "Son of Man" is vast, with endless (and fruitless) debate. Most of it is derailed by the disbelief expressed about the historicity of the sayings in the Gospels, and this is compounded by disbelief in the historicity of the book of Daniel. Guthrie presents five approaches to the question, none of which are acceptable for an inerrantist. He believes the sayings to be authentic. See his survey in Donald Guthrie, *New Testament Theology* (Downers Grove, IL: InterVarsity, 1981), 270-291.

84 The word "rightly" is not in the Greek text and ought to be omitted.

85 The author of Hebrews will cite Psa. 45:6-7 to establish Jesus as the Son of God (Heb. 1:8-9). See George H. Guthrie, "Hebrews," in *Commentary on the New Testament Use of the Old Testament*, eds. G. K. Beale and D. A. Carson (Grand Rapids: Baker, 2007), 938-939.

86 See the remarks on the Parable of the Vineyard in Lk. 20:9-19 above.

Pilate asks Jesus if He is a king, and he receives a response that hardly absolves Jesus of the charge (how could it? Jesus was indeed a king). But it seems to satisfy Pilate, and he sends Him to Herod Antipas (Lk. 23:1-12). John will record that when He is returned and interrogated by Pilate, Jesus is declared innocent by the Roman Governor (Jn. 18:38; 19:4, 6), saying three times, "I find no fault in Him." This means that Jesus was not crucified as a malefactor or criminal but for the sake of expedience.[87]

Jesus is Crucified between Two Thieves

I shall not linger here to comment on Calvary. But Luke does have a fascinating exchange between Jesus and the two men who were crucified with Him (Lk. 23:39-43). The first one mocks Jesus for not exercising His supposed messianic prerogatives to deliver them.[88] Along with the majority of onlookers, this man does not understand the magnitude of what is happening. After rebuking his fellow, the other thief plaintively addresses Jesus: "Jesus, remember me when you come into your kingdom" (Lk. 23:42).[89]

I think a major reason for Luke's inclusion of this interchange is because it expresses hope in the future of the promised covenanted Kingdom of God. That Kingdom was, as the believing thief testified, Jesus' Kingdom! It goes beyond credulity to imagine this man believing that Christ's Kingdom was in heaven and not on earth.[90] It is hard indeed to be convinced that the dying thief was the sole individual to regard Jesus' Kingdom as synonymous with the right hand of God in glory. No, his faith in both the Kingdom and in Jesus as the Heir of it would have been this-worldly in its orientation. Minimally, he would be thinking in covenantal terms of the Abrahamic and Davidic promises to Israel, which were understood as having their fulfillment in our world, not in heaven. I am unimpressed by attempts to turn the thief on the cross into the first spiritualizer of Scripture.

Joseph of Arimathea "was also waiting for the kingdom of God" (Lk. 23:51; cf. 2:25). The word translated "waiting" is *prosdekomai*, which, avers Marshall, "joins him with the pious Israelites described in the birth narratives."[91] Joseph, as a member of the Sanhedrin, would not be inclined to expect a heavenly kingdom.[92]

---

87 It is incorrect to claim that Jesus "was found guilty of a crime deserving capital punishment" (Paul F. M. Zahl, *Grace in Practice: A Theology of Everyday Life* [Grand Rapids: Eerdmans, 2007], 80). Christ's "trial" before Annas and Caiaphas was a mockery and could not be considered lawful (cf. Acts 13:28).

88 I say "supposed" because the Messiah could *not* save Himself without damning all others.

89 There is some disagreement about whether the original text has *eis* ("into") or *ev* ("in") your kingdom. Some scholars make something of the difference (e.g., Bock, *Luke 9:51–24:53*, 1869), but if "into your kingdom" refers to Jesus receiving the Kingdom, then not only is there little to choose between the prepositions, but it infers that Luke has included it to pair it with the future sense of *Basileia* throughout the passion narrative.

90 See e.g., George Eldon Ladd, *The Presence of the Future*, 136.

91 I. Howard Marshall, *Commentary on Luke*, 880.

92 While it is true that at this time (A.D. 30) the Sanhedrin was more prominently represented by Sadducees than Pharisees, this would not result in such spiritualization. "Sadducean theology was about the 'here and now' with a this-worldly eschatology of the first five books of the Bible" (Paul Barnett, *Jesus and the Rise of Early Christianity*, 140).

The Risen Jesus Opens the Scriptures: The Hermeneutical Value of Luke 24

After the crucifixion of Jesus (Lk. 23:44-56) comes a remarkable chapter that features five distinct episodes (depending on how one counts them): the angel messenger and the women (Lk. 24:1-11); Peter running to the empty tomb (Lk. 24:12); The Road to Emmaus story (Lk. 24:13-35); the appearance of Jesus to the disciples (Lk. 24:36-49); and the ascension (Lk. 24:50-53). My interest here is in the interpretive importance of these encounters.

In the first incident, the "man" (i.e., angel, v. 23) said to them, "He is not here, but is risen! Remember how He spoke to you when He was still in Galilee, saying, 'The Son of Man must be delivered into the hands of sinful men, and be crucified, and the third day rise again'" (Lk. 24:6-7, my emphasis). We are reminded of the statement so often repeated in this study, that God means what He says. Thus, they remembered what Jesus had said (Lk. 24:8; cf. Lk. 9:22). Among other things, what this tells us is that we need to keep in mind exactly what the Lord has told us, especially when circumstances take a turn for the worse.

I have divided Peter's response to the women's report because his action confirms the women's story about the empty tomb (Lk. 24:12; cf. Jn. 20:3-8). In the next section, two disciples are journeying from Jerusalem to Emmaus, conversing about the horrible tragedy of the trial and crucifixion of Jesus when Jesus (His identity somehow hidden from them) joins them and asks them what they are talking about (Lk. 24:18). The response Jesus gets is almost one of disbelief that He could not know about what had happened (Lk. 24:18-20). Then the speaker, Cleopas, says this: "But we were hoping that it was He who was going to redeem Israel. Indeed, besides all this, today is the third day since these things happened" (Lk. 24:21).

This statement reveals that the disciples were thinking along OT lines. They were waiting for the long-promised redemption of Israel (through the New covenant and the "re-activated" Abrahamic and Davidic covenants), showing their expectation of the prophesied Kingdom (e.g., Mic. 4:1-4; 7:14-20; Isa. 11:1-10; 26:2-4; Ezek. 36-37). Cleopas even mentions "the third day," but the penny does not drop. Had they not heard about what the women reported about the angel's words (Lk. 24:9-10; 22-24)?

Jesus' reaction to this testimony was unexpected. "Then He said to them, 'O foolish ones, and slow of heart to believe in all that the prophets have spoken! Ought not the Christ to have suffered these things and to enter into His glory?' And beginning at Moses and all the Prophets, He expounded to them in all the Scriptures the things concerning Himself" (Lk. 24:25-27).

He called them "fools" and accused them of being slow to believe the very prophets who had raised their expectations (Lk. 24:25). These men were believers in Jesus and were walking away disconsolately because they thought their hopes had been dashed. But in reality, they had not believed "all that the prophets [had] spoken." They had not connected the Suffering Servant with the Ruling Messiah, although both were in the Prophets. They needed a Bible study on the OT's witness to Christ's death (Lk. 24:26)! If the Lord had started in with a lot of typological and spiritual interpretation, these men might have understandably had a reason to feel aggrieved for being called fools. After all, it is hardly fair to call someone a fool for not spiritualizing your words and for not trusting in those spiritualized meanings. We must strenuously resist the impulse to turn Jesus' teaching on the Kingdom into something ethereal. No, Jesus did not engage in typological hermeneutics in Luke 24!

In verse 25 the Lord speaks of "the prophets" whereas in verse 27 Luke speaks of Jesus going through "the law and the prophets." No doubt these are synonymous, both referring to the Hebrew Scriptures. The "suffering" of Christ is to be found in Psalm 22 and Isaiah 53, with the Paschal lamb a prefigurement of it (Exod. 12:3-11; Num. 19:11-12). One might also want to throw in Psalm 41:9; Isaiah 50:6; 52:14-15; Daniel 9:26; Zechariah 11:12; and 13:6.

Luke stresses that Jesus "expounded to them in all the Scriptures the things concerning Himself" (Lk. 24:27), which would include all or most of the messianic prophecy of the OT from Genesis 3:15 onward. Even if He kept only to the prophecies fulfilled at His first coming, the list would be impressive. Besides all of the details of Psalm 22 and Isaiah 53, there are Genesis 3:15; 22:13-14, 18; 49:10; Deuteronomy 18:15; 1 Chronicles 17:11-14; Psalm 16:10; 34:20; 68:18; 69:21; Micah 5:2; Isaiah 7:14; 9:6; Daniel 9:25-26; Zechariah 9:9; 12:10b.[93]

A little further on in the narrative, we see Jesus with His disciples (Lk. 24:36-49). Again, Jesus explains the Scriptures' testimony about Himself, His decease, and His resurrection (Lk. 24:46). He added that "repentance and remission of sins should be preached in His name to all nations, beginning at Jerusalem" (Lk. 24:47). This is an important transitional verse for Luke as he proceeds to write the book known as the Acts of the Apostles, but I do not take it to be part of what was explained to the disciples from the Tanakh. After expounding the Scriptures, Jesus then told the disciples about their proclamation of Him to the world (Lk. 24:46-49). This requires some comment: "Then He said to them, "Thus it is written, and thus it was necessary for the Christ to suffer and to rise from the dead the third day, and that repentance and remission of sins should be preached in His name to all nations, beginning at Jerusalem" (Lk. 24:46-47).

This text informs us of the necessity of Christ's rejection and death so that He could rise from the dead and that "repentance and remission of sins" could be proclaimed throughout the world (see Acts 1:8). We are not to think that on this account the preaching of John the Baptist (Matt. 3:1-3), Jesus (Matt. 4:17), and the disciples (Matt. 10:5-7) was somehow disingenuous. The offer of the "at-hand" Kingdom was sincere and would certainly have come about if (and what a big "IF") Israel had received Christ as they ought to have done. We are up against the tension between the foreknowledge of a faithful God and the responsibility of rebellious man. In the same way the Gospel offer goes out to unsaved people today as a genuine offer that can and often is refused, so the offer of Jesus as Messiah and Lord of the Kingdom of God was

93 I have only provided twenty-five references (although Psa. 22 & Isa. 53 contain many prophetic details), yet this list would have taken some time to explain in full.

genuinely preached in Israel before Christ's rejection. The counterfactual question, "What would have happened...?" is as moot as Matthew 11:21 or 1 Samuel 23:10-13. It is a question that makes sense only if men were not sinners. The necessity of something may require the non-realization or insubstantiation of what might have been, but it does not obviate what might have been if matters had turned out differently.[94]

The preaching to the nations of repentance and faith (not just faith!) was part of the Creation Project from the beginning and was predicated on the death and resurrection of the Lamb of God (Jn. 1:29; cf. Rev. 13:18), which was in part a fulfillment of the third aspect of the Abrahamic covenant (Gen. 22:18; Gal. 3:8, 29). The Church, therefore, is not an afterthought or Plan B in God's program for history.

Finally, Luke gives a report of the ascension:

> And He led them out as far as Bethany, and He lifted up His hands and blessed them. Now it came to pass, while He blessed them, that He was parted from them and carried up into heaven. And they worshiped Him, and returned to Jerusalem with great joy, and were continually in the temple praising and blessing God. Amen (Lk. 24:50-53).

The risen Christ blesses the disciples He leaves behind. They are left in a savage and uncompromising world, and most of them will be martyred in it. Jesus goes to heaven until such a time as God the Father sends Him to claim the world and install the Kingdom of God, at least as Luke's Gospel has it, as the combined threads of eschatology and teleology in the Creation Project culminate in Him.

94 I feel I must apologize for the philosophizing tone of that sentence, but I wanted it to stand because it makes a brief point I wanted to insert. To illustrate it, think of Peter having an accident and not making it to the fire (Lk. 22:54-62), and therefore never getting into the pickle he got into which led to him denying Christ.

9

COVENANT AND KINGDOM IN MATTHEW

And the high priest answered and said to Him, "I put You under oath by the living God: Tell us if You are the Christ, the Son of God!" – Matthew 26:63

The Gospel of Matthew is usually thought to be heavily concerned with the Kingdom. This is true, but I think I have proved that the Gospel of Luke is just as heavily given over to the theme of the Kingdom. Nevertheless, of the five major divisions of this Gospel (Matt. 5–7; 10; 13; 18; and 23–25), all of them stress the Kingdom. What is more, as I shall briefly show, Matthew lays stress upon the name "Son of David."

Things that Require Attention

As one encounters this Gospel there are three things which require care and attention: Matthew's Parables, The Kingdom of Heaven and the Kingdom of God, and The Gospel of the Kingdom.

Matthew's Parables

The way Matthew's Gospel speaks of the Kingdom, especially in the Parables, is of particular interest. We can see that a strong vein of Jesus' teaching concerns matters of what we might call movement toward the consummation of the Kingdom. In particular, the introductory phrase "the kingdom of heaven is like," which is found only in the first Gospel, is usually followed not by a description of kingdom elements like peace, prosperity, and glory, or even vengeance, but by subtle descriptions of contamination (Matt. 13:24-25), and the growth together of good and evil (Matt. 13:31-33). Therefore, it addresses the need for sorting the wicked from the just when Christ returns (Matt. 13:47-50). Then again, the kingdom of heaven is illustrated in terms of a king who claims his debts and forgives a debtor, who then fails to show the same mercy to his debtor (Matt. 18:23-35). It is also pictured like a landowner who decides to be generous to certain laborers who, through no fault of their own, have worked less than others (Matt. 20:1-16), or in the story of another king who invites social outcasts to his son's wedding feast after being rejected by those who first received invites (Matt. 22:2-14).

This is all very mysterious.[1] In these passages, the properties of the Kingdom *prior* to its consummation are in view. The road to the eschatological Kingdom is long and encumbered.

The Kingdom of Heaven and the Kingdom of God

Matthew 3 begins with John the Baptist proclaiming, "Repent, for the kingdom of heaven is at hand!" (Matt. 3:1-2). It has him calling Pharisees and Sadducees "a brood of vipers" (Matt. 3:7), which hardly matched the exalted spiritual status they gave themselves. Later in this Gospel, we see Jesus calling Pharisees (and scribes) "hypocrites" and "fools and blind" (Matt. 23:13-19). In Matthew the religious leaders get called all kinds of names. Modern scholarship has tried to correct these supposed Matthean malapropisms, and we do know of Pharisees who became followers of Jesus (Acts 15:5). All in all, though, the portrait the Holy Spirit has left us in the first Gospel does them no credit at all.

After the temptation of Jesus, which I shall look at from Matthew's perspective soon, we find Jesus immediately preaching, "Repent, for the kingdom of heaven is at hand" (Matt. 4:17). This is of interest because it means there is a direct continuity between John's preaching and Jesus' preaching.[2] There was, therefore, a large swell of expectation of the "kingdom of heaven" in the early days of Christ's ministry wrought by the attention-grabbing efforts of the two men.[3]

Since Matthew is the only writer to use the designation "kingdom of heaven," and that often in the same situations as the other evangelists have "kingdom of God," it is evident that the two expressions are very similar, if not one and the same.[4]

But Matthew does employ "kingdom of God" in Matthew 6:33; 12:28; 19:24; 21:31, 43. So what is happening here? Why does Matthew use what appears to be a circumlocution for "God" most of the time but not all the time? Here are some thoughts.

In Mathew 5:33 we read, "Seek first the kingdom of God and His righteousness and all these things will be added to you." Quite clearly, if Matthew had inserted

1 Jesus Himself refers to "the mysteries of the kingdom of heaven" in Matt. 13:11.

2 This kind of similarity is what has encouraged some of the more liberal leaning scholars to hazard that Jesus was a disciple of John the Baptist. But John the Baptist's ministry makes little sense *without* Jesus.

3 The Gospel writers nowhere inform us that "the kingdom" in Jesus' early preaching means anything other than what the OT prophesied. See Alva J. McClain, *The Greatness of the Kingdom*, 276ff.

4 Some traditional dispensationalists, like Lewis Sperry Chafer and John Walvoord, adamantly held that there was a difference in meaning between the two terms. See the explanation in Stanley D. Toussaint, *Behold the King: A Study of Matthew* (Grand Rapids: Kregel, 1980), 65-68.

"heaven" for "God" in this place, he would have done away with the subject of the pronoun "His," so we can readily understand why "of God" would be preferable. The next instance is somewhat similar:

> But Jesus knew their thoughts and said to them: "Every kingdom divided against itself is brought to desolation, and every city or house divided against itself will not stand.
>
> If Satan casts out Satan, he is divided against himself. How then will his kingdom stand? And if I cast out demons by Beelzebub, by whom do your sons cast *them* out? Therefore, they shall be your judges. But if I cast out demons by the Spirit of God, surely the kingdom of God has come upon you." (Matt. 12:25-28).

Jesus is speaking about His incursions into the kingdom of Satan (Beelzebub). He explains that He expels demons "by the Spirit of God" (Matt. 12:28). It would sound a bit lame if, instead of speaking plainly about "the kingdom of God," Matthew had Jesus say, "kingdom of heaven." Heaven is not the antonym of Satan—God is!

In the next instance, in Matthew 19, the context involves the Rich Young Ruler, who is asked "Why do you call me good? No one *is* good but One, *that is*, God" (Matt. 19:17). The conversation is about moral qualifications, and *God,* not heaven, is the standard. It would be rather peculiar if, after mentioning God as the standard of goodness to inherit eternal life, Matthew then omitted His name when responding to His shocked disciples. Let us read His reply: "Then Jesus said to His disciples, 'Assuredly, I say to you that it is hard for a rich man to enter the kingdom of heaven. And again I say to you, it is easier for a camel to go through the eye of a needle than for a rich man to enter the kingdom of God'" (Matt. 19:23-24).

In Matthew 19:23 Jesus may be speaking either about going to heaven (i.e., inheriting "eternal life") or about the coming Kingdom itself. In verse 24 He is referring to *whose* Kingdom it is. Ergo, whose righteousness is the benchmark for entrance. In which case, the subject has to be "God."

Finally, in Matthew 21 we have two mentions of "kingdom of God": "'Which of the two did the will of *his* father?' They said to Him, 'The first.' Jesus said to them, 'Assuredly, I say to you that tax collectors and harlots enter the kingdom of God before you'" (Matt. 21:31). Notice that the Lord has introduced the character of a father. The first son in the story, who was recalcitrant at the beginning, repented and did his father's will. He was not the son who looked and sounded good but who was found to be disobedient. The first son was like the "tax collectors and harlots" who turned from their sin after considering the will of God through Jesus' preaching. Hence, the *Person* of God is the subject of the sentence.

The last time "kingdom of God" is used by Matthew is in 21:42-43:

> Jesus said to them, "Have you never read in the Scriptures: 'The stone which the builders rejected has become the chief cornerstone. This was the LORD's

> doing, and it is marvelous in our eyes'? Therefore I say to you, the kingdom of God will be taken from you and given to a nation bearing the fruits of it."

Here Psalm 118 is quoted and Yahweh ("the LORD") is the main Actor. It is God who has disposed history in such a way that "the builders" refused the true cornerstone. Very pointedly, Jesus stated that those kingdom-builders who professed to be in God's employ were building their own little kingdom. As God would take the rejection of His Son personally, the phrase "kingdom of heaven" would be too impersonal to suit the occasion here.

Those are my brief explanations as to why Matthew uses "kingdom of God" five times rather than his more usual designation, "the kingdom of heaven." Readers are free to disagree with these reasons, but there must *be* reasons. To recap then, "the kingdom of heaven" in Matthew is a circumlocution, where possible, of the name of God for His abode.

The Gospel of the Kingdom

The first Gospel records the temptation of Jesus at the start of Matthew 4. The main difference between Matthew's narrative and Luke's is in the order of the presentations. Most commentators hold that, whereas Luke was concerned about calling attention to Jerusalem in his third temptation, Matthew has preserved the original list, the worship of the Tempter being the most audacious and desperate attempt to deflect Jesus from His appointed mission.[5]

After recovering strength, Jesus moved from Nazareth to the seaside town of Capernaum (Matt. 4:13-16). The prophecy cited in connection with the move is from Isaiah 9:1-2. The use of the verses after Jesus' temptation indicates that the evangelist sees Jesus' mission beginning from Capernaum, even though Nazareth also lay within the old territories of Zebulun and Naphtali. As we have already seen, Matthew tells us that Jesus preached, "Repent, for the kingdom of heaven is at hand" (Matt. 4:17).[6] But a few verses later, when the calling of Andrew, Peter, James, and John is done, we read this: "And Jesus went about all Galilee, teaching in their synagogues, preaching the gospel of the kingdom, and healing all kinds of sickness and all kinds of disease among the people" (Matt. 4:23).

In the absence of any other clues, the only logical conclusion is that the message of the imminent Kingdom that John and Jesus have been proclaiming was the same

5 For example, see Donald A. Hagner, *Matthew 1–13*, 62.

6 The diversity of healings that are described in these verses may be seen as a pre-Kingdom overruling of the curse and sin coming through the one who will by His presence restrain the ravages of the Fall. Although I cannot find much agreement with his overall strategy, the following quote is certainly worth reproducing: "On the assumption that Jesus saw himself as working within the parameters of Isaiah's poetic logic, it follows that his acts of healing—whether involving the restoration of sight, hearing, the use of one's limb, or what have you—signaled the restoration of creation" (Nicholas Perrin, *The Kingdom of God: A Biblical Theology* [Grand Rapids: Zondervan, 2019], 157). I think this is a suggestive comment, although I prefer to think of these miracles and wonders as adumbrations of the world to come. They are eschatological pointers, not the introduction of the "already" aspect of the Kingdom in history.

"gospel of the kingdom" referred to in this verse. The phrase "gospel of the kingdom" is found elsewhere in Matthew in 9:35 and 24:14, as well as once in Mark 1:14. Of what did it consist? Well, we have said it was the message of John the Baptist before Jesus' baptism and anointing, as well as Jesus' message thereafter. We must come to terms with it. Try as one might, it is very hard to imagine John the Baptist declaring the death and resurrection of Christ before revealing Jesus as the Christ. We have seen that Luke 18:31-34 says that the disciples could not comprehend Jesus' prediction of His forthcoming demise and that the knowledge was "hidden from them." That assuredly entails that they did not go out and preach the Pauline Gospel as they were sent out in Luke 10:1ff. In Matthew this declaration of upcoming death does not come until Matthew 16:21. Peter clearly does not grasp its necessity (Matt. 16:22-23). The disciples are presented as having some superficial comprehension of Jesus' demise in Matthew 17:22-23.

I fully realize that even stating the obvious truth about this matter is not likely to be well received in some quarters. But my job is not to make up scenarios where John the Baptist, Jesus, and the disciples are all preaching the substance of 1 Corinthians 15:1-4 prior to Jesus' death and resurrection, especially in light of *clear evidence to the contrary* (just look at the ignorance of the disciples). Some things are what they are, however discomfited they make us feel. At such an early stage in His earthly career, Jesus simply was not telling anyone about His upcoming death and resurrection. And if neither He nor His disciples were proclaiming His death and resurrection, then as sure as "eggs is eggs" they were not proclaiming the need for faith in it either! The closest one comes to the notion is John 2:19-22, where Jesus told the Jews that if they destroyed "this temple," He would raise it up in three days. But John 2:22 is patently clear: "Therefore, *when He had risen from the dead*, His disciples remembered that He had said this to them; and they believed the Scripture and the word which Jesus had said" (Jn. 2:22, my emphasis).

The disciples did not put two and two together until after Christ was raised. Therefore, they were in no position to preach "Paul's Gospel" until they could look back at it all with the benefit of hindsight.

What is one to do with these facts? The standard procedure is to ignore the evidence and equate "the gospel of the kingdom" (and the preaching of "the kingdom of heaven/God is at hand") as if it did include belief in the crucified and risen Lord.[7] However, and to put it bluntly, it didn't![8] And if "the gospel of the kingdom" did include the details of Christ's passion and rising again, then not only was its meaning not understood by His disciples, but the general populace would have been left even more in the dark. It would have been "good news" that no one knew was good or why. There is no way to assert that Jesus publicly preached faith in His death and

7 E.g., Fred H. Klooster, "The Biblical Method of Salvation: Continuity," in *Continuity and Discontinuity: Perspectives on the Relationship Between the Old and New Testaments*, ed. John S. Feinberg (Wheaton, IL: Crossway, 1988), 159.

8 In my estimation, this one "problem" throws a spanner in the works of much biblical theology that has been and is being done.

resurrection prior to those events transpiring.[9] Any honest approach to the Gospels will be forced to admit that fact. The "gospel of the kingdom" is not the same "good news" as one finds in Paul.

One further question of interest is whether there is any significance to the fact that Matthew seems to indicate some sort of change in the preaching of Jesus after Matthew 12, the chapter following (Matt. 13) being His introduction of His parables. Personally, I believe that the argument for a change in Jesus' teaching activity is intriguing. On the other hand, I do not think it is conclusive. If one reads the two chapters (Matt. 12 and 13) there is no break in the action, and Matthew inserts no obvious theological marker to show that some "break" with the past ministry has taken place. We must remember that Matthew has structured his Gospel thematically and not necessarily chronologically. More to the point, when the phrase is seen again later in the book, no indication of a break from the past is inserted. In Matthew 24:14 Jesus does not say "the gospel of the kingdom I preached earlier" but rather refers to "*this* [*touto*] gospel of the kingdom" (my emphasis). The natural reply should be that for Him to say "*this* gospel..." would mean that Jesus was preaching the same "gospel of the kingdom" up until He delivered His Olivet Discourse.

Finally, if Jesus and the disciples were not preaching the gospel of the kingdom, and they were not preaching "Paul's Gospel," what were they preaching? I will take up this subject more later on.

The Sermon on the Mount

The Sermon on the Mount is one of the greatest—perhaps the greatest—speeches ever recorded. Three whole chapters of Matthew's Gospel are given over to it.[10] Because it was given in the early part of Jesus' ministry, the question of its application to the post-ascension Church has been debated. Dispensational writers have, not surprisingly, offered several opinions on the subject. I think that most of it does apply today.[11] Like the Ten Commandments, the Sermon on the Mount contains much universal truth; truth that always matters and always guides.

The sermon was actually a piece of instruction for the twelve (Matt. 5:1-2). Christ begins with eight "beatitudes" (Matt. 5:3-10) with a sort of postscript (Matt. 5:11-12). All of them start with the word "Blessed (are)" (*makarioi*) and ends with a reward

9 Carson says "the 'good news' concerns God and the inbreaking of his saving reign in the person of his Son the Messiah" (D. A. Carson, "Matthew," 121). With all due respect, Jesus was not preaching "the inbreaking of his saving reign." He was preaching the imminent approach of the Kingdom.

10 Critical scholarship has often tried to pull the "Sermon" apart using source and form criticism. It is framed by an *inclusio* (Matt. 5:1 and 7:28–8:1), which only looks fabricated if one really wants it to be. I therefore have no sympathy at all with those efforts and their disregard of what is placed right in front of their noses.

11 As usual, Vlach provides the best outlook: "In sum, the Sermon on the Mount of Matthew 5–7 reaffirms that the kingdom of heaven is future and earthly (5:5). We pray for its coming (6:10) and it will be established in connection with coming judgment (7:21-22). True believers possess a positional relationship to the King before the kingdom is established. They are to live by Jesus' kingdom ethic" (Michael J. Vlach, *He Will Reign Forever*, 304-305).

(e.g., "they shall..."). The first (Matt. 5:3) and the eighth (Matt. 5:10) both end with the promise "theirs is the kingdom of heaven," forming an *inclusio.* The overall concern is for those who, in their search for righteousness, encounter forms of resistance from the world. The rewards are plainly eschatological—the promises of relief and a return for their patience acting to promote perseverance. Again, the credibility of the Speaker is at issue. Does the Lord mean what He says? The whole sermon depends on an affirmative answer to that question. The various rewards: the Kingdom of heaven, comfort, inheriting the earth, filling, obtaining mercy, seeing God, becoming the sons of God—these are not separate from one another. Rather, they are to be the happy lot of the humble, the mourners, the meek, the persecuted, etc. The gifts of God outnumber the trials of faith.

In Matthew 5:17-20 Jesus talks about His relationship to the Law. He begins by claiming, "Do not think that I came to destroy the Law or the Prophets. I did not come to destroy but to fulfill" (Matt. 5:17).

Given what was said in the Introduction about Christ's relationship to the New covenant,[12] it might come as a surprise to hear Him say that He did not come to destroy the Law[13] and the "old [Mosaic] covenant" it represented.[14] When Jesus says He hasn't come to destroy the Law or the Prophets, He employs the verb *kataluein,* which is best understood as meaning "to annul,"[15] to do which would be to strike at the heart of Jewish faith. What the Lord is doing here is preparatory to the six antitheses that will follow (i.e., Matt. 5:21-48).[16] The formula "You have heard...But I say unto you," which characterizes the coming antitheses, requires some qualification.

With that said, however, that Jesus *can* respond with "But I say..." means that He assumes a level of authority as a teacher far above that claimed by the teachers of the day. And this could only be so if, indeed, He "fulfilled" the OT.[17] But how? As Michael Vlach astutely recognizes:

> Not all theologians mean the same thing when they refer to "fulfillment" in Jesus. When we speak of "fulfillment" of kingdom promises in Jesus we assert that Jesus literally brings to fulfillment *all* that was predicted in the OT. Some erroneously hold fulfillment in Jesus means OT promises are absorbed into Jesus in such a way that literal fulfillment of OT promises and covenants is no longer necessary.[18]

---

12 See the Introduction under "The New Covenant and Jesus Christ."

13 Many take the reference to the Law here to entail the whole Hebrew Bible. This is the view of Wayne G. Strickland, "The Inauguration of the Law of Christ with the Gospel of Christ: A Dispensational View," in *Five Views on Law and Gospel*, ed. Stanley N. Gundry (Grand Rapids: Zondervan, 1996), 258. I think this is correct. My thanks to Ian A. Hicks for this reference.

14 On this passage, see the booklet by Michael J. Vlach, *The New Covenant Lawgiver: Jesus and Law in Matthew 5:17-48* (Cary, NC: Theological Studies Press, 2022).

15 John Nolland, *The Gospel of Matthew*, 217.

16 Ibid. See also the comments by I. Howard Marshall, *New Testament Theology*, 99.

17 Jesus uses the phrase "the Law or [ἢ] the Prophets," which shows that He viewed them as having equal weight (which was often not the case in Judaism).

18 Michael J. Vlach. *He Will Reign Forever*, 44.

This is well put. Not for the first time (and certainly not the last), eschatology will dictate the exegesis. There is a tendency among those who see the Story of the Bible in "redemptive-historical" terms to use it to redirect the plain meaning of words in a path more in keeping with their "Church equals the new Israel" reading. But if we do not introduce the ecclesial concerns into the Gospels unless and until they are specifically mentioned, it is possible to follow the inspired author to where he wishes to lead us and not think of him (as evangelical critical scholarship is wont to do) as writing from the perspective of his Church and its needs (which must perforce be imagined).

In Matthew 5:17-20 we find Jesus in His early ministry challenging the accepted *interpretation* of the Hebrew Bible,[19] pointing it at Himself. Hence, the "Law or the Prophets," viewed as they should be viewed, agree with Jesus' life and ministry, while being fulfilled in Him as the Coming One who will bring in a Kingdom of righteousness that will transcend them and the old covenant they represent. This movement from old to new is only made possible in Jesus the Christ, who lived out the Law's demands and, as Isaiah predicted and as Peter will go on to say, "by whose stripes [we] were healed" (1 Pet. 2:24; cf. Isa. 53:5).

How then does Jesus fulfill the OT? It refers to His ministry being in accord with what was predicted in the OT. It does not have to do with Jesus' New covenant instigation that would occur immediately before His passion (Matt. 26:26-28), but to the prophetic nature of His person and work.[20]

EXCURSUS: The Forbidding of Oaths

Nestled within the six antitheses of Matthew 5:21-48 is a section on oath-taking. Since this book and its predecessor are about covenants and their oaths, it would be remiss of me not to comment on this interesting section in relation to the oaths of God. Here is the passage:

> Again you have heard that it was said to those of old, "You shall not swear falsely, but shall perform your oaths to the Lord." But I say to you, do not swear at all: neither by heaven, for it is God's throne; nor by the earth, for it is His footstool; nor by Jerusalem, for it is the city of the great King. Nor shall you swear by your head, because you cannot make one hair white or black. But let your "Yes" be "Yes," and your "No," "No." For whatever is more than these is from the evil one (Matt. 5:33-37).

The genesis of this present Biblical Theology depends directly upon the fact that God Himself has placed His character and reputation under oath, and yet here we see Jesus telling His disciples never to take oaths.[21] The reason they (and we) are not to take an oath is because oaths are required as a sign of truth-telling, and we are to be

19 Interpretation is what verse 19 is all about.

20 See, e.g., the discussion of this passage by Douglas J. Moo, "The Law of Moses or the Law of Christ," in *Continuity and Discontinuity*, 204-206.

21 The context is not judicial where a person swearing to tell the truth is and ought to be a requirement, but of taking personal oaths.

truth-tellers and known to be such. This imitates God Himself, whose "Yes" is always "Yes" and "No" is always "No" (Matt. 5:37). The book of James, which takes its cue from the Sermon on the Mount,[22] echoes these words in James 5:12 but adds to it a warning of future judgment. From this I ask a simple question: would a God who is "very compassionate and merciful" (Jam. 5:11) threaten judgment on those taking oaths (and by extension covenants) when God Himself does this very thing? So why does God make oaths? Why does the Almighty One, who is Truth and upon whom all truth is predicated, make covenants? The author of Hebrews puts it best: "For men indeed swear by the greater, and an oath for confirmation *is* for them an end of all dispute. Thus God, determining to show more abundantly to the heirs of promise the immutability of His counsel, confirmed *it* by an oath" (Heb. 6:16-17).

In the first volume of this work, I wrote the following:

> Oaths require forethought and careful composition. Failure to think-through the words used may lead to tragic consequences, as the story of Jephthah drives home (Judg. 11). Along with solemnity, premeditation persuasively argues for clarity. For a covenant that isn't clear is hardly competent to do its job, particularly as time slips by... Since covenants include solemn oath-taking, they are not slapped together indiscriminately. Perhaps the single most important thing a covenant must address is the problem of ambiguity.[23]

God wants His creatures to believe Him. But we all have a deep-seated tendency to derive meaning independently of what God has said. God's covenants are gracious amplifications of plain speech about matters of great importance concerning the destiny of humanity. The reason God entered into covenant was because of our inability to believe that He means what He says. And what do we do to prove Him right? We ignore, reduce, alter, redirect, or subvert His covenant oaths!

The Kingdom to Come in the Lord's Prayer

We are accustomed to treating the so-called "Lord's Prayer" within our own "Church" context. And no wonder, for the guidance and hope it supplies are a great boon to our spiritual lives. But if we situate this model prayer in its setting in the Sermon on the Mount, we have to allow that it signified something a little different for the disciples, especially Matthew 6:10: "Your kingdom come. Your will be done on earth as *it is* in heaven."

In circa A.D. 30 Jesus' references to God's "kingdom" would, when combined with His messianic claims and miracles, summon up only one idea in the minds of His audiences: the covenanted Davidic Kingdom predicted in, for example, Isaiah 11:1-10 or Jeremiah 23:5-6. Just recall Jesus being called "Son of David" in texts like Matthew 9:27; 12:23; 20:30; 21:9, 15; and 22:42, which is a reference to the Davidic

22 See Virgil V. Porter, Jr., "The Sermon on the Mount in the Book of James, Part 1," *BSAC* 162 (Jul 2005), 344-60.

23 Paul Martin Henebury, *The Words of the Covenant,* Vol. 1, 46-47.

heritage. No one could envision the Church at such an early date, and passages like Acts 1:6 persuasively combat any argument from silence.[24] No, the Father's Kingdom, which is to be prayed for, is the New covenant Davidic Kingdom of the OT Prophets. We also notice that this coming Kingdom is to be "on earth," *not* in heaven.[25] This too accords with the Prophets. The fact that Jesus instructs His disciples to pray for the Kingdom, and that they would be praying for the Kingdom of Messiah, surely tells us that Yahweh will stick to the words of the covenant He made with David, and also those covenants He made with Abraham and Phinehas! Covenants that can only be literally fulfilled in the coming messianic Kingdom.

There is a further consideration we need to make with reference to Christ's words, for their anticipatory nature suggests that the Kingdom for which we pray will be synonymous with its portrayal *in the prayer*. This is to say, in praying "Your will be done on earth as *it is* in heaven" we are asking (sometimes without thinking) that the Kingdom will not be present *until* this happens!

Similar to the teaching in Luke 19:11 that staves off any hopes of an imminent arrival of the Kingdom of God, Jesus' instruction here essentially does the same thing, at least in the sense that we now ought to realize that the Kingdom which was then preached as being "at hand" at the start of Jesus' ministry was put off until the second advent.[26] Matthew 6:10 precludes any notion of the Kingdom of God being established in a world yet under the thrall of Satan and the governance of the wicked. To put it in the words of John the Apostle, only when "The kingdoms of this world have become *the kingdoms* of our Lord and of His Christ" (Rev. 11:15) could it be said that the Kingdom of Heaven/God is present upon the earth and that the second and third petitions of the "Lord's Prayer" will be answered.

The Context of the Proclamation

Toward the end of the Sermon on the Mount, Jesus issues a warning about false professors: "Not everyone who says to Me, 'Lord, Lord,' shall enter the kingdom of heaven, but he who does the will of My Father in heaven" (Matt. 7:21).

We must remind ourselves that at the time when this was taught, Jesus and the disciples were proclaiming the message that "the kingdom of heaven is at hand" (Matt. 4:1; 10:7). There was a sense of urgency about the coming of the New covenant Kingdom that later would no longer be present as Jesus neared Jerusalem.[27]

24 As I have already indicated, a way around this is simply to claim that the Gospel writers (particularly Luke) were writing in the 60's to 80's A.D. and wrote their Gospels from an ecclesiological perspective. I find such claims untenable.

25 A little further on, Jesus says to "lay up for yourselves treasures in heaven" (Matt. 6:20). By this we are not to think that heaven is the permanent home of the saints. Treasures and rewards for the next life cannot be stored on earth in this life. According to Heb. 12:27, the earth (and heaven) will be shaken so that any place one might think to store treasures will be "removed."

26 This postponement of the Millennial Kingdom should not cause any consternation. The two "advents" of Christ are brought together in numerous passages in both Testaments, which means they will need to be separated, not just in time, but in our understandings. This is why postponement-theory is a hermeneutical necessity.

27 Hence, the Lord's resigned words in Lk. 19:42: "If you had known, even you, especially in this your day, the things *that make* for your peace! But now they are hidden from your eyes."

When the Lord proclaimed the Sermon on the Mount, the Kingdom of Heaven was proclaimed as being just around the corner. Therefore, the admonishment about doing the will of the Father in Matthew 7:21 resonates with John the Baptist's heralding of bearing "fruits worthy of repentance" (Matt. 3:8/Lk. 3:8).

Here again the Kingdom is in the future. It is to be entered only by the righteous; therefore, it cannot come into a world ruled by sin and unrighteousness. If there is to be a different notion of the Kingdom later in the NT, it will be discussed when and where it arises.[28] But that different notion, if it exists, is not found in the Sermon on the Mount.

The Centurion and the Sons of the Kingdom

The next passage I wish to consider is the healing of the centurion's servant in Matthew 8 and what Jesus says in relation to it. Luke also records the incident (Lk. 7:1-10), but without the observations given in Matthew 8:5-13. After the centurion expressed faith in Jesus' power and authority to just "speak a word, and my servant will be healed" (Matt. 8:8), the Lord spoke both about the faith of the Gentile soldier and the fate of those whom He referred to as "the sons of the kingdom."

> When Jesus heard *it,* He marveled, and said to those who followed, "Assuredly, I say to you, I have not found such great faith, not even in Israel! And I say to you that many will come from east and west, and sit down with Abraham, Isaac, and Jacob in the kingdom of heaven. But the sons of the kingdom will be cast out into outer darkness. There will be weeping and gnashing of teeth" (Matt. 8:10-12).

Let us consider the faith of the centurion; of what did it consist? He is a Gentile who is aware of what Jesus is doing and saying. Jesus has made a deep impression on him. He calls Him "Lord." As a centurion, he knows men, and he knows Jesus is no ordinary man. In the culture of the time, many believed that words could carry power, especially if they were associated with a deity. It is safe to assume the centurion had witnessed Christ's mighty works and he came to believe, not that Jesus *might* have the power to heal his servant, but that He *did* have it. Moreover, he was convinced that the power of Jesus' words was sufficient to affect the world dynamically and authoritatively. In sum, the centurion was sure that Jesus was who He claimed to be. His trust in Jesus was grounded in the words of Jesus, supported by the works.

Now consider Jesus' application of the centurion's faith: "I say to you that many will come from east and west, and sit down with Abraham, Isaac, and Jacob in the kingdom of heaven" (Matt. 8:11). The various points of the compass serve to indicate the far-reaching impact of the work of God in which Jesus is central. As the Abrahamic covenant includes a provision for the nations (Gen. 12:3; 22:18), Jesus would not be saying anything controversial about the Gentiles. But putting it the way He does,

28 I shall give some consideration to the matter in my treatment of the Parables of the Kingdom in Matt. 13.

that Gentiles will come into the Kingdom while some Jews (very religious Jews no less) would be excluded, would be guaranteed to raise the ire of some of His listeners. In the passage, the phrase "sons of the kingdom" refers to Israelites, who are party[29] to the Abrahamic and Davidic covenants, and who, therefore, expected to enter the Kingdom.[30] Jesus' highlighting of the centurion's *faith in Him* showed what would be the deciding factor.[31] Mere ancestry was not a sufficient qualification.

Yet there will be believing Jews in the Kingdom.[32] Israel will not be replaced, nor does the passage say that Israel will be expanded to become mainly Gentile in complexion. Faith in Messiah Jesus is the road to covenantal blessing. Israel's covenants do not bypass Jesus, they pass *through* Him.[33]

Matthew 9 mostly concerns reports of Jesus' amazing healings and exorcisms. All these reports are grouped together to show how Christ overcame the effects of the curse and the deleterious consequences of sin upon the body. These include the healing of the Paralytic (Matt. 9:1-8/Lk. 5:17-26), the restoration of the young girl and the healing of the woman with the issue of blood (Matt. 9:18-26/Lk. 8:40-56), the healing of two blind men (Matt. 9:27-31), and the expulsion of a demon which had rendered a man mute (Matt. 9:32-34). These mighty reversals of the different effects of the Fall, of which nothing equal had been seen in Israel (Matt. 9:33), are linked to the proclamation of the Kingdom (Matt. 9:35).

The Bridegroom Taken Away

Also included in the chapter is a short interaction with the Pharisees about fasting (Matt. 9:14-17). The Pharisees wanted to know why the disciples of Jesus did not fast. The answer they got is worth pondering: "Jesus said to them, 'Can the friends of the bridegroom mourn as long as the bridegroom is with them? But the days will come when the bridegroom will be taken away from them, and then they will fast'" (Matt. 9:15).

A question arises about why the disciples do not fast when they are with Jesus. The figure of the bridegroom is used for illustrative purposes. But the sting in the tail is in the second half of the verse when Christ says that the bridegroom will be taken away from them. This is an oblique reference to Christ's removal by death. The reason for not fasting in Christ's presence is because it is inappropriate. But why? I think

---

29 When I say "party," I mean here that these covenants are Israelite covenants (although the last promise of the Abrahamic covenant covers the nations). But faith is required to enter the blessings of the covenant. This does not make the covenants conditional in the sense that God can cancel His sworn promises. It does introduce a condition outside the oath which must be met (and will be met via providence) for Israelites to secure the promises.

30 D. A. Carson argues that the context forbids equating the "sons of the kingdom" here with the NT Church (Carson, "Matthew," 325-326).

31 Again, it should be noted how entrance into a future Kingdom is at issue.

32 As I have tried to show and will show, the coming Kingdom is the New covenant Kingdom.

33 The other unilateral covenants converge upon Jesus and diverge from Him having been given the green light to be fulfilled upon those saints with whom the covenants are realized. This is a main plank of Biblical Covenantalism.

because of who He is and what He can bring. He is the Lord whose works restore and even bring life. Hence, mourning is out of place.[34]

In the first volume and the Introduction to this volume, I endeavored to show that Messiah is the embodiment of the New covenant.[35] I hope this will become more apparent as we continue, but the upshot of this understanding is that in His miracles of power and works of compassion, Jesus the Christ was offering foretastes of His restraining influence over creation, which will be displayed in full in His Kingdom. I say "restraining influence" because it is my understanding that the first part of the Kingdom of God will be conducted on this cursed earth, and that, therefore, the powerful presence of the Great King will quell the curse's power and retard the doleful tides of sin before the onset of the New Creation.[36] So when the bridegroom is here, there is no room for mourning and fasting.

The two pictures that follow of patching an old garment with new cloth and of putting new wine into old bottles (Matt. 9:16-17) imply the same incongruity as fasting when the bridegroom is present. What Jesus brings is "new" and cannot be incorporated into what already exists (for instance, Second Temple Judaism). Jesus brings discontinuity because He brings the New covenant![37] However, it ought to be stated that His presence secures continuity in the Creation Project as a whole. Just as, for example, old cloth and new cloth are still cloth, Christ's transcendent Kingdom work improves upon what came before.[38]

Interpreting Matthew 10

Jesus dispenses power to vanquish demons and sicknesses to His disciples in Matthew 10:1 in preparation for them going throughout Israel, heralding the impending Kingdom of Heaven (Matt. 10:1-10). The wonders they are to perform in the sight of their countrymen demonstrate the unsuitability of putting new wine in old wineskins. The Kingdom they are preaching as "at hand" will introduce a new aeon, one that will outdo this aeon as a combine-harvester outdoes a scythe. The miracles should not be seen only as signs that attract attention, but as portents of the kind of realm the Kingdom of God will be.

But it is a striking fact that Matthew tells us that this powerful witness was to be confined.

34 Carson links the image of the bridegroom to the Jewish messianic hope of the time (D. A. Carson, "Matthew," 227).

35 Paul Martin Henebury, *The Words of the Covenant*, Vol 1, 64-67.

36 Aspects of this power were gifted to the disciples as they went to "the lost sheep of the house of Israel" (Matt. 10:1-8). I shall be saying more on this in my comments on 1 Cor. 15.

37 Carson's comments on this pericope are sensible and accurate (D. A. Carson, "Matthew," 227-228). However, it appears to me that so far in Matthew's Gospel, the Kingdom has been presented as a future reality. Jesus and the Kingdom are a joint package. This is not to say that there is no continuity between "this age" and "the age to come," only that the difference of Christ's kingship over against the rulers of this world is so vast that everything is affected.

38 The illustration can't be pushed too far as old wine is often preferable to new wine. But that aspect of similarity is not what is being discussed.

> These twelve Jesus sent out and commanded them, saying: "Do not go into the way of the Gentiles,[39] and do not enter a city of the Samaritans. But go rather to the lost sheep of the house of Israel. And as you go, preach, saying, 'The kingdom of heaven is at hand.' Heal the sick, cleanse the lepers, raise the dead, cast out demons. Freely you have received, freely give" (Matt. 10:5-8).

No other Gospel writer includes this saying, but Matthew felt that it was important to put it in, in all probability for contextual reasons. The road to the Gentiles could mean the actual roads to Tyre and Sidon, or to the Decapolis, but is better interpreted as any route that takes you to where Gentiles are. Carson offers a balanced explanation of the prohibition, citing the attitude of the disciples in Luke 9:52-56 and adding that Jesus did not wish to invite "premature offense" at this stage of His ministry.[40] But that does not go far enough, in my opinion. There is a focus on Israel that is legitimate, harkening all the way back to Genesis 12 and Exodus 19. It respects the covenants God made with Abraham, Isaac, and Jacob and the fact that Jesus is first the Jewish Messiah.[41] His ministry was, in Paul's later language, "to the Jew first" (Rom. 1:16; 2:10).

Then there is a section about persecution (Matt. 10:16-23). The first part of it is straightforward enough, although even there the sayings crop up in Luke and Mark in eschatological settings (Mk. 13:9-13; Lk. 21:12-17). The real difficulty enters in with Matthew 10:21-23. Verse 21 is found in Mark and Luke in proximity to "tribulation" passages (of which more later). Verse 22 includes the well-known "But he who endures to the end will be saved." Its use in Mark 13:13 is placed right next to, and looks to be consonant with, the end times discourse of Jesus (which is where Matthew will also place it in unmistakable terms in Matthew 24:13-14). If one is not dead set on finding immediate first-century correspondences to these sayings, it begins to look as if Matthew 10:21-23 leaps the centuries, landing us in the days just prior to the Lord's return in power.

This impression is only cemented by verse 23: "When they persecute you in this city, flee to another. For assuredly, I say to you, you will not have gone through the cities of Israel before the Son of Man comes" (Matt. 10:23).

Many attempts have been made to make sense of this difficult verse in a first-century setting, but in my opinion, they all fail. Let us pick apart the ingredients:

> 1. The Son of Man was the one speaking to the disciples. They were not waiting for Him to come; He was already there.
>
> 2. Although Israel was and is a small territory, there is no evidence that Christ's disciples covered the whole land in their evangelistic efforts.

39 A unique study contrasting this passage with the Great Commission of Matthew 28:18-20 is James I. Fazio, *Two Commissions: Two Missionary Mandates in Matthew's Gospel* (El Cajon, CA: Southern Evangelical Seminary Press, 2015).

40 D. A. Carson, "Matthew," 244.

41 See Ed Glasscock, *Matthew*, 222-223.

3. Soon after the death of Jesus, the scattered disciples were given a wider field of evangelism and most of them, either to avoid persecution or for ministry's sake, began to work further afield.

4. If the disciples had completed their task of going through every town in Israel, they would have falsified Jesus' words. Jesus predicted that they would not complete the task before He came.

The first and the fourth points are the most difficult to get around. To my mind, the only plausible view is that the words are proleptical, that is, anticipatory. The setting has shifted to the time of the end, the period running up to and including the second coming (i.e., "before the Son of Man comes").[42] This portion of the chapter might be thought about as telescoping out from post-ascension persecution (Matt. 10:16-17) to wider persecution throughout Christian history (Matt. 10:18-20), reaching into the times and events surrounding the second advent (Matt. 10:21-23). This position means the "you" in Matthew 10:23 refers to those who will be ministering for Christ prior to His return. There is nothing particularly strange about this; one finds the same idea in John 14:1-3. Whether or not one agrees with this interpretation, what cannot be escaped is that the coverage of Israel and the coming of Christ belong together.[43]

If Matthew 10:23b causes headaches for scholars, Matthew 11:12 comes a close second: "And from the days of John the Baptist until now the kingdom of heaven suffers violence, and the violent take it by force."

Since we are studying Jesus' teaching on the Kingdom of God/Heaven, we must tackle this verse. Once more, various attempts have been made to make sense of the passage. The attention is grabbed by the word "the violent" (*biastes*) who take the Kingdom by force. What kind of force can take the Kingdom of Heaven? If the Kingdom of Heaven is eschatological, the answer from the text itself is that nothing can take it, for no human violence disturbs the entrance of those whom God permits to enter, nor perturbs the Kingdom upon entering it. Bunyan famously had one of his characters in *Pilgrim's Progress* cut through the swathe of guards before the king's gate, but the exegetical basis for the image is dubious.[44] One approach that I think has a lot of merit looks at the verse, in particular the verbs *biazetai* and *biastai*, negatively,

42 It is also plausible to view Matt. 10:40-42 as eschatological.

43 Some interpreters try to get round this problem by theorizing that Matt. 10:23 is based upon a non-extant source that has found its way into the text. See e.g., John Nolland, *The Gospel of Matthew*, 428. Carson calls the verse "the most difficult in the NT canon" (D. A. Carson, "Matthew," 250). He runs through seven interpretations and chooses the last, where the coming of the Son of Man refers to the coming judgment against the Jews (Ibid., 252). But this leaves points 1 and 4 above untouched and therefore is unsatisfactory. For more analysis see Ryan E. Meyer, "The Interpretation of Matthew 10:23b," *Detroit Baptist Seminary Journal*, 24 (2019), 45-62. Also, Richard L. Mayhue, "Jesus: A Preterist Or A Futurist?" *MSJ* 14 (Spring 2003), 75-77.

44 John Bunyan, *The Pilgrim's Progress*, many editions. See also Thomas Watson, *Heaven Taken By Storm: Showing the Holy Violence A Christian is to Put Forth in the Pursuit After Glory* (Ligonier, PA: Soli Deo Gloria, 1992). Although they do not get Matt. 11:12 right, I strongly recommend both of these works!

as teaching that religionists want to press into the Kingdom and react violently against those who are righteous. Hence, they attack the Kingdom instead of surrendering to its preconditions.[45] This understanding of the verse fits well with the oppositional content in Jesus' discourse, especially Matthew 11:15-26.[46] It would also presage what appears to be a turning point in Jesus' proclamation in Matthew 12 and 13.

Changes Afoot in Matthew 12

As Matthew 12 begins, we find Jesus answering the Pharisees regarding the matter of His disciples plucking the heads of grain to eat on the Sabbath (Matt. 12:1-8). Luke and Mark also record this encounter, but I take note of Matthew's report because he includes a statement by Jesus about Him being "greater than the temple" (Matt. 12:6). This is in addition to His claim that "the Son of Man is Lord even of the Sabbath" (Matt. 12:8). These two statements constitute direct challenges to the Pharisees' religion. There were scarcely any more important institutions of Pharisaic Judaism than the temple and the Sabbath (even though, much to their chagrin, the temple was overseen by the Sadducees). Who was this Galilean to exalt himself above these pillars of Judaism?

Certainly, what Christ is doing here is bold, but it is not arrogant. How else is the true Son of Man of Daniel 7, the Messiah, nay, the co-Creator, going to get across to these "doctors of the Scriptures" that He transcends all those things which, in one way or another, epitomize Him? What is the Law without the covenant? What is the Sabbath without the Creator's cessation of the first creation week (cf. Exod. 20:11)? If the Messiah will inaugurate the New covenant and Jesus has been announced by John the Baptist as He, and Jesus' mighty miracles and impeccable character more than corroborated John's announcement, should not the eyes and ears of all those near to God be open to His message? The question is of course rhetorical, for in God's purposes, these men and their religious neighbors (the scribes and Sadducees) would head up the opposition against Jesus. But the signs were there, and word and deed pointed the Pharisees in the right direction.

As if these already present clues were not enough, Jesus quotes Hosea 6:6 to them: "But if you had known what *this* means, 'I desire mercy and not sacrifice,' you would not have condemned the guiltless" (Matt. 12:7).

On the basis of the aforementioned clues, the Pharisees should have cottoned on to who Jesus was (i.e., "God with us," Matt. 1:23). This, in turn, ought to have informed their understanding of what the disciples were doing. Mercy is better than sacrificial duty, according to Yahweh, who, in His Son, is greater than the temple or

45 This negative take on verse 12 is favored by Craig Blomberg, *Matthew*, 187-188. A commentator who thinks Jesus intended a kind of double entendre is Daniel M. Doriani, *Matthew*, Vol. 1 (Phillipsburg, NJ: P & R Publishing, 2008), 470-471.

46 After reviewing several options, George Eldon Ladd prefers to take the verb as a middle so that it is the kingdom itself that is "making its way powerfully" and dynamically through history. See Ladd, *The Presence of the Future*, 158-164. This of course fits his system, but it is not very persuasive.

the Sabbath.[47] This is underlined in the very next section, where the Pharisees' gross neglect of mercy meant they could not stand to see a man's withered hand restored on the Sabbath (Matt. 12:9-14). Hence, we see that an ethical starting point may prevent correct biblical hermeneutics from being employed.

Behold My Servant

After healing the man on the Sabbath, Jesus knew that the Pharisees wanted Him dead. He did not contend with the vendetta but moved on, warning His followers not to make Him widely known (Matt. 12:15-16). It is worth noting Matthew's comment on this incident, which takes the form of an OT quotation:

> Behold! My Servant whom I have chosen,
> My Beloved in whom My soul is well pleased!
> I will put My Spirit upon Him,
> And He will declare justice to the Gentiles.
> He will not quarrel nor cry out,
> Nor will anyone hear His voice in the streets.
> A bruised reed He will not break,
> And smoking flax He will not quench,
> Till He sends forth justice to victory;
> And in His name Gentiles will trust (Matt. 12:18-21).

Matthew provides the first word of the quotation: "Behold!" He wants to bring attention to Jesus as the Servant of Yahweh.[48] This Servant is "beloved" and has been given God's Spirit, and He will see to it that justice thrives in the world. Unfairness and injustice will not prevail. So yes, He is greater than either the temple or the Sabbath.

This long quotation is taken from Isaiah 42:1-4, which, of course, is a Servant Song. Isaiah 42, together with Isaiah 49, includes a key reference to the Servant (Messiah) who will be made "as a covenant" to bring salvation (see Isaiah 42:6 and 49:8). This "covenant" must be the New covenant (as most scholars recognize) because that covenant is the only one that deals with redemption and salvation.

I cannot stress this last point too much. Let the reader examine the Noahic covenant (Gen. 6, 9), the Abrahamic covenant (Gen. 12–22, 26, etc.), the covenant God made with Phinehas (Num. 25), and the Davidic covenant (2 Sam. 7; 1 Chron. 17; Psa. 89, etc.), and see if you can find the concept of redemption from sin in any of

47 This way of putting the matter owes much to the excellent comments of Robert H. Gundry, *Commentary on the New Testament* (Peabody, MA: Hendricksen, 2010), 49-50. Hosea 6:6 is followed by recrimination "Like men, they have transgressed the covenant..." (Hos. 6:7). Though admittedly a difficult verse, the transgression of the covenant (in all probability the Mosaic covenant) was because mercy, which reflects "the knowledge of God," was forgotten, just as in the case of the Pharisees.

48 Leon Morris, *The Gospel According to Matthew* (Grand Rapids: Eerdmans, 1992), 310.

them.[49] It is just not there! But there *is* a covenant that deals directly with redemption and salvation—the New covenant (e.g., Jer. 31; Ezek. 36).

The quotation is notable for its emphasis on salvation being brought to the nations (or Gentiles). Is this the major point of the quotation and of Matthew's use of it? I don't believe so, although the fact that he does include the reference to Gentiles must be considered. The main focus of the evangelist is upon the humility or lowliness of the Servant. The passage is expansive, and Matthew wants his reader to notice it. The religious leaders of Israel may have rejected Jesus, but He is going to receive not just believing Jews, but believers from the nations too. The inclusion of the nations at this juncture is no surprise to the attentive reader. In Matthew 8:11 Jesus states, "Many will come from east and west, and sit down with Abraham, Isaac, and Jacob in the kingdom of heaven." As many New covenant passages, including Isaiah 42, refer to God's salvation going out to the nations (e.g., Isa. 49:6; 54:5; 66:19; Mic. 4:2; Zech. 8:7-8, 20-23; Mal. 3:12), Matthew is simply following the logic of the New covenant and connecting it with the humble Servant of God, Jesus Christ.[50]

A Turning Point

Matthew 12:22-30 relates the story of Jesus' miracles being ascribed to Beelzebub (Matt. 12:24). Jesus' response to this accusation is to reason with His detractors. Messiah Jesus is stronger than Satan, so He can raid Satan's domain and free those whom the evil one has bound (Matt. 12:29). The Lord claims, "But if I cast out demons by the Spirit of God, surely the kingdom of God has come upon you" (Matt. 12:28).

This verse is jumped upon by those who believe the Kingdom began in the first century, but it fails to pay due attention to the fact that Jesus' preaching and miracles so far in Matthew are fully consistent with OT expectations. Because Christ is the Son of God, He has the power (through the Spirit) to "bind the strong man." That is part of His missional identity. But just here, that identity is rejected in no uncertain terms; therefore, the reader must pay attention to what happens next. As one writer has said, "This act of blasphemous unbelief on the part of the Jewish religious authorities was the turning point of Jesus' ministry."[51] Hence, the meaning is that the King is present, and the Kingdom of God[52] is, or has been up until this point, present in the person of the King, and that Kingdom is around the corner, awaiting the Jews' acceptance of Messiah.[53] But the King is rejected and the realization of the Kingdom He has been

49 Even the bilateral Mosaic covenant doesn't deal with salvation because it requires perfect conformity, which is impossible (unless you are Jesus Christ).

50 The chapter ends with Jesus' family waiting for Him while He ministered, with the Lord replying, "whoever does the will of My Father in heaven is My brother and sister and mother" (Matt. 12:50). This also hints at the universality of His work.

51 Ronald N. Glass, "The Parables of the Kingdom: A Paradigm for Consistent Dispensational Hermeneutics," *MTJ* 5 (Spring/Fall 1994), 111.

52 This is one of the few places Matthew uses "Kingdom of God." This is probably to contrast Jesus' Kingdom with the Satanic one He is being associated with.

53 This way of interpreting the verse allows the normal use of the aorist verb *phthano,* and not subject it to a proleptic meaning. However, a proleptic aorist remains a good option. See Daniel B. Wallace, *Greek Grammar Beyond the Basics: An Exegetical Syntax of the New Testament* (Grand Rapids: Zondervan, 1996), 564 n. 32.

proclaiming is pushed back in history. It was not set up because the King was not received (cf. Lk. 19:11ff.).

The Parables of the Kingdom

In any study of the Kingdom, "the parables of the kingdom" are critical, with seven (or eight, depending on one's reckoning) located in Matthew 13.[54] Although this is not a Bible commentary, it is important to take a look at these parables because they provide important information about the progress of God's Kingdom program.[55] We should remind ourselves that although the majority of OT texts refer to the eschatological Kingdom, there are verses such as Psalm 103:19, which declare, "The LORD has established His throne in heaven, and His kingdom rules over all." There is then a sense in which God has a kingdom up in heaven (naturally enough), which equates to His sovereign control over the affairs of history down here. But this is not the same as the Kingdom on earth described in such vibrant predictive terms by the Prophets, the eschatological Davidic-New covenant Kingdom.[56]

Prior to chapter 13, Matthew has employed the term "kingdom of heaven" mainly in a futuristic sense. The Kingdom is something ahead but imminent (Matt. 3:2; 4:17; 5:3, 10, 19-20; 7:21; 8:11; 10:7; 11:11-12). In several instances, the passages plainly speak of the coming new aeon (Matt. 5:19-20; 8:11), although I submit that all those references ought to be taken in that way. The last mention of the Kingdom before the parables of the kingdom is in Matthew 12:28: "But if I cast out demons by the Spirit of God, surely the kingdom of God has come upon you." There the exorcisms of Jesus are related to the Kingdom because they preview the eradication of the malevolent spirits once the King (who is present) takes the reins of power. However, things change in Matthew 13.

Parables as a Response to Hostility and Message Amendment

Before looking at the parables themselves, we must ask about this change. Matthew writes his Gospel around five discourses, of which Matthew 13 is the third. But Matthew 13:1 shows that chapter 13 is connected to what happened in chapter 12. There the rejection of Jesus' Kingdom message, which centered on Himself, becomes intensified; so much so that many commentators refer to it. Hagner, for instance, speaks about "the rejection and hostility themes and... the apparent failure of the kingdom that dominate chapter 12."[57] Matthew 13 opens with Jesus going "out of the house" and speaking to the multitudes by the sea, beginning with the Parable of the Sower (Matt.

54 Though differing in places, I recommend the exemplary two part study by Mike Stallard, "Hermeneutics and Matthew 13," *Conservative Theological Journal* 5.15 (Aug 2001) and 5.16 (Dec 2001).
55 Often the nuances within these parables are not dealt with adequately.
56 As we have seen previously, *that* Kingdom is very much a part of the theology of Luke as well.
57 Donald A. Hagner, *Matthew 1–13*, 366-367.

13:3-9).[58] Unlike many dispensationalist writers, I see nothing significant about Jesus leaving the house. If one reads the narrative from Matthew 12:1 to 13:1, one sees that at the start of Matthew 12 He is in the fields with His disciples (Matt. 12:1-8). In Matthew 12:9-14 He is in a synagogue, which He withdraws from, and is with the multitudes until He appears to be in a house (Mark reports that His family members were "standing outside," Mk. 3:31). It is just narrative scene-setting, accurate but vague.

However, I do think there is something to the switch to parables of the kingdom in this chapter. This is highlighted in the disciples' question about this very thing in Matthew 13:10: "And the disciples came and said to Him, 'Why do You speak to them in parables?'"

Listen to Jesus' answer: "Because it has been given to you to know the mysteries of the kingdom of heaven, but to them it has not been given... Therefore I speak to them in parables, because seeing they do not see, and hearing they do not hear, nor do they understand" (Matt. 13:11, 13).

Jesus continues by citing Isaiah 6:9-10, which shows that the parables are connected to a judgment upon those who reject plain speech.[59] The reader should recall that the preaching of John the Baptist and Jesus were fully in line with OT covenant expectations of the Kingdom. These, plus the signs and miracles that corroborated Jesus' ministry as Kingdom-foreshadowing events, provided clear evidence of Jesus' identity as the prophesied coming One.

I think it is instructive to notice what Jesus does *not* say here. He does not indicate that the reason for His parables is because He has been rejected, at least not obviously. Mark records this conversation seemingly early in Jesus' ministry (Mk. 4:10-12), as does Luke (Lk. 8:9-10). If Matthew is telling us that Jesus' Kingdom message begins to change from an imminent Kingdom to a far-off eschatological one, it is quite obliquely done. And yet, there is a change. As I will show below, the imminence of the Kingdom is pushed into the background in the parables of chapter 13, with the growth of the Kingdom (or at least of Kingdom-related matters), coming to the foreground. Let us turn to the Parables of the Kingdom then, and after we have looked at them, I will return to this matter of whether a transition in Jesus' earlier teaching has occurred.

1. The Parable of the Sower

The first parable, the famous Parable of the Sower (Matt. 13:1-9; 18-23), is the key parable in that it calls our attention to interpretation (hearing).[60] This parable does

58 I have heard some dispensationalists say that this "house" is the temple, but that is plainly not so.

59 This is essentially the teaching of Matt. 13:11-13. Note also Mk. 4:34: "But without a parable He did not speak to them. And when they were alone, He explained all things to His disciples." See Mark Saucy, *The Kingdom of God in the Teaching of Jesus*, 331-332; and Alva J. McClain, *The Greatness of the Kingdom*, 322-323.

60 "In many ways...this is the quintessential parable that opens up our understanding of all Jesus' parables" (Andreas J. Köstenberger, *The Jesus of the Gospels: An Introduction* [Grand Rapids: Kregel, 2020], 92). This perhaps goes a little too far. The next parable, the Parable of the Wheat, and the Tares is the main parable of the Kingdom.

not contain the formula "the kingdom of heaven is like," which is seen in the other parables in chapter 13.

The first parable acts as a sort of interpretive guide to the rest of the parables in the chapter. At its close, we see that the parable is all about how one hears. "He that has ears to hear, let him hear" (Matt. 13:9). The ear has been made to hear rightly. Matthew 13:14-16 (which cites Isaiah 6:9-10) relates the misuse of eyes and ears, the problem emanating from the heart! We see this in Jesus' interpretation of the first parable, where He notes that the seed (i.e., the word) does not find receptive ground. In Matthew 13:19 the person does not understand the word, and the cause is in the heart. In Matthew 13:20-21 the word is gladly received, but there is no depth for it to take root. That is, the heart is not prepared for the word. The way Jesus puts it is interesting: "He has no root in himself" (Matt. 13:21). This indicates that although the word was accepted, it was accepted rather like a lover of fiction accepts a pile of books, only to discover that nothing in the pile strikes his fancy. Or rather, the books received require more than a mere foray of the imagination. In Matthew 13:22 the third kind of hearer is too enamored with the world for the word to change their heart.[61] At last we come to the hearer who "understands" (Matt. 13:23). Hearers of this sort produce "fruit," probably in accordance with their abilities and circumstances. A true hearer will understand the word. That is what the Parable of the Sower is about. Hopefully now we will be in a better position to be attentive to the other parables.

EXCURSUS: "The Kingdom of Heaven is like"

Before proceeding, I think we have to be clear on what is meant by the repeated phrase, "the kingdom of heaven is like" (Matt. 13:24, 31, 33, 44, 45, 47, 52).[62] To do that we have to connect it to "the mysteries of the kingdom," which refers to the content of the parables themselves (Matt. 13:11). If we understand the phrase to refer to "the word of the kingdom," we may be misled. In contrast to the Parable of the Sower, where the "word of the kingdom" is the proclamation of the Kingdom signified *by* the seed (Matt. 13:3, 4, 19), in the Parable of the Wheat and Tares "the word of the kingdom" is *not* the seed, but instead *produces* the seed (Matt. 13:26), the seed being "the sons of the kingdom" (Matt. 13:38).[63] The Sower is Christ who proclaims the word that produces the "seed."

In light of the differing meanings of "the word of the kingdom," depending on its parabolic setting, I think it best not to consider it alongside the sayings "the mysteries of the kingdom" and "the kingdom of heaven is like." That said, when deciding about "the kingdom of heaven is like," we can go one of two ways. We can assume that the proclamation of the word by Jesus' followers throughout what will become Church

61 Of course, we are to understand that the "heart" does not refer just to the emotional side of man, but to his driving impulses.

62 The phrase also appears in Matt. 18:23; 20:1; 22:2; and 25:14.

63 In Matt. 8:12 the term "sons of the kingdom" is applied to Jews who are excluded from the eschatological Kingdom. This reminds us that every parable must be studied for how words are used within its own story.

history is meant, in which case the Church proclaims the Kingdom. But that view, as we have just seen, is problematical.[64]

Alternatively, we can concentrate on identifying just what "the mysteries of the kingdom" are in these parables, and we shall have our answer. Up until this time in Matthew, Jesus was preaching a particular message, about the immanence of the next age ("the kingdom of heaven is at hand"). However, this proclamation ceased in the ministry of Jesus. Moreover, it seems to have ceased before Matthew 13.[65] Perhaps, though, it will be resumed when that message is again relevant? In light of Matthew 24:14, where the "gospel of the kingdom" is said to be proclaimed, this second position looks to have something going for it. If the gospel of the kingdom equates with the message of the imminent Kingdom ("the kingdom of heaven is at hand"), then its ceasing before Matthew 13, when the message of imminence changes, and its re-proclamation in the eschaton makes a lot of sense. In fact, when one compares Matthew 4:17 with the Great Commission (Matt. 28:19-20), the idea of the near onset of the Kingdom has vanished.

To be clear on what I am saying so far, I think that the announcement of the approaching Kingdom ("the kingdom of heaven is at hand") by John the Baptist and by Christ prior to this chapter is the same as "the word of the kingdom" referred to in Matthew 13:19.[66] But since the heralding of "the kingdom of heaven is at hand" stops here, it cannot be fitted within Jesus' refrain "the kingdom of heaven is like," which speaks of growth (Matt. 13:36, 32, 33, 48). Hence, in this latter phrase we see a *kingdom in the making* and its progress as such from that time up to the second advent.

We must recall that Jesus is teaching about "the mysteries of the kingdom," and that these mysteries concern its progress toward final consummation, not the consummation per se. For instance, it cannot be that the devil sows false disciples in the messianic Kingdom itself (Matt. 13:38-39), since in any end times scenario the devil is incapacitated (however Revelation 20 is interpreted). Given the growth theme that dominates Matthew 13, the phrase "the kingdom of heaven is like" must refer to an aspect or aspects of it that run from the first advent *to* the coming of the covenanted Kingdom at the second advent.

2. The Parable of the Wheat and the Tares

The Parable of the Wheat and the Tares tells us something crucial about "the kingdom." It shows us that the "kingdom" is something that is "planted" and is growing, and that it is vulnerable to assault from the enemy. This ought to put us on our mettle; we are not to think of the final eschatological Kingdom here. The "kingdom" in the repeated phrase "the kingdom of heaven is like" is something else.

In His explanation of the parable in Matthew 13:36-43, Jesus identifies Himself as the Sower of the good seed (Matt. 13:37), the devil as the enemy who sows bad seed

64 See D. A. Carson, "Matthew," 316-317, 324-326. It is also worth noting that the Church has not proclaimed the kingdom, at least not in a major way, unless one wishes to equate the kingdom to the Roman Catholic Church that is!

65 See below.

66 This is not controversial. See e.g., John Nolland, *Matthew*, 539.

(Matt. 13:39), the field as the world (Matt. 13:38), the wheat as "the sons of the kingdom" (Matt. 13:38), the tares as the "sons of the wicked one," and the reapers as the angels who come at the end of the age (Matt. 13:39).[67]

What Jesus is presenting in these parables is *a kingdom in the making*, not consummated. For instance, both the "sons of the kingdom" and the "sons of the wicked one" are seen as growing (Matt. 13:30, 38). Some believe this means that the kingdom of heaven is seen as beginning at the start of Jesus' public ministry and extending through the visible Church till the "end of the age" (Matt. 13:39, 49).[68] That is a common understanding, especially among Reformed commentators. But it has problems. Firstly, we are expressly told that "the field is the world," not the Church (Matt. 13:38).[69] This must be carefully pondered, for it means that "the sons of the kingdom," who are represented by "good seed" (Matt. 13:38), cannot be synonymous with Christians, who, of course, make up the Church. And if that is the case then, "the sons of the wicked one" cannot be false Christians. Who, then, are they? Perhaps the safest answer (although admittedly frustratingly indeterminate) is that these godly and ungodly "sons" represent two strands of sinners since the time of Jesus (Matt. 13:37). The first saved by grace and the second enslaved by the devil.[70] But surely the age to come (inferred here, though see Matt. 12:32; cf. Matt. 19:28) is the true new age of the Kingdom (cf. Matt. 13:43), as it has uniformly been prior to this point in the book. Cutting the kingdom of heaven into two strands; one future and Davidic,[71] one spiritual and non-Davidic, does not do full justice to what Jesus says.

The eyes have to be fully open. For example, one thing that ought to grab the attention but may slip by is that "the sons of the wicked one" in Matthew 13:38 are not connected to the Kingdom, while "the sons of the kingdom" are. But in light of the question about what the kingdom is in the parables, we have to decide if the eschatological Kingdom is meant, or the more understated form is in view. I think the context weighs in favor of the former.

One should notice how "His kingdom" (Matt. 13:41) equates to the return of Jesus, not to His present session in heaven. The "angels" in the parable correspond to the angels in Matthew 24:30-31 at Christ's coming. "The kingdom of their Father" in Matthew 13:43 is the New covenant Kingdom after it has been purged of the wicked (cf. Matt. 25:31-46). It is the nuances in the parables that make them challenging. Let us keep reading.

> Therefore as the tares are gathered and burned in the fire, so it will be at the end of this age. The Son of Man will send out His angels, and they will gather out of His kingdom all things that offend, and those who practice lawlessness, and will cast them into the furnace of fire. There will be wailing and gnashing

67 What follows is not an exposition of the parable but an examination of crucial terms.

68 This is the position of George Eldon Ladd, *A Theology of the New Testament* (Grand Rapids: Eerdmans, 1983), 93.

69 This is before any mention of the Church.

70 I do not mean that the "sons of the wicked one" necessarily include all lost men, but rather those who grow alongside the saints. Remember, the evil one plants these people.

71 In the sense of a dynasty reigning over Israel.

> of teeth. Then the righteous will shine forth as the sun in the kingdom of their Father. He who has ears to hear, let him hear (Matt. 13:40-43)!

The close of the parable deals with eschatological issues. The Son sends out His angels "to gather out of His kingdom all things that offend" (Matt. 13:41, my emphasis). This has to mean that there is an expression of the Kingdom that predates the full realization of "the age to come."[72] This expression is the onset of the covenanted Kingdom in its initial cleanup phase.[73] As indicated above, the sending of the angels is a second advent event.

Christ returns and gathers the wicked out of His Kingdom, and the full Kingdom of the Father is then launched. The new aeon, "the kingdom of their Father" (Matt. 13:43), will be mediated by the Son.[74] It is a New covenant Kingdom.

We see then that the phrase "kingdom of heaven" is somewhat elastic in Matthew 13. In Matthew 13:41 and 43 it refers to the eschatological Kingdom, but the phrase "the kingdom of heaven is like" refers to aspects or even portents of the kingdom already taking place, not to the future messianic Kingdom *in toto*.

3. The Parable of the Mustard Seed

The other five (or six) parables are shorter. The Parable of the Mustard Seed (Matt. 13:31-32) speaks of the "kingdom of heaven" beginning almost imperceptibly like a tiny seed but growing until it becomes a tree that can hold bird's nests. Does this depict positive or negative growth? The wheat or the tares? It is hard to say, but I side with the majority who see it as positive growth.[75] The "mystery" here is the slow, gradual growth toward completion. This may refer to the progress of what I have designated as "the Creation Project," or more accurately, a stage of it as it moves from Christ's first to His second advent.[76] It is not the growth of the Kingdom itself (i.e., its OT Davidic covenant aspect), but the growth of elements that will become central pieces of the consummated Kingdom.[77]

---

72 That is to say, the eschatological Kingdom.

73 Just to be clear, when Christ says that His angels will one day "gather out of His Kingdom all things that offend" (Matt. 13:41), He is probably referring to an event that happens right after Christ has returned to the earth. In which case, the "kingdom" in that place is the eschatological Kingdom in its infancy, though perhaps ahead of its formal inauguration.

74 To these considerations, we might add the Parable of the Workers in Matt. 20:1-16 and the Parables in Matt. 21:28-32 and 22:1-12. Of course, many writers insist upon relating that parable to the Church. E.g., Joachim Jeremias, *Rediscovering the Parables* (New York: SCM Press, 1966), 24-27.

75 This is not the same as saying the parable illustrates the success of the Gospel. I am just saying that positive elements of growth are in view.

76 Some argue that there is an emphasis on the "shining" of the righteous when the Kingdom finally comes. See Robert L. Saucy, *The Case for Progressive Dispensationalism*, 100-101.

77 Some dispensationalists believe that the growth of evil is portrayed in this parable. For example, Andrew Woods, *The Coming Kingdom*, 79-83. Woods relies heavily on Arthur W. Pink's *pre*-amillennial work.

4. The Parable of the Woman Hiding Leaven

The Parable of the Leaven (Matt. 13:33) has, of course, been interpreted as illustrating the private growth of the "kingdom" or Gospel in the world throughout history. But this way of thinking about it would be foreign to the initial hearers of the message. "Leaven" is not equated with good things in the Bible. Jesus Himself consistently uses leaven as a negative figure elsewhere (Matt. 16:6, 11-12; cf. Mk. 8:15). Paul does the same (1 Cor. 5:6-8; Gal. 5:9). When we come to the OT, things do not change (e.g., Exod. 12:15, 19; 34:25; Lev. 2:11; 10:12; Deut. 16:4; Amos 4:5). Are we now to believe that this word would be understood positively in this single case?[78] No, the growth of the leaven, which is "hid" (linking it with the devil's surreptitious sowing in Matthew 13:25, 39), refers to the "tares" of the second parable. In my opinion, it is best to understand this as illustrating the hidden growth of evil in history, not simply as the general impact of the unrighteous, but of a certain line of often powerful men and their minions whose ambition and greed make them foils in Satan's hands. It is something like this that John is alluding to when he writes about the whole world being "under the sway of the wicked one" (1 Jn. 5:19).

5. The Parable of the Hidden Treasure

The next parable is the Parable of the Hidden Treasure (Matt. 13:44), where a man sells everything once he discovers treasure in a field. The treasure isn't his until he owns the field! The joy of the man and the value of the treasure shows that this relates to the positive aspect of the "kingdom." Is this the Kingdom in a mystery form? After all, one can scarcely find a "kingdom" that is yet to be seen but lies ahead of us when Christ comes back. It is not easy to decide. One possibility is that since Christ embodies the Kingdom, coming to understand who He is makes every other thing secondary. In this sense the treasure is not the Kingdom but is the message about Christ. Another possibility is that the treasure signifies the "kingdom-in-the-making."[79] In this case, the man finds that the Kingdom is being formed among the followers of Jesus but is not to be realized until Christ returns.

6. The Parable of the Pearl of Great Price

Likewise with the parable which follows: a man finds "a pearl of great price" (Matt. 13:45-46). Since a pearl is a thing of beauty, it seems natural to infer that this depicts a positive aspect of the "kingdom," perhaps the truth of the message preached?

7. The Parable of the Dragnet

Finally, we read the Parable of the Dragnet (Matt. 13:47-50). In this parable we see good and bad (clean and unclean) fish pictured, which reminds us of the Parable of the Wheat and the Tares. The fishermen are pictured as sitting down to sort through

78 This is the view of Craig L. Blomberg in his *Preaching the Parables: From Responsible Interpretation to Powerful Proclamation* (Grand Rapids: Baker, 2004), 123-124.

79 Clearly, there is not a huge difference between the two.

the full net, and Jesus interprets this as the angels' separating "the wicked from among the just" (Matt. 13:48-49). This occurs around the time of Christ's return.

8. The Parable of the Householder

After He has recited the seven parables of the kingdom, Jesus closes with a parable likening the good listener, the one who comprehends Him, to a householder who can produce old and new treasures from what he has learned (Matt. 13:52). Right hearing was the subject of the Parable of the Sower that introduced the chapter. The application is that right hearing will produce right action. This suits the disciples turned Apostles who bring truth out of both the OT and the teachings of Jesus.[80]

Back to the Question of a Transition in Jesus' Kingdom Teaching

It is clear that some alteration in the preaching of Jesus after Matthew 12 and (at least as Matthew presents it) a different presentation in the form of the parables of the kingdom began.[81] The animosity towards Jesus' person had reached a crescendo in chapter 12. The explanation given by Jesus concerns judgment upon those who would not entertain His message (Matt. 13:11-15). It seems their rejection of Him was quite definitive (e.g., Matt. 12:14, 24, 31-32, 39).[82] Therefore, the parables He taught, which began "the kingdom of heaven is like," which started in Matthew 13 (and continued into Matt. 18, 20, 22, and 25), signified a subtle shift in His proclamation. This shift concerned the timing of the covenanted Davidic Kingdom but not its essential eschatological nature. The eschaton was being pushed back.[83] As I shall show later, this is something that Luke (in Acts) and Paul understood and incorporated into their theology.

80 Andreas J. Köstenberger, *The Jesus of the Gospels*, 93.

81 "For Matthew, then, the antecedent of Jesus' original message and ministry is clear. In every way Jesus' "gospel about the kingdom" was the gospel of the Old Testament prophets." – Mark R. Saucy, "The Kingdom-of-God Sayings in Matthew," *BSAC* 151 (Apr 1994), 181. The whole article is recommended.

82 One might object that it was the leaders who rejected Jesus, not the people generally. Additionally, He was still healing the multitudes (Matt. 12:15). But take note of Jesus' words in Matt. 12:41-42: "The men of Nineveh will rise up in the judgment with this generation and condemn it, because they repented at the preaching of Jonah; and indeed, a greater than Jonah *is* here." Perhaps because of the influence of the leaders on the people Jesus knew they would follow these men and not Him. In other words, Jesus knew the exasperating and tragic penchant of most people to follow blindly and unthinkingly (Matt. 15:14). At any rate, Matthew 11 gives examples of the rejection of Jesus by the crowds (see Matt. 11:20-24).

83 "While the unconditional Abrahamic Covenant prevents Israel from forfeiting ownership of the covenanted promises, first-century Israel's lack of response to the offer of the kingdom prevented the nation from possessing these blessings. From the time of Christ up to the present hour Israel remains only the owner rather than the possessor of the covenanted promises. Although not cancelled, the messianic kingdom remains in a state of Postponement" (Andrew Woods, *The Coming Kingdom*, 44). This is well put; however, I do not agree Israel is the owner of all the covenant promises. The third part of the Abrahamic covenant, though through Israel, belongs to the nations (Gen. 12:3). Likewise, the New covenant in Christ is not the sole property of Israel (cf. 1 Cor. 11:25). See further in my treatment of the epistles of Paul.

But doesn't that open a can of worms? If the mysteries of the kingdom concern its *growth*, that must mean that some aspect of the Davidic Kingdom announced by John the Baptist and Jesus is present in the Church. This is what Progressive Dispensationalists have been asserting for a while. Am I therefore confessing to be among their number?

My answer is no, but it is a measured no. While I do not hold to any view that claims that Christ is ruling from heaven now, as in the work of Blaising and Bock,[84] I do believe that Robert and Mark Saucy are correct to identify certain markers of the coming Kingdom in the ministry of the Holy Spirit and the priestly work of Christ in heaven on our behalf. This is because of the connection of the Spirit with the New covenant. Here I think their more moderate version of Progressive Dispensationalism is of real help.[85] Mark Saucy's stimulating work, *The Kingdom of God in the Teaching of Jesus*, especially his own contribution at the end of his book, sets forth solid exegetical argumentation for viewing the priestly work of Christ as connected with the parabolic mystery-form of the kingdom.[86] More will be said, but it would be helpful if my reader keep in mind the four references to the Spirit in Matthew 12:18, 28, 31, and 32.

Finally, if my understanding of the phrase "the kingdom of heaven is like" is accurate, that it refers to a kingdom-in-the-making through the present session of Christ as High Priest, then it sheds light upon Luke's use of the phrase in Paul's ministry in Acts 28:23 and 31, plus its use by Paul in his epistles.

A Summary of the Parables in Matthew 13

What one is left with after studying these parables is the crucial importance of hearing correctly (paying attention), the joint growth of lookalike good and evil (true and false) followers, the secret insidious growth of what Satan has sown within the sphere of the growing "kingdom" (cf. Matt. 15:13), the surpassing value of having found the truth, and the job of separating the true followers from the false that is given to the angels at the second coming. In this chapter, "the kingdom of heaven" does not refer to the eschatological reign of peace but to the mysterious progress of the Christ message in conflicting circumstances accompanied by some deposits of the effect of Jesus and the work of the Spirit (cf. Matt. 12:28) that will end in the eschatological Kingdom. We are left with the following:

1. The "word of the kingdom" is not necessarily the same as the announcement "the kingdom of heaven is at hand." The latter was certainly "the word" that had been proclaimed up until this time, but Jesus is projecting ahead to a new period starting in Matthew 13 when that message will not be proclaimed.

84 See Craig A. Blaising and Darrell L. Bock, *Progressive Dispensationalism* (Grand Rapids: Baker, 1993), 232-283.

85 Not that I buy into all their arguments. For example, the meaning of *musterion* in the NT.

86 See Mark Saucy, *The Kingdom of God in the Teaching of Jesus in 20th Century Theology* (Dallas: Word, 1997), esp. 328-346.

2. The phrase "the mysteries of the kingdom" relates to the several aspects or perspectives about the *progress* of the kingdom *before* its consummation in the messianic age to come.[87] The parables refer to the Kingdom-in-the-making, not to the inaugurated messianic Kingdom itself, although that goal is mentioned (Matt. 13:43).

3. This means that the majority of Jesus' usages of "the kingdom of heaven" in these parables, as well as the other parables where we come across the phrase "the kingdom of heaven is like" (i.e., Matt. 18:23; 20:1 ff.; 22:2; 25:14) do not refer to the eschatological Kingdom but rather to the growth activity toward that Kingdom.

4. All the parables that include the introductory formula "the kingdom of heaven is like" (which is peculiar to Matthew) describe either positive or negative characteristics of this growth or both.

5. The fact that Jesus speaks of what the kingdom of heaven is like means that some features of the Kingdom are present and growing even today. This growth is related to Jesus' present session in heaven as our High Priest and the work of the Holy Spirit.[88]

6. However, in Matthew 13:41, 43 and 44 the kingdom of heaven is the eschatological Kingdom either just before its proper inception or in its consummation.

It is exceptionally difficult to decide exactly what form the progress of the kingdom of heaven takes since the message "the kingdom of heaven is at hand" is not the message of the Church. In my view, the best option is to understand these Matthean parables as describing participation or pilgrimage of the elect, whether in the Church or not (e.g., Tribulation saints[89]), as they travel towards the coming age of fulfillment.[90]

---

87 "Thus, these mysteries cover the time period between Israel's formal rejection of the kingdom and the Second Advent (13:40-42, 49-50). The kingdom mysteries represent new truths concerning the kingdom that were undisclosed in the Old Testament" (Andrew Woods, *The Coming Kingdom*, 72).

88 There is more to say about this point. The present chapter would be overly long if I were more expansive.

89 By saying this, I am showing my hand. It lies ahead of me to try to prove that the NT distinguishes Church saints from pre- and post-Church saints (e.g., Israel and the nations). Unless we insist upon spiritualizing Revelation 21:23-26, we can readily see a distinction of peoples in the New Creation. It will also be my job to argue tentatively for the removal of the Church before the Tribulation period.

90 Another less discussed yet glaring issue is the stubborn fact that the Kingdom message of Jesus in the Gospels is not the same as the "Pauline" message of the Church. Like it or not, the crowds were not hearing about the pending substitutionary death and resurrection of the Lord from either Him or His (clueless) disciples. I shall seek to establish this fact later in this book.

Several Incidents

In the chapters that follow, several incidents call for attention. Matthew 14 includes the Feeding of the Five Thousand (Matt. 14:1-21) and Jesus' walking on the water (Matt. 14:22-33). In one the Lord produces an abundance of food from a mere pittance. In doing so, He shows Himself to be the Master of the material realm, the great Provider of the creature's sustenance, Yahweh Jireh (Gen. 22:14). In walking atop the waves, the Lord is the One who transcends creation, utterly above and beyond any element, law, or force. Other examples one will come across are Jesus' healing every manner of disease and ailment (Matt. 15:29-31), the Transfiguration (Matt. 17:1-9), money out of a fish's mouth (Matt. 17:24-27), and the withering of the Fig Tree (Matt. 21:18-19). Whether driving out demons, cursing trees, or revealing His true glory, all these acts underline the absolute Lordship of Jesus.[91] Of course, John's Gospel makes a major contribution to this as we shall see.

In Matthew chapter 15 Jesus goes into the region of Tyre and Sidon, a pagan region. There He is approached by "a woman of Canaan" (Mark calls her "Syrophoenician," Mk. 7:26) whose daughter is possessed. Jesus' answer to the woman is quite startling: "I was not sent except to the lost sheep of the house of Israel" (Matt. 15:24). This statement reminds us of what Jesus said to His disciples before He sent them out in Matthew 10:5-6: "Do not go into the way of the Gentiles, and do not enter a city of the Samaritans. But go rather to the lost sheep of the house of Israel" (my emphasis).

I believe these are highly significant statements, especially when considered together. We must remind ourselves that they come in a "Jewish" Gospel. Why would Jesus say such a thing? A number of matters arise. In the first place, we should note that Jesus deliberately ventured outside Israel. Did He do it to meet this woman? Matthew doesn't say. But it provides Him with an opportunity. He is the Jewish Messiah, and the Messiah will also bring blessing to the Gentiles (Isa. 49:6). And yet, she calls Him "Lord, Son of David" (Matt. 15:22), a direct reference to the Davidic covenant. Therein may be a clue: the covenant with David does only lie with Israel, and this woman is indicating that she is aware of that. But she is confident that His mercy extends beyond the ethnic bounds of the covenant.[92] Jesus receives honor from her far above that which He was used to receiving from many in Israel. She may not be associated with the Davidic covenant, but she is connected to Christ by other means (cf. Jn. 1:29).

91 Later, the risen Jesus will state, "All authority has been given to Me in heaven and on earth" (Matt. 28:18). This truth refers to Christ's risen human nature and our connection to it. More will be said about this further on.

92 I realize this is rejected on the grounds that Jesus and the Church are the New Israel. That will be studied later.

EXCURSUS: The "Son of David" in Matthew

This raises an interesting question about the careful use of the title "Son of David" by Matthew.[93] Matthew records the term "Son of David" in reference to Jesus more than any other writer. But he does so by usually having the phrase upon the lips of the outliers of the community, like the blind (Matt. 9:27; 15:22; 20:30-31; 21:15). In his opening chapters, "Son of David" refers to the Davidic line assured through the Davidic covenant (Matt. 1:1, 20). It is sure that the very same meaning is implied by those upon whose lips it is found in the rest of this Gospel. The Davidic covenant is very much alive and well in Matthew.

Additionally, as Kyle Dunham has shown, men such as noted Matthean scholar Jack Kingsbury, as well as William Loader, have called attention to the fact that in this Gospel, the title "Son of David" is employed selectively in tandem with Jesus' Davidic claims to accompany His messianic signs like healings and exorcisms. Dunham writes:

> Based upon Kingsbury's insights, we may conclude that the title "Son of David" in Matthew emphasizes more fully the fact that Jesus is the harbinger of the Messianic kingdom as the royal Davidide promised to Israel. Matthew's purposeful use of the nomenclature reinforces the proposition that Jesus initially is announcing the messianic kingdom, which later is placed in abeyance as the shadow of Jesus' passion looms over the latter stages of his ministry.[94]

So, for example, after Jesus drove out a demon from a man who was blind and mute so that he spoke and regained his sight, the people asked each other, "Could this be the Son of David?" (Matt. 12:21-22). Here the two elements of the title come together: the powerful works and the recognition of the true identity of Jesus.

Everyone is well aware that Matthew concludes his Gospel with what is called the Great Commission, in which Jesus tells His disciples to "make disciples of all the nations" (Matt. 28:19), showing that the Gentiles are invited to believe in Him. However, here in Matthew 15 the focus is still very much on His mission to Israel. Not until the next chapter does He begin to tell His disciples of His coming rejection and death (Matt. 16:21). Finally, in Matthew 21:12-17 Jesus, the "Son of David," cleanses the temple by overthrowing the tables of the moneychangers. It is remarkable that the real Heir to the throne (cf. Matt. 21:38) takes it upon Himself to cause a commotion in the temple. This is better understood once we realize that the Messiah will combine both the crown and the high priesthood in Himself (Zech. 6:12-13).

---

93 I have been greatly helped by the ThM thesis of Kyle C. Dunham, "The Kingdom of Christ and of God: A Traditional Dispensationalist Argument for Inaugurated Eschatology," 56-58.

94 Ibid., 58.

The First Mention of the Church

In Matthew 16:18 Jesus predicts the Church:[95] "On this rock I will build My church, and the gates of Hades shall not prevail against it." The "rock" to which Jesus refers is not Peter, and (I surmise) not Peter's testimony, but the opening of Peter's understanding by God the Father. Without that, Peter would not have put the pieces together.

Jesus' words here are predictive. As He will next tell His disciples about His pending trial and death (Matt. 16:21), this prediction of the Church makes good sense. A chapter of the Creation Project is about to close, and a new chapter, the chapter of the Church, is about to open. Later we will discuss the Church's relationship to the Abrahamic covenant, particularly its third prong—the blessing of the nations—and the Church's necessary (instead of shadowy) connection to the New covenant, as well as its essential connection to the resurrection.

The Message of Christ's Transfiguration

At the end of Matthew 16 and the start of chapter 17, the author records the episode of the Transfiguration. This is also given by Mark (9:1-13) and Luke (9:27-36). These two latter Gospels explicitly tie the event to Jesus' language of taking up the cross and following Him by recording the Lord's words about shame at His coming: "For whoever is ashamed of Me and My words, of him the Son of Man will be ashamed when He comes in His *own* glory, and *in His* Father's, and of the holy angels" (Lk. 9:26).

Another odd feature of the Synoptics is how Matthew and Mark say the Transfiguration happened "six days" after Jesus said this (Matt. 17:1; Mk. 9:2), whereas Luke has "about eight days" (Lk. 9:28). Perhaps there is no mystery here as both are approximations, but couldn't one of them just have said "seven days later"? I will leave the reader to his speculations. What is not speculative is that the voice of God the Father alludes to the first Servant song in Isaiah 42:1.[96] Considering Isaiah's connecting of the Servant with a covenant in Isaiah 42:6, this should not be missed. And certainly, the covenant overtones of the Transfiguration are many.

1. The revelation of Jesus' divine status on the mount emphasizes anew the wonder of the incarnation, which is so central to the whole mission of God. The Son of God, which is a key messianic term in Matthew,[97] became human for the purpose of saving His people Israel, but also of saving the Gentiles. Although the Abrahamic covenant speaks about Yahweh's "blessing" to both groups, it stops short of telling us how that blessing is to come about. The

95 To jump ahead to a crucial fact about the Church which is commonly ignored, the Church is necessarily and unalterably tied to the resurrection of Jesus Christ. Hence, the Church could not (read did not!) exist before circa A.D. 30.

96 See e.g., F. F. Bruce, *The Book of Acts*, NICNT (Grand Rapids: Eerdmans, 1977), 88.

97 Kyle C. Dunham, "The Kingdom of Christ and of God," 58.

Gospels tell us that the incarnate Son of God will initiate the New covenant in His own blood (Matt. 26:28).[98]

2. The presence of Moses and Elijah showed that covenantal matters were foremost in the event. Moses stands for the covenant at Sinai, while Elijah, the archetypal prophet, upheld the covenant in the face of massive declension.

3. The last verse of Matthew 16 plainly connects the Transfiguration with the Kingdom (Matt. 16:28; cf. Mk. 9:1).

4. In Matthew 17:9 Jesus says, "Tell the vision to no one until the Son of Man is risen from the dead." This link to the resurrection is a link to the covenanted new life in Him as well as to the coming Kingdom of God.

5. Finally, the voice of God alluding to Isaiah 42 connects the event to the Servant of the New covenant.

All three Synoptics connect the Transfiguration with the second coming, even if it is implicit rather than explicit. Although he does not associate it with shame as Luke does (Lk. 9:26), Matthew does relate Jesus' words:

> For the Son of Man will come in the glory of His Father with His angels, and then He will reward each according to his works. Assuredly, I say to you, there are some standing here who shall not taste death till they see the Son of Man coming in His kingdom (Matt. 16:27-28).

From what happens next, we realize that the "coming" Jesus refers to here is the Transfiguration, not His actual second advent. But that is noteworthy, for the way Jesus worded it surely means that the Transfiguration of Messiah on the mount was a pre-signification of His coming. Peter seems to indicate this in his second epistle. Recalling the Transfiguration, he writes: "For we did not follow cunningly devised fables when we made known to you the power and coming of our Lord Jesus Christ but were eyewitnesses of His majesty" (2 Pet. 1:16).

So not only does the context encourage us to understand this event as a pre-enactment of the second coming, Peter's interpretation of it does too. This means that the "kingdom" to which Christ refers in this passage is the eschatological Kingdom (Matt. 16:28). I also think it very reasonable to infer that the presence of Moses and Elijah with Jesus on the mount must be kept in mind once we reach the two witnesses in Revelation 11:3-6.[99]

Certainly, it appears that the Lord Jesus laid a great deal of stress upon His coming Kingdom. We must always remember that His Kingdom stems from the Davidic covenant. While many covenant theologians tell us that the Davidic covenant is no

98 Although the critical text omits the word "new" from the verse, we know from Luke and Paul that this word was spoken.

99 Mal. 4 is about the second coming. Is it just coincidence that the last three persons mentioned are the "Sun of Righteousness" (Mal. 4:3), Moses (Mal. 4:4), and Elijah (Mal. 4:5)?

longer in force, such a statement can only be made because the covenants of God are not being taken seriously.

Twelve Thrones

> Jesus said to them, "Assuredly I say to you, that in the regeneration, when the Son of Man sits on the throne of His glory, you who have followed Me will also sit on twelve thrones, judging the twelve tribes of Israel" (Matt. 19:28).

In answer to Peter's remark that His disciples had left everything to follow Him, Jesus spoke these words of encouragement. Of interest to us in this biblical theology is the time reference that Jesus places on the rewards. He explicitly speaks of the time "when the Son of Man sits on the throne of His glory." This is not a reference to the throne in heaven, where Jesus sits at the Father's right hand (Acts 5:31; Rom. 8:34; Heb. 1:3; Rev. 3:21), for Jesus is not said to sit *on* the throne. And it is not referring to a throne He will be seated on immediately after ascending to heaven. No, this is a clear reference to the Davidic throne of His coming messianic Kingdom. Jesus will, in a future day, reign on this earth (Psa. 2:8; Jer. 23:5; Zech. 14:9).

But in His reply to Peter, the Lord promises that when He sits upon "His throne of glory" (cf. Isa. 24:23 NASB; 66:18; Dan. 7:14; Zech. 6:13; see also Psa. 24:8-10) the disciples will sit upon twelve thrones and judge the tribes of Israel.[100] This will happen in what Jesus calls "the regeneration," or *palingenesia.* The word "regeneration" suggests a remaking of the world, which is precisely what the OT Prophets foretold, and what the New covenant (in unison with the Noahic covenant[101]) will fully bring about (e.g., Isa. 32:15-17; 35:1-10; 55:12-13).

Despite how some schools of theology argue around it, this verse makes it manifestly obvious that the tribes of Israel, hence the nation of Israel, will be in existence in the coming messianic Kingdom.[102] This fully confirms the wording of the OT and its covenants. Texts such as this pose enormous problems for those who want to insist that the Church is the New Israel. Attempts to quietly expunge the plain sense of this passage so that it will not threaten realized eschatology take us from what God has spoken.[103]

100 See D. A. Carson, "Matthew," 425-426. Carson believes the "judgment" given to the twelve is for Israel rejection of Messiah. This is unlikely as the scene is after the new aeon has begun, not prior to that Kingdom. These are not temporary thrones.

101 The Noahic covenant was made with all creation. The New covenant does not only replace the Mosaic covenant, it has the power through Christ and His resurrection to transform the world (cf. Rom. 8:20-22).

102 Indeed, from an OT covenant perspective, how could there be a messianic Kingdom without the nation of Israel in their own land?

103 Joshua Jipp claims that this same promise is extended to "all of his followers" in the next verse (Matt. 19:29). See Jipp, *The Messianic Theology of the New Testament*, 53. But this is patently untrue, as any reader of verse 29 can verify for themselves.

"The Kingdom of God will be taken from you"

"Replacement theology" or "supersessionism" is the name that has been given to certain theologies whose protagonists assert that the covenant promises to national Israel given in the OT are fulfilled in Jesus Christ and the Church in Him. It needs to be emphasized that the majority of those who hold to this teaching in one form or another repudiate the moniker, preferring to call their views "fulfillment theology."[104] I will not labor the point here, but this text in particular acts as a touchstone text for understanding what is really going on.

The text sits just below the Parable of the Wicked Tenants (Matt. 21:33-42) and is connected with it. Jesus is speaking to the chief priests and elders (Matt. 21:23). Here are the verses: "Therefore I say to you, the kingdom of God will be taken from you and given to a nation bearing the fruits of it" (Matt. 21:43).

The key thing to understand about this verse is the question of whether Jesus is speaking of two distinct parties or groups. The one group being the nation of Israel, the second group would be the Church. This would result in the first group (Israel) having the kingdom of God taken away from them and it being given to another "nation," the Christian Church. In any fair understanding of the transaction, a replacement of one party with another party would be taking place. For the label "replacement theology" to stick we would need to see that different writers interpret this verse in the sense given above. Here are a few examples:

> 1. "Luke 21 reiterates and expands on this prediction of Jerusalem's judgment (vv. 20-24), specifically the destruction of the temple. That this destruction will also indicate a judgment of rejecting ethnic national Israel as God's true people is expressed in Matt. 21...In [Matt. 21:43], which interprets the conclusion of the parable in verse 41, again the psalm quotation is seen as the supporting reason for Israel's rejection from being God's steward... This verse interprets the conclusion of the parable... Israel's stewardship of God's kingdom will be taken away from it, and the gentiles will be given the stewardship."[105]
>
> 2. "Matthew 21:41, 43 say that this new form of the kingdom (and by implication of the temple) will be the gentiles, though we know from elsewhere that a remnant of ethnic Jewish believers will also identify with Jesus and join with the gentiles as the new form of the kingdom and temple, which is the church."[106]
>
> 3. "It is Matthew's assumption, probably unconscious at this point, that the life of God's people will continue in the life of the discipleship community, which allows him to identify the destroyed tenant farmers as the Jewish religious leaders but the replacement tenant farmers as the leaders of the Christian

104 A misnomer if ever there was one.
105 G. K. Beale, *A New Testament Biblical Theology*, 680-681.
106 Ibid., 681.

community. The continuing existence of the Jewish community that has not become Christian remains out of sight..."[107]

4. "Possibly the form of the language of this saying has been modified by tradition, but the central idea appears to be sound. The Jewish nation which has rejected the offer of the Kingdom of God has therefore been set aside as the people of God and is to be replaced by a new people."[108]

Although many interpreters state that the "you" in Matthew 21:43 refers to the religious leaders of Israel, there are those like Beale who are bold enough to say the "you" is the nation of Israel.[109]

Historic premillennialist Craig Blomberg has stated, "The church does not replace Israel without remainder...but it comes close, overlapping with the roles and functions once reserved for the Jewish nation."[110]

The proper interpretation is, I believe, more prosaic. Just as the outcasts who were brought in from the highways and byways in the Parable of the Wedding Feast (which follows in the next chapter), the fruit-bearing "nation" is Israel, but not the religious leaders of Jesus' day.[111] They would be replaced.[112] Joel Willits observes, "Matthew 21:45 makes clear that the intended audience got the message."[113]

The Odd Man Out

The parable that begins Matthew 22 pictures a king who invites the expected guests to his son's wedding, only to be turned down and, in some cases, treated with the utmost disdain. The king, therefore, sends servants out to gather a set of unexpected outcasts to attend. Upon entering the wedding hall, the king notices a man who has not bothered to put on a proper wedding garment. He is in attendance, but he shows as much contempt for the occasion as those who stayed away. No one gets into the kingdom without being prepared.

"O Jerusalem!"

Moving now to the end of Matthew 23, we run into these emotive words from the Lord:

---

107 John Nolland, *Gospel of Matthew*, 876.

108 George Eldon Ladd, *The Presence of the Future*, 249.

109 G. K. Beale, *A New Testament Biblical Theology*, 673. Charles L. Quarles is among many who believe that the tenants are apostate Israel, not just the leaders, and the new tenants are the Church (Quarles, *Matthew*, 542-543). In a footnote (543 n. 681), Quarles is clear that his interpretation is in no way antisemitic. I absolutely agree, but it is supersessionist.

110 Craig L. Blomberg, *A New Testament Theology*, 376.

111 See here Alva J. McClain, *The Greatness of the Kingdom*, 297: "The difference between the two nations is spiritual and moral, not racial."

112 Ed Glasscock, *Matthew*, 423.

113 Joel Willits, "Zionism in the Gospel of Matthew," in *The New Christian Zionism*, ed. Gerald R. McDermott (Downers Grove, IL: InterVarsity, 2016), 127.

> O Jerusalem, Jerusalem, the one who kills the prophets and stones those who are sent to her! How often I wanted to gather your children together, as a hen gathers her chicks under *her* wings, but you were not willing! See! Your house is left to you desolate; for I say to you, you shall see Me no more till you say, '*Blessed is He who comes in the name of the LORD*!' (Matt. 23:37-39).

This exclamation by Jesus at the end of His castigation of the scribes and the Pharisees is at once poignant and full of portent. Jesus is not speaking here merely as a prophet. A prophet does not gather people to himself but to God. Jesus is speaking both as Messiah and God. Of note also is how greatly prized Jerusalem is to Jesus. This accords with the prophetic witness, not to say with the expectations aroused by the New covenant. Here in this heartfelt cry, we can see that the covenant program has not been derailed, not even by Jesus' rejection by the religious movers and shakers. This is why Jesus' use of "until" is crucial. He is not thinking at all about rejecting Jerusalem, not to say Israel. His "until" anticipates the repentance of Israel with their consequent acceptance of Jesus as Messiah.[114] This awaits His second advent (cf. Zech. 12:10; Rev. 1:7).

The Olivet Discourse

We come at last to the Olivet Discourse in Matthew 24–25. The main descriptive section comes in Matthew 24, with an addendum at the end of Matthew 25, before which are two parables.

Matthew 24:1-2 belong on their own. What Jesus says prompts what follows. They provide the setting for the discourse that follows in that they refer to the glories of Herod's temple.[115] Jesus does not even acknowledge the great structure, which by His time was famous throughout the Empire. Instead, He predicts its devastation, which came upon it in A.D. 70.

Some are tempted to confine the verses that follow to the first century, but I think this is a mistake. Verse 3 is critical to what will follow: "Now as He sat on the Mount of Olives, the disciples came to Him privately, saying, 'Tell us, when will these things be? And what *will be* the sign of Your coming, and of the end of the age?'" (Matt. 24:3).

Jesus and His disciples have arrived at the Mount of Olives outside Jerusalem. The disciples, moved to further inquiry by Jesus' prophecy of the destruction of the temple, come to Him with more questions. Two questions are put to Jesus. The first refers to the overthrow of the temple that Jesus had just spoken of. The second question concerned Christ's coming (which He had already spoken about: Mk. 8:38; Lk. 12:40; 17:24[116]; 18:8; cf. Matt. 16:28; 19:28). This coming was understood to take

114 Cf. Romans 11:25-27.

115 Herod's temple was essentially a rebuilding of the temple built under Zerubbabel. Hence, both edifices are usually referred to as the Second Temple.

116 Jesus appears to have used the analogy of a lightning flash to speak of His second coming before Matt. 24.

place at the time of "the end of the age." If one pays close attention to the words recorded by the evangelist, it quickly becomes clear that the first question does not receive an answer (at least none is reported). Matthew's focus is upon the answer to the second question, the one about Christ's return and the end of the age. This can be decided by noticing the phenomena of men claiming to be Christ (Matt. 24:5, 24), false prophets abounding (Matt. 24:11, 24), the setting up of Daniel's "abomination of desolation" (Matt. 24:15), greatly intensified tribulation reminiscent of Daniel 12 (Matt. 24:21-22), and the signs of the second coming itself (Matt. 24:29-31), with its depiction of Christ judging the nations to determine who goes into life and who faces punishment (Matt. 25:31-46). These particulars are not to be swept away with the magic word "apocalyptic." They direct our attention away from the first century and onto events just prior to and including the second advent. This conclusion is reinforced by the repetition of the term "the end" in the first half of the discourse (Matt. 24:3, 6, 13, 14). This also corresponds to the employment of "the end" in Matthew 10:22; 13:39-40, 49, cf. 28:20.

The Sign of Christ's Coming and the End of the Age

Since Jesus' remarks concern the second question of the disciples, their question about Christ's coming and the end of the age, it is vital we get the setting of these remarks right. First, "the beginning of sorrows" (Matt. 24:8) includes what appears to be world upheaval, both societal and natural (Matt. 24:6-7). Of course, there have always been "wars and rumors of wars." Hence, the only way to make sense of this would appear to be in terms of an undeniable explosion of war and mayhem. This concentration of wars is combined with false prophesying and "many" people falsely claiming to be Christ (Matt. 24:4-5).[117] We must look for wars, widespread civil unrest, natural calamities, disease, false Messiahs, and false prophets occurring *together*. People will be alarmed and fall prey to deception. This will precede the end, but "the end is not yet" (Matt. 24:6), meaning, I believe, that before Christ's second coming, the world (or at the very least the Middle East[118]) will be thrown into confusion and chaos amid claims of pseudo-messiahs.

In this time period, the saints will be persecuted (I take the "you" here as anticipatory, referring to Christ's followers in that future time). The general alarm will be exploited by false prophets (Matt. 24:9-12), who will encourage the persecution. It is within this context that we must fit the warning, "He who endures to the end shall be saved" (Matt. 24:13).

What does the saying mean? I think the very first question to be asked is, Does the phrase "the end" in verse 13 mean the same as it does in verses 3, 6, and 14? Or does it mean something like "the end of one's life" or "the end of one's trial"? I see no

117 Not many men in history have made this claim. The most famous was Simon Bar-Kokhba, who was overthrown by Rome in A.D. 135. Rabbi Akiba believed he was the Christ (see https://www.jewishhistory.org/bar-kochba/).

118 It is unclear whether these end time predictions of Jesus have the entire world in view or just the area covered in His time by the Roman Empire, West and East.

reason to believe that this second answer is correct. The end should mean "the end of the age," as it does in the rest of its usages in the discourse. If this is correct, we may paraphrase verse 13 as, "He who makes it through to the return of Christ." To bring in Matthew 25:41-46, it would mean that those *saints* who survive the persecution will be ushered into the Kingdom.

But doesn't this create a tautology? Am I simply stating that the ones who make it through the final torrid days of this age are the ones who escape death? Of course, the question of what the verb "saved" means in this verse is critical. If it means the salvation of the soul, then the problem of tautology vanishes, but the possible problem of works raises its head. Does one have to endure to have their soul saved? If so, how is this connected to the matter of justification? If, however, "saved" equates to survival, the tautology reappears. Or does it? What if we paraphrase things a bit? What if it means "the believer who gets through the Tribulation will be rescued and will enter the peaceable Kingdom"? Glasscock writes, "Contextually, the salvation being discussed here was not eternal redemption but deliverance from the persecutions and wretchedness of the world."[119]

Which is it? Unless one is intent on removing the contextual markers that place the passage in an eschatological and Tribulational setting, the two options I have just set out remain. My own position is that the second option is preferable. Saints who somehow make it through the coming Tribulation (which I equate with Daniel's seventieth week, Dan. 9:24-27) will be ushered into the Kingdom of Christ. They may be the same as "the righteous" of Matthew 25:46.

The Gospel of the Kingdom and the End of the Age

I have said that it is essential to interpret the Olivet Discourse in light of the way Jesus answered the *second* question that He was asked in Matthew 24:3.[120] So far, I have tried to show that the whole direction of the discourse points to the end times and not to the first century A.D. This impression only deepens as the chapter proceeds. In the next verse, Jesus remarks, "And this gospel of the kingdom will be preached in all the world as a witness to all the nations, and then the end will come" (Matt. 24:14).

This statement is immediately followed by the warning about seeing "the abomination of desolation spoken of by Daniel the prophet" (Matt. 24:15). That verse, as well as what has gone before, places the preaching of the "gospel of the kingdom" at the time of "the end." As hard to take as it may be for many, the plain fact is that the Gospel of Matthew does not know anything about the good news involving Christ's substitutionary atonement and His resurrection for our justification (cf. Rom. 4:25; 1 Cor. 15:1-4).[121] The "gospel" of Matthew's narrative is "the kingdom of heaven is at hand" (Matt. 3:2; 4:17; 10:7), and when Matthew 4:23 and 9:35 speak of "the gospel

119 Ed Glasscock, *Matthew*, 466-467.

120 Most scholars believe that the destruction of the temple in A.D. 70 is addressed by Jesus in Lk. 21:12-24. As can be seen from my comments on that passage, I respectfully disagree.

121 Most commentators routinely conflate this "gospel of the kingdom" with the gospel of Paul without considering the contextual problem. Cf. Charles Quarles, *Matthew*, 608-609.

of the kingdom," it appears that the message of the soon arrival of the kingdom is what is being spoken of.[122] As a matter of fact, although Jesus does mention His forthcoming death and resurrection in Matthew 16:21, 17:23, and 26:31-32, it was not done openly, and the disciples are not portrayed as fully comprehending His meaning. One may fairly ask then, aside from the dissonance that these facts may produce within us, is it not true that the gospel of the kingdom presented in Matthew is *different* in content than the gospel in Paul's letters?[123] The blunt but unwelcome answer is yes!

What then are we to do with this prediction by Christ about the gospel of the kingdom being preached for a "witness" before the end comes? One thing we must say is that this text has nothing to do with present world missions, laudable as they are.[124] A point that follows hard on its heels is that the gospel of the kingdom, viz., "the kingdom of heaven is at hand," which made sense at the first coming before Christ's rejection, begins to make sense again, only in light of Christ's imminent second coming. This is just what we see in Matthew's narration. My conclusion again is that Matthew 24:14 refers to the time of the Tribulation.[125]

The Image and the Great Tribulation

It is usual for dispensationalists to divide the seventieth week of Daniel 9—a week that lasts for seven years—into two halves of three and a half years each. There are good reasons for this, which I shall discuss, but this clean division is not as apparent when one concentrates solely on the Olivet Discourse. After the verse about the preaching of "the gospel of the kingdom," the passage continues like this:

> "Therefore when you see the '*abomination of desolation*,' spoken of by Daniel the prophet, standing in the holy place" (whoever reads, let him understand), "then let those who are in Judea flee to the mountains. Let him who is on the housetop not go down to take anything out of his house. And let him who is in the field not go back to get his clothes. But woe to those who are pregnant and to those who are nursing babies in those days! And pray that your flight may not be in winter or on the Sabbath. For then there will be great tribulation, such as has not been since the beginning of the world until this time, no, nor ever shall be And unless those days were shortened, no flesh would be saved; but for the elect's sake those days will be shortened" (Matt. 24:15-22).

122 In Matt. 24:14 the pronoun "*touto*" is to be translated as "this," which refers the reader back to the proclamation of Jesus and His disciples about the coming Kingdom.

123 One must face the fact that the word *euangelion* ("gospel" or "good news") does not possess a technical meaning in the four Gospels like it does in the later NT.

124 Pauline references to the Gospel going out to all the world (e.g., Col. 1:5-6, 23) are clearly hyperbole. In any case, the "gospel of the kingdom" in the context of Matthew's narrative does not include Christ's vicarious death and resurrection.

125 Cf. Heb. 4:1-2; Rev. 14:6-7.

Jesus refers to Daniel as a prophet who predicted something called "the abomination of desolation" (Dan. 11:31; 12:11).[126] Whatever it is, it *stands* "in the holy place." The name "the holy place" is an OT term designating the temple. That is to say, this abomination will stand in the temple! To Jesus' hearers the temple means only one thing: the Jerusalem temple. Yet for Jesus, Daniel's prophecy is still future. The reaction of "those in Judea" is to flee. They flee because some *thing* is "standing" in the temple in Jerusalem.[127] That "abomination of desolation" is the signal for intense persecution at the end.

But what could the abomination be? The natural conclusion is that it is some sort of statue or image.[128] There is another place in the NT where this imagery is cited. In Revelation 13 a person called "the beast" is worshipped by the "earth-dwellers" (Rev. 13:3-9). He has an accomplice called "the false prophet" who seems to act as his agent and mouthpiece, but who possesses supernatural powers that enable him to deceive with great signs and wonders and to persuade men to make an *image* of the beast, which then comes alive (Rev. 13:11-15).[129] Those who will not worship the image are persecuted and killed (Rev. 13:15).

One further text that may have a bearing on the image of Matthew 24:15 is mentioned by the Apostle Paul in 2 Thessalonians 2:3-4 where someone called "the man of sin/son of perdition" goes into "the temple of God" and "sits" in it "as God." Since the beast receives worship, it is not a far stretch to suppose that he would enter a temple of worship. Nor is it supposing too much to envisage him placing an image of himself in the same temple.[130] But which temple? Well, if it is the same temple that Jesus speaks about as "the holy place" in Matthew 24:15, it would be situated in Jerusalem in Judea.

This setting up of "the abomination of desolation" is linked to "the great tribulation" (Matt. 24:21). Hence, most dispensational premillennialists have identified the great tribulation as beginning at the mid-point of the seventieth week mentioned in Daniel 9, and I believe that they are right. I have made comments on this in Volume One,[131] but something should be said about it here.

---

126 In Dan. 9:27 there is a reference to "the wing of abominations" and making "desolate." This passage is hard to understand and may not be what Jesus is speaking about in Matt. 24. See however, the detailed exegesis of J. Paul Tanner in his *Daniel*, EEC (Bellingham: WA: Lexham Press, 2020), 590-596. Tanner's commentary cannot be overlooked.

127 The prophetic context is so crucial to getting the interpretation right. Jesus is still answering the question about the end time. This ought to dismiss out of hand attempts to locate the "abomination" in the first couple of centuries A.D. See e.g., Charles Quarles, *Matthew*, 612-615. The passage hones-in upon Israel: Judea, holy place, rooftop, Sabbath. It is not concerned so much with worldwide trouble, but rather Israel's trouble—"Jacob's Trouble" (Jer. 30:7).

128 For example, the altar raised up by Antiochus Epiphanes in 168 B.C. had an abomination "set up" or "built" upon it according to 1 Macc. 1:54.

129 More will be said about this when we consider the book of Revelation.

130 I shall of course say more about this "Beast" in the course of this book.

131 See *The Words of the Covenant*, Vol 1, 315-317.

The Seventieth Week of Daniel and the Great Tribulation

Although I intend to say more about this and related themes later in this volume, the occurrence of it in the Olivet Discourse affords an opportunity to try to connect the period of intense trouble spoken about in the Prophets with Jesus' words here.

Taken as weeks of years, the seventy heptads or weeks of Daniel 9:24 total up to 490 years. But Daniel 9:25 refers to the completion of just sixty-nine weeks, or 483 years. The seventieth week is mentioned in verse 27 in a fascinating, if obscure, passage:

> Then he shall confirm a covenant with many for one week;
> But in the middle of the week
> He shall bring an end to sacrifice and offering.
> And on the wing of abominations shall be one who makes desolate,
> Even until the consummation, which is determined,
> Is poured out on the desolate (Dan. 9:27).

The "he" of the verse logically refers back to "the prince" or "ruler" (*nagid*), whose people are mentioned in the previous verse.[132] This prince is said to make a covenant, or possibly force a covenant of seven years duration.[133] The seven-year period is the final week of the seventy weeks determined upon Daniel's people and Jerusalem (Dan. 9:24). Note where the focus is: upon Israel, just as in Matthew 24:16-20.

The covenant that this prince will make is not described.[134] It is enough to know that this prince does something "in the middle of the week" (i.e., after three and a half years) that is related to the covenant—he stops the sacrifices and offerings. The very fact that sacrifices and offerings are being made indicates strongly that a temple is present and a sacrificial system is in full swing. Along with other premillennial interpreters, I believe that we are obliged to see a close connection between the seven-year covenant and the rebuilding of the temple at Jerusalem in the closing years of our era before the return of Christ.

Matthew then is focused upon Israel, just as was Daniel (Dan. 9:24). Christ's description of catastrophic events in Matthew 24/Mark 13 also calls to mind what Jeremiah calls "the time of Jacob's trouble" (Jer. 30:7), about which the prophet says, "Alas, for that day is great, so that none is like it," and after which Israel will serve Yahweh their God, and "David their king." Jeremiah 30:7 is very close in meaning to Jesus' words, "For then there will be great tribulation, such as has not been since the beginning of the world until this time, no, nor ever shall be" (Matt. 24:21). It is also close to Daniel's words, "And there shall be a time of trouble, such as never was since

132 Those who try to force it to mean the Messiah are not following the author himself. See J. Paul Tanner, *Daniel*, 590-591. Tanner includes a footnote (297) in which he notices several amillennial scholars who agree that this "prince" is the future antichrist.

133 Ibid., 592-593.

134 Tanner thinks it is most likely the Mosaic covenant. I am not so sure. Unbelievably, Riddlebarger thinks it is the covenant of grace! Kim Riddlebarger, *A Case for Amillennialism: Understanding the End Times* (Grand Rapids: Baker, 2003), 155.

there was a nation" (Dan. 12:1), which concerns "the time of the end" according to Daniel 12:8.

There is then to be a time in history when the rage and violence against the Jews and Jerusalem will be worse than at any other time in their history. This prophecy is not referring to the Holocaust, as terrible as that was, since it does not match the prophetic picture. No, this "great tribulation" is yet to come. It is concentrated in the last half of the seventieth week and is associated with the coming evil potentate who enters a rebuilt temple in Jerusalem, erects a statue of himself, and claims to be divine.[135]

But why does this "man of sin," this "son of perdition" (2 Thess. 2:3) turn on the Jews and their capital city? An obvious answer is that they will not accept his claims to be God. That may well be, but one has to remember that the OT does present Messiah as having divine attributes (Isa. 7:14; Mic. 5:2; Zech. 14). One can imagine how passages like Isaiah 2:3-4 and Malachi 3:1 could be recontextualized and applied to the false messiah. I, therefore, think something more than this will be in play.

Jesus' Olivet Discourse picks up the note of latter-day tribulation for Israel, adding revelation to the OT picture. With respect, the person who wants to cram the seventieth week into the first century is not attending to what these passages are saying. What is clear is that the persecution will be so ferocious that "unless those days were shortened, no flesh [i.e., in Israel] would be saved" (Matt. 24:22).

EXCURSUS: Alternative Views of the Seventieth Week[136]

Because the idea of a rebuilt temple and sacrifices is impossible to some people (based often upon a misreading of Hebrews 8–10), they dismiss this construction out of hand. What they offer in its place appears to me to involve a combination of a flight of the imagination coupled with a determined resistance to the details of this passage and those verses that overlap with it. Basically, there are two alternatives to the interpretation I have given. The first is to pack the whole seventieth week into the first century A.D., which requires dividing it in half with a gap of forty years in between. The second is to elongate the second "half" of the week so that it stretches out for nearly two thousand years! Those scholars who see a fulfillment of this prophecy in the first revolt of the Jewish War in A.D. 66–70 point to a number of facts which, they say, account for the details in Daniel and Matthew.

There are substantial problems with this view. Firstly, and fatally, it ignores the subject under discussion, which is *not* the destruction of Herod's temple in A.D. 70 but the "sign of [Christ's] coming and of the end of the age" (Matt. 24:3b; 6, 14, 15, 27-31). As we have seen and will continue to see, Jesus is prophesying about the end times and the circumstances surrounding His second coming. Secondly, the actual siege of Jerusalem began in the summer of A.D. 68 but was not prosecuted in full

135 One perceived problem with this is that these "signs of the times" disqualify any notion of an anytime coming of Jesus Christ. But this is not necessarily true. The doctrine of imminence, if it is true, regards the perspective of the Church. Therefore, a pretribulationist can easily assert an immanent rapture while allowing for these signs of distress in the seventieth week.

136 For a good summary of the various positions on the Seventieth Week, see now the Appendix in Tanner, *Daniel*, 774ff.

until the following year.[137] This means that it took at most two years for Jerusalem to fall, not the three and a half years needed for the first or last halves of the seventieth week.[138] Thirdly, this position also ignores the fact that the entire seventy weeks are determined upon Israel and Jerusalem, as foretold in Daniel 9:24.

This brings us to another problem, which is that the destruction of the temple occurred forty years after the crucifixion and resurrection of Jesus and into the era of the Church. A gap in time is therefore not averted. Either there is a forty-year gap between the first half of the seventieth week or another way to account for the last three-and-a-half-year period must be created. Amazingly enough, the novel position of those who cannot bring themselves to see that the seventieth week begins "after Messiah the Prince is cut off" (Dan. 9:26) is to elasticize the second half of the week and turn it into the entire period of Church history from the ascension to the second coming![139] They do this while taking the first half of the seventieth week literally, together with all the other 483 years of the prophecy. Apart from it producing an outrageous hermeneutical chimera, this position ignores (yet again) the resolute fact that the seventy weeks' prophecy concerns Israel, *not* the Church.

False Christs and the True Christ

Jesus continues His answer to the disciples' second question by repeating the assertion that although there will be many false Christs and false prophets and many attention-grabbing supernatural happenings in that time, one ought not to be fooled (Matt. 24:23-24). We should take note that, contrary to the scientistic naturalism so prevalent among "intellectuals" in our day, the Tribulation will be charged with spectacular supernatural manifestations and calls to worship. It will be an extremely "spiritual" time, with no room for cool rationalism.

Matthew 24:27 says that the real coming of Christ will be so singular and incontrovertible that nobody could mistake it. It will be like a blast of sheet lightning across the sky. Therefore, during this short period, one can expect news outlets to work overtime in disseminating their propaganda and false flags, "signs and wonders" distracting the masses, groupthink fomenting "the madness of crowds," and the label "conspiracy theorist" and the like aimed at any who will not accept the "fact" that God has come to earth in the person of the future "prince."

137 L. L. Grabbe, "Jewish Wars with Rome," in *Dictionary of New Testament Background*, eds. Craig A. Evans and Stanley E. Porter (Downers Grove, IL: InterVarsity, 2000), 586-587.

138 Hence, if Jerusalem was under siege for two years rather than three and a half years, it means that one cannot connect it with the seventieth week. There is another position which teaches that the seventieth week began at Christ's baptism and ended around the conversion of Paul in Acts 9, but the latter half of the seventieth week does not fit this scenario.

139 E.g., "The final three-and-one-half years of the seventieth week as interpreted by John is symbolic of the church on earth during the entire time of its existence. It also is a reference to the tribulation depicted in Daniel" (Kim Riddlebarger, *A Case for Amillennialism*, 156).

The Return!

> Immediately after the tribulation of those days the sun will be darkened, and the moon will not give its light; the stars will fall from heaven, and the powers of the heavens will be shaken. Then the sign of the Son of Man will appear in heaven, and then all the tribes of the earth will mourn, and they will see the Son of Man coming on the clouds of heaven with power and great glory. And He will send His angels with a great sound of a trumpet, and they will gather together His elect from the four winds, from one end of heaven to the other (Matt. 24:29-31).

The second coming of Christ is the beginning point of the real New World Order, not the utopian nightmare of the elite classes. Jesus' coming again into the world that He made but that crucified Him is not, as I understand it, the second part of a two-part drama, but better the second phase of a single work, sandwiching the pre-decreed time of the Church.

In His continuing narrative on the Mount of Olives, Jesus predicts that right on the heels of the Tribulation, great cosmic signs will be beheld, involving the sun, the moon, and the stars. That is, the "firmament" of Genesis 1 will start to work erratically. Providence, which through Christ upholds the normal functions of the sky (cf. Col. 1:17; Heb. 1:3b), will falter, thus declaring to blind humanity (the "earth-dwellers" of Revelation 3:10; 6:10; 11:10; 13:8, etc.) the reality of his dependent creaturehood and the imminent shift in the control of the world-system. Jesus refers to a sign: "The sign of the Son of Man will appear in heaven" (Matt. 24:30). Whatever it is, this "sign" will be in contrast to the malfunctioning of the heavens that presages it. Some suppose the sign is the Shekinah-glory of Ezekiel 43:1-5, but that cannot enter until the Millennial temple has been built, which will not happen until after the second advent (see Zech. 14:4).

According to the passage, the earth will witness not just intense suffering, whether localized around Israel or spread out throughout all lands, but it will have become familiar with remarkable manifestations of spiritual power. But nothing will compare to what happens next! Jesus, the Danielic Son of Man, will appear "on the clouds of heaven" (Matt. 24:30). His countenance will be terrible, His grandeur intoxicating, His evident power devastating.

At the sight of the returning Christ, a loud trumpet sound is heard, and angels descend for the purpose of gathering up the elect. The "elect" in view are most likely believing Jews (Isa. 65:9) but might perceivably include all Tribulation saints, although this would require a widened context. One thing they are not is the Church.[140] We are not told where the saints are taken, but as earth becomes the scene of the Kingdom, it seems likely that they are carried to a place of safety ahead of the vengeance of a wrathful Christ (Isa. 61:1-2; 63:1-6; 2 Thess. 1:6-9; Rev. 19:11-16).

---

140 See below.

"This Generation"

In Matthew 24:34, after providing all of this detail concerning the Tribulation, Jesus says these words: "Assuredly, I say to you, this generation will by no means pass away till all these things take place."

It ought to be easy enough to divine from what has been said about Christ's visible (second) coming in the preceding verses that the "generation" being referred to is the end time generation who will witness it.[141] However, those who wish to cram all of this language into fulfillment in A.D. 70 go ahead and spiritualize the "all these things" Jesus has just mentioned so they can teach an invisible *parousia* involving a thorough revision of the Lord's words. This is a good example of man's default of independence in top gear in the minds of some of the saints. There is no middle ground between these "re-interpreters" and ourselves. They will interpret the words of God one way and we will interpret them another way, and "never the twain may meet." I do not wish to be uncharitable, but this teaching demonstrates a decided refusal to follow an argument (Matt. 24:3c, 6, 13, 14, 15-22, 27, 29-31).

"As in the Days of Noah"

I cannot expound every verse in Matthew, or any other book for that matter, so I jump to Mathew 24:36, where Jesus picks up the thread of verses 15-31. He refers to a "day and hour" that remains unknown to all but God the Father.[142] This reminds us that "the Creation Project," which God began "in the beginning," is still running and will run until the new heavens and new earth are fashioned. This "day and hour" is too specific to mean the entire second half of the Tribulation. It relates to the advent itself. Thus, immediately before Christ comes, people will be going about their business, which is what is meant by "eating and drinking, marrying and giving in marriage" (Matt. 24:38), but then the day and hour will be upon them. Just as the rain began falling once God shut Noah in the Ark (Gen. 7:1-10), so the intervention in the affairs of life by the returning Christ will take place all of a sudden.

But doesn't this way of putting things ignore the terrible sufferings that will be experienced during this time? How can life go on as normal with "people eating and drinking, marrying and giving in marriage" (Matt. 24:38) in the midst of so much upheaval?[143]

My answer is somewhat tentative since I do not believe the Scriptures furnish us with enough information to construct the end times picture with the degree of detail we would like. But the fact is that there have always been many whose lives were only

141 I should say something about the "fig tree" illustration in Matt. 24:32. The fig tree is just used for the analogy (like e.g., Jn. 12:24) and possesses no more significance than the "carcass" and the "eagles" in Matt. 24:28.

142 Mk. 13:32 says that not even Jesus knows this information. We must parse such sayings carefully. The Lord is saying that as the Servant of God He is unaware of the exact timing of His return. This is because He has willingly set aside His divine prerogatives such as omniscience and omnipresence in order to become who He had to become for us. (cf. Phil. 2:5-8; Heb. 10:9-10).

143 This is the question put by John F. Hart. See part 2 of his "Should Pretribulationists Reconsider the Rapture in Matthew 24:36-44?" *JOTGES* 21 (Spring 2008), 47.

tangentially affected by evil times, especially the rich and powerful. In what may well be an allusion to the same Tribulation, the Apostle John records the black horse rider ordered not to touch the oil and the wine; products consumed by the wealthy (Rev. 6:5-6). In a similar manner, Paul, when speaking of the Day of the Lord, says that unbelievers will be celebrating "peace and safety" just before "sudden destruction comes upon them" (1 Thess. 5:3). These passages at least indicate that life's patterns can continue in evil times, at least for some, and often the "some" number many more than one might think. But I am, of course, reading this group of "elites" into the passage!

Another thing to consider is the extent and intensity of the "time of Jacob's trouble." I think it is very possible that the "Great Tribulation" will impact some areas a lot more than others, particularly in the Levant. I am not saying that it will not be felt on other continents, but perhaps not to the same extent.

Then Jesus mentions the two men and two women in Matthew 24:40-42: "Then two *men* will be in the field: one will be taken and the other left. Two *women will be* grinding at the mill: one will be taken and the other left. Watch therefore, for you do not know what hour your Lord is coming." I have made comments about this saying already in my chapter on Luke. Are these verses speaking of the rapture or removal of the saints before God's wrath? If we examine verse 42 first, we see that Jesus is issuing a warning. But is the warning about being taken or being left? It is not easy to be definite, although as with Luke, the example of Noah tilts the interpretation toward those taken being carried to safety (Luke also includes Lot, Lk. 17:28-29).[144] Glasscock writes:

> It might be best to understand the taking of these as the collecting of the elect of v. 31 (not the rapture of the church, but the gathering of the sealed Jews and faithful Gentiles of the Tribulation) and leaving the others behind for the judgment about to come on the earth.[145]

Matthew 13:41-43 and 13:47-50 appear to have the angels gathering the unbelievers to judgment with the saints being left to enter the Kingdom. This *may* mean that my position given above needs reversing. But I still feel justified in my interpretation, for I do not believe Matthew 13 precludes the saints being carried to safety before the ungodly are dealt with. Moreover, the separation in Matthew 13 appears to take place *after* Jesus has returned (see below the separation of "the sheep and the goats" in Matthew 25:31ff.), and thus describes a different situation than Matthew 24:40-42.

144 I do think that an argument can be made for a "rapture" in Matt. 24:40-41 when it is combined with Rev. 14:14-16, but it is not decisive. Moreover, I cannot see the Church in either context.

145 Ed Glasscock, *Matthew*, 477.

EXCURSUS: Is the Church in Matthew 24?

So far in our study of Matthew, we have only come across the Church once,[146] in the famous prediction of Matthew 16:18. In that context, Jesus is not speaking of the presence of the Church in His day. He was telling His followers of what was to be in the future. The Church was not yet in existence![147]

Since the two mentions of the Church in Matthew clearly point to it being a future reality from the point of view of the narrative, it should be asked whether there are good reasons to think that the Church is in view in the Olivet Discourse. Granted, the chapters are prophetic, but that does not in itself mean that the Church ought to be read into them.

From our survey of Matthew 24 (and Luke 21) we have seen that the focus is upon Israel, Jerusalem, and the Jews (e.g., Matt. 24:15-20; Lk. 21:20-24[148]), and this matches Daniel 7:21-27, where "the saints of the Most High" are Jews.

Some interpreters like to point to the Great Commission, where the last verses in the book states: "Go therefore and make disciples of all the nations, baptizing them in the name of the Father and of the Son and of the Holy Spirit, teaching them to observe all things that I have commanded you; and lo, I am with you always, *even* to the end of the age. Amen (Matt. 28:19-20).

Utilizing this verse, which does reach to the Church age, and bringing it into Matthew 24, which apparently does not, the words "to the end of the age" mirror the disciples' question in Matthew 24:3. The reasoning is then that since these words are in both chapters, and the Great Commission concerns the Church (that is, these men will be the first participants in the Body of Christ), one is justified in seeing the Church in the Olivet Discourse.

The trouble with this is that whether the Church was there or not would make no difference. This is because if the Church is absent during the seventieth week,[149] the Great Commission in Matthew 28 would still be pertinent.[150] So, although the phrase "to the end of the age" is the same, the contexts are not the same. Those who claim the Church is in the Olivet Discourse can only do so on the basis of other passages from Scripture, not from Matthew 24–25, Luke 21, or Mark 13.

Added to this, we must take seriously the fact that Jeremiah 30:7 calls the Tribulation (or at least the last half of it) "the time of Jacob's trouble," not the time of the Church's trouble or even the earth's trouble. And in Daniel 7 and 12 the people in view are in Israel. Finally, the tribulational chapters in the book of Revelation (Rev.

---

146 It is very probable of course that the discipline text in Matt. 18:17 concerns the future Church. That passage only makes sense once Jesus has departed, and the disciples form the foundation of the Church (Eph. 2:20).

147 I commit a whole chapter to the necessity of the Church being a post-resurrection reality later in this book.

148 I have already given reasons for believing this passage does not primarily refer to A.D. 70.

149 My position on the removal of the Church (the rapture) is cautiously pretribulational. This is something I will discuss later in the book.

150 Please note that I am not fallaciously arguing that since the pretribulational rapture is fact, the Church is not present in Matthew 24–25. The Great Commission is quite generic and fits both Church-age and Tribulation settings.

6 to 19) do not mention the Church either. Although these absences are no more than circumstantial proof for pretribulationism, those mid-trib, prewrath, and post-trib proponents who have the Church going through some or all of the seventieth week must provide solid arguments for their views that are not plagued by circular reasoning.

The Parable of the Ten Virgins

The two parables that begin chapter 25 both have lead-ins that state, "The kingdom of heaven is like" (Matt. 25:1, 14). The second of these, the Parable of the Talents (Matt. 25:14-30),[151] is about stewardship in honoring the King. Glasscock hits the nail on the head:

> The Lord's point was that the kingdom ... was calling servants to honor and glorify its King. Those who failed to do so demonstrated they were not true servants but wicked, lazy, and useless usurpers of the prerogatives of the kingdom ... primarily this parable relates to Israel, who claimed a desire to serve their King but in reality squandered His blessings. Any temptation to relate this to the church or associate the "talents" with skills or abilities, especially spiritual gifting, is eisegesis.[152]

The first parable is about the wise and foolish virgins and concerns "the day [and] the hour" of Christ's coming (Matt. 25:13; cf. 24:36). The story is simple. Ten virgins (sort of maids in waiting who have not yet been married) are looking out for the bridegroom. Only five virgins prepare their lamps for the coming night, and when it comes, five are away buying oil while the bridegroom arrives and leaves. Five virgins were unprepared for the bridegroom's coming (cf. Matt. 24:44). In this parable, we find more support for those "taken" in Matthew 24 being the saints, while the unprepared remain.

The Sheep and the Goats

The Olivet discourse closes with Jesus depicting a scene that happens *after* His second advent. Again, it should not escape notice that since Jesus began to answer the disciples' question in Matthew 24:4, the focus has been upon the end time and the second coming. Let us look at how the section begins:

> When the Son of Man comes in His glory, and all the holy angels with Him, then He will sit on the throne of His glory. All the nations will be gathered before Him, and He will separate them one from another, as a shepherd divides *his* sheep from the goats. And He will set the sheep on His right hand, but the goats on the left (Matt. 25:31-33).

---

151 Although some writers hold that the Parable of the Talents is repeated in Mark 13 and Luke 21, I am one of those who demur. There are too many dissimilarities between Matthew's account and the other Gospels. See Ed Glasscock, *Matthew*, 484ff.

152 Ibid., 488.

This judgment appears to complement the Parable of the Talents. In that passage too, the King returns and deals with people and their service (or lack of it) toward Him. Note that whereas the parable has the King interacting with individuals (e.g., Matt. 25:24-27), the "Sheep and Goats Judgment" pictures Him addressing and being addressed by groups ("those on His right hand," "the righteous," "those on His left hand," Matt. 25:34, 37, 41). We are not told how the wicked among "the nations" remain after the second coming, but nothing contradicts what we have already been told in Matthew 13:41-43 and 49-50 as long as one allows this passage in Matthew 25 to throw light on those parables. What we are told here must mean that, for example, the dividing off of "those things that offend" in the Parable of the Dragnet (Matt. 13:47-50) occurs subsequent to the Lord's return. Clearly King Jesus has some house-cleaning to do before He can begin His rule of *shalom* in earnest.[153]

The passage indicates that it is "the nations" that are being judged (Matt. 25:32). This word *ethnos* usually signifies Gentiles in contrast to Jews. The entry in Balz and Schneider is unambiguous: "Matthew describes the Son of Man's judgment of 'all ἔθνη.' According to Matthew's usage and the context and content of the pericope, 'all ἔθνη' must refer to those peoples (outside Israel!) to whom the message of Christ has not reached or rejected it."[154]

Granted that "the nations" equal the Gentile nations, are we justified in maintaining that those Jesus refers to as "My brethren" are Jews? It appears that may be so, although it should be admitted that taking "My brethren" (Matt. 25:40) as meaning "My fellow Jews" is more than a short stride. It may well refer to all believers in that day.[155]

The treatment of the "goats" is as severe as it could be. Those at Christ's left hand depart to "everlasting punishment"; a fate which corresponds to the "everlasting life" of those on His right (Matt. 25:46). There can be no doubt that if the "sheep" enter eternal bliss, then the "goats" enter eternal punishment. There is no room at all in this verse for the notion of a temporary hell, still less for annihilationism.[156]

Further Covenantal Episodes

The final three chapters of the Gospel of Matthew are mainly taken up with the betrayal,[157] death, and resurrection of our Lord. Jesus' death is linked to the New covenant (just as in Luke), although Matthew places the emphasis upon the remission

153 This calls to mind the mysterious time delay one reads about in Dan. 12:11-12, where the difference between the length of days in those verses many indicate the time needed for this "shake up" immediately after Christ's arrival.

154 N. Walter, "ἔθνος" in *Exegetical Dictionary of the New Testament*, eds. Horst Balz and Gerhard Schneider, Vol. 1 (Grand Rapids: Eerdmans, 1999), 383.

155 There is an element of works in the verdict: "Assuredly, I say to you, inasmuch as you did not do *it* to one of the least of these, you did not do *it* to Me" (Matt. 25:45). Perhaps this is because the circumstances will require true faith to reveal itself through good works? Compare Heb. 11.

156 It is my opinion that the Lord's question, "Serpents, brood of vipers! How can you escape the condemnation of hell?" in Matt. 23:33 effectively annihilates "annihilationism."

157 On a side note, it is interesting to read how Judas had the gall to ask Jesus "is it I?" after he had already agreed to betray Him (Matt. 26:14-16, 25).

of sins (Matt. 26:28). After the institution of the Lord's Supper, Jesus is arrested after being picked out by Judas (Matt. 26:47-51). The violent reaction of Peter, though understandable, evinced ignorance of the larger Project:

> Jesus said to him, "Put your sword in its place, for all who take the sword will perish by the sword. Or do you think that I cannot now pray to My Father, and He will provide Me with more than twelve legions of angels? How then could the Scriptures be fulfilled, that it must happen thus?" (Matt. 26:52-54).

The thing that was on Jesus' mind was the obedient carrying out of the crucial part of the Creation Project: the plan for the self-sacrifice of the Son of God on behalf of the sins of man and of the regeneration of creation through His resurrection in the cursed world. Peter's sword, or all the swords in the world for that matter, would not have sufficed to keep God's covenant on track. The only path ahead was the cross.[158] Avoidance of Golgotha through either the perpetual holding off of His enemies or by their destruction—which would have been the result had twelve legions of angels been sent to His aid (Matt. 26:53)—would have produced the same effect as if Jesus had succumbed to Satan's temptation in the wilderness (Matt. 4:1-11). The Scriptures had to be fulfilled, and that meant literally![159]

"If He is the King of Israel"

We have seen that Matthew employs the idea of the Kingdom in two basic ways. At the beginning of his Gospel, "the kingdom" is the eschatological Kingdom of OT expectation. In the parables, however, the introductory phrase "the kingdom of heaven is like" points to images of the progress of the kingdom program as it wends its way to final fulfillment; only now and then is the age to come in view. Now that He is in the hands of His foes, it looks to most onlookers as though this man cannot be the Messiah. He is powerless against those who wish Him dead, being fully submitted to the non-exercise of divine prerogatives or authority, even though He once appeared as the "Commander of the army of Yahweh" (Josh. 5:14).

Matthew 27:26-50 is one of the most intensely stirring recitals ever penned. From one angle it seems to give the lie to all the grand expectations of the OT of the great Coming One. Surely, we are mistaken about Jesus. He is defeated. He goes to meet death, having barely made a splash in the world, never mind reigning over it in justice and peace! That was the perspective of many at the time, and they doubtless thought they had good scriptural reasons for their opinions. They are represented by those who cried, "If He is the King of Israel..." They believed that something miraculous had to happen to realign reality with covenant expectation. Ergo, Jesus could not be the long-expected King.

158 This was confirmed in God's answer to Jesus' plea in Matt. 26:39.

159 The same can be said about the prediction of Peter's denial (Matt. 26:69-75), and of Christ's resurrection and His meeting with them in Galilee (cf. Mk. 16:7).

Matthew 27:26-50 runs through the mockery of the Roman soldiers to the mockery of the thieves crucified with Him, to the mockery of the chief priests and scribes and the crowd before the cross. The soldiers cried, "Hail, king of the Jews!" (Matt. 27:29) after they had placed a crown of sharp thorns on His head, which they proceeded to mercilessly beat down into His skull. Jesus, beaten and bloody, is their temporary sport. A "king" without the authority of a steward, a criminal brought under the heel of one small part of the massive machinery of Rome. Jesus is jeered by those who were crucified along with Him (Matt. 27:44). This lasted for some time before one thief saw the truth about who He was, and it was no small triumph and vindication in the midst of His rejection that this soul called Him "Lord" (Lk. 23:42). But the disdain continues with the baying crowds:

> If You are the Son of God, come down from the cross.... If He is the King of Israel, let Him now come down from the cross, and we will believe Him. He trusted in God; let Him deliver Him now if He will have Him; for He said, "I am the Son of God" (Matt. 27:40, 42-43).

There is no doubt about what is happening here; the King is utterly rejected; so much so that the Jews around the cross call down an imprecation upon themselves (Matt. 27:25). These rejectors of the proffered Messiah understood Who Christ would be; the Son of David, the Son of God. But as far as their eyes could see, this Jesus was not He. He was not their King because He was not the Messiah. Their reason worked part way. They knew the prophecies. But it could not alight upon the right object—Jesus of Nazareth! Reason was not guided by faith, and so it was offended (Matt. 21:42).

Jesus is still thought of as a deceiver, a false messiah by the majority of Jews. Yet the same OT that furnished ancient Judaism with fervent expectations of the coming of the Great King is clear also about the truth that He must meet with death due to being rejected by His people. Throughout his passion narrative, Matthew contents himself with only one small citation from the First Testament:[160] "They divide My garments among them, And for My clothing they cast lots" (Psa. 22:18).

If the people did not see the soldiers cast lots for Jesus' clothing, there was plenty that they did see that ought to have called Psalm 22 to mind. And not Psalm 22 only, but several other OT messianic texts should have had them looking for a Suffering Servant (cf. Isa. 53). I want to remind the reader of these texts, but must first take note of what I might properly call an Abrahamic covenantal text, picking up on the third promise of that covenant (Gen. 12:3), although it's close proximity to the suffering One in the psalm implies a New covenant context at the end of the psalm:

> All the ends of the world
> Shall remember and turn to the LORD,
> And all the families of the nations

160 He had earlier cited a prophecy from Jeremiah that is not found in his Book, but which closely resembles Zech. 11:12-13. We must not be so naïve as to believe that Matthew was so unintelligent as to get his source wrong. It is far more reasonable to assume that Jeremiah did indeed speak this prophecy, but that it was given to the later prophet to write it down.

> Shall worship before You.
> For the kingdom *is* the LORD's,
> And He rules over the nations (Psa. 22:27-28).

The sufferer in this psalm exclaims that one day every nation will worship Yahweh, because He will exercise rule over them (cf. Psa. 2:6-8). Hence, the psalm mixes the twin roles of the Servant of Yahweh as we meet Him in Isaiah. The prophet Isaiah wrote thus about the Suffering Servant: "Who has believed our report?" (Isa. 53:1a).

After reading the passion narratives of the Gospels, one can see how apropos that question is. The reference to this Servant (Isa. 52:13) growing up "as a tender plant, and as a root out of dry ground" (Isa. 53:2) warns the Jews of this man's lowly beginnings, but this same individual will be "exalted and extolled and be very high" (Isa. 52:13), but only once He has "sprinkled many nations" (Isa. 52:15; cf. 53:11).

Daniel predicted that Messiah would be "cut off and [would] have nothing" (Dan. 9:26 NASB), and Zechariah foretold how "they" (Israel) would one day "look on Me whom they pierced" (Zech. 12:10; cf. Psa. 22:16). There was plenty of witness to the rejection of Messiah in the Hebrew Scriptures. But they could not see their King on the cross.

I locate the source of the unbelief in what I have called man's default setting, the lurch to independence that now is motivated by our sin nature. It is this default in man that prepares us to shrug off the authority of God's word, even if it is acknowledged as an authority.[161]

Another Answer

But then, there are a multitude who have come *after* who see things another way. They too ask themselves, "If He is the King of Israel..." but they answer in a different way. They know Jesus is the King of Israel, but quite contrary to Matthew, they redefine "Israel." For these believers, the cross and the resurrection are the focal point of everything, and God's Word must be interpreted on the basis of it and the subsequent events in the Church. Jesus is the King, but He rules from heaven.

Although this position fully recognizes the divinity of Jesus and accepts Him as the Messiah, I want to be a little bit controversial here in claiming that this second group, good men as they are, have not entirely allowed Jesus to be the Messiah He undoubtedly is! Jesus "Christ" has been redefined along with "Israel."[162] They have done this because they have chosen the wrong perspective from which to look at His messianic role, and they have constructed an ingenious story where the terms "Christ/ Messiah" and "Israel" have been adapted to fit the new story well.

161 See my *The Words of the Covenant*, Vol 1, 101-104.

162 I am not ingratiated with the contemporary penchant for seeing Jesus as the new Adam or Israel (or many others one could mention). He is the "second man" (1 Cor. 15:47) and the "last Adam" (1 Cor. 15:45), but He is not called "the new Adam" by Scripture. For an example of this tendency see, e.g., Patrick Schreiner, *Matthew, Disciple and Scribe: The First Gospel and Its Portrait of Jesus* (Grand Rapids: Baker Academic, 2019), 239.

The Creation Reacts to the Creator's Death

Matthew is the writer and first-hand witness who tells us about some extraordinary physical disturbances that happened when Jesus died. "God with us" passed out of this life in the extremity of torment, and several "signs" accompanied His demise.

First, there was the veil of the temple, which was torn from the top to the bottom (Matt. 27:51a). It is impossible to say unequivocally which curtain is meant: the inner curtain separating the Holy of Holies from the holy place, or the more public one separating the holy place from the outer court. The majority of interpreters are content with either possibility. If it was the inner curtain, it could not have been kept secret.[163] John Nolland cites the interesting possibility that this rending of the temple veil from top to bottom may have signified God breaking out in reaction to what had occurred. This is also seen in the quaking of the earth and the splitting of the rocks.[164] It is tempting to imagine such a response, but one could also envisage the locality being affected by the decease of Him who upholds "all things by the word of His power" (Heb. 1:3). The rending could also be God tearing the curtain to signify that Christ's death had made a way into heaven possible for sinners.

Be that as it may, the sighting of many saints who had been dead coming to life after Christ's resurrection (Matt. 27:52-53) had another meaning: perhaps it signified that the New covenant was in effect or coming into effect?[165]

Setting A Guard

It is one of the interesting aspects of the religious leaders' request for a guard over Jesus' tomb that it made even more sure the corroboration of the miracle of His resurrection. They inadvertently underwrote the validity of His victory over death. It is also of interest to see Matthew refer to the earlier claim of Jesus to raise up the temple in three days if it were destroyed (Matt. 27:40/Mk. 14:58). This saying is not actually recorded in the Synoptics but occurs in the Gospel of John in John 2:19. It is what has been called an undesigned coincidence in the Four Gospels.[166]

Jesus is Raised

I shall be commenting more on the resurrection when I turn to John's Gospel. In Matthew 28:2 another earthquake is reported, this time connected with an angel moving the stone covering the grave. This angel frightened the guards so much that they froze (Matt. 28:3). Matthew makes us aware that there was a good deal of supernatural ruckus surrounding the passion and resurrection. The angel informs the women that

---

163 D. A. Carson, "Matthew," 580.

164 John Nolland, *Matthew*, 1211-1213.

165 I would admit this only if the sightings of these risen saints occurred after Jesus had ascended to the Father (Jn. 20:17). It is clear from Matthew's chronology that there was a delay of several days between Matt. 27:51 and 52-53. See Eckhard J. Schnabel, *Jesus in Jerusalem: The Last Days* (Grand Rapids, Eerdmans, 2018), 336.

166 For more on these undesigned coincidences, see now Lydia McGrew, *Hidden in Plain View: Undesigned Coincidences in the Gospels and Acts* (Chillicothe, OH: DeWard Publishing, 2017).

Jesus is going ahead of the disciples to Galilee. Moreover, the Lord Himself repeats the message to the women as they are in the way (Matt. 28:5-10).[167]

The Encouraging Words of the Risen Christ

I want to say something about some of the words of the risen Christ. In Matthew 28:9 He says, "Rejoice!" And in verse 10, "Do not be afraid..." Then He claims, "All authority has been given to Me in heaven and on earth" (Matt. 28:18).[168] Finally, in verse 20 are words of reassurance: "Lo, I am with you always, *even* to the end of the age."

I have picked these sayings out because they all convey a message of encouragement and hope. The completion of Jesus' "work of humiliation," as I may call it, has produced a fantastic result. Isaiah prophesied that Yahweh's suffering Servant would "see the labor of His soul and be satisfied" (Isa. 53:11). In this opening greeting, Jesus projects that deep satisfaction with everything that has resulted from His torments. The victory over death is not His alone because He has done it at the Father's behest for us! Life as God knows it, as it was meant to be communicated to God's image; the Life of God experienced by His saints, unfettered by the curse, and unbowed by sin. There is good reason to "rejoice!"

Since one cannot rejoice truly if there is any feeling of doom hanging over one's head, Jesus tells the women not to fear. In fact, this word of comfort, "Fear not," characterizes the speech of heaven to God's people (Gen. 26:24; 46:3; Judg. 6:10, 23; Dan. 10:12; Matt. 1:20; Lk. 1:13, 30; 2:10; Rev. 1:17).

Why is there no cause to fear and every reason to rejoice? It is because Jesus, the resurrected man, the King of the coming world, has been given "all authority" in all creation ("heaven and earth"). Thus, when He returns, He will use that power to influence the entire fallen state. He will rule with an iron rod, but in justice, love, and peace. The resurrection is the signal for the great realities ahead. This clarifies His last words in this Gospel: "I am with you always, even to the end the age" (Matt. 28:20).

Because Jesus and His authority is with us as we pass through this life, as He has been with all believers since His resurrection, it is logical that His "presence" with the saints will connect His first and second comings. This is to say, Jesus being with the saints from the first to the second coming (whether, for sake of argument, they be Church age believers or Tribulation saints) connects the two and, in essence, makes them one. We ought also to take note of Jesus' words "even to the end of the age"

167 As many other writers have pointed out it is astonishing that women, whose witness was not considered reliable in the ancient world, were chosen to be the first witnesses to the resurrection.

168 Many cite these words as proof that Jesus is now reigning as King. E.g., Herman Ridderbos, *The Coming of the Kingdom*, 507; Willem VanGemeren, *The Progress of Redemption* (Carlisle, UK: Paternoster, 1995), 357. But we must be careful not to make them say more than they say. Jesus, for example, is not to be construed as claiming that He alone has this power and authority. The Father and the Spirit too! Therefore, the limitation of this *exousia* is to the *Man* Christ Jesus. He bears this power with special reference to the mission of His people (who would shortly comprise the Church) in the world. He is not now reigning upon the earth as predicted in the OT and the Gospels. Psalm 2:6-9 is not being fulfilled today. The book of Revelation places this in the future (Rev. 2:25-27; 12:5; 19:11-15). The power of Christ comes, in this sense, when He sets up His Kingdom (Lk. 12:35-46; Matt. 13:41; 19:28).

because they tell us not to expect this age to "come to completion" for some time. The second advent was not just around the corner.

Summary of Part Four

Luke

•The theme of the Kingdom of God in Luke should not be read in reference to the post-advent Church. The Synoptic Gospels in particular are historical reports of what Jesus said and did prior to the beginning of the Church, and the Church is out of context in the narrative aside from a few future references.

•At the synagogue in Nazareth in Luke 4, Christ is careful to separate the first and second advent contexts in His quotation from Isaiah 61. This is an important hermeneutical marker.

•At least until Luke 17 the Kingdom of God is the literal Davidic New covenant Kingdom predicted by the OT.

• Even when one arrives at Jesus saying, "The kingdom of God is within you" (Lk. 17:21), the Kingdom is represented by the King who is speaking. Jesus was the King in His first coming, but His kingship was rejected. Hence, the Kingdom was rejected and thus postponed, only to come irresistibly at the second coming of the King.

• Luke locates the coming Kingdom upon earth, not in heaven. The miracles, for example, promote a this-worldly eschatology.

• Owing to Him being rejected, Jesus' Parable of the Pounds (Lk. 19) was told explicitly to disabuse the disciples of the notion of an immediate appearance of the Kingdom of God.

• Luke 21 refers to "the Days of Vengeance" of Isaiah 34, 61, and 63, which shows that Luke acknowledges a future for Israel after the second coming that is predicted in those chapters.

• "The times of the Gentiles" refers to Israel's subordination under Gentile rule and the consequent loss of the kingly line from the Babylonian Captivity to the second advent.

• Luke's record of the institution of the Lord's Supper in Luke 22 stresses the importance of Christ's blood as vitally connected to the New covenant.

• Since the disciples with whom Jesus observed the first Lord's Supper were to be foundational to the Church (Eph. 2:20), this logically entails that the Church commemorates and participates in the New covenant (1 Cor. 11:25).

• Luke's emphasis on the Spirit and the New covenant needs to be traced in both of his books (Luke and Acts).

• Jesus' words on the road to Emmaus pointed out to His companions that they had not read the Prophets carefully. If they had done so, they would have known that He would be rejected.

• Jesus did not engage in typological interpretation after the resurrection.

Matthew

• Matthew's usual references to the Kingdom of Heaven are simply a way of speaking of the Kingdom of God via circumlocution.

• When he does speak of the Kingdom of God, it is in contexts where it is necessary to differentiate God in the discussion.

• The Gospel of the Kingdom in Matthew refers to the prophesied Kingdom of the Prophets, which John the Baptist, Jesus, and the disciples were preaching, especially in the first part of Jesus' mission.

• After Matthew 12 there appears to be a shift in Jesus' mode of teaching the crowds. He begins to teach in Parables, etc.

• The Sermon on the Mount records Jesus' Kingdom ethic in view of the arrival of the Kingdom of God.

• The Parables of the Kingdom all highlight a facet of the coming Kingdom, which is now pushed back to the eschaton. Some facets are positive, and some are negative.

• Jesus' phrase, "The kingdom of heaven is like," appears in most of the Matthean parables and indicates what could be called a "kingdom in the making," progressing to the second advent.

• The meaning of "kingdom" in the parables is quite tricky to define with exactitude. Hence, His words should be read carefully.

• Matthew includes "Son of David" sayings in connection with Jesus' miracle-working, combining his Kingly rights with those of His messianic mission.

• When the Church is mentioned (only in Matthew), it is in a future context.

• Jesus' remark to the disciples that they would rule with Him on twelve thrones judging the tribes of Israel is a sure indicator of a future for the elect nation corresponding to the OT covenants.

• The Olivet Discourse is about Israel in the "end" (time), including the Tribulation and the second advent. It does not refer to the Church.

• The "generation" Jesus refers to in Matthew 24:34 is the generation of the "end."

PART FIVE:
COVENANT IN MARK AND JOHN

10

COVENANT AND KINGDOM IN MARK

Now they were on the road, going up to Jerusalem, and Jesus was going before them; and they were amazed. And as they followed they were afraid. Then He took the twelve aside again and began to tell them the things that would happen to Him.
- Mark 10:32

Frank Thielman writes, "Like many first-century Jews, Mark believed that the Scriptures told of a future king who would come and rule God's people Israel with justice."[1] It needs to be understood that these writers and those they write about lived within the cultural setting of God's covenants with Abraham, Moses, and David, and in anticipation of the promised New covenant.

Similarities and Differences (First Coming Hermeneutics)

But Thielman, along with most evangelicals, believes that Jesus fulfilled these promises (especially through Isaiah) at His first coming.[2] He asserts that:

> For Mark, therefore, Jesus' proclamation of the kingdom of God and his establishment of this reign through exorcisms, healings, and feedings were all signs that through Jesus, God had visited his people to effect the restoration Isaiah had promised.[3]

The glaring difficulty with this view and the interpretation of the Isaianic texts upon which it stands is that if those texts are taken at face value, they contradict

1 Frank Thielman, *Theology of the New Testament: A Canonical and Synthetic Approach* (Grand Rapids: Zondervan, 2005), 59.
2 Ibid., 64.
3 Ibid., 66.

Thielman's thesis.[4] Taking just one example, here is what he says about the Isaianic fulfillment in the first century:

> Therefore, like God in Isaiah 40-66, whose arm is bared as a warrior's to do battle against the enemies of his people (Isa. 40:10; 42:13-17; 49:24-26; 51:9-11; 52:10) and to lead them "along the way" out of exile and back to Jerusalem (Isa. 35:8-10; 40:3; 42:16; 43:16, 19; 49:9, 11; 57:14), Jesus conquers the demons in [Mk]1:16-8:26 and then in 8:27-11:1 leads his disciples along "the way" to Jerusalem. Similarly, just as God in Isaiah 35:5-10 restores sight to the blind, hearing to the deaf, and strength to the lame prior to the jubilant return of Israel to Zion along the "Way of Holiness" Jesus gives sight to the blind (8:22-26; 10:46-52), hearing to the deaf (Mark 7:31-37; 9:13-29), and strength to the lame (2:1-12) prior to and during his journey with his followers along the "way" to Jerusalem.[5]

This way of matching specific prophecies of the OT with basic similarities in the NT and calling them "fulfilled" is standard procedure in academia.[6] But it simply will not satisfy any student of Scripture who believes that in order to exercise faith in what God says, God has to mean what He says. One cannot simply brush aside the massive *dissimilarities* between the OT and NT passages.[7] Let me unpack what I mean by that statement. For that, we must turn to Isaiah.

Isaiah 40:5 declares, "The glory of the LORD shall be revealed, and all flesh shall see *it* together." This did not happen in the first century, but will happen at the second coming and thereafter (cf. Mk. 13:26; Rev. 1:7; Isa. 35:2; 66:18). One cannot just quote Isaiah 40:10 without noting this context (see Isa. 40:9). Similarly, the other passages Thielman cites from Isaiah 42, 49, 51, and 52 refer to Yahweh acting in power on behalf of Israel prior to redeeming the nation. For instance, Thielman cites Isaiah 51:9-11, but he ignores much of the wording of verse 11: "So the ransomed of the LORD shall return, and come to Zion with singing, with everlasting joy on their heads. They shall obtain joy and gladness; Sorrow and sighing shall flee away" (Isa. 51:11, my emphasis).

In no sense could this prophecy be fulfilled in the first century ministry of the "Suffering Servant." This is to occur after the second coming. But scholars who insist upon employing a first coming hermeneutic are forced to cram it into a first century fulfillment that it cannot all be pushed into (because the covenants won't allow it).

It is the same with those passages that Thielman says refer to God bringing His people "out of exile and back to Jerusalem (Isa. 35:8-10; 40:3; 42:16; 43:16, 19; 49:9,

4 I use Thielman as an example of the majority of interpreters who employ a first coming hermeneutic that cuts right across the specific wording of the covenants.

5 Ibid., 66. Thielman, as many contemporary scholars, relies much on the book by Rikki E. Watts, *Isaiah's New Exodus in Mark* (Grand Rapids: Baker, 2001).

6 This is compounded by a misreading of Paul in my opinion. E.g., Richard B. Gaffin Jr., *In the Fullness of Time: An Introduction to the Biblical Theology of Acts and Paul* (Wheaton, IL: Crossway, 2023), 291ff.

7 One thing one must always keep a sharp eye out for in any form of "this-is-that" assertions are the dissimilarities! They are often given short shrift.

11; 57:14)." These either concern the second advent (Isa. 40), or the establishment of the New covenant Kingdom after Christ's return (Isa. 35; 42; 43; 49), or the promise to save Israel by those means (Isa. 57). They do not refer to the first coming, except, as we have seen and shall see, as we understand the offer of the Kingdom as a bona fide offer that was rejected.[8] And only then is Isaiah 40:1-3 in full view.

Finally, Thielman's quotation above appeals to the miracles recorded in Isaiah 35:5-10 as fulfilled in Jesus' miracles and His journey to Jerusalem. Certainly, Jesus as Messiah did heal the blind, the deaf, and the lame, and He did go to Jerusalem. But He did *not* make "waters shall burst forth in the wilderness, and streams in the desert" (Isa. 35:6; cf. 35:1). He did *not* "come with vengeance" (Isa. 35:4). The road to Jerusalem was not a "Highway of Holiness," since in nobody's imagination could first century Jerusalem be thought of as holy. And unclean and wicked people did tread that road, not just the redeemed (Isa. 35:8-9). Lastly, "the ransomed of the LORD" did not "return," and no one came "to Zion with singing, with everlasting joy on their heads." The disciples of Jesus did not "obtain joy and gladness," and although they rejoiced later when they saw the risen Jesus, their "sorrow and sighing" did not "flee away" (Isa. 35:10).[9] The healing ministry of Jesus was a foreshadowing of the transformative power of the coming Kingdom. The King had come, but He was rejected and will return "in vengeance" upon His enemies, bringing eternal salvation with Him in His Kingdom of restorative peace.[10]

What I am saying here is that a reader of the Bible can choose to ignore these differences or to creatively lend them spiritual meanings, but he will have to pick and choose which verses to take literally (e.g., the healing of the blind and deaf) and which to spiritualize away. All of the Isaianic texts cited by these men are covenantally tied, and their full realization in redemption and restoration will come through the New covenant when it is brought in for Israel at the second coming.

Covenantal Threads

The widespread anticipation of Jews about the Messiah was grounded in God's covenants. Marshall observes, "For Mark the kingly associations of the term *Christ* indicate that it carries the sense of the person through whom God establishes the kingdom."[11] The term "Messiah/Christ" is itself strongly associated with the idea of covenant. This becomes clear once we ask, "What was Jesus anointed to do?" When we consider that the burden of His preaching concerned the Kingdom of God (cf. Mk. 1:14-15), and that He spoke of "the age to come" (Matt. 12:32; Mk. 10:30/Lk. 18:30)

8 The interested reader can look at the way I try to fit these texts (or those around them) into the developing covenant picture of the coming Kingdom in my *The Words of the Covenant*, Vol. 1, 250-260.

9 These "nots" are the crucial dissimilarities that, no matter the similarities, must be respected.

10 See here Harry Bultema, *Commentary on Isaiah* (Grand Rapids: Kregel 1981), 319. Thanks to Ian Hicks for the source.

11 I. Howard Marshall, *New Testament Theology*, 82 (italics in original).

and "the end of the age" (Matt. 13:39-40), which refers to the Kingdom to come (cf. Matt. 6:10), the Davidic links show through.[12]

The covenantal threads are woven throughout the fabric of the Gospels but are not always obvious to the modern reader. But this shall be dealt with in another chapter. Let me begin this study with a great proclamation: "The time is fulfilled, and the kingdom of God is at hand. Repent, and believe in the gospel" (Mk. 1:15).

These are the words of Jesus after John the Baptist was imprisoned. If we only had this verse in isolation, we might think that "the gospel" that Jesus was urging people to embrace was "Paul's gospel," but that is not the case. Mark 1:14 tells us that Jesus was preaching "the gospel of the kingdom of God." This means that the "gospel" of Mark 1 was the good news about the imminent messianic Kingdom. Hence, when He said "the time is fulfilled," Jesus was referring to the time of messianic expectation, an expectation which had been stirred particularly by the Prophets. The "Kingdom" was the New covenant Kingdom, a culmination of the Abrahamic and Davidic covenants.[13] This implies the strands of the Abrahamic and Davidic covenants find concrete fulfillment because they are filtered through the New covenant redemption in Jesus.

I have already stated the unpopular view that the Synoptic Gospels present us with a bona fide offer to Israel of the messianic Kingdom predicted by the Prophets and the rejection of that offer by the vast majority of the religious leaders and the people.[14] The Gospel of Mark, with its famous depiction of the secret identity of Jesus, certainly adds its weight to this understanding.

In contrast to the way I have approached the other Gospels, my treatment of Mark will be more thematic. I choose to do this because I do not wish to bore my reader who reached this place by wading through my comments on Luke and Matthew, but also because I believe isolating Mark's themes helps me give another perspective on the covenantal genius of the Gospels.

Everyone knows about the tireless movement in Jesus' ministry that is described by Mark. The first chapters especially are breathtaking in their portrayal of Jesus' work ethic. The breaking through of the Kingdom of God in His miracles and wonders and the authority and wisdom in His teaching was not cataclysmic or classically apocalyptic. The coming of the Kingdom was written large in the Person and ministry of Jesus, but it was vulnerable too. God, in His wisdom, sent Messiah as a Persuader,

12 Marshall also considers "Lamb of God" to likely be a messianic title. See I. Howard Marshall, *New Testament Theology*, 496.

13 See under "The Kingdom of God as a Covenant Kingdom" in the Introduction.

14 I really do not see why people have a problem with this. For example, outside of Hyper-Calvinism, it is a demonstrable fact that today people are offered Christ in the Gospel and reject it, yet it is a "well-meant offer." Again, God's offer to Jeroboam in 1 Ki. 11:37-38 was sincere, even though God knew it would be rejected. Other examples are Jeremiah's warning to the nobles not to resist the Babylonians in Jer. 27, or his warning to the Jews about going to Egypt in Jer. 42–43. The same principle is at work in the NT with the good news offer of the King and Kingdom upon condition of repentance in the Gospels.

not as a Commander. Jesus is the servant (Mk. 10:45), prophesied by Isaiah (Isa. 42; 49; 53). He must therefore be rejected (Isa. 53:3; Mk. 8:31; 12:10; cf. 1 Pet. 2:4).

Major Covenantal Themes in Mark

The Messianic Titles

Mark speaks of Jesus as the Son of God three times, with four additional variations (Mk. 1:1; 3:11; 15:39; cf. 5:7; 9:7; 12:6; 14:61-62). Mark 3:11 is uttered by a possessed man who is instantly told to keep quiet. The other two instances at the beginning and the end (or close to the end) of the Gospel act as bookends for the gradual emergence of Jesus' identity through the Markan vignettes. "Son of God" is a royal, messianic name (Psa. 2; cf. Matt. 26:63),[15] associated both with heaven and with the Davidic covenant.[16]

It is notable that the third mention of Christ as the Son of God comes from the lips of a Roman soldier at the final moments of Jesus' life (Mk. 15:39). One might have thought that a more appropriate time to include this recognition would be after Jesus was raised from the dead, say in Mark 16:6. This shows that Mark is focused upon the work of Christ as God's willing Servant.[17]

The instant quotation of Malachi 3:1 and Isaiah 40:3 in Mark 1 links Jesus with Yahweh and the Messenger of the covenant, while John the Baptist's speech concerning Him connects Jesus to the New covenant through His baptizing with the Holy Spirit (Mk. 1:7-8). This is a strongly New covenant-oriented opening! I say this because a study of the prophesied role of the Holy Spirit in the OT shows that His activity is closely connected with salvation and regeneration (e.g., Isa. 11:2; 32:15; 44:3; Ezek. 36:26-27; 39:29; Joel 2:28-29; Zech. 12:10), and Mark groups together OT New covenant texts (Mal. 3:1; Isa. 40:3). But then Mark quickly moves to Jesus' activity among the people and the emerging portrait takes over, but not before we are told that "the Spirit drove Him into the wilderness" to be tempted by Satan (Mk. 1:12). Mark does not record the Temptation itself, but I might say here that his questions, "If you are the Son of God..." indicates that Satan understood it as a messianic title.

Likewise, Mark has Jesus referred to as the "Son of David" just twice (Mk. 10:47-48 and 12:35). Mark 12:35 is of interest because it is an abridged version of the more famous query the Lord put to the Pharisees in Matthew 22:41ff:

> Then Jesus answered and said, while He taught in the temple, "How *is it* that the scribes say that the Christ is the Son of David? For David himself said by the Holy Spirit: 'The LORD said to my Lord, "Sit at My right hand, Till I make Your enemies Your footstool."' Therefore David himself calls Him

15 Frank Thielman, *Theology of the New Testament*, 57ff.

16 Andrew T. Le Peau, *Mark Through Old Testament Eyes* (Grand Rapids: Kregel, 2017), 31.

17 In that sense, the older NT Introductions are right to make Jesus the Servant the key theme of Mark's account.

> 'Lord'; how is He *then* his Son?" And the common people heard Him gladly (Mk. 12:35-37).

The way this is put casts the attention upon the onlookers and not the Pharisees. It places the emphasis upon the impressions of "the common people" rather than upon Jesus' opponents. Mark's comment about "the common people" draws a dividing line between them and the "experts." Jesus leaves the latter group to ponder His Davidic credentials.

Upon His return from the wilderness temptations, Jesus began preaching "the gospel of the kingdom of God," claiming, "The time is fulfilled.[18] The kingdom of God is at hand" (Mk. 1:14-15). The rest of the chapter is filled with miracles and deliverances which stagger those witnessing them. In fact, Mark concludes his incident-filled first chapter by saying that because of His notoriety, Jesus could no longer enter the townships openly (Mk. 1:46; cf. 3:8; 6:53-56).

In Mark 3:21-30 Jesus is accused of being "out of his mind" and being empowered by Beelzebub (Satan). In response, He warned that the accusation meant that the Holy Spirit's good work was being ascribed to Satan and would never be forgiven (Mk. 3:29-30). Such an ascription of God's work in Jesus to "the ruler of the demons" (Mk. 3:22) effectively negates the New covenant work that Christ is doing in anticipation of the New covenant Kingdom that He is announcing.

The Commands to Tell No One

On several notable occasions in Mark's Gospel, Jesus commands that His true identity, or something about Him, is not to be made public knowledge.[19] In fact, it has been remarked that "Mark employs the secrecy theme in order to teach that until the cross Jesus cannot be rightly known for who he is."[20] It is worthwhile examining a few of these occasions because they speak to the matter of the progress of revelation. The first instance is in chapter one:

> Now there was a man in their synagogue with an unclean spirit. And he cried out, "Let *us* alone! What have we to do with You, Jesus of Nazareth? Did You come to destroy us? I know who You are—the Holy One of God!" But Jesus rebuked him, saying, "Be quiet, and come out of him!" (Mk. 1:23-25).

This incident occurred when Jesus had been teaching at the Capernaum synagogue (Mk. 1:21). Although the Lord's command for the demon to "shut up!" could be interpreted as Him not willing for it simply to speak, I think the fact that it correctly identified Him as "the Holy One of God" might constitute another reason. This epithet, "the Holy One," is a favorite term of Isaiah, and always refers to God (Isa. 29:23;

18 In a similar vein see Gal. 4:4-5.

19 I am not including those occasions when Jesus told people who were healed not to spread it abroad (e.g. Mk. 1:40-45).

20 James R. Edwards, *The Gospel of Mark* (Grand Rapids: Eerdmans, 2002), 19.

30:15; 43:3; 48:17; 54:5; 55:5; 60:9).[21] Isaiah 29:17-24 is a New covenant renewal passage. Isaiah 30:15 is also included in a New covenant context (Isa. 30:15-26). As for Isaiah 43:3; 48:17; 54:5; 55:5; and 60:9, let the reader study each context and he will see the eschatological and soteriological content in them all; they all have to do with the New covenant, the true covenant of redemption.

> And the unclean spirits, whenever they saw Him, fell down before Him and cried out, saying, "You are the Son of God." But He sternly warned them that they should not make Him known (Mk. 3:11-12).

These demonic spirits do obeisance and call Jesus "Son of God."[22] It is a matter of surprise that the Lord comes to earth, the domain of evil, and one of the things He must do is to quieten the testimony to Him from the demonic realm. There seems little doubt that Jesus did not wish such abrupt testimony. Mark particularly brings this out. The proclamation of John the Baptist was enough. Now seeing and hearing Him was the way to knowing Him.

> Now as they came down from the mountain, He commanded them that they should tell no one the things they had seen, till the Son of Man had risen from the dead (Mk. 9:9).

After Peter, James, and John had witnessed the incredible manifestation of God's behind-the-scenes program on the Mount of Transfiguration, Jesus instructed them not to tell anyone about what had just transpired. His transformation in Mark 9:2 and the attendance of Moses and Elijah (Mk. 9:4-5) showed them the greatness of Jesus by orders of magnitude, but this truth was to be hidden for the time-being. The incarnation and the testimony of good deeds and unparalleled teaching would suffice. Jesus did call attention to Himself, but subtly (Mk. 2:8-12; 5:19; 8:38, etc.). He knew He must die. He knew also that the great manifestation of His power and majesty lay far ahead for Him (Mk. 13:24-27).[23]

In Mark 15:43 we read that Joseph of Arimathea was "waiting for the kingdom of God." His bold request for the body of Jesus and his burial of Him in his own tomb strongly suggest that Joseph saw the way into the future Davidic Kingdom through Jesus, even though He was dead.

The Question, "Who Can This Be?"

Corresponding to the hidden identity motif in Mark is the open question, voiced several times in the narrative, about that identity. Either explicitly or implicitly, Jesus produced responses from people who wanted to get behind who He really was (see

21 See also Jer. 51:5; Hos. 11:9, 12; and Hab. 3:3. The Habakkuk passage is especially noteworthy as it may be a prophecy of the second advent (it shares certain similarities to Isa. 63:1-6).

22 In Mk. 5, "Legion" calls Him "Jesus, Son of the Most High God" (Mk. 5:7). Contrast this with what some of His countrymen were saying about Him. See Mk. 6:1-3.

23 Admittedly, some of these commands to stay silent might have had different reasons (e.g., Mk. 8:22-26).

Mk. 4:35-41; 2:12; 6:51; 7:37; 11:18; 12:17; 15:39). These appraisals of Christ's impact upon His hearers reflect a lot more than a native power of oratory.

Jesus' Baptism

God the Father's announcement when His Son was baptized included references to both of His comings: "You are My beloved Son, in whom I am well pleased" (Mk. 1:11). Martin says the verse "is a striking linkage of two Old Testament passages (Ps. 2:7 and Isa. 42:1)—a coronation formula for the messianic Son and a portrayal of the Suffering Servant of God."[24] He also believes there may be "a possible underlying motif in the wording, which recalls Genesis 22."[25] This is a lot to get out of a few words, but it is an intriguing thought all the same. It is enticing to contemplate both comings in this divine speech as Jesus becomes the Christ!

A more certain observation is Stuhlmacher's pairing of Mark 1:1-11 with Mark 11:27-30,[26] where the assembled religious leaders ask Jesus, "By what authority are you doing these things?" (Mk. 11:28). Jesus takes them back to the baptism of John: "The baptism of John—was it from heaven or from men? Answer Me" (Mk. 11:30). This was ingenious because if they had answered in the affirmative, not only would they be authenticating John, but they would also tacitly be authenticating the baptism of Jesus as the baptism of the Messiah!

The "Messianic Secret"

In 1901 a work was published that coined the term "messianic secret" of Mark. The author was a higher critical German scholar named William Wrede. Much of Wrede's scholarship has been debunked, but his insights into four "silence" motifs remain very helpful. These motifs are listed by Lane as:

1. Jesus silencing the demons (Mk. 1:23ff., 34; 5:6ff.; 9:20).

2. Jesus commanding those he healed to be silent about Him (Mk. 1:44; 5:43; 7:36; 8:26).

3. Jesus instructing the disciples privately (Mk. 4:10-20, 34; 7:14-23; 8:30ff.; 9:28ff.; 10:32-34; 13:3ff.).

4. The failure of Jesus' disciples to understand Him (Mk. 4:13, 40ff.; 6:5-52; 7:18; 8:16-21; 9:5ff., 19; 10:24; 14:37-41).[27]

---

24 Ralph P. Martin, *New Testament Foundations: A Guide for Students*, Vol. 1 (Eugene, OR: Wipf & Stock, 1999), 179. Also, Peter Stuhlmacher, *Biblical Theology of the New Testament*, 77. He adds Isa. 44:2.

25 Ibid., 179-180.

26 Peter Stuhlmacher, *Biblical Theology of the New Testament*, 77.

27 William L. Lane, "*Theios Aner* Christology and the Gospel of Mark," in *New Dimensions in New Testament Study*, eds. Richard N. Longenecker and Merrill C. Tenney (Grand Rapids: Zondervan, 1974), 144.

Although many of these references have some question over them, I think these categories, particularly the first two, are worthwhile to explore for my purposes too. Let's start with the first motif, the words of demons.

"Now there was a man in their synagogue with an unclean spirit. And he cried out, saying, 'Let *us* alone! What have we to do with You, Jesus of Nazareth? Did You come to destroy us? I know who You are—the Holy One of God!'" (Mk. 1:23-24). What I find interesting about the words of the demon(s) to Jesus is the note of surprise. The question, "What have we to do with You...?" most probably means, "Why are you interfering with us?"[28] It is as if the timing was not right. The demons appear to expect a coming judgment (cf. Mk. 5:7; we see this more clearly later), but not at *that* time.[29] I do not think it a large leap of the imagination to say that the demons know that there is a Creation Project ongoing. This impression is given more credence by this passage from Matthew: "And suddenly they cried out, saying, 'What have we to do with You, Jesus, You Son of God? Have You come here to torment us before the time?'" (Matt. 8:29, my emphasis).

What is meant by "before the time"? In my opinion, the demon(s) referred to the second advent and its fallout. We cannot know for sure when the destruction of the demons will occur, but we can say more securely that it will be after Christ's return. In Mark 1:23-24 the question "Why are you interfering with us?" would be a stupid question for a demon to ask the Son of God, unless, of course, the implication was, "Why are you interfering with us before the yet distant time of judgment?" This infers that the demons know the difference between the first and the second comings of Christ. Or at least that they know that the avenging Messiah was not due to close out history until much later.[30]

What about the name "the Holy One of God" (Mk. 1:24)? It identifies Jesus as the one whom Yahweh would one day send into the world. In the OT the term "Holy One" often refers to Yahweh Himself (e.g., Job 6:10; Psa. 71:11; 89:18; Isa. 1:4; 10:20; 17:7; 29:18, 23; 41:14, 16; Jer. 51:5; Ezek. 31:7; Hos. 11:9, 12; Hab. 1:12), sometimes in an eschatological setting as we have seen (cf. Ezek. 39:7; Hab. 3:3).

In Mark 1:24 Jesus is called "the Holy One of God," as in the special Servant of Yahweh whom He has sent into the world. Jipp writes, "The demon's reference to Jesus as "the Holy One of God" is likely a messianic title which originated out of the practice of sanctifying and anointing the Davidic king with holy oil."[31]

These incidents with demoniacs are instructive. By calling Jesus "the Holy One," the demons used a title associated with the New covenant. But they were surprised and afraid by His appearance before them. Could it be that the demonic realm

28 Andrew T. Le Peau, *Mark Through Old Testament Eyes*, 48; James D. G. Dunn, *Jesus Remembered*, 675.

29 "The demons recognize—far more clearly than synagogue congregation—the role of judgment in the ministry of Jesus" (Walter W. Wessel, "Mark," in *EBC*, ed. Frank E. Gaebelein, Vol. 8 [Grand Rapids: Zondervan, 1984], 627).

30 The reaction of surprise among the demons is seen also in e.g., Mk. 9:20.

31 Joshua W. Jipp, *The Messianic Theology of the New Testament*, 62.

understands the coming of God's Messiah is a two-phase coming? Or were they caught off-balance by His "early" appearance in the first century A.D.?

The next category in which the "messianic secret" is seen is in Jesus telling those He healed to keep quiet about Him. Mark 1:40-45 is about the leper who Jesus touches and heals.[32] Mark 5:34-43 is the story of the young girl Jesus raised from the dead. Mark 7:35-37 records the Lord healing the deaf and dumb man.

These examples are fascinating. If the miracles bear witness to the covenanted Kingdom, what would make Jesus strictly charge these people to be quiet about what He did for them? Mark does not tell us. The most obvious reason is that He did not want to attract the wrong kind of attention based upon what might be considered hearsay. He wanted people to believe His words, not His deeds apart from His words. Still, the healing miracles do remind us of Isaiah 53:4 ("He has borne our griefs"), and that passage is related to the New covenant work of the Servant. Mark wants us to know that Jesus is the Son of God (Mk. 1:1; 3:11; 15:39). But he wants us to join in on the discovery too. Although he tells us up front who Jesus is, his narrative invites us to come to that conclusion ourselves.

But there is another motif noted by Wrede and others that should be explored. They are the texts in which Jesus' own disciples do not comprehend Him (e.g., Mk. 6:51-52; 7:18; 8:16-21, 32; 9:9-10; 14:37-40). As I have shown in my remarks on Luke and Matthew, the teaching of Jesus about the good news was not a proclamation of His death, resurrection, and ascension in the mode of Paul in his epistles (e.g., Rom. 4:23-25; 6:1-10; 1 Corinthians 15:1-6; Gal. 1:1, 4; cf. Gal. 2:20). The reader will have to forgive me because I want to hammer this point home. Let us take a look at two of these passages:

> Now Jesus and His disciples went out to the towns of Caesarea Philippi; and on the road He asked His disciples, saying to them, "Who do men say that I am?" So they answered, "John the Baptist; but some *say*, Elijah; and others, one of the prophets."
>
> He said to them, "But who do you say that I am?" Peter answered and said to Him, "You are the Christ."
>
> Then He strictly warned them that they should tell no one about Him. And He began to teach them that the Son of Man must suffer many things, and be rejected by the elders and chief priests and scribes, and be killed, and after three days rise again.
>
> He spoke this word openly. And Peter took Him aside and began to rebuke Him. But when He had turned around and looked at His disciples, He

32 It is most notable that Jesus chooses to touch the leper rather than just speak words of healing. The touch of Christ witnesses to His compassion on one who had not been touched for who knows how long? This touch represents God better than many miracles!

> rebuked Peter, saying, "Get behind Me, Satan! For you are not mindful of the things of God, but the things of men" (Mk. 8:27-33).

As I have said above, this occurrence at Caesarea Philippi is a narrative highpoint in Mark's account. Peter pointedly confesses his clear persuasion that Jesus is the Christ, to which Jesus characteristically warns the disciples not to let that be known. Jesus next informs His disciples that He, the Christ, will die after His ministry because He will be rejected by the Jewish leaders. Peter immediately counters the prophecy. He does so, according to Wilkins, because "that is incongruent with Peter's still-developing conception."[33] That is to say, at that time, Peter's understanding of Jesus and His mission did not entail his Master, who he had just identified as the longed-for Messiah, having to "be killed," never mind rise again.

It is more than a little interesting that just at the time that Jesus is speaking to His disciples about His true identity, Satan is there trying to influence matters. Satan is aware that "Christ" is the Christ of the covenants, and that, therefore, He must suffer and die in accordance with the OT Scriptures (Isa. 53; Psa. 22).[34] This means that Peter's contradiction of Jesus ought to be seen as a corollary to Satan's temptations, especially the temptation for Jesus to have the Kingdom without the cross (Lk. 4:5-8). And that means Satan was keeping a sharp eye out for language that implied fidelity to God's covenants.

> Now as they came down from the mountain, He commanded them that they should tell no one the things they had seen, till the Son of Man had risen from the dead. So they kept this word to themselves, questioning what the rising from the dead meant (Mk. 9:9-10).

Of course, this text follows directly from Mark's account of the Transfiguration (Mk. 9:1-8). There, Peter, James, and John experience the unveiling of Jesus' true glory as the Son of God. The prohibition not to talk about the experience is probably because *that* Messiah, the Lord of Glory, is not the Messiah of the first coming, the first stage of the one work of the coming King of the covenants.

The text also brings up the matter of the ignorance of the disciples concerning Christ's coming passion.[35] Since they would have been familiar with a general resurrection at the end of time (Dan. 12:2-3; Jn. 11:24), we can sympathize with the questioning of the disciples in Mark 9:10. But once again, it demonstrates that they could not have been preaching faith in Jesus' death and resurrection as the basis of God's forgiveness of sin. That was not the gospel they knew at the time![36]

---

33 Michael J. Wilkins, "Peter's Declaration concerning Jesus' Identity in Caesarea Philippi," in *Key Events in the Life of the Historical Jesus*, eds. Darrell L. Bock and Robert L. Webb (Tübingen: Mohr Siebeck, 2009), 366.

34 Not long after, Jesus will emphasize that He is the Servant of Yahweh by saying "For even the Son of Man did not come to be served, but to serve, and to give His life a ransom for many" (Mk. 10:45). This was said in a similar context where He had predicted His death (Mk. 10:33-34).

35 In this sense, Mark's Gospel is in the form of an irony in that the reader is more clued into what's going on than the disciples appear to be.

36 Sadly, not a word about this is found in some amillennial writings. E.g., Benjamin Gladd, "Mark," in *A Biblical-Theological Introduction to the New Testament: The Gospel Realized*, ed.

With all this said, here is what some respected authorities say about Mark's "secrecy motif." The first is James Edwards:

> Mark employs the secrecy theme in order to teach that until the cross Jesus cannot be rightly known for who he is...Only at the cross can Jesus be rightly known... At the cross Jesus is revealed as the suffering Son of God, whose rejection, suffering and death reveal the triumph of God. Only at Golgotha can Jesus be rightly known as God incognito who reveals himself to those who are willing to deny themselves and follow him in costly discipleship.[37]

Did you catch that? People, even pious believers, could not know Jesus truly until Golgotha. Let us remind ourselves of what the apostle Paul wrote concerning the gospel he preached: "For I delivered to you first of all that which I also received: that Christ died for our sins according to the Scriptures, and that He was buried, and that He rose again the third day according to the Scriptures" (1 Cor. 15:3-4).

The apostle goes further than Edwards and includes the resurrection in what is to be known about Jesus. Here is another scholar's opinion: "Mark distinctively highlights the frequent failures and misunderstandings of Jesus's earthly followers. Specifically, they fail to understand that the very purpose of Jesus's mission...is for him to suffer and die for sinners."[38]

I think this sums up the pre-ascension situation well. It was only after Christ returned to heaven that the Spirit came upon them in power (Jn. 38-39; 16:13; Acts 1:4-5). Therefore, it is a mistake to view the pre-ascension gospel as being the same thing as the post-ascension gospel. Both are about Jesus and require faith in Him, but the former is focused on the coming covenanted Kingdom, and the other is centered on Jesus' death and resurrection. While the second proclamation can accommodate the coming Kingdom in its message, the first proclamation could not include Christ's death and resurrection within it, for the reasons given above and elsewhere.

It is not my aim in life to rain on anyone's parade, but we have to face facts. Mark is telling us, even louder than the other Gospels, that nobody before the crucifixion (at the earliest), and not really until after the resurrection (which is integral to Paul's gospel), trusted in Jesus as their dead and risen Lord! Ergo, the gospel preached by Jesus and His disciples in the Four Gospels was *not* the same as the gospel we Christians believe and by which we are saved. Let that sink in. It may be hard to keep down, but it is essential that we receive it. If there is an explanation of this data that can logically and contextually conclude that Jesus preached "Paul's gospel," I have not met with it.

True Identification

Peter's confession of Jesus, "You are the Christ" (Mk. 8:29), forms a watershed in the Gospel.[39] But it is followed with a typical statement of secrecy by Jesus (Mk. 8:30).

Michael J. Kruger (Wheaton, IL: Crossway, 2016).

37 James R. Edwards, *The Gospel of Mark*, 19.

38 Andreas J. Köstenberger, *The Jesus of the Gospels*, 157.

39 See e.g., Peter Stuhlmacher, *Biblical Theology of the New Testament,* 581.

This reminds us that the confession of Peter in Mark serves a literary as well as a historical purpose. Christ equals Messiah, the promised King, Servant, and Savior (Gen. 49:8-10; Isa. 42:1-7; 49:1-9; 52:13-15; Mic. 5:2). But His work will be in two phases (Isa. 9:6-7; 61:1-3; Zech. 10:9-10; Mal. 3:1-3). Because the attention is mainly on the righteous reign of this Promised One in the OT, most Jews did not equate the coming King Messiah with the Suffering Servant of Isaiah 53:1-12. Peter's confession, which according to Matthew was prompted by the Father (Matt. 16:17), stated the truth about Jesus' identity, just as the loud cries of the demoniacs (Mk. 1:24; 3:11; 5:7) and the words of the centurion at the cross (Mk. 15:39) did. However, none of these witnesses, not even Peter, seemed to contemplate the death of Jesus as the first stage of His mission—a mission wrapped in covenant promises. We must recall that Messiah is "the Messenger of the *covenant*" of Malachi 3:1 in His first coming!

Again, we must not think that this dilatoriness was Jesus' fault. Mark 8:38 records Him as saying, "For whoever is ashamed of Me and My words in this adulterous and sinful generation, of him the Son of Man also will be ashamed when He comes in the glory of His Father with the holy angels." What Peter made of this statement is anyone's guess, but another "coming" is plainly stated.

Yet because of Mark's way of soft disclosure and his record of the disciples' slowness to keep up, this moment of clear testimony by Peter, coming right in the middle of Mark's narrative, is an important juncture in the story. It is an insider's response to the question, "Who is this?" (Mk. 4:35-41), which plays a significant part in this Gospel.[40] If He is the predicted Messiah, then in Peter's mind, and in the minds of his fellow disciples, the covenants with Israel (the Abrahamic, Priestly, and Davidic in particular) were very close to being brought to pass.

"Assuredly, I say to you, whoever does not receive the kingdom of God as a little child will by no means enter it" (Mk. 10:15). I call attention to this saying because little children do not indulge in typological and/or symbolic interpretation or spiritual hermeneutics. And while one could object that the verse does not concern itself with interpretation, I reply that in order to "receive the kingdom," a child must know what it is. Edwards thinks that the emphasis in the context is upon the helplessness and vulnerability of a little child.[41] In this view, the child is picked up and carried into the kingdom. However, Jesus says they "receive [*dechomai*] the kingdom," not that they are carried into it. They, therefore, must *accept* it in some way. How do they accept it? They do it simply. I believe I am within my rights to point out that children believe what they are told and do not seek out hidden or obtuse meanings. Hiebert says, "Jesus was not thinking of children per se but of the qualities they typify: the spirit of receptivity, dependence, and trustfulness."[42] In the parables of Mark 4, the kingdom is growing as in Matthew 13. In Mark 9:1 it refers to the phenomena witnessed at the

---

40 I. Howard Marshall, *New Testament Theology*, 67.

41 James R. Edwards, *The Gospel of Mark*, 306-307; also C. E. B. Cranfield, *The Gospel According to St. Mark* (Cambridge: University Press, 1966), 323-324.

42 D. Edmond Hiebert, *The Gospel of Mark: An Expositional Commentary* (Greenville: Bob Jones University Press, 1994), 282.

Transfiguration. In Mark 9:47 the "kingdom" is something to be entered into by radical means if necessary. In that text, the future Kingdom is probably in view.[43]

What then is the kingdom that children receive? Is it "the present rule of God in the lives of men"?[44] I don't think this is what Mark is saying, absent some Pauline assumptions. Mark never emphasizes the inwardness of the Kingdom. Unlike Matthew and Luke, Mark's Gospel does not stress the Davidic core of the Kingdom of God. It is hard to say whether the kingdom in Mark 10:14-15 is that future Kingdom (as it assuredly is in Mk. 11:10, 14:23, and probably 10:24-25 and 15:43). I have my doubts. In any case, especially in Mark, to receive the Kingdom is to identify and receive the King.

More Covenant Elements

Mark 11:17 quotes Isaiah 56:7: "My house shall be called a house of prayer for all nations." Isaiah 56:1-7 is certainly covenantal. Isaiah 56:4, 6 refers to the Mosaic covenant, while Isaiah 56:7 itself alludes to the New covenant with its inclusion of "all nations" coming to God's house (cf. Isa. 2:2-3). As in Matthew 21:23-27 and Luke 20:1-8, Mark's report of Jesus questioning the chief priests, the scribes, and the elders (Mk. 11:27) turns on its covenantal meaning; the essence of it being that John the Baptist (Mk. 11:30) was the predicted "voice" who would go before Messiah (Isa. 40:3), the Messenger of the covenant (Mal. 3:1).

In Mark 12:18-23 the Sadducees set forth a riddle concerning a woman who marries seven men.[45] The answer they got back was one of profound simplicity: "I *am* the God of Abraham, and the God of Isaac, and the God of Jacob" (Mk. 12:26). This response cites Exodus 3:6 and the episode of the Burning Bush. In that context, the land aspect of the Abrahamic covenant is at the forefront (Exod. 3:8). This is the first time that the familiar triplet is used in the Bible (cf. Exod. 2:24), and it is extremely covenantal.[46] So, Jesus answers the Sadducees' bad theology by calling attention to the covenant commitment of Yahweh.

Then Jesus asks His accusers a question about the Christ predicted by David in Psalm 110 (Mk. 12:35-37). His reference to Psalm 110:1 is to cause them to think about Messiah as not only the greater Son of David, but also as the Son of God (Psa. 2:7, 12; cf. Psa. 45:6 with Heb. 1:8). Psalm 110 is concerned with the reign of the future Davidic Priest-King. I hope the reader can see how thoroughly saturated the Gospels are with the notion of "covernance"!

In Mark 14:22-26 we get a truncated version of the institution of the Lord's Supper. In his treatment of this passage, referencing Exodus 24:8, Zechariah 9:11,

43 Ibid., 44; see also Morna D. Hooker, *The Gospel According to Saint Mark* (Peabody, MA: 1991), 239.
44 Hiebert, *The Gospel of Mark*, 283.
45 See also Matt. 22:23-28; Lk. 20:27-33.
46 See Daniel I. Block, *Covenant*, 426.

Jeremiah 31:31, and Isaiah 53:2, Peter Orr explains, "the [New] covenant blood initiates the relationship and is the grounds of God's rescue."[47]

There is no way around the fact that the blood that Christians are redeemed by—the blood that all sinners are redeemed by—is New covenant blood! What this entails is not that every saved sinner is incorporated into the Church, which is an error of Covenant Theology. It simply means that all saints from every era, both before and after Calvary, were saved by grace through faith by the instrumentation of the blood of the cross. They were saved into the eventual New covenant Kingdom of Christ by New covenant blood.[48]

What I find interesting about this short version is where Mark places the emphasis:

> And as they were eating, Jesus took bread, blessed and broke *it,* and gave *it* to them and said, "Take, eat; this is My body." Then He took the cup, and when He had given thanks He gave *it* to them, and they all drank from it. And He said to them, "This is My blood of the new covenant, which is shed for many. Assuredly, I say to you, I will no longer drink of the fruit of the vine until that day when I drink it new in the kingdom of God" (Mk. 14:22-25, my emphasis).

What intrigues me about this passage is how it is shaped to point toward the fulfillment of God's covenantal project through the New covenant in Christ. The underlined text shows where the emphasis is placed.

Finally, in Mark we get an unambiguous declaration of the culmination of the covenantal Creation Project. For the most part, this Gospel has been concerned with Jesus as Son of God at His first coming. But now, the second phase of Christ's work of reconciliation comes into view, if only briefly.

When He is crucified, Mark simply tells us that the inscription above Jesus read, "The King of the Jews" (Mk. 15:26). Then the chief priests mockingly (but correctly) refer to Him as "the Christ, the King of Israel" (Mk. 15:32). The whole scene is brought to its climax by the confession of the centurion: "So when the centurion, who stood opposite Him, saw that He cried out like this and breathed His last, he said, 'Truly this Man was the Son of God!'" (Mk. 15:39).

"Son of God" is, as we have seen, associated with Messiah.[49] Mark, after all, opens up his Gospel with the words: "The beginning of the gospel of Jesus Christ, the Son of God" (Mk. 1:1; cf. Psa. 2). This confession, along with the other identity statements in Mark 14 and 15, opens up a new possibility of a future return of this Son of God to reign on earth from Jerusalem in the New covenant Kingdom.

47 Peter Orr, *The Beginning of the Gospel: A Theology of Mark* (Wheaton, IL: Crossway, 2022), 156.

48 This may take a little time to settle in, especially for some dispensationalists. But the blood of the New covenant is the only way to Glory, no matter who you are. See further remarks in my treatment of 1 Cor. 11:25 below.

49 Joshua W. Jipp, *The Messianic Theology of the New Testament*, 57-58. Jipp later teaches that Jesus' enthronement is ironically portrayed in His crucifixion (Ibid., 80-81). This thesis has received a book-length treatment in Jeremy R. Treat, *The Crucified King: Atonement and Kingdom in Systematic and Biblical Theology* (Grand Rapids: Zondervan, 2014). I disagree with this conclusion.

11

COVENANT THEMES IN JOHN

If God is glorified in Him, God will also glorify Him in Himself, and glorify Him immediately.
– John 13:32

At first blush, the Gospel of John does not appear to be promising ground for studying God's covenants. And in a direct sense, that is correct. John seems to be the least interested of the evangelists in the covenants.

Yet, as a matter of fact, what he has to say about Jesus relies heavily upon those covenants. These covenantal links are to be discovered slightly under the surface of John's message, but they stand behind his most outstanding motifs. The picture of the coming King from the OT makes Him divine (Isa. 7:14), the pre-existent One (Mic. 5:2; cf. Prov. 8:22-23), the Prophet (Deut. 18:15-18), Israel's Priest-King (Psa. 110:1, 4), and, therefore, the Son of David (1 Chron. 17:11-12). All of these designations are incorporated into John's portrait of Jesus Christ, and all of them are tied to the covenants of Yahweh in the OT.

Another indicator is John's use of the word for love, *agapao*, which is a covenant-related term. Daniel Block maintains, "The notion of covenant underlies the word *agapao*, which is usually translated with a single word, 'love.' However, like the Hebrew word *'ahab*, which Greek *agapao* represents, this word suggests 'covenant commitment demonstrated in action in interest of the other person.'"[1]

Since John's Gospel is often associated with this word, I think it is worth mentioning that his *agapao* texts can be profitably studied within a covenantal context. This goes for other inspired authors as well, but because John's style is to hint at things and let his reader make the proper connections, or to even assume the connections are

1 Daniel I. Block, *Covenant*, 399. Block very perceptively observes "This meaning explains Peter's preference for *phileo*...when Jesus asked him, 'Do you love [*agapao*] me?' (Jn. 21:15-16)."

made, his use of the covenant-related term *agapao* requires that we read it with potential covenant associations.

A Bold Start

John's Gospel comes right out of the blocks with the proclamation of Jesus' divinity and His central role in the creation of the world. It maximizes the antithesis, or better, "contradiction" between He who was in the world and the world that did not recognize Him. The word for "covenant" (*diatheke*) does not appear in his Gospel, and only once in John's writings, in Revelation 11:19, where it refers to "the ark of His covenant" in heaven. This Gospel is often considered to reflect a lawsuit motif, and Andrew Lincoln, in particular, has made a good case for that view.[2] However, a Roman Catholic Indian scholar, Rehka Chennattu, claims that John 13–17 especially has a deliberate covenantal structure. Neither of these works teaches the covenant continuity I am investigating, but Chennattu's book does at least show that the Beloved disciple thought covenantally.[3] As she says, "One needs (sic) not look for exact parallels between John's narrative and any single OT tradition, but rather identify the essential elements of the OT covenant traditions appearing in John 13–17."[4]

In addition to this, Nicholas Perrin has examined Jesus' seven "I Am" statements in John and has, among other things, concluded, "The seven 'I Am's' are relevant to a study of the Kingdom because through them, Jesus is asserting the arrival of the Kingdom through himself."[5] If right, this means that the "I Am's" are rooted in the covenants.[6] Below I shall show that this is at least partially true.

John's main attention is not upon Jesus' eschatological claims and not on the covenants per se, but as John Pryor stated, "even though the word 'covenant' is never used in [John's] gospel, covenantal notions are of *primary* importance."[7]

John's Gospel was written, "that you may believe that Jesus is the Christ, the Son of God, and that believing you may have life in His name" (Jn. 20:31). The identity of Jesus as God's beloved Son working among sinners and dying for them and being raised for them is the burden of this account. The eschatology of John is more personal than general.

---

2 Andrew T. Lincoln, *Truth on Trial: The Lawsuit Motif in the Fourth Gospel* (Eugene, OR: Wipf & Stock, 2019).

3 Rekha M. Chennattu, *Johannine Discipleship as a Covenant Relationship* (Peabody, MA: Hendricksen, 2006).

4 Ibid., 69.

5 Nicholas Perrin, *The Kingdom of God*, 131.

6 Another study that argues for the apostle's immersion in the OT covenants is Sherri Brown, *Gift Upon Gift: Covenant through Word in the Gospel of John* (Eugene, OR: Pickwick, 2010).

7 John W. Pryor, *John: Evangelist of the Covenant People* (Downers Grove, IL: InterVarsity, 1992), 157 (my emphasis).

Some Initial Covenantal Hints

This does not mean that John is bereft of useful information that throws light on the Creation Project. For instance, John the Baptist's statement, "I have seen and testified that this is the Son of God" (Jn. 1:34), is momentous. The presence of God's Son in the world indicated a real moment of "crisis" in the history of creation.[8] The importance of this is summed up by John himself, whose proclamation, "Behold the Lamb of God who takes away the sin of the world" (Jn. 1:29), was dependent upon it. The Lamb of God is the Son of God. The personal presence of God's Son as the one who "takes away the sin of the world" (Jn. 1:29) bespeaks a covenant of salvation to replace the Mosaic covenant. John does not say it in those terms, but that is where his statements lead (see Jn. 1:10-14, 17). John Pryor, for instance, believes that the most powerful of the covenantal images in this Gospel is found in John 1:14: "And the Word became flesh and dwelt among us, and we beheld His glory, the glory as of the only begotten of the Father, full of grace and truth."[9] What Pryor sees in this verse is the motif of the pervasive covenant presence of Yahweh in the OT (e.g., Exod. 25:8; 29:45-46; 33:7; Num. 14:14; Deut. 1:42; 12:11; 31:17; 1 Ki. 18:36).

The name "Lamb of God" is connected by many with the Passover Lamb, which links Jesus to the deliverance of His people, and with the Abrahamic covenant, which was the cause of Yahweh's remembrance of Israel (Exod. 3:6-8). As surprising as it may seem, the Passover Lamb was not offered to atone for sins. The blood of the animal was smeared on the doorposts of the Jewish houses in Egypt as a sign for the avenging angel to pass over those dwellings (Exod. 12:1-13), but it is never called an atonement. Stuhlmacher observes, "It must be furthermore remembered that the Passover lamb was not an atoning sacrifice in ancient Judaism; the Passover blood was not interpreted in terms of atonement theology until rabbinic times."[10]

Since John the Baptist said the Lamb of God would take away the sin of the world, it is doubtful that the Passover Lamb was in John's mind when he spoke this. Further to this is the fact that a lamb was not often offered at Passover. Although questioning the view of Jeremias (and Stuhlmacher) above, Leon Morris considers this second objection to be fatal.[11] We should recall that John was the son of a priest (Lk. 1:5, 13), so he would not make the mistake of thinking the paschal lamb was to make atonement. But as Morris suggests, perhaps by his time it was considered sacrificial. One idea is, therefore, that the name "Lamb of God" better equates to the Servant of Yahweh in Isaiah 52:13–53:12. If this view is correct, then Jesus' death at the approximate time when the Passover lambs were sacrificed[12] signaled a change from Passover to the

8 See here the suggestive work by G. Campbell Morgan, *The Crises of the Christ.*

9 John W. Pryor, *John: Evangelist of the Covenant People*, 158.

10 Peter Stuhlmacher, *Biblical Theology of the New Testament*, 672. Earlier (668) he cites Joachim Jeremias, *The Eucharistic Words of Jesus*, 225-231, as an authority.

11 Leon Morris, *The Apostolic Preaching of the Cross*, 133.

12 According to Jn. 19:14, Jesus was crucified on the Day of Preparation for the Passover, but John intended his readers to make the connection. See James D. G. Dunn, *Jesus Remembered*, 772-773.

beginning of something new; the death of Messiah for sin,[13] and perhaps a new deliverance or exodus.[14] I think this opinion has a lot of biblical merit, but it is far from conclusive.[15] Perhaps the reference is to the several lamb offerings made to Yahweh in ancient Israel.[16] If that is the case, then Israel's covenant bonds to God are in sight.[17] From this short survey, it is clear that one cannot be dogmatic about equating John the Baptist's identification of Christ as "the Lamb of God" with Jesus being the Passover Lamb, even if the sacrificial meaning of the cross is of vital importance.

John the Baptist understood that the Spirit anointing and remaining on Jesus (which is not a phenomenon seen in the OT) singled out Jesus as the Christ. But he understood as well that the ability of Christ to baptize with the Holy Spirit (Jn. 1:32-33) moved Him apart from the righteousness of the Law (cf. Rom. 3:21); that is, it was a practice that was alien to the old covenant but was promised under the New covenant (cf. Ezek. 36:26-27; Heb. 8:6). This is why John announced that Jesus must increase and John himself must decrease (Jn. 3:30), because John was in the line of OT prophets (cf. Matt. 11:13), and was, therefore, tied to the old covenant, hence his baptism with water.

We can piece together the Baptist's "Christology" by observing he knew that the One he announced pre-existed him (Jn. 1:15), that He was divine (Jn. 1:34), and that, by implication, He became God's Christ at His baptism (Jn. 1:32-34). Christ, therefore, is a divine figure. John knew that Jesus' ministry surpassed his own and all those who had gone before Him, including Moses (e.g., Jn. 1:7-8, 23, 27, 29 and 34), so "John goes out of his way to emphasize the messiahship of Jesus."[18]

Jesus certainly made a very big impression on those aware enough to see Him with the right eyes. If we move a bit further in John 1, we come across this statement by a startled Nathaniel: "Nathanael answered and said to Him, 'Rabbi, You are the Son of God! You are the King of Israel!'" (Jn. 1:49).

The episode began, at least for Nathaniel, when Phillip found him and made what must have been a perturbing announcement: "We have found Him of whom Moses in the law, and also the prophets, wrote—Jesus of Nazareth, the son of Joseph" (Jn. 1:45).

There is no beating around the bush with Phillip. He tells Nathaniel what he knows. As far as he was concerned, Jesus of Nazareth was the Messiah, the coming King, the Seed of the woman (Gen. 3:15). This statement tells us that men like Phillip

13 Ibid., 672.

14 By speaking of a "new exodus," I do not mean what amillennial interpreters mean. Only in the sense that Christ delivers sinners through His sacrifice and thus breaks the connection with Moses' law by being the Prophet like Moses (Deut. 18:15, 18-19) who brings salvation through the New covenant. This salvation is to be completed by entrance into the eschatological Kingdom. This appears to agree with the author of Hebrews (Heb. 3:1-6; 4:1, 8-9; 9:28; 12:25-28).

15 See, e.g., I. H. Marshall, "Lamb of God," in *Dictionary of Jesus and the Gospels*, 432-434.

16 See Leon Morris, *The Apostolic Preaching of the Cross*, 141-143.

17 Arnold G. Fruchtenbaum believes the term "Lamb of God" connects Jesus "with two Old Testament concepts: first...with the paschal lamb of Exodus 12, and, second, the messianic lamb of Isaiah 53" (Fruchtenbaum, *Yeshua: The Life of Messiah from a Messianic Jewish Perspective*, Vol. 1, 522).

18 John W. Pryor, *John: Evangelist of the Covenant People*, 131.

understood that these prophesied ones were one and the same Man. Nathaniel's outburst (if I may call it that) showed that people also knew that the promised one would be the Son of God.

But look at what he does next: Nathaniel equates the Son of God with the Davidic King (Jn. 1:49)! He thought that the heir of the Davidic covenant was to be the Son of God (cf. Jn. 11:27)! This not only shows us that these first disciples thought in covenantal terms, but that they had brought together the significance of the person of Messiah and combined it with the covenants. Rounding things off in John 1, Jesus adds to the list of His titles that of the Danielic "Son of Man" in John 1:51.

John's Statements About the Kingdom

When Jesus is interrogated by Pilate, He is asked if He is a king. The answer Pilate receives is in the affirmative (Jn. 18:37), but Pilate asks because of the cryptic statement that Jesus had spoken moments before: "My kingdom is not of this world. If My kingdom were of this world, My servants would fight, so that I should not be delivered to the Jews; but now My kingdom is not from here" (Jn. 18:36).

It is critical to acknowledge the fact that the only kingship connected to the role of Christ is that associated with the covenant with David, and that covenant stipulates a this-worldly reign in Jerusalem (cf. Psa. 47:8-9; Isa. 9:6-7; Zech. 8:3; 14:9, 16; Lk. 1:32-33). He is "Immanuel," "God with us" on earth, not God up in heaven. By stating that His kingdom was not of this world, Jesus was not saying it was a heavenly kingdom.[19] Rather, He was saying that His Kingdom upon the earth is not a kingdom in succession to every other kingdom of man throughout history. Hays comments, "Jesus implicitly accepts the title of 'king' but insists that his kingship is grounded in otherworldly authority and that he exercises kingly power not through military might but through his testimony to the truth (18:37)."[20] Hays thinks Jesus is redefining the kingdom, but I disagree. It is more likely that Jesus means that "His kingdom does not take its origin or draw its power from the unbelieving world."[21] Furthermore, His Kingdom is implemented from above.[22] History starts again when King Jesus begins to reign (cf. Rev. 11:15).

Instead of opting to say that Jesus' "kingdom" is in heaven, some have claimed that when He spoke these words to Pilate, Jesus was speaking of the provenance of His kingship. The idea then would be that He was cryptically telling the Roman governor that His authority to rule came from God.[23] But this interpretation of John 18:36-37 does nothing to further the discussion since everyone accepts it. Then the

19 E.g., William Hendriksen, *A Commentary on the Gospel of John* (London: Banner of Truth, 1964), 408-409.

20 Richard B. Hays, *Echoes of Scripture in the Gospels*, 325.

21 J. Carl Laney, *John*, 331.

22 Similarly, in Jn. 8:23 Jesus tells the Jews, "You are from beneath; I am from above. You are of this world; I am not of this world." His meaning was not that He didn't belong on earth, nor was it that He would not rule upon earth. Jesus meant that He was not a product of this world.

23 This is the position of George Eldon Ladd, *The Presence of the Kingdom*, 193-194; and Daniel Block, *Covenant*, 578-579. Block appears to believe that Jesus was crowned king at His Passion.

interpretive turn is made to make Jesus King during these events. Not only does this go against the grain of the Davidic covenant, it fails to distinguish between the purposes of the first and second comings. As I have shown in Volume One, the messianic prophecies place more emphasis upon what, from our perspective, is the second coming of Christ than the first, and the stress falls very much upon Christ's reign at that time, not at the time of the first coming.

Jesus' mention of the kingdom in John 18 prompts me to look at John 3:3 and 5, where the only other uses of the term are found in this Gospel.

> Jesus answered and said to him, "Most assuredly, I say to you, unless one is born again, he cannot see the kingdom of God" (Jn. 3:3).

> Jesus answered, "Most assuredly, I say to you, unless one is born of water[24] and the Spirit, he cannot enter the kingdom of God" (Jn. 3:5).

What does Jesus mean by "the kingdom of God" here? Is He being coy? And what would Nicodemus, a Pharisee, think He meant? We should recall that this was early in Christ's ministry and not long after the witness of John the Baptist to Him. Nicodemus did not seem to understand Jesus' statement in verse 3 because he asked, "How can a man be born when he is old? Can he enter a second time into his mother's womb and be born?" (Jn. 3:4).

Our tendency is to read this interchange from a Pauline perspective. That is, we read it post-ascension and post-Pentecost. By doing this, we are tempted to equate being "born again" with the kingdom, as if Jesus was saying, "Unless you are regenerated, you cannot go to heaven" or "... have eternal life." But is that accurate? One recent work confidently asserts, "In the Synoptic Gospels, the phrase 'kingdom of God' occurs frequently to refer to the state of being in right relationship with God through Christ... but [in John] he speaks of having abundant and eternal life as equivalent to being in the kingdom of God."[25] In this view, the "kingdom of God" equals salvation ("everlasting life," Jn. 3:36).[26]

It should have been no surprise to Nicodemus that a new birth would be required to enter the coming Kingdom. Deuteronomy 30:6 and Ezekiel 36:26-27 ought to have come to mind, even if the expression "born again" was foreign.[27] The point is that Nicodemus would have thought that "the kingdom of God" was the eschatological Kingdom, and the Lord does *nothing* to disabuse him of that notion. The fact that one must be born again to be a part of the Church (future when Nicodemus came to Jesus) does not mean that Jesus was speaking *about* the Church in John 3. The OT New covenant texts presuppose the same idea.

24 It is my position that the "water" here is a reference to physical birth.

25 Karen H. Jobes, *John Through Old Testament Eyes* (Grand Rapids: Kregel, 2021), 78. It ought to be evident that "kingdom of God" in the Synoptics signifies a good deal more than simply "right relationship to God through Christ," but I'll let that slide.

26 Ibid., 79.

27 See e.g., Craig Blaising, "Biblical Hermeneutics," *in The New Christian Zionism*, ed. Gerald R. McDermott (Downers Grove, IL: InterVarsity, 2016), 85; and Michael J. Vlach, *He Will Reign Forever*, 27, 277.

Given the rare occurrences of "kingdom of God" in John, the three usages ought to be considered. Here in John 3:3 and 5 the Kingdom of God should be seen as the content of what Jesus was teaching at the time, which prompted Nicodemus to remark as he did (Jn. 3:2). For context, we are forced to repair to the other Gospels where we can readily see Jesus proclaiming the Kingdom of God (e.g., Mk. 1:14-15; Lk. 4:43; 8:1; cf. Matt. 4:17). It was this theme in Jesus' preaching, reinforced by His supporting miracles that brought Nicodemus to Jesus. This Kingdom must be seen (Jn. 3:3) or entered (Jn. 3:5) through the new birth by the Spirit (Jn. 3:7-8). Well, doesn't Isaiah 32:15-18 say the same thing in a different way? This is the New covenant Kingdom anticipated in Joel 2:28-32; Isaiah 11:2; 11:1-10; 59:20-21; Ezekiel 36:27; and Zechariah 12:10. So when Christ tells Nicodemus that he must be born from above in order to enter the Kingdom, and when He tells Pilate "My kingdom is not of this world" (Jn. 18:36-37), He is speaking about the future earthly New covenant Kingdom ushered in by the Holy Spirit. The fact that the same Spirit-produced change is true of entering His Church only shows that New covenant work is being wrought in both contexts.

"Destroy this Temple..."

In John 2 Jesus is asked for a sign by the Jews. In tune with places like Matthew 12:39, the Lord announces a sign, but not one that "an evil and adulterous generation" is going to pick up on. "Jesus answered and said to them, 'Destroy this temple, and in three days I will raise it up'" (Jn. 2:19).

This is a text that amillennialists like to pounce on to "prove" that Jesus has replaced the Jerusalem temple and that the Church is the temple in Him.[28] Clearly this goes far beyond anything in the text itself. Jesus was referring to His physical, pre-glorified body (Jn. 2:21-22). The NT applies the word "temple" not only to the physical body of Jesus, but also to the Church, Christ's mystical body (cf. 2 Cor. 6:16; 1 Cor. 12:27), to the individual Christian (1 Cor. 6:19), and, last but not least, to the actual temple in Jerusalem (Acts 5:20-25). Nothing in the passage and nothing in John's writings suggests that Jesus is alluding to His physical body *replacing* the temple in Jerusalem. He is deliberately equivocating so that the Jews would think one thing and His disciples would come to see something else. This is not the usual communication practice of the Lord but is deliberately adopted because of their willful blindness.[29] It simply would have been futile doing a miracle for them (Jn. 2:23-25).

Reading this Gospel, it becomes clear that John's main focus is on believing in Jesus and receiving salvation (e.g., Jn. 3:16-17; 4:13-14; 5:24; 6:29, 32-36, 47; 11:25, etc.). But there are passages that fit well within the OT picture of the Coming One which we ought to notice.

> Most assuredly, I say to you, the hour is coming, and now is, when the dead will hear the voice of the Son of God; and those who hear will live. For as the

28 N. T. Wright, *Jesus and the Victory of God*, 335, 495.

29 I remind you that the reason given for the parables is for a judgment against those who reject the plain truth (Matt. 13:10-15).

> Father has life in Himself, so He has granted the Son to have life in Himself, and has given Him authority to execute judgment also, because He is the Son of Man (Jn. 5:25-27, my emphasis).

John 5 is full of statements by Jesus that one should reflect on. In the speech above, Jesus claims dead people who hear His voice will yet live. The means by which this will be accomplished is through the power of "life" that the Father has granted to His incarnate Son. Christ is not only the Son of God but is also the Son of Man.[30] As the Son of God, He is equal to the Father. But it is as the Son of Man that He judges the dead. As the Son of Man, He is the great Servant (cf. Matt. 12:8-18) through whom the world is reconciled in every way to the Father. "Son of Man," of course, refers to Daniel 7:13-14 and the One who comes to rule the world for God. In Daniel 7 it refers *to the second coming and rule*, but Jesus has claimed the title at His first coming.[31] This signifies the harmony between the incarnate Jesus of the first coming and the resurrected Jesus of the second coming—the one great work of Messiah. Seeing as the Son of Man figure in Daniel comes to reign (second coming), this tells us that the first and second comings are one "event" or one work broken up into two phases. Hence, when John's Gospel speaks about Jesus' "time" (Jn. 7:6, 8, 30), it speaks of His demise. Thus, the "Son of Man" title covers both major episodes in Christ's career: His sacrificial death and His coming reign.[32]

Verse 27 explains why Jesus performed His great signs and wonders. It was *because* He was the Son of Man, and the Son of Man will bring this world to heel. The miracles of Jesus are Him "acting out the kingdom"[33] in His first advent.

But there is another clear allusion to Daniel in John 5:28-29: "Do not marvel at this; for the hour is coming in which all who are in the graves will hear His voice and come forth—those who have done good, to the resurrection of life, and those who have done evil, to the resurrection of condemnation."

The unmistakable recollection of Daniel 12:2 projects the meaning into the time around the second advent. When asked whether He was the Christ, and thus the one to bring in the expected new aeon, "Jesus answered them, 'I told you, and you do not believe. The works that I do in My Father's name, they bear witness of Me'" (Jn. 10:25).

Before this, Jesus had appealed to Moses to verify who He was (Jn. 5:39-47). But as Hays puts it, "Jesus' adversaries, despite their earnest scrutiny of Moses' writings, lapse into interpretative failure because they reject Jesus' astonishing claim to the true

30 There has been a great deal of discussion about the title "Son of Man" in the scholarly literature. See e.g., Donald A. Hagner, "Excursus: Son of Man," *Matthew 1–13*, 213ff., and I. Howard Marshall, *Jesus the Saviour*, 73-120.

31 As J. Paul Tanner, *Daniel*, 441.

32 This can be easily demonstrated from a comparison of Matt. 18:11 with 19:28, and 20:28 with 25:31.

33 I owe this way of putting it to I. Howard Marshall, *New Testament Theology*, 77. In Marshall's words, "We could say that Mark's theme is the Messiah and Son of God who proclaims the kingdom and who acts it out in ways that express who he is." Although Marshall is referring to Mark's Gospel, this description of Christ acting out the kingdom suits all the Gospels.

and ultimate referent to whom Moses' words point."[34] They did not follow the logic of the covenantal hermeneutic of the OT.

Life in the Son

What follows in John 5:31-47 is an extraordinary passage wherein Jesus places Himself right at the center of God's revelatory and salvific activity, contrasting it in opposition to the feigned piety and knowledge of the Jewish leadership. But I must limit myself to a few verses in which the joint themes of word and life come to the fore: "But you do not have His word abiding in you, because whom He sent, Him you do not believe. You search the Scriptures, for in them you think you have eternal life; and these are they which testify of Me. But you are not willing to come to Me that you may have life" (Jn. 5:38-40).

John, the foremost preacher of the day, bore witness concerning Jesus (Jn. 5:33, 35), and Jesus' marvelous works also testified about Him (Jn. 5:36). But none of these availed because these religious men would not believe the Scriptures. At the end of the day, failure to believe that the OT testified to Jesus as the Christ meant that their searching the Scriptures was all in vain. "Life" was in the One that the Word of God pointed to ("they testify on My behalf," Jn. 5:39), and He was speaking to them. But instead of coming to Him for life, they sought to kill Him (Jn. 5:16). They wanted to put Life to death!

This passage also says that God has placed life eternal in His incarnate Son (cf. Jn. 5:24-26, 40). "The Old Testament Scriptures are nowhere considered dispensable, but they are secondary insofar as...they point to Jesus rather than turn faith upon themselves."[35] In my opinion, this focus on the Christocentricity of Scripture needs to be considered covenantally. God is giving life through the covenant Servant ("I have come in My Father's name," Jn. 5:43), whom Moses, the old covenant representative, anticipates (Deut. 18:18).

John 6:33 says that Jesus has come down from heaven to give "life to the world." This "life" is associated with resurrection in John 6:40 and 44 and is mediated to believers by Christ our High Priest (Heb. 7:16), whose High Priesthood relies upon "a better covenant," that is, the New covenant (Heb. 7:20-22; 12:24). The connection with the New covenant via the book of Hebrews illustrates the validity of relating the theologies of separate NT authors. It shows also that the New covenant is always in the background of the NT's affirmations. In a remarkable passage, Jesus claims to be the source of "the food which endures to everlasting life... because God the Father has set His seal on Him" (Jn. 6:27). This saying deserves to be explored further.

According to Block, "God the Father had stamped Him with His own seal."[36] This is the only place in the Gospels where "God the Father" is used. God has "sealed" Christ. The meaning is that the Father shows His approval of Christ's person and

34 Richard B. Hays, *Echoes of Scripture in the Gospels*, 283.
35 James M. Boice, *Witness and Revelation in the Gospel of John*, 35.
36 Daniel I. Block, *Covenant*, 558.

message. But the verse also refers to Christ's gift of Life, so the validation includes authority to forgive sin and bestow eternal bliss. This is what the book of Hebrews means when it makes Jesus the Mediator of the New covenant (Heb. 9:15; 12:24).[37]

Earlier in the same chapter, John records the Feeding of the Five Thousand (Jn. 6:1-13). John then adds a comment on what happened next:

> Then those men, when they had seen the sign that Jesus did, said, "This is truly the Prophet who is to come into the world." Therefore when Jesus perceived that they were about to come and take Him by force to make Him king, He departed again to the mountain by Himself alone (Jn. 6:14-15).

This is remarkable because it shows that ordinary men equated "the Prophet who is to come," who harks back to Moses' prophecy in Deuteronomy 18:15, 17-18, with the coming King, or at the very least with a kingly figure. Why else would they seek to make Jesus king after concluding that He was the Prophet who Moses had spoken about? Further, their intuition to make Jesus a king was borne out of OT expectations. That Jesus evaded their intentions was not an indication that He believed Himself to be a different kind of king (a heavenly king). It was only evidence that His time to reign had not come.

An Example of Subtle Messianic Allusions in John's Gospel

I want us to look at a fascinating interchange in John 7:14-24. The background to this exchange is the healing of the man at the Pool of Bethesda in John 5:1-16.

As Jesus was teaching in the temple, the Jews (the Jewish religious leaders) were impressed by His knowledge, even though they were aware that He had never attended one of their schools (Jn. 7:14-15). Here is Jesus' reply: "My doctrine is not Mine, but His who sent Me" (Jn. 7:16).

Impressed as they are with His grasp of the Scriptures and His ability to synthesize their teaching, they are not prepared for His answer. Jesus does not refer to a teacher but to a Sender—God! This makes Him a herald or messenger, and therefore might call to mind the Prophet of Deuteronomy 18:18 ("He shall speak to them all that I command Him"), and perhaps Malachi's "Messenger of the covenant" (Mal. 3:1). Jesus then continues,

> If anyone wills to do His will, he shall know concerning the doctrine, whether it is from God or whether I speak on My own authority. He who speaks from himself seeks his own glory; but He who seeks the glory of the One who sent Him is true, and no unrighteousness is in Him (Jn. 7:17-18).

He states that the proof not only of His command of the Scriptures but of the divine provenance of His doctrine was in accepting and doing it. Jesus is constantly depicted

37 I realize that in making this connection I could be accused of reading covenant into the passage. My method is not to presuppose covenant everywhere but to acknowledge its presence "behind the scenes."

as pointing to the One who sent Him.[38] But He is a reader of the human heart (Jn. 2:24-25), so He asks them directly, "Why do you seek to kill Me?" (Jn. 7:19).

John provides a response from "the people," which appears to be a reference to those allied with the Pharisees and scribes: "The people answered and said, 'You have a demon. Who is seeking to kill You?'" (Jn. 7:20). This is disingenuous as we discover just a few verses further on: "Now some of them from Jerusalem said, 'Is this not He whom they seek to kill?'" (Jn. 7:25). So, the Prophet is in their midst, and they are impressed with what He says, but their hearts are not attuned to it nor to the God whose doctrine it is.

The way Jesus ends this exchange is most suggestive. He tells them, "Do not judge according to appearance, but judge with righteous judgment" (Jn. 7:24). If His hearers were paying attention, they would have made the connection with Isaiah:

> His delight is in the fear of the LORD,
> And He shall not judge by the sight of His eyes,
> Nor decide by the hearing of His ears;
> But with righteousness He shall judge the poor...
> (Isa. 11:3-4a, my emphasis).

In this little section of John, Jesus alludes to the Prophet of Deuteronomy 18 and to the coming Davidic Ruler of Isaiah 11. There is no doubt that He is confronting the people with His credentials.

The Promise of the Spirit

As I have stated before, the promise of the bestowal of the Holy Spirit is strongly connected with the onset of the New covenant. John is the only evangelist who records Jesus' teaching about the Spirit in relation to salvation.[39] The first instance of this is found in John 7. Jesus cried: "He who believes in Me, as the Scripture has said, out of his heart will flow rivers of living water" (Jn. 7:38). And John's commentary on this is important to notice: "But this He spoke concerning the Spirit, whom those believing in Him would receive; for the Holy Spirit was not yet *given* because Jesus was not yet glorified" (Jn. 7:39).

To what OT passage was Jesus alluding when He spoke of "rivers of living water" flowing out of the heart? Leon Morris writes that the best reference is Isaiah 58:11:[40]

> The LORD will guide you continually,
> And satisfy your soul in drought,

38 Jesus makes this claim over thirty times in John's Gospel.

39 The Synoptics do not link the Holy spirit to personal salvation other than to report John the Baptist's statement that the Christ would baptize with the Holy Spirit (Matt. 3:11; Mk. 1:8; Lk. 3:16).

40 Leon Morris, *The Gospel According to John* (Grand Rapids: Eerdmans, 1979), 424. Contrariwise, Hays believes Jesus is mainly referencing Ezek. 47:1-2 and Zech. 14:16, but this requires a lot of spiritualizing and seems far-fetched. See Richard B. Hays, *Echoes of Scripture in the Gospels*, 315-316.

> And strengthen your bones;
> You shall be like a watered garden,
> And like a spring of water, whose waters do not fail.

Morris supplies several other references, Isaiah 44:3 among them:

> For I will pour water on him who is thirsty,
> And floods on the dry ground;
> I will pour My Spirit on your descendants,
> And My blessing on your offspring...

These are clear New covenant settings, and though the affinity between Jesus' statement and these texts is somewhat indirect, there is enough correlation to understand the point He is making. Notice the mention of the Spirit in Isaiah 44:3. The theme of transformation and even regeneration is present in both contexts. It should also be noted that these prophecies concern eschatological Israel, not the Church. But what about John 7:39 and its remark about the Spirit not yet being given "because Jesus was not yet glorified"? This points us to Pentecost (Acts 2). I shall have to put forward a case for the Church being formed with the descent of the Holy Spirit in Acts 2, but for the present, I ask that we concentrate upon the reason given by the Apostle for the delay in the Spirit's coming. After the Lord ascended to heaven (Acts 1:11), there was a hiatus before the Spirit came. For what it's worth, I believe that the same thing will occur after the second coming regarding Israel (cf. Zech. 12), but just now, what I wish to point out is that this is the first indication that *the Church could not come into being before the death and resurrection and the descent of the Spirit*!

As we saw above with John 5:25-27, the dispensation of the New covenant through and by Christ began with the first coming. But the two advents are actually one work in two phases; or, if you like, two New covenant eras, one involving the Church and the other the predicted OT era centered on Israel and flowing out from it to the nations.

As one moves further on in John, the Lord speaks of the Holy Spirit in relation to His departure: "Nevertheless I tell you the truth. It is to your advantage that I go away; for <u>if I do not go away, the Helper will not come to you; but if I depart, I will send Him to you. And when He has come</u>, He will convict the world of sin, and of righteousness, and of judgment" (Jn. 16:7-8, my emphasis).

This is an important text because it tells us that the Holy Spirit could not come to us unless Jesus went back to glory.[41] Jesus could not send the Spirit until He returned to heaven. This means that the presence and work of the Spirit post-Calvary was different than His work before then. It is difficult to comprehend how sinners before Acts 2 (the descent of the Spirit at Pentecost) were regenerated and indwelt by the Spirit. In his book, *The Divine Comforter,* Pentecost highlighted John 14:17 as distinguishing a change in the work of the Holy Spirit from before to after Christ's

41 Of course, other verses tell us the same kind of thing.

passion.[42] The verse states, "I will ask the Father, and He will give you another Helper, that He may be with you forever; *that is* the Spirit of truth, whom the world cannot receive, because it does not see Him or know Him, *but* you know Him because He abides with you *and will be in you*" (Jn. 14:16-17, NASB, my emphasis).

In the Hebrew Bible, the coming of the Spirit to change hearts is connected with the New covenant (e.g., Isa. 59:21; Ezek. 36:26-27; Zech. 12:10a; cf. Jer. 31:33). In the NT, the sending of the Spirit is linked with the finished work of Christ and His ascension back to heaven, and this coincides with the institution of the New covenant. This is critical to keep in mind as one reads the NT, because if the Holy Spirit was not "in" believers before Acts 2,[43] then there was no Church before Acts 2. And salvation, or rather the results of salvation, was not the same before and after Calvary.[44]

Abraham's Seed? Yes and No!

In the middle of John 8 there is an exchange between Christ and the Jewish leaders where they challenge Jesus' assertion that to believe in Him is to be free (Jn. 8:31-33). Within the exchange is an interesting interplay of ideas about what it means to be a child of Abraham. The Jews had stated in John 8:33 that they were free already on the basis that they were Abraham's descendants. Jesus countered by shifting the ground on them so that they were forced to look at their spiritual connection to the patriarch, not just their physical derivation: "I know that you are Abraham's descendants, but you seek to kill Me, because My word has no place in you. I speak what I have seen with My Father, and you do what you have seen with your father" (Jn. 8:37-38).

On the one hand, Jesus acknowledges the Jews' claim to be descended from Abraham, while on the other, He links them to another "father." This is cleverly done with the words "you do what you have seen with your father" in verse 38. Feeling perhaps misunderstood, they retort that "Abraham is our father" (Jn. 8:39). This gives Jesus the upper hand. Having set aside their genealogical credentials as a mere truism, He can now concentrate on their spiritual lineage. This is going to reach its crescendo in verse 58, with Jesus declaring, "Before Abraham was, I Am." The meaning of this

42 To quote Pentecost: "The Lord Jesus, in revealing truth concerning the Holy Spirit in the upper room, divided the Holy Spirit's ministry into two parts: that before the day of Pentecost and that following the day of Pentecost" (J. Dwight Pentecost, *The Divine Comforter: The Person and Work of the Holy Spirit* [Chicago: Moody Press, 1977], 51). See also, James M. Hamilton, Jr., *God's Indwelling Presence: The Holy Spirit in the Old and New Testaments* (Nashville: B&H, 2006). Hamilton admits that the Spirit did not indwell believers in the OT period, and he is to be commended for taking Jn. 14:17 seriously. I think he makes too much of the OT materials, and his examination of Johannine texts would have benefitted from thinking through the implications of the arrival of Christ in history, and the requirements of faith that may have demanded. But he provides a thoughtful study of the issues.

43 We must recall that from the vantage point of Jn. 16 the question was "when" the Spirit would come (cf. Jn. 16:13). In Jn. 20:22 the risen Jesus breathed on the disciples, saying "Receive the Holy Spirit." In and of itself this was proof-positive of the deity of Christ and of His extraordinary authority upon earth, but it was not the new birth. It seems that the disciples were given the Spirit to enable them in some way.

44 Inclusion into the Body of Christ is one example.

statement was both that Jesus is divine (Exod. 3:14), which the Jews understood very quickly (Jn. 8:59), and that Abraham's faith guided him to see Jesus' "day" and rejoice (Jn. 8:56). But before the confrontation ends, the Lord has made a distinct separation between Abraham and the Jews. That separation was in the realms of spirituality and faith. Abraham was of God and therefore anticipated Jesus the Christ (Jn. 8:39-40). These Jews were of the devil (Jn. 8:44), and so were a million miles from being properly related to Abraham in the way that mattered.

This passage throws light upon the matter of what constitutes a true Jew. No Gentiles were present. The conversation was held between rival Jewish men. Both were children of Abraham, Isaac, and Jacob physically.[45] But only one (Jesus) was connected to Abraham in faith.[46] This same distinction between two kinds of Jews, the merely physical versus the physical *and* the spiritual, is seen in Romans 2:28-29 and 9:6-8. I shall revisit the subject of being a true Jew once we arrive at the book of Romans.

The "I Am" Statements in John

The seven "I Am" statements (with the predicate) are unique to John's Gospel.[47] He also employs the identification four additional times in the absolute sense without the qualifier in John 8:24, 28, 58, and 13:19. These statements by Jesus combine His Person and His mission. Jesus' identity is as much in what He does as who He is.[48] Stuhlmacher has a helpful section where he runs through these titles.[49] Although he does not refer to the covenants, his brief exposition has deep covenantal and salvific[50] undercurrents.

I Am the Bread of Life (Jn. 6:35, 48)

Twinned with this expression is Jesus' claiming to be "the living bread" in John 6:51. This saying not only highlights Jesus' claim to be deity (cf. Exod. 3:14), which is present in all these sayings, but it calls to mind the provision of manna in Exodus 16 and Numbers 11. In John 6:32 Jesus makes this very connection. The Mosaic covenant, under which the manna was given in the wilderness journey, could only sustain physical life. The Mosaic code could never provide spiritual salvation; therefore, it could only help in *this* world. Hence, Jesus provides "grace and truth" (Jn. 1:17), something that Moses could not provide.[51]

45 Jesus' ethnic link to Abraham came through His mother, Mary.
46 Although actually Abraham was connected to Him by faith.
47 The Synoptics record one similar usage in Matt. 24:5; Mk. 13:6, and Lk. 21:8.
48 Larry R. Helyer, *The Witness of Jesus, Paul and John*, 312-313.
49 Peter Stuhlmacher, *Biblical Theology of the New Testament*, 675-679.
50 Thomas R. Schreiner, *The King in His Beauty: A Biblical Theology of the Old and New Testaments* (Grand Rapids: Baker, 2013), 516.
51 Moses did of course provide truth, but "truth" in John's Gospel is located in the person of Jesus. It is the bigger truth about creation and existence.

I Am the Light of the World (Jn. 8:12)

The two great New covenant Servant passages in Isaiah 42:6 and 49:6 provide the background for this saying. They both refer to the Servant of Yahweh as "a light to the Gentiles." These same contexts both call the Servant "a covenant to the people," so Jesus is consciously drawing attention to the covenantal significance of Himself as the "Light." As "the true Light" (Jn. 1:9) and "the Logos" (Jn. 1:1-3, 14), Jesus brought order out of the chaos that sin had sown in mankind.

It is characteristic of John not to point to overt OT references but to provide images that call OT passages to mind.[52] We should, therefore, think twice if we are tempted to say that John is not covenantally aware.

I Am the Gate for the Sheep (Jn. 10:7, 9)

According to Stuhlmacher, "The metaphor can be explained by Psalm 118, which was interpreted messianically by early Judaism and early Christianity. Psalm 118:20 speaks of 'the gate of the LORD' through which 'the righteous shall enter,' and this is precisely how Jesus presents himself."[53] By passing through Him, one exits the old life and "will go in and out and find pasture" (Jn. 10:9). Jesus is the "turnstile" to salvation, New covenant salvation. The sinner leaves behind the old covenant as a rule of life and enters into the life-giving sphere of the New covenant.

I Am the Good Shepherd (Jn. 10:11, 14)

In John 10:11 Jesus refers to Himself as the Good Shepherd "who gives his life for the sheep." Here, to quote Ridderbos, "The Son's knowledge of and love for the Father is directed to that self-offering, in which God's eternal love in Jesus forces itself into the world."[54] The picture of a shepherd is a stock image in the OT. David spoke of Yahweh as his shepherd in Psalm 23:1. Ezekiel inveighed against false shepherds in Ezekiel 34 and commended the true shepherd who would one day take care of God's sheep (Ezek. 34:1-10). Zechariah acted out the roles of a faithful shepherd and a wicked shepherd in Zechariah 11.

By speaking about Himself this way, Jesus was deliberately reminding His audience that He was God's shepherd, and perhaps also saying that He was Yahweh, David's shepherd, although before the incarnation. It is beyond dispute that Jesus attributes roles to Himself that are unique. He is the *only* Good Shepherd (Jn. 10:11, 16) who lays down His life on behalf of the sheep (Jn. 10:11, 15). Yet in laying down His life, Jesus is not abandoned to death. He has authority to come back to life (Jn. 10:18).

This power to give up life and reclaim it goes far beyond any ability known among the greatest saints of the OT. But it is not for show. Recall that in His description of

52 On this phenomenon see Richard B. Hays, *Echoes of Scripture in the Gospels*, 284ff.
53 Peter Stuhlmacher, *Biblical Theology of the New Testament*, 677.
54 Herman Ridderbos, *The Gospel of John: A Theological Commentary* (Grand Rapids: Eerdmans, 1992), 362.

Himself as "the door" or "gate" (Jn. 10:7-9), Jesus declares, "If anyone enters by Me, he will be saved, and will go in and out and find pasture" (Jn. 10:9).

It turns out that going "in" through Christ "the door" is paradoxically an entrance "out" into somewhere else. In the next verse, He states, "I have come that they may have life, and that they may have *it* more abundantly" (Jn. 10:10).

So, Christ's power over His death and return to life brings with it abundant life for all His saints (the sheep). In the context of His mission, Christ has entered the world, will die here, and will vanquish death here.

At the close of the mission, "there will be one flock and one shepherd" (Jn. 10:16). The mention of "one flock" seems to some interpreters to prove their contention that there is and always has been only one people of God. But is that really what Jesus is saying? It may be that those interpreters are projecting the future of the Church onto Jesus' statement, whereas He might be looking at the future of Israel. Or it may be that He is saying that every saved human being from whatever age is one humanity, however they might be divided by covenantal promises in the eschaton. Of course, He *might* be saying what covenant theologians and progressive covenantalists think he is saying: that there really is just one people of God. Of the three alternative views, I think the last is the least likely. My reason for saying this is that it is *anti*-covenantal in that it goes against what the divine covenants affirm. It also creates a contradiction—inherent in older Covenant Theology—that the Church has always existed. After all, one cannot claim to believe in only one people of God and in the same breath declare that the saints before the death and resurrection of Jesus were not part of the Church.

The covenants curb the intuition to interpret the "one flock" of John 10:16 as one people of God for the ages. In the context of John 10, the "other sheep" refers to the Gentiles, to whom the Servant is sent "as a light" (Isa. 49:6).[55] Therefore, the reference to "one flock" is best seen as anticipatory of the Jew-Gentile Church (cf. Eph. 2:15), especially in light of Christ's prediction of His death (Jn. 10:11).[56]

I Am the Resurrection and the Life (Jn. 11:25)

Death and dissolution are part and parcel of life under the sun. They are irreconcilable with the existence of God in heaven. According to J. A. Schep in his book, *The Nature of the Resurrection Body: A Study of the Biblical Data*, the Greek word *anastasis* always means resurrection of the body.[57] Here Jesus uses the term as a title for Himself. He therefore is the Giver of life (cf. Deut. 32:39; 1 Sam. 2:6). This parallels what Jesus had said of Himself in John 5:26-29. According to Jesus, God "has granted the Son to have life in Himself" (Jn. 5:26). In John 11:25 the Lord says He is the resurrection *and* the life. The life is new life with the Creator, the life that a human being rightly related to God will have in the Kingdom of God. If we compare this with Isaiah 49:6 and 8, we see a New covenant connection. How could the Servant "raise up

55 Hence the imperative "I must" in verse 16.
56 J. Carl Laney, *John* (Chicago: Moody, 1992), 191.
57 J. A. Schep, *The Nature of the Resurrection Body: A Study of the Biblical Data* (Grand Rapids: Eerdmans, 1964).

the tribes of Jacob, and... restore the preserved ones of Israel" (Isa. 49:6) if He was not endued with resurrection life? Resurrection life is essential to the Creation Project as a whole, for unless it could be given to sinners, the Project could not be completed.

I Am the Way, the Truth, and the Life (Jn. 14:6)

Perhaps the most famous and plainly redemptive of the "I Am" statements is this one in John 14:6. In this self-identification by Jesus, He gives Himself three separate names, although I think they make up one title. The context of this remark came after Thomas had asked, "Lord, we do not know where You are going, and how can we know the way?" (Jn. 14:5). The "way" is the way to "My Father's house" (Jn. 14:2), which is heaven. Leon Morris stated:

> "Way" speaks of a connection between the two, the link between God and man. "Truth" reminds us of the complete reliability of Jesus in all that He does and is. And "life" stresses the fact that mere physical existence matters little. The only life worthy of the name is that which Jesus brings, for He is life itself.[58]

How does a human being find his way to his Creator and His heaven? Jesus is that way, and He is the only way. He is not a pathway we can tread. He is a Savior who will take us. And He is the Truth, "the one who is what he says he is and does he says he will do."[59] And as the one who will defeat death, He is the giver of life! What is of interest is that these three names, "Way," "Truth," and "Life," are associated with the purpose behind God's covenants, the New covenant in particular. For example, Isaiah 42:7 speaks of the Servant whose role is to "open blind eyes." As I have pointed out many times in this book and its predecessor, Messiah is to be made "a covenant to the people" (Isa. 42:6; 49:8) for the means of salvation. Hence, He is the way to Yahweh through salvation. But He is also the faithful and righteous Servant (Isa. 53:11-12), who, as a covenant of salvation (the New covenant), represents the truth of God to men.

I Am the True Vine (Jn. 15:1, 5)

The final "I Am" in John 15 picks up on the imagery of Israel in Isaiah 5, where Judah is depicted as a vineyard that does not produce. The purpose of the illustration is to highlight the importance of abiding in Christ, because from Him derives everything that counts in the spiritual life. In fact, Jesus asserts, "Without Me you can do nothing" (Jn. 15:5). The metaphor is not to be pushed into service of those with supersessionist tendencies who wish to reduce covenant Israel down to Jesus and remake Israel as the Church in Him.[60]

---

58 Leon Morris, *The Gospel According to John*, 641. In a footnote Morris notes that Jesus is claiming to be the source from whence all other truths, light, life, etc. comes (Ibid., n. 16).

59 See Herman Ridderbos, *The Gospel of John*, 493.

60 As for example, Brent E. Parker, "The Israel-Christ-Church Relationship," in *Progressive Covenantalism* (Nashville: B&H, 2016), 62ff. Parker notices the role of Psa. 80 behind Jesus'

Summary

In these seven "I Am" statements, one does not have to look too far, at least in several of them, to find covenant overtones. The very term *ego eimi* ("I Am") signifies the covenant God (cf. Exod. 3:16). Jesus gives bread that lasts, which indicates something better than what was provided under Moses. He is the Light, just as Isaiah predicted He would be (Isa. 49:6. Cf. 2:5). This same Light is also made as a covenant in the same verse. The shepherd motif is common in the OT, and such passages as Ezekiel 34:1-31 make it plain that God's faithful Shepherd will bring God's people to Him. In my view, Ezekiel 34:11ff. describes a New covenant context. And indeed, Ezekiel 34:25 mentions "a covenant of peace," which transforms the earth and animal life upon the earth. This is a New covenant blessing.[61]

The four addition "I Am" statements also have covenantal traces in them. In these texts Jesus points to Himself as the "I Am" without qualification (Jn. 8:24, 28, 58; 13:19). In the most famous of these uses, Jesus states, "Jesus said to them, "Most assuredly, I say to you, before Abraham was, I AM" (Jn. 8:58). The conversation in this place is with the Pharisees (Jn. 8:13) and probably others (Jn. 8:22), and Abraham holds a central place in it (Jn. 8:33, 37-40, 52-53, 57-58). Hence, the covenantal role of Abraham runs through the interchange.[62]

Christ is the Son of God

Back in John 10, as Jesus walked in Solomon's Porch, He was accosted by the Jews who state, "How long do You keep us in doubt? If You are the Christ, tell us plainly" (Jn. 10:24). Jesus answered that He had told them and that His works prove it, but a little further on—after Jesus declares, "I and the Father are one" (Jn. 10:30)—Jesus responds to them with these words: "Do you say of Him whom the Father sanctified and sent into the world, 'You are blaspheming,' because I said, 'I am the Son of God'?" (Jn. 10:36).

Notice that Jesus connects the title Christ with His standing as the Son of God. Thus, the Jewish leaders have their answer, but their false expectations, which were based on their bloated sense of self-importance, mar their ability to comprehend Him. However, in the next chapter, we find Martha, the sister of Lazarus, expressing, "Yes, Lord, I believe that You are the Christ, the Son of God, who is to come into the world" (Jn. 11:27).

---

illustration, but he spiritualizes the prayer (e.g., "Restore us, O God; Cause Your face to shine, and we shall be saved!" Psa. 80:3). The "we" of the psalm includes the tribes of Israel (Psa. 80:1-2) who were brought out of Egypt (Psa. 80:8).

61 I might include here Ezek. 34:17, which says: "And as for you, O My flock, thus says the Lord GOD: 'Behold, I shall judge between sheep and sheep, between rams and goats.'" This reminds us of Matt. 25:31-46, where the returned King Christ judges the nations.

62 I should add to this the fact that two of the signs which John records relate to Jesus as the resurrection (healing of a blind man, Jn. 9:1-7) and giving life from the dead—though not here eternal life—(the raising of Lazarus, Jn. 11:38-44).

Martha makes the connection that the Jewish leaders, with all their "expertise," cannot make.[63] She knows that the Messiah will be the Son of God. This being so, Jesus' title of "Son of God" pertains not so much to His pre-existent state as God the Son (which He is at all times) but to His role as the Servant who would become King.[64]

The eleventh chapter records Jesus groaning or "bristling" within Himself at His friend Lazarus' death (Jn. 11:33, 38). As John has portrayed Him as "Life" (e.g., Jn. 1:4; 10:10; 11:25), this is all the more understandable. Life is troubled when it meets its opposite, but Life wins out (Jn. 11:25-26, 43-44).

Jesus the King

In the next chapter, we see Jesus coming to Jerusalem for the last time (Jn. 12:12-15). John's treatment of the Triumphal Entry is brief but interesting. He notices that the crowds were shouting, "Hosanna! 'Blessed *is* He who comes in the name of the LORD!' the King of Israel!" (Jn. 12:13).

It seems that the people in the crowd recognized Jesus as the rightful King of Israel *because* they saw Him as their Messiah. John does not offer commentary on this other than to cite Zechariah 9:9: "Fear not, daughter of Zion; Behold, your King is coming, sitting on a donkey's colt" (Jn. 12:15). Then he tells us that the disciples did not catch on to what this meant until after Christ's resurrection and ascension (Jn. 12:16). In the ferment of the situation, their senses were perhaps overloaded. But whatever the explanation, it did dawn on them that their Lord, who they knew to be God's Son, had entered Jerusalem as prophesied, but not to a city with open arms. He did not bring peace to the nations (Zech. 9:10). Rather, He came to the city of His death.

This is not the first time John has signaled Jesus' role as the true King of Israel. Nathanael, remember, had exclaimed it in John 1:49, and after the Feeding of the Five Thousand, the people wanted to make Him King (Jn. 6:15); a move which Jesus avoided. At the trial of Jesus, the Jews claimed that He had made Himself a king (Jn. 19:12, 21), even going so far as to step beyond their own messianic views and show allegiance to the Emperor. Jesus' impact upon Pontius Pilate was pronounced, with Pilate declaring "Behold your King" (Jn. 19:14), and even having a banner written which spelled out "JESUS OF NAZARETH, THE KING OF THE JEWS" (Jn. 19:19).

Remarkably, the name of David only appears in one place in this Gospel, in the context of a discussion between the people after Jesus had taught and performed miracles in the Temple in John 7.

> Therefore many from the crowd, when they heard this saying, said, "Truly this is the Prophet." Others said, "This is the Christ." But some said, "Will the Christ come out of Galilee? Has not the Scripture said that the Christ comes

63 This statement should be qualified slightly because it seems they did have some idea of who Jesus was but didn't like what they saw. See Matt. 26:62-64 (but see 1 Cor. 2:8).

64 What Paul says in Phil. 2:5-11 reflects this also.

> from the seed of David and from the town of Bethlehem, where David was?" So there was a division among the people because of Him (Jn. 7:40-43).

Two things are of note here. First, some of the crowds, at least, are so impressed by what they hear that they entertain the thought that Jesus may be the Prophet like Moses predicted in Deuteronomy 18:15-18. Others were certain that He was the Messiah. But there were doubters (as there always are). They know that Jesus hails from Galilee, and they are correct to say that Christ will come from Bethlehem. What they don't know is that Jesus was born in Bethlehem. In the second place, they also state that "Christ comes from the seed of David." This is the only verse in John where David is referred to, yet from what we have studied, it is clear that the Davidic covenant is presupposed throughout this Gospel, so we should be on the lookout for covenantal links.

If we read down in John 12 there are two texts that I think ought to grab our attention:

> But although He had done so many signs before them, they did not believe in Him... (Jn. 12:37).

> He who rejects Me, and does not receive My words, has that which judges him—the word that I have spoken will judge him in the last day (Jn. 12:48).

John singles out two main reasons why Jesus should have been believed. One was the "mighty signs" which were done by Him wherever He went. These extraordinary miracles demonstrated in the clearest way that Jesus was sent by God. Through healings of the sick, the lame, and the blind; through exorcisms, the raising of the dead, the provision of wine and food and money seemingly out of nowhere, the stilling of the storm, and even walking upon the water, these works which attended Jesus' every day were never seen in such quantities nor demonstrated with such power (Jn. 14:11). They showed proof in the extended world that the great Prophet had come. If Jesus could bring such wonderful changes locally, why could He not bring true harmony to the whole world? This is why John cites Isaiah 53:1 (Jn. 12:38), because of the overwhelming evidence to His Person (Jn. 7:31).

But then there were His words, of which it was said, "No man ever spoke like this man" (Jn. 7:48). Christ's words were God's words, and they, therefore, bore the full demand of compliance from any who heard them. Together, the works and the words of Jesus formed a powerful witness to Israel that the long-awaited Coming One was here!

Jesus and His Betrayer

All of the Gospels refer to Jesus' betrayal by Judas Iscariot, but John's account is the most riveting. As John tells us, the announcement of the coming betrayal came right after Jesus had demonstrated unprecedented humility in washing the feet of all His disciples (Jn. 13:1-17). In beginning the disclosure, Jesus quotes Psalm 41:9, "He who eats bread with Me has lifted up his heel against Me." In its context, the verse fits amid a catalog of maladies that David has been afflicted with, but Jesus picks it out and gives it a new application; or should I say, gives it a new prophetic significance.

Jesus had chosen His disciples, including Judas Iscariot (Jn. 6:70-71).[65] Judas is unusual in that he has several cryptic texts related to him. In the text just cited, Jesus calls him a "devil." Then, in John 17:12 Jesus refers to Judas as "the son of perdition," the exact same name Paul later calls the "man of sin" (2 Thess. 2:3). This figure's blasphemies recall the "little horn" of Daniel 7:25, who will persecute the saints. Is this a mere coincidence? I hardly think so, although what one makes of it is another question altogether. Another mysterious thing about Judas is that, rather than saying he went to the grave or to Hades, Peter refers to him going "to his own place" in Acts 1:25. Whichever way one deals with these cryptic references, Judas was an odd fellow.

One more matter of note concerning Judas Iscariot is that, according to John 13:27, after Jesus gave him the bread, Satan entered him. Then Jesus spoke to him, saying, "What you do, do quickly." Verse 28 reports that none of the others picked up on this, which shows that Satan can enter a person without others being aware of it. One thing is clear: Judas was an agent of the Devil. He was sent to disrupt the covenant plan that Messiah was born to implement.

Preparing a Place for Us

The opening verses of John 14 are among the most well-known by all Christians. They have brought hope and encouragement to all God's saints. I want to look at them here because this is a good place to ask about the relation of heaven and the coming kingdom as a home. I have been saying a lot about the coming kingdom of Christ in this book and its prequel, but doesn't the fact that Jesus says He is preparing places for us in heaven do away with the idea that we shall dwell on a new earth, both "Millennial" or eternal? Let us remind ourselves of the passage:

> Let not your heart be troubled; you believe in God, believe also in Me. In My Father's house are many mansions; if *it were* not *so,* I would have told you. I go to prepare a place for you. And if I go and prepare a place for you, I will come again and receive you to Myself; that where I am, *there* you may be also (Jn. 14:1-3).

These words are wonderful, and I would not want to wrest them away from believers for the sake of teaching a novelty. The verses say what they say, and I know that if I die before the Lord's return I shall go to heaven because heaven is where He is (Acts 1:11; 3:20-21; 2 Cor. 5:8). Moreover, Jesus says in this very passage that He will return "and receive you to Myself; that where I am...you may be also" (Jn. 14:3). It appears then that Jesus is saying that He will one day come and waft us all to heaven forever.

65 The name "Iscariot" or "Ish-Kerioth" means "man of Kerioth." Kerioth was in Moab in modern Jordan (Jer. 48:24-25; Amos 2:2).

As apparent as that thought may be, there are good reasons to question that view. First, as others have noted, John 14:17-18 seems to qualify John 14:3 in its reference to the Spirit. That is, Jesus will come in the arrival and indwelling of the Spirit. This means that the "coming" of verse 3 is not necessarily a reference to the physical second coming.[66] Second, if Jesus is referring to His second advent, He would have to be speaking proleptically of those believers who will be alive when He comes; he cannot be referring to the disciples who would join Him in glory much sooner. I will assess whether the passage can be applied to the doctrine of the rapture further in this book, but I will say that a taking out of the saints before the second coming, and even before the Tribulation (or at some point in it) makes good sense. Third, Christians have been going to the "mansions"/"rooms" for nearly two millennia, so there has been ample time for the words to be experienced as true. But this does not mean that Jesus will not return to earth; and therefore, it does not mean that Jesus will not reign in the Kingdom of God on earth.

The Resurrection of the Messiah

I said earlier that I would discuss the resurrection in John. John's account includes several interesting stories that highlight facets of the theology of the risen Messiah. I call Him "Messiah" because I want to keep our minds attentive to the fact that *Christos* is not to be thought of as Jesus' last name, but is rather His covenant appointment as the Servant of Yahweh, the Branch, and the Seed of the woman. John has already noticed the resurrection on Jesus' lips, most notably in John 2:19 and again in John 11:25. In the latter, the power of Jesus to resurrect the dead is prominent. But in the former, Jesus' own resurrection is in view (Jn. 2:21-22).

John's account of the risen Jesus is in his final two chapters. The first story in John 20 is about Mary Magdalene's arrival at the tomb early in the morning. She reports that the tomb is empty (Jn. 20:2). Peter and John rush to the site and confirm her witness (Jn. 20:3-10). The Gospel also records their ignorance of the resurrection: "For as yet they did not know the Scripture, that He must rise again from the dead" (Jn. 20:9).

This, of course, agrees with the Synoptic writers. So once more, I have to press the matter, if His own disciples did not fathom the resurrection of Jesus until after they saw Him (in Jn. 20:19-29), then how could it have been a part of the gospel they proclaimed before that event? As painful and untidy as this glaring piece of information is, we must think through its ramifications. For one, it means the message Jesus and His disciples preached publicly did not include His impending death and resurrection from the dead. This is just true whichever way you want to slice it.

66 I realize that Jn. 14:3 is commonly cited by premillennialists as a reference to the "rapture." See, e.g., Wayne Brindle, "Biblical Evidence for the Imminence of the Rapture," *BSAC* 158 (April-June 2001), 138-151. As I point out below, this may be true. My purpose at present is to explore exegetical options available to answer the question of whether the passage nullifies a this-worldly expectation of the kingdom.

Saying this emphatically does not mean there is a strict division between the Gospels and the Epistles. The majority of those who believed in Jesus as the Messiah would go on to believe He was crucified for their sins. We know that Paul speaks to this moral continuity in 1 Timothy 6:3-4a: "If anyone teaches otherwise and does not consent to wholesome words, even the words of our Lord Jesus Christ, and to the doctrine which accords with godliness, he is proud, knowing nothing." Here the continuity in view is the humble disposition and character of the saint who has Jesus as his great Exemplar (1 Thess. 1:6; cf. 1 Pet. 2:21; 1 Jn. 2:6). But one cannot avoid the fact that the Church was not formed until Acts 2, and the Spirit was not given to indwell believers until then (Jn. 7:37-39; Acts 1:8).

Another matter is that those who trusted in that pre-Golgotha message and died prior to the proclamation of Christ's death and resurrection were saved on the basis of that event, even though it did not form the content of their faith in Christ. In the third place, we must not construct understandings of the Gospel histories that pass over this truth. I, for one, wish things could be tidier, but it is not for me to rewrite the sacred text for the sake of settling my nerves.

As the chapter continues, we encounter the beautiful story of Mary Magdalene's meeting with the risen Lord (Jn. 20:11-18). Jesus forbade her to touch Him, for He told her, "I have not yet ascended to My Father" (Jn. 20:17). This obviously meant something. Jesus seems to say He must present Himself to His Father in heaven. What comes to my mind in this connection is Hebrews 9:11-12:

> But Christ came *as* High Priest of the good things to come, with the greater and more perfect tabernacle not made with hands, that is, not of this creation. Not with the blood of goats and calves, but with His own blood He entered the Most Holy Place once for all, having obtained eternal redemption.

If we join this passage together with John 20:17, then we may interpret Christ's words to Mary Magdalene as indicating His imminent return to heaven to present Himself (and some of His blood?) to God at the altar of the tabernacle in heaven (Heb. 8:2, 5). I see no reason not to believe that heaven has a literal temple in it. Away with the silly idea that heaven is like a blank film set with nothing in it. It has a mountain and a city (Heb. 12:22). The risen Jesus resides there in a glorified human body (Acts 1:11; 3:20-21; Col. 3:1). So yes, there is a temple there, and Jesus ascended there as the spotless Lamb of God (1 Pet. 1:19) and then returned to appear before and be handled by His disciples in John 20:24ff. This indicates that Jesus was a covenant sacrifice. As a covenant sacrifice, He must present Himself to God as the conqueror of death for humankind, in essence, so that humans could stand vindicated in Him (cf. Jn. 17:24-26).

When He comes to the disciples in John 20:19ff. His first words are, "Peace be unto you." This peace has been hard won for them by Christ Himself, and He is eager to pronounce it. But it is not given in word only. Jesus' next words are, "Receive the Holy Spirit" (Jn. 20:22). The Spirit is a gift of the *risen* and vindicated Christ. This gift of the Spirit is not the indwelling of the Spirit experienced at Pentecost and thereafter, but was a special empowerment given, probably to help them in their witness until they received power from on high (Lk. 24:49; Acts 1:4-5). Previous to Pentecost (Acts 2), the disciples were not regenerated.

Chapter 20 closes with John's testimony to Jesus: "These are written that you may believe that Jesus is the Christ, the Son of God, and that believing you may have life in His name" (Jn. 20:31). He wants us to know that Jesus is both Messiah and Son of God, and that "life" was available through faith in His name. This "life" was, of course, connected to His resurrection. The resurrection is the first installment and trigger of the New Creation. It is the foundation of everything that will occur in the coming Kingdom of God.

A Final Lesson in Hermeneutics

Before I examine the book of Acts there is one more thing that I want to call attention to. It concerns the conversation between Jesus and Peter about the Beloved Disciple (John) in John 21:

> Then Peter, turning around, saw the disciple whom Jesus loved following, who also had leaned on His breast at the supper, and said, "Lord, who is the one who betrays You? Peter, seeing him, said to Jesus, "But Lord, what *about* this man?"
>
> Jesus said to him, "If I will that he remain till I come, what *is that* to you? You follow Me."
>
> Then this saying went out among the brethren that this disciple would not die. Yet Jesus did not say to him that he would not die, but, "If I will that he remain till I come, what *is that* to you?" (Jn. 21:20-23).

Prior to this passage, Peter is told that when he is old, he will be led away to death (Jn. 21:18-19). Curious about the fate of John, Peter asks about him. The answer Peter gets back is basically a "that's not your business" rejoinder. However, the precise words of Jesus are important here: "If I will that he remain till I come, what *is that* to you? You follow Me" (Jn. 21:22).

From John's comment in the next verse, we find out that a false rumor circulated about John not seeing death. If we ask why the rumor started, the answer is that Jesus' words were misinterpreted and given a meaning that they did not support. The error was due to nothing else but a faulty hermeneutic. Jesus meant exactly what He said, but some read a foreign meaning into His words.

To correct the misinterpretation and to fortify the correct one, John repeats Jesus' words verbatim: "If I will that he remain till I come, what *is that* to you? You follow Me." We have here a great example of the importance of believing that God means what He says. This is a hermeneutical shot across the bow. The passage constitutes a kind of touchstone for proper interpretation, a warning not to deduce meanings not supported by the plain words of Scripture. I acknowledge the caution with gratitude.

John's method could be described as insinuation (in the positive sense). Others have written persuasively about how John shows acquaintance with the Synoptics.[67] He knows the Synoptics and seems to rely on them, albeit somewhat obliquely. He has his own purpose, and his portrait of Jesus is intended to draw people to faith and keep faith in Him. But John has not forgotten Israel. And he has not forgotten the covenant bond between Israel and God. Covenant is very much a part of the world of John's Gospel. In the words of Johannes Pedersen, "One is born of a covenant and into covenant, and wherever one moves in life, one makes a covenant or acts on the basis of the already existing covenant."[68] In other words, for John, as for all Israelites of his time, the very atmosphere of their lives was covenantal. And this can be seen in the fabric of John's writings.

Covenant Associations in the Epistles of John

John's three short epistles are too brief to have much covenantal content, but that does not mean they are totally devoid of contributions. In the first place, the book of 1 John opens with a reference to the "Word of life" (1 Jn. 1:1). Commentators go back and forth about whether John is referring to the witness to Jesus. John Stott and many others believe it refers to the message about Jesus.[69] It is hard to decide, and so is best left to one side.[70]

What is easier to ascertain is the strong emphasis on love (*agape*) in these letters. As I have already said, *agapao* has covenantal overtones. God's faithfulness to His people should certainly be seen covenantally (cf. Jer. 31:1-3, 31-34).[71] As such, *agapao* overlaps the idea of covenant love in the Hebrew words *hesed*[72] and *ahab*.[73] And the embodiment of covenant love is Jesus Christ (cf. Isa. 42:6; 49:8).[74] John at least hints at this by telling us that Jesus not only provided propitiation through His blood, but that "He Himself is the propitiation for our sins" (1 Jn. 2:2; 4:10). In 1 John 4:10 this is

67 See especially chapters 1 and 2 in Lydia McGrew, *Hidden in Plain View: Undesigned Coincidences in the Gospels and Acts.*

68 Johannes Pedersen, *Israel: Its Life and Culture* (London: Oxford University Press, 1964), 308, as quoted in Rekha M. Chennattu, *Johannine Discipleship as a Covenant Relationship,* 59.

69 John R. W. Stott, *The Epistles of John* (Leicester: InterVarsity, 1990), 64-65.

70 I. Howard Marshall believes the phrase is a name for Jesus. See his *New Testament Theology*, 568, 572.

71 Leon Morris, *The Apostolic Preaching of the Cross*, 82.

72 For a wonderful practical exposition of *hesed* using the book of Ruth see Paul E. Miller, *A Loving Life: In a World of Broken Relationships* (Wheaton, IL: Crossway, 2014).

73 As said previously (Vol. 1, 259), God's *hesed* has strong covenantal overtones. See also Daniel I. Block, *Covenant*, 370-371, where the author shows that God's *ahab* is behind the covenant with David. "Indeed, *ahab* was an action word, fundamentally *signifying covenant commitment demonstrated in action in the interest of the other person*, a meaning that carries over into New Testament *agapao*" (Ibid., 138, italics his). In a footnote (n. 10) Block gives "John 3:16; 14:15, 21, 23-24; 15:13; but esp. 1 Cor. 13:1-8." God's love is covenantal.

74 Ibid., 83.

directly connected with God's love for us. The pervasive love concept in these letters might reasonably be tied in with our New covenant relationship.

Hence, we read that Christians can cleanse themselves with the blood of their Savior: "But if we walk in the light as He is in the light, we have fellowship with one another, and the blood of Jesus Christ His Son cleanses us from all sin" (1 Jn. 1:7).

Although John does not say so, I do not think he would object at all with Paul's doctrine of the blood as New covenant blood (1 Cor. 11:25), especially because he was present when the Lord designated His blood as "the blood of the New covenant" (Lk. 22:20). Christ's blood is the means through which the saint can stay in good relationship with God in the New covenant. Not that the Christian's inclusion in the New covenant is jeopardized by unconfessed sin, but his rewards may well be (2 Jn. 1:8). Thus, the Christian's manner of life may lead in and out of sin, but the general tendency will show evidence of heart transformation, such as was predicted in the New covenant (e.g., 1 Jn. 4:7; 5:18; cf. 2 Cor. 3:3; Ezek. 36:27).

Moreover, even if this is lacking, Jesus Christ is our Advocate.[75] There is a possible allusion to Isaiah 53:11 in 1 John 2:1: "We have an Advocate with the Father, Jesus Christ the righteous."[76] Again, therefore, we are circling close to covenant themes. We know that God sees life with Him in terms of covenant (cf. Matt. 22:32; cf. Mal. 2:5). The New covenant guarantees life with God because it brings the forgiveness of sins (Jer. 31:31, 34; 2 Cor. 3:6). John echoes this when he writes, "He who has the Son has life; he who does not have the Son of God does not have life" (1 Jn. 5:12).

First John has a lot to say about "life." On the positive side, "God has given us eternal life, and this life is in His Son" (1 Jn. 5:11). These references support the view that "the Word of life" in 1 John 1:1 refers to the Son Himself.

John's Teaching About Antichrist

John's epistles are also notable for their mention of Antichrist, a subject not broached in his Gospel. The apostle certainly believed in a future personal Antichrist: "You have heard that the Antichrist is coming" (1 Jn. 2:18).

A personage will arise who will exert massive influence in the world. It is logical to conclude that this "Antichrist" is one and the same as Daniel's "little horn" (Dan. 7:8), "willful king" (Dan. 11:32ff.), and Paul's "man of sin" (2 Thess. 2:3). And since John is interested in this individual, it is not surprising that he reappears in the prophetic book of Revelation (Rev. 13). I should at once say that the Epistles of John do not develop the doctrine in any significant way. They do, however, inform us of something that Paul had also spoken of when he writes about "the mystery of lawlessness is already at work" (2 Thess. 2:7). Similarly, John refers to "the spirit of the Antichrist, which you have heard was coming, and is now already in the world" (1 Jn. 4:3).

75 In fact, it is noteworthy the number of times the name "Jesus Christ" is used in 1 and 2 John. See Herbert W. Bateman, *Jesus the Messiah*, 340-341. "Christ," as I have shown, is a covenant title.

76 Peter Stuhlmacher, *Biblical Theology of the New Testament*, 672.

John relates this "spirit of the Antichrist" with the doctrine that "Jesus Christ has come in the flesh" (1 Jn. 4:3), but what does he mean? Clearly there is much more to it than that. Today, a few men like Robert Price and G. A. Wells deny that such a person as Jesus Christ existed.[77] This is a marginal and, frankly, idiotic point of view. Clearly John was not warning about misconstruing someone whom he had never known. Not even post-Jamnia Judaism denied that Jesus existed. There must be more to it.[78]

I think the answer is in the name and significance of "Jesus Christ." "Christ" refers, of course, to Messiah, the coming King prophesied in the OT (Gen. 3:15; 49:8-10; Psa. 2; Mic. 5:2; Isa. 9:6; Dan. 9:25-26; Zech. 9:9). "Jesus" is the one who is the Messiah and who has come into the world. Therefore, I think the denial that the Christ has come in the person of Jesus is the basic claim of the spirit of Antichrist. But this leads to the teaching that since Jesus was not the Messiah, then Messiah is still to come. Hence, we might surmise that the denial that Jesus was the promised Messiah, with all that entails, opens up the possibility that when Antichrist comes, he will claim to be the real Christ.[79]

This understanding covers all of the ways John speaks about the Antichrist and antichrists. In 2 John we are told, "For many deceivers have gone out into the world who do not confess Jesus Christ as coming in the flesh. This is a deceiver and an antichrist" (2 Jn. 7). The incarnation of Jesus the Christ and all that it means for man's relationship with the Creator is the Truth that is spurned by those who teach minimally what the Antichrist will proclaim maximally.

77 Many good books debunk this view. E.g., Craig S. Keener, *The Historical Jesus of the Gospels*; and the four replies to Price in *The Historical Jesus: Five Views*, eds. James K. Beilby and Paul R. Eddy (Downers Grove, IL: IVP, 2009).

78 This way of summing things up in basic terms with the suggestion that there is more to it is quite common with John.

79 The question of when the Antichrist claims to be Messiah is of interest. To my mind, the claim comes at the start of the seventieth week, which is why the Jews make a covenant with him and build the temple of Matt. 24; 2 Thess. 2; and Rev. 11. When Antichrist (the Beast) claims to be God and demands worship (Rev. 13:4) the Jews will refuse to follow him and will be persecuted (Matt. 24:15ff/Mk. 13:14ff; Rev. 12:12-17).

12

THE COVENANTAL BACKDROP OF THE GOSPELS

Likewise He also took the cup after supper, saying, "This cup is the new covenant in My blood, which is shed for you."
– Luke 22:20

When thinking through the "covernance" of the Gospels, or indeed of the NT generally, several crucial components have to be understood:

1. Israel as an ethnic, national people group was a historical and covenantal reality, and the terms of the Abrahamic covenant and its consequences concern real things in real time as its effects. Therefore, the "seed/descendants" part of the Abrahamic covenant was not open to question. While it was certainly true to say that "not all Israel [was] Israel" (Rom. 9:6) in terms of true spirituality, it was nevertheless a settled fact that Israel *qua* Israel was in existence, and the covenants settled its continued existence. Israel was the covenant nation of Yahweh, as the early portions of Matthew and Luke especially make clear.

2. The Davidic promise was the subject of widespread expectation in Second Temple times. This expectation was, of course, bound together with the anticipation of the Messiah. As testified to by diverse religious and even political movements in the first century A.D. (such as the Essenes, Pharisees, and Zealots) and even afterward (the followers of Simon bar Kochkba), this zeal for the restoration of the Davidide dynasty was a powerful undercurrent in NT times. As Larry Helyer says, "The Gospels must be read against the backdrop of a strong expectation that God would soon act to reestablish the Davidic Dynasty."[1]

1 Larry R. Helyer, *Exploring Jewish Literature of the Second Temple Period*, 59.

The Irrevocable Covenants

These two engines, Abrahamic and Davidic, were perpetually running in the background even when they were not explicitly mentioned, but they directed the mindset of most Jews. Rather like the East–West standoff during the Cold War (circa 1960–1980), the covenantal backdrop was a known constituent of the worldview of Israel in the time of Jesus and the Apostles.[2] There was no reason to continually make reference to the Abrahamic and Davidic covenants. It was taken for granted in ancient times that any talk of Israel or Israel's Messiah presupposed God's covenants (e.g., Matt. 2:2; 3:8-11; 8:11; 20:30-31; 21:9, 15; Mk. 10:48; Lk. 1:67-79; 22:20; Jn. 8:53-56).

Having said this, I must make a sort of concession. My refusal to alter covenant meanings to force them into first coming fulfillment is a minority position. In my commitment to the univocal character of Yahweh's covenant oaths in the OT, I have projected a course that few wish to take. Here, for example, is a recent work in which the author commits himself to find the core of NT theology in (mostly) first century fulfillment:

> In sharp contrast, every NT book states (usually quite explicitly but once in a while only implicitly) that the age of the fulfillment of these promises has arrived. The Messiah has come. Israel's savior has appeared. Their spiritual exile can be over. The people of Israel are being reconstituted among Jesus' followers. A new age has been inaugurated that will embrace all people and all peoples of the world on equal terms. While not every last prophecy of the OT has come to pass, the last days have begun that will climax in the completion of everything that yet remains unfulfilled. In fact, we can go further and say that in every writer and even in every individual book of the twenty-seven NT books, this conviction (either in these words or others) shines through at the very heart of what the writer and document are trying to express.[3]

While Blomberg's views regarding redemptive-historical fulfillment at the first advent are the norm, I, for one, am quite unsatisfied with how this method undercuts the covenant promises of the OT. I do not believe that "The people of Israel are being reconstituted among Jesus' followers," no matter how credentialed the author happens to be or how assertively one puts it. What did Yahweh say?

> If those ordinances depart
> From before Me, says the LORD,
> *Then* the seed of Israel shall also cease
> From being a nation before Me forever (Jer. 31:36).

2 In his important book on covenants Daniel Block writes concerning Genesis 12–50: "like the operating system in a computer, which constantly runs in the background, the covenant was the driving force in the entire narrative" (Daniel I. Block, *Covenant,* 105). In view of what we have seen in our survey of the Gospels, there is no reason to believe this was not still the case in Jesus' day.

3 Craig L. Blomberg, *A New Testament Theology* (Waco, TX: Baylor University Press, 2018), 11.

The ordinances referenced are the sun, the moon, and the stars in the previous verse. The idea is that these are fixed. Yes, even these heavenly bodies will be dissolved at the end of the Millennium (Rev. 20:11), but not before that time. God has made a permanent "deal" with Israel, which shall last even into the new heavens and earth (Isa. 65:17-18).

I believe that not even Yahweh (especially not Yahweh, actually) is free to alter an oath He has sworn. If He has covenanted with Israel that it will always be a nation before Him, then that is the end of it, and the NT cannot change this truth. This is an example of what I have said before: if our interpretations of Scripture go against the words of the covenant that God made, then our interpretation is incorrect and must change. The covenant doesn't and indeed can't change!

Psalm 105 proclaims:

> O seed of Abraham His servant,
> You children of Jacob, His chosen ones!
> He is the LORD our God;
> His judgments *are* in all the earth.
> He remembers His covenant forever,
> The word *which* He commanded, for a thousand generations,
> *The covenant* which He made with Abraham,
> And His oath to Isaac,
> And confirmed it to Jacob for a statute,
> To Israel *as* an everlasting covenant,
> Saying, "To you I will give the land of Canaan
> As the allotment of your inheritance" (Psa. 105:6-11).

Could anything be clearer? The word for covenant, *berith*, appears twice in the passage (Psa. 105:8, 10) and is supplied a third time by implication in verse 9. The oath Yahweh took regarding the Abrahamic covenant is there in Psalm 105:9. On top of this, the specific part of the Abrahamic covenant being emphasized is the land promise (Psa. 105:11). This is in contrast to the NT, where Paul emphasizes the third part of the covenant, the blessing to the nations (Rom. 4:13, 17[4]; Gal. 3:8). Although all can admit that Gentiles come into blessing through the covenant with Abraham as stipulated in Genesis 12:3 and 22:18, this does not abrogate nor change what the psalmist declares in Psalm 105 or what the Prophets predict in places like Hosea 2:19; Micah 4:7-8; Isaiah 9:6-7; 60:21; Jeremiah 7:7; 17:24-26; 31:26; and Ezekiel 43:7.

If we return to the opening sentence of the Blomberg quote above, he claims that "every NT book states (usually quite explicitly but once in a while only implicitly) that the age of the fulfillment of these promises has arrived. The Messiah has come. Israel's savior has appeared."

---

4 In Rom. 4:18, Paul applies Gen. 15:5 to "the nations." Although the original context speaks of physical descendants, it is not inappropriate for the apostle to extend the promise to the "heirs through faith" in the nations since his point is that Gentiles have been joined to Abraham (though not to Isaac and Jacob) through faith.

In brief, my response to this claim is that I think it shows how two men can read the same passages and come out with very different views. This is not a problem with the texts themselves but with us, the readers, and our assumptions. In an important sense, it is quite true to say that "Israel's savior has appeared." Of course, He has. But in another important sense, we must recall Zechariah 12:10: "Then they will look on Me whom they pierced." When is the "then"? Is it the first advent of Christ? Absolutely not, for right before that statement in the same verse, we read, "And I will pour on the house of David and on the inhabitants of Jerusalem the Spirit of grace and supplication." The whole context of Zechariah 12 (and indeed the section Zechariah 12–14) tells us that Israel does not come to salvation until Christ's return, and the NT agrees with this (Rom. 11:15, 25-27; Rev. 1:7).[5]

So, there is an important decision to be made about what one is to do with God's covenants. Either those oaths of God are irrevocable (cf. Rom. 11:29), or they are pliable, and God is free to claim that the words He used never meant what they appeared to say.[6] I realize that those who advocate for the second option would never want to say it in those terms. But if one is going to teach fulfillment of covenant oaths in totally unexpected ways, I do not see how this conclusion can be avoided.

The truth is that the Gospels do *not* tell us that the covenants that God made with Abraham, Phinehas, or David have been altered to fit the requirements of the Church, still less that they found their fulfillment in the first century. The presence of royal allusions in relation to Messiah/Christ throughout the Gospels (and the NT generally) has been viewed from a first coming perspective, but this has been to the detriment of what the text is actually saying. The patently eschatological language of much of the kingdom teaching of the Synoptics has been shoehorned to fit the first coming. This is done in the face of Yahweh's covenants in the First Testament, and the fact that the majority of the messianic prophecies in the OT focus upon the second advent, not the first.[7] Such clues are forgotten in the rush to read Jesus and the Apostles as if they believed the covenants were satisfied at the cross, the resurrection, and in the Church. Peters said it well:

> If a strictly logical history of Jesus is ever written, it must embrace something like these divisions: (1) The offered Messiah and His claims, how evidenced; (2) the rejected Messiah and His utterances from the time the representative men conspired to put Him to death; (3) the crucified and resurrected Messiah, showing how covenant and prophecy can still be fulfilled...[Christ's] life has been too much considered *isolated* from a previously presented Divine Purpose, from covenants understood in their plain, grammatical construction, from a relationship to an elect nation, from a tender of the Kingdom, its

5 Because Jesus died before Jewish witnesses, John can use Zechariah's prophecy in that situation (Jn. 19:37), but the wider context of Zechariah is a second advent reality.

6 "Perhaps one of the most striking features of Jesus' kingdom is that it <u>appears not to be the kind of kingdom prophesied in the OT and expected by Judaism</u>" (G. K. Beale, *A New Testament Biblical Theology*, 431, my emphasis).

7 Added to this is the oft-cited fact that the first coming prophecies were fulfilled literally (e.g., virgin birth, Bethlehem, Son of David, miracles, manner of death, etc.).

> rejection and subsequent postponement, and the result has been that, while all these are given by the evangelists as necessary to preserve the unity and claims of that life, the omission introduces defects that mar the otherwise *self-evident coherency* of the gospels. The more the gospels are contemplated in the light of the covenants and of the facts as they existed at the First Advent, *the more logically consistent, the more connected and admirably adapted to secure the design intended, will they appear.*[8]

That quotation should be mulled over for some time. We may now summarize our discussion. The importance of covenant in the Gospels is seen in the following:

1. The stress upon the Abrahamic and Davidic covenants in Matthew and Luke.

2. The proclamation of the Kingdom in the early ministry of Jesus.

3. Jesus referring to His throne that He will sit upon when He returns in power.

4. The teaching that the disciples will judge the tribes of Israel after the second coming.

5. The meaning of the title "Christ" and its covenantal associations.

6. The covenantal associations of God's love.

7. The sacrificial, and therefore covenantal meaning of the crucifixion.

8. Christ's institution of the New covenant in His own blood.

The above shows the importance of the Abrahamic and Davidic covenants in the Gospels. But it is the hugely significant New covenant that divides the new aeon from "this present evil world" (Gal. 1:4). As one writer has said, "The covenant is central to [Jesus'] teaching. Jesus preached the kingdom of God throughout his ministry, and the kingdom cannot be understood apart from the covenant."[9] Williamson adds, "Although the 'new covenant' is mentioned explicitly only in connection with the Last Supper, the Gospels are replete with associated ideas."[10]

I have demonstrated above the pervasiveness of "covernance" in the Four Gospels and how it is wise to read them in light of the OT covenants and not in spite of them.[11] There is no doubt in my mind that covenant is the structural and hermeneutical key to reading the Bible. I am, of course, referring to the biblical covenants that Yahweh made, the Noahic, Abrahamic, Mosaic, Priestly, Davidic, and New. These covenants,

8 George N. H. Peters, *The Theocratic Kingdom*, Vol. 3, 349-350.
9 John H. Walton, *Covenant: God's Plan, God's Purpose* (Grand Rapids: Zondervan, 1994), 151.
10 Paul R. Williamson, *Sealed with an Oath*, 183.
11 It is because the covenants of God and their influence upon the evangelists has rarely been noticed that this work is necessary.

especially the Abrahamic, Davidic, and the New, underpin the Gospels, providing a subtheme for the ministry and words of Jesus the Messiah.

Summary of Part Five

Mark

- "First coming hermeneutics" fails to divide the OT prophetic witness correctly and so looks for fulfillment at the first coming, which, if the covenants are taken seriously, cannot occur until the second coming.

- Mark's mention of the title "Son of God" at strategic points in his narrative (the beginning, middle, and end) is each related to a covenant theme.

- On a number of occasions in Mark, the question "Who can this be?" is asked. This prods the reader to investigate the Gospel for an answer.

- Mark includes a motif called "the Messianic secret," where either Jesus commands that His identity not be disclosed, or the disciples fail to comprehend Jesus after being instructed by Him.

- It appears that only at Golgotha the truth about Jesus as the Servant of Yahweh comes into view.

John

- John may not spring to mind as an author concerned with covenants, but a little exploration proves otherwise. There are various indicators of the influence of covernance upon the evangelist, including the underlying covenant associations of the word *agapao.*

- The covenant idea as an influence upon John has been carefully examined by several scholars. Even the Gospel's stated reason for being written reflects New covenant life through Christ.

- In all probability, John the Baptist's phrase about Jesus as "the Lamb of God" did not have the Passover in mind.

- John's sparse mentions of the Kingdom of God all refer to the coming New covenant Kingdom.

• The style of John's writing is to point to certain truths and to allow the reader to piece things together. For instance, the Gospel's teaching about the coming of the Spirit (Jn. 7:39; 14:17) involves a demarcation line drawn between the ministry of Jesus at His first coming and the later ministry of the Spirit after the ascension.

• The "I Am" sayings of Jesus usually strike covenantal notes.

• The signs and discourses in John's Gospel are chosen to impress upon the reader the indisputable truth of His divinity and His mission.

• John 21 closes the narrative with a timely lesson on how to interpret Jesus. We must beware of our tendency to infer things from His words that He did not say, and to carefully attend to what He did say.

The Epistles of John

• Once again, John's use of *agapao* has covenantal associations.

• A person's manner of life in Christ, as depicted by John, has New covenant overtones.

• John teaches that the Antichrist will deny that Jesus as Christ ever came in the flesh. Perhaps this is so he can falsely claim to be Christ?

The Covenantal Backdrop of the Gospels

• The hopes of national Israel are treated as alive and well (and literal) in the Gospels.

• This contradicts the usual position of Evangelical scholarship that Israel's covenant hopes are to be reinterpreted in accordance with the first century Christ-event.

• Particular emphasis in the Four Gospels is upon the Abrahamic, Davidic, and New covenants.

• Owing to the prevalence of covernance in the Gospels, it is a mistake to interpret them without reference to God's covenants.

PART SIX:
ACTS AND THE EPISTLES OF PAUL

13

COVENANT AND KINGDOM IN ACTS

You are sons of the prophets, and of the covenant which God made with our fathers, saying to Abraham, "And in your seed all the families of the earth shall be blessed."
– Acts 3:25

The Transitional Character of Acts

Before delving into the covenant-related teaching of Acts, I should say a word about its transitional nature. At the start of the book, Jesus is with His disciples, teaching and fellowshipping with them. He then ascends to heaven. The Feast of Pentecost is in swing in Acts 2, and Jerusalem is filled with Jews and proselytes from all over the Mediterranean world. As Peter addresses these Jews and proclaims the death and resurrection of Jesus the Messiah, they are told to believe in Him and be baptized "for the remission of sins" (Acts 2:38). No one today receives remission of sins at baptism but rather at the moment they trust in the substitutionary merits of the cross. In the next chapter, Peter appears to re-offer the Kingdom to the Jews upon condition of repentance (Acts 3:19-21). In Acts 8 we are told about the Ethiopian eunuch, who, upon asking what hinders him from being baptized, is told by Philip that if he believes he can (Acts 8:36-38). It appears that the baptism of Acts 2 differs from this baptism.

Then, in Acts 10 Peter is given a vision wherein he is taught that it is now okay for him to eat meats that were previously designated unclean under the Mosaic codes (Acts 10:9-16; cf. 15:6-10). In Acts 19:1-7 Paul finds disciples of John the Baptist who are ignorant of Jesus as the Christ, and after laying hands on them, they receive the Holy Spirit.

It might be uncomfortable to point such things out, and it would be easier for me to pretend that they are not there, but I would rather face the music and try to fathom out what is going on in these passages.[1] As far as Acts 2:38 is concerned, I believe it is possible to understand Peter in such a way as to connect the remission of sins with the Jews' repentance and faith, of which the subsequent baptism would be a confirmation. That is the position of many respected commentators.[2]

As for the other instances just mentioned, my view is that God working in time among groups of disparate people would preclude Him acting in so cut-and-dried a manner as to deal in a singular fashion with all. The vicissitudes of life require more latitude in such transitional days as those of the death of Jesus, His resurrection and ascension, the descent of the Spirit, and the empowerment of the apostles.[3] The disciples of John in Acts 19 were, for instance, doubtless pious men who had not yet learned of the identity of the Messiah that John preached about. If it be protested that John pointed to Jesus and proclaimed Him the "Lamb of God" (Jn. 1:29), I would answer that these disciples were evidently not present when that was done. Hence, the need for the preaching of Jesus as Messiah to be accompanied by the laying on of Paul's hands (to verify him as an apostle) and the gift of tongues (to verify the new birth through Christ, see Acts 19:6).

The Disciples' Question About the Restoration of the Kingdom

We have already seen how Luke lays heavy stress upon the Kingdom of God. Although it does not receive half as much notice from commentators as it deserves, Luke is very interested in the matter of continuity between the OT and the Apostolic writings that would become the NT.

This continuity is quickly seen in the opening of the first chapter of Acts. There we see the risen Lord teaching His disciples over the course of forty days. Luke tells us that the main burden of Jesus' teaching was "speaking of the things pertaining to the kingdom of God" (Acts 1:3). Interestingly, Luke finishes Acts with Paul preaching the Kingdom (Acts 28:23, 31).[4] Without any qualifying distinction, the meaning of the phrase "kingdom of God" in Acts 1 should be determined via reference to the Gospel of Luke, the first volume of Luke's two-volume history.[5] As my study of Luke's Gospel has shown, Luke employs the term purposefully to refer to the eschatological Kingdom promised in the covenants. Aside from reading the NT retrogressively,

1 Just as it would be easier for me to take for granted that Jesus publicly preached His coming death and resurrection as part of the good news in the Gospels. But the fact of the matter is that He did not.

2 E.g., F. F. Bruce, *The Book of the Acts* (Grand Rapids: Eerdmans, 1977), 68-69.

3 We might recall the incident of Ananias and Sapphira in Acts 5:1-11 in support of this. In those early days of the Church, the drastic measures taken against them by God was to ensure the health of the nascent Church.

4 Michael J. Vlach, *He Will Reign Forever*, 401.

5 If I may insert a note here about Luke's ethnicity, I believe there is good reason to think that Luke was a Hellenistic Jew. See David L. Allen, *Lukan Authorship of Hebrews* (Nashville: B&H, 2010), 261-323. Also, G. Scott Gleaves, *Did Jesus Speak Greek? The Emerging Evidence of Greek Dominance in First-Century Palestine* (Eugene, OR: Pickwick, 2015), 117-121.

there is no reason to think his use of "the kingdom of God" changed in the opening of Acts.[6]

With this assumption in hand, I venture to say that the "kingdom" that Jesus was teaching the disciples about during the forty days after His resurrection was the covenanted kingdom prophesied in the OT and expected by the faithful in Jesus' day. The understanding of the meaning of the Kingdom of God in Acts 1:3 as being fully in step with the OT covenants is given more encouragement by the interchange we encounter a few verses later:

> Therefore, when they had come together, they asked Him, saying, "Lord, will You at this time restore the kingdom to Israel?"
>
> And He said to them, "It is not for you to know times or seasons which the Father has put in His own authority. But you shall receive power when the Holy Spirit has come upon you; and you shall be witnesses to Me in Jerusalem, and in all Judea and Samaria, and to the end of the earth" (Acts 1:7-8).

This is the last question put to Jesus before His ascension. Jesus had just reminded the disciples of the ministry of John the Baptist (Acts 1:4-5), which must have stirred hopes of the coming "kingdom" about which John had preached (Matt. 3:1-2). Therefore, their question in verse 6 was quite natural. After so much instruction about the Kingdom of God from the Master Teacher, we cannot be so narrow as Calvin and believe that the disciples didn't grasp Jesus' meaning.[7] In a similar vein, N. T. Wright tries to set this episode up as a contest between Jesus and "the satan" as he insists on calling him.[8] Wright thinks the disciples did not grasp "the nature of Jesus' agenda."[9] I believe that it is Wright's agenda that gets in the way. The disciples' inquiry, "Lord, will You at this time restore the kingdom to Israel?" (Acts 1:6), was *based* on the teaching they had been receiving both before and after Christ's resurrection (cf. Matt. 19:28). It was not a pitiable misconstrual of it. The disciples' question to Jesus was loaded with anticipation. David Burggraff comments: "Now that He was alive again, having just demonstrated His power to overcome death itself, surely the *time* to restore the Jewish kingdom...on earth in all its glory must be close at hand. Their question was simply one of *timing*."[10] Burggraff is right. The question of the disciples, which they seem to have repeated, was about "when" the expected Kingdom would be restored, not about its character. They certainly had that understanding down pat after all the time they had spent with Jesus!

How did Jesus respond to the inquiry? Did He immediately take it upon Himself to correct their deeply ingrained yet erroneous understanding of the Kingdom? Did

6 Darrell L. Bock, *Acts*, BECNT (Grand Rapids: Baker, 2007), 62.
7 John Calvin, *Commentary upon the Acts of the Apostles*, Vol. 1 (Grand Rapids: Baker, 1981), 43.
8 N. T. Wright, *Jesus and the Victory of God*, 459.
9 Ibid., 463.
10 David L. Burggraff, "Augustine: From the 'Not Yet' to the 'Already,'" in *Forsaking Israel: How It Happened and Why It Matters*, ed. Larry D. Pettegrew, 2nd ed. (The Woodlands, TX: Kress Biblical Resources, 2021), 42 (emphasis his); cf. also James D. G. Dunn, *Beginning From Jerusalem* (Grand Rapids: Eerdmans, 2009), 144.

He (as on other occasions),[11] confounded by their dilatoriness, retort, "How can you still think the kingdom concerns just Israel?" He did not do that because their expectation was anchored not only in His teachings but also in the OT[12] and the Davidic covenant. Let us remind ourselves of His answer:

> He said to them, "It is not for you to know times or seasons which the Father has put in His own authority. But you shall receive power when the Holy Spirit has come upon you; and you shall be witnesses to Me in Jerusalem, and in all Judea and Samaria, and to the end of the earth" (Acts 1:7-8).

There is no trace of a rebuke in these words. He was telling them that the "when" of the restoration of the Kingdom to Israel was not for them (or us) to know.[13] That restoration will come. Indeed, it must come, for God has covenanted to do it. Whatever we do with that information from our historical vantage-point, we had better make peace with the fact that the covenants will not bend to our theological preferences.[14]

The Ascension of Jesus

The ascension of Jesus Christ back to where He was before (Jn. 6:62) was not simply "a return from the wars," as it were. We must remember that the eternal *Logos* (Jn. 1:1-3) came to our fallen world and grew up and lived in it as a human being, like one of his creatures; one of those who so imperfectly reflected His image. His ascension into heaven was *as a man.* He had succumbed to the full cruelty of human beings, and He had been taken by Death. He was changed. His arrival in Glory was the arrival of the great Savior of the Creation Project—the Man who put it all right. Victory was not yet claimed, but it was and is assured. Jesus entered "the greater and more perfect tabernacle not made with hands, that is, not of this creation" (Heb. 9:11), and there, in some mystical way that I cannot explain, He came into the Most Holy Place with His own blood and expiated our sins (Heb. 9:12). Acts 1:9-11 is the record of the ascension:

> He was taken up, and a cloud received Him out of their sight. And while they looked steadfastly toward heaven as He went up, behold, two men stood by them in white apparel, who also said, "Men of Galilee, why do you stand gazing up into heaven? This *same* Jesus, who was taken up from you into heaven, will so come in like manner as you saw Him go into heaven."

This took place at the Mount of Olives (Acts 1:12), which is the very mountain that will be wrenched apart when He comes again in great power and majesty, according

11 E.g., Matthew 16:11; Mark 4:40; 8:21.

12 See here Darrell L. Bock, *Acts*, 60-63.

13 Rightly, Frank Thielman, *Theology of the New Testament: A Canonical and Thematic Approach* (Grand Rapids: Zondervan, 2005), 133.

14 These verses are another touchstone of interpretation. It is not only premillennial commentators who should recognize the nature of Israel's Kingdom, as understood by the disciples, was a live option at this juncture.

to Zechariah 14:4. The touch of the risen Christ's feet upon this mountain will set off a chain-reaction that will impact the entire Middle East; perhaps the whole world (cf. Isa. 2:19-21; Heb. 12:26). The return of Christ will eventuate in the world's inhabitants not opposing but embracing and projecting the will of the Father through the reign of the Son. He will come bodily, in the clouds, to lay claim to what was first given to Him by His Father (cf. Col. 1:16). And He comes as the Mediator of His New covenant (Heb. 9:15), to fulfill all the unconditional covenants that God made in the OT with Noah, Abraham, Phinehas, and David.

The Day of Pentecost

Jesus had told the disciples to remain in Jerusalem until they received the Spirit (Lk. 24:49; Acts 1:8). The beginning of Acts 2 finds them together in a room when all of a sudden, a heaven-sent wind blew around them and fire-like tongues came upon them (Acts 2:1-3). They were filled with the Holy Spirit, who the tongues may have symbolized. As a result, they each began to speak in a language (for that is what is meant) that they had never previously learned (Acts 2:4).

Luke supplies us with a logical reason for this: it was the day of Pentecost, the high point of the feast, and Jerusalem was swarming with Jews from all over the Roman Empire. The native tongue of these Jews was not Hebrew—even Jews living in Israel spoke mainly Aramaic and Greek—but reflected the varied places they lived (Acts 2:7-11). It is readily apparent that spoken languages are in view here and not supposed "heavenly" languages insisted on by some charismatics and Pentecostals. It is very clear that these "tongues" were given to communicate with these foreign-speaking Jews.

Peter's First Sermon

The commotion caused by this miracle of languages made some utter disdainful remarks about the disciples being drunk (Acts 2:13). This gave Peter the pretext he needed to speak to the crowd. After dismissing the accusation, Peter announced that what was happening was "what was spoken by the prophet Joel" (Acts 2:16). He then quoted Joel 2:28-32 (cf. Acts 2:17-21). But what was this? Joel did not mention the gift of tongues. Moreover, none of the phenomena spoken about by the prophet were manifested in Acts 2![15] Was this Peter getting ahead of himself again (cf. Matt. 17:4)?

This speech by Peter presents every interpreter with a challenge. Even those who push their way past the details and glibly state that, in fact, Joel 2 was fulfilled in Acts 2. In its context, Joel 2:28-32 is an eschatological prediction of the end of the age. It speaks of the coming of the Spirit upon "common people" in all parts of society. It is preceded by a prophetic call to national consecration (Joel 2:15-17), followed by the response of Yahweh in terms of divine pity, decisive action against Israel's enemies, and New covenant blessings upon their land (Joel 2:18-27). Joel 2:26-27 is key here:

15 See Craig L. Blomberg, *A New Testament Theology*, 104.

> You shall eat in plenty and be satisfied, and praise the name of the LORD your God, Who has dealt wondrously with you; and My people shall never be put to shame. Then you shall know that I *am* in the midst of Israel: I *am* the LORD your God and there is no other. My people shall never be put to shame (Joel 2:26-27, my emphasis).

Notice carefully the language of final reconciliation between God and His people. Yahweh is dwelling in the land as Israel's God and His people are safe in perpetuity. This is where we must fit Acts 2:28-32. This is what was uppermost in Peter's mind at Pentecost!

In Acts 2 no one is seeing visions, no one is dreaming, no one is prophesying, no great apocalyptic signs formed in the sky, and the Spirit was poured out on a few men in a room. Further, in Joel 2 no one is speaking in tongues. What was Peter thinking? The single thing in common between the two passages is the coming of the Holy Spirit.

It is the coming of the Spirit that is the clue. And covenantally speaking, from Peter's vantage-point, the descent of the Spirit is an eschatological portent. But is this a confusion of the first and second advents? We cannot entertain the idea! What then? We are either thrown back to the total fulfillment hypothesis, however bizarre that looks when the two texts are compared, or we are constrained to look for more clues. And clues can be found in the next chapter and Peter's next recorded sermon. I, therefore, want to skip ahead briefly and come back to this context with the help I think Acts 3 furnishes.

The Return of Jesus and the Restoration of All Things

> But those things which God foretold by the mouth of all His prophets, that the Christ would suffer, He has thus fulfilled.
>
> Repent therefore and be converted, that your sins may be blotted out, so that times of refreshing may come from the presence of the Lord, and that He may send Jesus Christ, who was preached to you before, whom heaven must receive until the times of restoration of all things, which God has spoken by the mouth of all His holy prophets since the world began.
>
> For Moses truly said to the fathers, "The LORD your God will raise up for you a Prophet like me from your brethren. Him you shall hear in all things, whatever He says to you" (Acts 3:18-22).

This is a complicated passage, but I shall try to prise apart its main teachings. Peter first calls the Jewish crowd to repentance because their Messiah has come and has been killed. Peter speaks about the prophecies concerning Christ's suffering as though they should have been readily apparent,[16] and we may assume there was enough knowledge of the requisite texts for Peter to strike a connection to (whatever our fragmentary knowledge of the time tells us).[17]

However, things take a remarkable turn in verses 19 to 21, where Peter promises that if they will repent and believe his message, three world-changing events would occur: (1) Their sins would be "blotted out," basically removed from them. (2) What he calls "the times of refreshing" and "the times of the restoration of all things" would happen. (3) God would send Jesus their Christ back to earth.

The mention of those three events in Acts 3 ought to stop us in our tracks. Peter is preaching the coming of the New covenant Kingdom around A.D. 30! Why then did Christ not come back? Why didn't the predicted Kingdom of peace come about? Many would say that the promised Kingdom, though expected by the Jews, arrived in a different way than was projected, and that the "kingdom" is found in the Church.

There is a way forward. There is an answer—and a fairly straightforward one at that. It is this: *the promised kingdom of peace and glory and the return of Christ as King would have occurred if the conditions of restoration had been met.* They were not!

One can hear the howls of protest come across the airwaves: "Are you saying that since Christ was rejected before and after the crucifixion, God had to move to Plan B?" "Are you claiming that the Church was potentially unnecessary?" The answer to both questions is a dogmatic "No!" To illustrate, Reformed systematic theologians distinguish between the "well-meant offer" of the gospel to all sinners indiscriminately and the offer to those whom God knows will be regenerated.[18]

This illustration shows that God can know what will happen because He has decreed it will happen (however one understands the decree) even though a contradictory state of affairs (a version of a counterfactual) is proffered. Peter is proclaiming in Acts 3:19-21 exactly what he appears to be proclaiming. Jesus would come, and the "times of refreshing" would arrive if Israel repented and trusted Jesus as the Christ. They didn't, and God knew that they wouldn't. The rejection was foreknown and decreed by God. Unbeknownst to Peter, there was no way Christ would be accepted; therefore, the advent of the Church was determined just as much as the time of Jesus' birth (Gal. 4:4) or the crucifixion (Psa. 22; Lk. 24:44; cf. Jn. 15:25).

Returning to Acts 2

If we understand Peter's bona fide offer of Christ and the kingdom in Acts 3 and reread his use of Joel 2 in Acts 2, the proclamation starts to take meaningful shape before our eyes. The phenomena described in Joel 2:28-32, which had to do with the coming of "the great and awesome day of the Lord," concerns the end of days. That is to say that Peter fully expected that the descent of the Holy Spirit at Pentecost would

16 I must include a note of caution here. Acts 3:17 will speak of the ignorance of both people and (surprisingly) the rulers (which may explain the offer in Acts 3:19-26). This ignorance may well have been mainly caused by the traditions of the rabbis (Mk. 7:6-12).

17 What every scholar is willing to admit is that the first part of the first century A.D. was filled with messianic hope. The Feast would have only heated up the fervor.

18 See Robert Letham, *Systematic Theology* (Wheaton, IL: Crossway, 2019), 651-668.

trigger all these events leading up to the return of Christ and the setting up of His great Kingdom—the anticipated "Kingdom of God" (cf. Acts 1:3, 6)!

It is crucial to realize that Peter was still thinking within the basic framework of OT eschatology and Jewish expectation that we find in the Gospels and Acts 1:6. His immediate concern in this setting was to point to the cross and (especially) the resurrection as the eschatological breaking-in of God into Israel's history. In Acts 2:15 the term "this" refers to Jesus' resurrection throughout Peter's speech (Acts 2:24, 30, 31, 32), which demonstrates that Jesus is "both Lord and Christ' (Acts 2:36)."

The reference to the outpouring of the Spirit (Acts 2:17-18, 33) is intended to show the Jews that the New covenant has been inaugurated and that there is still opportunity for them to repent and believe (in this sense, the baptism of verse 38 may be seen as a partial fulfillment of John's baptism). Of course, the nation did not believe this message. They rejected it again in Acts 3:12-26, where the expectation of the arrival of the Davidic Kingdom was still patently in the air (esp. Acts 3:19-21). In other words, these were good-faith offers of the Kingdom, which were rejected by all but a relative few.

Viewed this way, the one work of Christ in its two phases of cross and crown are still held together in Acts 2 and 3. If so, the "signs and wonders" of Acts 2:19 are at the doorstep pending national acceptance of Jesus as Messiah; not only the crucified Messiah, but risen Messiah—bringing the two phases into close proximity. In God's Creation Project, this was not due to human sin. A final climactic intervention would be needed. This intervention (as Christ's rejection) is seen in the Prophets (Isa. 61:1-3; Zech. 14:3-4; Mal. 3:1b-2) and restated in the NT (Matt. 24:29-30; 2 Thess. 1:6-10; Rev. 19:11-16).

In Acts 3:22-23 Peter cites Deuteronomy 18 about the Prophet like Moses (Acts 3:15, 18-19). There is a line in there that says, "And it shall be that every soul who will not hear that Prophet shall be utterly destroyed from among the people" (Acts 3:23; cf. Deut. 18:19). Peter quotes this passage to his Jewish audience in the same setting as his words about the sending (again) of Christ (Acts 3:20-21). This is because the Deuteronomy passage goes together with the return of Christ. Acts 3 closes with these words:

> Yes, and all the prophets, from Samuel and those who follow, as many as have spoken, have also foretold these days. You are sons of the prophets, and of <u>the covenant which God made with our fathers</u>, saying to Abraham, 'And in your seed all the families of the earth shall be blessed' (Acts 3:24-25, my emphasis).

It is quite clear that Peter is thinking covenantally in these sermons in Acts 2 and 3. Here he alludes to the Abrahamic covenant. What is fascinating to me is the part of the Abrahamic covenant he calls their attention to. It is the third plank of the covenant, which promises, "And in your seed all the families of the earth shall be blessed" (Acts 3:25).

Why would he say that? I think the answer is that, although he was speaking to Jews at a Jewish Festival, Peter knew that what Jesus had said in Acts 1:8: "But you shall receive power when the Holy Spirit has come upon you; and you shall be witnesses to Me in Jerusalem, and in all Judea and Samaria, and to the end of the earth." To those words we need to add the following:

> Thus it is written, and thus it was necessary for the Christ to suffer and to rise from the dead the third day, and that repentance and remission of sins should be preached in His name to all nations, beginning at Jerusalem. And you are witnesses of these things (Lk. 24:46-48).

> Go therefore and make disciples of all the nations, baptizing them in the name of the Father and of the Son and of the Holy Spirit (Matt. 28:19).

As these texts show, the disciples were well versed in the attitude of the Good News being for all peoples. Jesus had been rejected by His own (cf. Jn. 1:11), but the message about Him was not limited to Israel; certainly not by the Abrahamic or New covenants. Hence, we must conclude that, even though Peter offers Christ's return from heaven to Israel in Acts 3:19-25[19] (clearly an offer was made), he is aware of the fact that the Gospel must be spread to the Gentiles too. Just how that would be done and how much time Peter thought would pass between his words and Jesus' return is impossible to know, but it does appear reasonable to think that it would all occur in their generation.

If we take a look at the last verse in Acts 3, we shall see another covenantal overtone: "To you first, God, having raised up His Servant Jesus, sent Him to bless you, in turning away every one *of you* from your iniquities" (Acts 3:26). Peter here refers to Jesus as God's "Servant." The word "Servant" is only employed in a messianic sense by the prophet Isaiah (Isa. 42; 49; 50; 52–53). Peter is deliberately calling his audience's attention to Isaiah's Servant, more particularly to the salvific portions of the Servant Songs (e.g., Isa. 49:6 and 53:1-12). Isaiah's Servant is made "as a covenant to the people; to restore the earth" (Isa. 49:8, the context is salvational), so that God's covenant work is the prime activity of the Servant.

EXCURSUS: The Throne of David and the Present Session of Christ

Scholars advocating what is called Progressive Dispensationalism have called attention to Peter's teaching in Acts 2:22-40 to prove that the ascended Jesus is now enthroned as King in heaven. Foremost is the Lukan scholar, Darrell Bock. A person must be a slow learner indeed if he cannot benefit from Bock's output. I think Bock deserves credit for tackling a tough text, even if I have to disagree with his solution.

---

19 Hence, the phenomena of Joel 2:28-32a, which Peter preached about in Acts 2:16-21, would have come about through the Spirit's influence had his message been believed. Another way to put this is that *both Acts 2:16-21 and 3:19-25 would have taken place if the Jews en masse had believed that Jesus was their Messiah* whom they had crucified but God had raised from the dead.

Bock's Question

I had the opportunity some time back to dialogue a little with Bock about the matter.[20] He asked me:

> How can a dispensationalist see the current application of the Abrahamic Covenant and the New Covenant (see the Last Supper in procuring forgiveness we now experience) and not see the Davidic covenant being initially realized by what Jesus has done, as Luke 3:16 predicts and Acts 2:14-36 proclaims?

My reply to him was a tad long and meandering, so I will try to reshape it below for the purposes of this book. The main point can be stated in a few words: the dynamics of the one work of Christ in two comings requires that we allocate fulfillments carefully between the two. Just as David was anointed king by Samuel (1 Sam. 16) but was not made king until after the death of Saul (2 Sam. 2), even so, Jesus is the anointed messianic King but has not yet been enthroned.

An Answer

Permit me to expand upon that answer here. First, Bock asked about Luke 3:16 so I will begin there. In Luke 3:16 John the Baptist announces that One will come after him who will baptize with the Holt Spirit. The Spirit-transformation of believers is a prediction of the presence of the New covenant (e.g., Ezek. 36:27). In the context, Jesus has not yet been baptized and presented as the Christ. John's announcement of the coming One includes elements of the first coming (i.e., the baptism with the Spirit of Lk. 3:16) and the second coming (the judgment language of Lk. 3:17). The two phases of Christ's work are bundled together in typical OT fashion. Importantly though, the context is prior to Christ's rejection, so I take the baptism with the Holy Spirit to be the New covenant promise of the Spirit's vitalizing coming to Israel with the Kingdom that was being proclaimed (Matt. 3:1-2; Mk. 1:14-15). There is no Church yet in view as far as the revelation goes. Once Jesus is rejected by Israel, the promised Kingdom is pushed back to the second advent. But He *has* come. That cannot be reversed, and it changes everything.

At His coming, Jesus inaugurated the New covenant (Lk. 22:14-20), yet in a context in which the Kingdom is now driven into the future (Lk. 22:29-30). Hence, the first phase of John's prediction, the baptism with the Spirit (Lk. 3:16) in the New covenant, is made with those disciples who would go on to be foundational to the Church (Eph. 2:20). This operation of the New covenant explains the use of Spirit language in Acts 2. Still, the full realization of that blessing as it pertains to Israel (per John's audience and context) awaits the second advent when Jesus comes in judgment,[21] after which He brings the New covenant to the repentant remnant of Israel in line with the OT pattern.

20 See "3 Premillennialists Duke it Out" at http://mydigitalseminary.com/3-premillennialists-duke-it-out/.

21 Notice the "fire" and "winnowing" language in Lk. 3:16-17.

That there is some sort of "already" aspect in Acts 2:14-36 is true, yet I would want to lay stress upon the object of that "already"—the "new man," the Church, not Israel. Here is where there is some chronological transition between "the Church age" and the "times of restoration" that Peter was holding out to Israel in Acts 3 (and Acts 2 for that matter). Both were "in play" at this time. I take Acts 3:19-21 as referring to the Davidic/New covenant Kingdom, so if we link Acts 3:19-21 with Acts 1:6 (see above), we better understand Peter's mindset in Acts 2.

In Acts 2 we face several issues, none of which I will pretend to give the final answer to. In Acts 2:14-21 there is the debated use of the Joel prophecy preceded by the "this is that" formula (Acts 2:15). The first thing to say is that whichever interpretation is brought to the use of Joel 2, few people believe that these extraordinary happenings of vv. 19-20 actually occurred at Pentecost.[22] Further, the Holy Spirit was not poured out on "all flesh" (Acts 2:17).

So, what was Peter doing? My answer is that Peter was still thinking within the basic framework of OT eschatology and Jewish expectation that we find in the Gospels and in Acts 1:6, the full spiritual-material manifestation of Paradise under King Jesus as per Isaiah 11:1-11.

Assessing Bock's Argument for Christ Ruling from Heaven

Bock marshals a formidable-looking argument for his view that Jesus is reigning now on David's throne. His case centers on the links between Peter's use of Psalms 16, 110, and 132 in Acts 2:22-36.

> (1) Since Peter connects the ascension in Acts 2:34 and 35 to Psalm 110:1, Bock thinks Christ has been enthroned, although the text does not say as much. In the setting, I think it makes better sense to see it as an explanation as to why He is not there reigning as the OT predicted He would do.
>
> (2) He believes the allusion to Psalm 132:11 in Acts 2:30 relates to the Davidic throne.[23] But in the context of Acts 2, this is not what Peter is doing. Peter has to explain the resurrection and its tie to Jesus' messiahship. In Acts 2:30-31 that is exactly what Peter says, "He [David], foreseeing this, spoke concerning the resurrection of the Christ" (Acts 2:31). We must take Peter at his word.

22 E.g., Darrell L. Bock, "The Reign of the Lord Christ," in *Dispensationalism, Israel and the Church: The Search for Definition*, eds. Craig A. Blaising and Darrell L. Bock (Grand Rapids: Zondervan, 1992), 48. Bock understands the "This is that" formula in the Joel prophecy as "this is the beginning of that," although he appears to contradict himself on page 51. But if Joel's prophecy only began to be fulfilled at Pentecost, it is right to ask, with Woods, "Why did Peter quote both sections from Joel 2 if only one of them was fulfilled on Pentecost? It seems more likely that he would have only quoted the section that was to be fulfilled on the Day of Pentecost rather than both" (Andrew Woods, *The Coming Kingdom*, 202). R. N. Longenecker, "Acts," in *EBC*, ed. Frank E. Gaebelein, Vol. 9 (Grand Rapids: Zondervan, 1981), 276. Elliott Johnson believes that the Joel prophecy was preached to indicate coming judgment. See *A Dispensational Biblical Theology*, 383-384.

23 *Dispensationalism, Israel and the Church*, 48-49.

(3) Linking Acts 2:30 up with Luke 1:68-79, Bock declares, "This passage and Luke 1:68-79 also counter the claim that no New Testament text asserts the present work of Jesus as a reigning Davidite sitting on David's throne."[24] Again, I don't find such an argument satisfying. Zacharias' speech in Luke 1 is uttered within the environment of the coming of Christ in the early Lukan chapters, which I have covered in my chapter on Luke above. Christ as Christ is rejected, and the Kingdom is put in the eschaton (Lk. 19:11). To me, Bock, even though he is aware of Luke's "until" passages (Lk. 13:35; 17:27; 21:24; 22:16, 18; Acts 3:21), does not make use of them, and it blunts his point.

(4) Bock also asks, "Now how can one allow the fulfillment of Melchizedekian priesthood for the present age from Psalm 110 and then deny the present rule of Jesus, which is also tied to the language of the same psalm?"[25] My answer is simply that the book of Hebrews does not stress the enthronement of Jesus, but it *does* stress His priesthood (Heb. 5:5-10; 6:13-20; 7:9-28). One may point to Hebrews 7:1-4 and the emphasis of the meaning of Melchizedek's name. Yet the context resolves the issue, because the writer uses this to illustrate the greatness of Melchizedek (Heb. 7:4) in building his argument.

(5) In the fifth place, Bock states, "Jesus' rule is present in the salvation benefits he bestows as part of the initial phase of his rule. The kingdom is invisible in the sense that he does not rule over every person directly, but in those who share in the benefits he offers, especially in the provision of the Spirit"[26] I reply, "But He doesn't even do that!" If He did, we would not need to be admonished constantly to walk in the Spirit and not in the flesh (Gal. 5:16). Again I must call attention to our default mode of independence from the Word of God. In this sense, the prediction of total obedience we find in Deuteronomy 30:1-6 and the Prophets has not yet come about (cf. Rom. 7:21-25).

(6) Bock holds that confessing Jesus as the Messiah is "a regal confession."[27] I believe he is right in one sense and not right in another. He is right to say that "Messiah/Christ" is a Davidic title, but he is incorrect to equate it solely with Davidic rule. David himself was anointed king by Samuel long before he became king (1 Sam. 16:11-13), so the equation of Messiah = rule is not airtight.

---

24 Ibid., 49.
25 Ibid., 51.
26 Ibid., 53.
27 Ibid., 52.

The Main Thrust of Peter's Sermon

Peter's immediate concern in this setting was pointing to the cross and (especially) the resurrection as the eschatological in-breaking of God into Israel's history. As already noted, the pronoun "this" of Acts 2:15 is answered by the references to the resurrection throughout Peter's speech (vv. 24, 30, 31, 32, cf. 36). Peter's emphasis throughout is not on Christ's enthronement in fulfillment of the Davidic covenant, but on His resurrection from the dead and His ascension to the right hand of God (Acts 2:24, 27, 30-35). As the Messiah, Jesus shall therefore sit on David's throne (Acts 2:30). But to answer this by maintaining that "Solomon, as Davidic king, sits on the Lord's throne (1 Chron. 29:23; 2 Chron. 9:8)"[28] is to forget that the Davidic dynasty rules for Yahweh in His stead (1 Sam. 16:1; 2 Sam. 7:16). But the roles cannot be reversed. A Davidic ruler, not even Jesus, can rule in Yahweh's stead from heaven. No, the Davidic throne in view here is earthly, not in heaven. Jesus spoke to His disciples about returning to the Father (Jn. 14-16), but He never once indicated that He would sit upon David's throne in heaven.

In Conclusion

The two phases of cross and crown are still held together in Acts 2 and 3. Allowing this line of reasoning helps us with Joel's prophecy. How so? Because the "signs" and "wonders" that Jesus did prior to Calvary (Acts 2:22) portend the "signs" and "wonders" of Acts 2:19, which speak to the second coming. Here I again appeal to Acts 3:19-21 for help.

Let me proceed to Acts 2:25-35 and try to fit it into the picture. Jewish national acceptance in the risen Christ ought to have come because the OT predicted it (Acts 2:25-28; cf. Psa. 16). For present purposes, I shall forego verses 25-29 and pick it up in Acts 2:30. As I have said, the resurrection was uppermost in Peter's mind in this sermon. The next verse proves this by saying that David "spoke concerning the resurrection" (Acts 2:31). In verse 33 the emphasis is now on the ascension "to the right hand of God," which I do not take as a reference to the throne of David, for otherwise Acts 3:19-21 makes no sense to me. Would the throne of David be sent with Jesus as He traveled back to earth?

Acts 2:33 appeals to the coming of the Spirit, yet actual fulfillment of Joel's New covenant prophecy awaits the condition of national repentance, which was not forthcoming. The quotation of Psalm 110:1 refers then to the present continuing priestly session of Christ in heaven awaiting the fulfillment of the Davidic New covenant Kingdom announced, first by John the Baptist, and then by Peter. I hope this rather convoluted explanation will be seen as viable. Whichever position is taken on Acts 2 and 3, it is easy to get one's wires crossed. This is my attempt to sort them out, and I think it preserves the meaning of the OT covenant testimony better than Bock's already-not yet reading.

28 Ibid., 51.

Persecution Starts

Acts 4 and 5 relate the beginning of persecution against the Apostles and believers. But in these chapters, there are many covenant references. As Acts 4 opens, we see the Sadducees trying to push their weight around. These men were "greatly disturbed that they [the apostles] taught the people and preached in Jesus the resurrection from the dead" (Acts 4:2). The Sadducees stuck only to the five Books of Moses, which meant that they denied things like angels, the immortality of the soul, and the resurrection (Lk. 20:27), things that are not found in the Torah.[29] Also, "They expressed no messianic expectation, which tended to make them satisfied with their wealth and political power."[30] As can be easily imagined, this combination made them antagonistic towards the disciples on many levels. What would have riled them up even more was the preaching of the resurrection and its necessary connection to the name of Jesus, and the fact that it was being boldly claimed that Jesus had been resurrected *already*, not even waiting for the general resurrection, which the Pharisees believed in.

Peter's proclamation the following day, when he pointed his finger at the "rulers, elders, and scribes" (Acts 4:5), as well as the family of the high priest (Acts 4:6), for killing Jesus (Acts 4:10), was occasioned by the miraculous and incontrovertible healing of the lame beggar in Acts 3:1-11. Peter impressed upon the assembled dignitaries that the miracle was done in the name of (i.e., the power of) Jesus of Nazareth, the resurrected one. Thus, the healing proved the resurrection, which, in turn, proved Jesus to be the Messiah. To this Peter added, "Nor is there salvation in any other, for there is no other name under heaven given among men by which we must be saved" (Acts 4:12). The name of the risen Jesus Christ not only brought restorative power, it also brought the authority to save. This signifies that *Christos* is not a last name but a title. Here the salvific and regenerative power of the New covenant are set before the assembly. The quotation from Psalm 118:22 in Acts 4:11 is apt. God has signaled a new beginning, a new creation even, in reversing the condemnation of Jesus Christ. He has become "the chief cornerstone."

After they had been released (Acts 4:23), the saints lifted their voices to God in praise, citing Psalm 2 (Acts 4:24-26). The quotation seems somewhat exaggerated since the religious authorities in Jerusalem, as intimidating as they were, did not amount to the "nations" and "kings of the earth" mentioned in Psalm 2:1-2. Still, the sentiment was spot on, and the resistance of the Jewish leaders epitomizes the attitude of authorities generally. The reality of the resurrection meant that all worldly authority would be done away with eventually. The fact that David is invoked strikes me as significant, and this along with the double mention of "Your holy Servant Jesus" (Acts 4:27, 30), introduces once more the New covenant overtones.

More diverse healings performed by the apostles in Jesus' name (Acts 5:12-16) led to them being arrested, imprisoned, miraculously freed, and let go with a warning. During the exchange, Peter told the high priest and others assembled, "Him God

29 We do of course find many mentions of the Angel of the LORD in Genesis–Deuteronomy.

30 Michael J. Wilkins, "Matthew," in *Zondervan Illustrated Bible Backgrounds Commentary, Volume 1, Matthew, Mark, Luke*, ed. Clinton E. Arnold (Grand Rapids: Zondervan, 2002), 25.

has exalted to His right hand *to be* Prince and Savior, to give repentance to Israel and forgiveness of sins" (Acts 5:31, my emphasis).

Peter refers to Christ as a "Prince" (*archegos*). He had done this once before when he called Jesus "the Prince of life" in Acts 3:15. The most obvious influence is surely Daniel 9:25, where in the middle of the Seventy Weeks prophecy, there is a reference to "Messiah the Prince." The next verse declares that "Messiah will be cut off" (Dan. 9:26), but Peter here reverses the sentiment and calls Him the "Prince of life." The other relevant passage is, of course, Isaiah 9:6, where the final epithet given to the coming Davidic Ruler is "Prince of peace." Since these two texts highlight two aspects of Jesus' Lordship—His messiahship and His being the Source of *shalom*—Peter's skillful use of "Prince" is calculated to impress both of these facets of the One whom the religious elites have just murdered. Isaiah 9:7 connects this "Prince of peace" with God's covenant with David, while Peter in Acts 3:13 ties in the Abrahamic covenant and the Isaianic Servant, a Servant who, not so coincidentally, is referred to *as a covenant* in Isaiah 42:6; the covenant under discussion being, as I have argued, the New covenant.[31]

We witness Peter bringing together the Abrahamic, Davidic, and New covenants and relating them to Jesus in the early chapters of Acts. He nowhere relates these covenants in a supersessionist or "fulfillment theology" way, wherein we need look no further than the first advent for the spiritual realization of those covenants.

The Arrest and Speech of Stephen

Stephen was one of the six men of faith who were chosen as deacons[32] in Acts 6. Among the accusations brought against him was, "We have heard him say that this Jesus of Nazareth will destroy this place and change the customs which Moses delivered to us" (Acts 6:14). This charge causes me to speculate about what was involved in the "change" in the Mosaic customs. Was Stephen pointing away from the Jerusalem Temple[33] and perhaps the hopes wrapped up in the cultic parts of the Mosaic covenant associated with it? Was he replacing it by preaching the New covenant in Christ? We cannot be sure, but such an understanding looks to be accurate (cf. 2 Cor. 3:6).[34]

Most commentators agree that Stephen must have quoted Jesus words about destroying "this temple" (His body) and Him rebuilding it in three days (Jn. 2:19), and it does seem as though these words, or rather a distortion of them, were still ringing in the ears of many people (see Mk. 14:38). The destruction of Christ's body was

31 See my *The Words of the Covenant*, Vol. 1, 254, 256.

32 When the NT uses the word "deacons" (*diakonos*, e.g., 1 Tim. 3:8-13) for an office within the local church, it takes on a specific meaning (just as e.g., *christos*, *apostolos*, or *angelos*). This has to be kept in mind when seeking to address questions about who may qualify to bear the office.

33 Dunn makes a good case for the main emphasis of Stephen's teaching to involve the temple. See James D. G. Dunn, *Beginning From Jerusalem*, 260-262, 268-72.

34 Some believe that Stephen was preaching against "the whole Jewish system of civil and religious life." See Richard Belward Rackham, *The Acts of the Apostles: An Exposition* (London: Methuen, 1922), 91. Certainly, the New covenant has temple connections, but those connections are eschatological (e.g., Ezek. 37:27-28).

connected to the New covenant transaction (Lk. 22:19-20). Strictly speaking, the New covenant was in Christ's blood, but the body had to be part of the offering (see Heb. 10:5). Since the charges against Stephen included the changing of the "customs" of Moses, it is not a long shot to suggest that Stephen would want to tell his fellow Israelites that the New covenant had been made through the ugly circumstance of Jesus' murder. The resurrection validated both Jesus' words and His mission.

Stephen's sermon is crammed full of OT citations and allusions, many of which are rooted in the covenants. The epic of Abraham is described in brief terms (Acts 7:2-8), where Stephen refers to "the covenant of circumcision" that God gave to Abraham in Genesis 17 (Acts 7:8). Circumcision was, strictly speaking, the sign or token of the covenant,[35] but Stephen's point is that Israel as a special people was given the covenant. Circumcision is a constant reminder of it. The narration then skips over to Joseph and then on to the time of Moses, where the link with Abraham, Isaac, and Jacob is noted (Acts 7:32). From the time of Moses, Stephen calls attention to Deuteronomy 18:15 and the prophecy of the future Prophet (Acts 7:37). After receiving the "living oracles" (the Ten Commandments, Acts 7:38) the quick apostasy in the incident of the golden calf is recited (Acts 7:39-41) and treated as an ongoing undercurrent of heart-defection by the quotation of Amos 5:25-27 some 700 years later (Acts 7:42-43).

In the quotation from Amos, what Stephen chooses is very striking. Acts 7:43 records:

> You also took up the tabernacle of Moloch,
> And the star of your god Remphan,
> Images which you made to worship;
> And I will carry you away beyond Babylon.

It is not an exact quotation of the Hebrew of Amos 5:26-27a, but is close to the LXX rendering. The names of the pagan deities in the Hebrew are *Sikkut* (*Sakkut*) and *kiyun* (*Chiun* or *Kaiwan*[36]). Both refer to the god Saturn.[37] Another name would be the familiar *Moloch*.[38] Whatever the name, this underworld deity was truly an abomination and is closely associated with child-sacrifice. In Stephen's speech, he cites the "tabernacle" and the "star" as symbols of this rebellion.[39] It is telling that for so long in OT times many Israelites seem to have carried around such symbols even while claiming to be in covenant with God.

35 On occasion, the token of a covenant is identified with the covenant itself as a sort of shorthand for the covenant bond. See Daniel. I. Block, *Covenant*, 428-430.

36 See e.g., James Luther Mays, *Amos* (Philadelphia: Westminster Press, 1969), 112.

37 Hosea 3:1 condemns Israel for worshiping false deities, although it does not name them.

38 Also known as Molech/Milcom. See Lev. 18:21; 20:2-5; 2 Ki. 21:3-5; 23:10; Jer. 32:35; Isa. 57:9; Ezek. 16:21; 23:37-39.

39 It is of note that the Bible nowhere speaks of a star of David. It appears on the front of the Leningrad Codex (A.D. 1008).

Further Instances of Kingdom and Covenant

The preaching of the deacon Philip in Acts 8 is described as relating to "the things concerning the kingdom of God and the name of Jesus Christ" (Acts 8:12), which resulted in many baptisms. There is no reason to deny that Philip preached about the coming eschatological kingdom. Christ has come, and the kingdom of Christ *will* come. The mix of *telos* and *eschatos* furnishes a strong worldview message about the sterility of religion and the hopeless vagaries of paganism.

Baptism and the New Covenant

Acts 8:26-40 tells the story of the conversion and baptism of the Ethiopian eunuch, who was probably a proselyte.[40] This man was reading from Isaiah 53, a New covenant chapter.[41] He was told that he could receive baptism (which was either by immersion or effusion) if he believed the Gospel of Jesus that Philip had expounded to him from the prophet. It must be a no-holes-barred belief (Acts 8:37), because baptism was seen as the token of the New covenant in Jesus, with the Gospel of His death for sin and resurrection being the content of that faith. Whether Philip explained baptism in covenant terms is impossible to say. However, it cannot be dismissed since the eunuch would have been a strict adherent to the Mosaic covenant, and would surely have needed to have had Christ's shed blood explained to him in New covenant language.

Another important consideration is the fact that the coming of the Holy Spirit is a phenomenon associated with the New covenant (e.g., Isa. 32:15; Ezek. 36:27; Zech. 12:10), and when one considers Peter's question in Acts 10:47 in such light, there is more than a suggestion that he thought of baptism in that way. I am not saying that baptism as a sign of the New covenant is necessary (see 1 Cor. 1:17). We know it is a sign, and that it signifies belief in Christ's death and resurrection. I am venturing to say that baptism and the New covenant are linked by virtue of this fact. This means that baptism has to be for believers only. The theological construct that is the covenant of grace is a poor replacement for God's revealed New covenant.[42]

Coming to Acts 10, we have the episode of Peter's vision of the great sheet filled with unclean animals and the subsequent ministry to Cornelius. This was a watershed event for Peter, which he reported upon in Acts 11:1-18 (cf. Acts 15:6-11). The vision admonished Peter to accept what he had previously deemed to be unlawful (Acts 10:11-16; 11:7-9). This could not have occurred had Peter been under the old Mosaic covenant, which forbade eating such things. Notice then that Peter was released from the requirements of the Torah and must, therefore, have been under a

40 Eckhard J. Schnabel, *Early Christian Mission*, 685.

41 This is said in so many words by e.g., Paul Williamson, *Sealed with an Oath*, 159; and Thomas Schreiner, *Covenant*, 102.

42 Although I will look more into it later, I want to say that I am perplexed by those who hold that Christians have no part in the New covenant. Surely every time we celebrate the Lord's Supper and read from 1 Corinthians 11:23-26 we tacitly admit our participation in the New covenant?

new requirement. Are we to believe that having been brought out from under one covenant, Peter was now clear of a replacement covenant?

Paul's First Speech

Acts 13 is grounded in God's covenants. When Paul addresses the synagogue in Pisidian Antioch in Acts 13:13-41,[43] we find him referring to the Abrahamic covenant in 13:17 and 26. The Mosaic covenant is implied in 13:17-20, and the Davidic covenant in 13:21-22, 33 (with a quotation of Psa. 2:7). Then Jesus is introduced as the Davidic/New covenant Savior in 13:23 and 34ff. (with quotes from Isa. 55:4 and Psa. 16:10), until the New covenant itself enters in Acts 13:38-39. One book puts it this way, "The covenants provide a substructure for Paul's understanding of Israel's history in Acts 13."[44] Unfortunately, these authors believe that "Paul's sermon presents Jesus the Messiah as the culmination of Israel's history. The earlier covenants were designed to be fulfilled in and through the Messiah, Jesus, who inaugurated God's new covenant promises."[45]

But this totally misreads Paul and utterly misconstrues the "design" of the covenants. Paul is in a Jewish service (Acts 13:14-15, 26) reciting Israel's covenant history, moving from the promise to David to Jesus and John the Baptist (Acts 13:22-25). His point is that Jesus is the Davidic Messiah who brings New covenant salvation. It is certainly not that every covenant promise to Israel is being fulfilled in his day. Because of the dictates of their first coming hermeneutic and their acceptance of a wholly non-exegetical typological interpretive motif, the authors come to the wrong conclusion about Paul's sermon.[46]

When the next Sabbath comes around, the Gentiles want to hear Paul, and he cites Isaiah 49:6 (Acts 13:47),[47] a verse and context with which we have become familiar. There is nothing incongruous about salvation coming to the Gentiles since that is what the Prophets predicted.[48] But we are given no license to conclude that "Jesus the Messiah is the culmination of Israel's history" or that "The earlier covenants were designed to be fulfilled in and through the Messiah, Jesus." No! Jesus is the *start* of Israel's covenant hopes, not their fulfillment![49]

---

43 It is worth noting that this is the first place where we hear Paul's teaching. Cf. Bruce W. Longenecker, "Moral Character and Divine Generosity: Acts 13:13-52 and the Narrative Dynamics of Luke-Acts," in *New Testament Greek and Exegesis: Essays in Honor of Gerald F. Hawthorne*, eds. Amy M. Donaldson and Timothy B. Sailors (Grand Rapids: Eerdmans, 2003), 142-143. On pages 146-147 the author gives nine foci which suggest that Paul has Israel in mind in this first speech.

44 Chris Bruno, Jared Compton, and Kevin McFadden, *Biblical Theology According to the Apostles*, 69.

45 Ibid., 71.

46 In actual fact, they came to the wrong conclusion before they interpreted the passage.

47 A good argument for the messianic understanding of Isaiah 42:6-7 here, see Brian J. Tabb, *After Emmaus: How the Church Fulfills the Mission of Christ* (Wheaton, IL: Crossway, 2021), 150-154.

48 Cf. Acts 13:27.

49 For more on Acts 13, see under "Paul in Acts" below.

James at the Jerusalem Assembly

In Acts 15:13-21 we get James' proposal for how Gentile Christians relate to the Law. He is responding to testimonies of Paul, Barnabas, Peter, and their experiences.[50] James goes to the book of Amos to prove his point.

> Simon has declared how God at the first visited the Gentiles to take out of them a people for His name. And with this the words of the prophets agree, just as it is written:
>
> 'After this I will return
> And will rebuild the tabernacle of David, which has fallen down;
> I will rebuild its ruins,
> And I will set it up;
> So that the rest of mankind may seek the LORD,
> Even all the Gentiles who are called by My name,
> Says the LORD who does all these things' (Acts 15:14-17).

The passage James is citing is from Amos 9:11-12 (LXX). If we look at the theme James has in mind, it is that God is going to "call out a people for His name" from the Gentile nations. There is nothing controversial about this. But why go to Amos 9? I think the answer lies somewhere with the passage's acceptance of Gentile inclusion in salvation and its relative antiquity (8th century B.C.). But there is another part to it. The mention of the rebuilding of David's tabernacle, which alludes to the eschatological temple, is an acknowledgment of God's marvelous work in the coming of Christ and His initiation of the New covenant and its offer to Israel. And although Israel has remained obdurate, change has been brought about, and a new eschatological process has been set in motion. So no, the promised neo-Davidic Kingdom of Christ has not appeared (and James nowhere declares Amos 9:11-12 fulfilled). But Israel's King has come, been rejected, and now awaits His second coming to fulfill the ancient prophecies of restoration.

Because Christ has now come to Israel but has been rejected by them, there is an unavoidable "incongruity" that has surfaced between what has been brought to pass by Jesus' ministry and passion and what awaits to be fulfilled. Amos 9 suffers from this "incongruity" insofar as the pieces were put in place for its realization, yet ignorance and hard-heartedness have delayed important elements of the promise. As McClain observed, "Peter is only saying that the miraculous testimony of Pentecost was something to be expected prior to the establishment of the Messianic Kingdom."[51] Hence, once more we observe the phenomenon of the two comings having to be parsed if one is going to rightly interpret the entire work of Christ.

50 Peter is emphasized as the one to whom the acceptance of the Gentiles without the entailments of the Law is revealed (in Acts 10). See Acts 11:7-10.
51 Alva J. McClain, *The Greatness of the Kingdom*, 400.

EXCURSUS: The Book of Acts and Dispensational Change

There is a good deal of continuity between the Gospel of Luke and Acts.[52] However, because Acts records the ascension of Jesus (Acts 1:11), the day of Pentecost (Acts 2), the conversion of Saul and his commission to the Gentiles (Acts 9), Peter's vision of the lowered sheet filled with animals previously considered unclean, and his errand to the house of the Gentile Cornelius (Acts 10), the "council" of Jerusalem (Acts 15), and the meeting of the followers of John the Baptist with Paul (Acts 19), there is much in Acts where events of a transitional nature transpire. These events, including the descent of the Holy Spirit at Pentecost and the beginning of the Christian Church, must be thought about soberly. This is where the concept of "dispensation" can help. Although I believe "dispensations" are not of primary importance, it is true that the birth of the Church ought to be seen as a new dispensation (*oikonomia*) in the outworking of the Creation Project.[53]

Having said this, we don't want to veer off course by drawing a line between early Acts and late Acts. There are those who thrust added "dispensations"—as if there weren't enough already!—into the Acts period (circa A.D. 30–62), and who divide the Church into two: an Acts 1–8 Jewish Church where baptism was practiced, and an Acts 9–28 Church where it was not required. Some teach that the 70th week of Daniel 9 began in Acts 1 and ended with the Gospel going to the Gentiles in Acts 10.

As for the first, it is totally implausible to suggest a cleavage in post-Pentecost doctrine on the thin veneer of ultra or hyper-dispensationalism.[54] The Church began in Acts 2 before Paul was converted. Furthermore, at the very start of Paul's ministry, his teaching is said to have edified and comforted the churches "throughout all Judea, Galilee, and Samaria" (Acts 9:26-31). These churches already existed as part of the Body of Christ before the Apostle was saved (cf. Rom. 16:7; Acts 5:11; Gal. 1:13). No difference is made between a pre-Pauline "Jewish Church" and a post-Pauline Church. Paul himself told the Galatians and the Corinthians that, as an unbelieving Jew, he "persecuted the church of God" (Gal. 1:13; 1 Cor. 15:9).

Hyper-dispensationalists say that the Church predicted by Christ in Matthew 16:18 is different than the one Paul preached, but he gives no indication of this at all. Neither does he give any indication that the Church he taught about was separate from the Church Christ predicted. They also claim the "mystery" of the Church was revealed only to Paul, but in fact, in Ephesians 3:5 Paul tells us that not only he, but *all* the apostles, taught the same "mystery" regarding Christ and the Church. He also warns Christians at the end of his life to give heed to the words of Jesus Christ (1 Tim.

---

52 Craig L. Blomberg, *A New Testament Theology*, 384-385.

53 "Although the Lord is the founder of the church and the One who laid the groundwork during His earthly life, the church did not come into existence until the day of Pentecost" (Charles C. Ryrie, *Biblical Theology of the New Testament*, 109). Also, Walter C. Kaiser, Jr., *The Promise-Plan of God*, 323.

54 On this see e.g., Ernest Pickering, "Distinctive Teachings of Ultra-Dispensationalism," *CENQ* 4 (Winter 1961), 39-44; Charles C. Ryrie, *Dispensationalism*, 197-208; and Norman L. Geisler, *Norman L. Geisler, Systematic Theology: Church/Last Things*, Vol. 4 (Minneapolis: Bethany House, 2005), 680ff., and Gary Gilley's brief but helpful review of C. Stam's *Things That Differ*, at https://tottministries.org/things-that-differ-the-fundamentals-of-dispensationalism/.

6:3-4). Although Jesus did not publicly proclaim the content of 1 Corinthians 15:1-4 prior to His death, He did predict the coming of the Church, which is never said to be a separate entity from the pre-Pauline Church. When I speak about transitions in the book of Acts, I am simply referring to the dynamics of gradual revelation in the early Church.

Paul in Acts

The Apostle Paul was the first theologian of the Church. He was not a disciple of Jesus, and he never had the advantage of living and working with the Lord in his earthly sojourn. But Paul did have first-hand training from the risen Christ, according to Galatians 1:11-12, 15-18, and 2:2. With an excellent background in the Law and traditions (Acts 22:3), personal instruction from Jesus and a special commissioning from the Holy Spirit (Rom. 1:5; Gal. 2:8), Paul was fully prepared for his writing as well as his missionary activities.

Our first real encounter with Paul's apostolic teaching is in Acts 13, his first missionary journey with Barnabas. His lesson in the synagogue at Pisidian Antioch (Acts 13:13-41) begins with the Exodus (Acts 13:17) and quickly comes to David and then to Jesus (Acts 13:22-23). The way he takes is curious. He does not refer directly to the Davidic covenant or its terms but instead announces Jesus this way: "From this man's seed, according to *the* promise, God raised up for Israel a Savior—Jesus—after John had first preached, before His coming, the baptism of repentance to all the people of Israel" (Acts 13:23-24).

As a reminder, the Davidic covenant does not contain any note of a promise of salvation from sin in its terms. But Paul here is drawing a natural and no doubt common inference that the covenant implied such a salvation would come, and the Scriptures indicated that it would come through a Savior (Gen. 22:18; Psa. 22:31; Isa. 9:6-7; 49:5; 53:6). The ministry of John the Baptist (which presumably was known about even in Pisidia) is mentioned by Paul because he preached repentance to Israel in view of the Coming One. The Abrahamic note is struck in Acts 13:26. Then he proceeds to assert that the Jewish scholars at Jerusalem were ignorant of Jesus because they were ignorant of their own prophetic literature (Acts 13:27)—quite a charge! Thus, the promised One was killed, but God raised Him up again (Acts 13:30-33). Now the theme of kingship is brought up via Psalms 2:7 (Acts 13:33) and 16:10 (Acts 13:35) while applying Isaiah's "I will give You the sure mercies of David" (Isa. 55:3) to God's justification of Jesus in raising Him up (Acts 13:34). It is through Jesus that forgiveness of sins is now available to Israel (Acts 13:38-39). A final quotation from Habakkuk 1:5 warns against unbelief (Acts 13:40-41).[55]

This sermon presupposes the covenants with Abraham, David, and, since salvation comes through it, the New covenant in Jesus.[56] Sadly, the majority of the Jews

55 The use of Hab. 1:5 with its language of wonderworking was apposite even though the original was concerned with the impending Babylonian conquest. See F. F. Bruce, *The Book of Acts*, 279.

56 Paul does not refer to Him as the Christ here, although some of his arguments in his epistles depend upon that title—e.g., the many uses of the name "Christ Jesus" throughout the Pauline

rejected Paul's message and reacted to it with hostility (Acts 13:45). It seems they did not much care for Paul sharing the good news with the Gentiles. In his rebuke, Paul cites Isaiah 49:6—a covenant text (see Isaiah 49:8). Yet despite this unpromising response, he always held on to hope for the twelve tribes, even after the establishment of the Jew/Gentile Church (cf. Acts 26:7).

Paul's Preaching of the Kingdom of God

On several occasions we read of Paul preaching about the Kingdom of God. In Acts 14:22 it is clear that for the apostle, the Kingdom is yet future. It is the messianic or New covenant Kingdom. In Acts 17:7 the Jews from Thessalonica accused Paul of saying that a king other than Caesar, that is to say, Jesus, should be served. It may be that all that was being preached was that Jesus is Lord, and this was spun by the Jews to make Paul into a revolutionary, but it is possible that he was preaching the coming Kingdom of God. In Acts 19 we read of the apostle, "reasoning and persuading concerning the things of the kingdom of God" for three months in Ephesus (Acts 19:8). Without Luke telling us more, we cannot be certain whether this preaching concerned the future Kingdom or its appearance in the form of Jesus at His first coming (or indeed in some other form). We have seen that in the majority of cases, Luke has in mind the eschatological Kingdom.[57] As he was teaching in a synagogue, it seems safe to assume that he was not equating the Kingdom with the Church!

If I leave aside the passage in Acts 20 for the moment, the last time the Kingdom of God is found in Acts is at the end of the last chapter. There we read, "So when they had appointed him a day, many came to him at *his* lodging, to whom he explained and solemnly testified of the kingdom of God, persuading them concerning Jesus from both the Law of Moses and the Prophets, from morning till evening" (Acts 28:23). In the last verse of Acts, Luke leaves Paul "preaching the kingdom of God and teaching the things which concern the Lord Jesus Christ with all confidence, no one forbidding him" (Acts 28:31).

In these places we see that Paul's teaching of the Kingdom is consonant with his teaching about Jesus. Has the Kingdom arrived? Yes and no. No if what is meant is the great Kingdom in which Messiah reigns from Jerusalem and Israel is blessed above all nations. But yes, if what is meant is that Messiah has indeed come. Yet since the King has gone until His return in glory, it is plausible to think that the Kingdom is held in abeyance until that return. The preaching of the Kingdom by the apostle would then be the eschatological leaning of his message.

Acts 20 has the scene of the gathering of the Ephesian elders at Miletus and Paul's farewell. He refers to "the ministry [he] received from the Lord Jesus, to testify to the gospel of the grace of God" (Acts 20:24). This is, of course, a reference to the Gospel (cf. v. 21). But then he mentions the kingdom: "And indeed, now I know that you all,

---

literature.

57 E.g., Lk. 1:33; 4:43; 6:20; 7:28; 9:62; 11:2; 12:31-32; 13:18, 29; 14:15; 18:17; 19:11; 21:31; 22:16, 18, 29-30; Acts 1:6; 14:22.

among whom I have gone preaching the kingdom of God, will see my face no more" (Acts 20:25).

This statement is followed up by Paul's reminder that he has declared to these pastors "the whole counsel of God" (Acts 20:27). The word translated "counsel" in verse 27 is *boule*, which is rendered "purpose," "plan," or "will" of God in Acts 4:27-28, 5:38-39, and 13:36. In this setting, "counsel" fits well since God's "purpose" has been revealed, but we should retain the notion of intent. The *boule* is not the Gospel only but the entire project within which Jesus makes sense.[58] I take it then that the preaching of the Kingdom of God" here is the Creation Project that incorporates Eden and the Fall, the covenants with Noah, Abraham, Moses, and David, the messianic prophecies that accompany and give mutual support to them; and, of course, the incarnation, death, and resurrection of Christ and its eschatological meaning.[59]

In Acts 20:28 Paul admonishes the Ephesian elders, "Therefore take heed to yourselves and to all the flock, among which the Holy Spirit has made you overseers, to shepherd the church of God which He purchased with His own blood."As well as stressing the work of Christ's vicarious sacrifice as a fully divine work, the verse tells us something important about the Church. Marshall explains:

> This strongly suggests that the church is something new, and that suggestions that Luke simply envisaged a continuing people of God, enlarged by the inclusion of Gentile believers, are not altogether accurate. There is in fact a new people of God, in continuity with the old but now composed of believers in the Messiah. The coming of Christ marks a new beginning.[60]

I would have to disagree with what Marshall says about a people of God "in continuity with the old," because he does not see an Israel/Church distinction, but he is exactly right to tie the Church with recognition of Jesus as Messiah. The Church is a "new man" (Eph. 2:15) and, as I shall show, is indelibly correlated with the death and resurrection of Christ.

Paul and God's Promise to Israel

I want to end this chapter by noticing Paul's defense before Agrippa in Acts 26. Let us remind ourselves of his speech:

> I think myself happy, King Agrippa, because today I shall answer for myself before you concerning all the things of which I am accused by the Jews, especially because you are expert in all customs and questions which have to do with the Jews. Therefore I beg you to hear me patiently. My manner of life from my youth, which was spent from the beginning

58 It is well for pastor-teachers to make sure that the Gospel is set in a framework or story in which it makes the best sense, and this includes not only the biblical worldview but also the atmosphere most conducive to its telling.

59 Hence, the "whole counsel of God" includes both teleology and eschatology.

60 I. Howard Marshall, *New Testament Theology*, 167-168.

> among my own nation at Jerusalem, all the Jews know. They knew me from the first, if they were willing to testify, that according to the strictest sect of our religion I lived a Pharisee. And now I stand and am judged for the hope of the promise made by God to our fathers. To this *promise* our twelve tribes, earnestly serving *God* night and day, hope to attain. For this hope's sake, King Agrippa, I am accused by the Jews (Acts 26:2-7).

Here at the end of his two-part history, Luke informs us that the great apostle did not see the preaching of Christ as altering or nullifying what God had promised Israel in the OT, but as leading to its literal fulfillment. Vlach says:

> Paul's message has roots back to the patriarchs of Israel and what God revealed to them. The promise God made to Abraham, Isaac, and Jacob is the same promise Paul is proclaiming. There is no indication this "promise" has been transcended or spiritualized or refined into something different. This is the literal hope to Israel as found in the Abrahamic Covenant...[61]

One has to wonder why commentators who depreciate the disciples for their question about the Kingdom being restored to Israel to Jesus in Acts 1:6 do not give the same treatment to Paul in this place. Did Paul not "get it"? Or did he believe that God's oaths concerning his people were utterly secure, and that rather than proclaiming a mostly Gentile "new Israel," he knew that the physical "remnant" of Abraham, Isaac, and Jacob would one day attain precisely what God has promised?[62] Some cite Acts 13:32-33 and 26:22-24 as proof of the fulfillment of Paul's stated hope, but in both passages Paul is referring to the death and resurrection of the Jewish Messiah, alluding to the New covenant verse in Isaiah 49:6. This again is a failure to take God's oaths seriously. Paul did not, and neither should we. With that said, let us turn to examine Paul's letters.

61 Michael J. Vlach, *He Will Reign Forever*, 428.

62 Darrell L. Bock, *Acts*, 714. It should come as no surprise to discover that Acts 26:6-7 is avoided by most a- and post-millennialists. An exception is G. K. Beale, who believes that Paul's epistles teach that Christ is "the true Israel" and that, therefore, the Church inherits the promises in Him. See G. K. Beale, *A New Testament Biblical Theology*, 140.

14

PAUL: AN APOSTLE OF THE NEW COVENANT (1)[1]

Paul, a bondservant of Jesus Christ, called to be an apostle, separated to the gospel of God which He promised before through His prophets in the Holy Scriptures, concerning His Son Jesus Christ our Lord, who was born of the seed of David according to the flesh, and declared to be the Son of God with power according to the Spirit of holiness, by the resurrection from the dead. – Romans 1:1-4

Although he did not write systematic expositions, and the majority of the words we have from him are in the form of occasional letters to churches on the mission field, Paul qualifies as the greatest theologian of the Christian Church.[2] His thought is profound and multilayered. I am not going to do full justice to it here.[3] My interaction with Paul is more modest.[4] I am interested in investigating how the covenants of God

1 In giving my treatment of covenant in Paul this title, I realize that some will be a little wary about reading on. Those who have read Volume One will have been prepared for my emphasis on the New covenant and its essential use as the covenant to ensure the literal fulfillment of the other covenants. An overview of my reasoning about the New covenant is to be found in the fourth chapter of this book under the heading, "The New Covenant and Jesus Christ." I ask anyone who has turned straight to these pages to first read over that little section to gain a better understanding of my approach to the subject.

2 James D. G. Dunn, *The Theology of the Apostle Paul* (Grand Rapids: Eerdmans, 1998), 2.

3 I should say that there are several different approaches to Paul, which, although they can learn from each other, do not end up on the same page. My position is very conservative, yet in this study I have cited a lot of authors who differ quite widely from me. This is because most conservative scholars have written very little on "covenant" in relation to Paul. There has been good work done by those whom I might call "semi-conservative" authors like Wright, Dunn, Hays, etc., which, even though I arrive at different conclusions than they do, have helped me think through the text in profitable ways.

4 Sad to say I know of no dispensational work on Paul and his theology. It has often been my complaint that Dispensationalism, which I generally respect, has failed to produce works in many areas where other theological approaches have excelled.

affected his thought, although that influence is vast.[5] And I am also interested in how he understood the doctrine of the Church against the background of the OT covenants, and the role the Person of Jesus Christ plays in that understanding.

Paul as an Apostle of the Covenant(s)

In treating the Epistles of Paul, I have decided to follow a thematic rather than a chronological scheme.[6] I want to treat Paul as an author like I have treated Luke or Isaiah. I am not of the opinion that the inspired apostle once thought one way and, ten or so years after, thought quite differently. To say it another way, I do not believe that the inspired letter to the churches in Galatia (c. A.D. 48–50) evinces a less mature theological mind than we find in Romans (A.D. 56) or in 2 Timothy (c. A.D. 65).[7] We are talking about a mere fifteen years after all, and what often holds true for you and I as we study and ruminate on Scripture cannot be considered analogous to Paul's inspired understanding.[8]

The occasional nature of Paul's correspondence does not furnish enough data to theorize about the state of his doctrine by comparisons of his letters. The same holds true for Paul in the book of Acts. There is but one theology of Paul, not a naïve theology and a mature theology.[9]

I should also say that I am not persuaded by the resolve of many modern "critical" scholars like Douglas Campbell[10] and J. Christiaan Beker,[11] who urge upon us an "apocalyptic Paul."[12] By this term, they have in mind Paul's doctrine of God's radical

5 Normally, it is contemporary non-dispensational scholars who call attention to the pervasive influence of "covernance" in Paul. Naturally, they tend to find premature fulfillment of the covenants with Abraham, David, and even the New covenant in the Church without looking for literal fulfillment for the nation of Israel (or the nations) in the coming Kingdom. E.g., David B. Capes, Rodney Reeves, and E. Randolph Richards, *Rediscovering Paul: An Introduction to His World, Letters and Theology* (Downers Grove, IL: InterVarsity, 2007), 172-183, 257-263.

6 I should add here that I take all thirteen letters traditionally ascribed to Paul. I have no time for dithering about the disputed authorship of Ephesians, the Pastorals, etc. All the Greek copies we have of these letters ascribe them to Paul. For a clear affirmation of the Pauline authorship of all thirteen NT Letters ascribed to Paul, see D. A. Carson and Douglas J. Moo, *An Introduction to the New Testament*, 2nd ed. (Grand Rapids: Zondervan, 2005), 337-350; and Stanley E. Porter, *The Apostle Paul: His Life, Thought, and Letters* (Grand Rapids: Eerdmans, 2016), 156-178.

7 It is for this reason the works of Paul can be read profitably in canonical order. See e.g., Andreas J. Köstenberger and Gregory Goswell, *Biblical Theology*, 520-521.

8 This statement demands a study in itself, but I cannot allow myself to get sidetracked. I, therefore, should say that my understanding of the authors of Scripture being led into all truth (Jn. 16:13), and "borne along by the Holy Spirit" (2 Pet. 1:21), inevitably results in a fully matured inscripturation of God's words (2 Tim. 3:16). See B. B. Warfield, *The Inspiration and Authority of the Bible* (Phillipsburg, NJ: 1948), 351-410.

9 I have no hesitation in applying Jesus' promise in Jn. 16:13 to Paul (cf. Gal. 1:16b).

10 Douglas A. Campbell, *The Deliverance of God: An Apocalyptic Rereading of Justification in Paul* (Grand Rapids: Eerdmans, 2013).

11 J. Christiaan Beker, *The Triumph of God: The Essence pf Paul's Thought* (Minneapolis: Fortress, 1990).

12 See a review and augmentation of this theme in Brant Pitre, Michael P. Barber, and John A. Kincaid, *Paul: A New Covenant Jew: Rethinking Pauline Theology* (Grand Rapids: Eerdmans, 2019), 64-94. The term "apocalyptic," as John Barclay has said, seems to mean different things to different people.

intervention into world affairs through His resurrection and the proclamation of the new birth, concluding with His second coming (although that minimizes the views). For reasons I have gone into elsewhere, I reject using the notion of apocalyptic in this way, for it always ends up getting in the way of what the text appears to be saying. So, for example, we end up with an "apocalyptic gospel,"[13] not a straightforward Gospel with natural teleological and eschatological elements.[14] What I want to try to show is that Paul *thought* covenantally. "Covenant" was a part of his Jewish milieu.[15]

The coming of the Son of God into the world and His death and resurrection formed a new reality. What He left behind shapes revelation and instructs our theological view of the world. We look backward and forward in light of the Christ event and its sequel at the second advent. This is certainly what Paul did.

But God's covenants are never forgotten in Paul. The Noahic, Abrahamic, Mosaic, and Davidic covenants are all important to him, especially as seen through the New covenant. They always undergird the message. The New covenant, in particular, provides the continuity between the Testaments. With that said, it's time now to turn to the theme of covenant in Paul.[16]

Paul and the Concept of Covernance

Like the other NT writers, Paul does not speak explicitly about the biblical covenants in many places. Having said that, the presence of covenant language is easy to find, and the influence of the covenants is also not hard to detect. As a matter of fact, the idea of covernance is everywhere presupposed. One has only to consider the following examples to see this clearly:

> And we have such trust through Christ toward God. Not that we are sufficient of ourselves to think of anything as *being* from ourselves, but our sufficiency *is* from God, who also made us sufficient as ministers of the new covenant, not of the letter but of the Spirit; for the letter kills, but the Spirit gives life (2 Cor. 3:4-6, my emphasis).

> And this I say, *that* the law, which was four hundred and thirty years later, cannot annul the covenant that was confirmed before by God in Christ, that it should make the promise of no effect (Gal. 3:17, my emphasis).

13 E.g., Anthony C. Thiselton, *The Living Paul: An Introduction to the Apostle's Life and Thought* (Downers Grove, IL: InterVarsity, 2009), 17.

14 I also detect a subtle equivocation in the meaning of the word "apocalyptic." When applied to Paul's message, it more closely concerns the literal sense of the term as a "revelation" rather than a genre of literature.

15 See Paul R. Williamson, *Sealed with an Oath*, 186. "The idea of covenant was central to Judaism in this period...covenantal ideas were totally common and regular at this time" (N. T. Wright, *The New Testament and the People of God*, 260; Idem, *Paul: In Fresh Perspective* [Minneapolis: Fortress, 2005], 26).

16 In what follows the reader will constantly encounter the New covenant. This will hardly surprise anyone familiar with Volume One. *The New covenant furnishes most of the continuity between the Testaments.*

> For these are the two covenants: the one from Mount Sinai which gives birth to bondage, which is Hagar— for this Hagar is Mount Sinai in Arabia, and corresponds to Jerusalem which now is, and is in bondage with her children— but the Jerusalem above is free, which is the mother of us all (Gal. 4:24-26, my emphasis).

Statements such as these could not be made unless the covenant concept was in the air Paul breathed, as it were. The word may not occur many times in his writings, but "covenant" was fundamental to Paul's thought-world.[17]

I shall be examining these and other scriptures in due course, but permit me to point to one or two matters as we begin. In 2 Corinthians 3 (A.D. 56) Paul tells us that he comprehends his whole ministry in terms of the New covenant,[18] and in true New covenant fashion (e.g., Isa. 32:15; Ezek. 36:27), he highlights the work of the Spirit in this ministry (2 Cor. 3:3, 6, 8).[19] In Galatians 3:17 he refers to "the [Abrahamic] covenant that was confirmed before [the Law] by God in Christ." In Galatians 4 he speaks of the symbolism of two covenants: the one signified by Ishmael and the bondage to the flesh; the other signified by Isaac and the freedom through the grace promise, the promise of the covenant with Abraham (which Ishmael was not party to, Gen. 17:18-19)[20] transcended the requirements of the Mosaic Law. We also see his concern for the covenant theme illustrated at the beginning of Romans, where he speaks of Jesus as "born of the seed of David according to the flesh" (Rom. 1:3). Although it is often missed, the apostle Paul thought along covenantal lines, and we would do well to follow him along those same lines.

Paul's Understanding of God's Covenants

I debated with myself about doing this, but I think we should dive right in and begin with that lightning rod statement in 2 Corinthians 3:6: "[God] also made us sufficient as ministers of the new covenant, not of the letter but of the Spirit; for the letter kills, but the Spirit gives life."

In this massively important chapter, the apostle Paul styled himself as a minister of the New covenant.[21] That declaration might stick in the craw of some readers, but,

17 Even Paul's thoughts about Jesus were covenantally influenced, for as scholars have increasingly recognized, Paul recalibrates the *Shema* of Deut. 6:4 to include Christ (e.g., 1 Cor. 10:6). "As a Jew," Capes observes, "Paul was a monotheist, but now...he understands that Jesus somehow must be reckoned within God's unique covenant identity" (David B. Capes, *The Divine Christ: Paul, the Lord Jesus, and the Scriptures of Israel* [Grand Rapids: Baker, 2018], 80).

18 Mark A. Seifrid, *Christ Our Righteousness: Paul's Theology of Justification* (Downers Grove, IL: IVP Academic, 2000), 112.

19 Is it then assuming too much to read the "Spirit-chapters" of Rom. 8 and Gal. 5 as New covenant influenced?

20 We must distinguish between a straight promise and a covenant promise. Gen. 17 proves that Ishmael was the recipient of the former but not of the latter.

21 In the chapter, Paul is comparing his New covenant ministry with Moses' old covenant ministry. See Johannes Munck, *Paul and the Salvation of Mankind* (Richmond, VA: John Knox Press, 1959), 174; and Andreas J. Köstenberger and Gregory Goswell, *Biblical Theology*, 554.

as they say, "it is what it is."[22] It must be allowed to sink in. One of the main theses of the present work is that the unequivocal covenants of God are supplied with the guarantee of their literal fulfillment *because* of their encounter with the New covenant in Christ.[23] And even though he rarely refers to it by name, it has become clear to many scholars that Paul's theology is steeped in the New covenant.[24] This will become evident in many of the passages I will discuss below.[25] The Person of Jesus the Christ may, in numerous instances, stand for the New covenant in Him. I think it is true to say that without this comprehension of his mission, Paul's theology is difficult to pull together.[26] When one thinks of the matter-of-factness with which the apostle speaks about the Church, his future hopes for the nation of Israel, the sacrificial and atoning nature of the cross, and his characterization of the OT Law, the New covenant work of God in Christ brings it all into focus.

Our multifaceted union with Christ is a covenantal one. In fact, the title *Christos* is itself covenantal,[27] and the Spirit who unites us to His resurrection is covenantally given.[28] This is the conclusion I believe one should arrive at by comparing, for example, 2 Corinthians 3:16-17 with 3:3-6.[29] The Christian is in that blood bond as well as in Jesus through the Spirit (Rom. 8:10-11; 1 Cor. 12:13; Eph. 2:12-13; Col. 1:27; 2 Thess. 2:13).[30]

---

22 Dispensationalists have argued about whether the New covenant is for the Church. But there are many who have no trouble with the Church being full parties to the New covenant alongside of Israel. These include John MacArthur, Michael Vlach, and Tony Garland.

23 See e.g., *The Words of the Covenant*, Vol. 1, 57-58.

24 See, for example, while not always agreeing with them fully, Paul R. Williamson, *Sealed with an Oath*, 182-201; Bruce A. Ware, "The New Covenant and the People(s) of God," in *Dispensationalism, Israel and the Church*, 84-91; Peter J. Gentry and Stephen J. Wellum, *Kingdom through Covenant,* 512, 607; Brant Pitre, Michael P. Barber, John A. Kincaid, *Paul, A New Covenant Jew: Rethinking Pauline Theology*; James P. Ware, *Paul's Theology in Context*, esp. 104-110; Mark A. Seifrid, "Unrighteous by Faith: Apostolic Proclamation in Romans 1:18-3:20," in *Justification and Variegated Nomism, The Paradoxes of Paul*, eds. D. A. Carson, Peter T. O'Brien and Mark A. Seifrid, Vol. 2 (Grand Rapids: Baker, 2004), 135; David B. Capes, Rodney Reeves, and E. Randolph Richards, *Rediscovering Paul: An Introduction to His World, Letters and Theology*, 161-162; Ian J. Vaillancourt, *The Dawning of Redemption: The Story of the Pentateuch and the Hope of the Gospel* (Wheaton, IL: Crossway, 2022), 107-109.

25 Many dispensationalists insist that God's covenants were made *only* with Israel. They point to Rom. 9:4 as proof of this. But this says too much. Paul is very clear in Gal. 3 that the Gentiles in the Church are included within the third aspect of the Abrahamic covenant (Gal. 3:15-29). The Noahic covenant is not an Israelite covenant. As I try to show, the New covenant is behind the preaching of the gospel (2 Cor. 3:1–4:6), and Christians celebrate (sadly sometimes unknowingly) the New covenant blood that bought them in the Lord's Supper (1 Cor. 11:25). What are the two elements of the Lord's Supper if not tokens of the New covenant? See e.g., 1 Cor. 10:16 with 11:23-29.

26 It has recently been plausibly asserted that seeing Paul as "a New covenant Jew" helps to integrate the apostle's thought. See Brant Pitre, Michael P. Barber, John A. Kincaid, *Paul, A New Covenant Jew*, 62. I sympathize with this portrayal, although while not denying his Jewishness, I would prefer to call him "a New Covenant apostle."

27 This is necessarily the case if one takes a Christological view of Isaiah 49:8.

28 See, for example, the remarks of Larry L. Helyer, *The Witness of Jesus, Paul and John*, 259, 267.

29 It is Christ who takes the veil away (2 Cor. 3:16) for those "in Christ" (2 Cor. 3:14) to whom "the Spirit gives life" (2 Cor. 3:6) through the New covenant message of Paul and his co-laborers.

30 F. F. Bruce, *Paul: Apostle of the Heart Set Free* (Grand Rapids: Eerdmans, 1989), 209-211.

This qualifying distinction is all-important for Pauline thought on the subjects of law and grace. If we return to the three passages above, we can see this. In Galatians 3:17 he says, "The law ... cannot annul the covenant that was confirmed before by God in Christ, that it should make the promise of no effect." What is this "covenant" that is said to be "confirmed" in Christ and that the law, due to our habit of breaking it, "cannot annul"? It is, of course, the covenant with Abraham that Paul has introduced in Galatians 3:5-9 and 14. The Abrahamic covenant has three branches to it: the promise of literal descendants through Abraham, Isaac, and Jacob, the promise of a homeland, and finally, that through Abraham all the families of the earth would be blessed (cf. Gen. 12:1-3, 7). It is crucial that we get the proper piece of the covenant right. Paul is not talking in Galatians 3 either about the physical seed or the land promises. He is focused on the third branch, the blessing upon the nations.[31] The blessings of this third branch of the covenant are said to be "in Christ" (Gal. 3:14, 17).

What we read here is Gentile Christians being told that they are children of Abraham through the promise that "all the families of the earth would be blessed" (cf. Gal. 3:8). Paul is *not* saying here that Gentiles have entitlement to the other two parts of the Abrahamic covenant.[32] He *is*, however, saying that our inheritance is covenantal. Hence, all aspects of the Abrahamic covenant are to be fulfilled through Christ, but the Christ-connection—and this is crucial—is a New covenant connection (Isa. 49:8; 1 Cor. 11:25; Heb. 9:15).

But I digress. If we return to 2 Corinthians 3, we must perforce talk about the New covenant.[33] Paul begins this great epistle by speaking about suffering and the consolation of God (2 Cor. 1:3-11), and then refers to what he calls "the day of the Lord Jesus" (2 Cor. 1:14), by which he seems to point to the judgment seat of Christ (2 Cor. 5:10).[34] This day concerns a judgment of our faithfulness (1 Cor. 3:11-15).

The opening two chapters of 2 Corinthians are quite self-referential (2 Cor. 1:8-10; 2:1, 4, 10, 12-17), with the apostle saying much about his circumstances and attitude to the ministry. In chapter 3 he turns this focus from afflictions and such to appeal to the Church at Corinth concerning his credentials as an apostle. The Spirit of God has made His mark in them (2 Cor. 3:3), and it is the same Spirit who enables

31 The same thing is to be seen in Rom. 4, although Rom. 4:18 does quote Gen. 15:5 and applies it to Abraham being the father of many nations (linking it up with Gen. 17:5 in Rom. 4:17). We should note, however, that this particular promise is not part of the covenant oath(s) of Yahweh to Abraham. Paul is employing these texts to illustrate justification by grace through faith.

32 In light of this, it is vain to freight in 2 Cor. 1:20, "For all the promises of God in Him are Yes, and in Him Amen, to the glory of God through us." God promised very many things in the Bible. He promised to save Noah and his family in the Ark (Gen. 7:1-5). He promised abundance of food to the starving Jews (2 Ki. 7:1-16). Clearly the apostle did not have these and many other promises in mind. In the same way, it is a mistake to believe that God's promises to Israel of land and descendants, etc. are inherited by the Church. This rips 2 Cor. 1:20 out of its context.

33 David Woodall, "2 Corinthians," in *The Moody Bible Commentary*, eds. Michael Rydelnik and Michael Vanlaningham (Chicago: Moody, 2014), 1812. I should also note here that I use the capital 'N' for "New covenant" because in the NT it can be preceded by the definite article (Lk. 22:20; 1 Cor. 11:25), which contextually indicates a name.

34 Even if we accept the critical text reading "judgment seat of God," many still refer to it as the *Bema* seat.

Paul and his helpers to pursue their New covenant ministry (2 Cor. 3:6). In keeping with this, Paul's ministry is called "the ministry of the Spirit" in verse 8! This is a clear New covenant marker.[35] Hence Paul's contrast of the "old covenant" (*palaios diathekes*)[36] with the New covenant in the second half of the chapter makes perfect sense (2 Cor. 3:7-18).[37] Fee makes our case:

> In contrast [to the old covenant], the new covenant, by means of the life-giving Spirit, is written on "tablets of human hearts" (2 Cor 3:3); its rite of "circumcision" is that "of the heart" (Rom 2:29). The gospel and its ministry are accompanied by a much greater and more enduring glory, the ministry of the Spirit himself (2 Cor 3:8). *The new covenant is life-giving, because its content, Christ,* is administered by the Spirit...The promised new covenant has replaced the old, and the gift of the Spirit proves it.[38]

This is an excellent summary of the data. Fee manages to provide a digest of 2 Corinthians 3 while highlighting the content of the New covenant, who is Christ.[39] Therefore, we are justified in equating the Gospel Paul preached with the proclamation of the New covenant.[40] The ministry of the New covenant is "the ministry of reconcilia-

---

35 In 2 Cor. 1:22 he says of God, "who also has sealed us and given us the Spirit in our hearts as a guarantee." This "guarantee" in the NKJV (*arrabon*) is better rendered "earnest" or "pledge." It is paired with "seal" (*sphragizo*), which speaks of God's ownership of us. Schreiner astutely remarks "The seal authenticates and documents God's people as his own" (Thomas R. Schreiner, *Paul, Apostle of God's Glory in Christ*, 275). This calls to mind Paul's own language of the Corinthian Christians being "an epistle of Christ" (2 Cor. 3:2-3). Another writer puts things well: "Thus, in the present the Spirit is simultaneously a portion of the life and power of the future age, and a sign pointing beyond the present, telling believers that the fullness of the messianic age has not yet arrived" (T. Paige, "Holy Spirit," in *Dictionary of Paul and His Letters*, 411). If we connect this with Jesus' sending of the Spirit after His ascension (Jn. 16:7), and Paul's doctrine of spiritual circumcision in Phil. 3:3, then it is tempting to draw the conclusion that the apostle viewed the gift of the Spirit as a token of the New covenant for the Church from the divine side. Furthermore, we might add to this the baptism with the Spirit of 1 Cor. 12:13, wherein spiritual baptism is part of what qualifies us to be "in Christ" (cf. 1 Cor. 15:22). For more on the metaphors of "down payment" and "sealing," see Gordon D. Fee, *God's Empowering Presence: The Holy Spirit in the Letters of Paul*, 806-808, although without the insistence that the gift of the Spirit means that "the eschatological promises of Paul's Jewish heritage have been fulfilled" (808). For the locative sense of baptism with the Spirit see Ibid., 178-182.

36 I realize that many take this phrase in 2 Cor. 3:14 to mean the OT, but this spoils the contrast. The correct translation of *diatheke* in that place is "covenant" not "testament." See e.g., NASB, ESV, NET. Also, Daniel Block, *Covenant*, 484-485, 520; James D. G. Dunn, *The Theology of Paul the Apostle*, 725; Richard B. Hays, *Echoes of Scripture in Paul*, 134; Douglas J. Moo, *A Theology of Paul and His Letters*, 170-171. To translate *diatheke* as "testament" in 2 Cor. 3:14 completely messes up the contrast between the Mosaic covenant and the New covenant that Paul is plainly wanting to make in the entire chapter.

37 See Philip Edgcumbe Hughes, *Paul's Second Epistle to the Corinthians* (London: Marshall, Morgan & Scott, 1962), 110-115.

38 Gordon D. Fee, *God's Empowering Presence*, 813. My emphasis.

39 Again, we should remind ourselves that Jesus Christ is not only the sacrifice for sin, He is the focal point of the New covenant terms, which are not firstly about something, but about Someone (1 Cor. 15:1-4; 11:25; 2 Cor. 4:3-6). "Paul identifies the 'new covenant' as the gospel of Jesus Christ" (Paul R. Williamson, *Sealed with an Oath*, 192).

40 One can simply state that Paul in 2 Cor. 3 is contrasting the gospel (of the New covenant) with the old covenant. E.g., John Howard Schutz, *Paul and the Anatomy of Apostolic Authority* (Louisville: John Knox Press, 2007), 210.

tion," of which he speaks in 2 Corinthians 5:18. This both supports our exegesis of the chapter and helps emphasize our equation of Christ and the New covenant!

The Sacrificial Nature of the Cross

Another indication of the presence of the New covenant is the recognition of the cross as a sacrifice. Although he only employs the term once in reference to the crucifixion of Christ, Paul concurs with the writer of Hebrews that Jesus' death on the cross was a sacrificial act. Hebrews 9:26 speaks of the crucifixion as putting away sin "by the sacrifice of Himself." Paul echoes this when he states, "Christ also has loved us and given Himself for us, an offering and a sacrifice to God" (Eph. 5:2). Acceptable sacrifices in the Bible are always made in connection with one of God's covenants. The Mosaic system obviously involved multiple sacrifices in its provisions (e.g., Lev. 1–9). Therefore, the Priestly and Davidic covenants established during this period were connected to those sacrifices. The Noahic (Gen. 8:21; 9:20-21) and Abrahamic (Gen. 15:9-11) covenants have conspicuous sacrifices associated with them. The sacrifice of the New covenant is the Lamb of God (cf. Jn. 1:29; 1 Pet. 1:19; Rev. 5:6, 12), whose blood both Christ and Paul call New covenant blood (Lk. 22:20; 1 Cor. 11:25). This means that if we are going to speak of Christ's cross as a sacrifice, we must also speak of it as a covenant sacrifice.[41] In regard to the Christian's union with the risen Christ, we ought to understand the ongoing consecration of ourselves to God as a New covenant sacrifice (Rom. 12:1).

In view of these things, the Christian's relation to the redemptive act of Christ is "overtly and fundamentally covenantal."[42] In fact, Christ's atonement is a New covenant atonement, in that without His death on the cross, the New covenant would not have come into being.[43] This underscores how deeply the theme of covernance lay behind Paul's thoughts.[44]

A Covenant Hope of Salvation

In the book of Romans, Paul's argument up until Romans 4 has been that all men are sinners, Jews and Gentiles alike, and that God's forgiveness and salvation are beyond

41 James P. Ware, *Paul's Theology in Context*, 116-117.

42 Brant Pitre, Michael P. Barber, John A. Kincaid, *Paul, A New Covenant Jew*, 159.

43 This is the thesis also of Michael J. Gorman's *The Death of the Messiah and the Birth of the New Covenant: A (Not so) New Model of the Atonement* (Eugene: Wipf & Stock, 2014), 5. I only notice it in passing, and believe Gorman blurs the lines between justification and sanctification. But his work is important, and from the perspective of my purpose in tracing out the development of God's covenants with man throughout the Bible, I see it as a natural consequence of funneling the other divine covenants through the New covenant. One can hardly reach the conclusions I have reached without believing that Christ's atonement for sin is closely connected to the New covenant in Him. I do agree with Gorman (Ibid., 20-21) that the New covenant connection necessitates a participatory relationship with the risen Christ in the New covenant. However, I hesitate to label this as a part of our justification. I see justification as a judicial declaration of "not guilty" in the sinner's favor. That said, I do think justification and sanctification belong together. Where you find one you will find the other.

44 I shall return to the theme of the New covenant in Paul further on.

the reach of any man through the means of law-keeping and good deeds (Rom. 1:18–3:6). He lists a group of indictments in Romans 3:10-14, drawing upon texts (mainly in the psalms), several of which contain strong covenant declarations within them. The first text in Romans 3:10 probably cites Ecclesiastes 7:20. Romans 3:11 and 12 employ Psalm 14:2-3, a text which ends on a ringing covenantal note, "Oh, that the salvation of Israel *would come* out of Zion! When the LORD brings back the captivity of His people, Let Jacob rejoice *and* Israel be glad" (Psa. 14:7). Romans 3:13 quotes Psalm 5:9, which speaks of rebellion against God and invokes the covenant name in verses 10-11 in contrast to the transgressors. The last part of Romans 3:13 cites Psalm 140:3, a psalm that resounds with covenanted hope of salvation and divine presence in verses 7, 12, and 13. Romans 3:14 is from Psalm 10:7, which pleads with Yahweh in verses 12, 16, and 17. Then Romans 3:15-17 is drawn from Isaiah 59:7-8, a beautiful passage which is completed by a clear New covenant promise.[45] Lastly, Romans 3:18 quotes Psalm 36:1, a psalm that includes the line, "For with You *is* the fountain of life; in Your light we see light" (Psa. 36:9), a sentiment inconceivable outside the OT idea of covenant relationship.

I do not say all this to be drearily pedantic. My reason for pointing it out is to demonstrate how a Second Temple Jew, such as Paul (a former Pharisee), *cannot have missed the covenantal associations in the passages he was quoting*, even if they go over the heads of most Gentiles. He took the notion of the covenant God for granted.

Declared Righteous

The apostle follows up these indictments by concluding:

> Now we know that whatever the law says, it says to those who are under the law, that every mouth may be stopped, and all the world may become guilty before God. Therefore by the deeds of the law no flesh will be justified in His sight, for by the law *is* the knowledge of sin (Rom. 3:19-20).

Any attempt to impress God that one is good enough to be granted eternal life and avoid condemnation for wrongdoing and wrong thinking will be scuppered on the rocks of God's righteous justice (Gal. 3:10; 2 Tim. 1:9; Tit. 3:5). All that "the law" can do, whether written on scrolls or on the conscience (Rom. 2:12-15), is to pronounce our guilt (Gal. 2:16, 21). Therefore, if sinners are to have hope of salvation, it is plain enough that God must do it, and He must do it without contradicting His own holiness. What we need is to be *declared* innocent by God, to be justified instead of condemned. Here Paul's language is decisive, but requires a careful reading:

45 "'The Redeemer will come to Zion, and to those who turn from transgression in Jacob,' Says the LORD. 'As for Me,' says the LORD, 'this *is* My covenant with them: My Spirit who *is* upon you, and My words which I have put in your mouth, shall not depart from your mouth, nor from the mouth of your descendants, nor from the mouth of your descendants' descendants,' says the LORD, 'from this time and forevermore'" (Isa. 59:20-21).

> But now the righteousness of God apart from the law is revealed, being witnessed by the Law and the Prophets, even the righteousness of God, through faith in Jesus Christ, to all and on all who believe. For there is no difference; for all have sinned and fall short of the glory of God, being justified freely by His grace through the redemption that is in Christ Jesus ... (Rom. 3:21-24).

This way of salvation has been made. The sinner is given "the righteousness of God" (Rom. 3:22) that justifies him (Rom. 3:24). Nevertheless, something happens to the believer. The declaration of a sinner as justified through faith in Christ is not the end of the matter. Let us continue with the above quotation:

> ... whom God set forth *as* a propitiation by His blood, through faith, to demonstrate His righteousness, because in His forbearance God had passed over the sins that were previously committed, to demonstrate at the present time His righteousness, that He might be just and the justifier of the one who has faith in Jesus (Rom. 3:25-26).

Paul declares that redemption is available in only one place: "in Christ Jesus" (Rom. 3:24).[46] But why is this? It is because Christ has been "set forth" by God to *propitiate*[47] God on the sinner's behalf. Paul says the way in which God is propitiated is through Jesus Christ's own blood! This means that, as he says, Christ *is* the propitiation Himself (Rom. 3:25a; cf. 1 Jn. 2:2; 4:10). But if the sinner is declared righteous *through the blood of Christ*, then his righteousness (not to mention his justification) must surely be covenantal (cf. Lk. 22:20; Heb. 13:20).

Back to the Blood

And so, we are back to the blood of Christ; and Christ's blood is, says the apostle, "the blood of the new covenant" (1 Cor. 11:25). When an animal was killed to propitiate God for sin, all of its blood was used.[48] *All* of the blood was covenant blood, either from the peace and sin offerings, or the burnt offering (e.g., Lev. 4:30, 34; 5:9; 8:15; 9:9; Deut. 12:16, 27; 15:23). Since Jesus was "the Lamb of God" (Jn. 1:21) who acted as our sin-substitute (1 Pet. 3:18), and "He is our peace" (Eph. 2:14a), the sin and peace offerings are relevant to our thinking about the cross. My point is that all the blood was covenant blood, regardless of how it was used. *If Christ's blood is "the blood of the new covenant," then it is all New covenant blood.* There is no such thing in God's economy as sacrificial blood that is non-covenantal. The attempt by well-meaning

46 By inverting the usual pronouncement of the Lord's name, the apostle is highlighting Jesus' messiahship. It is as the covenant Christ that Jesus brings redemption.

47 The NT employs the terms "propitiate" and "propitiation" to refer to the turning away from the transgressor the righteous wrath of God. It never means what it means when applied to pagan gods, whose all-too-human character traits required them to be appeased for any number of petty and unrighteous demands. See the classic presentation and defense of propitiation in Leon L. Morris, *The Apostolic Preaching of the Cross*, 144-213.

48 See R. E. Averbeck, "Sacrifices and Offerings," in *Dictionary of the Old Testament: Pentateuch*, eds. T. Desmond Alexander and David W. Baker (Downers Grove, IL: InterVarsity, 2003), esp. 716-725.

scholars, especially some dispensationalists, to detach the blood of Jesus Christ from God's covenant is, therefore, misguided.

But this recognition entails another; for the promise of the New covenant, which Paul himself applies to Christians, is that God will change the heart (Ezek. 36:26; 2 Cor. 3:3; cf. Rom. 2:29). If an effect of the New covenant is a change of heart (even if it is not complete in this life, cf. Rom. 7:25), then the "righteousness" of the Christian cannot solely be of a forensic variety. Here the present and the eschatological aspects of the New covenant come into focus.[49] Due to the present condition of Christians as justified but not yet glorified, the total transformation of the sons of God has not occurred. Sanctification is, in an important sense, progressive.[50] And Paul's correspondence, in large measure, directly addresses this state of affairs. Although Paul does not use John's language about the blood of Christ cleansing the Christian from sins committed after he has been justified (1 Jn. 1:9), he does speak of Christ's blood making peace for us (Col. 1:20) and calls Christ "our peace" (Eph. 2:14). One does not have to hold to a sacramental view of the Lord's Supper to understand that the communion or bond which congregations experience when taking the elements together has a spiritual dimension which includes the Lord (1 Cor. 10:16). Hence, the fact that Christ's "blood of the New covenant" is still active in our sanctification, along with the Holy Spirit (Rom. 8:10-11; Gal. 5:16, 22-25), points to the blessed truth that we are dealt with under the auspices of our participation in the New covenant.

Strangers from the Covenants of Promise

I want to move on to consider another passage that elucidates the importance of the New covenant to Paul's theology:[51]

> Therefore remember that you, once Gentiles in the flesh—who are called Uncircumcision by what is called the Circumcision made in the flesh by hands— that at that time you were without Christ, being aliens from the commonwealth of Israel and strangers from the covenants of promise, having no

49 Yes, justifying faith calls forth imputed righteousness (Gal. 2:20-21; Phil. 3:4-5, 9), but the apostle can also speak of a righteousness given to the saints. In Rom. 6:13-19 the believer is charged to place himself under the dominion of righteousness. 2 Cor. 9:10 implores us to increase the fruits of our righteousness (cf. Phil. 1:11). In the Pastorals, Paul says we are to "pursue righteousness" (1 Tim. 6:11; 2 Tim. 2:22), and the Scriptures are given with that in mind (2 Tim. 3:16-17). Of course, the work of God's Spirit within us is key to all of this (Gal. 5:16-18). I shall say a bit more about this further on.

50 I am not sure "progressive" is the best term. Most Christians, me included, make embarrassingly meager progress in becoming like Christ. This is perhaps because the concept of dying to self and suffering for Christ has not been emphasized as it ought to be. The apostle's words, "For we who live are constantly being handed over to death because of Jesus, so that the life of Jesus may also be revealed in our mortal flesh" (2 Cor. 4:11), seem foreign to many believers in the West. See Richard B. Gaffin, Jr., "The Usefulness of the Cross," *WTJ* 41 (Spring 1979), 228-246.

51 If the reader is asking themselves why the author keeps returning to the New covenant, it is not because I am riding a hobby-horse. Far from it! It is because I am convinced from both Testaments that it is the key that opens up many weighty issues in NT theology.

> hope and without God in the world. But now in Christ Jesus you who once were far off have been brought near by the blood of Christ (Eph. 2:11-13).

Two elements from the verses surrounding this passage deserve special mention. These are the inclusion of the Spirit (Eph. 2:18) and the fact that two "peoples" are made one in verse 16. Paul's reminder to these Gentile Christians is how Gentiles (the uncircumcision) were outside of two blessings: "the commonwealth of Israel" and "the covenants of promise" (Eph. 2:12).[52] Let us examine each one in turn.

A commonwealth consists of nations that are allied through colonial ties. The commonwealth of the United Kingdom, for example, includes Canada, Australia, and New Zealand, among other countries. Those countries are independent of the UK and are assuredly not identical with it, but they are part of the British Commonwealth. The Greek word Paul employs here is *politeia* which means "citizenship" or indicates one who is a member of a people group with all its privileges and protections.[53] If granted, it was a real privilege.[54] If "commonwealth" is the correct rendering, as I believe it has to be,[55] then Paul is saying that, although Gentiles are not members of Jewish society, they are, with believing Jews, now members of the heavenly society (cf. Phil. 3:20).

The other item of inclusion that Gentile Christians access in Christ is "the covenants of promise." Does this mean that Gentiles are incorporated within *all* of the unilateral covenants God made with Israel: the Abrahamic, Priestly, Davidic, and the "New"?[56] Let us briefly look at each in turn.

As far as the Abrahamic covenant is concerned, the answer is, as we have said many times, that Gentile believers are included within the third aspect of the covenant, the blessing upon all nations (Gen. 22:18). This is brought out most clearly for the Church in Galatians 3. As for the Priestly and Davidic covenants, Gentile believers are not party to them since Christ is our High Priest after the order of the non-Jew

---

52 "This points to the hereditary antipathy cherished, or the sacred recoil felt toward [Gentiles] on the part of the covenant people, so long as they were in their heathenish state; for to be called *Uncircumcision* by them was all one with being accounted reprobate or profane" (Patrick Fairbairn, *The Revelation of Law in Scripture* [Phillipsburg, NJ: 1996], 454, emphasis his).

53 See Ceslas Spicq, *Theological Lexicon of the New Testament*, Vol. 3, trans. and edited by James D. Ernest (Peabody, MA: Hendrickson, 1996), 125-129.

54 Stanley E. Porter, *The Apostle Paul: His Life, Thought, and Letters*, 19-20.

55 The apostle is not saying that Gentiles become Jews or even Israelites, but rather that they will enter into the privileges of being God's people.

56 At this place, covenant theology really comes a cropper. CT identifies the "covenants of promise" with the single "covenant of grace." See e.g., Guy Prentice Waters, "Covenant in Paul," in *Covenant Theology: Biblical, Theological, and Historical Perspectives*, eds. Guy Prentice Waters, et al. (Wheaton, IL: Crossway, 2020), 238. This makes no sense. Harold Hoehner's remark about fitting the covenant of grace in this context deserves quoting in full: "This is a concocted theological covenant derived from many proof texts from various contexts but has no real basis in Scripture. Scripture does not have a covenant called the 'covenant of grace.' Also, why would the gentiles be 'strangers' to the covenant of grace since [it] has nothing to do with national distinctions?... This theory should not be taken seriously for it is an example of theology controlling exegesis rather than exegesis controlling theology" (Harold W. Hoehner, *Ephesians: An Exegetical Commentary* [Grand Rapids: Baker, 2003], 358). Any theology that cannot handle Paul's language in Eph. 2:12 needs to go back to the drawing board.

Melchizedek (Heb. 5:1-10), and the main thrust of the covenant with David is Israel-centric. Besides, regarding the Priestly covenant, the Church is said to be a temple within the framework of Ephesians 2:19-22. Thus, Christians constitute a different spiritual temple than the temple in Jerusalem, which is an object of the Priestly covenant and is allied with the line of Phinehas and Zadok.[57] The covenant with David concerns his kingship over Israel, which will be extended over the nations (Psa. 2:6-8; 22:28; Isa. 2:4; Jer. 4:2; Zech. 14:16). This universal reign is to be fulfilled by Jesus at His second coming (1 Tim. 6:15; Rev. 19:16). Gentiles, therefore, will be reigned over by King Jesus (though not as Israelites). In that sense *only* it could be said that Gentiles enter into the eschatological benefits of the Davidic covenant,[58] because Jesus does not reign as King until after His return.[59]

We must recall that in Ephesians 2:12 Paul said "covenants" (plural), not "covenant" (singular). So far, we have seen that Gentiles in Christ are party to the third branch of the Abrahamic covenant, and that, in a secondary sense, they could be said to be beneficiaries of the Davidic covenant on account of their presence in the coming Kingdom.

What then about the New covenant? That is also a covenant of promise. And since it alone brings with it the means of salvation, isn't it the *main* covenant of promise upon which all the rest of the unconditional covenants depend? Were the Gentiles yet "aliens" from it? Certainly. This bringing together of Gentile and Jew fits the ministry of the New covenant (2 Cor. 3:6ff).

To this writer, at least, the fact that dispensationalists are all over the place on this question is nothing short of exasperating. I don't wish to disrespect anyone, and I uphold the right for anybody to disagree with me, but it appears that many good and able men have not asked the most fundamental question: "What *is* the New covenant?" They also seem to have overlooked the fact that revelation is progressive. I am fully behind the standard dispensationalist view that the Church cannot be found in the OT, either in existence (since it is dependent upon the resurrection) or in anticipation (since it is never hinted at).[60] Hence, it is not to be expected that Jeremiah will mention the Church in Jeremiah 31. But does the OT *limit* the New covenant to Israel? It assuredly does not! Although we may grant Jeremiah 31 and Ezekiel 36 to be addressed only to Israel,[61] that is not true of other New covenant passages in the OT, like Isaiah 42, 49 and 52:13-53:12.[62]

57 Saying this does not mean that Gentiles cannot come to the millennial temple (Ezek. 40-48; Zech. 14), only that the two do not exclude each other.

58 It could not be said that Gentiles are parties to the Davidic covenant, unless, of course, one employs a first coming hermeneutic.

59 I made a case for this in *The Words of the Covenant*, Vol. 1, e.g., 358, 362. The messianic emphasis in the OT is predominantly second advent and after.

60 My position on the Church as a "mystery" is that it was not disclosed in any way in the OT.

61 Although, it is recognized that Jer. 31:31, 33-34 influences Paul's statement about Israel's future salvation in Rom. 11:26-27. See Brant Pitre, Michael P. Barber, John A. Kincaid, *Paul, A New Covenant Jew*, 56-57; Thomas R. Schreiner, *Romans*, 619.

62 "The New Covenant expands the promise to Abraham of blessing 'to all the families of the earth.' Here is revealed the means by which man can have his sins forgiven in order to enjoy eternal fellowship with the holy God" (C. E. Piepgrass, "A Study of the New Testament

Paul, the Law, and the New Covenant

The New covenant cannot sit alongside the old Mosaic covenant. Its purpose is to replace it (2 Cor. 3:7-11; Heb. 8:13). The saint who is under the covenant in Christ is not under the old [Mosaic] covenant. The reason for this is twofold. First, Paul, in the spirit of Jesus' earlier statement in Matthew 5:17-20, declares that faith in Christ does not void the law but rather establishes it in the act of Him keeping it for us (Rom. 3:26-31).[63] The second reason comes as a logical consequence of my insistence that Christ embodies the New covenant. That is, having a right relationship with Christ by faith necessarily includes entrance into New covenant status for the saint. And *one cannot be a party to two conflicting covenants, one dealing with 'works,' the other dealing with grace.*[64] We may grant that the Mosaic covenant was a gracious gift and, at the same time, stand with the apostles, John (Jn. 1:17) and Paul (Gal. 3:12), in insisting that its "instruction" was commanded (cf. Eph. 2:15).

To be quite clear, because a Christian is under the New covenant, he is not under the Law. When we take the "cup" in the Lord's Supper, we are proclaiming (whether we realize it or not) that we are parties to the New covenant and, to use Paul's words, "Christ has made us free" (Gal. 5:1; cf. 5:4).

Neither those who hold that the New covenant is restricted to future Israel nor those who believe that the Church has some sort of tangential relationship to the New covenant can point to covenant transference[65] as a major reason for why the saint is not under the Law. However, they *can* point to the fact that Christ has rendered moot the requirements of the Law *in terms of justifying righteousness*. The NT is clear on this issue. Christ came "to redeem those who were under the Law" (Gal. 4:5). Henceforth, a person who is redeemed from being under the Law must now perforce no longer be under its thrall. Yet, in 1 Timothy 1:8 Paul says, "The law is good if one uses it lawfully." That is, if one uses the law to remind oneself of God's standards, and especially if one judges the immorality of the world by it.[66] The Law as an external standard has absolutely no authority over the Christian (e.g., Gal. 2:16, 19; 3:1-3, 11-12).

The Christian's Relationship to the Law

Having made such a declaration, we must ask about the saint's relationship to the Law. It is plain to see that the Law exists, for Paul still appeals to it on occasion (e.g., with women keeping silent in the assembly, 1 Cor. 14:34). If the Law is not operative in some sense today, how can Paul say, "Every mouth will be stopped, and all the world will be guilty before God"—the standard being God's Law (Rom. 3:19)? And

References to the Old Testament Covenants," ThD diss., [Dallas Theological Seminary, 1968], 174). With acknowledgements to Ian Hicks for the reference.

63 See e.g., Ronald E. Diprose, "A Theology of the New Covenant: The Foundations of New Testament Theology," *EMJ* 17 (Summer 2008), 60.

64 The whole conception of what constitutes "the works of the law" and "grace" has been challenged in the last thirty or so years. However, the classic treatments are still reliable.

65 I.e., the believer being transferred from being under the Mosaic Law to the New covenant in Christ.

66 Gordon D. Fee, *1 and 2 Timothy, Titus* (Peabody, MA: Hendricksen, 1988), 45.

what is Paul doing in Romans 13:9 where he states, "For the commandments, 'You shall not commit adultery,' 'You shall not murder,' 'You shall not steal,' 'You shall not bear false witness,' 'You shall not covet,' and if there is any other commandment, are all summed up in this saying, namely, 'You shall love your neighbor as yourself'"?

In Romans 13:8-10 we can see how Paul enjoins Christian love by referring to the Law! This is because the Ten Commandments (well, nine of them[67]) are divine disclosures of ethical norms rooted in the attributes of God. If it is correct for an apostle to base moral teaching on the Law, then it must be correct to include the Law as a standard for Christian conduct.[68] I believe that is unavoidable, but I must immediately qualify that statement. First, these commandments reflect God's own character (e.g., He is truthful, just, faithful, etc.), and as such, they possess normative moral authority over a Christian who images Him. Therefore, if one is to be "conformed to the image of Christ," he will be conformed more and more to the Decalogue. This is important to notice since the Law cannot regulate behavior as a "rule of faith" because we are taken from under its rule (Rom. 8:2-4; Gal. 5:18; Eph. 2:15). Paul says, "The Law is not faith" (Gal. 3:12), and, "We were kept under guard by the law, kept for the faith which would afterward be revealed. Therefore, the law was our tutor *to bring us* to Christ, that we might be justified by faith" (Gal. 3:23-24).

If we examine Romans 6:1, we come across a most important question: "Shall we continue in sin that grace may abound?" If we return Paul's strong negative answer, then the question for the Christian ethicist is, "Well then, what *ought* we to do?" How do we explicate a passage like, say, Romans 6:11-19 for the people of God? This involves us in the setting forth of *positive* ethics. We know *Who* the standard is (Rom. 8:29; Phil. 3:14), and we know that the Commandments, correctly understood, point to His moral perfection. Therefore, we may use the Law lawfully (1 Tim. 1:8), as Paul does, to adjust our conduct accordingly. This is to say that the present application of the Ten Commandments (minus the 4th) *derives from their universal normativity and application.*[69]

What If Christians Had No Relation to the Law?

Think of this example: the Bible tells us not to bear false witness (Exod. 20:16; Rom. 11:9). This is a NT use of the Eighth Commandment, which some say they are not obliged to obey in any sense since the Law is not a norm for Christians. But if one

67 The Fourth Commandment is never repeated in the NT. In fact, it is directly contradicted in Rom. 14:5-6.

68 Look, for instance, at Eph. 6:1-3. See how the apostle uses the Sixth Commandment for its normative force of his injunction for children to obey their parents.

69 That is, in normal circumstances. I shall not enter into the debate about whether for instance lying to protect an innocent life is affected. In such circumstances, I believe one is faced with a situation where it is impossible to treat the subjects as ends in themselves (i.e., as the Golden Rule commands) because there is no "good" alternative, and one must choose the most righteous "means to an end." This might appear to be a pragmatic approach, however, readers should consult Robert Kane, *Through the Moral Maze: Searching for Absolute Values in a Pluralistic World* (Armonk, NY: North Castle Books, 1996), 13-30. Sometimes people's lives are at stake.

does not hold himself accountable to the Eighth Commandment (even though it is in a NT epistle written to Jews *and* Gentiles), he may believe that he need not trouble himself on this point, at least until he fixes his hermeneutics. Until he does, this leaves such people on the horns of a dilemma. If a person believes they are not *commanded* to tell the truth, that is, if they believe "*you shall not lie or bear false witness*" (Deut. 5:20) is not an authoritative command to them because: (1) they are a Gentile, and (2) they are sanctified by faith alone; then clearly, they can ignore Paul's clear teaching which roots itself in the Law. If the rejoinder comes back that Christians are under the law of Christ (Gal. 6:2), I reply that the law of Christ is love and that love compels us to observe God's universal commandments as they are delineated in the Decalogue.[70]

Let us compare two Pauline passages to further elucidate my point:

> Circumcision is nothing and uncircumcision is nothing but keeping the commandments of God *is what matters* (1 Cor. 7:19).

> For Christ *is* the end of the law for righteousness to everyone who believes (Rom. 10:4).

In the 1 Corinthians 7 verse, "the commandments of God" assuredly refer to the Law in some way, and that way is set in opposition to the cultic requirements of the Law as seen in circumcision. This means that Paul is offsetting *one* aspect of the Law with another. The first aspect, what Paul calls "the commandments of God" (1 Cor. 7:19), involves the universal ethics entailed in the Ten Commandments (minus the 4th). The second aspect is the cultic-ethnic aspect tied to the token of the Abrahamic and Mosaic covenants (circumcision).

Pointing this out does not mean that it is okay to divide the Law into moral, civil, and ceremonial components. The Fourth Commandment is ethnocentric and concerns Israel, just like circumcision (cf. Jn. 7:22-23). But it is nevertheless true to say that while the rule of male circumcision is for Jews, and is therefore not universal, the rule concerning idolatry is for all of God's worshipers. Hence, in 1 Corinthians 7:19, "the commandments of God" have to do with the universal and unchangeable realities reflecting God's majesty and character and so are fully in force for Christians, even if they are not in themselves a means of justification, seeing as they play no part in the content of the Christian gospel.[71] The Commandments reflect the character of God and are normative for the saint on *that* basis! In Romans 10:4, where justification

70 "Owe no one anything except to love one another, for he who loves another has fulfilled the law. For the commandments, 'You shall not commit adultery,' 'You shall not murder,' 'You shall not steal,' 'You shall not bear false witness,' 'You shall not covet,' and if *there is* any other commandment, are *all* summed up in this saying, namely, 'You shall love your neighbor as yourself.' Love does no harm a neighbor; therefore love *is* the fulfillment of the law" (Rom. 13:8-10).

71 Tony Garland rightly observes, "In a strict sense, yes. But the law does play an important part in highlighting the "good" in good news. So to the degree that our condemnation under the law and inability to satisfy its requirements underwrite the "good" of the gospel, it wouldn't be far off to say it contributes to a fully-rounded gospel understanding" (Personal communication with Garland).

of the sinner *is* at issue (Rom. 10:3, 5), Christ is the *telos*, and the goal of the Law is achieved in Him.

These admonitions from Paul (and others such Eph. 1–5:21 and 1 Thess. 4:1-7) can all be subsumed within the Ten Commandments as expounded by writers like Jochen Douma and John Frame (again, minus the Sabbath command).[72] A person who will not be ethically accountable to the Ten Commandments cannot, without serious contradiction, consider themselves obligated to obey Paul's injunctions either. They are of one fabric. This also accounts for those New covenant passages which speak of God's "law" being internalized in the saints (cf. Ezek. 36:26-27; 2 Cor. 3:3).

In summary, the Law is not a rule of life for the Christian because we are under the New covenant. Whereas the Mosaic covenant contained many commandments, ordinances, and stipulations as part of its oath (i.e., Exod. 20–24),[73] the New covenant for the Church is the simple Gospel of justification by faith in Jesus Christ and His finished work. There is nothing to do but believe (wholly depend upon) the merits of the crucified and risen Lord. The Christian is not, in that sense, "under the law" (Gal. 5:1-4, 17). Because of the Christian's involvement in the New covenant "in Christ," he *cannot* be "under the law" as a rule of life—Christ having lived that life. But the Christian should realize that it is always wrong to have other gods, to dishonor God's name, to commit adultery, or to steal. These are universal ethical norms because they reflect the character of God Himself, or they have implications one must draw from it. They impress a moral imperative upon human beings at all times and in all places. This is why the apostle can refer believers to the commandments of God while teaching us that "we are not under law but under grace" (Rom. 6:14), because "Christ is the end of the law for everyone who believes" (Rom. 10:4).

The New Covenant and the Church

I appreciate that not everyone who reads these words will agree with me on this, but there is more to say about the question of the Church's relation to the New covenant. Let us give it fuller consideration,[74] for I am convinced that we Christians must be full parties to the New covenant if we are to be at all related to the covenant God. God does nothing eschatological outside of His covenants.

One should not hold to two or more peoples of God[75] in an unbalanced way, for example, Israel being in covenant with Yahweh and the Church being adrift of the covenants of God but tethered to Him in some inexplicable way. I wish to, therefore, return to 2 Corinthians 3:

72 Jochen Douma, *The Ten Commandments: Manual for the Christian Life* (Philipsburg, PA: P&R, 1996). This is the best treatment of the Decalogue in my opinion. See also John M. Frame, *The Doctrine of the Christian Life* (Philipsburg, NJ: P&R, 2008) and Jerram Barrs, *Delighting in the Law of the Lord: God's Alternative to Legalism and Moralism* (Wheaton, IL: Crossway, 2013). All are Reformed treatments, so naturally I do not agree with every assertion these authors make.

73 This could be expanded to the whole book of Deuteronomy.

74 Of course, I give sustained attention to this matter throughout.

75 This will receive development when we reach the book of Revelation.

> Clearly you are an epistle of Christ, ministered by us, written not with ink but by the Spirit of the living God, not on tablets of stone but on tablets of flesh, that is, of the heart...but our sufficiency is from God, who also made us sufficient as ministers of the new covenant, not of the letter but of the Spirit; for the letter kills, but the Spirit gives life (2 Cor. 3:3, 5-6).

Who cannot see the continuity and semblance of thought here? The Holy Spirit is the cause both *of* the new life of the Corinthian Christians and the ministry of the New covenant *to* them! If, as some insist, the apostle did not believe the New covenant was for the Gentiles, then why did he tell them he was ministering it? Why speak of it to them? And supposing as some do, his "New covenant ministry" was a separate ministry from the one Paul had in Corinth, why did he draw so close a connection between this supposed non-covenantal Corinthian ministry and his supposed "other" ministry (i.e., of the New covenant)?[76] One would only *minister* the New covenant to the *party* involved, and only at the suitable time! With all due respect to those who wish to snip off the "New covenant" from Paul's ministry as apostle to the Gentiles—this beggar's belief! What has happened to the "plain sense"? Pray, what is the difference in the context between what Paul calls "the ministry of the Spirit" in verse 3 (cf. 2 Cor. 3:9) and "the ministry of the Spirit" in verse 6?[77] If Paul wished to create befuddlement in the minds of his Corinthian readers, inserting the notion of the New covenant into their minds when it was irrelevant to them would certainly be a great way to do it![78] And if we read on a little to the beginning of chapter 4, we can see that he continues undaunted, "since we have this ministry" (2 Cor. 4:1).[79] The "ministry" surely hasn't changed since he last spoke of it in 2 Corinthians 3:1-9.[80]

Furthermore, as several scholars have observed, 2 Corinthians 3:3 almost certainly alludes to Jeremiah 31:33 and Ezekiel 36:26-27 by referencing "tablets of stone" and "tablets of flesh." Douglas Moo thinks this allusion is obvious.[81] Hays expands upon this link persuasively:

> The reader who follows these echoes will be led back into a thesaurus of narrative and promise; only there, in the company of Moses and Jeremiah and Ezekiel, does Paul's metaphor of the Corinthians as a 'letter from Christ' disclose its true wealth.[82]

---

76 Or even of some eschatological ministry of which he would not be a part?

77 For a fine running exegesis of this chapter, I recommend Victor Paul Furnish, *II Corinthians*, 195ff.

78 I do not say this to belittle those with whom I disagree. I am simply trying to ask penetrating questions.

79 Notice also the correlation between 2 Cor. 3:18 and 4:3-6.

80 "Now all things are of God, who has reconciled us to Himself through Jesus Christ, and has given us the ministry of reconciliation" (2 Cor. 5:18). Surely this is the same ministry he is discussing in chapters 3 and 4?

81 Douglas J. Moo, *A Theology of Paul and His Letters*, 168-169.

82 Richard B. Hays, *Echoes of Scripture in the Letters of Paul*, 127-128.

In their book on Pauline Theology, Pitre, Barber, and Kincaid stress that, "For Paul, depending especially upon the prophets Jeremiah and Ezekiel, the old covenant was never intended to be permanent but to be renewed by a covenant involving God's Spirit..."[83]

We do not have to agree with the conclusions these authors draw from this observation, but we ought not to ignore it either. If the apostle is relying on Jeremiah 31 and Ezekiel 36 when writing to Gentiles in 2 Corinthians 3, then I cannot see how it can be maintained that the Church is not a full party to the New covenant!

But it could be argued (and has been argued) that all Paul is doing in 2 Corinthians 3:6 is drawing a kind of parallel. The argument goes that the phrase "ministers of the new covenant" does not mean that Paul and his companions are actually *ministering* the New covenant, only that their ministry *resembles* the future New covenant dispensation.[84] I struggle a bit here. The New covenant work of the Spirit at the second advent is a complete work resulting in complete obedience (e.g., Deut. 30:6; Ezek. 36:25-27; Zeph. 3:13), which is quite unlike what we experience today. Still, if that is what Paul is doing, one has to ask in interrogative tones, "Why even say such a thing?" How is the apostle to the Gentiles helping matters by dropping a "by the way, our ministry is sort of like what the New covenant ministry *will* be like" in verse 6? Why make a comparison of covenants here at all when one of them is still future? How does that help the saints in Corinth? (Or in London? Or New York? Or Timbuktu?). It surely looks like Paul views "the ministry of the Spirit" (2 Cor. 3:8) as synonymous with his present work "as [a] minister of the new covenant, not of the letter but of the Spirit" two verses earlier. And even if the definite article is missing, so that it actually reads, "*a* new covenant," in verse 6, how far does that take us? The contrast is between the Mosaic covenant and *some* covenant—a covenant involving the Spirit's gift of new life. Which covenant could that be? The Abrahamic, Priestly, and Davidic covenants do not include the Spirit's saving action in their terms. The answer is staring us in the face.[85]

Another Pauline New Covenant Text

> We then, *as* workers together *with Him* also plead with *you* not to receive the grace of God in vain. For He says:
>
> "In an acceptable time I have heard you,
> And in the day of salvation I have helped you."
> Behold, now *is* the accepted time; behold, now *is* the day of salvation (2 Cor. 6:1-2).

83 Brant Pitre, et al., *Paul, A New Covenant Jew*, 42 (the original is in italics).

84 "The New Covenant provides a metaphor to explain his letter of commendation of his ministry to the Corinthians" (Elliott Johnson, *A Dispensational Biblical Theology*, 440). But where in the context is this even hinted at? Are we still here reading the text with our vaunted literal hermeneutic?

85 Cf. David K. Lowery, "2 Corinthians," in *Bible Knowledge Commentary: New Testament*, eds. John F. Walvoord and Roy B. Zuck (Grand Rapids, MI: Victor Books, 1997), 560-561; Paul R. Williamson, *Sealed with an Oath*, 192-193.

The OT passage that Paul is quoting is Isaiah 49:8. Here is the original passage:

> Thus says the LORD:
> "In an acceptable time I have heard You,
> And in the day of salvation I have helped You;
> I will preserve You and give You
> As a covenant to the people,
> To restore the earth,
> To cause them to inherit the desolate heritages..."

This passage (2 Cor. 6:1-2) functions similarly to 2 Corinthians 3:6. Paul unmistakably refers to himself and his coworkers with this New covenant reference. Isaiah 49:8 is a familiar verse to readers of Volume One. It includes a reference to the Servant (Messiah) as "a covenant to the people." The apostle does not quote the phrase, but it is safe to say he was aware of it. Is this a mere coincidence? Hardly. Schnabel has drawn attention to Paul's habit of reaching for Isaiah's Servant Songs to understand and articulate his own mission. In fact, I believe Schnabel is right when he declares that the apostle saw himself as fulfilling the work of the Servant of the Lord.[86] This can be seen in Paul's speech in Pisidian Antioch in Acts 13:46-47, where he quotes Isaiah 49:6 and applies it to his ongoing work among the Gentiles. As envoys of Jesus, Paul and his coworkers are extending the Servant's mission. We can readily appreciate the link if we allow that Jesus the Servant is made a covenant of salvation (Isa. 49:8), and we connect this with Paul's declaration in 2 Corinthians 3:6.

Again, in Acts 26:16-18 Schnabel points to the allusion to Isaiah 42:6-7 and 21.[87] As Isaiah 42:6 also refers to the Servant as "a covenant to the people," the evidence that Paul saw his work in strongly covenantal ways is beginning to stack up. If Isaiah 42 and 49 portray Messiah as the covenant Servant of Yahweh, and Paul is himself seeing his ministry as an extension of the Servant's work, then the "Apostle to the Gentiles" is doing covenant work in the Church![88]

It takes just a little fitting of the pieces together to conclude that Paul clearly understood his mission to the Gentiles in *New covenant terms.* Hence, in 2 Corinthians 6:1-2 we can infer his meaning as, "Today is salvation offered to you Gentiles through Christ the Servant, through whom God has made the [New] covenant with those who believe in Him."[89] What ought not be missed here, as in all Paul's letters, is how covernance lies behind his thought.

---

86 See Eckhard J. Schnabel, *Early Christian Mission: Paul and the Early Church*, Vol. 2, 942-944.

87 Ibid., 943.

88 N. T. Wright believes that Isa. 42:6 (and 49:5-6) refer to Israel as the Servant of Yahweh in Isaiah, and only apply to Christ through the designation of Him as Israel by Paul in the NT. See N. T. Wright, *Paul and the Faithfulness of God*, 805-806. I do not agree with this view. To me and many others, it is obvious that these texts cannot refer to Israel and are deliberately messianic.

89 Schnabel does not make the connection with the New covenant that I am making. Nevertheless, I think it is hard to evade once it is pointed out. Indeed, I am sure that he would hold the view that Paul was a New covenant emissary to the Gentiles.

Paul's Allegory of the New and Old Covenants in Galatians 4

Paul's teaching at the end of Galatians 4 is one of the trickier parts of his correspondence. It is well to print the text in full:

> Tell me, you who desire to be under the law, do you not hear the law? For it is written that Abraham had two sons: the one by a bondwoman, the other by a freewoman. But he *who was* of the bondwoman was born according to the flesh, and he of the freewoman through promise, which things are symbolic. For these are the two covenants: the one from Mount Sinai which gives birth to bondage, which is Hagar—for this Hagar is Mount Sinai in Arabia, and corresponds to Jerusalem which now is, and is in bondage with her children—but the Jerusalem above is free, which is the mother of us all. For it is written:
>
> "Rejoice, O barren,
> You who do not bear!
> Break forth and shout,
> You who are not in labor!
> For the desolate has many more children
> Than she who has a husband."
>
> Now we, brethren, as Isaac *was,* are children of promise. But, as he who was born according to the flesh then persecuted him *who was born* according to the Spirit, even so *it is* now. Nevertheless what does the Scripture say? "Cast out the bondwoman and her son, for the son of the bondwoman shall not be heir with the son of the freewoman." So then, brethren, we are not children of the bondwoman but of the free (Gal. 4:21-31).

The fact that Paul wrote this to a group of churches so early on in his ministry demonstrates the depth of theological instruction within these churches. Here the apostle resorts to allegory (which is unusual) to get across a point about the "two covenants," namely the Mosaic covenant and another covenant.[90] The question is, which cove-

90 Michael J. Vlach opts for this other covenant being the Abrahamic covenant, owing to the previous mention of that covenant in Galatians 3. See his *The Old in the New: Understanding How the New Testament Authors Quoted the Old Testament* (The Woodlands, TX: Kress Biblical Resources, 2021), 270. Vlach says in a footnote, "This is not to say that the New covenant is not also in view by Paul since the New covenant is an extension and outworking of the Abrahamic covenant" (Ibid., 270 n. 2). See also Donald K. Campbell, "Galatians," in *Bible Knowledge Commentary: New Testament*, eds. John F. Walvoord and Roy B. Zuck (Grand Rapids, MI: Victor Books, 1983), 604. In my opinion, Paul is more likely referring to the New covenant. I lean this way because making it just the Abrahamic covenant ignores what Paul says about "Jerusalem above" and its implication of Mt. Zion above (Heb. 12:22), which has nothing to do with the Abrahamic covenant. It also fails to acknowledge that the Abrahamic covenant cannot save unless it is directed *through* Christ and the New covenant (see my treatment of Gal. 3 under "The Abrahamic Covenant and Paul's Argument in Galatians 3:1-16" below). In Gal. 4 please note the mention of the Spirit in Gal. 4:6 and the fact that Isa. 54, which is quoted in Gal. 4:27, is a New covenant text. On this passage, see Ben Witherington III, "Paul, Galatians, and Supersessionism," in *God's Israel and the Israel of God: Paul and Supercessionism*, eds.

nant is in view? The two proposals are the Abrahamic covenant or the New covenant. It is difficult to decide between the two. Some are adamant it is the Abrahamic covenant.[91] Let's look a bit closer.

The apostle begins with a question: "Tell me, you who desire to be under the law, do you not hear the law?" The point here is whether or not it is wise to "desire to be under the law" (i.e., the old covenant). The allegory is about Ishmael and Isaac, sons of Abraham by Hagar and Sarah, respectively. Isaac is the son of covenant promise, a promise of perpetuity that could not exist within "Mosaic conditions." Paul links the first to the Law at Sinai, which is then connected to "Jerusalem which now is." On the other hand, Isaac is related to "the Jerusalem above," as he is to the Abrahamic covenant (Gen. 17) and the New covenant because of its salvific provisions. Paul says we Christians "are children of promise" and are free (from the old covenant). His argument is that this alternative covenant, which I believe to be the New covenant in Christ, is bringing fulfillment of the third aspect of the Abrahamic covenant to us. That is to say, the third part of the Abrahamic covenant, the blessing upon the nations, is mediated to us in the New covenant, which has dispensed life and freedom in Christ.[92]

Paul's Use of the Last Supper in 1 Corinthians 11

If there is one passage that ought to show that the "Apostle to the Gentiles" believed the Church has entered into the provisions of the New covenant (and by it one of the provisions of the Abrahamic covenant), it is 1 Corinthians 11. Let me reproduce the argument in full:

> For I received from the Lord that which I also delivered to you: that the Lord Jesus on the *same* night in which He was betrayed took bread; and when He had given thanks, He broke *it* and said, "Take, eat; this is My body which is broken for you; do this in remembrance of Me." In the same manner *He* also *took* the cup after supper, saying, "This cup is the new covenant in My blood.

Michael F. Bird and Scot McKnight (Bellingham, WA: Lexham, 2023), 76-77; Paul R. Williamson, *Sealed with an Oath*, 199; cf. I. Howard Marshall, *New Testament Theology*, 683. However, this is not a hill I am willing to die on.

91 E.g., Matthew S. Harmon, "Allegory, Typology, or Something Else? Revisiting Galatians 4:21–5:1," in *Studies in the Pauline Epistles: Essays in Honor of Douglas J. Moo* (Grand Rapids: Zondervan, 2014), 149 n. 26. Also, Richard B. Hays, *Echoes of Scripture in the Letters of Paul*, 114.

92 In Gal. 5 Paul speaks of the Holy Spirit as the main instrument of our freedom. E.g., "But if you are led by the Spirit, you are not under the law" (Gal. 5:18; cf. Gal. 5:5, 16-18, 22-25). In my opinion, this indicates a focus on the New covenant. The Spirit is not connected to the covenant with Abraham. I fully realize that some good people will claim that I have run off the rails in saying that Christians are parties to the New covenant, but this does look exactly like what Paul is saying, and I must also say that the counter explanations that I have come across look like excruciating circumlocutions of the plain arguments Paul is presenting, both in these passages and elsewhere. Once again, I call attention to 2 Cor. 3:6: "who also made us sufficient as ministers of the new covenant, not of the letter but of the Spirit; for the letter kills, but the Spirit gives life." The "liberty" and "freedom" of Gal. 5:1 is found in the New covenant.

> This do, as often as you drink *it*, in remembrance of Me." For as often as you eat this bread and drink this cup, you proclaim the Lord's death till He comes. Therefore whoever eats this bread or drinks *this* cup of the Lord in an unworthy manner will be guilty of the body and blood of the Lord.
> But let a man examine himself, and so let him eat of the bread and drink of the cup. For he who eats and drinks in an unworthy manner eats and drinks judgment to himself, not discerning the Lord's body (1 Cor. 11:23-29).

The reason I have supplied the larger context will become clear as we proceed. Let us notice a few things at the beginning. In the first place, Paul says that he received this information from the Lord (1 Cor. 11:23). Therefore, he is relaying the Lord's teaching. Next, the phrase "do this in remembrance of Me" is found after the token of the bread in 1 Corinthians 11:24 and the cup in verse 25. This implies that the bread and the cup cannot be separated; they both serve as symbols of one thing. Just as the bread signifies Christ's body, the wine symbolizes His blood. Third, the cup symbolizes "the new covenant in My blood" (1 Cor. 11:25). If we believe the cup refers to Christ's blood, we must believe—if we employ literal interpretation—that the cup refers to the new covenant blood of Jesus! I see no way around it unless we do hermeneutical alchemy. This means that the cup of the Lord's Table, and probably the bread too, are New covenant tokens! The Lord's Supper is not a humdrum religious artifact, but the active memorial of the cost of our salvation and the celebration of our participation in the New covenant in Christ!

After the symbolism is supplied, Paul tells the Gentile Corinthians (and us) that when Christians repeat this ordinance, they are both looking back to the cross and forward to the second coming (1 Cor. 11:26). He then issues a warning to any who ought not to partake of the tokens lest they "be guilty of the body and the blood of the Lord" (1 Cor. 11:27), thereby underlining the inseparability of the two elements. The final two verses (1 Cor. 11:28-29) continue the warning but also invite worthy participants to "eat of the bread and drink of the cup" (v. 28). Paul ends by claiming that an unworthy taker "eats and drinks judgment to himself, <u>not discerning the Lord's body</u>" (1 Cor. 11:29, my emphasis).

What does it mean to *not* discern the Lord's body? What is meant by the "body" here? Craig Blomberg,[93] J. D. G. Dunn,[94] and I. Howard Marshall[95] agree that *soma* in verse 29 refers to the Body of Christ, the Church.[96] Viewing the "body" in 1 Corinthians 11:29 as the Church appears to be the best interpretation since interpreting it as not discerning the body of Jesus smacks of sacramentalism. But if the "body" in verse

93 Craig L. Blomberg, *A New Testament Theology*, 292.

94 J. D. G. Dunn, *The Theology of Paul the Apostle*, 59-60.

95 I. Howard Marshall, *New Testament Theology*, 275.

96 Others demur. For example, Leon Morris, *The First Epistle of Paul to the Corinthians: An Introduction and Commentary* (Grand Rapids: Eerdmans, 1975), 163-164, who takes it as referring to the body of Jesus. See also Robert H. Gundry, *Commentary on the New Testament*, 668.

29 is the Church, then the New covenant of verse 25 must logically be *for* the Body of Christ.

If it be objected that Paul was loosely citing the words of institution of the Lord's Supper in Luke 22, which was made with Jewish disciples, I would refer such people to Ephesians 2:19-20: "Now, therefore, you are no longer strangers and foreigners, but fellow citizens with the saints and members of the household of God, having been built on the foundation of the apostles and prophets, Jesus Christ Himself being the chief corner*stone...*" (my emphasis).

As we have already seen with Ephesians 2:11-13, the subject is the inclusion of the Gentiles into the "commonwealth of Israel" and "the covenants of promise." This inclusion occurs in the Body of Christ, the Church. According to Ephesians 2:20 the foundation of the Church is formed by "the apostles and [NT] prophets." I shall have to revisit this passage later, but if the Church is built upon the apostles, eleven of whom partook of the establishment of the Lord's Supper in Luke 22:14-23, and Paul cites that event in his Corinthian correspondence, then it seems dead-to-rights that the Gentiles partake of the very same "Table" as the disciples did. And what was initiated was "the new covenant in My blood" (Lk. 22:20)!

EXCURSUS: Assessing the Arguments for Restricting the New Covenant to Israel

For theologians of many persuasions, the question of the Church's relationship to the New covenant is a moot point. But for dispensationalists, the question rages on. Michael Vlach has identified no less than six different points of view among dispensational interpreters on the New covenant.[97] Michael Stallard put together a very handy book with several scholars debating the matter.[98] The most common views are as follows: (1) The Church bears no relation at all to the New covenant.[99] The New covenant is for Israel alone. (2) The Church benefits from the New covenant even though Israel alone is the true party. (3) The Church is a full party in the New covenant alongside Israel.

I have already set forth arguments for why I take the third position. More reasons will be added below. But I want to survey the other positions quickly.[100]

97 http://mikevlach.blogspot.com/2019/07/six-views-on-new-covenant-fulfillment.html

98 Mike Stallard, ed., *Dispensational Understanding of the New Covenant* (Regular Baptist Press, 2012). Another book with several contributors who deny any relation of the New covenant to the Church is Christopher Cone, ed., *An Introduction to the New Covenant* (Hurst, TX: Tyndale Seminary Press, 2013). The book is a sterling effort by good men, but it fails to convince. It does not weigh evenly the supposed objections against what is being plainly asserted and so avoids drawing the conclusions that the inspired authors seem to be at pains to draw.

99 This is the shared view of the writers in the book cited above.

100 For more on this issue see Chapter 3, "The Terms of the New Covenant and Its Parties."

(1) The Church is Not Related to the New Covenant

This position has its able defenders, but its chief weaknesses, in my estimation, are first its over-reliance upon Jeremiah 31:31-34 to define the New covenant,[101] even though there are clear New covenant texts that predate Jeremiah. Then there is the seeming reluctance to consider how the Church as a mystery would require inspired apostolic connections to be made with OT messianic prophecies, including covenantal connections.[102] Third, there is the problem, at least as I see it, of an in-principle conflict with plain-sense hermeneutics. Hermeneutical gymnastics are required if 1 Corinthians 11:25 and 2 Corinthians 3:3-6 are *not* to be applied to the Church directly. Last but not least is the matter of Christ's blood being wholly "the blood of the New covenant" (Lk. 22:20). If we are saved by New covenant blood, then we are New covenant saints.

As for my first problem with this viewpoint, it is an error to base one's understanding of the New covenant on Jeremiah 31:31-34[103] (and by extension, Hebrews 8:8-12).[104] As I showed in the first volume, and as many have shown before me, the *concept* of the New covenant goes all the way back to the book of Deuteronomy (Deut. 30:6) and comes into focus before the time of Jeremiah (Isa. 49:8; 54:10; 55:3; 59:21; 61:8; Hos. 2:18). Everyone will agree that a doctrine can be present in the Bible before it is named. But even when we arrive at Jeremiah 31, it has to be clearly said that he does not *name* the covenant. This "new covenant" (Jer. 31:31) is not given its name until Luke 22:20/1 Corinthians 11:25,[105] where the definite article is used. Paul uses this phrase in 1 Corinthians 11 with the article in teaching about the Lord's Supper. Earlier in the book, Paul explicitly links the blood of Christ to the Church in 1 Corinthians 10:16.[106] From then on, whether the article is supplied or not, the subject is the same: *the* New covenant.[107]

---

101 Technically, Jer. 31 refers to *a* new covenant not *the* New covenant. Passages like Deut. 30:1-6; Isa. 42:1-7; 44:1-5; 49:1-10 predate Jeremiah but are accepted as New covenant texts. What Jer. 31 does is to associate Yahweh's eschatological salvation-work through the Spirit with a covenant.

102 After all, nowhere in the OT is the Church said to be related to the Abrahamic covenant, and for the same reason, it is not spoken of prior to Matt. 16.

103 We may throw Ezek. 36:26-27 in the mix here as well.

104 I do grant that the passage may be used as "a control passage" to study the New covenant, as e.g., David Gunn, "An Overview of New Covenant Passages, Ostensible and Actual," in *An Introduction to the New Covenant*, ed. Christopher Cone (Hurst, TX: Tyndale Seminary Press, 2013), 41. However, just because the context of Jer. 31 (and some other NC texts) refers to Israel only, it does not mean that it is *confined* to Israel. Clearly, there are New covenant passages which include the nations too (e.g., Isa. 49:6-8; 54:5; Mal. 3:12).

105 "In the words of institution of the Lord's Supper, Jesus sees his impending death as the sacrifice that inaugurates the new covenant promised by Jeremiah. In the version preserved in Matt 26:28/Mk 14:24 Jesus, as he takes the cup, says, 'This in my blood of the covenant,' clearly referring to the sacrifice that inaugurated the Sinai covenant in Exod 24:8. The version preserved in 1 Cor 11:25 and Luke 22:20...speaks of 'the new covenant in my blood,' clearly echoing the Jer 31 promise of a new covenant" (Charles H. H. Scobie, *The Ways of Our God: An Approach to Biblical Theology* [Grand Rapids: Eerdmans, 2003], 495-496).

106 "The cup of blessing which we bless, is it not the communion of the blood of Christ? The bread which we break, is it not the communion of the body of Christ?" (1 Cor. 10:16).

107 "This view, likewise, must be rejected. The evidence from the New Testament indicates that several of the provisions of Jeremiah's new covenant are directly related to the church" (R. Bruce Compton, "Dispensationalism, the Church, and the New Covenant," *Detroit Baptist*

Paul's fullest discussion is found, of course, in 2 Corinthians 3:1–4:6. To try to reduce this extended argument down to an analogy or metaphor, which would be utterly meaningless to the Greek recipients to the point of confusion, is to seek to undo the "damage" that the apostle is otherwise perceived to be doing to an Israel-only New covenant.[108] The hard fact is Paul did *not* say he was practicing a "new covenant type ministry."

When we get to Hebrews, this view is faced with the difficulty of claiming its doctrines apply to Christians while at the same time asserting that its central doctrine, the New covenant in Christ's High Priestly blood, does not apply to Christians (see the chapter on Hebrews below).

In a rather different take on this matter, John R. Master believes that the New covenant cannot be related to the Church because Christians are not living fully sanctified lives like the New covenant passages predicted.[109] But this reason falls away once one admits that Christians have been given the Holy Spirit and "new hearts" in connection with a covenant (2 Cor. 3:3, 6ff.). If we are not yet perfected, that does not contradict anything in the OT. Christians celebrate the New covenant in Christ (1 Cor. 11:25) and approach the throne of God on that basis (Heb. 4:14-16; 10:19-25). The tension created by living between the two comings of Christ needs to be considered. Further, if the Church is not related to God's New covenant, it is extremely hard to reconcile how it can be *bought* with New covenant blood and our hearts sprinkled with it (cf. 1 Cor. 6:19-20; Heb. 10:19-22).

(2) The Church Benefits from the New Covenant

J. Dwight Pentecost is a respected dispensational scholar who wrote a fine book entitled *Thy Kingdom Come.*[110] The main passages Pentecost cites as referring to the New covenant are Isaiah 61:8; Jeremiah 31:31-34; 32:37-42; Ezekiel 16:60-62; 36:24-32; and 37:26. He believes that the New covenant was made with Israel, and the Church benefits from it.[111] He gives several reasons for his position. The first reason for restricting the New covenant to Israel (with the Church getting some of the salvific benefits) is that it was said to be made with "the house of Israel and the house of Judah"

Seminary Journal 8 [Fall 2003], 39). I would press this a little more and say that, since the phrase "the New covenant" is a NT phrase, it has more claim to be taken at face value.

108 See the valiant effort of George Gunn, "Second Corinthians 3:6 and the New Covenant," in *An Introduction to the New Covenant*, 201-35.

109 John R. Master, "The New Covenant," in *Issues in Dispensationalism*, eds. John R. Master and Wesley R. Willis (Chicago: Moody, 1994), 108.

110 J. Dwight Pentecost, *Thy Kingdom Come: Tracing God's Kingdom Program and Covenant Promises Throughout History* (Grand Rapids: Kregel, 1995). In this work, he covers the New covenant on pages 164 to 177.

111 Ibid., 175. An impressive article that arrives at the same conclusion is R. Bruce Compton, "Dispensationalism, the Church, and the New Covenant," *Detroit Baptist Seminary Journal* 8 (Fall 2003), 3-48. Compton comes close to saying the New covenant is also made with the Gentiles (and the Church) but backs off of making the Church a party to the New covenant. He does include Isa. 45:10 as a New covenant text (Ibid., 21). For similar conclusions to Compton, see Renald E. Showers, *There Really Is a Difference: A Comparison of Covenant and Dispensational Theology* (Bellmawr, NJ: Friends of Israel, 1993), 103-106.

(Jer. 31:31; Heb. 8:8).[112] The second reason is that "it must of necessity be made with the same people with whom the original Mosaic Covenant had been made."[113] Third, Israel will not receive the benefits of the New covenant until the second coming.[114]

I have the utmost respect for Dr. Pentecost and have personally much to thank him for, but I do not think he goes as far as the passages indicate he should. It is true that Jeremiah (and the author of Hebrews) limits his New covenant prophecy to Israel and Judah, and that is because, in that OT setting, Yahweh was referring to them. But as said above, that fact does not mean that other New covenant passages do not *include* the Gentiles. Pentecost's selective choice of New covenant passages looks cherry-picked. Many interpreters, dispensationalists among them, identify as New covenant texts those that include Gentiles.[115] There are many other passages that, although they do not name the covenant as the New covenant, are rightly considered to be important OT New covenant passages. These texts include Deuteronomy 30:1-6; Isaiah 32:9-20; 42:1-7; 49:1-13; 52:10-53:12; 54:10; 55:3-5; 59:15b-21; 61:8; Jeremiah 32:36-44; Ezekiel 16:53-63; 36:22-38; 37:21-28; Hosea 2:18-20; Joel 2:28–3:8; Micah 7:18-20; Zechariah 9:10; and 12:6-14. These passages contain many of the same elements within Pentecost's group of texts mentioned above, but some of them bring the Gentiles into the covenant.

The next reason for restricting the full blessings of the New covenant to Israel is that it must be coextensive with the "old" Mosaic covenant. But this does not follow, for if Yahweh were to reach out to the nations in the OT, He would have had to do it through the Law. There would be no other conceivable way to do it. But that would fail. Ergo, if the Gentiles are to be saved, it must be through a New covenant. Since the New covenant is in Christ's blood, and it is *that* blood that gives all sinners access to the grace of God (Acts 20:28; Rom. 3:24-25; Eph. 1:7; 2:13), there appears to be a major disconnect with those who wish to deny the Gentiles complete entry into the New covenant. And this only intensifies once 1 Corinthians 11:25 and 2 Corinthians 3:6 are recalled to the discussion. While it is easy to say that the Church benefits from the New covenant (while not being party to it), it is difficult to demonstrate how said benefits come to the Church without being channeled *through* the New covenant.

As for the third reason, that Israel will not benefit from the New covenant until the second coming, it is readily granted. But what difference does that make? If salvation going out to the Gentiles is one way "to provoke [Israel] to jealousy" (Rom. 11:11), then the Gentiles entering into the benefits of the New covenant before the nation of Israel would be a good way to do just that.

---

112 J. Dwight Pentecost, *Thy Kingdom Come*, 171. He is a little vague on the "how" of this arrangement.

113 Ibid., 172.

114 Ibid., 172-173.

115 See the article by Compton cited above, especially 39-40. Also, I recommend parts 1 and 2 of Rodney J. Decker, "The Church's Relationship to the New Covenant," *BSAC* 152 (Jul 1995) and 152 (Oct 1995). Cf. Michael J. Vlach, *He Will Reign Forever*, 407, 461. See Chapter 3, "The Terms of the New Covenant and Its Parties." By "terms" I mean those things that God promised in New covenant texts; specifically, those promises that were not already covered by the oaths of the other unconditional covenants.

A major problem here is that Pentecost has not perceived that the New covenant is *the* salvation covenant—there is no other![116] Further, he has not sufficiently understood the affinity of the New covenant with the person of Jesus Christ and His blood. Finally, although he cites them, he does not engage with 2 Corinthians 3:6 or 1 Corinthians 11:25.

To repeat, the question that arises is whether Pentecost's passages *alone* refer to the New covenant or whether there are other very similar texts that have been omitted solely because they make reference to the Gentiles. I have already been at pains to assert that the New covenant is *the* salvation covenant. None of the other covenants deal with soteriological matters. In Volume One of this work, I wrote:

> I believe that if we allow redemption passages like Isaiah 49:6; 54:5; 66:19; Micah 4:2; Zechariah 8:7-8, 20-23; Malachi 3:12 to be New covenant passages, just as those we have listed above (e.g. Deut. 30:1-8) then we simply cannot restrict the New covenant to Israel. Surely the smiting and expanding stone of Daniel 2:35 and 44, and the "Son of Man" character of Daniel 7:13-14 presuppose salvation among the nations? As I have tried to demonstrate in my comments on Isaiah 42 and 49, the Servant who is made a covenant is Christ, and He is made a covenant of salvation. In Isaiah 49:6-8 the One who saves Israel and the nations and who is made a covenant cannot be a covenant of salvation only to Israel, while the nations are saved in a different way.[117]

Another, less delicate way of saying this is that dispensationalists especially, since they so adamantly advocate for a literal hermeneutic, need to reevaluate the New covenant passages in both Testaments, particularly in Paul.

(3) The Church is a Full Party in the New Covenant Alongside of Israel

All writers know that the New covenant blessings of completed salvation await the eschaton (cf. 1 Jn. 3:2). This covenant promises salvation (i.e., redemption, forgiveness, restoration). But it is also embodied in Jesus Christ, His body and blood, His mediation. He is made "a covenant for the people" (Isa. 49:6-8). As I have argued previously, Jesus is the New covenant![118] It therefore follows that to be attached to Christ is to be attached to the New covenant.[119] To escape this conclusion, one would have to prove that the blood of Jesus with which the Church is redeemed is not the blood

116 Related to this is the matter of including the land promise within the provisions of the New covenant itself, rather than seeing it as pertaining to the Abrahamic covenant (e.g., Gen. 12:7). The land promise becomes fulfillable once it is brought into contact with the salvific provisions of the New covenant.

117 Paul Martin Henebury, *The Words of the Covenant*, Vol. 1, 273.

118 Just to remind the reader, I say this not only because of Isa. 42:6 and 49:8, but because He *is* the Lamb of God (Jn. 1:29), whose blood is the blood of the New covenant (Lk. 22:20), making Him the New covenant sacrifice (cf. Heb. 9:15-17 NASB) as well as the High Priest who mediates the New covenant (Heb. 12:24).

119 Although I do not go as far as he does regarding OT regeneration, Zane C. Hodges catches the idea in "Regeneration: A New Covenant Blessing," *JOTGES* 18 (Autumn 2005), 43-49.

of the New covenant, and I honestly do not know how that can be done, especially by those espousing literal hermeneutics.[120]

Admitting that the Church is also a party to the New covenant does nothing at all to the OT promises to Israel in Jeremiah 31, Ezekiel 36, etc. Isaiah wrote before these men, and he plainly declares this covenant includes the Gentiles (Isa. 49:6-8). Besides, the augmentation of detail concerning the New covenant follows what we witness in messianic prophecy and the other covenants. What allowing the Church to be a full party to the New covenant does is magnify Jesus Christ. It makes His work on the cross so much more poignant. Equating Jesus as the New covenant makes Him the *pou sto*, the fulcrum of the Creation Project.

A narrow reading of Jeremiah 31:31-34 has been allowed to blinker many fine dispensational interpreters into assigning the New covenant to Israel alone. My plea is that they would come to realize that the main ingredient in the New covenant is salvation, or more broadly, reconciliation in the form of redemption and restoration. Everything else that is purported to be found in the New covenant is, in actuality, several aspects of the other unilateral covenants of God—promises that have been revived because of the transforming power of Christ, which will come to fruition in a literal way by passing through the New covenant in Him.

The Abrahamic Covenant in Paul

I have given arguments above for the Church being a party to the New covenant. We are redeemed by New covenant blood and celebrate our Lord's death and return with New covenant emblems. Paul's ministry was characterized by himself as a "ministry of the New covenant" (2 Cor. 3:6ff.), and as we shall see when we get to the book of Hebrews, Jesus is our New covenant High Priest.

Now, we must ask about the status of the Abrahamic and Davidic covenants. As we shall see, Paul does not neglect either, and his theology reserves an important role for both covenants after the death and resurrection of the New covenant Christ.

The Church's Relation to the Covenant with Abraham

At the start of Romans 4, Paul introduces Abraham to illustrate his point and to bolster his argument about how a person is justified. In Romans 4:1 Paul asks a rhetorical question about Abraham "in the flesh"; that is to say, on his own merits. But as Genesis 15:6 shows (Rom. 4:3), righteousness was not something that Yahweh recognized in Abraham, but it was reckoned to him on the gracious premise that he believed God. Yahweh "credited" righteousness to Abraham. What is more, He did this before Abraham had been circumcised (Rom. 4:10-11). The apostle's reasoning relies

120 I do appreciate the concern of dispensationalists to avoid all connections with supercessionism. But claiming the Church is not under the New covenant is not the way to do it. In fact, its question-begging appearance may become a factor in people abandoning Dispensationalism in favor of a theology with a more forthright understanding of the New covenant. I believe Biblical Covenantalism, while ardently anti-supersessionist, can hold to a robust approach to the New covenant.

upon the grace of God being shown to the patriarch before he "worked" for God by being obedient.[121] This is summed up in a preparatory assertion in Romans 4:4-5.[122] What promises came to Abraham were not based one iota on his own inherent worth.

In his discussion of God's promise, Paul nowhere mentions the land aspect of the Abrahamic covenant, neither does he speak of the promises to Israel that were a part of that covenant. His interest is solely in God's grace being shown in response to Abraham's faith (cf. Rom. 4:16-18).

In Galatians 3:14 the apostle wants his Gentile audience to know that they have received "the blessing of Abraham," to which he also ties in the gift of the Holy Spirit. This does not imply that the gift of the Spirit is connected to the Abrahamic covenant, for that connection is never mentioned in the relevant texts. But it does mean that the "blessing of Abraham" comes through the New covenant—the covenant that does promise the Spirit (2 Cor. 3:6; cf. Gal. 4:6). It is a mistake to keep the Abrahamic covenant apart from the New covenant in Christ.

Abraham as "Heir of the World"

But then, in Romans 4 comes verse 13: "For the promise that he would be the heir of the world *was* not to Abraham or to his seed through the law, but through the righteousness of faith" (Rom. 4:13).

It ought to be clear that the only covenant promise in the chapter that might concern Abraham being "the heir of the world" was the third part of the covenant dealing with the blessing of the nations through him (e.g., Gen. 12:3c; 22:18). It is not a part of the land pledge plainly set out in Genesis 15:17-21. Interpreters who employ Romans 4:13 as a proof-text for expanding the land promise over all the earth and giving it to the Church are pursuing a theological agenda and are not observing the apostle's argument.[123] If they are to prove the land promise has been converted into something different[124] and handed to the Church, they need to do a lot more than appeal to this verse. Context is king, and contextually, Romans 4 is not about land at all. Numerous commentators have been explicit that Romans 4:13 is *not* concerned with the land promise.[125] The context is justification to salvation, not Israel's land grant.[126] A more

121 Pitre, Barber, and Kincaid launch a penetrating assault on this position in chapter 5 of their *Paul, a New Covenant Jew*. Some of their argumentation is thought-provoking, but their main point, that justification includes personal righteousness, fails in my view to follow the argumentation of Paul closely. Their treatment of Rom. 4 in particular is not persuasive (Ibid., 183-190).

122 "Now to him who works, the wages are not counted as grace but as debt. But to him who does not work but believes on Him who justifies the ungodly, his faith is accounted for righteousness" (Rom. 4:4-5).

123 E.g., Constantine R. Campbell, *Paul and the Hope of Glory* (Grand Rapids: Zondervan, 2020), 214-215; Thomas Edward McComiskey, *The Covenants of Promise*, 204-205.

124 More territory—the entire earth's surface—just none for the nation of Israel to whom the oath was made.

125 See e.g., F. F. Bruce, *Romans: An Introduction and Commentary*, TNTC, rev. ed. (Downers Grove, IL: IVP Academic, 2008), 110-111; Frederic Godet, *Commentary on the Epistle to the Romans* (Grand Rapids: Zondervan, 1956), 176. Cf. Michael J. Vlach, *The New Creation Model*, 371.

126 Even John Murray, *Romans*, 141-142, recognizes this.

recent commentator writes, "...in speaking about God's promise, he [Paul] does not include any reference to the territorial aspect of the promise given to Abraham and to his descendants."[127]

But there are others who read the verse as if Paul were combining all three elements of the covenant and applying it to Jew and Gentile salvation in Christ.[128] Even some messianic Jewish scholars opt to see both spiritual and geographical intent in Romans 4:13.[129] But there is no warrant for doing this, especially here where the apostle is arguing that God reckoned Abraham as righteous before the covenant sign of circumcision was given, which therefore means that through faith in God's words (which Paul infers is the Gospel, Rom. 1:16; 3:24), the same imputed righteousness is available irrespective of ethnic identity.

The word "world" (*kosmos*) appears once in Romans 4, so we must look at what Paul is speaking about to determine what he means by it. As anyone can see from Romans 4:1-5, the apostle is thinking in terms of the dual concept of justification and righteousness. Faith, not works, is the bridge from one to the other (hence the insertion of Gen. 15:6). David is then used to illustrate the point at issue (Rom. 4:6-9). Next, we get a question about whether this imputed righteousness is only for the Jews (circumcision, Rom. 4:9), which is answered by the fact that Abraham was justified before he was circumcised (Rom. 4:10). This means that his faith-justification to righteousness is not bounded by circumcision, so that those not circumcised may receive justification through faith the same way Abraham did (Rom. 4:11-12). Those not circumcised would be the rest of the peoples of the world. So far, not a word about the physical land! Paul is still on the theme of righteousness, which he will go on to argue for in the rest of the chapter. There is no reason to think that Paul switched theological topics in verse 13. The "world" he is speaking of is people, not land (cf. Rom. 3:6, 19; 12:2; 1 Cor. 1:20-21, 27-28, etc.).

The Abrahamic Covenant and Paul's Argument in Galatians 3:1-16

There are similarities between Romans 4 and Galatians 3. In the beginning of Galatians 3, Paul again contrasts law and faith with one another (Gal. 3:1-5). Again, he quotes Genesis 15:6 (Gal. 3:6) because he wants to establish the primacy of faith over works when it comes to justification, which he says is imputed (*logizomai*). Nowhere in the chapter does he speak about the land promise. F. F. Bruce, for instance,

127 R. N. Longenecker, *The Epistle to the Romans*, 510.

128 This is the position of Thomas R. Schreiner, *Romans*, BECNT (Grand Rapids: Baker, 1998), 227-228. Schreiner provides a list of OT passages which he claims proclaim "the universal character of the promise." But these passages clearly concern the future kingdom, not the Church. The only way they can validate Schreiner's point is if they are spiritualized. The use Schreiner makes of these OT texts betrays the fact that he is reading both them and Rom. 4:13 within a first coming frame of reference.

129 See e.g., David Rudolph, "Zionism in Pauline Literature," in *The New Christian Zionism*, 173-177. Nevertheless, this is a fine essay.

explicitly declares, "The reference to the land...plays no part in the argument of Galatians."[130] This is essential to understand once one comes to Galatians 3:16.[131]

Paul is well aware of the ambiguity in the word "seed." The question is, how can he relate it to Christ in Galatians 3:16 and yet preserve the collective meaning he knows is clearly there in the original context he is citing? As Galatians 3:29 makes clear, Paul has not lost sight of the collective meaning of the word.[132] I believe that here the corporate dimension is included by Paul in the One—Jesus Christ. In Paul's mind, fulfillment was always understood to require Christ the Fulfiller. Once this is acknowledged, one must choose between several hermeneutical options.

In the first option, Paul employed some kind of semi-apocalyptic interpretation through which he could summon any OT passage to take on a new meaning in his argument. This is the position of Richard B. Hays.[133] It posits a change of meaning under the influence of Paul's supposed hermeneutic. The second option is that, although he never said it, Paul intended us to infer that the Genesis texts he referred to (whichever ones they were) had intended meanings beyond those found on the surface of the passages in their original setting. Paul was only now declaring to us what God had hidden behind those OT promises.

This would be the position of many of those who believe the NT is necessary to rightly interpret the Old.[134] A clear implication of this position is that there is hermeneutical, or at the very least, linguistic *discontinuity* between the two Testaments. The meaning of a particular term or phrase in the original context without recourse to the NT would procure a different sense than it would once the NT was consulted.

Another outcome of this approach would be to separate the original author's intended meaning from that of the Holy Spirit. While this possibility should not be ignored, the burden of proof for such a claim is on those who make it, whether they are aware of it or have to be made aware of it by others.

Then there is a third option. Paul understood that the term "seed" could not be legitimately confined to a singular noun referring to Messiah, since the word is a collective noun and is used as such many times in the OT (especially in Genesis), and, indeed, by Paul himself (e.g., in Gal. 3:29). In which case the singular and the corporate

130 F. F. Bruce, *The Epistle to the Galatians*, NIGTC (Grand Rapids: Eerdmans, 1982), 172.

131 As for which particular passages Paul is citing in Gal. 3:16, one cannot be that exact. I tend to think Genesis 22:18 is the best choice since it contains the needed room for both singular and plural meanings within the Abrahamic narrative.

132 "And if you *are* Christ's, then you are Abraham's seed, and heirs according to the promise" (Gal. 3:29).

133 Richard B. Hays, *The Conversion of the Imagination* (New Haven: Yale University Press, 1989), 43.

134 E.g., "The notion of Christians being part of God's Israelite family is expressed well in Galatians...Paul views Christ to be the summation of the true Israel and understands all, whether Jew or gentile, whom Jesus represents to be true Israel... The identification in Gal. 3:29 that both believing 'Jew and Greek' (3:28) are 'Abraham's seed' is, then, a reference to them as the continuation of true Israel" (G. K. Beale, *A New Testament Biblical Theology,* 671). Or, "Earlier expressions point to things beyond themselves that are greater than the meaning that would have been perceived by those receiving these earlier expressions" (Graeme Goldsworthy, *According to Plan*, 123).

must be closely related; the corporate fulfillment being predicated on the coming "Seed," Messiah.[135]

Only this third view preserves the integrity of the OT contexts, not to mention the specificity of God's covenant promises to Israel. Promises which Paul elsewhere says are inviolable (Rom. 11:25-28). Only on this view can we avoid the treacherous waters of hermeneutical and philosophical ambiguity upon which the first two views implicitly lean. This third way would be my understanding. To demonstrate it, one must try to show that there is no need for an OT passage to be considered a "shadow" or "type" of a NT reality, but rather that the witness of both Testaments can be hermeneutically aligned to allow all the relevant verses to speak in their own words.

A Short Tour of Galatians 3:1-16

If we look at Galatians 3, we will find Paul reasoning about the role of faith in God's saving economy. We will not find him saying anything about God's covenants with the people of Israel and the land grant God promised them. Of course, those who wish to expand the land promise realize this. Their contention is that because the apostle speaks of OT texts that not only refer to Christ as the "seed" (e.g., Gen. 17:7) but also contain promises about the "land," it only stands to reason that the word "seed" in Genesis (and the rest of the OT?) is not a reference to the nation of Israel ("descendants"), but only ever to Christ; and the "land," likewise, is not Canaan (or the portion described in Gen. 15), but heaven.[136] What the Apostle has done, so the thinking goes, is to offer an inspired interpretation of terminology only dimly understood before Paul wrote Galatians circa A.D. 50 (see Option 2 above).

I want to show how one can understand Paul's pedantic insistence on a single seed and yet not have to employ a tough verse (Gal. 3:16) to infer an altering of the original land grant to the corporate seed—Israel. But first, we shall examine Paul's argument in Galatians 3.

Galatians 3:1-5

Paul is distressed that the churches in Galatia have been taken in by those who emphasize justification and sanctification through "works of the law."[137] He, therefore, contrasts faith from the works of the law which certain Judaizers were insisting on. The Holy Spirit, he reminds them, was received by faith in Paul's Gospel and not at all by works (Gal. 3:2). And since the Spirit was received by faith, it is unreasonable to think that one should not continue to walk in faith (Gal. 3:3), especially since the Spirit works in response to faith (Gal. 3:5).

135 See Michael Vlach, *The Old in the New*, 231-234.

136 Some would say the whole land surface of Earth.

137 I agree with Moo that this phrase basically means "doing what the law requires" (Douglas J. Moo, *A Theology of Paul and His Letters*, 69). This is a broad enough definition to embrace the data. The phrase "the works of the law" and its supposed emblematic meaning is associated with the New Perspective.

Galatians 3:6-9

Abraham is now introduced, together with the quotation of Genesis 15:6, to prove that justification is by faith alone (Gal. 3:6). And just as Abraham's faith was declared sufficient for justification,[138] so we too must exercise faith in God's Word to us in the Gospel (Gal. 3:7). The next verse quotes from the promise of blessing to all nations through Abraham by faith (Gal. 3:8). This connects salvation to the Abrahamic covenant (expanded in Romans 4).[139] The verse says the Scripture foresaw this salvation of the Gentiles. Paul shows this by simply bringing Genesis 15:6 and Genesis 12:3 together. Righteousness is what man most needs, and that is what God imputed to Abraham in Genesis 15:6 upon his faith in God's promise. In line with the third aspect of the Abrahamic covenant (Gen. 12:3), the Gentile nations will be blessed. This begins with imputed righteousness, by their faith-connection with Abraham via the covenant (Gen. 12:3; Gal. 3:9). Thus, there is a corporate identity via a provision of the Abrahamic covenant (Gen. 12:3). *But there is no clear provision in the Abrahamic covenant itself to provide the salvation needed for our entering into the blessings upon Gentiles.* This would mean the Abrahamic covenant (and the Davidic and Priestly covenants too, for that matter) would require supplementing with a specific salvific promise to bring about their success. That "supplement" is, as I have said, the New covenant in Jesus Christ.

Galatians 3:13-16

In verses 10-12 Paul demonstrates the demanding requirements of the law over against faith. Christ is now introduced as the One who redeems us "from the curse of the law" (Gal. 3:13) and connects us to Abraham and the reception of the Spirit "through faith" (Gal. 3:14). Verse 15 refers to a mere covenant between men[140] as binding and not open to annulment or the addition of a codicil changing the terms (i.e., "adds to it"). The illustration of a man's covenant[141] is being used to show the incontrovertibility of such covenants, something to be revisited in Galatians 3:17 (cf. Rom. 11:28-29), where the Abrahamic covenant is the subject.

In Galatians 3:16 the apostle writes: "Now to Abraham and his Seed were the promises made. He does not say, 'And to seeds,' as of many, but as of one, 'And to your Seed,' who is Christ." In order to connect Abraham and the covenant to the promised salvation through faith, Paul fastens on the messianic implications of the

138 This statement must be qualified somewhat. I shall deal with this qualification further on.

139 There is a definite concentration of Abrahamic material in Gal. 3–4 and Rom. 4, 9–11. Cf. Matthew V. Novenson, *Paul, Then and Now* (Grand Rapids: Eerdmans, 2022), 84.

140 This again will be discussed in more detail because some scholars believe that Gal. 3:15 (and 2 Cor. 3:6 and Heb. 9:16-17) refers to a "last will and testament," not a covenant (e.g., James D. G. Dunn, *Beginning From Jerusalem*, 740 n. 381). I will just say here that I find these interpretations of *diatheke* do violence to their contexts.

141 For clear and persuasive arguments for translating *diatheke* as "covenant" in Gal. 3:15, see Paul R. Williamson, *Sealed with an Oath*, 195-199. Block disagrees with this but offers little by way of substantiation (*Covenant*, 395). Besides, he contradicts himself later when he claims, "Gal. 3:15 is not about God's covenant with Abraham, but a generic statement about how human covenants operate" (Ibid., 435, my emphasis).

"seed-promise" to Abraham in Genesis 12-22. He is well aware of what he is doing. We must recall that he does not dispense with the collective sense, which he needs to ground his argument (Gal. 3:29).

What he is doing here is including the collective sense within the singular (Christ).[142] It is through Christ that the promises—all the promises—of the Abrahamic covenant will find their fulfillment and consummation. Believers from Abraham to the end of the age are connected to the Abrahamic covenant through the Seed, Jesus Christ; and this connection is forged through the New covenant!

Though the New covenant is not explicitly mentioned in Galatians 3, I believe it is securely in Paul's mind. In fact, this becomes clearer when, in Galatians 4:22ff., he sets off the New covenant (Sarah, Mt. Zion) from the old (Mosaic) covenant (Ishmael, Mt. Sinai).[143] We Gentiles enter into the promised blessing of Genesis 12:3 through the New covenant in Christ (cf. 1 Cor. 11:25-26). The Abrahamic, Priestly, and Davidic covenants all depend on the *mediation of Christ in the New covenant* (cf. Heb. 12:24). Despite the awkward vacillation of many dispensationalists over the New covenant,[144] the words of the institution of the Lord's Supper prove that Christ has made the New covenant with the Church. What is more, *that is the only way the Church accesses the Abrahamic covenant*! Every covenant blessing runs through Jesus Christ and the New covenant in Him.

In order for the Abrahamic covenant to be tied to the Church (especially its Gentile contingent), that covenant must be connected to the New covenant in Christ. If that is true, then Paul is thinking along these very lines when he cites the four words "and to your seed" from Genesis. He most probably does not have an exact reference in mind, as he did with his earlier quotation of Genesis 15:6, but rather has in view the repeated use of the phrase through the Abrahamic narrative.

If one accepts this thesis, then the corporate dimension of the Abrahamic covenant, which Paul needs to complete his argument in Galatians 3:29, remains intact; but is fed through the "Mediator of the New covenant"—the one "Seed" of Galatians 3:16. Thus, because the Church is a participant in the Abrahamic covenant via the promises in Genesis 12:3 and 22:18, it does so because of its participation in the New covenant in Christ.

The Davidic Covenant in Paul

The Davidic covenant concerns itself with the subjects of King and Kingdom. The details involve reigning from Jerusalem over a restored and blessed Israel but also extend the rule over all the nations of the earth (see Psa. 67; Isa. 2:2-4; Zech. 14:9).

142 This of course is understood by most expositors, although contrary to them, I hold that the Abrahamic covenant emerges from Christ to be fulfilled literally in all of its three aspects.

143 "The discussion in Gal 4:21-31 presupposes the concept of a new covenant versus and old one, without either phrase actually being used" (Victor Paul Furnish, *II Corinthians: A New Translation with Introduction and Commentary*, Anchor Bible [Garden City, New York: Doubleday, 1984], 198).

144 Not every dispensationalist has trouble making the Church a party to the New covenant.

Therefore, the rule is neither parochial nor universal to the exclusion of national and ethnic identities. In expounding the covenant with David in Paul (or the rest of the NT), it is remarkable how many studies fail to uphold the specific words of the covenant God made. This is important for us to note because, as Alva McClain said, "There is no epistle of the New Testament addressed to the saints in 'the kingdom of heaven.'"[145] What this means is that we cannot make the Church and the Kingdom the same thing, and therefore, we cannot convert Davidic promises into Church promises.

Saying this does not mean that the Davidic covenant is absent from Paul.[146] One does not have to look very far to confirm this. First of all, Romans 1:3 says that Christ "was born of the seed of David according to the flesh."[147] Romans 11:9-10 quotes from Psalm 69:22-23, which ends on a Kingdom note (Psa. 69:35-36). In Romans 15:12 Paul quotes from Isaiah 11:10, a very strong Kingdom passage.[148] Although his main focus is upon God's reaching out to the Gentiles (Rom. 15:7-13), the Isaiah quotation, which is the last of four OT references in the context, is followed by, "Now may the God of hope fill you with all joy and peace in believing, that you may abound in hope by the power of the Holy Spirit" (Rom. 15:13). This "hope" is plausibly interpreted in context as the Kingdom of Christ (although Romans 14:17 is the only place in the book where Paul uses the word).

Speaking of the Kingdom, we have seen that Paul's preaching in Acts had much to do with the Kingdom of God (Acts 14:22; 19:8; 20:25; 28:23, 31; cf. Col. 4:11; 2 Thess. 1:5; 2 Tim. 4:1, 14). We see him still clinging to the OT hope for the twelve tribes of Israel in his defense before Agrippa in Acts 26:7. It is difficult to read such an appeal if, as we are told, he believed that both the idea of "Israel" and their national hope was transmuted to the Church. From his epistles, it seems that he was concerned about inheriting the Kingdom of God (1 Cor. 6:9-10; 15:50; Gal. 5:21; Eph. 5:5; 1 Thess. 2:12; 2 Thess. 1:5). Since the Kingdom of God in the Gospels and Acts is frequently a reference to the future Kingdom, and, to my mind, most of the Pauline mentions of it are too, all of these verses are linked with the covenant God made with David.

EXCURSUS: The Davidic Covenant and the Church

But that raises the question of how the Church relates to the coming Kingdom (I discuss the "already-not yet" position further on). My answer is that the Church will be a part of the wider messianic Kingdom, although it will not be a part of the renewed Kingdom of Israel. Thus, as far as the initial promise to David in 2 Samuel 7 is concerned, the Church is not a party to the Davidic promise.

145 Alva J. McClain, *The Greatness of the Kingdom*, 431.

146 Block, for instance, has a very brief section of the Davidic covenant in Paul. See his *Covenant*, 604-605.

147 See also 2 Tim. 2:8.

148 See Craig Blaising, "A Theology of Israel and the Church," *Israel, the Church, and the Middle East: A Biblical Response to the Current Conflict*, eds. Darrell L. Bock and Mitch Glaser (Grand Rapids: Kregel, 2018), 94.

With that said, there is Acts 15 to consider. In Acts 15:13-21 James makes a speech that includes a reference to the Gospel going out to the Gentiles (Acts 15:14) and a quotation of Amos 9:11-12 indicating that the raising up of David's line in Jesus Christ will cause the Gentiles to seek the Lord (Acts 15:15-17). In the context of Amos 9, this passage seems attached to the "Day of the Lord."[149] In Acts 15, however, James cites this text to prove that salvation is now offered to the Gentiles.[150] Toussaint is correct to point out that "James did not say Amos 9:11-12 was fulfilled in the church; he simply asserted that what was happening in the church was in full agreement with the prophets."[151] However, that does not answer why James chose that particular passage. Why did he go to Amos? I don't think there is much inscrutability to it. The Church is not spoken of in the OT. So, *any* passage which refers to God saving the Gentiles has to be linked to the coming of Messiah, and this inevitably calls forth the matter of the messianic prophecies in the OT not drawing a distinction between the first and second comings. Since Messiah is closely tied to the Davidic dynasty, it is expected that OT prophecies would link the two comings together since most of them projected one coming of Messiah to rule on earth.[152] Ergo, Amos 9 is as good as any reference to refer to the New covenant outreach to the Gentiles in the Church.[153]

Then there are those passages in Paul with clear messianic connotations, such as 1 Corinthians 15:22 (new life); 2 Corinthians 5:10 (judgment); Ephesians 1:10, 21 (dominion); 1:19-20 (resurrection); and Philippians 3:7-9 (righteousness). As an honorific[154] (which Paul often uses), "*Christos*" certainly has Davidic kingly implications.[155] So much so that Wright provocatively translates *Christos* as "King" in some places.[156] Hays observes, "Jesus is David's heir, who is to reign not only over Israel but

149 See *The Words of the Covenant*, Vol. 1, 231.

150 James cites the LXX, which differs quite a bit from the Hebrew OT. In my opinion, James opted for this reading because it better supported his argument and agreed with the OT prophecies on the matter. Still, the fact that he does not claim Amos 9:11-12 was fulfilled is significant.

151 Stanley D. Toussaint, "Acts," in *Bible Knowledge Commentary: New Testament*, eds. John F. Walvoord and Roy B. Zuck (Grand Rapids, MI: Victor Books, 1983), 394.

152 Vlach calls the Davidic covenant "'a charter for mankind,' meaning Gentiles will be blessed by it too" (Michael J. Vlach, *He Will Reign Forever*, 574). See Vlach's treatment of the Davidic covenant in Ibid., 569-579.

153 Peter Goeman has argued that in Acts 15 James is also alluding to Isaiah 45:21 and Zechariah 8:22 (both covenantal texts). For the details of his argument, see Peter J. Goeman, "The Role of the LXX in James' Use of Amos 9:11-12 in Acts 15:15-18," *Journal of Dispensational Theology* 18 (Summer/Fall 2014), 107-25.

154 N. T. Wright, *Paul and the Faithfulness of God*, 824.

155 This is argued at length by Joshua W. Jipp in his *Christ is King: Paul's Royal Ideology* (Minneapolis: Fortress, 2015), although I do not share his eschatological position.

156 Wright is quite assertive; "The royal meaning of *Christos* does not disappear in Paul's writings. It is present, central and foundational" (N. T. Wright, *Paul and the Faithfulness of God*, 824, cf. 822, 835). Unfortunately, this recognition of the kingly status of Messiah, when mixed with a first coming hermeneutic can produce outlooks like that which claims that faith in Christ involves implicit allegiance to Jesus the King. See e.g., Matthew W. Bates, *Salvation By Allegiance Alone: Rethinking Faith, Works, and the Gospel of Jesus the King* (Grand Rapids: Baker, 2017). For instance, Bates writes, "With regard to eternal salvation, rather than speaking of belief, trust, or faith in Jesus, we should speak instead of fidelity to Jesus as cosmic Lord or allegiance to Jesus as king" (Ibid., 5). He says, "The gospel is not primarily about the necessity of the human response of 'faith' in Jesus's saving work, but rather about how Jesus came to

also over the gentiles (Rom. 1:3),[157] as Paul proclaims in the climactic peroration of Romans: 'The root of Jesse shall come, the one who rises to rule the Gentiles; in him the Gentiles shall hope' (Rom. 15:12)."[158]

That being the case, we should not be surprised by the fact that, for Paul, *Christos* retains its Davidic significance:

> Indeed, the title [*Christos*]... often thought to have become for Paul merely a proper name, has by no means lost its messianic connotations, as hinted by several passages where he uses it with the definite article: 'Welcome one another, therefore, just as (lit., the Christ) has welcomed you (Rom 15:7; cf. Rom 9:5; 15:3; 2 Cor 1:5; 2:14; Phil 1:15, 17; 3:7; Col 2:6; 3:1, 4). Wherever in Paul's letters we read the name "Christ," the suggestion that he is the royal Son, Israel's expected King, is not far in the background.[159]

Here we should recall the Gospels and how they emphasize the Davidic aspects of the title (Matthew and Luke, in particular). Nevertheless, even granting overtones of the Davidic covenant in the title or honorific *Christos,* I must agree with Vlach when he concludes:

> Paul did not view the Davidic covenant as being fulfilled in the present... Paul's lack of discussion on the Davidic covenant may coincide with the picture presented in other Scripture passages in which Jesus will assume the Davidic throne in connection with His Second Coming to earth (Matt. 19:28; 25:31; Rev. 3:21).[160]

I am persuaded that it is essential to recall the tension created by the bifurcation of the singular arrival of Christ into first and second advents. We must endeavor to make sure that we include this phenomenon within our hermeneutical investigation of the appropriate NT texts.

---

be enthroned as Lord of heaven and earth" (Ibid., 13). Again, "the gospel is the power-releasing story of Jesus's life, death for sins, resurrection, and installation as king...good news about the enthronement of Jesus the atoning king..." (Ibid., 30). It is clear from these quotations that Bates employs a "first coming hermeneutic" which assigns fulfillment of second coming prophecies to the first century A.D. Nevertheless, I do not want to dispatch Bates' book with a few simple remarks. He is an excellent writer, and portions of the book reflect contemporary scholarship well (e.g., into the meanings of *pistis,* "Messiah," and the topic of participation). For a good response to Bates and others (though sadly lacking interaction with M. Gorman) see Kevin W. McFadden, *Faith in the Son of God: The Place of Christ-Oriented Faith within Pauline Theology* (Wheaton: Crossway, 2021).

157 I have supplied the book reference in places where Hays omits it.

158 Richard B. Hays, *Reading with the Grain of Scripture* (Grand Rapids: Eerdmans, 2020), 153.

159 Ibid., 153-154. Likewise, "It should be noted that 'Christ' is not for Paul the last name of Jesus; it retains its meaning 'Messiah'" (Michael J. Gorman *Cruciformity: Paul's Narrative Spirituality of the Cross* [Grand Rapids: Eerdmans, 2001], 19 n. 2).

160 Michael Vlach, "The Eschatology of the Pauline Epistles," in *The Return of Christ: A Premillennial Perspective,* eds. David L. Allen and Steve W. Lemke (Nashville: B&H, 2011), 244.

The Already-Not Yet Kingdom?

> He has delivered us from the power of darkness and conveyed us into the kingdom of the Son of His love, in whom we have redemption through His blood, the forgiveness of sins (Col. 1:13-14).

There is an important matter to which I must give attention before moving on, and that is the correlation between the Davidic covenant, the "kingdom," and the Church. I must confess to a certain reticence to use the popular phrase "already-not yet"[161] because of the things that come with it. I should probably just get over it and employ the term in a qualified sense. But I want to state outright that I do not believe the Bible teaches that Jesus is presently sitting upon the Davidic throne and ruling from it in heaven. In fact, He is not actually sitting on any throne in heaven but is "at the right hand" of the Father's throne (Acts 7:55-56; Col. 3:1; Heb. 1:3; 12:2).

Yet, Jesus is the Christ, the King, and those two titles are associated with each other (although they are not synonymous). "Christ" is not just the King, but He is the coming Ruler predicted by the Prophets.

The question though is whether Christ is ruling as Davidic King now. In Colossians 1:13-14 the term "kingdom" is used of the Church now. Christ *has* delivered us (*errusato*, aorist tense) "from the power of darkness," so what about Christians now being in the "kingdom"? One writer gives this explanation: "Christ exercises 'mediatorial sovereignty' that will one day be 'merged in the eternal kingdom of God' when Christ hands over his kingdom and it becomes the future kingdom of God."[162]

In this approach, Jesus is reigning from heaven in anticipation of His second advent when, according to the author, He delivers up creation to the Father (see 1 Cor. 15:23-28).[163] George Eldon Ladd claims that this passage applies now, though he is careful to say that "This 'Kingdom of Christ' cannot be equated with the church."[164] He says, "The Kingdom of Christ here is the invisible sphere of Christ's reign into which men enter by faith in Jesus Christ."[165] I am fine with this definition because Christ is Head of the Church (Col. 1:18; Eph. 1:22; 5:23), but is He King of the Church? My answer is "No." Not only does the NT not make such a statement, but the Church is not a geopolitical entity that can be reigned over as a king reigns over a nation. Ladd believes "the church is the custodian of the kingdom" through the Spirit.[166] This I deny because the Church is a body of "lights" in a dark world (Phil. 2:15) to which we do not belong (Col. 2:8; 1 Jn. 2:15-17). It is not our job to watch over the Kingdom in

---

161 The term is associated with the work of C. H. Dodd and George E. Ladd, but the idea is found earlier. For example, Geerhardus Vos, *The Pauline Eschatology* (1930 reprint; Phillipsburg, NJ: P&R, 1979), 36-41.

162 Adam Copenhaver in Adam Copenhaver and Jeffrey D. Arthurs, *Colossians and Philemon: A Commentary for Biblical Preaching and Teaching*, Kerux (Grand Rapids: Kregel, 2022), 71.

163 See my treatment of this passage in, "*When Christ Delivers Up the Kingdom to the Father*" in the next chapter.

164 George Eldon Ladd, *A Theology of the New Testament*, 410-411.

165 Ibid., 411.

166 George Eldon Ladd, *The Presence of the Future*, 273-274.

Christ's stead, as if it were some fragile relic that needed guarding. On the other hand, Michael Vlach comments:

> The church is not the kingdom, but it relates to the kingdom program in several important ways...believers in Jesus are "sons of the kingdom" (Matt 12:38). This means the kingdom belongs to them and they are members of the kingdom even though the kingdom's actual establishment awaits Jesus' return.[167]

In this view, the "kingdom" of Colossians 1 is yet future even though it belongs to them now. This understanding matches other verses that state truths about Christians that lie in their futures. Philippians 3:20 says, "our citizenship is in heaven," yet we are not in heaven. Ephesians 2:6 says Christ has "raised us up together, and made us sit together in the heavenly places in Christ Jesus." But we are here on earth. The argument is then one of prolepsis; that future things can be stated as if they were present. I don't want to be seen as splitting hairs on this issue, especially since the phrase "already-not yet" is hardly precise.[168] Indeed, it is a wax nose if ever there was one. One may eagerly say "Yes" to it in one guise and vehemently say "No" in another. To my mind, I graduate to Vlach's way of thinking over Copenhaver's and Ladd's.

To be clear, Colossians 1:13 and such statements refer to the fact that, as Acts 26:18 puts it, we have been turned "from darkness to light, and from the power of Satan to God," to await "an inheritance among those who are sanctified by faith in [Jesus]." We have been transferred from Satan's thrall and are under Christ as we anticipate His return to set up His Kingdom.[169] If there is a kingdom on earth right now, it is ruled over by Satan, "the prince of the power of the air" (Eph. 2:2), who is "the god of this age" (2 Cor. 4:4), "the ruler of this world" (Jn. 12:31). He is so powerful that, according to John, "the whole world lies under the sway of the wicked one" (1 Jn. 5:19). And yes, it does have geopolitical dimensions (cf. Dan. 10:12-13, 20; Rev. 2:13), as difficult as it may be to comprehend such matters. Jesus is at the Father's right hand. His throne is messianic and, therefore, earthly, and that is its glory.

---

167 Michael J. Vlach, *He Will Reign Forever*, 540-541.

168 See Elliott E. Johnson, "Prophetic Fulfillment: The Already and Not Yet," in *Issues in Dispensationalism*, eds. John R. Master and Wesley R. Willis (Chicago: Moody, 1994), 187-192. This essay is recommended.

169 As I said in my comments on the four Gospels, Jesus' first coming was His presentation of Himself as Messiah and hence as King. But He was rejected (according to the foreordination of God) and has gone to receive the Kingdom from God (Lk. 19:11-12) and return as "King of kings" (1 Tim. 6:15; cf. Rev. 17:12-14, 17-18).

15

PAUL: AN APOSTLE OF THE NEW COVENANT (2)

Who was delivered up because of our offenses, and was raised because of our justification. - Romans 4:25

The Church, the Holy Spirit, and the Resurrection of Christ

If there is one subject that I think has not received the attention that it deserves in Paul's thought, it is the vital relationship the Church bears to the resurrection of the Lord Jesus Christ. To me, this is what philosopher Alvin Plantinga calls a "defeater" for the claim that there is only one people of God in Scripture, the Church.[1] My reason for saying this is because the Church as the Body of Christ bears a special relation to the resurrection that saints in the OT did not enjoy (cf. Rom. 6:1-11).[2] We are going to inspect the data of the Pauline literature and see if it is possible to disengage the Church from the resurrection.[3] But I begin with John 7:38-39:

> "He who believes in Me, as the Scripture has said, out of his heart will flow rivers of living water." But this He spoke concerning the Spirit, whom those believing in Him would receive; for the Holy Spirit was not yet *given,* because Jesus was not yet glorified (Jn. 7:38-39).

1 Most covenant theologians who are a- or post- millennial believe that the Church is in the OT. E.g., Francis Turretin, *Institutes of Elenctic Theology*, trans. G. M. Giger, ed. J. T. Dennison, Vol. 3 (Phillipsburg, NJ: P&R, 1997), 18.6.II, 30; see also 18.5.IV, 27. However, some amillennialists I have conversed with have told me that they do not believe the Church is in the OT, but they are very fuzzy about what to call "the people of God" before the NT era. Of course, unless they admit that the Church is not in the OT (i.e., the Church being believing Israel), they run straight into the charge of replacement theology. This sticks because they aver that there is one people of God for all time, and yet some say that OT Israel should not be called the Church.

2 OT saints were saved by grace through faith but nowhere are we told that they were indwelt by the Holy Spirit in the way Christians are.

3 By this I mean Christ's resurrection. There remains a resurrection ahead for Christians. See e.g., 1 Cor. 15:13ff.; Phil. 3:11; 2 Tim. 2:18.

In this text John tells us that the Holy Spirit would be received by the saints after Jesus had been glorified. Jesus entered into His glory when He ascended to heaven in Acts 1:9-11 (cf. Lk. 24:26). This refers to the descent of the Spirit in Acts 2.[4] John 7:39 was written by the apostle long after the fact to explain the cryptic words of the Master. Those in the Church, Christ's spiritual body, are the ones to whom the Spirit was given.

> And being assembled together with them, He commanded them not to depart from Jerusalem, but to wait for the Promise of the Father, "which," He said, "you have heard from Me; for John truly baptized with water, but you shall be baptized with the Holy Spirit not many days from now" (Acts 1:4-5; cf. Acts 11:15-16).

This text links baptism with the Spirit and the gift of the Spirit.[5] There is a definite connection between the Holy Spirit and the New covenant. In that oft-underappreciated verse, Paul writes that God "made us sufficient as ministers of the new covenant, not of the letter but of the Spirit; for the letter kills, but the Spirit gives life" (2 Cor. 3:6).

The pouring out or giving of the Holy Spirit to the saints is a mark of the New covenant (e.g., Isa. 32:15; 44:3; 59:21; Ezek. 36:27; 37:14; 39:29; Joel 2:28-29; Zech. 12:10; Matt. 28:19; Lk. 11:13; Jn. 7:37-39; 14:17; Rom. 5:5; 8:9-11; 1 Cor. 2:12; 3:16; 6:19; 12:3, 11; 2 Cor. 1:21; 3:3, 18; 5:5; Gal. 3:14; 5:25; Eph. 1:13; 2 Tim. 1:14; Tit. 3:5). *None of the other divine covenants address the subject of the Spirit.* One might ask whether the gift of the Spirit as indwelling presence is connected to covenants at all. But as a matter of fact, the promise of the Spirit *is* bound to covenant. Further, the coming of the Spirit is bound to the Passion and resurrection of Jesus. Jesus said, "If I do not go away, the Helper will not come to you; but if I depart, I will send Him to you" (Jn. 16:7). If Jesus had not ascended back to heaven, the Holy Spirit would not have come to indwell us. But the cross of Christ is all about the reconciling blood of Christ (Eph. 1:7; 2:13; Col. 1:20), and that blood is, as we have seen, New covenant blood (1 Cor. 11:25). So, there is a convergence of factors: the gift of the Spirit producing a "new heart," the fact that the Spirit's work *in this respect* is connected to the New covenant, and the relation of those two factors with the blood of Christ.

The Resurrection Link

The resurrection of Jesus Christ from the dead is an eschatological event. His risen glorified body, which proclaimed in itself the defeat of death, is a beautiful anachronism, a flame of hope from which all believers can draw strength. Life blazes in a world of death, signaling the coming victory of Life (cf. 1 Cor. 15:54-57; 2 Cor.

4 Once more, this means that believers prior to the ascension of Jesus were not indwelt by the Holy Spirit as they would be after Pentecost. A change occurred that we must face and adapt our theologies to.

5 The book of Acts could well be called "the book of the Spirit," especially its first half.

5:4). Although I disagree with his "apocalyptic" reading, I like the way Beker puts it: "Resurrection language is eschatological language...For this reason the resurrection of Christ, the coming reign of God, and the resurrection of the dead belong inseparably together."[6]

To Paul, the resurrection of Christ is the promise of history.[7] This is why it takes up so much of the proclamation in the first part of Acts. It is also essential to our understanding of the birth of the Church.

I continue this section by being a bit provocative. Here it is: there could be no Church before the resurrection of Christ for the simple reason that the organism that is made up of Christians is essentially connected to the life of the resurrected Lord.[8] Therefore, without the resurrection, there could be no Church. I realize that such a statement will upset anyone who believes that saints before the cross were indwelt by the Spirit and that there is only one people of God for all ages, but there it is, and I think it is quite easy to demonstrate.

In the first place, we have seen that the gift of the Holy Spirit is a gift associated with the New covenant.[9] This is seen in many OT New covenant passages such as Isaiah 59:20-21; Ezekiel 16:59-62; 36:25-32; and Joel 2:2-29. But the New covenant could not be inaugurated until Christ's covenant blood had been shed. Further, it is the *ascended* Christ who sent the Spirit (e.g., Jn. 14:25-28). That is to say, the glorified Jesus sent the Spirit (Jn. 7:39). This seems to be what the apostle is saying in Galatians 4:4-6:

> But when the fullness of the time had come, God sent forth His Son, born of a woman, born under the law, to redeem those who were under the law, that we might receive the adoption as sons. And because you are sons, God has sent forth the Spirit of His Son into your hearts, crying out, "Abba, Father!"

There is a chronological development here. God sends His Son, the Son redeems, then God sends forth the Spirit of His Son. The Spirit is sent after the Son is sent, which is to say, the reference to the Spirit in Galatians 4:6 is in consequence of what was accomplished by the sending of the Son. Hence, the Holy Spirit is sent *after* the death and resurrection of Christ to apply the results of the Son's work to sinners. The Church is "a dwelling place of God in the Spirit" (Eph. 2:22). With that foundation laid, we can move on to the link with Christ's resurrected life.

---

6 J. Christiaan Beker, *The Triumph of God*, 66-67.

7 Ibid., 127.

8 In saying this, I am not asserting that we are raised now. I only mean that the Church's union with Christ in new life is a union not with the dead Christ but with the exalted living Christ.

9 "Paul's claim that the church is the place where God's new covenant is being enacted is especially clear in his claim that believers enjoy distinctive new-covenant blessings. Primary among those blessings is the gift of the Spirit" (Douglas J. Moo, *A Theology of Paul and His Letters*, 465). See also David Gunn, "An Overview of New Covenant Passages: Ostensible and Actual," in *An Introduction to the New Covenant*, 52, 54. Although not agreeing with the whole piece, I commend this article for its careful analysis.

In Pauline theology, Christians have "died with Christ" (Rom. 6:8; Col. 3:3), but they have also been vitally linked to the risen Christ.[10] In the first place, there is a definite link with our justification: "Who was delivered up because of our offenses, and was raised because of our justification" (Rom. 4:25).

If Christ had to be raised for our justification, then it follows that the body comprised of justified believers (the Church) is a post-resurrection organism, and there is a dynamic relationship between Christ's resurrection and our new life "in Christ" through the Holy Spirit. This New covenant gift of the Spirit is what provides just a small foretaste of the resurrection life that awaits us. Hence, "He who raised Christ from the dead will also give life to your mortal bodies through His Spirit who dwells in you" (Rom. 8:11).

Similarly, Paul asserts that "we were buried with Him through baptism into death, that just as Christ was raised from the dead by the glory of the Father, even so we also should walk in newness of life" (Rom. 6:4). If we must be "buried with Him through baptism into [His] death," having been "crucified with Christ" (Gal. 6:14), then Christ had first to die for it to occur (even analogously).

The covenant dimension is essential to all of this. Paul saw himself and his co-workers as ministering "not... the letter but... the Spirit; for the letter kills, but the Spirit gives life" (2 Cor. 3:6 my emphasis). The New covenant is "the Holy Spirit covenant." It is the covenant that gives life (cf. Tit. 3:7).

The conclusion is inevitable; Christ had first to die to instigate the New covenant, then be raised from the dead "for our justification," and the Spirit of the New covenant had to come in a new way before the Church could exist! The Church has to be a resurrection-New covenant entity.[11]

Union with Christ

This truth, that the Church is a post-resurrection body, can be supported tangentially by other doctrines, such as our union with Christ. As we have already seen, the phrase "in Christ" and its variations, although it can have a number of meanings depending on the context, always signifies the close bond between the justified sinner and his Savior. This is seen in the Epistle to the Philippians (e.g., Phil. 1:11, 14; 3:9-10; 4:21). Marshall notes that in Philippians 3:10 "there is a great emphasis on the powerful effects of this union with Christ, in which the resurrection life of Christ is shared with Paul, now and after physical death."[12] The book of Colossians also speaks to this:

> If then you were raised with Christ, seek those things which are above, where Christ is, sitting at the right hand of God. Set your mind on things above, not

10 Interestingly, a search of Paul's use of the term "resurrection" (*anastasis*) reveals him looking forward to either comprehending it (Phil. 3:10-11), or else participating in its glory (Rom. 6:5; cf. Rom. 8:11; 10:9; 1 Cor. 6:14).

11 The Church is not the only New covenant entity. There is also the future remnant of Israel and the redeemed nations from the Tribulation, plus the redeemed from the Millennium. More of that later.

12 I. Howard Marshall, *New Testament Theology*, 354.

> on things on the earth. For you died, and your life is hidden with Christ in God. When Christ *who is* our life appears, then you also will appear with Him in glory (Col. 3:1-4).

This crucial text states the reality of Christians being "raised with Christ" (Col. 3:1), who is referred to as "our life" (Col. 3:4), and looks forward to our glorification. How could a believer be raised with Christ and be given His life before Christ had come to earth and lived and died and risen? Ephesians says, "Blessed *be* the God and Father of our Lord Jesus Christ, who has blessed us with every spiritual blessing in the heavenly *places* in Christ" (Eph. 1:3).

Our spiritual blessings are said to be in the heavenly places "in Christ" (cf. 1 Pet. 1:4). The prepositional phrase *en Christo* here refers to the sphere of those blessings,[13] as well as the *source* of blessings.[14]

> I have been crucified with Christ; it is no longer I who live, but Christ lives in me; and the *life* which I now live in the flesh I live by faith in the Son of God, who loved me and gave Himself for me (Gal. 2:20).

This passage is valuable not only as a summation of our new life in Christ but of our participation in His death ("crucified with Christ"). It also tells us that Christ lives in us; hence, this reflects the "Christ our life' language in Colossians 3:4. Paul's life is joined by faith to Christ's resurrected life. As George Beasley-Murray observes:

> For Paul, the former Pharisee who sought to live in total obedience to the Law and experienced it as a tyranny that held him in thrall, it was an inexpressible relief to know that in Christ's death and resurrection he was released for life in the new age. That element of the theology of redemption became for him an existential reality: his life under the domination of Law had ended, and life henceforth was a fellowship with the risen Christ; or, otherwise expressed, the risen Christ was the continuing source of his life.[15]

Again, how could all this be possible before the resurrection of the Son of God? This subject seems not to have been given the attention it deserves, perhaps because it fits very awkwardly into a one-people-of-God scenario.

After stating that Gentile believers have been "brought near" by Christ's blood (Eph. 2:13), Paul asserts that "the middle wall of separation" between Jews and Gentiles has been "broken down" at the cross so that Christ has created "in Himself one new man from the two, thus making peace" (Eph. 2:14-15). The context

13 I allow for that inasmuch as the spiritual dimension is not delimited by spatial considerations. Of course, the one does not exclude the other. 1 Cor. 15:22 is crucial here. See Herman Ridderbos, *Paul: An Outline of His Theology*, 60-64, although I do not espouse federal theology since I reject the theological covenants.

14 It is not a metaphor but a reality. Cf. James P. Ware, *Paul's Theology in Context*, 80-82.

15 G. R. Beasley-Murray, "Dying and Rising with Christ," in *Dictionary of Paul and His Letters*, 221. The author takes a universalist approach to some NT passages (e.g., 2 Cor. 5:14-17) which I cannot endorse. However, the above quote makes our point well.

is inescapable. The Body of Christ is "post-resurrectional," and therefore, the "new man," the Church, *cannot exist prior to the cross and resurrection.*

Although there might be some wiggle-room in Paul's language about the Church as a "mystery" not previously revealed (cf. Eph. 3:3-6), there is no ambiguity at all in Colossians 1:26—unless one wishes to dispute the fact that "Christ in you" (Col. 1:27) does not require us to be "in Christ." But that would, in any case, defang the contrary argument and would fly in the face of Paul's mention of "His body, which is the church" (Col. 1:24). Also, the Church is connected through the Spirit to Christ's resurrection life. This is Paul's point in Romans 6:4-11. It is augmented in Ephesians 1:15-23 and 2:4-6, 10.[16]

The only way around the conclusion that the Church is a post-resurrection "body" is to claim that OT saints somehow get freighted into the Church once it is established (thus preserving the one-people-of-God idea). But this means employing fictive exegesis of the pertinent texts and it cannot stand on its own two feet without a theological "just-so" story to support it. No, the Christian's life comes through the Spirit who connects us with the resurrected Jesus and baptizes us into His body, the Church (1 Cor. 12:13). The propitiation of our sins is dependent upon Christ's resurrection: "If Christ is not risen, your faith is futile; you are still in your sins!" (1 Cor. 15:13). And since the Church is a new thing not revealed in the OT, it cannot be read into the OT as if it comprised pre-resurrection saints as well as post-resurrection saints.

Dying and Rising with Christ

When he was a Pharisee, Paul (Saul of Tarsus) believed himself to be spiritual and God-focused (Phil. 3:4-6), but he was terribly mistaken. So much so that he acquiesced to the stoning of Stephen (Acts 22:20). But that is not how he saw himself after he trusted Jesus as the Christ (cf. Phil. 3:7-8). As a born-again child of God, he had a different opinion: "Therefore, from now on, we regard no one according to the flesh. Even though we have known Christ according to the flesh, yet now we know *Him thus* no longer" (2 Cor. 5:16).

This verse is not saying that Paul did not view human beings as physical beings, or that he paid no attention to the sin nature. Rather, as someone who had experienced a spiritual rebirth, he now understood both Jesus and humanity from another perspective. Coming to Christ "meant a turnaround in his perception of all things, including Christ," as Moo puts it.[17] This change in perception is because a real transformation has occurred: "Therefore, if anyone *is* in Christ, *he is* a new creation; old things have passed away; behold, all things have become new" (2 Cor. 5:17).[18]

16 OT saints are not said to be linked to the resurrection of Christ in this way.

17 Douglas J. Moo, *A Theology of Paul and His Letters*, 176-177.

18 This concept of dying with Christ and rising with Him as an ongoing experience is vital for Christian sanctification. As the apostle states in 2 Cor. 4:10, we are "always carrying about in the body the dying of the Lord Jesus, that the life of Jesus also may be manifested in our body." Thus, we are called to enter into His sufferings (Phil. 3:10; cf. 1:29). This is well brought out in Paul E. Miller, *J-Curve: Dying and Rising with Jesus in Everyday Life* (Wheaton, IL: 2019).

This great text declares the blessed and incontrovertible fact that the Christian is a "new creation" or "creature" as the KJV has it. This is not the same as saying that the New Creation has dawned, which I think is jumping to conclusions.[19] But as we have been removed from our connection to Adam ("in Adam all die," 1 Cor. 15:22a) and reconnected to Christ, the true image of God (2 Cor. 4:4; Col. 1:15), we are new in Him—in His life. We are being worked on (2 Cor. 3:18; Col. 3:10; cf. Eph. 2:10; Phil. 2:12-15; Tit. 2:14), and eventually we shall display the fully restored image (Rom. 8:29; 1 Cor. 15:49). But this progressive conformity of ourselves to the image of God in Christ is made possible by our connection to the death and resurrection of Christ, especially the latter. Accordingly, the Christian *ekklesia* is dependent on the resurrection. It follows then that this "one new man" of which the apostle speaks in Ephesians 2:15 is a post-resurrection entity and did not exist before the resurrection of Jesus.

To drive this home a little more, even though it is common to hear people say that sinners are saved by Christ's death, that is not strictly true. Paul clearly states that "if Christ is not risen, your faith *is* futile; you are still in your sins!" (1 Cor. 15:17), which means that the sacrificial death of Jesus on its own may save the believer from God's wrath, but it does not save us from our sins unto eternal life. This is where Christ's resurrection life comes in: "For if when we were enemies we were reconciled to God through the death of His Son, much more, having been reconciled, we shall be saved by His life" (Rom. 5:10, my emphasis).

The death of Christ reconciles the sinner to God so that he need not fear God's punishment of his sins, but the sinner still needs to be attached to the life of the risen Christ to enjoy everlasting bliss.[20] We are "saved by His life."[21]

Of course, it could be argued that all believers from all past ages before the empty tomb have now been connected to the resurrection and hence incorporated into the one Body, the Church. But as stated above, that is a mere assertion without proof.[22]

More academically see Michael J. Gorman, *Cruciformity: Paul's Narrative Spirituality of the Cross* (Grand Rapids: Eerdmans, 2001). As Gorman puts it in another publication, "Participation is not merely one aspect of Pauline theology and spirituality, or a supplement to something more fundamental; rather, it is at the very heart of Paul's thinking and living. Pauline soteriology...is inherently participatory and transformative" (Michael J. Gorman, *Participating in Christ: Explorations in Paul's Theology and Spirituality* [Grand Rapids: Baker, 2019], xviii). This does not indicate wholesale endorsement of Gorman, but the matters he raises have been too often lost in out post-Enlightenment world. Living out the death and resurrection of Jesus in our lives, which are often disfigured by hurt and pain and plain unfairness, brings Christian discipleship back to earth. Important aspects of this teaching are to be found in some Puritan writers like Joseph Hall, Henry Scougal, and John Bunyan.

19 As e.g., Thomas R. Schreiner, *Paul: Apostle of God's Glory in Christ*, 144.

20 Herman Ridderbos, *Paul: An Outline of His Theology*, 538-539.

21 Hence, it is incorrect to claim that the sinner was saved at the cross *if complete salvation is in view*. The sinner is pardoned in light of the cross, but Christ's resurrection-life is the necessary precondition for Christians to be glorified.

22 In my opinion, OT Jewish saints will be part of the reconstituted nation of Israel in the Kingdom. OT non-Jewish saints will be part of the saved nations in the Kingdom, and the Church will make up a third part of humanity. As will be made clearer when we get to Revelation 21–22, I hold to a triad of saved humanity in the Kingdom and New Creation: Israel, the Nations, and the Church. This reflects the Divine Trinity so that the constitution of humanity will mirror the three-in-one Creator.

The natural way to take Paul's teaching is to understand it as referring to the creation of a *new organism* made up of all those who have believed subsequent to His resurrection from the dead (cf. Col. 2:12). This corresponds to Colossians 1:18, where Christ is called "the firstborn from the dead," where Paul's focus is the Church ("He is the head of the body, the church").

Water Baptism

Any consideration of water baptism in the NT will run into the issue of its proper subjects and mode. Advocates of Covenant Theology divide into two camps over this. Dutch Reformed and Presbyterian believers hold that an infant is included in the covenant of grace on the basis of solidarity with believing parents.[23] Reformed Baptists rightly stress that the NT only recognizes saved people as recipients of baptism, but they also hold to a covenant of grace (although they understand it slightly differently).[24] In either case, they both believe that water baptism is a figurative expression of the subject's union with the death and resurrection of Christ.[25]

Although both types of Covenant Theology wrongly tie baptism to the covenant of grace, which is not a covenant explicitly found in Scripture, they at least recognize its relation to the baptism with the Holy Spirit, even though their theologizing of the covenants does not permit more than a single people of God from Eden to New Creation.[26] From the point of view of our understanding of the New covenant in Christ, water baptism is not only a figure of Spirit baptism (1 Cor. 12:13),[27] but it images the Christian's connection to the resurrection, and, in so doing, shows that the Church is a resurrection organism.[28]

Inheritors of the Kingdom

In an anticipatory passage in John 14, Jesus promises His disciples (or, more accurately, those who are alive when He returns) that He is preparing a place for us. This place is in heaven since it is to heaven that Jesus ascended in Acts 1:11. Jesus stated, "If I go and prepare a place for you, I will come again and receive you to Myself; that

23 O. Palmer Robertson, *The Christ of the Covenants*, 280.

24 See Pascal Denault, *The Distinctiveness of Baptist Covenant Theology* (Birmingham, AL: Solid Ground, 2016), 32.

25 See Gerald Bray, *God Is Love: A Biblical and Systematic Theology* (Wheaton, IL: Crossway, 2012), 635.

26 For a critique of Covenant Theology, see Paul Martin Henebury, *Deciphering Covenant Theology* (forthcoming).

27 In line with many others, I interpret the baptisms of Rom. 6:1-5; Eph. 4:5; Gal. 3:27; and Col. 3:5 as baptism with the Spirit. For more in-depth treatments I recommend *Believer's Baptism: Sign of the New Covenant in Christ*, ed. Thomas R. Schreiner and Shawn D. Wright (Nashville: B&H, 2007), although I do not hold to Baptist Covenant Theology. See also Matt Waymeyer, *A Biblical Critique of Infant Baptism* (The Woodlands, TX: Kress Biblical Resources, 2008); and Peter Goeman, *The Baptism Debate: Understanding and Evaluating Reformed Infant Baptism* (Raleigh, NC: Sojourner Press, 2023).

28 See Charles C. Ryrie, *Biblical Theology of the New Testament* (Dubuque, IA: ECS Ministries, 2005), 176, 183.

where I am, *there* you may be also" (Jn. 14:3). But how does that fit with Paul's language about Christians being inheritors of the Kingdom to come, if that indeed is a valid inference?[29]

The first thing to say is that when the NT writers refer to the Kingdom, they usually have in mind neither the present age nor the New Heavens and New Earth. Although many would object to that statement, I do not think it is difficult to prove. As to the first assertion, that the Kingdom is not the present age, this can be shown by texts such as 1 Corinthians 4:8: "You are already full! You are already rich! You have reigned as kings without us—and indeed I could wish you did reign, that we also might reign with you!"

What could be clearer than the fact that the apostle Paul did *not* think that the Kingdom had come? If we are to one day reign with Christ (2 Tim. 2:12; cf. Rev. 5:10), then the apostle was being ironic, sarcastic even, in addressing the Corinthians as if they were reigning now.

A little further on in the epistle,[30] Paul implies that they (and we) shall inherit the Kingdom (seen as future) so long as they are not hypocrites, which will come out in their lives. He says something similar in Galatians 5:21 and Ephesians 5:5. Then, in 1 Corinthians 15:50, he says that "flesh and blood[31] cannot inherit the kingdom of God; nor does corruption inherit incorruption." We have not yet received "incorruption," so by Paul's logic, neither have we inherited the Kingdom.[32]

Inheritance in Heaven?

It might be argued from Colossians 1:12 that our inheritance is in heaven.[33] This would make "the kingdom of the Son of His love" in the next verse (Col. 1:13) a reference to heaven also. But the context indicates a possible eschatological sense (see Col. 1:27-29).[34] In light of the fact that the NT routinely teaches a future Kingdom of Christ on earth (Matt. 13:41-43; 19:28; Mk. 14:25; Lk. 13:29; 19:11; 21:31; 22:16, 18; Acts 1:6; 1 Cor. 4:8; 2 Thess. 1:5; Jam. 2:5), it is unlikely the apostle is opposing that testimony. And this opinion is given extra support from Romans 8:

> For I consider that the sufferings of this present time are not worthy to be compared with the glory which shall be revealed in us. For the earnest expectation of the creation eagerly waits for the revealing of the sons of God. For the creation was subjected to futility, not willingly, but because of Him who subjected it in hope; because the creation itself also will be delivered from the

29 It should be noted that every time Paul relates inheritance and kingdom, it is a negatively charged passage (e.g., 1 Cor. 6:9-10; Eph. 5:5; Gal. 5:21). Even 1 Cor. 15:50 does not positively state we will inherit the Kingdom of God.

30 1 Cor. 6:9-10.

31 By "flesh and blood" I understand him to mean our mortal bodies as explained in 1 Cor. 15:42-49.

32 This is close to what we see also in Eph. 1:14, 18 and Col. 3:24.

33 "Giving thanks to the Father who has qualified us to be partakers of the inheritance of the saints in the light" (Col. 1:12).

34 Michael J. Vlach, *He Will Reign Forever*, 448-450.

> bondage of corruption into the glorious liberty of the children of God. For we know that the whole creation groans and labors with birth pangs together until now. Not only that, but we also who have the firstfruits of the Spirit, even we ourselves groan within ourselves, eagerly waiting for the adoption, the redemption of our body (Rom. 8:18-23).

This is an extremely important eschatological passage because it teaches that there is a this-earthly glory both for the Christian and for the earth itself. It meshes perfectly with passages like Matthew 19:28 and Acts 3:19-21. Clearly it is not referring to the new heavens and new earth which replace this one (2 Pet. 3:12-13; Rev. 20:11; 21:1; cf. Matt. 24:35). It is a matter of debate as to when this earth "will be delivered from the bondage of corruption" (Rom. 8:21). In this writer's view, either Paul is writing hyperbolically in anticipation of the coming Millennium, or he envisages a two-stage transformation which will see the curse eventually lifted.[35] I side with the former position because the New Creation is not this one, and Paul is writing about this creation. During the Millennial Kingdom, the power of King Jesus that was displayed in miniature in His miraculous healings (Mk. 1:21-45), His overturning the claims of death (Mk. 5:21-44), and His stilling of the wind and the waves (Mk. 4:35-41) will be extended throughout the whole world, suppressing the effects of the curse while refitting the earth to display its Edenic beauty (see e.g., Psa. 50:2; Isa. 11:6-9; 32:16-17; 51:3; Hos. 2:18-23; Amos 9:11-15; Mic. 4:1-4; Ezek. 36:35). This imposed *shalom* will usher in universal joy (Isa. 35:1-2; Psa. 48:1-14).[36]

The Judgment Seat of Christ

Paul's eschatology is notable for certain passages that speak about a judgment of the Christian's works.

> For no other foundation can anyone lay than that which is laid, which is Jesus Christ. Now if anyone builds on this foundation with gold, silver, precious stones, wood, hay, straw, each one's work will become clear; for the Day will declare it, because it will be revealed by fire; and the fire will test each one's work, of what sort it is. If anyone's work which he has built on it endures, he will receive a reward. If anyone's work is burned, he will suffer loss; but he himself will be saved, yet so as through fire (1 Cor. 3:11-15).

This passage is written to Christians (whose foundation is Christ, v. 11) and concerns their "work" (mentioned four times). Those who have not built well (i.e., whose service for Christ has been poor) will still be saved, but only just (v. 15). Those who have built well (whose service has been good) will be rewarded (v. 14). It appears that this

35 For a good exposition of this passage see Matt Waymeyer, *Amillennialism and the Age to Come*, 139-145.

36 In the New Heavens and Earth, Christ's power will not be needed to constantly overcome the forces of the curse, thus sustaining the Peaceable Kingdom. According to Rev. 22:3 there is no curse in the New Creation.

bema as Paul calls it in 2 Corinthians 5:10 (NASB),[37] is where rewards are received or lost. In 2 Timothy 1:18 Paul hopes that the Lord will have mercy on Onesiphorus (cf. 2 Tim. 1:16) "in that Day." What "Day" is that? The link with the *bema* of 2 Corinthians 5 is plausible, as is the link to 1 Corinthians 3.[38] It appears that Paul is teaching that Christians will be judged by Christ around the time He returns. Whether this "appearing" (*parousia*) refers to the pretribulational rapture or to the second coming proper is uncertain.[39] My guess is it will occur while the seven-year Tribulation is happening on earth. I do not think we are helped by going to Revelation 4 and identifying the twenty-four elders as representing the Church (vv. 4, 10).[40] To me, this is an unprovable theory (even if it turns out to be true).

This judgment seat of Christ is where we Christians "must appear" to give account for our service to God. I have made the claim throughout that Christians are parties to the New covenant. Therefore, it seems that our loyalty to the terms of the New covenant will be the basis for our judgment.

Teleology and Eschatology in Paul

Scripture reveals a continuous movement from creation to New Creation, with God's providential guidance and governance directing everything that comes to pass or will come to pass, particularly the covenantal trajectory of history. In the Bible, teleology (purpose/goal) and eschatology (the movement towards the goal, especially the end of things) are intertwined and ought not to be disconnected. We can see this in Paul.

The Plan of God "From the Foundation of the World"

In Ephesians 1:3-4 the apostle uses a phrase which crops up in several other places in the NT. These verses include the expression "from the foundation of the world" in connection to the believer's sanctification. The phrase "before the foundation of the world" can mean something like "from ancient times," as it appears to do in Luke 11:50 or Hebrews 9:26,[41] although it can also mean "before the world was created" (Jn. 17:24; cf. 1 Cor. 2:7; Eph. 3:9). Here are some representative verses from elsewhere in the NT:

> He indeed was foreordained before the foundation of the world, but was manifest in these last times for you (1 Pet. 1:20).

37 *Tou bematou tou Christou* ("the judgment seat of Christ"). Rom. 14:10 is similar but refers to the judgment seat of God.

38 Another text comes to mind: "Finally, there is laid up for me the crown of righteousness, which the Lord, the righteous Judge, will give to me on that Day, and not to me only but also to all who have loved His appearing" (2 Tim. 4:8). In this passage, the timing of "the Day" coincides with the Lord's appearing.

39 On balance I am a pretribulationist, although not a dogmatic one.

40 My thoughts on the matter are well stated in Robert L. Thomas's analysis of the 24 elders in *Revelation 1-7: An Exegetical Commentary* (Chicago: Moody, 1992), 344-349.

41 See also e.g., Jn. 9:32; Acts 3:21; Rom. 16:25.

> All who dwell on the earth will worship him, whose names have not been written in the Book of Life of the Lamb slain from the foundation of the world (Rev. 13:8; cf. Rev. 17:8).

> Then the King will say to those on His right hand, "Come, you blessed of My Father, inherit the kingdom prepared for you from the foundation of the world" (Matt. 25:34).

When approaching eschatology, it is good to be alert to one's presuppositions. The presuppositions of the present writer are grounded in the covenants of God, firstly as understood from an OT perspective and then into the NT in continuum with that perspective, although with consideration given to the tension between the first and second comings (cf. Matt. 12:28). Again, I want to point out that those covenants cannot be reinterpreted, transformed, typologized, redirected, or spiritualized. They are dug in and stubbornly resist the hermeneutical jazz that they have been subjected to. If we proceed in tune with them, we shall have our interpretive bearing.

What then are we to make of the phrase before or from "the foundation of the world"? I am interested in Paul's use here, but it may not be out of place to survey the other uses. In 1 Peter 1:20 the idea is that Christ was projected to be incarnated in this fallen world at a specific point in earth's history. This reminds us of Paul's words in Galatians 4:4, "When the fullness of the time had come, God sent forth His Son, born of a woman." This coming of the Son of God as the God-man was the key piece of the Creation Project that was foreknown in every detail before the world began. The revealing of this truth to humanity is what Paul speaks to in 1 Corinthians 2:7, where he speaks of a mystery that was revealed, "which God ordained before the ages for our glory." This, in turn, dovetails with the mention of Christ as a "Lamb slain since before the foundation of the world" (Rev. 13:8). Our "glory" was achieved through the willing self-sacrifice of Jesus and His subsequent resurrection.[42] In the same manner, the Kingdom that was prepared for the saints (Matt. 25:34) is another piece in the same comprehensive purpose. Hence, "the dispensation of the fullness of times" in Ephesians 1:10 seems to be a way of referring to this cumulative purpose coming to pass.

The Church's Goal "in Christ"

The book of Ephesians contains a number of passages describing the *telos* of the Church. In Ephesians 1:3-6 Paul writes:

> Blessed *be* the God and Father of our Lord Jesus Christ, who has blessed us with every spiritual blessing in the heavenly *places* in Christ, just as He chose us in Him before the foundation of the world, that we should be holy and without blame before Him in love, having predestined us to adoption as sons

42 If we take this truth and combine it with what Paul says in Rom. 8, we get a better understanding of why he so confidently asserts what he does in Rom. 8:1, 11, 15-18, 23, 28-30, and 31-39.

> by Jesus Christ to Himself, according to the good pleasure of His will, to the praise of the glory of His grace, by which He made us accepted in the Beloved.

In this passage, we are given a purpose of the Church.[43] In The apostle raises an invocation to the Father who chose the Christian saints to be set aside through righteousness to participate in loving fellowship as adopted sons. But he adds a location or sphere "in" which this new life is to be lived: *en Christo* or "in Christ." Porter writes, "The most likely explanation of what Paul means by being "in Christ" is that one falls within the sphere, power, or control of Christ."[44]

This all has more cosmic implications, which again point to how indispensable Christ is to the Creation Project.[45] Without Him, the whole plan would collapse into incoherence. Verse 10 makes it clear that the term comprehends "all things in heaven and earth," of which the Church is but one piece. We as Christians have been predestined to participate in this great purpose,[46] although our entrance into it is not all ahead of us; it concerns us now. Therefore, we ought to see ourselves as working out a little part of the grand scheme in our own lives. As "sons" we represent our Father by our pursuit of Him in this world. There is an election to "work out" (cf. Phil. 2:13)[47] and a direction to go in. The believer is a stranger and a pilgrim in this world, and he lives his life by the Son of God, trying to walk in the Spirit, not in the flesh (Heb. 11:13; 1 Pet. 2:11; Gal. 2:20; 5:16).

From 1 Thessalonians 4:16 we hear about "the dead in Christ." Paul means that those believers in the Church who have died and gone to be with Him in heaven are situated in Him still. This throws light upon Paul's language about "the whole family in heaven and earth" (Eph. 3:15). The "family" is the Church, and it is made up of those Christians now in heaven and those presently living on the earth.[48]

---

43 Paul in Ephesians is not concerned with the local church but with its universal character; the big scheme as it were. It is well known that Eph. 1:3-14 constitute one long sentence in the Greek. The sentence turns to each Person in the Godhead (the Father [1:4-6]; the Son [1:7-12]; the Spirit [1:13-14]). I cannot go into the intricacies of the passage in this work, but it deserves careful examination.

44 Stanley E. Porter, *The Apostle Paul: His Thought, and Letters*, 101.

45 "The divine purpose for creation, redemption and the consummation of all things is comprehended within the "sphere" of Christ (Eph. 1:3-10)" (M. Seifrid, "In Christ," in *Dictionary of Paul and His Letters*, 434).

46 This passage has been used by Calvinists to teach election to salvation. However, whatever the merits of that view (and there are some), it does not appear that Paul had that in mind here. The election is to those things entailed by our salvation: "that we should be holy and without blame before Him in love" (Eph. 1:4). God "predestined us to adoption as sons by Jesus Christ to Himself" (Eph. 1:5), not salvation itself. That is, the election is to things awaiting us in Christ not to getting us there.

47 Phil. 2:13 is directed to those already saved. It does not address how one becomes saved. Verse 14 ought to make Paul's meaning clear. He is speaking about the believer's sanctification.

48 It is worth mentioning that nowhere is the term "in Christ" applied to OT saints. This no doubt is connected to the differing work of the Spirit between pre- and post-advent economies (cf. Jn. 14:17).

"The Dispensation of the Fullness of the Times"

I made reference to this phrase from Ephesians 1:10 above. Paul is extremely concerned about where everything is heading, about where God will bring His Creation Project and what that consummation will be. Yet he also sees clearly that the Creation Project is in motion as we speak. Before the Athenian intellectuals at Areopagus, he upset the apple cart by stating, "And He has made from one blood every nation of men to dwell on all the face of the earth, and has determined their preappointed times and the boundaries of their dwellings" (Acts 17:26).

This pronouncement, which would have been quite insulting to Athenian ears, portrays God as the sole determiner of the rise and fall of kingdoms and epochs, including Greece. First, in contradiction to Athenian belief that they were somehow preeminent among the races of the earth, the apostle told them that they were just one part of one human race, no matter what color, caste, economic status, or educational level they may be. The earth is made for mankind to dwell on. This statement raised the status of all men and harkens back to our original creation as those made in the image and likeness of God (Gen. 1:26). But Paul continued by saying that God has also "determined their pre-appointed times and the boundaries of their dwellings." This must not be interpreted as a limitation on travel or even immigration, but it does show that, for the most part, people groups are where God has appointed them. Hence, there is a purpose, though mysterious, to the places and the times that people find themselves in. This reveals that an inscrutable Reason lies behind history.

But Paul's main emphasis was on the future reconciliation of all things to God. This was signaled by Christ's resurrection, a new creation in the old world. One of the best expressions of this eschatological purpose is in Ephesians 1:10: "That in the dispensation of the fullness of the times He [God] might gather together in one all things in Christ, both which are in heaven and which are on earth—in Him."

The "Christocentricity" of this verse is as complete as it can be. In some time that the apostle calls "the dispensation of the fullness of times," God the Father has purposed to bring together everything in creation, both in heaven and upon earth, "in Christ." The future of the created order is not merely a picture of Christ sitting upon a throne and ruling and subduing land, sea, and sky, great and small, as satisfying as that is to our mind's eye. It is something entirely more focused and deliberate. It is, as far as I can comprehend it, the mind-blowing truth that the entire created realm will be so vitally connected to Jesus Christ, the Son of God, that He will be the heart of it all, from Sun and stars to mountain glen and bordered garden, from the gigantic ocean beasts to the smallest insect, it will all answer to Him in some way. A Creation for Christ in which we shall dwell, imaging Him.

This is the biggest possible understanding of a Christological world. Not a world where all is Christ, for every man and woman is made to be who they are and to express their lives as individual children of God. But a world suffused *with* Christ in some tangible but inexpressible way. The Jewish Messiah and King, the Ruler of the nations, the Head of the Church. God receives glory not just through the cross, but through the life of the God-Man coursing through the fibers of creation.

This, therefore, is not a verse that can be confined to the Church. Yes, Paul has the Church's participation in this coming era at the forefront of his mind (e.g., Eph. 1:22-23; 2:4-7, 19-22; cf. Col. 1:18), but here especially, the vision is wider and all-comprehending; it includes the whole creation of God of which the Church is but a part.[49]

What then is "the dispensation of the fullness of times" (Eph. 1:10)?[50] Is it a reference to the Millennial Kingdom?[51] It is not easy to say. In the coming "mediatorial" Kingdom that will be set up when Jesus returns in fulfillment of specific OT prophecies, the situation is blissful yet not perfect. Sin and death will be present, although not in such overwhelming power as they are today (e.g., Isa. 65:20; Zech. 8:4-5). At the close of the thousand-year Kingdom, Satan, who has been imprisoned for the duration, will be released and will gather a large army to march against Jerusalem (Rev. 20:7-10), being utterly defeated in the process (cf. Gen. 3:15).

Alternatively, "the dispensation of the fullness of times" might well be Paul's way of referring to the New Heavens and Earth (Rev. 21-22). Few could dispute the appropriateness of the designation. The Creation Project culminates in the sinless and eternal New Creation. From then on, we enter a brand-new created realm. The "times" in this scenario would refer to the history of the world, from the Fall to the final defeat of Satan and the ending of the curse. Therefore, the term "dispensation" in these scenarios either speaks of the Millennial Kingdom or the New Creation. If it is the latter, then the phrase really does not have within it a meaning like "a period of time."

Of course, "the dispensation of the fullness of times" could also be Paul's way of speaking about the new era inaugurated by the messianic reign, which extends from the Millennium into the eternal state. If this view is correct, then what was just said about the word "dispensation" applies here too. Even more so, because we would have two phases combined the final "dispensation."[52] Whatever the phrase refers to, it is a time in the future when the Father pulls everything within the sphere of the Person and work of Christ, the *Logos* (Jn. 1:1-3).

The Teleology of the Church

This book is centered on the covenants of God and the structure that they provide for understanding the Bible. As I have said in the Introduction, once we come to the NT, and particularly when we arrive at those books which presuppose the death and resurrection of Jesus, one covenant comes to dominate—the New covenant. This is not to suggest that the Abrahamic and Davidic covenants are absent from these books (contra many Reformed biblical theologians). The main theme is salvation in Christ

49 See e.g., Robert L. Saucy, *The Case for Progressive Dispensationalism*, 154, 165.

50 Harold W. Hoehner sees it as "talking about God's activity of administration, as all the verbs describing his activities make clear. Hence, God purposed in Christ, in the administration (or carrying out) of the fullness of times, to unite under one head all things in Christ" (*Ephesians*, 218). Notice that on this view, the standard dispensational conception of a "dispensation" as a stewardship that a man (or men) are under breaks down.

51 This is the view of e.g., Elliott Johnson, *A Dispensational Biblical Theology*, 490.

52 This again shows up the uncertainty connected to the term "dispensation" and casts doubt on the technical sense required by Dispensationalism, at least here.

and its corollaries like inheritance, glory, and kingdom. Salvation is required for the other aspects to be fulfilled.

Just to be clear, I am not saying the New covenant *replaces* the other unilateral divine covenants,[53] but it does eclipse them in that it is the covenant that provides the condition upon which the promises of the other covenants can be brought about. Hence, my position is that the NT writers are preoccupied with the New covenant's effects, even if they do not always refer to it directly. My contention is that the close affinity between Jesus Christ and the New covenant makes it the avenue along which the *telos* or purpose of the Church runs. Notwithstanding those who resist the implication, the Church is the first New covenant society. The remnant nation of Israel will be the second New covenant institution, even though the New covenant itself was predicted in direct relation to them in Jeremiah 31, etc.

As a New covenant institution, the Church is set upon the rails of the teleology and eschatology of the New covenant. This is to say, it is being directed towards its goal in Christ. This goal is first realized in the Kingdom of God as it is experienced in Christ's subduing of the cursed earth in the Millennium and then in the New Heavens and Earth where there will be no more curse (Rev. 22:3). More will have to be said about this, but I think this is the place to briefly enter into the subject of the Church's function in the Creation Project as far as I understand it.

The Church and the Creation Project

I want to state emphatically that I do not hold to a conception of the Church[54] that makes it a parenthesis in the Bible's story. Some of the confusion about this may stem from laying out the wrong map of the story itself. Let me explain.

The biblical narrative does not start with Israel but with two people and their progeny, from whom all of us come. After the great flood, God narrows this line of descendants down to Noah and his family, and the covenant program is born. From the Table of Nations, which is created out of successive generations of men (Gen. 10), God selects Abraham and the seed of promise through Isaac, Jacob, and the tribes of "Israel" that are related to them. Israel is God's elect nation (Deut. 7:6-9; Isa. 45:4; cf. Isa. 41:8; 44:1; Rom. 11:5), and the covenants God has made with Israel will be fulfilled just as God has promised. On the timeline of Scripture, these peoples and events do not all begin together. Israel's timeline does not kick everything off. It comes at the time predetermined by God in the Creation Project. So it is with the NT Church. It could only come into being after the death of Christ. Its "startup" was also predestined in the grand plan of God, just as Israel's was earlier. The dawn of the Church ought to be seen as another phenomenon along the great timeline of the Bible, not a parenthesis in the ongoing story of Israel. In Christ the two temporarily overlap (cf. Eph. 2:14-16), but they will separate again in respect to the covenant blessings to be inherited by each society of saints.

53 I think it does replace the Mosaic covenant, though again, there are aspects of that covenant that are universal.

54 See in chapter 1, "Is the Church a Parenthesis in the Plan of God?"

The Christian Church then was integrated into the Creation Project in its time, not to replace Israel, nor to extend Israel, nor to digress from the story of Israel, but as another manifestation of God's expression of His glory in man.[55] First of all, the Church was foreordained:

> Blessed *be* the God and Father of our Lord Jesus Christ, who has blessed us with every spiritual blessing in the heavenly *places* in Christ, just as He chose us in Him before the foundation of the world, that we should be holy and without blame before Him in love (Eph. 1:3-4).

The "us" in this passage refers to Christians in the Church. To be "in Christ" is to be in the Church in Pauline parlance.[56] Paul is saying that Christian holiness in love is what God chose us for "in Him" (i.e., in union with Christ).[57] The blessings, plainly enough, are "spiritual" (*pneumatikos*), kept for us "in the heavenlies," although we should note that they are "in Christ" (Eph. 1:3). But our election to blamelessness is also "in Christ." What this means is that there is an alignment in God's preordained plan for our lives to the spiritual blessings that await us—a *telos*.

The Bride of Christ

Linked to the above is the concept of the *ekklesia* as espoused to Christ (cf. 2 Cor. 11:2). In Revelation 19:9 reference is made to "the marriage supper of the Lamb." This *appears* to be between Christ and the Church, although not everyone sees it that way. Two chapters later, we come across the New Jerusalem, the new city that descends from heaven to the new earth, and of this city it is said, "Then one of the seven angels who had the seven bowls filled with the seven last plagues came to me and talked with me, saying, 'Come, I will show you the bride, the Lamb's wife'" (Rev. 21:9). Scholars have identified "the Lamb's wife" as the Church, although technically speaking, if the connection is right, New Jerusalem is the city that accommodates the Church.[58] Paul's concern in 2 Corinthians 11 is pure doctrine and pure life for those espoused to Christ.

---

55 I shall contend that there are three such expressions: Israel, the Church, and the nations, representing a triad of peoples which are also a people reflecting God's triunity.

56 For example, Richard C. Gamble, *The Whole Counsel of God: Volume 2, The Full Revelation of God* (Phillipsburg, IL: P&R, 2018), 600.

57 I do not in all good conscience think that this passage is rightly used to by those who interpret the "choosing" to be about who is <u>*to be*</u> in Christ. The apostle's concern here is with how those in Christ are to reflect God's character.

58 Many dispensationalist scholars disagree. Walvoord believes that the New Jerusalem "will have among its citizens not only the church... but also Israel, or the saints of other ages, whether in the Old Testament or in the tribulation period" (John F. Walvoord, *The Revelation of Jesus Christ* [London: Marshall, Morgan & Scott, 1966], 322). But if all the saints of all the ages are citizens of New Jerusalem (as he appears to say), who are the "nations" who dwell on the new earth? His comments about the "kings" and "nations" of Rev. 21:24-26 seem confusing to me (Ibid., 326-328). A more thorough analysis, which parses out this approach, is Tony Garland, *A Testimony of Jesus Christ: A Commentary on the Book of Revelation*, Vol. 2 (Camano Island, WA: SpiritAndTruth, 2004), 159, 166-169. I shall say more about this matter when I comment on the book of Revelation.

Another text which is useful for this teaching is Ephesians 5:22-33. This text is often used in marriage counseling to draw a comparison between the husband-wife bond and the Christ-Church bond. That is to say, it has been asserted that the Church is (or will be) related to Christ as the wife is related to her husband. I agree that this is strongly implied in the passage, and it helps to tie the Church and Christ together in a marriage relationship, although the marriage is yet to be, according to John in Revelation 19:7-9 (and perhaps Rev. 21:2, 9-10).

If it is right to believe the Church is the Bride of Christ, several suggestive things follow. The first is that of privilege. Christians are a part of a society of people who will have a special relationship with the second Person of the Trinity. But on the heels of this statement, another matter rushes in. That second issue is the question of whether the marriage of Christ—and there is to be a "marriage supper" (Rev. 19:9)—is to be equated with the marriage of Yahweh to Israel in the OT.

There are several problems with equating these two "marriages." The chief one is that the Hebrew Bible declares that Yahweh was already married to the nation of Israel (who are literal descendants of Abraham, Isaac, and Jacob) and means to remarry Israel.

> "Return, O backsliding children," says the LORD; "for I am married to you. I will take you, one from a city and two from a family, and I will bring you to Zion" (Jer. 3:14).

> For your Maker *is* your husband,
> The LORD of hosts *is* His name;
> And your Redeemer *is* the Holy One of Israel;
> He is called the God of the whole earth (Isa. 54:5).

Reading these texts, along with Hosea's prophecy,[59] shows that Israel was indeed "married" to Yahweh, at least at one point (cf. Exod. 24; cf. Ezek. 16:8), and that He fully intends to remarry Israel for all time (God hates divorce).[60] In the meantime, there are plenty of words of condemnation about Israel's shameful spiritual adultery. The main thing not to be missed here is that, unlike Israel's marriage relationship with Yahweh in the OT, the Church's relationship to Christ is not yet one of "husband and wife" but rather of an engagement *to be married* in the future.

I conclude, therefore, that Yahweh's marriage to the harlot wife Israel (who will be fully forgiven and restored) is not and cannot be one and the same as the upcoming marriage of Christ and the Church. We must face the fact that Yahweh, God the Father, has a bride, the remnant of ethnic Israel as per the covenants, and that Christ has a different bride, the Jew-Gentile Church. While it is true that both entities are related eternally to God through the New covenant, this does not mean that the entities merge into one another. I argue that the New covenant brings salvation ("Jesus"), but salvation does not erase the Israel-Church distinction in the age to come.

59 See my *The Words of the Covenant*, Vol. 1, 232-233.
60 See Isa. 54:6-8.

One more thing. Those interpreters who believe that God's marriage to Israel in the OT is the same as Christ's marriage to the Church do so because they hold that the Church has either replaced national Israel or (more commonly in our day) that the Church is Israel extended as a people—it is the "new Israel." The problem with the two views is that they have not come to terms with the crucial association of the Church with the resurrection of Jesus. Nor have they taken seriously the truth that the Church is not remarried, whereas the nation of Israel is to be remarried (Jer. 3:6-10; Hos. 2:1-23).

When Christ Delivers Up the Kingdom to the Father

There is a strategic passage in 1 Corinthians that bears upon both the eschatology and teleology of the Bible. That text is found in 1 Corinthians 15:20-28. It requires a little time to think through, although I will confess at the outset that the passage may act as an exemplar of the influence of theological predispositions in hermeneutics.[61] Because the thought is condensed, it is easy to jump to conclusions about what each verse means. It starts with a theological preamble: "But now Christ is risen from the dead, *and* has become the firstfruits of those who have fallen asleep. For since by man *came* death, by Man also *came* the resurrection of the dead. For as in Adam all die, even so in Christ all shall be made alive" (1 Cor. 15:20-22).

Paul tells us that the resurrected Christ is only the first to rise among a host of others who have met death, euphemistically referred to as having "fallen asleep." The OT idea of "firstfruits" was that the first and best of the crop was given to God the Provider. It symbolized both the pledge of a full harvest to come and the honor of God's sovereignty over the harvest. Paul says death is linked to Adam while resurrection life is linked to Jesus. All that are in Adam will die and remain in death. All who are counted in Christ will be "made alive." A saint may be connected physically to Adam and the curse, but because they are counted righteous in Christ, death cannot hold them.

It is crucial to the Christian Gospel and the whole Creation Project that the resurrection of the dead, procured as it is by the sufferings on Calvary's cross, be accomplished by a man. Jesus was and is the Christ, and the Christ is a man for men. Despite His eternal provenance and His spectacular accomplishments, which go far beyond anything done by Abraham, Moses, David, or Elijah, this Man died cruelly, detested by the powerful, misunderstood, feared, or even ignored by the majority; yet by Him (and Him alone) comes the resurrection of the dead!

I shall look more deeply into the cosmic implications of the resurrection further on, but I want to note here how death through a man (Adam) is reversed and

61 Exegesis is not an exact science. This statement may easily be tested against any number of passages as they are interpreted by an equal number of scholars. In this case, I am using Gordon Fee and N. T. Wright as "counter exegetes" to my position. In doing this, I am well aware that where I differ from them (and them from me) I am encouraged in my line of thinking by my adoption of a certain premillennial eschatology. The best I can do, therefore, is to provide exegetical reasons for my interpretation of the passage. I cannot be too dogmatic. That will settle nothing.

augmented (by glorification) through a Man. "But each one in his own order: Christ the firstfruits, afterward those *who are* Christ's at His coming" (1 Cor. 15:23). Paul speaks about a resurrection order.[62] Jesus Christ is the first, and His resurrection prefigures ours, although it happened many centuries ago. As indicated above, the OT concept of the "firstfruits" of the crop is used by the apostle here. Firstfruits is "the first sheaf of the harvest which guarantees that there will be more to come."[63] Hence, the health of the firstfruits signals the health of the whole crop to come. As Paul will elaborate at the end of the chapter, the glory that comes to the saints upon their resurrection corresponds directly to the glory that was Christ's when He was raised.[64] This translates into the sort of status befitting sons of God (however unworthy). Paul declares, "We shall...bear the image of the heavenly *Man*" (1 Cor. 15:49). This "bearing" refers to a new way of existence: the eschatological real us! The completed saint!

Then we get a mention of the "end," which is qualified by the way of instrumentation: "Then *comes* the end, when He delivers the kingdom to God the Father, when He puts an end to all rule and all authority and power. For He must reign till He has put all enemies under His feet" (1 Cor. 15:24-25, my emphasis). Christ's giving up of the Kingdom to His Father occurs after He has reigned and "put all enemies under His feet." I take this to include not only Death, but the great archenemy of God, Satan.

Now, the real question is about the Kingdom. Is Paul saying that Jesus is ruling now? That is the interpretation of most exegetes. Fee dogmatically claims the passage proves that Christ is reigning now.[65] But is such confidence justified? Verse 25 says, "He must reign till..." There is an imperative here. It is essential for Christ to reign. The reason Paul gives is that He must bring all His enemies (actual persons or beings) into submission. The allusion is to Psalm 110:1-2: "The LORD said to my Lord, sit at My right hand, till I make Your enemies Your footstool. The LORD shall send the rod of Your strength out of Zion. Rule in the midst of Your enemies!" (my emphasis).

Notice how the Psalm locates the place of Christ's rule: "Zion" or Jerusalem. This ought to cause us to think and ask some questions:

1. Can "Zion" mean the right hand of God in Heaven?

2. Since the OT indicates that Christ will rule in the midst of His enemies, does Paul negate it?

---

62 For a good premillennial exposition of the passage, I recommend Michael J. Vlach, *He Will Reign Forever*, 436-444. I do not believe there is an iron clad argument for a three-stage interpretation of 1 Cor. 15:20-28 that wins the day for premillennialists, but it does mean that the passage fits into the larger premillennial outlook very well. There exists a strong reciprocal relationship between our interpretation of this text and many other passages in the Old and New Testaments.

63 N. T. Wright, *The Resurrection of the Son of God*, 333.

64 It is understood that this glory differs among the saints, doubtless depending on their service, but all glory is glory indeed, and if it is connected with the glory of the risen Jesus, it will far excel our expectations.

65 Gordon D. Fee, *Pauline Christology: An Exegetical–Theological Study* (Peabody, MA: Hendrickson, 2007), 109-112.

> 3. What kind of reign is Christ involved in now if the world is just as evil and messed up as ever, with none of His enemies being defeated for two millennia?
>
> 4. If Christ's present reign is restricted to the saints in heaven, isn't that a rather inane rule? God the Father is on the throne (Psa. 11:4; Matt. 23:22; Rev. 4–5). He rules in heaven. The ascended Son is at the right hand of God's throne (Acts 2:33-34; Rom. 8:34; Heb. 1:3; 8:1; 1 Pet. 3:22). What sort of reign is it when a king does not even sit on his throne?

The majority of commentators teach that Christ is indeed reigning in heaven right now and has done so since His ascension. As so often in amillennial and postmillennial interpretation, the little details are brushed aside. We are told that "Zion" on earth cannot be the place of His rule even though numerous prophecies tell us quite the opposite (e.g., Psa. 2:6; 48:1-14; 50:2; 102:13-21; Isa. 2:3; 12:6; Joel 3:16-21; Mic. 4:1-7). "Zion" does not appear to be a synonym for Heaven. Furthermore, the reign of Christ in Heaven, as envisioned by those who believe He is ruling now, must be of a rather unusual variety. It is very unlike the reign predicted in the Hebrew Scriptures, or indeed asked about by the disciples in Acts 1:6. In fact, it seems to differ imperceptibly from God's ongoing providential care of creation. Certainly, there has been a marked absence of anything that might resemble what typically would count for a kingly reign over the whole earth. We still witness the crushing of the weak under the heel of the ungodly, the elevation of pride and vanity, the suffering of God's people, plus the fact that Satan is still styled "the god of this world" (2 Cor. 4:4), who "walks about like a roaring lion, seeking whom he may devour" (1 Pet. 5:8)! Let us be frank. If Jesus is reigning over the world and has been for nigh on two thousand years, it has been a singularly ineffective "hands-off" approach! And as for Him reigning in Heaven, well, how is that any different than the Father's ongoing rule?

Added to all this is the way Psalm 110 is employed in other places in the NT. Michael Vlach notes:

> In reference to Psalm 110:1, the author of Hebrews says Jesus is "waiting" at the right hand of the Father (see Heb. 10:12-13). When the heavenly session is over, God installs His Messiah on the earth to reign over it. From our current historical perspective, Jesus is currently at the right hand of God the Father, but this will be followed by a reign upon the earth. Thus, Jesus "must" reign from earth because Psalm 110 says this must happen. In Acts 3:21, Peter also uses "must" in regard to Jesus and His heavenly session before He returns to earth to restore everything.[66]

Vlach adds, "Jesus the Son and Messiah must have a sustained reign in the realm where the first Adam failed (see Gen. 1:26, 28; 1 Cor. 15:45)."[67]

---

66 Michael J. Vlach, *He Will Reign Forever*, 441.
67 Ibid., 442.

"The last enemy *that* will be destroyed *is* death" (1 Cor. 15:26). Satan is not the last enemy, Death is. We know that the future reign of Christ will have death in it, for Isaiah 65:20b says, "For the child shall die one hundred years old, but the sinner *being* one hundred years old shall be accursed."

If it is allowed to stand without being manipulated via typology or spiritualization, then Zechariah 14:16-19 speaks of Yahweh meting out punishments against nations who refuse to honor Him in Jerusalem. Zechariah 8:3-5 should also be recalled because it refers to old and young in the streets of Zion at a time when "Jerusalem shall be called the City of Truth" (Zech. 8:3). These facts, uncomfortable as they are for amillennialists and postmillennialists alike, demand either that we manipulate these OT texts to fit the way we think they *ought* to read, or we leave space in our systems for the insertion of a future Kingdom where Jesus Christ will reign, but where sin and death are still present, and where He therefore must rule with a rod of iron (Psa. 2:6-9; Rev. 2:27; 12:5; 19:15).

So, 1 Corinthians 15:24-25 fits with the view that the new heavens and earth, where Christ delivers up the Kingdom to His Father, and wherein there shall be no more curse (Rev. 22:3), will be preceded by a "Millennial Kingdom," where Christ must reign until He has dealt with every enemy, Death being the last one.

"For 'He has put all things under His feet.' But when He says 'all things are put under Him,' it is evident that He who put all things under Him is excepted" (1 Cor. 15:27). It must not be forgotten that Jesus in both his first and second advents, not to mention His coming rule, is the Servant of Yahweh.[68] The whole Creation Project is built on His willingness to humble Himself and come into His own creation to suffer and die in it and to bring it under His dominion. Here the apostle quotes from Psalm 8 and lends it a Christological interpretation, one that it does not appear to support in its original setting. But the interpretive move is justified on account of the Incarnation. The *man* Christ Jesus (1 Tim. 2:5) is the key to the Creation Project, and He accomplishes it covenantally.

"Now when all things are made subject to Him, then the Son Himself will also be subject to Him who put all things under Him, that God may be all in all" (1 Cor. 15:28). If I understand this verse correctly, Paul teaches here that Jesus cannot assume the role of absolute Sovereign of creation until He has delivered everything up to the Father.[69] But is Paul saying that the Son will forever be subject to the Father? I think we must tread carefully here. This cannot be an ontological submission of the Son to the Father since that would mean there is an eternal ontic superiority within the Trinity. The only way an eternal hierarchical order within the Godhead is possible is in the loving *relationship* between the three Persons; something that cannot be exactly duplicated in human relationships but which the best Father-Son relationships represent.

68 As a side note, although it is common nowadays to think of Jesus as a Servant-Leader, it would be more accurate to think of Him as a Servant-Ruler. He is our undisputed Lord and Master.

69 It could be that there is an interval between when everything is made subject to the Son and the Son Himself being subject to the Father.

To Sum Up

How might I summarize my understanding of 1 Corinthians 15:20-28? If I have caught the gist of the great apostle's thought here, the verses express the marvelous truth that the resurrection of Jesus on behalf of His saints is the first installment in the full reconciliation of all things to God (cf. Col. 1:19-20). This process is to be drawn out over several thousand years. Christ rose and ascended two thousand years ago, and His return will begin (not continue) His reign on this earth, an earth that has relentlessly gone its own way in defiance of God (Prov. 14:12). Christ's initial rule (which I believe will last for a thousand years, Rev. 20), is to bring His creatures to heel and to order and beautify the world so that it is fit to be presented *back* to His Father as rescued and restored. It will also justify God's righteous dealing with fallen man because, as we shall see, given the most perfect political situation in a serene environment, and with Satan under lock and key, humanity will still chafe under the beneficent rule of King Jesus, and will finally rejoin the briefly emancipated Satan to seek His overthrow (Rev. 20:7-10).

If I may supplement this portrait with more NT data, the rationale for the dissolution of the present heaven and earth and the bringing into being the New Heavens and Earth is that only in the New Creation will there be no more sin (Rev. 21:4, 27) or curse (Rev. 22:3), and hence no more Death (2 Cor. 5:4).

The Return of Christ in Paul

The earliest letters of Paul are the Epistle to the Galatians and the two Epistles to the Thessalonians (c. A.D. 48-50). Every attentive reader knows that the theme of the second coming is found in every chapter but one in 1 and 2 Thessalonians. The teaching also features strongly in 1 Corinthians (chs 3, 15), Philippians 3:20, the letter to Titus, and both 1 and 2 Timothy. Different verbs are used, but the same idea is in view. To these texts we may add Romans 8:19. These passages do not serve only as anticipations of a great event; they speak of the culmination of something.

If we take the Thessalonian epistles as our starting point, we can see the different uses to which the apostle puts the doctrine of Christ's second advent. First, there is the aspect of patient waiting (1 Thess. 1:9-10). The coming of Christ "delivers us from the wrath to come" (1 Thess. 1:10). What this wrath is, we are not told outright. It may be the wrath of the second coming or the "revealing" itself as per 2 Thessalonians 1:5-9, or it may be "the Day of the Lord" (1 Thess. 5:1-3, 9). It may also denote the Tribulation, if one allows that Paul might have had that in mind.

Paul also relates the coming (*parousia*)[70] of Christ to our sanctification (1 Thess. 3:13; 5:23). In 1 Thessalonians 2:19 he writes, "For what *is* our hope, or joy, or crown of rejoicing? *Is it* not even you in the presence of our Lord Jesus Christ at His coming (*parousia*)?"

70 From Paul's usage of the two verbs here, I believe the "revealing" and the "coming" of Christ are the same event.

As I understand the passage, Paul is saying that the saint's fellowship in the presence of the Lord will be an ample reward for his endeavors when we all participate in Christ's "kingdom and glory" (1 Thess. 2:12; 2 Thess. 2:14).

Titus 2:13 is a famous passage concerning Christ's return: "Looking for the blessed hope and glorious appearing of our great God and Savior Jesus Christ." Writers have gone back and forth about whether this "blessed hope' is the second advent itself or the rapture of the Church.[71] Paul's main emphasis in the context is on godly living in this life (Tit. 2:12, 14). Whether the rapture is in view or the second advent itself entirely depends on which position is taken on the timing of the rapture. I have admitted to being pretribulational in my orientation; therefore, I equate the "blessed hope" with the removal of the Church before the Tribulation. It is also possible that the apostle conflates both events, as pretribulationsists often do when expressing their wish for Christ's return. But it is possible that Titus 2:13 does lend support for a postribulational rapture. The text is ancillary to other passages. There is no definitive way to prove any of the claims.

First Thessalonians 4:13-18 is a little unusual amid the other references. For one thing, there seems to be a difference between 1 Thessalonians 4:13 and 5:1-2. In the latter text, the believers are well aware of Paul's doctrine, but in chapter 4 they appear to be informed of something new ("I do not want you to be ignorant..."). Therefore, it seems best to look at this text separately (see below).

Paul wrote about the return of Jesus as the great hope of the saint (Tit. 2:13). But he also saw it as the great hope of the earth. These two things are brought together in Romans 8, where he envisages a transformation of the saints that, in turn, triggers environmental changes, thus bringing the believer's hope into the realm of the larger Creation Project: "For I consider that the sufferings of this present time are not worthy *to be compared* with the glory which shall be revealed in us. For the earnest expectation of the creation eagerly waits for the revealing of the sons of God" (Rom. 8:18-19).

Here the apostle is contrasting the troubles of life with "the glory which shall be revealed in us." He personifies the created order as straining in expectation for something he calls "the revealing of the sons of God" (Rom. 8:19). So, Paul says that the humanity which in Adam originally came from the earth (Gen. 2:7) now becomes the locus from where the earth's chances of regeneration come once the glorification of saved humanity occurs.[72]

> For the creation was subjected to futility, not willingly, but because of Him who subjected *it* in hope; because the creation itself also will be delivered from the bondage of corruption into the glorious liberty of the children of

71 Examples are George Eldon Ladd, *The Blessed Hope: A Biblical Study of the Second Advent and the Rapture* (Grand Rapids: Eerdmans, 1990), who argues from a posttribulational perspective, and John F. Walvoord, *The Blessed Hope and The Tribulation: A Historical and Biblical Study of Posttribulationism* (Grand Rapids: Zondervan, 1976). Walvoord takes a pretribulational approach. I always think Walvoord is at his best when answering opponents.

72 This earthly regeneration is guaranteed by its connection with the glorification of believers, which is locked-in by the decree of God. See Rom. 8:30.

> God. For we know that the whole creation groans and labors with birth pangs together until now. Not only *that,* but we also who have the firstfruits of the Spirit, even we ourselves groan within ourselves, eagerly waiting for the adoption, the redemption of our body (Rom. 8:20-23).

Paul's reasoning is "that the creation was subjected to futility" as a consequence of the Fall. When one looks at Genesis 1, it becomes clear that the first five days of creation and the first half of the sixth day were all preparation for the creation of man in Genesis 1:26-27.

What God does next brings home to us the connection that Paul refers to between human glorification and the world's regeneration. God explicitly puts the responsibility for creation into the hands of man as His image in Genesis 1:28-30. The fact that the fortunes of man and the fortunes of his natural environment are intertwined with the second coming is important to notice. But someone might ask, "Where is the second coming in the passage?" It is found in the doctrine of "the redemption of the body" in verse 23. To see this more clearly consider two texts from 1 Corinthians 15:

> But each one in his own order: Christ the firstfruits, afterward those *who are* Christ's at His coming (1 Cor. 15:23).

> The first man *was* of the earth, *made* of dust; the second Man *is* the Lord from heaven. As *was* the *man* of dust, so also *are* those *who are made* of dust; and as *is* the heavenly *Man,* so also *are* those *who are* heavenly. And as we have borne the image of the *man* of dust, we shall also bear the image of the heavenly *Man* (1 Cor. 15:47-49).

The context concerns the resurrection body. In 1 Corinthians 15:23 we are told that we shall receive a body similar to Christ's resurrection body "at His [second] coming."[73] Hence, "the glory which shall be revealed in us" and "the revealing of the sons of God," which Romans 8:18-19 speaks about, occurs when Jesus returns.[74] In 1 Corinthians 15:47-49 many read verse 47 as a reference to the first coming, but the eschatological note is unmistakable. We "shall...bear the image" of the resurrected Jesus. Again Philippians 3:20-21 says:

> For our citizenship is in heaven, from which we also eagerly wait for the Savior, the Lord Jesus Christ, who will transform our lowly body that it may be conformed to His glorious body, according to the working by which He is able even to subdue all things to Himself.

The Christian has been born into "this present evil world" (Gal. 1:4), but he no longer belongs to it. We possess the right to enter heaven, a right bought for us by Jesus Christ. According to Philippians 3:21, it is Christ who will "transform our lowly

73 Although I shall not argue for it here, I believe pretribulationists are right to relate this transformation with the rapture (cf. 1 Cor. 15:51-54).

74 In light of what is said in 1 Cor. 15:51-52, my position is that the "coming" here refers to the rapture. I understand that this is not an exegetical conclusion.

body" by glorifying it. The apostle John will echo this truth later in the first century (1 Jn. 3:2).

We do well to take stock of the importance that Paul places on Christ's second coming. He pins all of our hopes upon it. Therefore, it is simply untrue to assert that "the linchpin of Paul's eschatology is the proclamation of Jesus of Nazareth as the Messiah."[75] This is not borne out by the preceding passages or the weight of hope they bear. Yes, Jesus is the Messiah, but it is what He achieves *as* Messiah that we look for.

The mention of the transformation of our bodies calls to mind the mystery of 1 Corinthians 15:50-52:

> Now this I say, brethren, that flesh and blood cannot inherit the kingdom of God; nor does corruption inherit incorruption. Behold, I tell you a mystery: We shall not all sleep, but we shall all be changed—in a moment, in the twinkling of an eye, at the last trumpet. For the trumpet will sound, and the dead will be raised incorruptible, and we shall be changed.

The language of transformation is linked to the kingdom of God in this text. Paul says that "flesh and blood" cannot inherit this kingdom—a kingdom that is in the future. What does he mean by this? The apostle is saying that our present earthly frame is not prepared for the glories in heaven. As Schreiner puts it, "The bodily flesh of this age is subject to weakness and death...our corruptible earthly body cannot enter the future kingdom."[76]

Paul tells us that we shall all be changed, that is, we shall become immortal and glorious. And this transformation will happen instantaneously. It will occur "at the last trumpet" (1 Cor. 15:52). I wish he had elaborated a little more on the trumpet! Which "trump" is he referring to? The book of Revelation refers to seven trumpets that are blown by angels, with the seventh recorded cryptically in Revelation 10:5-7 and finally blown in Revelation 11:15. There is a sense of finality that comes with this blowing, but is this what Paul had in mind when he wrote about "the last trump" some forty years earlier? I think this is doubtful. In ancient times, trumpets were used to get people's attention and to summon them (e.g., Exod. 19:13, 16, 19; Lev. 25:9; Neh. 4:20). Sometimes the trumpet raised the alarm (Joel 2:1; Amos 3:6; Zeph. 3:16). Jesus Himself taught that a trumpet would be blown when the angels were sent to gather up the saints at his second coming (Matt. 24:30-31), which may be synonymous with the seventh trumpet of Revelation, although to me that appears doubtful.[77]

---

75 L. J. Kreitzer, "Eschatology," in *Dictionary of Paul and His Letters*, eds. Gerald F. Hawthorne and Ralph P. Martin (Downers Grove, IL: InterVarsity, 1993), 256.

76 Thomas R. Schreiner, *Paul, Apostle of God's Glory in Christ: A Pauline Theology* (Downers Grove, IL: IVP, 2001), 142. "The resurrection will involve somatic existence, although not *fleshly* existence. 'Flesh and blood,' that is, our present fleshly bodies, cannot inherit the Kingdom of God (1 Cor. 15:50)" (George Eldon Ladd, *A Theology of the New Testament* [Grand Rapids: Eerdmans, 1983], 465).

77 See the exposition of Rev. 11 later in this volume.

It is preferable to think of "the last trumpet" in this passage as the final blast in a succession of trumpet calls that precede the transformation of our bodies, although there is no way of nailing it down more than that. For Paul, then, the coming of Christ is the time when we appropriate the glory of the resurrection which Christ has procured for us.

Instant Change and the Rapture?

The next question that arises is whether 1 Corinthians 15:50-52 is connected with the "snatching up" (*harpazo*) described in 1 Thessalonians 4:12-18. Here is the part of the passage that describes the "rapture":

> For this we say to you by the word of the Lord, that we who are alive *and* remain until the coming of the Lord will by no means precede those who are asleep. For the Lord Himself will descend from heaven with a shout, with the voice of an archangel, and with the trumpet of God. And the dead in Christ will rise first. Then we who are alive *and* remain shall be caught up together with them in the clouds to meet the Lord in the air. And thus we shall always be with the Lord (1 Thess. 4:15-17).

I am approaching the text as neutrally as I can, which means that I am not as concerned with *when* the snatching away will occur, but *what* will occur and its connection, if any, with the "change" described by Paul at the end of 1 Corinthians 15. The first thing that I have to point out is the rather obvious fact that this passage nowhere pinpoints the timing of the *harpazo*. This is not the reason Paul wrote the words. Some writers have referred to inscriptions on the tombs of famous men of the past where *harpazo* is used as a euphemism for death; thus, they were "snatched up" by death.[78] That cannot be the meaning here because the living are contrasted with those who have "fallen asleep," and both will be caught up together (1 Thess. 4:15-17). The link between this passage and 1 Corinthians 15:50-52 is the trumpet that is blown (1 Thess. 4:16). At the blast of this trumpet, things happen to the saints—they are transformed and glorified. And this change is one reason why I believe the snatching up of the saints cannot be post-tribulational, for then who would go into the Millennial Kingdom, have children, and grow old as per Isaiah 11, 65, and Zechariah 8? Glorified people will not procreate nor age. It, therefore, looks like the "rapture" of 1 Thessalonians 4:17 and the corresponding transformation of 1 Corinthians 15:51-52 must occur before the second advent. It is natural to believe that they occur simultaneously. This brings the rapture back to either pretribulational, mid-tribulational, or prewrath.

78 E.g., Constantine R. Campbell, *Paul and the Hope of Glory*, 112-113.

Paul and the "Day" of the Lord

If we take a look at the varied mentions of "the Day of the Lord" and associated phrases in Paul, we encounter a lively expectation of Jesus' coming and reign. In 1 Thessalonians 5:2-4 "the Day of the Lord" signifies His coming in judgment, bringing with Him "sudden destruction" (1 Thess. 5:3; cf. Rom. 2:5). Since the devastation of the Tribulation will make it absurd to speak of "peace and safety" (think the Four Horsemen, Rev. 6:1-8), it seems likely that the sudden onset of this "Day" refers to the Tribulation.[79]

In 2 Thessalonians 2:1-3 the emphasis seems to be on the Lord's return to gather His saints (cf. 2 Thess. 1:10), but he says, "that Day will not come" until a great *apostasia*[80] occurs, or "until the Man of Sin is revealed, the son of perdition" (2 Thess. 2:3). This *may* mean that Christians at this time will see this "Man of Sin" (Antichrist), although verses 6 and 7 indicate that the removal of "the Restrainer," whom I take to be the Holy Spirit in the Church,[81] happens just before "the lawless one will be revealed" (2 Thess. 2:8), which if other evidence were not forthcoming would seem to place the "rapture" of 1 Thessalonians 4:17 at that time.[82]

In 1 Corinthians 1:7-8 the apostle refers to the "revelation of our Lord Jesus Christ" and then speaks of Christ confirming the saints "to the end," which he equates with "the day of our Lord Jesus Christ." Here the second coming seems to be in his mind, as it does in 1 Corinthians 15:24, where he speaks of Christ "at His coming."

Then we have a group of texts that refer to "the Day" of Christ or of the Lord Jesus, etc. First Corinthians 5:5 and 2 Corinthians 1:14 are two examples, whereas Philippians 1:6 has "the day of Jesus Christ" and Philippians 1:10 "the day of Christ." In 1 Corinthians 5:5 and 2 Corinthians 1:14, the passages could be taken to refer to the Judgment Seat of Christ spoken about in 1 Corinthians 3:11ff.,[83] to the rapture, or the second coming proper.[84] All the possibilities crowd together in the End Times.

1 Corinthians 1:7-8 appears to point to the second advent, although it *could* point to the rapture.[85] I say the same thing about the twin references in Philippians 1. For my part, and in the absence of any qualifying language, I believe the most likely view is that both Philippians 1:6 and 1:10 ought to be understood as referring to the second coming. The same goes for Paul's hope of rejoicing "in the day of Christ" in

79 See the reasons stated concisely by Kevin D. Zuber, "1 Thessalonians," in *The Moody Bible Commentary*, eds. Michael Rydelnik and Michael VanLaningham (Chicago: Moody, 2014), 1888-1889.

80 This *apostasia* I take to be a "falling away" from Truth.

81 "Since this 'lawless one' and his power derive from Satan, it seems reasonable to suppose that only One powerful enough to restrain Satan is the One in view. Since the work of restraint is attributed elsewhere to the Holy Spirit (cf. Gn 6:3), it seems reasonable to suppose that He is the restrainer Paul had in mind here" (Kevin D. Zuber, *The Moody Bible Commentary,* 1893).

82 That is, at the beginning of the Tribulation or just before it.

83 That would be my preference (cf. 2 Tim. 1:18).

84 Cf. Acts 17:31.

85 I don't think insisting on technical meanings for Greek verbs is all that helpful, but "revealing" or "manifestation" is a strong word to use if the rapture alone is in view. But perhaps I am over-analyzing things? Pretribulationists are well within their rights to understand this verse within that outlook.

Philippians 2:16. These verses should not be forced into service of any rapture position. Although I grant that it is not illegitimate to fit them into a wider rapture teaching, in my opinion, none of them *corroborate* the different views.

Finally, in Ephesians 4:30 we are instructed not to grieve the Holy Spirit who has "sealed" us "for [or 'unto'] the day of redemption." Where this "day of redemption" is to be situated on the timeline of the last things depends on one's positioning of the "rapture," of course. Bringing the transformations written about in 1 Corinthians 15:51-57 and 1 Thessalonians 4:17 alongside Ephesians 4:30 is eminently reasonable, as our being snatched up to meet Christ and our "change" signify "the redemption of our body" (Rom. 8:23).

From this survey of the main passages which have to do with the "Day" of the Lord or of Christ, it appears that "the Day of the Lord" in Paul *covers the period from the rapture (providing the pre-trib view is correct) to the second coming.*[86] It may speak to specific events like the *Bema* Seat, but without telling us exactly when that event occurs. In my opinion, the covenants themselves have something to say about the issue of the timing of the taking out of the Church from this "present evil age" (Gal. 1:4). But I shall refrain from giving my views on that until later in this book.

Premillennialism in Paul (not A- or Post-Millennialism)

I have stated already that this study in the biblical theology of the NT assumes a premillennial eschatology. The reasons it does so are found in the first volume as well as in the expositions in this volume. The covenants of God, if they are left alone to say what they say, promote a premillennialist scheme. Although most readers of these pages will know what the various views of the Millennium[87] in relation to the second coming are, I shall give them in brief:

> Amillennialism is the belief that the "thousand-years" is not literal and encompasses the time between the first and second advents. Since this is so, there is no millennial reign of Christ after the second coming. It holds to one people of God in eternity. This is the majority view in contemporary evangelical scholarship.

86 "Many Bible students believe the Day of the Lord will be a long period of time rather than a single day–a period when Christ will reign throughout the world before He cleanses heaven and earth in preparation for the eternal state... The day would be a time of judgment (Is. 13:6, 9; Jer. 46:10), as well as restoration (Is. 14:1; Joel 2:28-32; Zeph. 1:7, 14-16; 1 Thess. 5:2; 2 Peter 3:10)" (Ronald F. Youngblood, "Day of the Lord," in *Nelson's New illustrated Bible Dictionary* [Nashville: Thomas Nelson, 1995], 335). For more on this matter see Thomas R. Edgar, "An Exegesis of Rapture Passages," in *Issues in Dispensationalism*, eds. Wesley R. Willis and John R. Master (Chicago: Moody, 1994), esp. 205-207, 209-210. Another good survey of the material, which helps to pick through the subject, although rejecting pretribulationism, is Ben Witherington III, *Jesus, Paul, and the End of the World: A Comparative Study in New Testament Eschatology* (Downers Grove, IL: InterVarsity, 1992), 159-169.

87 Viz., Christ's thousand-year reign mentioned in Rev. 20.

Postmillennialism is the view that the "thousand-year" kingdom, which may or may not be literal, will be brought about at some time before the second advent. Stated this way, one may see that Amillennialism differs little from Postmillennialism in its overall outlook; the main difference being that the former declares we have been in the "thousand-years" since the ascension, whereas postmillennialists await a great period of major positive Church influence over the world before Christ's returns. Aside from this, the two positions utilize the same theological arguments. Postmillennialists believe in one people of God in the eschaton.

Premillennialism comprises a variety of views which all hold that the thousand-year reign of Christ will happen after the second coming. "Historic" or "Covenant" premillennialists hold that this reign may or may not be literally one thousand-years in duration. They believe there will be one people of God after the second advent, which means that they can quite often agree with amillennial or postmillennial exegesis of covenantal passages, especially in the OT. Dispensational premillennialists believe that the thousand-years is literal and usually believe that since the covenants with Israel cannot be altered, there must be at least two peoples of God (although vitally connected in fellowship): Israel and the Church.

James Dunn has stated that if one is to understand the faith of the first Christians, one must seek to discover "the eschatological temper and perspective of the first believers."[88] Dunn believed these first Christians expected the any-moment return of Jesus to restore the earth as per Acts 3:19-21.[89] Acts 3:19-21 certainly makes a lot of sense in a premillennial structure. Granted, it is not a Pauline passage, but when wedded to Paul's expressions in Romans 8:19-23 and 11:19-29, they forge a strong triad of verses for premillennialism. If the "earnest expectation of the creation eagerly waits for the revealing of the sons of God" (Rom. 8:19), this means that the great transformation of the earth occurs subsequent to the second coming. Likewise, if the blindness of Israel is to be reversed when "the fullness of the Gentiles has come in" (Rom. 11:25), this has to mean that God's dealing with the Gentiles through the Church does not auger in the Kingdom at least until "all Israel" (i.e., the remnant) is saved (Rom. 11:26). And this salvation for Israel seems to trigger "times of refreshing...from the presence of the Lord," according to Acts 3:19.

Now if we turn to 2 Timothy, we find another verse to support Premillennialism. Paul declares, "I charge *you* therefore before God and the Lord Jesus Christ, who will judge the living and the dead at His appearing and His kingdom" (2 Tim. 4:1).[90] Here the coming of the Kingdom is dependent upon and coterminous with Christ's second

88 James D. G. Dunn, *Beginning From Jerusalem*, 536.

89 Ibid., 223ff. Dunn, of course, believed that this view was changed in light of Christ's non-appearance.

90 In 2 Tim. 4:18 Paul elicits the hope that God will "preserve *me* for His heavenly kingdom." This probably means only that once Rome has done him to death, he will enter heaven (cf. 2 Cor. 5:8; Phil. 1:23). It could, however, be his way of contrasting this "present evil age" (Gal.

advent. As McClain rightly saw,[91] this order is the same as we see in our Lord's words in Matthew 25:31: "When the Son of Man comes in His glory, and all the holy angels with Him, then He will sit on the throne of His glory."

This clearly indicates an *earthly* reign of Christ after He comes back to earth. It is in line with OT expectations. It is also confirmed when the apostle chides the Corinthians, "You are already full! You are already rich! You have reigned as kings without us" (1 Cor. 4:8a). The sarcasm is not subtle here. Paul is pointing out the irony of thinking that one has everything now. If that were indeed so, it must mean the saints are reigning now and the much-anticipated Kingdom has dawned.[92] And indeed Paul wishes it had: "And indeed I could wish you did reign, that we also might reign with you!" (1 Cor. 4:8b).

This, of course, is nonsense. Suffering comes before reigning (2 Thess. 1:5; 2 Tim. 2:12). Believers reign with Christ once "the kingdoms of this world have become *the kingdoms* of our Lord and of His Christ" (Rev. 11:15). Any notion that we are actually reigning with Christ now is a pious fiction.[93] These passages, therefore, strongly favor reading Paul in line with premillennial eschatology.

The Man of Sin and the Tribulation

Paul is primarily a Church theologian. He mentions the hopes of Israel out of understandable concern for his people and for God's solemn word vouchsafed to them. He believes in the remnant. When Israel's blindness is removed (Rom. 11:25), God will save the *nation* (see Acts 26:4-8).

But the OT predicts a time of upheaval spoken of variously as "the time of Jacob's trouble" (Jer. 30:7), or "time of trouble such as never was since there was a nation" (Dan. 12:1), after which Israel will be delivered (Jer. 30:7c; Dan. 12:1b). If we add into this the prospect of the "little horn" of Daniel 7:21-22 and the self-exalting king of Daniel 11:36ff., we can see that the OT has given us a time of Tribulation that resembles Daniel's descriptions (cf. Matt. 24:21-30), and which comes before the second advent of Jesus.[94]

Putting the pieces of this jigsaw together, it looks as though after "the fullness of the Gentiles has come in" (Rom. 11:25), there will be a time of peril for Israel in which an evil protagonist who will "speak *great* words against the most High, and

1:4) with the "age to come" (cf. Eph. 2:7). In either case, it is not grounds for spiritualizing the "kingdom" of 2 Tim. 4:1.

91 Alva J. McClain, *The Greatness of the Kingdom*, 433.

92 C. K. Barrett, *The First Epistle to the Corinthians* (Peabody, MA: Hendricksen, 1985), 108-109.

93 "Worse than that: it provides support for skeptics of Christianity in their assertion that 'Christians believe whatever they want—regardless of reality.' To say we are presently reigning is akin to Christian Science's denial of the physical reality of disease. Why should anyone believe our testimony that Christ died and rose again when we embrace goofy ideas like we are reigning in the here-and-now?" (Tony Garland, personal communication).

94 See e.g., *The Words of the Covenant*, Vol. 1, 316-319, 360-361.

shall wear out the saints of the most High" (Dan. 7:25), will have his time. After this, the people whom he persecuted shall inherit the Kingdom (Dan. 7:27).

The question before us is, does the apostle Paul refer to any of this in his letters? The answer is yes, and it is surprisingly detailed. For Paul's take on this, we must turn again to the Thessalonian correspondence. Let us turn first to what he has to say about the mysterious "man of sin" in 2 Thessalonians 2:

> Let no one deceive you by any means; for *that Day will not come* unless the falling away comes first, and the man of sin is revealed, the son of perdition, who opposes and exalts himself above all that is called God or that is worshiped, so that he sits as God in the temple of God, showing himself that he is God ... And now you know what is restraining, that he may be revealed in his own time. For the mystery of lawlessness is already at work; only He who now restrains *will do so* until He is taken out of the way. And then the lawless one will be revealed, whom the Lord will consume with the breath of His mouth and destroy with the brightness of His coming (2 Thess. 2:3-4, 6-8).

The "Day" is "the day of Christ" in verse 2. Before the day of Christ can materialize, certain intervening events have to occur. Something called "the falling away" (*apostasia*) must happen. Some pretribulationists believe that this *apostasia* is the rapture. I do not. I retain the view that this "falling away" is the defection of the visible Church from Christ and His Truth. The "Church" may maintain confessional items like the deity of Christ and even justification by faith, but the "hard content" (e.g., sin, repentance, sanctification, dying to self, etc.) is not pressed and a self-centered entertainment-based form of teaching replaces it, thereby presenting a false Jesus and a false gospel (2 Cor. 11:4). This lapsed "Church" will even be speaking of things like homosexuality and "common-law marriage" as if they are acceptable to God.

The next intervening event is the appearance of "the man of sin," who is given another name: "son of perdition" or "son of destruction." This individual matches the character of the "little horn" in Daniel 7 and calls to mind John's depiction of "the beast" in Revelation 13. The fact that Paul simply refers to this person as "the man of sin" suggests that he expects his audience to know who he is referring to. This is the coming great foe of Israel who goes by many names in Scripture.[95] Daniel calls him the "little horn" (Dan. 7:24-27) and the willful king (Dan. 11:36). Zechariah speaks of him as "the worthless shepherd" in Zechariah 11:15-17.[96] Paul's designation, "the man of sin," is most appropriate.[97] But Paul's other name, "the son of perdition," is

95 I shall give attention to this individual (the "Antichrist") when we study Rev. 13.

96 Some writers believe that the "one who comes in his own name" in Jn. 5:43 is a veiled reference to Antichrist. For example, G. H. Pember, *The Antichrist, Babylon, and the Coming of the Kingdom* (London: Hodder and Stoughton, 1888), 6.

97 Reformed scholar Kim Riddlebarger believes that the label fits many individuals down through Church History, but that it culminates in an end time villain. He fits this into an amillennial framework. See his *The Man of Sin: Uncovering the Truth About the Antichrist* (Grand Rapids: Baker, 2006), 13-14.

perhaps more interesting as it is the exact same name that Jesus called Judas Iscariot in His prayer to the Father in John 17:12!

Some interpreters have thought that the two names denote the two halves of the seven-year career of the Antichrist. But that is mere conjecture. The structure of 2 Thessalonians 2:3-4 does not encourage such a division. The "man of sin" or "lawlessness"[98] appears to be the same villain who "exalts himself" and sits in God's temple proclaiming himself a deity (2 Thess. 2:4).[99] That he is given another name (hardly unusual in the Bible) should not carry any meaning beyond what is clearly stated.

The characteristic that links this man most clearly to the sinful ruler of Daniel is, of course, his over-inflated ego. Daniel says that the coming persecutor will "speak *pompous* words against the Most High" (Dan. 9:25a), and as the willful king, "shall exalt and magnify himself above every god, shall speak blasphemies against the God of gods" (Dan. 11:36). According to Daniel 7:26-27 this individual's reign will be halted after "a time, times, and half a time" (i.e., three and a half years),[100] when the Kingdom of peace is ushered in. For Paul, the "man of sin/son of perdition" will oppose God, sitting "as God in the temple of God, showing himself that he is God" (2 Thess. 2:4).

What this surely means, if it means anything, is that at some time right before the Kingdom of God comes to earth, a malevolent ruler will arise who will secure great power over at least the biblical world, and quite possibly over the whole world (Rev. 13:3, 13). He will be an intensely religious figure, but a very vocal blasphemer of Yahweh. His hubris will be such that he will enter "the temple (*naos*) of God," which, for all the imaginative readings of our amillennialist friends, cannot mean the Church.[101] The *ekklesia*, as these writers very well know, is not a building one can sit in. But the "man of sin" "sits" (intransitive verb) in the *naos* of God. This denotes a temple structure, its holy place. Is this a rebuilt temple in Jerusalem? Very probably. From Jesus' own warning in Matthew 24:15-16, we know that a temple is required for the "abomination of desolation" to be "set up" in.

As startling as this is, we are confronted with a biblical truth that we should not shy away from. A man of great wickedness will someday sit in a temple (very probably in Jerusalem) and will proclaim himself to be God. That naturally means that he will demand worship, for only God can demand worship.

Second Thessalonians 2 goes on to refer to a "restrainer" who will be "taken out of the way" (2 Thess. 2:7), to allow this "man of sin" to be revealed "in his own [very

98 Man of "sin" (*hamartia*) is what the Majority Text reads, while man of "lawlessness" (*anomia*) is the reading of the Nestle-Aland and Tyndale House Texts.

99 Because he wants and receives worship (cf. Rev. 13:4, 12), some good Bible teachers believe that he will not present himself as Christ, but would Jesus warn of "false christs" (in Matt. 24:24/Mk. 13:22) and neglect to inform us of a greater threat who will not be a false christ (i.e., an anti-christ)? Messiah in the OT is a divine figure (Isa. 9:6-7; Mic. 5:2; Zech. 11:13), and a spectacular showing off of his claims as the true Christ in the Tribulation will be enough to persuade the masses. This is especially true if some claim to be, say, extraterrestrial was also made.

100 See *The Words of the Covenant*, Vol. 1, 311-312. I shall come back to this expression later in this book.

101 See, e.g., G. K. Beale, *A New Testament Biblical Theology*, 200-203.

particular] time." I believe this restrainer to be the Holy Spirit of God in His role within the Church. I cannot prove that thesis, but I think it is the most natural understanding (who or what else could it be?).[102] The restraining influence is what keeps in check "the mystery of lawlessness," which has been operating for nearly two millennia (2 Thess. 2:7; cf. 1 Jn. 2:18). Again, this restricting power fits the Spirit well. The result of the restrainer's "removal" is that this eschatological bogeyman can finally be revealed, and so, it appears, can the release of spectacular demonic powers (2 Thess. 2:9). This is where the apostle has arrived in his warning:

> The coming of the *lawless one* is according to the working of Satan, with all power, signs, and lying wonders, and with all unrighteous deception among those who perish, because they did not receive the love of the truth, that they might be saved. And for this reason God will send them strong delusion, that they should believe the lie, that they all may be condemned who did not believe the truth but had pleasure in unrighteousness (2 Thess. 2:9-12).

The reason for the great display of evil supernatural power is to deceive the masses. This deception will be worldwide and therefore very believable; unless a person has the light of Scripture to interpret it by. And the Scripture only gives its light to those who love its truth, which the masses never do. There is an indication that the truth is being put out there—"because they did not receive the love of the truth, that they might be saved" (2 Thess. 2:10). But the truth will be rejected because of the lying signs, and because they "had pleasure in unrighteousness" (2 Thess. 2:12). As with so many cases where discernment is wanting, the problem is not that the truth is unavailable, but that it contradicts what everybody else believes and wants to believe. The default setting of our hearts is to be independent of our Creator.[103] What Paul calls "the lie" in 2 Thessalonians 2:11 is not easy to divine right now, but it seems to me that a man proclaiming himself to be God and pointing to great demonstrations of power as proof would fit the bill nicely.

In this chapter, we have examined eschatological doctrines pertaining to the Church that are not explicitly tied to the divine covenants. However, this needed to be done because the Church is a covenant institution, and its future impacts the rest of God's covenant program. In the next chapter, we shall attend to Paul's teaching about Israel. But before we do, I want to say something about the "rapture."

102 Again, the wording seems to take for granted we know what he means. Since the Spirit's coming at Pentecost involved convicting the world "of sin, and of righteousness, and of judgment" (Jn. 16:8), His removal from that particular role will have a negative effect upon the world. It goes without saying that the Spirit of God can no more be absent the creation than the providence of God which He empowers.

103 *The Words of the Covenant*, Vol. 1, 102-104.

A Pretribulation Rapture?

The apostle Paul writes about the snatching away of God's people in the eschaton. This, therefore, is an opportune place to say something about the "rapture."[104]

The Meaning of *Harpazo*

To start things off, the Greek verb *harpazo* means "to snatch away, to seize, or steal (in the sense of grab)." Other than the central rapture text in 1 Thessalonians 4:17, *harpazo* is used in Acts 8:39 to refer to the relocation of Philip: "the Spirit of the Lord caught Philip away." It is also used by Paul in 2 Corinthians 12:2 and 4 to describe his (see 12:7) experience of being "caught up" to the third heaven. We see it again in Revelation 12:5 of the male child (Christ), "who was to rule all nations," Who was "caught up to God and His throne." In 1 Thessalonians 4:17 we read: "Then we who are alive and remain shall be caught up (*harpagesometha*) together with them in the clouds to meet the Lord in the air. And thus we shall always be with the Lord."

As the commentaries all recognize, the idea behind the verb implies force and suddenness. The big question is not whether this will happen, but *when* this snatching up will occur. As I will be at pains to show, the rapture is not a teaching that can be established by simply comparing proof-texts. The doctrine excites many passions, and this can lead to wishful thinking in exegesis. Some of the verses listed below are brought reluctantly to bear on the doctrine we are considering.

The Main Rapture Passages

We have already taken a quick look at 1 Thessalonians 4:17, but there are other salient passages. First Corinthians 15:50-58 is often brought in to help. Then Jesus' words in John 14:1-3 must be considered. Also joining the fray are 2 Thessalonians 2:3 and 13, Matthew 24:36-44, 1 Thessalonians 1:10, 5:9, and Revelation 3:10. Let's try to situate each one of these and clarify their roles in the discussion.

1 Thessalonians 4:14-18

The main purpose of this passage is to give comfort to the anxious saints who were concerned about loved ones dying off before the return of Christ. To do that, Paul tells the Thessalonians about something they seem not to have known (1 Thess. 4:13). This appears to contrast with what they knew very well, that is, the doctrine of the Day of the Lord (1 Thess. 5:1-2).

There is no doubt that the snatching away of the saints described in this passage is for the purpose of finalizing the work of salvation begun at regeneration. The Lord is described as coming from heaven amid the calls of a trumpet and the archangel.[105]

---

104 With apologies to those who disagree, I would have loved to do a deep dive into this subject, but the book is long enough already. Here I mainly give my reasons for being an 80% convinced pretribulationist.

105 It is unclear whether this will be audible to everybody or only to the saints. Because both the archangel and the trump of God (possibly blown by the same angel after he has cried out) my sense is that similar to the trumpet blasts at Sinai, all will hear the sounds.

The meeting of all Christians with their Lord, including those who had been deceased for a long time, takes place "in the air." Nothing is said about where Christ and His saints go from there, whether returning to heaven or continuing to earth. However, from the viewpoint of a "taking out" of people, this passage is a direct statement of a rapture.

1 Corinthians 15:50-58

This passage is included in Paul's resurrection chapter and comes after Paul has spoken about the logic of resurrection: "as we have borne the image of the man of dust, we shall also bear the image of the heavenly Man" (1 Cor. 15:49). This "must" language is then given a terminal point in the next section where the apostle writes, "Behold, I tell you a mystery: we shall not all sleep, but we shall all be changed, in a moment, in the twinkling of an eye, at the last trumpet. For the trumpet will sound, and the dead will be raised incorruptible, and we shall be changed" (1 Cor. 15:51-52).

The passage reveals something new (a mystery), surrounding the transformation of all Christians in an instant. This "change" refers to the receiving of our resurrection bodies—those which will "bear the image of the heavenly."

The language is clearly culminative, and one naturally connects it with Paul's rapture teaching in 1 Thessalonians 4. But there is no actual removal mentioned, only transformation. This is not problematical since it fits nicely with Paul's earlier argument. But it is at best supportive of 1 Thessalonians 4:17, adding some new information about what occurs at the rapture. Hence, if the text coincides with 1 Thessalonians 4, as it seems to do, it declares that a change happens in an instant as the saint is caught away.

John 14:1-3

This passage is proleptic in that the "you" to whom our Lord refers is not primarily the disciples, for He says, "If I go and prepare a place for you, I will come again and receive you to Myself; that where I am, there you may be also" (Jn. 14:3).

Jesus cannot only be referring to those to whom He spoke, but would intend His words to be taken in the context of His second advent.[106] But what does this passage have to do with the rapture? Well, notice that Christ is coming for "you," which I take to be His people. He comes to take them back to heaven (where He has been preparing places), although nothing is stated in regard to a transformation.

As for the timing of this gathering, it may appear cut and dried that it speaks to the second coming. But if so, there is a problem created by our being with Christ in heavenly mansions (or rooms, if you prefer) and Christ's earthly reign. If Christ is ruling on earth and we are in heaven, the latter part of John 14:3 cannot be true.

106 Rather like the Preterist 'proof-text' in Matt. 10:23.

Other Important Passages

Those are the major rapture passages, but there are several others that demand inclusion in the formulation of the doctrine.

1 Thessalonians 1:10

This verse says we "wait for His Son from heaven," who "delivers us from the wrath to come." The mention of Jesus coming from heaven matches 1 Thessalonians 4 and John 14, but the "wrath" must be identified. If it refers to the seven-year Tribulation (derived, as we shall see, from Daniel 9), then the verse favors a pre-trib rapture. However, if "wrath" bears a more restricted and technical sense, it could refer either to the last three and a half years of the Tribulation (in which case it would argue for a mid-trib rapture), or the last part of the Tribulation when the bowls of God's wrath are emptied out upon the planet (Rev. 16).[107] In any case, this verse must be retro-fitted to an already established teaching to be of any corroborative help.

1 Thessalonians 5:9

According to Paul, in this verse, God has not appointed us to "wrath," but the same question of identification as above needs to be addressed to utilize this verse well. It is not unfair, though, to mark the fact that this verse and the one above are written to the Church.

2 Thessalonians 2:7

I have commented on this text above. The thesis is that when the "Restrainer" is taken away (meaning the Holy Spirit), it is His role within the Church that is in view. Ergo, if He is removed, it makes a lot of sense that He does not leave the Church to itself but that the Church is likewise removed.

Matthew 24:36-44

This passage must be understood in context. The "coming" of verses 27, 30, 37, and 39 must inform the meaning of "coming" in verse 44. There can be no serious doubt that Christ is talking of His second coming in terms strongly reminiscent of OT prophecy (e.g., Dan. 7; Isa. 63) and the parables of Matthew 13, especially Matthew 24:40-43. This then is *after* the Tribulation.

The question is, what does the Lord mean by "one will be taken and the other left" in Matthew 24:40-41? Because of the close association with "the days of Noah" (Matt. 24:37-39), many expositors believe that the ones "taken" are whisked off to judgment. Is this really so? Is there enough in the passage to come down on one side? Furthermore, if those "taken" in verses 40-41 are actually raptured, doesn't that pretty much seal a post-trib rapture?

---

107 This would fit a prewrath position.

There is no doubt in my mind that this passage is a second coming passage. There is also no doubt in my mind that the language of "one taken...another left" in Matthew 24:40-41 is apposite to the present discussion. In the surrounding context, Jesus refers to a gathering up together of the elect (Matt. 24:31). So, Jesus does speak of a removal of saints. But is this "taking out" to be understood as the ones being "taken" a few verses later? I think there is a real possibility that it may.

Perhaps most dispensationalists say that those "taken" are taken to judgment. In Matthew 24:39 those who didn't make it into the Ark (because they couldn't be bothered to go) were taken away by the flood waters. But from my reading of the second coming passages in Isaiah 63:1-6, Malachi 3:2, 4:1-2, and Revelation 19:11-21, it does not appear to be such a good idea to be "left" hanging around. This agrees with the flood story, where it was infinitely preferable to be removed to safety in the Ark than to be left to face the elements. Further, in Revelation 14:14-16 the earth is reaped of the saints, "the harvest [which is a good image] of the earth," before the wicked are gathered to "the winepress of the wrath of God" in terms too reminiscent of Isaiah 63 to ignore. Thus, Revelation 14 should not be overlooked in the discussion of this passage.

John Hart of Moody Bible Institute argues that Matthew 24:29-35 is about the second coming proper, while verses 36-44 are about a pretribulational rapture.[108] His essay is quite ingenious, but like so much minute exegesis, rests upon *petitio principii.* The very reason for the investigation is to prove that the exegete's position is possible. This often relies on converting certain words into technical terminology. In short, Hart proposes that the shift in verse 36, indicated by the Greek phrase *peri de* (which seems to hark back to at least verse 21 and following), changes the outlook from the end of the Tribulation and (back to?) a pretribulational perspective. Hart also thinks the "normalcy" depicted in verses 38-41 is hard to reconcile with posttribulational circumstances, but easier to envisage prior to the Tribulation. My take is that life goes on pretty much as usual for a lot of folks in the Tribulation, even allowing for the awful conditions (cf. Matt. 24:48-51; Rev. 18:9-19), at least in terms of the items Jesus mentions.

Of course, if Hart's version is true, then Paul's rapture teaching in 1 Thessalonians 4:17 is no new doctrine (as Hart agrees); Paul just hasn't informed them about it yet. They know about the Tribulation well enough, but the apostle has not brought them up to speed on the rapture. I find these reasons completely unconvincing. I would class the *peri de* argument for pretribulationism as being too subtle to be persuasive, and it presupposes what it needs to prove. The circumstantial argument seems plausible on the face of things, but just because people will be living their lives as best they can at the end of the Seventieth Week does not mean all is well. This commits the Either/Or fallacy. It gains some purchase with 1 Thessalonians 5:3, but there is still work to do to link it strongly to just before the Tribulation. It is a possible inference.

108 John F. Hart, "Should Pretribulationists Reconsider the Rapture in Matthew 24:36-44, Part 1 of 3," *Journal of the Grace Evangelical Society* 20 (Autumn 2007), 47-70.

But then, I would argue, a posttribulational "taking out" is a stronger inference, especially when coupled with Revelation 14:14-16. For one thing, it does not read a hitherto unknown doctrine involving the as yet non-existent NT Church (cf. Jn. 7:39) into the context. And remember, these disciples asked Jesus if He was going to restore the kingdom to Israel in Acts 1:6. I can scarcely see them doing that if they knew about the rapture of the Church prior to that! So Jesus' teaching (in Hart's view) is too subtle for the disciples. I must move on, but I think a pre-trib interpretation of any verses in the Olivet Discourse is difficult to countenance.

2 Thessalonians 2:13

The rapture version of this seemingly soteriological verse comes about as a result of making "salvation" (*soteria*) mean something like "deliverance" in this context. But it is simply too obtuse to be considered a serious rapture passage. The excruciating lengths which have to be gone into to produce the possibility that Paul is referring to the rapture, plus its reliance upon a doctrine already supposedly proven, push the limits of credulity. Besides, this view sidesteps the pretrib problem text in 2 Thessalonians 1:5-10, which employs OT imagery and appears to naturally invoke the post-tribulational return of Christ in vengeance.

Revelation 3:10

I know there are other passages, and I'm sure we'll run into them, but this verse is often used to bolster pretribulationism. It reads: "Because you [the Philadelphian saints] have kept the word of My patience, I also will keep you from (*tereso ek*) the hour of trial which shall come upon the whole earth, to test those who dwell upon the earth."

If we allow, as is plausible, a proleptic application to Christians in the future, then the "keeping out" of the coming trial would fit a rapture, and, indeed, a pretribulational rapture. This is helped by the fact that this "keeping out" is connected to the "hour," and, therefore, the time of the event. I will investigate the timing of this event later, but I do want to address one "pretrib" text which is occasionally used.[109]

EXCURSUS: Is the Rapture in 2 Thessalonians 2:3?

Some dispensational writers have believed that the catching up of the saints is what is in view in 2 Thessalonians 2:3: "Let no one deceive you by any means; for that Day will not come unless the falling away comes first, and the man of sin is revealed, the son of perdition."

I shall return to this text further on in my remarks about the future Antichrist, but will focus briefly on the term "falling away" (*apostasia*). I personally cannot find where the noun ever refers to a physical separation. Even if, perchance, I am mistaken,

109 Whatever one makes of what I have just written, it is a fact that the Church is removed somewhere before Christ comes in wrath upon His enemies (2 Thess. 1:5ff. and Rev. 19:11ff.).

"physical separation" is undeniably not its main meaning. Hogg and Vine note that in the LXX, the term has a negative connotation for rebellion or defection.[110]

But is it possible that Paul employs the verb here in a positive sense to refer to the removal of the saints to "the air" as per 1 Thessalonians 4:17?[111] Personally, I think this is extremely doubtful.[112] Besides the basic problem of the lexical meaning of the term *apostasia*, why would the apostle make use of this word in 2 Thessalonians 2:3, when just a few months before he utilized the more precise term *harpagesometha* in 1 Thessalonians 4:17?[113] Reusing *harpazo* would be a clear reminder of what he had said in 1 Thessalonians 4:17 and would have been good pedagogy. If one adds to this the fact that Paul had indicated that this "seizing" of the saints was a *new* teaching, the switch from precision to ambiguity is even less intelligible. This detail ranks as a significant counterargument against equating the two texts.

More arguments against taking *apostasia* in 2 Thessalonians 2:3 as the rapture are simply replies to the several indecisive reasons given in its favor. For instance, although apostasies have been commonplace in Church History, it could be that a marked falling away from sound doctrine worldwide will precede the revealing of the man of sin (Antichrist). It could also mean that there will be a falling away from Truth as it has imposed itself upon most of the world due to Christian influence. That fits better into the context than a rapture hypothesis (cf. Lk. 14:34). Again, if it is asserted that 2 Thessalonians 3:1 refers to "the coming of our Lord Jesus Christ and our gathering together to Him," it begs the question to claim that the "coming" is pretribulational in that context. It is a non-sequitur.[114]

The fact of the matter is that a fool-proof exegetical presentation of a pretribulational "rapture" is not possible.[115] Neither is it possible for any of the other positions. Yes, exegetical reasons for the different viewpoints can be put forth, but in reality, the passages are not plain enough nor extensive enough to arrive at rigid conclusions about them. The best that can be argued for is an inference to the best explanation.[116]

---

110 C. F. Hogg and W. E. Vine, *The Epistles of Paul the Apostle to the Thessalonians* (London: Pickering & Inglis, 1929), 346-347.

111

112 Advocates for the view are E. Schuyler English, *Rethinking the Rapture* (Neptune, NJ: Loizeaux Brothers, 1954), and Andy Woods, *The Falling Away: Spiritual Departure or Physical Rapture? A Second Look at 2 Thessalonians 2:3* (Taos, NM: Dispensational Publishing House, 2018).

113 A future passive indicative of *harpazo.*

114 I believe it is, but the exegesis does not permit dogmatism.

115 Even though it has been enthusiastically defended by Michael J. Svigel, "The Apocalypse of John and the Rapture of the Church: A Reevaluation," *Trinity Journal* 22 (Spring 2001), 23-74. I remain completely Stoic about the "man child" in Revelation 12:6 being a double reference to Christ *and* the Church. Svigel places a lot of weight on the assertion that John is alluding to Isaiah 66:7 here. But he isn't! Isaiah 66:7 is a metaphor relating to the re-birth of Israel's kingdom in the next verse. Many fellow dispensationalists are rightly far from won over by such strained exegesis of Rev. 12.

116 On this, see my "Rules of Affinity" introduction at https://paulmhenebury.com/2012/04/03/rules-of-affinity/. Although I take the apostasy of the Church view because of the Gentile audience, I do want to mention the view that takes the apostasy as Jews signing of the covenant with the Antichrist in Daniel 9:27 (cf. Dan. 11:36 with 2 Thess. 2:4). I think this has several things to commend it.

16

PAUL: AN APOSTLE OF THE NEW COVENANT (3)

For the gifts and the calling of God are irrevocable.
– Romans 11:29

The Fortunes of Israel

From the time of Paul's dramatic conversion in Acts 9, he was called to represent Yahweh to the Gentiles (Acts 9:15; Gal. 1:16). Yet he never forgot he was a Jew (Rom. 9:1-3). Nor did he forget the covenant oaths Yahweh made with Israel. He would often begin a stint in a city by going into the synagogues and expounding Christ to the Jews (e.g., Acts 13:14; 14:1; 17:1-3). Paul's love for his people and his understanding of them in God's plan is exemplified in his apology before Agrippa in Acts 26:

> I think myself happy, King Agrippa, because today I shall answer for myself before you concerning all the things of which I am accused by the Jews, especially because you are expert in all customs and questions which have to do with the Jews. Therefore I beg you to hear me patiently. My manner of life from my youth, which was spent from the beginning among my own nation at Jerusalem, all the Jews know. They knew me from the first, if they were willing to testify, that according to the strictest sect of our religion I lived a Pharisee. And now I stand and am judged for the hope of the promise made by God to our fathers. To this promise our twelve tribes, earnestly serving God night and day, hope to attain. For this hope's sake, King Agrippa, I am accused by the Jews (Acts 26:2-7, my emphasis).

The man before whom Paul stood was well versed in Jewish beliefs. He therefore could judge whether the apostle was heretical in his teaching.[1] Paul appeals to the

1 "Agrippa's reputation is disputed, but he seems to have functioned in Rome as a spokesman for Jewish causes..." (James D. G. Dunn, *Beginning From Jerusalem*, 986 n. 134). See also F. Scott

widely known fact of his strict adherence to Jewish customs and teachings according to the sect of the Pharisees (Acts 26:4-5). Then he turns to the shared hope of Israel, in accordance with "the promise made to the fathers" (Acts 26:6), by which he meant the covenant promise stemming from Abraham, Isaac, and Jacob. Paul speaks of "our religion" (Acts 26:5), "our fathers" (Acts 26:6), and "our twelve tribes" (Acts 26:7). Assuredly, Paul was not one of those scholars who believe the tribes of Israel were lost in the two captivities!

Paul, it seems, held out the same "hope" that the other Jews in the room did. That hope was not for the immersion of the twelve tribes into the Christian Church but was for those tribes to experience the expected promises covenanted to Israel in the eschaton, centered on (but not solely on) the resurrection of the dead (Acts 26:8). As the apology continues, Paul introduces Jesus (Acts 26:15), who is the Christ (Acts 26:23). He would "proclaim light to the Jewish people and to the Gentiles" (Acts 26:23b).

The proclamation of "light" to both Jews and Gentiles doubtless recalls Isaiah 49:6.[2] Once again, we come across this great messianic text, in which Jesus is likened to a covenant, cited not just for Israel, but also for the Gentiles; meaning in this particular case, the recipients of Paul's New covenant preaching ministry.

But not everyone likes this interpretation. Amillennialist interpreters, for example, posit one people of God, the Church in Christ, in all ages, and therefore hold out no future hope to ethnic and national Israel of a Davidic Kingdom emanating from Jerusalem. God's covenants (Abrahamic, Priestly, Davidic, New) are reinterpreted and applied in their altered state to the Church, the "true Israel." We are, in fact, in the "millennial" kingdom now, they say.[3] What is to come next is the New Heavens and New Earth. Here is a typical expression of the view succinctly put: "Since Jesus is the corporate representative of Israel, God now recognizes as Israel all who respond in faith and obedience to the presence and will of God revealed in Jesus."[4]

To me, there are many problems with this point of view. How, for example, is one to explain Paul's plaintiff words to Agrippa in Acts 26:7? From the look of it, the apostle is undoubtedly thinking about the future of Israel as it is depicted in the OT covenants. He refers to this as " the hope of the promise made by God to our fathers" (Acts 26:6), and it is certain that King Agrippa would have thought about it that way. It is inconceivable that Paul's real meaning would match what Holwerda wrote in the above quote.

We may see this from another angle if we consider a passage in Isaiah 62:

> For Zion's sake I will not hold My peace,
> And for Jerusalem's sake I will not rest,

Spencer, *Journeying through Acts*, 235.

2 Joshua W. Jipp, *The Messianic Theology of the New Testament*, 109; Mark S. Kinzer, "Zionism in Luke–Acts," in *The New Christian Zionism*, 157.

3 G. K. Beale, *A New Testament Biblical Theology*, 427ff. Beale also holds that we are in the Tribulation (Ibid., 203).

4 David E. Holwerda, *Jesus and Israel: One Covenant or Two?* (Grand Rapids: Eerdmans, 1995), 56-57.

> Until her righteousness goes forth as brightness,
> And her salvation as a lamp that burns.
> The Gentiles shall see your righteousness,
> And all kings your glory.
> You shall be called by a new name,
> Which the mouth of the LORD will name.
> You shall also be a crown of glory
> In the hand of the LORD,
> And a royal diadem
> In the hand of your God.
> You shall no longer be termed Forsaken,
> Nor shall your land any more be termed Desolate;
> But you shall be called Hephzibah, and your land Beulah;
> For the LORD delights in you,
> And your land shall be married.
> For as a young man marries a virgin,
> So shall your sons marry you;
> And as the bridegroom rejoices over the bride,
> So shall your God rejoice over you (Isa. 62:1-5).

This poignant and impassioned declaration from Yahweh about Israel cannot be spirited away by the magic dust of post-Pentecost hermeneutics. This is the heart of God for His chosen people. "Zion" and "Jerusalem" are named (Isa. 62:1), and the "Gentiles" are brought in for contrast (Isa. 62:2). The righteousness of Israel will be witnessed by the nations of the world (Isa. 62:1-2), and Yahweh Himself will name them anew (Isa. 62:2b), in all probability once they are what He called them to be (Exod. 19:5-6; Isa. 44:8). New names are given in Isaiah 62:4: "Hephzibah" means "My delight is in her," while "Beulah" simply means "married." The new names match the divine opinion. Yahweh *will* delight in Israel (He doesn't now), and He *will* be married to the nation in their land (cf. Isa. 54:5; Jer. 31:32; Hos. 2:7, 16).

God will rejoice over redeemed Israel (Isa. 62:5; cf. Zeph. 3:17). Although these verses are not quoted in the NT, they encapsulate the hopes of Jews in Paul's day. They speak of the fulfillment of the Abrahamic covenant with Israel, of the bond that the covenant protects.[5] The latter half of the chapter brings in New covenant blessing (Isa. 62:8-12).[6] Dunn refers to Joseph Fitzmyer's citing of Isaiah 62:1-5 in connection with Acts 3:21 and the idea of "cosmic restoration."[7] I see no evidence in Acts or anywhere else to cause me to doubt the expectation of Peter in Acts 3 was shared by Paul and the Jews present in Acts 26. Hence, the expectation of Isaiah 62 is fully in accord with Acts 26:2-7, and nothing in Paul's defense suggests a spiritualization of these covenant promises ever entered his mind.

---

5 Robert L. Saucy, *The Case for Progressive Dispensationalism*, 184.
6 Paul R. Williamson, *Sealed with an Oath*, 43 n. 70.
7 James D. G. Dunn, *Beginning From Jerusalem*, 223 n. 259.

"The Israel of God"

I intend to give attention to Romans 11 further on, paying particular attention to the crucial "Olive Tree" metaphor.[8] In it we will see that God will again turn to deal with ethnic Israel (*not* the Church in Christ) once "the fullness of the Gentiles has come in" (Rom. 11:25). This statement is followed by the quotation of New covenant passages out of Isaiah. If an intervening system is not permitted access here, Paul means that once God has concluded His saving work with the Gentiles, doubtless through the Church, He will begin to save Jews *en masse* in a manner foretold in the OT Scriptures. Not independent of their national aspirations, but in full accordance with them as set out in the Abrahamic, Priestly, and Davidic covenants, mediated through the New covenant. This understanding helps with the interpretation of Galatians 6:16: "And as many as walk according to this rule, peace and mercy *be* upon them, and upon the Israel of God."

It is quite amazing how frequently this text is used by non-dispensationalists as a proof text for identifying the Church as "Israel."[9] I do not doubt the integrity of such men, but if one simply examines the passage, there is no reason to draw such a conclusion. Here is the wider context:

> As many as desire to make a good showing in the flesh, these *would* compel you to be circumcised, only that they may not suffer persecution for the cross of Christ. For not even those who are circumcised keep the law, but they desire to have you circumcised that they may boast in your flesh. But God forbid that I should boast except in the cross of our Lord Jesus Christ, by whom the world has been crucified to me, and I to the world. For in Christ Jesus neither circumcision nor uncircumcision avails anything, but a new creation. And as many as walk according to this rule, peace and mercy *be* upon them, and upon the Israel of God (Gal. 6:12-16).

Those who Paul mentions as wanting "to make a good showing in the flesh" (Gal. 6:12) are Judaizers who have brought into the Galatian churches the false teaching that Gentiles need to be circumcised to be right with God (Gal. 3:1; 5:1-6; 6:15). Obviously, this has covenant overtones, although the covenant being espoused in verses 12 and 13 is the Mosaic covenant, not the New covenant in Christ. However, the New covenant does, I believe, make a veiled appearance in verse 15: "For in Christ Jesus neither circumcision nor uncircumcision avails anything, but a new creation" (Gal. 6:15).

---

8 Romans 9–11 will be surveyed as a piece below.

9 Among authors who argue that Gal. 6:16 is referring to both Jew and Gentiles, see e.g., Ben Witherington III, *Jesus, Paul and the End of the World*, 107-108, 126-127; G. K. Beale, *A New Testament Biblical Theology*, 305-306, 309-310; Douglas J. Moo, *A Biblical Theology of Paul and His Letters*, 86-87. Gal. 3 is often the basis for their interpretations (see my exposition above). Oftentimes this position is simply taken for granted. See e.g., the first chapters of *Progressive Covenantalism* (27, 54), although they do footnote more extended treatments.

The reference to a "new creation" here is to the new birth (Gal. 4:6-7) through the Holy Spirit (Gal. 3:2; 5:25). As I have shown above, the reception of the Spirit is a New covenant blessing. Therefore, Jews and Gentiles *in the Church* have been made parties to the New covenant in Christ. However, it does not follow that the apostle has this in mind when he writes Galatians 6:16. One ought to recall the clear connection of New covenant blessings upon national Israel (Jer. 31:31-37; Ezek. 36:22-38; 37:15-28).

Replacing National Israel's Covenant Promises

G. K. Beale is at the forefront of what I, along with many others, identify as "replacement theology." In an essay on "The Eschatology of Paul," Beale writes:

> Christ's death and resurrection, along with the formation of the eschatological people of God, have ushered in the fulfillment of the OT's prophecies about the end times. In this initial eschatological phase, Christ and the church fulfill the promises concerning Israel's tribulation, deliverance from oppressors, and kingdom, since Jesus is seen by the NT as the true, spiritual Israel who represents his people as such (see Rom. 2:25-29; 9:6, 24-26; Gal 3:29; 6:15-16; Eph. 2:16-18; 3:6; 1 Pet 2:9; Rev 1:6; 3:9; 5:10).[10]

To respond in brief, Romans 2:25-29 refers to Jews who are unregenerate. Romans 9:6 refers to non-elect Jews. Romans 9:24-26 refers to Gentiles who are prepared for glory *along* with elect Israel. Galatians 3:29 concerns the Church's relation to the third part of the Abrahamic covenant. Galatians 6:15-16 concerns non-elect Jews, Gentiles, *and* elect Israel. Ephesians 2:16-18 and 3:6 both refer to the Jew/Gentile complexion of the Church. 1 Peter 2:9 refers to Jewish believers.[11] Revelation 1:6 and 5:10 speak of our future inheritance, but say nothing about Israel's Kingdom hopes. And finally, Revelation 3:9 seems to refer either to people who wrongly claim they are "spiritual Israel" (like Beale), or those who claim to be actual Jews but are not Jews.[12] Reformed Covenant Theology is heavily deductive in character, which results in wholesale spiritualizing of the covenants that Yahweh made. As clever as it undoubtedly is, Covenant Theology (and Progressive Covenantalism) contradict God.[13]

10 G. K. Beale, "The Eschatology of Paul," in *Studies in the Pauline Epistles: Essays in Honor of Douglas J. Moo*, eds. Matthew S. Harmon and Jay E. Smith (Grand Rapids: Zondervan, 2014), 202.

11 See the treatment of this passage in its place.

12 I expound most of these texts in the course of this book.

13 See, for example, David Rudolph, "Does Paul Eliminate Particularity for Israel and the Land in His Portrayal of Salvation Available to All the World?" in *The New Christian Zionism: Fresh Perspectives on Israel and the Land*, ed. Gerald R. McDermott (Downers Grove, IL: IVP, 2016), 167-194.

No Rapprochement

Before proceeding, I should say that views such as this tend to bring out what I believe to be the irreconcilable differences between Covenant Theology (and Progressive Covenantalism) and Dispensationalism (or, in my case, Biblical Covenantalism). The two approaches have different starting assumptions, and so end up in different places. We are brothers because we have believed that Jesus is literally the Son of God and that He literally died at Calvary for our sins and literally rose again so that we may have life eternal. This is why we have literally been given the Spirit, and we have been literally adopted into God's family. But when God's covenants are not taken literally by our brethren, we must lovingly but firmly oppose them. The following is my understanding of Paul's intention in Galatians 6:16:

For a start, it is important to note that Galatians is aimed primarily at Gentile Christians who have been unduly influenced by the high-sounding rhetoric of Jewish false teachers. For Paul, as a Jew who loves his people and his nation (Rom. 9:1-5; 10:1; 11:11-12), these false brethren were the very worst of combinations. Their twisted understanding of the Gospel and the place of Jesus Christ within it was a case of being so close yet so far away from the saving truth. And now they were infecting the churches with their doctrines. It is in that spirit that he pens his words.

He sees another motive in these Judaizers also. Paul says that the reason they so forcibly insist upon circumcision has to do with their avoiding persecution (probably from fellow Jews). If they can persuade Gentiles to be circumcised, they are closer to making proselytes out of them and bringing them under the auspices of the Law, not grace (cf. Gal. 3:3; 5:4). This is tantamount to avoiding the death of Jesus on the cross and the salvific benefits of His sacrifice. I do not say that these Judaizers rejected Jesus as the Christ, although I think that is distinctly possible. They may have pretended to be believers in Jesus as the Messiah in order to gain entrance to these assemblies.[14] Perhaps not. One thing is for sure: these men were a long way from being the kind of Jewish believers the apostle wished to encounter. His terse counter to their teaching is in Galatians 6:14: "But God forbid that I should boast except in the cross of our Lord Jesus Christ, by whom the world has been crucified to me, and I to the world."

If the cross of Christ is the sole instrument of separating the righteous from the world system, then what status does circumcision, or indeed the Law, still have (cf. Gal. 3:10-14)? This thought is found elsewhere. For example, in Colossians 2:14, Paul states that Jesus had "wiped out the handwriting of requirements that was against us, which was contrary to us." This He has removed completely, "having nailed it to the cross." Believers are not linked to the world. They are citizens of heaven (Phil. 3:20); new creatures "in Christ Jesus" (Gal. 6:15; cf. 2 Cor. 5:17). This is the truth that the Galatians should believe. Without it, there can be no "peace and mercy"[15] from God

14 Such is the way of self-deception that some of these false Christians may have thought they were true believers.

15 This order is unique in the Greek Bible. See Carl B. Hoch, Jr., *All Things New: The Significance of Newness for Biblical Theology* (Grand Rapids: Baker, 1995), 274-280.

to man. So, Paul declares, "And as many as walk according to this rule, peace and mercy *be* upon them, and upon the Israel of God" (Gal. 6:16).

The "many who follow this rule" are the true followers of Christ. But Paul's hopes for Israel, which are based in God's covenants, show themselves clearly in his adding "and upon the Israel of God" onto his statement in Galatians 6:16. In Romans 9:1-3 he says, "I have great sorrow and *continual* grief in my heart" (my emphasis), concerning Israel. This "continual grief" did not just start after he wrote Galatians. I firmly believe it was present when he wrote Galatians 6. Yes, Jews who corrupt the truth about Jesus have influenced the churches, and Paul calls them "accursed" (Gal. 1:8-9). But this does not mean that all Jews who speak the name of Jesus are false. There is "a remnant according to the election of grace" (Rom. 11:5), who are "the Israel of God" (Gal. 6:16). What could be a more natural thing for him to say? And why would anyone interpret the *kai* in verse 16 as anything but "and" when it makes perfectly good sense in the argument?[16] Unless, of course, their theology forced them into it.[17]

No, the "Israel of God" is elect Israel,[18] of whom there is always a remnant. They are "the twelve tribes scattered abroad," to whom James writes (Jam. 1:1). They are the actual descendants of Abraham, Isaac, and Jacob who have embraced the Gospel. They are also the eschatological Israel, who God will save after "the fullness of the Gentiles" has been brought in (Rom. 11:25).[19]

In order for a person to enter into the redeemed people of God, their sins must be propitiated. This means that, at a minimum, the sinner must be connected to Christ's propitiatory death on the cross. What is less clear is whether all sinners from *every age* are connected to Christ's life in the same way.[20] If, for example, Israel has covenant promises which guarantee its eternal existence as an independent nation "married" to God the Father (Jer. 3:14; Hos. 2:2, 7, 16), then union with Christ may look different for national Israel than it does for the Church, Christ's body.[21] Certainly the Spirit is

16 Indeed, as many have argued before, if he wished to equate those "who walk according to this rule" with "the Israel of God" why put a *kai* in there in the first place?

17 Many non-dispensational interpreters hold that "the Israel of God" in the passage is national Israel. E.g., H. D. Betz, G. C. Berkouwer, J. D. G. Dunn, E. DeWitt Burton, F. F. Bruce, F. Mussner, W. D. Davies, P. Richardson, B. Witherington, D. Yoon, etc. To use this disputed verse as a proof-text for the Church being "the true Israel" shows how meager the scriptural evidence is for this position.

18 It is far less likely to be the Judaizers who are troubling the churches.

19 See Ben Witherington III, "Paul, Galatians, and Supersessionism," in *God's Israel and the Israel of God*, 76-77.

20 This seems to be the assertion of Zane C. Hodges, "Regeneration: A New Covenant Blessing," *Journal of the Grace Evangelical Society*, 18 (Autumn 2005), 43-49. Hodges makes very similar statements to mine regarding Christ's "New covenant blood," but I do not go as far as he does in claiming that this implies regeneration, at least in the way it is experienced in the Church.

21 I understand how many people cannot bring themselves to consider the possibility that there is more than one people of God. With a world of variety all around them they believe that the variety stops at the people(s) of God. I do not believe that the biblical text justifies this position at all. In fact, the covenants stand in the way of it. This is why the covenants of God must be misshapen and reapplied so as to suit a presumed one people of God theology. This is one reason why I have had to devote so much space to address this prejudice.

prominent, and Israel's restoration is based in the New covenant (Jer. 31:31-34), but if the Church is Christ's bride (see Eph. 5:23, 32), and remnant Israel is the Father's bride (Jer. 3:14; Isa. 62:4), there will be similarities and differences—and the differences are not to be overlooked. There is a living hope for Israel as a nation guaranteed by the covenants of God, and that is what Paul is alluding to in Galatians 6:16.[22]

Paul's Concern for His People: What is Happening in Romans 9–11?

Romans 9 through 11 have been a bone of contention between different theological camps for hundreds of years. Often Romans 9 is utilized by Reformed writers to prove the doctrine of individual predestination to salvation (and damnation).[23] Whatever the merits of Calvinism as a soteriology, I believe that its adherents have here allowed their doctrine of salvation to come between themselves and the text. Paul here is not concerned with individual salvation per se, but with the sovereign[24] election of Israel as a group.[25] This is in line with OT thinking, where election is corporate (Exod. 19:5-6; Deut. 7:6; Isa. 45:4; 65:9; Jer. 31:9; cf. Rom. 11:28-29).[26] This corporate element is plainly in view in the divine covenants (e.g., Gen. 15; Exod. 24; Jer. 31:1, 7, 31-32; cf.

22 For more on this see e.g., S. Lewis Johnson, Jr., "Paul and 'The Israel of God': An Exegetical and Eschatological Case-Study," in *Essays in Honor of J. Dwight Pentecost*, eds. Stanley D. Toussaint and Charles H. Dyer (Chicago: Moody, 1986), 181-196. For a Reformed perspective, which calls into question the "spiritualizing interpretation" of the verse, see G. C. Berkouwer, *The Return of Christ*, Studies in Dogmatics (Grand Rapids: Eerdmans, 1972), 355-349.

23 E.g., John Piper, *The Justification of God: An Exegetical and Theological Study of Romans 9:1-23* (Grand Rapids: Baker, 1993). Boettner puts the matter bluntly: "The Reformed Faith has held to the existence of an eternal, divine decree which, antecedently to any difference or desert in men themselves, separates the human race into two portions and ordains one to everlasting life and the other to everlasting death" (Loraine Boettner, *The Reformed Doctrine of Predestination* [Phillipsburg, NJ: P & R, 1976], 83). But Dunn observes, "Even though the attempt has been made to interpret Rom. 9–11 in terms of individuals rather than peoples, it is clear enough that the chief concern for Paul was to affirm that the corporate entity Israel is still at the heart of God's purpose of salvation (11:25-26)" (James D. G. Dunn, "Paul's Theology," in *The Face of New Testament Studies: A Survey of Recent Research*, eds. Scot McKnight and Grant R. Osborne [Grand Rapids: Baker, 2004], 334). Although, I disagree with Dunn's equation of the Church with Israel.

24 God's sovereignty is His will in action over what He has made. This means that technically we cannot say "God is sovereign" in the same sense as we can say "God is love" (1 Jn. 4:8, 16). This is because "love" is essential to His being as God, whereas "sovereignty" is the exercise of God's will upon His external creation. God as Lord will exercise His sovereignty in accord with His essential attributes.

25 I do not deny an individual dimension to election. But I do not believe that is Paul's central concern in Romans 9–11.

26 This position flies in the face of the standard Reformed reading of these chapters. Greg Lanier, for example, in giving the fourteen OT quotations in Rom. 9–11 claims that, "While some of these examples evoke God's *corporate* election of Israel as a nation (Deut. 7:6-7), the main thrust is *individual* election, since Paul is arguing that some persons who seem to be part of 'Israel' are not actually part of it (Rom. 9:6)" (Greg Lanier, *Old Made New: A Guide to the New Testament Use of the Old Testament*[Wheaton: Crossway, 2022], 54). But Rom. 9:6 refers to the remnant of believers of Israel (cf. Rom. 9:27), not individual believers. Moreover, he doesn't even mention Gentiles until Rom. 9:24. He is speaking about elect and non-elect Israel. See Carl B. Hoch, Jr., *All Things New*, 272.

Rom. 11:25ff.). Yahweh is, of course, "the God of Israel" (Exod. 5:1; Num. 16:9; Josh. 24:23; 2 Sam. 7:27; Jer. 31:23). Paul is thinking corporately of Israel's remnant (Rom. 9:27; 11:5) and their covenanted hopes.[27] To cite Stephen Westerholm, "The notion that judgment could represent the final stage of God's dealings with his people proved unthinkable: how could a divine initiative end in failure?"[28]

In order to show that failure of Israel's calling and election, however nicely painted, is not an option, I shall run through Romans 9, linking it to OT texts and Paul's longer argument in Romans 10 and 11. The briefest outline of the section that helps as a basic guide is this: Romans 9 (Election); Romans 10 (Rejection); Romans 11 (Reception).[29]

In what follows, I set out a reading of the section that stresses the corporate Israel-centeredness of Paul's concerns. I know many who take a more corporate approach believe that he is teaching that the combination of both Israel and the Gentiles (i.e., the vast majority in the Body of Christ) in the Church is uppermost on the apostle's mind,[30] but I think the following Israel-focused approach has merit.

It doesn't take a genius to figure out that Paul has changed gears from Romans 8 to Romans 9. Unfortunately, many interpreters come to this section with an assumption that there can be only one people of God, the Church, and so they read the apostle in that light. This means that they may see more continuity between Romans 8 and 9 than is really there.[31] But that is to do him a disservice. They end up claiming that Paul's theme is the salvation of both Jews and Gentiles,[32] when on a plain

---

27 One can see the emphasis on corporate election from Rom. 9:3-5 ("my countrymen"); 6-7 ("in Isaac"); 11-13 (quoting Mal. 1:2-3); 23-24 (Jews and Gentiles), etc. Longenecker calls attention to the deliberate use of *sperma* ("seed," "descendants") in Rom. 9:6-8 and again in 9:29, plus the "roughly synonymous" noun *hypoleimma* ("the remnant") in Rom. 9:27, therefore forming an *inclusio*. See Richard N. Longenecker, *The Epistle to the Romans*, 811-813. This strongly suggests that the apostle does not change over from corporate to individual election then back to corporate election in the space of twenty-nine verses.

28 Stephen Westerholm, *Understanding Paul: The Early Christian Worldview of the Letter to the Romans* (Grand Rapids: Baker, 2004), 142.

29 Alva J. McClain, *Romans: The Gospel of God's Grace* (Chicago: Moody, 1986), 175.

30 See on this the detailed article by Brian J. Abasciano, "Clearing Up Misconceptions About Corporate Election," *Ashland Theological Journal*, 41 (2009), 59-90. One does not have to share the author's Arminian background to appreciate his arguments. See also the stimulating essay by William S. Campbell, "'Through Isaac Shall Your Seed Be Named' (Romans 9:7b): Israel and the Purpose of God in Romans," in *The Future Restoration of Israel: A Response to Supercessionism*, eds. Stanley E. Porter and Alan E. Kurschner (Eugene, OR: Pickwick Publications, 2023), 197-215; and Alva J. McClain, *Romans*, 175-184..

31 A good balance is struck by Ben Witherington III with Darlene Hyatt, *Paul's Letter to the Romans: A Socio-Rhetorical Commentary* (Grand Rapids: Eerdmans, 2004), 236-238. Naturally, this can be pressed too far in the other direction. The apostle's argument is not disconnected with what he has said before, but the question of Israel moves the conversation onto OT covenant ground.

32 This is stated succinctly by Schreiner: "the equality of the Gentiles with the Jews in the church is a truth that is not prominently featured in the Old Testament. When we think of the mystery of God's work relative to Jews and Gentiles, Paul's discussion of the whole matter in Romans 9–11 comes to mind..." (Thomas R. Schreiner, *Paul, Apostle of God's Glory in Christ*, 59). It is my opinion that the Church is not referred to at all in the OT. Further, Paul's concern in Rom. 9–11 is the fulfillment of God's covenants to Israel, and hence God's faithfulness to His word

reading of the chapters, his central concern has become the future of Israel.[33] Having proved that all are sinners and in dire need of God's grace in Romans 1–4, and shown that the sphere of God's grace is within Christ in Romans 5–8 (especially in the realm of the Spirit, Rom. 8:1-16), Paul reaches the *telos* of Christian salvation: glory and world-transformation in Romans 8:18-25, 30. Having concluded his outline of the Gospel, he is now in a place to proceed to the issue of God's covenant faithfulness to Israel in the next three chapters.

The opening refrain is enough to show that Paul is moving on from the doctrines of justification and sanctification in the Church and is now concerned with the fortunes of Israel. As he says: "For I could wish that I myself were accursed from Christ for my brethren, my countrymen according to the flesh" (Rom. 9:3). There is great intensity of feeling in these words. The reason for Paul's sorrow concerning Israel has to do with all that has been promised to that nation.

The apostle names six privileges that pertain to Israel: "who are Israelites, to whom *pertain* the adoption, the glory, the covenants, the giving of the law, the service *of God,* and the promises" (Rom. 9:4). Let us run through them quickly. First, he speaks of "the adoption." This is illustrated in texts like Ezekiel 16:3-14 (cf. Exod. 4:22; 19:5; Deut. 14:1; Isa. 64:8; Amos 3:2). Israel is depicted by Ezekiel as a baby who is left helpless right after birth, and God is described as taking pity on her, adopting her, and watching over her until adulthood (Israel is then described as going astray).

Next to be mentioned is "the glory," by which he means the glory of Yahweh that was shown to Israel during the wilderness wanderings (e.g., Exod. 16:7-10; 24:16-17; Lev. 9:23) and which entered the Tabernacle (Num. 14:10) and Solomon's Temple (1 Ki. 8:11). The third item mentioned is the covenants of God, the Abrahamic, Mosaic,[34] Priestly, Davidic, and New covenants.[35] Then comes "the giving of the Law," which refers to Exodus 19ff. (cf. Jer. 44:10). The fifth thing mentioned, "the service (of God)," refers initially to Exodus 19:6, which is yet to be realized (Isa. 43:10, 12), as well as the Levitical codes. Finally, we read of the "promises," which may be a generic reference to everything that Yahweh pledged to Israel, from the primacy of Jerusalem to the recombination of the tribes.[36]

(Rom. 9:1-5, 27-29; 10:1; 11:1-5, 11-12, 23-29), not the mystery of Jews and Gentiles in the Church!

33 The name "Israel" alone appears twelve times in these three chapters, and only here in Romans.

34 It is very possible that Paul places the Mosaic covenant under the next category, "the giving of the Law."

35 As I have shown, the New covenant is promised to Israel in Jer. 31:31ff., but it is also the property of the Church (1 Cor. 11:25). Of course, the third aspect of the Abrahamic covenant pertains to the Church and the nations. Finally, as the Davidic covenant refers to worldwide rule as well as a reign over Israel (Psa. 2:6-8; 66:4; 67:4; Isa. 26:9; Zech. 14:9), and as the Church will be present in the coming kingdom (2 Tim. 4:1), it means that the covenant with David *effects* the Church in the eschaton. For reasons such as these, I cannot agree with Johnson when he states, "the Biblical covenants are distinct because they are exclusively addressed to Israel as partners (Rom. 9:4)" (Elliott Johnson, *A Dispensational Biblical Theology*, 8). When one adds in the Noahic covenant, this statement is easily refuted.

36 "The Israel of God's call is still the Israel God called" (James D. G. Dunn, *The Theology of the Apostle Paul*, 520).

> But it is not that the word of God has taken no effect. For they *are* not all Israel who *are* of Israel, nor *are they* all children because they are the seed of Abraham; but, "In Isaac your seed shall be called" (Rom. 9:6-7).

The statement that "they are not all Israel who are of Israel" has been taken by many supercessionists as meaning that Gentiles can also be "of Israel" because they are "in Christ," who now represents Israel. But this utterly misreads the apostle's train of thought. It is a questionable assertion to claim that Jesus takes on Israel's mission. Israel's mission in the OT was not like modern Christian missions which spread out to different people groups. We do not see any call to Israel to spread their faith to the nations. Rather, they were more like a mirror for the nations to look at—an obedient people. They failed to do this but will succeed through the Spirit one day (Isa. 44:8-9).

Paul here is repeating an already acknowledged truth that simply being Jewish is not an automatic qualification, on its own, to share in the six blessings of verse 4.[37] Also, mere genetic relation to Abraham is nothing of itself (cf. Matt. 3:9). Notice that Isaac is introduced (Rom. 9:7). He is the child of promise, the child of faith (Gen. 21:12; cf. Gen. 17:18-19; Rom. 4:16-18). And the faith aspect is just as important to Paul as physical descent. The two must be combined. Then Jacob is introduced, with Paul reminding us that he was the subject of a prophecy, "the elder shall serve the younger" (Rom. 9:12/ Gen. 25:23), although the fact that the prophecy directly spoke of "two *nations*," not two individuals should be acknowledged![38]

This election was ordained that "the purpose of God according to election might stand" (Rom. 9:11). Here the verb *eklogen*, translated "election," refers back to verse 6 and an Israel within Israel (cf. Rom. 11:2-5).[39] As Ronald Diprose reminds us, "Esau never served Jacob (in fact, it was Jacob who bowed before Esau [Genesis 33:1-4])."[40] The idea is that Israelites are all related to Abraham through Isaac and Jacob, but not all are true believing Israel. God has "a remnant according to the election of grace" (Rom. 11:5).

The teaching of the Jewish remnant is familiar to any OT reader (2 Ki. 19:30-31; 2 Chron. 30:6; Isa. 1:9; 10:20-22; Ezek. 11:13-20; Zeph. 3:13). God has always preserved such a remnant. Right now, Jewish believers in Jesus are a remnant in the Church. Covenantally speaking, there has to be a remnant since there has to be a bloodline for eschatological Israel to claim. And not Jews only but God Himself must preserve Israel, or His oaths to the Fathers would fail.

---

37 This is brought out in places like Jer. 30:11 and Hos. 2.

38 "And the LORD said to her: 'Two nations *are* in your womb, two peoples shall be separated from your body; *one* people shall be stronger than the other, and the older shall serve the younger'" (Gen. 25:23).

39 I realize that not everyone likes to speak of "an Israel within Israel," but I see nothing inaccurate about the idea. For sure Israel, even in unbelief, are the people of the covenant (e.g., Neh. 9:32), but there is a Tribulation coming upon Israel and many will perish without receiving the New covenant blessing in Christ. The "all Israel" of Rom. 11:26 refers to the Jewish remnant.

40 I have been influenced here by Ronald E. Diprose, *Israel and the Church: The Origin and Effects of Replacement Theology* (Waynesboro, GA; Authentic Media, 2004), 15-21. Although I take issue here and there (e.g., I disagree that salvation was included within the terms of the covenant with Abraham, 16-17), I recommend this study.

The apostle then quotes another OT reference from Malachi 1:1-2: "Jacob have I loved but Esau I have hated" (Rom. 9:13). This saying is far removed in time from the Genesis narratives, being written in the fifth century before Christ. We see once more that the theme of the chapter so far is corporate Israel, not individual salvation. Israel is God's peculiar treasure (Exod. 19:5; Deut. 32:10; Zech. 2:8), while those from Esau (e.g., Edomites) were less favored.

Having put a theme in place, Paul asks a question: "What shall we say then? *Is there* unrighteousness with God? Certainly not!" (Rom. 9:14). This question is raised because the sovereign choice of Yahweh, independent of any good works, has been established. Israel is a chosen people, and that choice is not based upon their character or their deeds.[41] Paul supports this with a quotation from the book of Exodus: "For He says to Moses, 'I will have mercy on whomever I will have mercy, and I will have compassion on whomever I will have compassion'" (Exod. 33:19).

This, of course, is a divine prerogative. But it is not caprice. The very section this quotation comes from includes Yahweh's own description of Himself as "merciful and gracious, longsuffering, and abounding in goodness and truth" (Exod. 34:6). God is always just (Gen. 18:25; Deut. 32:4). Paul is not propounding a voluntarist God.[42] He states that God's gracious election of Israel was not unrighteous. Since all are sinners (Rom. 3:23; the one "lump" of Rom. 9:21), grace can operate where it deems fit. Our good efforts and wishes notwithstanding, sin bars the way. Hence, Paul is in agreement with John in asserting that God's decision comes before man's decision (Rom. 9:16; cf. Jn. 1:13).

Next, Paul illustrates this with the example of the Pharaoh of the Exodus (Rom. 9:17). Although he singles out an individual this time, it should be recalled that Pharaoh was the man who stood in the way of Israel. This man was fractious and proud, and God predicted that he would not allow Moses and Israel to go (Exod. 3:19). In the story of Yahweh's defeat of Egypt's gods that came from this (Exod. 4–12), we first hear of Pharaoh hardening his heart after the second and third plagues (Exod. 8:15, 32). This is before God hardened his heart after the sixth plague (Exod. 9:12), although it should be said that Yahweh had told Moses that He would harden Pharaoh's heart as far back as Exodus 4:21 (cf. Exod. 7:3).

God's hardening of the heart of someone who replied as Pharaoh did was fully justifiable.[43] Hence, Paul's polemical answer to one who questions how God can fault a person for doing His will is blunt and to the point: we need to remember Who is God and who is the creature (Rom. 9:19-21).[44]

---

41 When the life and character of Jacob is considered, this truth comes through loud and clear.

42 God cannot do anything He wants *because* He is the Creator. He only wants what is agreeable with His nature as good and veracious and just. In the same way, He cannot lie (Tit. 1:2) God cannot say something is good or just when it is not.

43 "Who is the LORD, that I should obey His voice to let Israel go? I do not know the LORD, nor will I let Israel go" (Exod. 5:2).

44 Although I have come down on one side of the issue, I do not wish to give the impression that the hardening of Pharaoh's heart should not be studied from all sides. I recommend Jerry M. Hullinger, "A Reexamination of Pharaoh's Hard Heart with Regard to Egyptian Religion," *JODT* 16 (Apr 2012), 23ff.; Gregory K. Beale, "An Exegetical And Theological Consideration Of The

What is one to make of this? I think what Paul goes on to say straightens out the confusion. He asks a question that does not portray human beings as hapless pawns of the voluntaristic Will, but as responsible agents under God's gaze (cf. Psa. 11:4; 33:13-15). He puts it this way:

> Does not the potter have power over the clay, from the same lump to make one vessel for honor and another for dishonor? What if God, wanting to show *His* wrath and to make His power known, endured with much longsuffering the vessels of wrath prepared for destruction, and that He might make known the riches of His glory on the vessels of mercy, which He had prepared beforehand for glory. even us whom He called, not of the Jews only, but also of the Gentiles? (Rom. 9:21-24).

This is a key passage in trying to understand election. It is not arbitrary in any sense. We may not know the precise *reasons* for God's selection of (and indeed creation of) Israel from among the nations of the world, but we can be sure that their election was not born out of irrationality or whim (cf. Dan. 4:37). God did not pick Israel to be His "special treasure" (Exod. 19:5) in the same way some Christians pick promises from the Bible, by closing their eyes and placing their finger on a page.

The first thing to notice here is that the two kinds of "vessels" came from the same "lump" (Rom. 9:21). Paul employs the word *phyrama,* which describes something that is mixed and kneaded together, like bread-dough. Hence, the "vessels" are fitted for their purpose after all the ingredients and the preparation had been done. The "one lump" is humanity. There is no hint here of God creating people to damn them.[45] No, Abraham was "a wandering Aramean" (Deut. 26:5 NASB), from whom the nation of Israel sprang; a part of the one lump from whom Yahweh formed His chosen people. Abraham, like everyone else, came from the nations who came from Noah, who came from Adam. So here is a man (Pharaoh, Rom. 9:17), whom Yahweh has "endured with much longsuffering" and who God has made a vessel of wrath (Rom. 9:22). This is the case with any sinner who defies God, or any nation for that matter. But out of that same "lump" Paul identifies a second type of vessel: those "prepared beforehand for glory" (Rom. 9:23). This is the remnant of Israel (cf. Rom. 9:4),[46] but it also extends to Gentiles in the Church (Rom. 9:24). This does not imply that *from now on into eternity* Israel and the Church are one people of God—the "theological Israel" as a recent book dubs it.[47] Rather, it accounts for why Jews and

Hardening Of Pharaoh's Heart In Exodus 4-14 And Romans 9," *Trinity Journal* 5 (Fall 1984), 129ff.; and Robert B. Chisholm, Jr., "Divine Hardening in the Old Testament," *BSAC* 153 (Oct 1996), 410ff.

45 As has been taught by many like John Calvin, John Owen, A. W. Pink, R. C. Sproul, and John Piper. Not all Calvinists have held to this position.

46 Although not connecting the "vessels of mercy" to the remnant of Israel, Moo does say of Rom. 9:14-23 that "Allusion in this part of the chapter to unbelieving Israel is muted but clear" (Douglas Moo, *The Epistle to the Romans*, 609). If unbelieving Israel is in view as the vessels of wrath, then believing Israel must be in view as vessels of mercy.

47 Chris Bruno, Jared Compton, and Kevin McFadden, *Biblical Theology According to the Apostles: How the Earliest Christians Told the Story of Israel* (Downers Grove, IL: InterVarsity,

Gentiles are *now* one people of God in the Church,[48] but it says nothing about the eschaton. I hope to show that the compelling witness of the NT (as that of the OT) is that the Church is an instantiation of the people of God, just as the remnant who will comprise the eschatological nation of Israel is another instantiation of the people of God.

Four Old Testament Quotations

From this point, Paul brings in two quotations each from Hosea and Isaiah. First up in Romans 9:25 is Hosea 2:23,[49] which in Hosea reads as follows:

> Then I will sow her for Myself in the earth,
> And I will have mercy on *her who had* not obtained mercy;
> Then I will say to *those who were* not My people,
> 'You *are* My people!'
> And they shall say, '*You are* my God!'

Paul's rendition of Hosea 2:23 is slightly different: "I will call them My people, who were not My people, and her beloved, who was not beloved" (Rom. 9:25). Particular notice should be given to the verb *kaleso* ("I will call"), which is inserted by Paul himself. Gentiles in the Church are God's "special people" (Tit. 2:14; cf. Rom. 15:9-11), called by Him (Rom. 1:6-7), and hence are "the vessels of mercy" (Rom. 9:23) along with Israel. But the mostly Gentile Church, which may be called "the new people of God,"[50] as long as supercessionism stays far away, will have its fruition (Rom. 11:25), and then God will turn once more to Israel (Rom. 11:26ff.). Hence, as far as the Church is concerned, Jews and Gentiles are one people (Eph. 2:15; Gal. 3:28). Because this is so, it is not drifting so far from the context to use Hosea to not only affirm the remnant's continuing access to grace through the Christian *ekklesia* (cf. Rom. 11:5), but the Gentiles too. However, as Paul will show in chapter 11, future Israel retains its covenant hopes independently of the Church.[51]

Paul's next quotation is from Hosea 1:10: "And it shall come to pass in the place where it was said to them, 'You are not My people,' there they shall be called sons of the living God" (Rom. 9:26). Paul's retention of the "place" of calling[52] warns us not to jump to hasty conclusions about his meaning. Since he had no problem adapting Hosea 2:23 for his purposes, the fact that he quoted Hosea 1:10 verbatim is significant. Hosea 2 is actually in keeping with Hosea 1, where the northern tribes of Israel are

---

2020), 126-129. Thomas R. Schreiner says, "The church is the renewed Israel and the arena in which God's promises find their fulfillment" (*Romans*, 528). The trouble is, Paul will go on to quote Hos. 1:10 (Rom. 9:26), which speaks not of a generic "arena" but of a specific "place" (i.e. the land of Israel) where Israel will again be called the sons of the living God.

48 Although Jews are still Jews.

49 In the LXX it is Hosea 2:25.

50 Thomas R. Schreiner, *Romans*, 527.

51 This means that while it is accurate to describe the Church as "the New People of God," it is a drastic mistake to call the Church "the New Israel." The "New Israel" will be the restored nation of Israel in the coming kingdom of God promised in the OT covenants.

52 Unlike the previous quotation, he leaves Hos. 1:10 untouched.

represented by the three children of the prophet conceived through Gomer; the second and third children are referenced in this context. The second child he is told to call Lo-Ruhama, which means "Not loved" (Hos. 1:6), and the other he calls Lo-Ammi, "Not my people" (Hos. 1:9). Straight after this episode about the children, there is a prophecy built upon the Abrahamic covenant of Israel's future blessing (Hos. 1:10-11). The two children symbolize the northern kingdom of Israel, which was taken into captivity by the Assyrians in Hosea's lifetime. The name Lo-Ruhama means that Yahweh's love and mercy have run out for Israel, while Lo-Ammi means that He has repudiated the northern tribes as being His covenant people (although it should be remembered that many people from those ten tribes came down to Judah rather than remain in apostate Israel, see 2 Chron. 15:9 and 19:4).

Paul's quotation of Hosea 2:23 and 1:10 in Romans 9:25 and 26 is usually thought to be the use of a principle of grace[53] rather than a strictly literal understanding of the Hosea passage, which in its original use refers to Israel and does not mention the Gentiles at all. But this creates a problem with Paul's use of Hosea, a problem which few interpreters take the time to discuss.[54] Surely if Paul wanted to find a passage that explicitly said that Gentiles would be saved together with Jews, he had the whole Hebrew Prophets before him. Why choose a passage that referred *only* to Israel? It makes no sense.[55] Unless, of course, one agrees with Hays that, "Paul deconstructs the oracle and dismantles Israel's privilege; with casual audacity he rereads the text as a prophecy of God's intention to embrace the Gentiles as his own people."[56]

But how can Paul "reread" a prophecy that does not include Gentiles as if it did? Well, I don't think he can, and I don't think he is. Perhaps then he is using the passage for the purposes of analogy?[57] That would fit the immediate context quite well, but one still wonders why he didn't simply go to Isaiah 49 or some other place.

A possible reason for Paul's use of Hosea 2:23 and 1:10 in Romans 9:25 and 26 is rooted in the Abrahamic covenant, in which Gentiles are included in the blessings to come through Abraham's seed (Gen. 22:18; Gal. 3:16, 29).[58] This view has the merit of sticking with the context (Rom. 9:24) while implying his "covenant consciousness" is at work (Rom. 9:4). It is an attractive view.

Finally, there is the suggestion that the apostle is not using Hosea for the purposes of analogy, to support a principle of inclusion for the Gentiles in eschatological Israel, or for an appeal to the covenant with Abraham, but rather he has one eye on Israel's covenants and promises while having to deal with the organism that is the Jew/Gentile Church. This is because his main purpose in the chapter is the election

53 That is, illustrating grace.

54 A notable exception is Douglas Moo in his *The Epistle to the Romans*, NICNT (Grand Rapids: Eerdmans, 1996), 612-614.

55 The position that Paul sees Gentile salvation as analogous to what Hosea was talking about looks just as unsatisfactory as an explanation. Why employ an obtuse analogy when he might have cited a text which would make his point more directly?

56 Richard B. Hays, *Echoes of Scripture in the Letters of Paul*, 67.

57 Michael G. Vanlaningham, "Romans," in *The Moody Bible Commentary*, eds. Michael Rydelnik and Michael Vanlaningham (Chicago: Moody, 2014), 1761.

58 This is the position of Richard N. Longenecker, *The Epistle to the Romans*, 822.

of Israel.[59] That is to say, the question of Gentile salvation (Rom. 9:24) is addressed in what comes immediately after, only to the extent that it is a *present* reality. He has already noted a Jewish remnant in the Church in Romans 11:5. It is an unavoidable context. Gentiles are indeed God's "people," where previously they were "aliens from the commonwealth of Israel and strangers to the covenants of promise" (Eph. 2:12; cf. Rom. 3:29; 9:30; Eph. 2:19). Paul is going to use Gentile salvation in his reasoning about Israel's ongoing unbelief (Rom. 9:30; 11:11ff.). In Romans 9:24 he mentions the Gentiles because they also have an election according to God's grace within the Church, and at Rome, there were many Gentiles, a majority perhaps, in the Church. But the Church included a remnant of Israel (Rom. 11:5).

But then he proceeds with his line of argument relating to Israel (the language of election in Rom. 9:6-23 pertains to the remnant, cf. Rom. 11:1-6, 25-29).[60] On the strength of this, one may suggest this paraphrase of verse 25a: "As He says also in Hosea (concerning the Jew/Gentile people of God)..."

I am well aware that the opportunity to read into a text what you want it to say is often afforded to the interpreter under the guise of "exegesis," and I may be guilty of doing just that, so perhaps few will follow me here.[61] But this interpretation is plausible, and I am persuaded that no violence is being done to the passage or Paul's argument.[62] Although I think it is preferable to identify Paul's focus as the promises to Jews and Gentiles in the Abrahamic covenant, I see some merit in this position,[63] especially when we consider Romans 9:27ff. (see below). However, once we come to Romans 9:27, things become clearer. Citing Isaiah 10, the apostle says:

> Isaiah also cries out concerning Israel:
>
> "Though the number of the children of Israel be as the sand of the sea,
> The remnant will be saved. For He will finish the work and cut it short in righteousness, because the LORD will make a short work upon the earth" (Rom. 9:27-28, citing Isa. 10:22-23).

59 Alva J. McClain, *Romans: The Gospel of God's Grace*, 183-184.

60 Of course, this point is disputed by those who believe the Church to be "spiritual Israel." E.g., Douglas Moo. *Romans*, 573ff.; Sam Storms, *Kingdom Come: The Amillennial Alternative* (Fearn House, Ross-shire, UK, 2015), 304. For a refutation of this view see the important appendix (B) in Carl B. Hoch, *All Things New*, 263-318.

61 To be clear, I believe a case can be made for a separation of Israel and the Church in the coming Kingdom even if Paul is using Hosea to speak of Jew/Gentile salvation. My argument does not depend upon the acceptance of my understanding of Rom. 9:25-26.

62 In fact, it perhaps explains why Paul should add the *kai* ("also, and") at verse 25a ("As He says also in Hosea...") but uses *de* ("also, but") in verse 27. If he meant to link Hos. 2:23 with the Gentiles of Rom. 9:25, why include the copula? It would be more direct and resonant to simply say, "As He [God] says in Hosea," and drop the particle. I suppose that the reply, "Because he didn't," is adequate. I simply pose the question.

63 I believe then that although it is very possible to read Rom. 9:25-26 as referring to the inclusion of the Gentiles in the redemptive cum elective plan of God, it is preferable to accord Paul the common sense not to try to prove it with two verses that have nothing to do with that particular point, and instead to read the verses as referring to his main theme in the section, which is the fate of Israel and its covenants. That is definitely the ground he is on in Rom. 9:27-29 where he quotes twice from Isaiah.

There can be no doubt that the apostle has chosen the right passage to support his point this time. The first line is Isaiah citing the Abrahamic covenant (Gen. 22:17; 32:12). The rest of the passage is Yahweh promising to save a remnant of Israel (not a remnant of Israel and the Gentiles as Isa. 10:20-22 makes clear). Has Paul switched back to Israel after dealing with the subject of Israel and Gentiles? Or has he been writing about Israel all this time, just mentioning the Gentiles in verse 24 in passing? I opt for the second view, or the view where the Abrahamic covenant is presupposed. These positions are underlined by the quotation of Isaiah 1:9 in Romans 9:29.

Romans 9:30-34 then asks and answers the question about Israel's failure to attain righteousness. Because they did not seek righteousness through faith (especially faith in Jesus as their Messiah), Israel "stumbled." Hence, the love that Paul has for Israel makes him sorrowful (Rom. 9:1-3) because they have rejected Jesus. Israel is God's elect nation (Rom. 9:13). Although Paul speaks of Gentiles, the accent is upon his people, Israel. The Gentiles have turned to God through Christ while, for the most part, the Jews have rejected Him.

This leads into Romans 10, where again, he states his theme right off the bat: "Brethren, my heart's desire and prayer to God for Israel is that they may be saved" (Rom. 10:1). In the next twelve verses (Rom. 10:2-13), Paul expands on what he had said at the end of chapter 9. The way of salvation for both the Jew and the "Greek" is through faith. But Israel has tried to follow the Law, which is impossible as a standard for justification (Rom. 10:5). The Jews should have known this, since it is the reason why a New covenant is needed (Jer. 31:31-34; cf. Ezek. 36:22-28).

Paul then asks, "How then shall they call on Him in whom they have not believed?" (Rom. 10:14). It is important to understand the identity of the "they" in the question. It is the Jews.[64] This is clarified more in Romans 10:16 and 19. This is rounded off by two quotations from Isaiah 65:1-2, verses 1 and 2 being split to drive home the point that the Gentiles have accepted God's offer while Israel remains in stubborn unbelief.

So we arrive at Romans 11 and Paul's question, "Has God cast away His people?" (Rom. 11:1a). "His people" certainly means Israel. Paul underscores his Jewish roots, "For I also am an Israelite, of the seed of Abraham, *of* the tribe of Benjamin" (Rom. 11:1b). This is not the language of someone who is seeking to explain the mystery of Jew/Gentile salvation. He does this in other places, but not here. If we follow him closely, we shall see how Paul first shows that God has always had a group of Israelites He has chosen for Himself (Rom. 11:2-5). At present, the Jews have been visited with a judgmental blindness from God (Rom. 11:7-10). The Gentiles are then reintroduced in Romans 11:11ff. (referred to as "you" in Rom. 11:17-25), to explain why the judicial blindness upon Israel has brought about the salvation of the Gentiles (Rom. 11:11). But God has a great eschatological plan for Israel, a plan which connects the chosen nation with the regeneration of the world.

64 Richard N. Longenecker, *The Epistle to the Romans*, 855.

> Now if their fall *is* riches for the world, and their failure riches for the Gentiles, how much more their fullness! (Rom. 11:12).

> For if their being cast away *is* the reconciling of the world, what *will* their acceptance *be* but life from the dead? (Rom. 11:15).

This draws in several strands from the Gospels (Matt. 19:21) and Acts (Acts 3:19-21) as well as the OT prophetic literature (e.g., Psa. 48:1-10; 134:3; Isa. 11:9-10; 49:14-23, etc.). The salvation and restoration of the nation of Israel will be the catalyst for the beautification of the whole earth.

The Olive Tree Metaphor in Romans 11

Some passages of Scripture have suffered under the myosis of its interpreters more than most. At the forefront of these abused passages is surely Romans 11:16-29. I realize there is much more in the book of Romans than this passage, and I shall be giving more attention to Romans, but right now, we are drilling down on Paul's covenantal understanding. For sure, there is a bit of deciphering of Paul's language to do, but all in all, I think the apostle's thrust is easy to grasp. The problem that many have who interpret these verses, especially those who like to employ the NT to interpret the OT, is that they tend to read their theology into the passage while ignoring the details. Here is one example:

> Paul's metaphor of the two olive trees (Rom. 11:16-24) also reflects this same perception: olive shoots from a wild olive tree, that is, Gentiles, are being grafted into the cultivated olive tree, that is, Israel, from which latter tree many natural branches, that is, Jews, had been broken off. This tree, Paul says, has a "holy root" (the patriarchs; see Rom. 11:28). Clearly, Paul envisions saved Gentile Christians as "grafted shoots" in the true "Israel of faith.[65]

Or this:

> In Rom. 11:17, 24 Paul refers to gentiles as a "wild olive tree" being "grafted into" the cultivated "olive tree" (*elaia*) of Israel. This probably continues the general image of Israel as an olive tree from the OT. Gentiles are now seen to be identified as part of this Israelite olive tree and thus a part of the continuation of true Israel.[66]

I believe this represents a fatal misreading of the apostle in this place. In order to counter this kind of interpretation, the best approach to the Olive Tree passage is to break it down into manageable portions.

---

65 Robert L. Reymond, *A New Systematic Theology of the Christian Faith*, 2nd ed. (Nashville: Thomas Nelson Publishers, 2002), 526-527.

66 G. K. Beale, *A New Testament Biblical Theology*, 674.

> For if the firstfruit *is* holy, the lump *is* also *holy*; and if the root *is* holy, so *are* the branches. And if some of the branches were broken off, and you, being a wild olive tree, were grafted in among them, and with them became a partaker of the root and fatness of the olive tree, do not boast against the branches. But if you do boast, *remember that* you do not support the root, but the root *supports* you (Rom. 11:16-18).

Paul mixes his metaphors in verse 16. The first figure links the quality of the "lump" (or whole dough) to the quality of its firstfruits (or sampling). Then he turns to the root (*rhiza*, i.e., of a tree, cf. Matt. 3:10) and its branches. The health of the branches will depend on the health of the root or stock of the tree. Romans 11:17 refers to branches "broken off" from the tree, which, by inference, is a tended tree in a garden (cf. Rom. 11:24). These branches refer to Israelites.[67] Then it speaks about "you, being a wild olive tree," being grafted in among them. The "you" refers to Gentile Christians. The kind of tree is now identified. The "Jewish" tree and the "wild" tree are olive trees. Notice also that the "root" is now "the root and fatness of the olive tree," ergo, the roots and trunk. The Gentiles are not to boast since they, as branches, are supported by the trunk (v. 18). Then the apostle imagines a question:

> You will say then, "Branches were broken off that I might be grafted in." Well *said*. Because of unbelief they were broken off, and you stand by faith. Do not be haughty, but fear. For if God did not spare the natural branches, He may not spare you either. Therefore consider the goodness and severity of God: on those who fell, severity; but toward you, goodness, if you continue in *His* goodness. Otherwise you also will be cut off. And they also, if they do not continue in unbelief, will be grafted in, for God is able to graft them in again. For if you were cut out of the olive tree which is wild by nature, and were grafted contrary to nature into a cultivated olive tree, how much more will these, who *are* natural *branches*, be grafted into their own olive tree? (Rom. 11:19-24).

Paul's retort is that faith is the key to inclusion in the olive tree (Rom. 11:20). Therefore, as a group, the Gentiles must continue in belief because if they don't (as a group), they too will be broken off (Rom. 11:21-22). Furthermore, God is able to graft the Jews back in again (Rom. 11:24). Now, this re-grafting of "Israel" is the predicted restoration of the nation under the auspices of the New covenant. Verse 24 signals the end of the Olive Tree metaphor, but it leaves unanswered the identity of the "root and fatness of the olive tree." It cannot be Israel because it is represented by the natural branches that remain (i.e., Christian Jews).[68] It cannot be the Gentile Christians

---

67 In Paul's time there were still a lot of Jews who made up the Church. It serves his purpose, therefore, to say "some" of the natural branches were broken off. In our day, Gentiles overwhelmingly make up the majority of the Church. That being the case, we can rightly say that the "natural branches" (see v. 24) represent the remnant of Israel (cf. v. 26).

68 A recent work which promotes this view says, "Ethnic Israel have pulled away from theological Israel and the Gentiles have been called into Israel..." (Chris Bruno, Jared Compton, and

because they are represented by the wild branches. It cannot be "the people of God" since they comprise the two kinds of branches, and it stops the apostle's argument prematurely.[69] We can discount, therefore, any interpretation that equates the olive tree with either Israel or the Church. What else is left? Let us keep reading:

> For I do not desire, brethren, that you should be ignorant of this mystery, lest you should be wise in your own opinion, that blindness in part has happened to Israel until the fullness of the Gentiles has come in. And so all Israel will be saved, as it is written:
>
> "The Deliverer will come out of Zion,
> And He will turn away ungodliness from Jacob;
> For this is My covenant with them,
> When I take away their sins" (Rom. 11:25-27).

Paul comes to the crux of his argument in these verses. In Romans 11:25 he refers to a "mystery," which is described as the partial blindness of (please take note) *Israel* until something called "the fullness of the Gentiles" has been consummated. The term "mystery" (*musterion*) refers here to something that could not be discovered[70] from the OT since the Israel/Church relation is not found there. But what of "the fullness of the Gentiles"? I have already linked this period to "the Times of the Gentiles" mentioned by Jesus in Luke's eschatological discourse (cf. Lk. 21:24). I will only say here that "the fullness of the Gentiles," as a phrase, fits logically in Paul's argument about the coming restoration of Israel (see Rom. 11:1-2, 11-12, 15, 23-24, 28-29). It is the termination of God's mission to the Gentiles through the Church, after which He will again turn to His covenant nation. Hence, in Romans 11:26a, he declares, "And so all Israel will be saved."

Now that the apostle has brought us around to the salvation of Israel, we should know that we are on New covenant ground. As Williamson observes, "When covenant is next explicitly mentioned (Rom. 11:27) in this important discussion of Israel's place in God's plan of salvation, it is not the covenants generally, but the new covenant that is brought into focus."[71]

This is so because in Jeremiah 31:31-34 it is made clear that future Israel is to be saved via the New covenant. But Paul does not go initially to Jeremiah 31 to establish his teaching. Instead, he repairs to Isaiah 59:20-21, then (possibly) to Jeremiah 31:34 for support[72] (although many scholars prefer Isa. 27:9 to Jer. 31:43).[73] The Isaiah

---

Kevin McFadden, *Biblical Theology According to the Apostles,* 140).

69 As e.g., Thomas R. Schreiner, *Covenant*, 110-111.

70 *Musterion* does not always bear this meaning. In Eph. 5:32 it simply means something hard to comprehend (cf. also Eph. 1:9).

71 Paul R. Williamson, *Sealed with an Oath*, 189.

72 Barry E. Horner, *Future Israel* (Nashville: B&H, 2005), 261. I do not think this reference is far-fetched.

73 See here Richard N. Longenecker, *The Epistle to the Romans*, 898-900; also, W. S. Campbell, "Covenant and New Covenant," in *Dictionary of Paul and His Letters*, eds. Gerald F. Hawthorne and Ralph P. Martin (Downers Grove, IL: InterVarsity, 1993), 181. Daniel Block's view

59 reference notably highlights the role of the Spirit coming upon the people (Isa. 59:21). The link to Isaiah 27:9b, which I think is a better bet than Jeremiah 31:34, is not as noticeable, but that text too sits within a restoration context. What is clear is that the "covenant" spoken of in Isaiah 59:21, which is associated with the Spirit, is the New covenant.[74]

Isaiah 59:20-21 (and 27:9) are New covenant passages, and in the Olive Tree illustration and its application in Romans 11, he rests the weight of his argument upon the New covenant. The New covenant is then the root and fatness of the tree since it is the only way of access to salvation ("When I take away their sins"). And since Jesus Christ's blood is the blood of the New covenant, and He Himself mediates it, this implies a messianic understanding of the Olive Tree.[75]

The passage continues, "Concerning the gospel *they are* enemies for your sake, but concerning the election *they are* beloved for the sake of the fathers. For the gifts and the calling of God *are* irrevocable" (Rom. 11:28-29). I have included these verses because they contribute to the overall understanding of the apostle's theme. The "gospel" here is, of course, the one that Paul has been expounding in the epistle (e.g., Rom. 1:15-17; 2:16; 15:16-20). Paul calls Israel "elect" on account of "the fathers." By this term, Paul has in mind the Jewish saints of the Hebrew Bible: e.g., Acts 13:17; 1 Cor. 10:1 (the Exodus generation); Acts 24:14 (Moses and the Prophets); Acts 26:6-7; Rom. 9:5; 15:8 (the Patriarchs); Acts 28:25 (hearers of the Prophets). In other words, the people of Israel are elect, although not all (Rom. 9:6). Paul is referring to the remnant who will compose "all Israel" (of Rom. 11:26a).[76] Israel's election is incomprehensible outside of the covenants that Yahweh made with them. God remembers what He has sworn to do, and He will perform it because He has sworn it. If that sentence verges on a tautology, I gladly keep it there to ward off any independent temptation to assert that God does *not* mean what He says. Paul makes his feelings clear about the matter by emphatically affirming "the gifts and calling of God are <u>irrevocable</u>" (Rom. 11:29, my emphasis); that is, "not to be repented of" (*ametamelaytos*). God has not and *will not* change His mind about His covenants etc. (cf. Rom. 11:4-5; Gal. 3:17). His saints ought to learn that lesson and interpret their Bibles accordingly.[77]

---

that Rom. 11:26-27 references Jeremiah is difficult to fathom. See his *Covenant*, 515. His brief exposition of the passage is disappointing.

74 Cf. Mark R. Saucy, "One Nation under God: Does the World Need an Israelite Theocracy?" in *The Future Restoration of Israel: A Response to Supercessionism*, eds. Stanley E. Porter and Alan E. Kurschner (Eugene, OR: Pickwick Publications, 2023), 134; Craig A. Blaising, "Biblical Hermeneutics," in *The New Christian Zionism*, 96-97.

75 Some have argued that the root and trunk of the olive tree is the covenants (plural), but that is not where Paul lands. Others insist that the Abrahamic covenant is indicated since there are provisions in it for Israel and the Church, but the Abrahamic covenant is not a salvation covenant. Rather, it is a promissory covenant which hints at coming salvation but does not supply the means of that salvation. That is the job of Christ in the New covenant. Cf. J. Lanier Burns, "The Future of Ethnic Israel in Romans," in *Dispensationalism, Israel and the Church: The Search for Definition*, eds. Craig A. Blaising and Darrell L. Bock (Grand Rapids: Zondervan, 1992), 206.

76 See the discussion in Robert L. Saucy, *The Case for Progressive Dispensationalism*, 252-256.

77 A useful cautionary article here is Robert Dean, "A Critique of O. Palmer Robertson's Interpretation of Romans 11," available at https://www.pre-trib.org/articles/all-articles/

Paul speaks of Israel's "calling" in Romans 11:29. What is Israel's calling? Surely it is expressed in Exodus 19:5-6. They are called to be "a special treasure to Me above all people" (Exod. 19:5; Isa. 43:3-4; Zech. 2:8). They are to be (re)married to Yahweh (see Hos. 2; cf. Isa. 54:5-6). This calling cannot be reconfigured and applied to the Church as the "New Israel." At least not without bringing God's words under suspicion, which is not an option.

The attentive reader of Romans 11 will see that the solution to this "reversal" problem is supplied by the apostle himself in Romans 11:12 and 15: "Now if their fall *is* riches for the world, and their failure riches for the Gentiles, how much more their fullness!... if their being cast away *is* the reconciling of the world, what *will* their acceptance *be* but life from the dead?"

By "life from the dead," we are not to understand the resurrection, since that is secured by Christ, not Israel. Rather, because "the regeneration," as Jesus calls it in Matthew 19:28, starts in the environs of Jerusalem (cf. Isa. 2:2-4; Jer. 33:15-16; Zech. 14:8; Acts 1:11; 3:21), Israel is the first place affected by this regeneration. Hence, the "fullness" of Israel is nothing less than their becoming "the head and not the tail" (Deut. 28:14; Isa. 46:13; Zeph. 3:20).

The whole section (Romans 9–11) closes with Paul's doxology extolling the wisdom of the divine plan for the ages. When Romans 11:33 asks rhetorically, "How unsearchable *are* His judgments and His ways past finding out?" it is not saying that God's way of communicating with men is an unsolvable riddle, or that some secret interpretive key only recently uncovered now lies in the hands of a handful of knowing scholars. It is an exclamation of the great and unfathomable wisdom of God from before the earth was formed, which is still operating and guiding history to its predetermined and preinterpreted *telos*. It is praising the Creation Project.

Does Paul Reverse OT Predictions of the Salvation of the Nations Through Israel?

One more question has to be asked of Romans 9–11 before we move on from it. That question has to do with the seeming reversal of the role of Israel as it pertains to the salvation of the nations in the OT.[78] Let us remind ourselves of what Paul said:

> For I do not desire, brethren, that you should be ignorant of this mystery, lest you should be wise in your own opinion, that blindness in part has happened to Israel until the fullness of the Gentiles has come in. And so all Israel will be saved, as it is written:
>
> "The Deliverer will come out of Zion,
> And He will turn away ungodliness from Jacob;

message/a-critique-of-o-palmer-robertson-s-interpretation-of-romans-11/read.

78 For an excellent study of this question, I recommend Robert L. Saucy's chapter, "Does the Apostle Paul Reverse the Prophetic Tradition of the Salvation of Israel and the Nations?" in *Building of the Foundations of Evangelical Theology: Essays in Honor of John S. Feinberg*, eds. Gregg R. Allison and Stephen J. Wellum (Wheaton, IL: Crossway, 2015), 66-90.

> For this is My covenant with them,
> When I take away their sins" (Rom. 11:25-27).

As can be seen, the apostle presents the salvation of Israel as something that happens subsequent to the salvation of the Gentiles in the Church. But doesn't this misread (or alter) the OT Prophets here? Numerous passages can be produced to show that Israel's cleansing and blessing would lead to God's blessing spreading throughout the world. Here are just some passages that come to mind:

> At that time Jerusalem shall be called The Throne of the LORD, and all the nations shall be gathered to it, to the name of the LORD, to Jerusalem. No more shall they follow the dictates of their evil hearts (Jer. 3:17).

> "And I will sanctify My great name, which has been profaned among the nations, which you have profaned in their midst; and the nations shall know that I *am* the LORD," says the Lord GOD, "when I am hallowed in you before their eyes" (Ezek. 36:23).

> Thus says the LORD of hosts: "In those days ten men from every language of the nations shall grasp the sleeve of a Jewish man, saying, 'Let us go with you, for we have heard *that* God *is* with you'" (Zech. 8:23).

Quite clearly, the Prophets are saying that Israel, though rebellious (note Ezekiel above), will be brought back to their God by Yahweh Himself, after which they will play a part in reaching the Gentile nations for Him (cf. Exod. 19:6; Isa. 43:9-15).

But we must also remember that these prophets foretold Israel's rejection of their own Messiah and God: "Then I said to them, 'If it is agreeable to you, give *me* my wages; and if not, refrain.' So they weighed out for my wages thirty *pieces* of silver. And the LORD said to me, 'Throw it to the potter'—that princely price they set on me" (Zech. 11:12-13a, my emphasis).

As Isaiah asked, "Who has believed our report?" (Isa. 53:1a). The rejection of Jesus by the Jews was foreknown (Lk. 24:25-27), something Paul himself declares (Rom. 9:32-33). But they were a people under covenant, and not just any covenant, but the kind of covenant that obligated God Himself to follow through. Thus, the Mosaic covenant gave God the obligation to judge His people, but the Abrahamic covenant, together with the Davidic covenant which sprang from it, gave God the obligation to rescue His wayward nation in the end.

Summary

I have not explored all of Paul's theology but have concerned myself mostly with how God's covenants find a conspicuous place within it. Both the Abrahamic and the Davidic covenants are alive and well in Paul's thought, but the main lens for his theological outlook for the Church is the New covenant in Christ. He saw himself as conducting a "ministry of righteousness" (2 Cor. 3:9), which he thought of as a ministry of the New covenant (2 Cor. 3:6), centering on preaching Jesus Christ (2 Cor. 4:5). Although I reserve the right to differ in my eschatology, I will let another sum things up for me:

The OT conception of the covenantal relationship of trust in YHWH looked forward to its fulfillment in this intimate relationship with the Son of God through faith. In Paul's theology, Christ is the foundation of the covenant, and Christ is the fulfillment of the covenant. *For Paul, the covenant is Christ.*[79]

Summary of Part Six

Acts

• Every interpreter must account for the transitions that happen in the book of Acts.

• Luke sets the disciples' question about the restoration of the Kingdom to Israel (Acts 1) in the context of the risen Christ's own teaching on the subject. This is done to emphasize that it has been postponed (from our point of view), but that it will come to pass at some future day.

• Attempts to get around the clear answer of Jesus to the disciples' question about the timing of the Kingdom place on display the biases of the interpreter against the future restoration of Israel.

• Christ's ascension to heaven was as a man forever to be the God-man for us.

• Peter's sermon in Acts at Pentecost must be understood in its historical setting. He was a Jew speaking to Jews about Messiah.

• Contrary to Progressive Dispensationalists and all non-dispensationalists, the throne of David has not been established and Jesus' present session in heaven does not include the initial realization of the Davidic kingship *in absentia.*

• Especially in the first part of Acts, the stress is put upon Jesus' resurrection and the Messiahship. "Christ," as in the Gospels and the Epistles, signifies His messianic status. "Christ" is not a last name.

79 James P. Ware, *Paul's Theology in Context*, 125 (my emphasis).

• Church baptism is associated with the New covenant gift of the Spirit.

• Paul's first speech in Acts 13 highlights the covenantal history of Israel. Paul does not claim that Jesus fulfills all of Israel's covenant hopes but rather ensures them.

• Paul's teaching about the Kingdom of God in Acts does not equate it with the Church.

Paul

• The concept of covenant in Paul's thought may be witnessed in his occasional yet pointed references to the covenants in his letters. He always builds something big upon them, the New covenant in particular.

• There should be no doubt that Paul saw his "ministry of reconciliation" as a New covenant ministry.

• Paul saw the cross of Christ as a New covenant sacrifice that purchased salvation for sinners.

• The blood of Christ, for Paul, is New covenant blood. Hence, when Christians celebrate the Lord's Supper, they should be celebrating their participation in the New covenant.

• Gentiles are no longer "strangers to the covenants" since, in Christ, they are included in the third part of the Abrahamic covenant through the New covenant.

• Attempts by Dispensational thinkers to either disassociate or at least distance the Church from the New covenant do not sit well with the apostle's language or the nature of Christ's atonement.

• The Kingdom of God in Paul's letters should be seen against its use in the Gospels and Acts. The Church's relation to the Davidic covenant enters in because Christ will rule Israel and the world.

• Jesus is not the King of the Church as is taught by the "already-not yet" approach so in vogue today.

- The Church is vitally connected to the resurrection of Christ. This means that the Church could not exist until the resurrection and the descent of the Spirit.

- The theology of Paul is both teleological and eschatological. He sees a movement and purpose to history.

- First Corinthians 15 includes a difficult section which, rightly understood, indicates an intermediate stage in God's Creation Project. This is the Millennium.

- The phrase "Day of the Lord" is used by Paul to refer to the beginning of the Tribulation to the second coming.

- The "Man of Sin" personage in 2 Thessalonians 2 is the same individual as the "Little Horn" of Daniel 7, the "Antichrist" of 1 John, and "Beast" of Revelation 13. He is obviously an individual. The temple in the context is not the Church.

- The apostle entertains a fixed hope for his people and nation.

- The disputed phrase "the Israel of God" in Galatians 6 does not refer to the Church but to the elect Jewish remnant who Paul believes still has and always has had a covenanted future.

- Although love and respect is owed to Christians who oppose taking the covenant hope at face value, the fact has to be faced that there can be no coming together over the details of eschatology between Covenant Theology and Progressive Covenantalists on one hand and dispensationalists and Biblical Covenantalists on the other. The assumptions of the two groups are never in agreement in these areas.

- Romans 9–11 is both a construction of the theological points of Romans 1–8 and also a needed digression for the purpose of answering a question about the fate of Israel.

- One's starting assumptions can get in the way of one's view of what Paul is talking about in Romans 9. We take the position that the apostle has indicated several times he is talking about Israel in the main.

- The Olive Tree metaphor in Romans 11 is best comprehended once the natural branches (Jews) and the wild branches (Gentiles) are acknowledged as *branches* of the tree and not the tree itself.

- Since Paul ends the metaphor by applying two New covenant passages to it, the best interpretation of the root and stock is that it is the New covenant and the other covenants (the Abrahamic covenant especially) that it connects to.

PART SEVEN:
HEBREWS AND THE GENERAL EPISTLES

17

THE ENIGMATIC BOOK OF HEBREWS

For men indeed swear by the greater, and an oath for confirmation is for them an end of all dispute.
– Hebrews 6:16

Reading Hebrews Aside from Paul

What I want to do in my treatment of this letter (or perhaps it is better to call it a sermon)[1] is to first set out its basic emphases and Christian teaching. After that, I want to look at how the author incorporates the covenants. Somewhat controversially, I will ask about the distinctively Jewish flavor of Hebrews and face the famous warning passages head-on, asking whether they can be reconciled with Pauline theology.[2]

Please do not misunderstand me. I am certainly not saying that the NT contradicts itself. What I am saying is that when one permits each NT author to say what he says, sometimes it becomes necessary to ensure that one is not trying to fit square pegs into round holes. This is apparent when the Gospels are compared to Paul's epistles, say when Matthew 10 is compared with Galatians 3, or when John the Baptist's and Jesus' cross-less and resurrection-less "gospel of the kingdom" (Matt. 4:23; cf. Matt. 3:2) is examined alongside Paul's gospel of 1 Corinthians 15:1-4. The reader must understand the contextual differences if he is not to run into difficulties. For example, if he does not look well to what he is doing, he will find himself forced to add Pauline doctrine into the early chapters of the Gospels in order to fill out John the

1 See especially the work done by Albert Vanhoye, *Structure and Message of the Epistle to the Hebrews*, Subsidia Biblica 12 (Rome: Gregorian & Biblical Press, 1989) and *The Letter to the Hebrews: A New Commentary* (Mahwah, NJ: Paulist Press, 2015).

2 Let me state that I am aware of the work of Ben Witherington III and his essay "The Influence of Galatians on Hebrews," *New Testament Studies* 37 (January 1991), 146-152. Interesting as this paper is, it does not materially impact my discussion here.

Baptist's and Jesus' messages. But once that is done, he will have to stay quiet about the ignorance of the disciples in Mark 9:31-32; 16:14; and Luke 18:31-34 (cf. Jn. 2:19-22),[3] or the fact that the Holy Spirit was not given to believers in Jesus until after His ascension (Jn. 7:37-39). We even run into this phenomenon in the transitional book of Acts, where in Acts 2, baptism seems necessary in order for the Spirit to be received (Acts 2:38).[4] This doesn't sit well with Paul distancing baptism from the essence of the Gospel in 1 Corinthians 1:17.

In a similar way, we must face anomalies between Paul and the author of Hebrews. The author of Hebrews writes in a fashion much more consistent with classical standards of the time. His arguments are very carefully structured and precise, not like the occasional nature of Paul's correspondence with their frequent digressions. Hebrews is, in the words of Harold Attridge, "the most elegant and sophisticated, and perhaps the most enigmatic, text of first-century Christianity...Its argumentation is subtle; its language refined; its imagery rich and evocative."[5]

Whoever wrote this work *knew what they wanted to say and how to say it.* Another difference from Paul is to be seen, for example, when the apostle's doctrine of eternal security is set alongside Hebrews' warning passages. I will have to do some explaining of the various approaches to these passages in the literature, but at the risk of sounding a little high-minded, none of them, in my opinion, adequately deals with all the details found in the paraenesis (i.e., warning, exhortation) passages, especially the major ones in Hebrews 2:1-4; 3:7-19; 5:11–6:12; 10:19-39; and 12:14-29. As we shall see, these warnings go way beyond divine saber-rattling.[6]

Hebrews is notable for its "constant alternation of instructional and hortatory passages"[7] and its negation of the *cultic aspects* of the Mosaic covenant.[8] It is also a prophetic book, urging its readers to look and strive for the coming messianic age. The warning passages play a major role in the exhortatory power of the message. There is a "rest" to enter (Heb. 4), a future that is as yet open-ended in the sense that many of the promises are still ahead.

---

3 In Matt. 16:20 Jesus "commanded His disciples that they should tell no one that He was Jesus the Christ." That would have made preaching Paul's gospel pretty hard to say the least.

4 I appreciate the efforts of those who wish to say that the Spirit is given upon repentance and baptism is included with repentance, but the verse does imply that "remission of sins" was not offered without baptism.

5 Harold W. Attridge, *Hebrews: A Commentary on the Epistle to the Hebrews* (Philadelphia: Fortress, 1989), 1.

6 It is notable that in the fine book, Herbert W. Bateman, ed., *Four Views on the Warning Passages in Hebrews* (Grand Rapids: Kregel, 2007). Grant Osborne (Classical Arminian) says, "It is interesting (undoubtedly by chance) that the two Arminian approaches were exegetical, going through the passages in order, while the two Calvinist approaches were more topical, going through the issues one at a time" (Ibid., 293). The present writer is not Arminian and holds to eternal security for the Christian, but he believes the exegetical approach is especially important in tackling the warning passages in Hebrews.

7 Peter Stuhlmacher, *Biblical Theology of the New Testament*, 528.

8 It does not negate the moral aspects.

Why "to the Hebrews"?

Without entering into the text-critical questions surrounding the book, we should note its title (which is found in the Greek manuscripts). What is one to make of this post-ascension (circa 64 A.D.) work being directed to "the Hebrews" and not to Christians generally? I grant that the vast majority of scholars hold that "Hebrews" is not its title. I do not believe that. To think that an ancient document like this began life without a title is too much for me to swallow. The book has always been known as "Hebrews" and not as anything else. Besides, the content of the work is plainly Jew-focused. We are all aware of the contrasts in the epistle between the "old [Mosaic] covenant" and the "New covenant" (e.g., Heb. 9:15) and between the Levite High Priesthood and the Melchizedekian High Priesthood (Heb. 7). But there is also a contrast between "Mount Sinai" and "Mount Zion" (Heb. 12:18-24). There is mention of entering into rest and its comparison with the Canaanite conquest (Heb. 3:18, 4:1-11) and the Sabbath (Heb. 4:4). There is also a contrast between the two "houses": those of Moses and Jesus (Heb. 3:1-6). Then there are the two sanctuaries (Heb. 8:2, 5) and the two High Priestly sacrifices (Heb. 9:6-28). When one sits back and really reflects on these things, the Israelite flavor of the book comes into prominence and needs to be taken seriously.

Stranger still, what about those continuous warning passages scattered throughout the book? Although many attempts have been made to dampen the wording, none of them are successful. Why such stark language about "an evil heart of unbelief" causing a fissure between them and God? Is it possible for a true Christian to depart "from the living God" (Heb. 3:12)? How is it that a person can find themselves in a position where there is "no place for repentance" (Heb. 12:17)? The nature of Hebrews 6:4-6 and 10:26-31 needs to be attended to with eyes that will see what the writer is really saying and not through the eyes of Paul. The author of Hebrews leaves nothing to chance, but is a very deliberate and skillful communicator. Let the chips fall where they may; both authors are equally inspired, and neither ought to be read through the other.

Mention of the author of Hebrews, whoever he may be, brings up another puzzle. This writer has left us a complex and carefully crafted piece of work in good Greek and with a well-developed structural dynamic. He knows what he wants to say, and he says it. The Catholic scholar Albert Vanhoye, one of the go-to scholars on the book, stated, "the author of the Epistle has structured his work with great care and has made use of fixed literary devices to indicate what he has done."[9] This intentionality of the author has to be kept in the mind of the reader of his book as it is read. If we won't face that fact, then we cannot say that we have done him justice, nor indeed the Holy Spirit who inspired the words.

9 Rodney J. Decker, "The Intentional Structure of Hebrews," *Journal of Ministry and Theology* 4 (Fall 2000), 98. Decker is citing Albert Vanhoye, *A Structured Translation of the Epistle to the Hebrews*, trans. James Swetnam (Rome: Pontifical Biblical Institute, 1964), 3. As a good introduction to these matters, I recommend Decker's article. As with all Decker's work, it maintains high standards of scholarship with faithful adherence to Scripture.

Then there is the particular "flavor" of the book. It is more "Jewish" than it is ecclesial, more homiletical than epistolary, more parenetic or hortatory than didactic. Decker agrees with Vanhoye, Guthrie, and Lane that the main thrust of the book is hortatory (that is, it is an extended exhortation). He writes: "This means that the exhortations (warning passages) are the primary thrust of the book. The expository sections serve as the doctrinal foundations for those warnings."[10] Thus, the difficulties with which the warning passages present the Christian interpreter must be faced head-on, not folded awkwardly to fit onto a Pauline shelf.

But also, as noted above, *Hebrews is prophetic.* As I hope to show, it would not be out of place (aside from the obvious teaching about Jesus) settling in with one of the Minor Prophets with its repeated rallying calls for perseverance and its eschatological bent.

For these reasons, I have called the book an enigma. There is a way forward that will not be found through Pauline assumptions, even if there are many affinities in the doctrine of the two authors. Like most things, the issue is not the similarities but the differences. As always, the devil is in the details. Therefore, as uncomfortable as it may be to stare at the chapters without calling Paul in to help, I shall be looking at Hebrews on its own as I expound the main covenantal teaching of the letter.

The Jewish Orientation of the Book

The first thing I want to notice is how Jewish the book is. Well, of course, someone will say. It is called "Hebrews," what else would one expect? But that is just it—why such a thoroughly Jewish book in the NT? If we leave aside the assumption that the book is written to Hebrew Christians (and that is what it is, however we may think it justified), and just allow it to address "the Hebrews," it may divulge one or two interesting facets. The book starts off with demonstrating, via several scriptures, that Jesus Christ is superior to any man or angel. He is the one through whom God speaks most fully. He is God's Son. This beginning is key to what will be said about Jesus throughout the book. Jesus is the divine Messiah who has taken on human form and has sacrificed Himself for us. He is our eternal High Priest who mediates the New covenant in His blood. All of this is thoroughly Jewish. It is as Hays says, "Our author gives no indication in his comments that this new covenant is meant for anyone other than 'the house of Israel ... the house of Judah' (8:8). The gentile church appears nowhere in the picture."[11]

This is not to say that Hays believes the epistle does not apply to Gentiles. It certainly does not mean that he believes that the New covenant is only for Israel. But Hays' point is important—Hebrews is aimed at, well, Hebrews! In the same essay, Hays observes, "In light of the pervasive "new exodus" imagery throughout Hebrews, it seems...probable that Hebrews represents a form of Jewish 'restoration eschatology,'

10 Ibid., 104.

11 Richard B. Hays, *Reading with the Grain of Scripture* (Grand Rapids: Eerdmans, 2020), 313.

indeed, the burden of proof would lie strongly on any other way of reading the text."[12] This "restoration eschatology" has, in my opinion, not been fully appreciated by students of Hebrews.[13]

A Premillennial Reading of Hebrews

The present writer has already stated his general agreement with what is now called Revised Dispensationalism—the Dispensationalism of Charles Ryrie and J. Dwight Pentecost. I go further and say that I find the work of Larry Pettegrew and Michael Vlach always to be excellent, even where we disagree. *That* we disagree is mainly down to me.[14] I prioritize the divine biblical covenants above the "dispensations." I have grave doubts about the viability of the "dispensations" to account for themselves and to hold up a biblical theology.

That said, I find the dispensational approach to Hebrews to be the best overall approach I have read. Therefore, I want to flesh out a reading of the book from a dispensational point of view but settled on the New covenant.[15]

The first chapter of Hebrews expounds the greatness of the Son. Jesus is given a dazzling array of attributes in the opening section. First, Jesus is the revelation of God above anything that came before (Heb. 1:2a). This is not to say that the author is teaching that what Jesus says in the Gospels is more authoritative and inspired than what God said in the OT. Not at all. His point is more specific. The incarnate Jesus is the greatest revelation of God. This understanding of Jesus as God's "speaking" par excellence elevates Him and His words as God's representative or sent one. And since the hearing of the word of God is such a crucial component of the book,[16] this will play into Jesus' role as the Mediator of the New covenant later on in the argument.

Then there is the expression that God the Father has appointed Jesus the "heir of all things" (Heb. 1:2b), a statement that sets up a specific eschatological anticipation, an anticipation that is covenant-guided. The author also says Jesus upholds "all things by the word of His power," which recalls what Paul said in Colossians 1:16 about everything being made "through Him and for Him."[17] Not only is this echoed in Hebrews 1:2, but it is expanded upon in the verses that follow. The crucified and risen Christ must surely reign upon this earth, and His word, His Torah, will go out to the ends of the earth and will be the final word in His Kingdom. The writer continues, "Who being the brightness of *His* glory and the express image of His person,

12 Ibid.

13 "Next to the Gospel of Matthew, the Letter to the Hebrews is theologically the most important Jewish Christian writing in the New Testament" (Peter Stuhlmacher, *Biblical Theology of the New Testament*, 522).

14 My reasons are set out in the first two chapters of Volume One.

15 There is no one dispensational understanding of the warnings of Hebrews, so I will do a bit of picking and choosing. Like Vlach, I also believe that some of the work by Progressive Dispensationalists is of real value, even if I cannot embrace that approach.

16 See, for example P. T. O'Brien, "God as the Speaking God," in *Understanding the Times: New Testament Studies in the 21st Century,* eds. Andreas J. Köstenberger and Robert W. Yarbrough (Wheaton, IL: Crossway, 2011), 197.

17 Hebrews also includes a reference to Jesus as "the Firstborn" (Heb. 1:6; cf. Col. 1:15).

and upholding all things by the word of His power, when He had by Himself purged our sins, sat down at the right hand of the Majesty on high" (Heb. 1:3).

Jesus is the exact image of God and shares His glory. Jesus had said, "He who has seen Me has seen the Father" (Jn. 14:6). Now risen and glorified, His word upholds His creation from the right hand of God's throne. But not before "He had by Himself purged our sins" (Heb. 1:3). Thus, we are only three verses in, and already the main lineaments of the Creation Project have been set out. This world has been created through and for the Son and is presently upheld by His word. He Himself is the Word,[18] who has sacrificed Himself in our stead, and He will one day return to reign over what is rightly His.

Hebrews 1:5-14 demonstrates the superiority of the Son to the angels, but verse 6 catches our attention because of its covenantal associations: "But to the Son *He says*: 'Your throne, O God, is forever and ever; A scepter of righteousness is the scepter of Your kingdom...'" The OT source is Psalm 45:6, and the writer continues it into the next verse. But clearly the mention of the "throne," "the scepter," and "Your kingdom" in connection with "righteousness" is covenantally loaded. Genesis 49:10 is the root of the Psalmist's thinking here. Therefore, the covenant with Abraham, which was in the mind of Jacob in Genesis 49, is behind the "scepter" imagery. But the inclusion of these three elements—throne, scepter, and kingdom—points us to the Davidic covenant, and the sphere of righteousness that surrounds them points to the New covenant. This again shows that the New covenant is the means of fulfillment for the other unilateral covenants of God.

We do not encounter the name "Jesus" until Hebrews 2:9, and the title "Christ" is not introduced until Hebrews 3:1. I believe this is because of a strategy of allowing the gradual realization of who the Son is to dawn on the reader. Not in the sense of revealing that the Son is Jesus, who is the Christ, but it is somewhat reminiscent of Mark's Gospel, bringing one truth into association with another truth as the picture is filled out. This strategy is aided by the collection of OT passages (Psa. 2:7; 2 Sam. 2:14; Psa. 97:7; Deut. 32:43 LXX; Psa. 104:4; 45:6-7; 102:25-27; capping it off with the Davidic reference in Psalm 110:1).

Hebrews 2:1-4 issues the first of the warnings in the book. If we are not careful to recognize the voice of the Lord and the teaching of His apostles ("those who heard Him," Heb. 2:3) and begin to "drift" (Heb. 2:1), how shall we escape?[19]

The great work of our salvation was done so that the Church could be brought into union with the Savior (Heb. 2:10-11). Since saved Gentiles[20] are the spiritual "seed of Abraham" (Heb. 2:16; cf. Gal. 3:29), we receive aid from Him who has

18 Some writers have tried to show a "Logos" theology in Hebrews. For example, Ronald H. Nash, *The Gospel and the Greeks: Did the New Testament Borrow from Pagan Thought?* (Phillipsburg, NJ: P&R, 2003).

19 We should understand that this warning was led up to by the buildup in Hebrews 1 and its exaltation of the Son.

20 Some writers would say that Hebrews is aimed mainly at Jewish Christians, who would thereby be motivated by the examples of their ancestors. See, e.g., Homer A. Kent, Jr., *The Epistle to the Hebrews* (Grand Rapids: Baker, 1972), 68.

assumed a High Priestly role for us (Heb. 2:17-18; 4:14-16). We have been brought by Jesus into His house, the Church, and are not under the Mosaic code (Heb. 3:1-6).

Then the author quotes Psalm 95:7-11 as the basis for a second warning that will culminate in a more expansive caution in Hebrews 4:1-11.[21] Hebrews 3:7-19 act then as a spur to Christians to stay faithful to Christ.

"The World to Come, of which we Speak"

It is crucial to read Hebrews 2:5 very carefully. In it, the writer states, "For He has not put the world to come, of which we speak, in subjection to angels" (my emphasis). The angels right now minister to the heirs of salvation" (Heb. 1:14; cf. 1:7). In "the world to come" (Heb. 2:5), of which the Son is the heir (Heb. 1:2), it seems as though the Son will be much more prominent, the coming age being subject to Him ("we do not yet see all things put under him," Heb. 2:8c).

Does this mean that a major theme of the book of Hebrews is "the world to come"? Has he been speaking about it already and we missed it? And what does the author mean by this designation? To answer the second question, I do not think there can be much objection to the view that it refers to the coming Kingdom after the return of Christ to earth. Some may view it as speaking of the Millennial Kingdom and others as the new heavens and earth. My own view is that it has both in mind as it savors leaving this present aeon behind forever. This possible theme is alluded to in Hebrews 1:8, 13, and we should be willing to count Jesus being called "the heir of all things" in Hebrews 1:2 and the mention of inheriting salvation in verse 14 as possible references to the new aeon. Hebrews 1:4 says, "He has by inheritance obtained a more excellent name" than the angels, which also suggests this theme since the "inheritance" may be seen as this-worldly and still to come. Hebrews 1:5 quotes from Psalm 2:7, in which David certainly refers to the messianic kingdom ("Yet I have set My King on My holy hill of Zion," Psa. 2:6). Then there is Hebrews 1:6 and its possible second coming reference: "when He again (*pallin*) brings the firstborn into the world" as in NKJV, NASB, NET, Westcott.[22] If these verses point to the coming kingdom—and there is more than a suggestion that they do—then the chances of it being a subject matter of Hebrews looks promising. And this reintroduces the divine covenants.

Right after the phrase "the world to come" appears, the writer appeals to Psalm 8, a psalm that speaks of the reason God made man. Man may have been made "a little lower than the angels" (Psa. 8:5; Heb. 2:7), but to obtain "glory and honor." As a race, we have not obtained anything approaching glory and honor, but Jesus has (Heb. 1:4, 8, 13; 2:9). In citing Psalm 8:5-6, Hebrews is explaining how Jesus has paved the way for those He has saved to inherit the dominion and glory planned for them. Hence, we read the contrast, "We do not yet see all things put under him. But we see Jesus..." (Heb. 2:8-9). Jesus brings "many sons to glory," according to Hebrews 2:10. He gives

---

21 Zane C. Hodges, "Hebrews," in *Bible Knowledge Commentary: New Testament*, eds. John F. Walvoord and Roy B. Zuck (Grand Rapids, MI: Victor Books, 1997), 785.

22 Coincidently, Psa. 2:8 refers to Yahweh giving His Son "the nations *for* Your inheritance."

"salvation" to man (Heb. 1:14; 2:3, 10; cf. 9:28[23]), but all things are rightfully His ("for whom *are* all things and by whom *are* all things," Heb. 2:10).

The reference to "the seed of Abraham" in Hebrews 2:16 appears to fit Israel more than the Church,[24] an impression which is strengthened in Hebrews 2:17 when it says that Jesus, as "a faithful and merciful high priest," makes "propitiation for the sins of the people," which would be a most peculiar way of talking about the Jew/Gentile Church.

Please do not misunderstand me here. I am not saying that Jesus is not the High Priest of the Church. God forbid. That would undo my entire teaching about the New covenant being for the Church as well as for Israel. I am simply trying to point out the somewhat uncomfortable fact that Hebrews is written to, well, Hebrews! We need to take that seriously.

Getting back to the first question I posed above, namely, is "the world to come" a major theme in the book? I think the Psalm 8 reference in Hebrews 2 reinforces this. The data looks like this:

1. Christ is "Appointed heir of all things" (Heb. 1:2).

2. He has "obtained an inheritance" (Heb. 1:4).

3. Psalm 2:7, in its context, refers to the reign of Messiah (Heb. 1:5).

4. If "again" connects to the verb "to bring in," the reference is to the second advent (Heb. 1:6).

5. A throne, a scepter, and a kingdom are mentioned in relation to His incarnation (Heb. 1:8).

6. Psalm 110:1, referring to the Davidic covenant, is cited (Heb. 1:13).

7. The author expressly says that he is speaking about "the world to come" (Heb. 2:5).

8. He then goes to Psalm 8, about man's dominion over creation (Heb. 2:6-8).

And we have not yet looked into the repeated use of the verb "rest" in Hebrews 3 and 4.

The "Rest" of God and the World to Come in Hebrews

Hebrews 3 speaks of God's "rest" twice in verses 11 and 18, and in both cases, it refers to the rest for Israel in the promised land after their wilderness wanderings

23 If we relate "salvation" to the "rest" of which the writer often speaks, there are hints that it refers in Hebrews as much to the kingdom as it does to the saving of the soul.

24 There is no argument for how believing Gentiles are Abraham's seed such as one finds in Gal. 3.

(Heb. 3:8-19).[25] This is the illustration (I did not say "type") that will be employed in chapter 4 for the "rest" (*katapausis*—a beautiful word denoting a ceasing from toil, repose). So, in the first verse of Hebrews 4, we read, "Therefore, since a promise remains of entering His rest, let us fear lest any of you seem to have come short of it" (Heb. 4:1).

The main commentaries all associate this "rest" with going to heaven, but let us allow the author to say what he wants to say. The first thing I want to call your attention to is the strong tone of the warning that is penned. Not to get technical, but the word is an aorist passive conditional (subjunctive) of *phobeo* and is rightly translated as "Let us fear lest" in the NKJV. There is a chance that some of those addressed will not make it into "rest." What was said above about the influence of the theme of "the world to come" in Hebrews should be applied here, as it flows out from that argument. It is the "therefore" of what was said in Hebrews 1–3. Notice next in Hebrews 4:2 that the word "gospel" is used to describe the message of hope that was preached to "us" as well as to "them." That is, the Israelites in the wilderness wanderings heard a gospel, but what was it? It was that God was taking them to a land flowing with milk and honey (Exod. 3:17; Lev. 20:22-24; Num. 14:7-8; Deut. 26:9; Jer. 11:5). Apart from a presumption (understandable as it may be) that this is applied to the Church in Pauline terms, why would we think that the "gospel" in Hebrews 4:2 is equivalent Paul's gospel?

The next few verses take some effort to get one's head around. The basic message is that although those unbelievers in the wilderness did not enter into rest (Heb. 4:2, 3, 5, 6, 8), there yet is a rest that some will indeed enter (Heb. 4:3, 6, 9). This rest is likened to the Sabbath day ("the seventh day," Heb. 4:4) and Yahweh's own cessation from His work of creation (Heb. 4:10).

I grant that my resistance to applying all of this to the Christian Church and accommodating it within Paul's doctrine risks disorienting the reader, but please stick with me. You see, in addition to being a day of rest (not necessarily of worship), what is special about the Jewish sabbath? The answer is found in Ezekiel:

> Moreover I also gave them My Sabbaths, to be a <u>sign</u> between them and Me, that they might know that I *am* the LORD who sanctifies them (Ezek. 20:12).
>
> I *am* the LORD your God: Walk in My statutes, keep My judgments, and do them; "hallow My Sabbaths, and they will be a <u>sign</u> between Me and you, that you may know that I *am* the LORD your God" (Ezek. 20:19-20).

---

25 In Heb. 3:2-6 the writer speaks of Moses and his "house," which is Israel, and Jesus and His own "house." Lane observes, "Moses stands among the covenant people and the whole retinue of God as 'honored servant'" (William L. Lane, *Hebrews 1–8* [Nashville: Thomas Nelson, 1991], 78). Moses occupies an exalted station in Judaism (Ibid., 74), but he is still only a "servant." Jesus, on the other hand is the "Son," and the people of God that He is over are His own house. Although in Jesus' case the "house" could be the Church, it must be conceded that, in this context, it could just as well be redeemed Israel.

The sabbath was a God-given sign for Israel. Of what was it a sign? The author of Hebrews links God's "sabbath" rest with the future "rest for the people of God" in Hebrews 4:9. Very interestingly, it just so happens that Ezekiel 20 goes over the exact same ground that the author of Hebrews is covering! And Ezekiel 20 is extremely covenantal. Seven times in the chapter, Yahweh mentions an "oath" that He took about the promised land. After rehearsing the history of the people's rebellion and excoriating them for their heathen practices and abominations, the prophet expresses a word of hope for the future of Israel in Ezekiel 20:33-44:[26] "Then you shall know that I *am* the LORD, when I bring you into the land of Israel, into the country *for* which I raised My hand in an oath to give to your fathers" (Ezek. 20:42). Just like the book of Hebrews, the prophet Ezekiel brings together the land promise and the sabbath sign (Heb. 4:8-10).

"Let us therefore be diligent to enter that rest, lest anyone fall according to the same example of disobedience" (Heb. 4:11). Notice how the author is pressing his readers toward something. They have not achieved it. Moreover, there is the threat that they may not achieve it. It is hard to place this doctrine next to Paul's doctrine of justification without feeling the disparity.

Again, what is this "rest" of which the author speaks? He says they must exert themselves (*spoudazo*, "hasten, labor diligently") to be certain of entering it. This is a rather heavy-handed way of promoting progressive sanctification if it is aimed at saints in the Church hoping for heaven. But heaven has not come into view. Everything points to the fact that "the world to come" is what this coming "rest" is about; that is, the Kingdom of God. The important passages are Hebrews 1:2, 6, 8, 12, 14; 2:3, 5, 8; 6:5, 12; 9:28; 10:13, 35-37; 11:10, 13-16, 39; 12:22, 28; 13:14.[27] But perhaps the impression will disappear?

Our High Priest

Hebrews 5 returns to the status of Christ as our High Priest and begins to develop it (Heb. 5:1-10), although more in preparation for the detailed complex of ideas associated with this theme later (Heb. 6:19–10:25). Christ is called by God to be our High Priest, but He is the High Priest from another order—the order of the non-Israelite king Melchizedek (Heb. 5:5-6). Jesus suffered, and His sufferings made Him "the author of eternal salvation to all who obey Him" (Heb. 5:7-9). This suffering is linked by the author with His calling to be High Priest after the order of Melchizedek (Heb. 5:10). As he will go on to say, the power of this new priesthood resides in two things: the permanence of the High Priest (Heb. 7:23-24) and His institution of a "better covenant" (Heb. 7:22).

The "better covenant" is, of course, the New covenant (Heb. 8:8, 13; 9:15; 12:24). Jesus, our High Priest, offered up Himself (Heb. 7:27b), and His resurrection—more

26 See also *The Words of the Covenant*, Vol. 1, 284-285.

27 These passages are seen as important Kingdom texts by Hutson Smelley, *Better With Jesus: A Mission 119 Guide to Hebrews* (Self-published, 2015), 5.

taken for granted than actually stated by the author (e.g., Heb. 9:11-12, 24-28)[28]—provides the grounds for His continuing office (Heb. 7:24).

If we go back a little to chapter 6, we come across a very stern warning in Hebrews 6:4-8. This, of course, is paralleled by the equally stern passage in Hebrews 10:26-31, but I shall come to that passage presently. The warning in Hebrews 6 is interpreted in various ways. Kent gives a summary of the views:

1. Saved persons who are subsequently lost.[29]

2. Professed believers who have never really been saved.[30]

3. Saved persons who backslide (but who nevertheless stay saved).[31]

4. A hypothetical case to illustrate the folly of apostasy.[32]

To be honest, and in light of the author's precision in Hebrews, I do not find any of these explanations entirely satisfactory. This feeling only intensifies when all the warning passages of Hebrews are brought together and read over. Here Attridge, though liberal, cuts to the chase:

> In the preceding verses [i.e., vv. 4-5] the description of the initial experience of conversion and life in the eschatological community had been elaborate, solemn, and somewhat ponderous. The next participle appears with dramatic abruptness. For those who have enjoyed the experience of Christian renewal and have "fallen away" ... the outlook is dire.[33]

And Stuhlmacher comments:

> Hebrews considers it unpardonable when anyone rejects the forgiveness of sins effected for him or her once for all by Christ. Inasmuch as this refers to final salvation, people do indeed lose their salvation by falling away from their baptismal confession.[34]

Whether one agrees with these assessments or not, it behooves us to think carefully about what the writer of Hebrews is saying. Unless one is coming to Hebrews with a dyed-in-the-wool Pauline dogmatism, it must be admitted that one often comes away

---

28 Though see Heb. 13:20.

29 He notes that Arminians generally take this view, naming Lenski (Homer A. Kent, Jr., *The Epistle to the Hebrews*, 111).

30 He cites Gleason Archer (Ibid., 112), although this has been the popular position of men like John Owen, William Gouge, and A. W. Pink. See also N. T. Wright and Michael F. Bird, *The New Testament in Its World*, 719.

31 Ibid., 112, giving Ryrie as an example.

32 Ibid., 113. This is Kent's choice (Ibid., 113-114). The approach advocated by Thomas R. Schreiner and Ardel B. Caneday in *The Race Set Before Us: A Biblical Theology of Perseverance Assurance* (Downers Grove, IL: InterVarsity, 2001), basically rehashes and expands this view.

33 Harold W. Attridge, *The Epistle to the Hebrews*, 170-171. He identifies the sin involved as "extreme apostasy" (the continued denial of Christ).

34 Peter Stuhlmacher, *Biblical Theology of the New Testament*, 540.

from the warning passages, especially Hebrews 6:4-6 and 10:26-29, with a certain feeling that the text has been conformed to a certain theology rather than listened to on its own terms. It ought to be noted also that for the writer of Hebrews, salvation is yet ahead of them, especially if the reference to "rest" is equated with it (esp. Heb. 4:1-11).[35]

Hebrews 7 takes us back to Melchizedek and gives us some tantalizing information about him. He was contemporary with Abraham (ca. 1850 B.C.) and was both king and priest of Salem (Heb. 7:1-2), the city that would become Jerusalem. This stirs interest as the OT had designated Messiah as both king and high priest, and in no clearer passage than Psalm 110:1 and 4. Hebrews 7:3 says Melchizedek was "made like the Son of God." "In what way?" we might ask. Certainly, in that Jesus as the Son has already been introduced as both king and high priest in the book (see Heb. 1:8; 2:17). The author then shows that the order of Melchizedek is actually superior to the order of Levi (Heb. 7:17). The Levitical priesthood, together with the office of high priest, was connected with the old covenant, the covenant made at Sinai and its reiteration in Deuteronomy.[36] Thus, we are introduced to the topic of covenant.

> For the law made nothing perfect; on the other hand, *there is the* bringing in of a better hope, through which we draw near to God. And inasmuch as *He was* not *made priest* without an oath (for they have become priests without an oath, but He with an oath by Him who said to Him: "The LORD has sworn And will not relent, 'You *are* a priest forever according to the order of Melchizedek'"), by so much more <u>Jesus has become a surety of a better covenant</u> (Heb. 7:19-22, my emphasis).

Christ has become the High Priest of "a better" covenant through the Melchizedekian order. This is quite something to say, for the Mosaic covenant established Israel as God's covenant people (Exod. 24:7-8; Josh. 3:14-17). Any move away from that covenant would constitute a grave threat to the identity of Israel as a nation. That is, unless Israel's covenant moorings were secured in the Abrahamic and Davidic covenants by another, greater way of righteousness and another superior intercessor. This is the very argument the writer of Hebrews is going to pursue. It begins with the oath of God to Messiah Jesus (Psa. 110:1), with which He "becomes a surety" for this superior covenant.

After the establishing oath, the second thing that is mentioned is Christ's eternal life. He "continues forever," a statement that takes the resurrection for granted,[37]

35 E.g., G. K. Beale. *A New Testament Biblical Theology*, 784-787.

36 As I showed in the first volume, the connection of the Levites to the Mosaic covenant will be transcended because of the Priestly covenant through Levi (Num. 25), and the representation of two layers of priests in Ezekiel's temple: Zadokites who trace their lineage to Phinehas and non-Zadokite "Levites," who nonetheless serve in a lesser capacity in the temple service. See *The Words of the Covenant*, Vol. 1, 167-168, 295, 351. However, the office of Levitical high priest is not renewed in Ezekiel 40-48. It seems that Christ will fill the high Priestly function by dint of His own greater sacrifice.

37 For the importance of the *fact* of the resurrection to the theology of Hebrews see N. T. Wright, *The Resurrection of the Son of God*, 457-461.

and so now "has an unchangeable priesthood" (Heb. 7:24).[38] The Melchizedekian order does not stress lineage (hence, no descendants for Melchizedek are named). No doubt this is because if ancestors were given, then Jesus would be tied to that ancestry. This shows the divine hand's involvement in what was divulged about Melchizedek in Genesis 14.

The Heavenly Tabernacle

With this argument made, the author reaches what he calls "the main point of the things we are saying" (Heb. 8:1). Being a High Priest forever, where does Jesus minister? The answer comes in the next verse: "a Minister of the sanctuary and of the true tabernacle which the Lord erected, and not man" (Heb. 8:2).

According to our author, there is a "sanctuary" or "tabernacle" in heaven! We know it cannot be on earth because we are told that the Lord built it, not man. This "true tabernacle" is the one after which the earthly tabernacle of Moses was designed (Heb. 8:5; cf. Heb. 9:11). It is at this heavenly tabernacle that Jesus ministers the "better covenant," a covenant that was prophesied in the OT.

The train of thought now leads to the longest quotation of an OT passage in the NT. The quotation is from Jeremiah 31:31-34 about the New covenant (Heb. 8:8-12). The establishing of the New covenant in heaven effectively does away with the old Mosaic covenant (Heb. 8:13). As Lane says, this fact "is amplified in the distinction between those gifts and sacrifices on earth (8:3-5; 9:9) and the eschatological high priest whose redemptive sacrifice was presented in heaven (8:3, 6; 9:14, 25, 28)."[39] Hebrews 9:12 tells us that Jesus entered this tabernacle "with His own blood" and offered it up there. But how could He do that if His blood was shed upon earth? My answer is that just as with the OT sacrifices, not all the blood was needed (e.g., Lev. 4), so Jesus only needed to offer some of His blood. I don't know how this was done, but I believe it actually *was* done because Hebrews says it was.[40]

Is there, then, a real tabernacle or temple in heaven? Many balk at this,[41] claiming that perhaps this is pictorial language used to get the point across. Another view equates the heavenly tabernacle with heaven itself, citing Hebrews 9:24.[42] But such a view looks to this author like an unwillingness to face the text. The tabernacle in the wilderness was made according to a strict pattern (Exod. 25:8, 40). Well then? Are we to be held in thrall by Platonic concepts of heaven? Or is it because we cannot bring ourselves to imagine heaven as having such a building? No commentary on the book

---

38 The word of the oath concerns the risen Jesus (Heb. 7:28).

39 William L. Lane, *Hebrews 1–8*, 203.

40 Perhaps the reticence of the risen Jesus not to be touched by Mary Magdalene in the garden, "for I have not yet ascended to My Father" (Jn. 20:17), was uttered in light of this? It is typical of John to only hint at this, but what other reason could there be?

41 E.g., Daniel P. Fuller, *The Unity of the Bible: Unfolding God's Plan for Humanity* (Grand Rapids: Zondervan, 1992), 381.

42 Homer A. Hent, *Hebrews*, 147. This seriously misreads the context, for the previous verse says, "Therefore it was necessary that the copies of the things in the heavens should be purified with these, but the heavenly things themselves with better sacrifices than these" (Heb. 9:23, my emphasis).

of Exodus worth its salt would omit to mention the representative aspects of the construction of the tabernacle or its minute attention to detail. Heaven has a city in it (Heb. 12:22); would a temple be out of place? Not according to Hebrews 8![43]

A New Covenant

The importance of the New covenant to the writer of Hebrews can hardly be overstated. Philip Edgcumbe Hughes observed, "The theology of the covenant belongs integrally to the argument of [the] central section of the epistle."[44] After quoting Jeremiah 31, the author is careful to refer to "a new covenant" (Heb. 8:13), but nobody doubts that the definite article is required in its other mentions in the book (Heb. 9:15; 12:23). Those interpreters who insist that the New covenant is not made with the Church, or that the Church is only tangentially related to the New covenant are, to my mind, once more in a hole of their own digging. To a man, these writers believe that Hebrews is addressed to Christians (it matters not if they claim Hebrew Christians are the recipients).[45] Therefore, they believe it is written to the Church or a segment of it (whatever that means). If that is so, then Christians are under the New covenant according to Hebrews, and Christ is our New covenant High Priest[46] (Heb. 2:17; 3:1; 4:14-15; 8:1, 6)![47] This tallies with the natural reading of 1 Corinthians 11:23-26 and 2 Corinthians 3:1-18. In the Bible, you can't be represented by a priest unless the priest is related to a covenant. Moreover, you can't call Christ's death on the cross a sacrifice unless you connect that sacrifice to a covenant.

After giving a brief description of the earthly tabernacle and the limitations connected with its service (Heb. 9:1-10), the author strikes a contrast with "the greater

43 I sometimes get the impression that many Christians view heaven as a vast empty plain or something like the Star Trek 'holodeck' and not as a physical place with topographical relief and structures.

44 Philip Edgcumbe Hughes, *A Commentary on the Epistle to the Hebrews* (Grand Rapids: Eerdmans, 1977), 364.

45 See Christopher Cone, "The New Covenant in Hebrews," in *An Introduction to the New Covenant*, 237. Cone advocates well for the view that only Israel is given the New covenant and that "no new teaching about the content of the NC" is found in Hebrews (Ibid., 255, 264, 268). He writes, "It would not be improper to say that the covenant has been validated, as long as there is no already not yet element read into the covenant" (Ibid., 254). Unfortunately, I am not convinced by the arguments. See below on the link between the High Priesthood of Jesus and the "better promises" with the New covenant itself. Also, the "you" of Hebrews 12:4, 7, 8, 17 clearly refers back to the "us" of 12:1 who are to "run with endurance the race that is set before us," and forward to the "you" who have come to Mt. Zion (Heb. 12:22), to "the general assembly and church of the firstborn who are registered in heaven" (Heb. 12:23), and, therefore, "to Jesus the Mediator of the new covenant" (Heb. 12:24). The relationship of the Church to the New covenant is made by the author himself. The style of argumentation has to kept in mind when looking for answers. See e.g., Lane, *Hebrews 1–8*, lxxvii-lxxxiv.

46 It is perilous to break the connection between Christ's High Priesthood for us and the covenant He mediates.

47 Compare especially Heb. 8:1 with 8:6: "We have such a High Priest, who is seated at the right hand of the throne of the Majesty in the heavens" and "But now He [Jesus as High Priest] has obtained a more excellent ministry, inasmuch as He is also Mediator of a better covenant, which was established on better promises." In Heb. 8:1-6 it is Jesus' function as High Priest that is in view, right after which the New covenant quotation from Jer. 31 is given.

and more perfect tabernacle not made with hands, that is, not of this creation" (Heb. 9:11), we then read this:

> For if the blood of bulls and goats and the ashes of a heifer, sprinkling the unclean, sanctifies for the purifying of the flesh, how much more shall the blood of Christ, who through the eternal Spirit offered Himself without spot to God, cleanse your conscience from dead works to serve the living God? (Heb. 9:13-14).

This section needs some exploration because there is a great deal within it. It begins by referring to three OT sacrifices, all of which were designed to provide cleansing in order to serve Yahweh. But that cleansing itself was only skin deep, it did not penetrate to the conscience (cf. Heb. 9:9). But the "blood of Christ" is different. It was offered in heaven (Heb. 9:11) "through the eternal Spirit" (Heb. 9:14). What does this strange phrase mean? The "eternal Spirit" is plainly the Holy Spirit, through whom Jesus was divinely enabled and upon whom He relied (see esp. Jn. 1:33; Lk. 4:1, 14, 18; and implied in Matt. 3:1; 12:31-32; Jn. 20:22).[48] But here the emphasis is not upon Jesus' ministry but upon His sacrificial death. The Spirit of God both upheld Jesus and raised Him from the dead (Rom. 1:4; 8:11). The onus in this context is upon the presentation of Jesus as the sacrificial animal offering Himself "without spot to God" (Heb. 9:14). His offering was Himself (Heb. 9:25-26). He too was the offeror—the High Priest (Heb. 9:25). Then also, of course, He is the Mediator of the New covenant (Heb. 9:15; 12:24), so that Jesus is the main participant in all three aspects of the covenant rite: offeror, sacrifice, and mediator/intercessor of the covenant (Heb. 7:25), the one who has authority to dispense its blessings.[49]

As indicated above, Jesus' death as an offering (the "Lamb of God," Jn. 1:29) was a sacrifice to God (Heb. 9:26; 10:12) as a New covenant sacrifice (cf. Heb. 10:26 with 10:29). Therefore, if the Church is to be connected to Christ's sacrificial death (Rom. 6:5-6), it is *ipso facto* connected to the New covenant (1 Cor. 11:25).[50]

The last part of the passage also calls for our attention because it says that our service to God springs from this New covenant sacrifice. Hence, we have an overlap with Paul's understanding of his teaching ministry as being a New covenant ministry (2 Cor. 3:3-6).

Chapter 9 ends with a reference to the second coming: "To those who eagerly wait for Him He will appear a second time, apart from sin, for salvation" (Heb. 9:28). This reminds us of the strong prophetic burden of the book. The "salvation" that the returning Jesus brings is a completed salvation, rather like the way Peter employs the

48 On this subject, see Gerald F. Hawthorne, *The Presence and The Power: The Significance of the Holy Spirit in the Life and Ministry of Jesus* (Eugene, OR: Wipf & Stock, 2003); J. Douglas MacMillan, *Jesus, Power Without Measure: The Work of the Holy Spirit in the Life of Our Lord* (Darlington, UK: Evangelical Press, 2015).

49 This being the case, I believe the view that translates *diatheke* as "covenant" instead of "testament" in Heb. 9:16-17 is correct. See the excursus, "The Meaning of *Diatheke* in Hebrews 9:16-17," below.

50 "For Hebrews the church lives under the sign of the new covenant" (Peter Stuhlmacher, *Biblical Theology of the New Testament*, 533).

term in 1 Peter 1:5, 9-10. But Hebrews must be understood to equate "salvation" with the coming "rest" of Hebrews 4:1, 3, 9, and 11, and "the world to come" of Hebrews 2:5. This can be accurately spoken of as the New covenant Kingdom.

EXCURSUS: The Meaning of Diatheke in Hebrews 9:16-17.

Most of our English Bible versions translate Hebrews 9:16-17 this way (I have provided vv. 15 and 18 for context):

> And for this reason He is the Mediator of the new covenant, by means of death, for the redemption of the transgressions under the first covenant, that those who are called may receive the promise of the eternal inheritance. *For where there is a testament, there must also of necessity be the death of the testator. For a testament is in force after men are dead, since it has no power at all while the testator lives.* Therefore not even the first covenant was dedicated without blood (NKJV, vv. 16-17 are in italics).

> Therefore he is the mediator of a new covenant, so that those who are called may receive the promised eternal inheritance, since a death has occurred that redeems them from the transgressions committed under the first covenant. *For where a will is involved, the death of the one who made it must be established. For a will takes effect only at death, since it is not in force as long as the one who made it is alive.* Therefore not even the first covenant was inaugurated without blood (ESV, vv. 16-17 in italics).

With the translation *diatheke* as either "testament" or "will" in vv. 16-17, the reader is led to conclude that these verses are not talking about the New covenant. In Hebrews 9:15 the Greek word *diatheke* is translated as "covenant." The same translation ("covenant") is repeated in v. 18.

If I were to give all the occurrences of *diatheke* in Hebrews, you would see that, apart from Hebrews 9:16 and 17, the word is uniformly translated "covenant." One doesn't have to think hard about why this word is rendered as "covenant" in these 16 other instances. The contexts make it very clear that the writer is referring either to the Mosaic covenant or Law, or to the New covenant which replaces it. And one doesn't have to seek too far for proof of this. Hebrews 9:15 contrasts the "first covenant" with the "new covenant," as does verse 18. The chapter itself reinforces the contrast and the appropriate translation of "covenant."

Why translate *diatheke*, which has been expressed as "covenant" everywhere else in the book, as "testament" or "will" in Hebrews 9:16-17? The answer is because it has been assumed that "the death of the one who made it" refers to a "testator" as per a modern "Last Will and Testament." We all know that when a person makes a will, it only comes into force when they are dead. Thus, one writer stated, "In the New

Testament the *diatheke* as a 'last will' is once brought into connection with the sacrifice of Christ..."[51]

But is Vos right? What is it in the context that demands the switch from "covenant" to "testament," other than this assumption that a will is being referred to simply because of "the death of the one who made it"? It seems to me that the whole case depends upon the supposition that *diatheke* can only mean "last will and testament" in Hebrews 9:16-17. There are several reasons for believing this to be a faux pas:

> 1. The meaning of *diatheke* in Hebrews 9:15 is "covenant." This is clear because the writer is referencing the Mosaic "covenant" in the preceding verses (vv. 11-13). If the word meant "last will and testament" in v. 15, the connection with the Mosaic covenant in vv. 11-13 would be lost, and the writer's whole argument rendered suspect. Such a switch would create an equivocation within the argument. That is, it would have the author mean two things by one word in a confusing way. This problem comes into sharp relief once chapter 8 is considered. The superiority of the "better covenant" (e.g., Heb. 8:6) demands it be contrasted with the Mosaic covenant, and hence, that it be itself a true covenant and not a last will and testament. This understanding is assured by the contrast in 8:7 (see comments there). Following on from this, Hebrews 8:8-12 gives the longest quotation of the OT by any NT writer. Is this quotation to do with a testament or a covenant? The answer is impossible to ignore. It is to a "covenant" (OT *berith*), not a testament!
>
> 2. The meaning "covenant" makes perfect sense in context. George H. Guthrie, an acknowledged expert on Hebrews, writes:
>
>> Interpreters often have read 9:16-17 in terms of "will" or "testament," but these verses should be read, in their context, as speaking of the establishment of a covenant... "The one arranging [*diatithemi*] it," occurring in participial form, in 9:16-17, refers to the sacrificial animal that must die for a covenant to be established... This fits perfectly with the argument of 9:18-22, which deals with Moses' inauguration of the Sinai covenant with the sprinkling of blood (Exod. 24:3-8).[52]
>
> 3. When one adds to this the critical observations of P. T. O'Brien, this position is weakened yet further.[53] I shall condense his argument below using several quotes:
>
>> a. "As we have seen, the context of v. 15 seems to demand the sense of 'covenant' because only covenants have mediators [underlining mine], while

51 Geerhardus Vos, "Hebrews, the Epistle of the *Diatheke*," *The Princeton Theological Review* 13 (1915), 601.

52 George H. Guthrie, "Hebrews," in *Commentary on the New Testament Use of the Old*, eds. G. K. Beale and D. A. Carson (Grand Rapids: Baker Academic, 2007) 973.

53 O'Brien's full discussion can be found in O'Brien, *The Letter To The Hebrews*, 328-332.

in v. 18 mention is made of the 'first diatheke', namely, the Sinai event and hence can only be a covenant."

b. "What our author says in vv. 16-17 does not correspond to 'any known form of Hellenistic (or indeed any other) legal practice.' A Hellenistic will was secure and valid when it was written down, witnessed and deposited, not when the testator died. Further, the distribution of the estate could occur when the testator was still living."

Indeed, don't we see this very thing in the Parable of the Prodigal Son, where the son took his inheritance before the father had died?

c. The wider context of Hebrews with our author's view of inheritance and his emphasis on the cult appears incongruous with the model of the secular Hellenistic testament.[54]

4. We must also remember what the author does with the work of Christ in this chapter: he calls it a "sacrifice" (Heb. 9:23, 26), which would not make sense if "testator" was what he meant in Hebrews 9:16.

I conclude from all this evidence, both internal and external, that there is no good reason for translating *diatheke* as "testament" in the sense of "last will and testament" in Hebrews 9:16-17. Thus, I commend the following translation of these verses as follows: "For where a covenant is, there must of necessity be the death of the one who made it. For a covenant is valid only over the dead, for it is never in force while the one who made it [the one who must die] lives."

It is by "the blood of Jesus (Heb. 10:19) that we can enter "the Holiest." Notice the reference to the New covenant in 10:15-17—New covenant blood! The blood of "the Lamb of God who takes away the sin of the world!" (Jn. 1:29).

Christ's Body a Covenant Sacrifice

The author of Hebrews chose as his go-to text the "Old Greek" of the OT, but it is not exactly what scholars mean when they say "LXX."[55] His singular use of Psalm 40:6-8, especially its translation of Psalm 40:6 as "a body you have prepared for me," is noteworthy. As Thomas Constable notes:

> Psalm 40:6 reads: "You have opened [i.e., cleaned out] my ears," whereas Hebrews 10:5 says: "You have prepared a body me." The idea is the same, the former expression being a figurative allusion (Exod. 21:6; cf. Isa. 50:4-5), and the latter a literal description. God had prepared His servant to hear His Word so that he would obey it.[56]

54 From Ibid., 329-330.

55 William L. Lane, *Hebrews 1–8*, cxviii.

56 Thomas L. Constable, *Notes on Hebrews* (2024 edition), 177, https://planobiblechapel.org/tcon/notes/pdf/hebrews.pdf.

After speaking of Christ's self-sacrifice, the author now turns to the physical body which God preordained for the Son of God to be incarnated in. I think that if we bring this passage into conversation with Genesis 1:26-27, we may say that the image of God, which I hold to be mainly spiritual, might include our physicality if we can say that the body of Jesus is the prototypical body after which Adam's body was fashioned. Be that as it may, in Hebrews 10, the source of our sanctification is by means of that body (Heb. 10:10). But this opens up a consideration when reading the words of the institution of the Lord's Supper in Luke 22:19-20 and 1 Corinthians 11:23-26. It appears that not only is the blood of Jesus a New covenant offering, but the body of Jesus was too. Therefore, when Christians partake of the elements of the Lord's Table, both symbols, the bread and the juice, signify our New covenant credentials, which is why Paul warns unworthy persons against taking both elements (1 Cor. 11:27-29).

Waiting for the Fulfillment of Psalm 110:1

In Hebrews 10:13 Christ is described as "waiting" in anticipation of something. But what is He waiting for? Once more, the eschatological bent of the book kicks in. He is "waiting till His enemies are made His footstool" (Heb. 10:13).

What is Jesus waiting for? According to Hebrews 10:13, He is "waiting till His enemies are made His footstool." This, of course, is in fulfillment of Psalm 110:1: "The LORD said to my Lord, 'Sit at My right hand, till I make Your enemies Your footstool.'" It appears, then, that God the Father will one day do this, without doubt, through the orchestration of events immediately prior to the second coming. Once this is done, what might be called "the Kingdom of the New covenant" will be set up. This explains the anticipatory language of "what is becoming obsolete and growing old [and] is ready to vanish away" (Heb. 8:13). Hence, "He takes away the first [Mosaic covenant] that He may establish the second [New covenant]" (Heb. 10:9). All indications are that this establishment will be accomplished after Christ returns.[57] Thus, "To those who eagerly wait[58] for Him He will appear a second time, apart from sin, for salvation" (Heb. 9:28).

This text locates "salvation" after Jesus comes "a second time." This salvation is the Sabbath "rest" in the Kingdom of God. Right now, Jesus acts as the High Priest whose self-offering abrogates the sacrifices under the old covenant (Heb. 10:10-18). This is why Christ is our High Priest *now*—which necessarily means that we are New covenant saints *now*.[59] If such were not true, Christ could not be our High Priest!

57 Although the New covenant was instigated at the first advent, and we enjoy its benefits, it is clear from both Scripture and experience that the New covenant age has not yet dawned. Christians have the Holy Spirit only as a pledge or "earnest" and not in His fullest expression in us. We are yet in our "earthen vessels" and not our glorified bodies. The voice of sin still calls within, and Satan and the world-system still exert their baleful influences every day.

58 The Greek word is *apekdechomai*, meaning "to wait expectantly." This matches the language of striving to enter rest in Heb. 4:11.

59 With due respect, I don't think this aspect of the New covenant has been fully considered by many dispensationalists.

Those interpreters opposed to premillennialism want to assign a present reign of Jesus from heaven, but that is not what the writer of Hebrews is doing here. The inspired author is telling us that the fulfillment of Psalm 110:1-2 (Christ's enemies becoming His footstool and Him ruling from Zion) *lies in the future*. This statement may create confusion in some readers' minds, for they might ask, how can Jesus be serving as High Priest of the New covenant if He is not yet reining in the New covenant Kingdom?

The answer is that the day of Christ's power has not yet arrived (Psa. 110:3), but having risen and ascended, nothing is stopping Him from exercising His priestly office. The two roles, High Priest and King, are not said to be coterminous. If this simple explanation is not sufficient for some, then I respectfully leave them to face Hebrews 10:13 in their quandary.

Hebrews 9:28 depicts believers as eagerly waiting for the second coming. Coupled with the anticipatory tones of the coming sabbath rest (Heb. 4:1-4, 9-10) and the stated intention of the author to write about "the world to come" (Heb. 2:5), we ought to carefully consider the rest of the book in this light. I believe this is the "something better" that we are told about in Hebrews 11:40.

In addition to those texts, we need to look at the last few verses in Hebrews 12:

> See that you do not refuse Him who speaks. For if they did not escape who refused Him who spoke on earth, much more *shall we not escape* if we turn away from Him who *speaks* from heaven, whose voice then shook the earth; but now He has promised, saying, "*Yet once more I shake not only the earth, but also heaven.*" Now this, "*Yet once more*," indicates the removal of those things that are being shaken, as of things that are made, that the things which cannot be shaken may remain. Therefore, since we are receiving a kingdom which cannot be shaken, let us have grace, by which we may serve God acceptably with reverence and godly fear. For our God *is* a consuming fire (Heb. 12:25-29).

The passage refers to the readers/hearers "receiving a kingdom which cannot be shaken" (Heb. 12:28). This is "the world to come," the millennial inheritance. The allusion in verse 25 is to the voice of Yahweh thundering from Mount Sinai in Exodus 19:18 (cf. Psa. 68:7-8). But a question comes up: does the author mean to tell us that God will speak once more in such a way? It appears so. The quotation from Haggai 2:6 needs to be studied in its context. Here are the surrounding verses:

> "*According to* the word that I covenanted with you when you came out of Egypt, so My Spirit remains among you; do not fear!" For thus says the LORD of hosts: "Once more (it *is* a little while) I will shake heaven and earth, the sea and dry land; and I will shake all nations, and they shall come to the Desire of All Nations, and I will fill this temple with glory," says the LORD of hosts...The glory of this latter temple shall be greater than the former,' says the

> LORD of hosts. "And in this place I will give peace," says the LORD of hosts (Hag. 2:5-9).

Through the prophet, Yahweh cites the Mosaic covenant at Sinai, which, because of His grace and its connection to the Abrahamic covenant, He continued to remember His oath.[60] But true to form, the emphasis shifts to the coming kingdom restoration when "the Desire of all nations" (Hag. 2:7) is present.

Who or what is this "Desire"? A messianic interpretation has been popular in Church History, of which the fourth verse of Charles Wesley's hymn "Hark! The Herald Angels Sing" is a famous instance.[61] Hengstenberg bluntly states that the messianic interpretation cannot be correct. He asserts, "The only admissible rendering... is 'the beauty of all the heathen.'"[62] In his opinion, this refers to the Gentiles coming with their possessions.[63] Peters was of a similar opinion.[64]

Another equally valid understanding construes the "Desire" as the kingdom temple.[65] My slight resistance to this interpretation is that the "house of Yahweh" does not become a magnet to the nations until the kingdom is in full swing. Whichever position is taken on Haggai 2:7, the context admits to a strongly premillennial outlook when the later temple is built after Yahweh has shaken creation and He is in a position to give *shalom* (Hag. 2:9).[66] Hence, the writer of Hebrews has the second coming of Christ and the Kingdom of God in his sights in Hebrews 12:25-29. The intriguing verses just before it encourage this conclusion.

A Stern Warning Against Turning Away

Having clarified the divine intent in sending the incarnate Son into the world to remit sin through the New covenant (Heb. 10:5-18), there follows a verbal blast that unsettles all who read it.[67] The reader is warned that to go back on his profession is to tread on Christ (who has just been described as making His enemies His footstool) and to treat as common "the blood of the covenant by which he was sanctified" (Heb. 10:29). The blood of the New covenant has set this person apart, so it must have been

60 When the text says "My Spirit will yet remain among you [Israel]" we are to call to mind the end of the Babylonian exile and Yahweh's providential presence in the throes of rebuilding.

61 The lyrics of this fourth verse read as follows: Come, Desire of nations, come; fix in us Thy humble home. Rise, the woman's conqu'ring Seed; bruise in us the serpent's head. Now display Thy saving pow'r; ruined nature now restore. Now in mystic union join Thine to ours, and ours to Thine..

62 E. W. Hengstenberg, *Christology of the Old Testament*, Vol. 2 (Edinburgh: T&T Clark, 1861), 942-946.

63 Ibid., 944-945.

64 Cf. George N. H. Peters, *The Theocratic Kingdom*, Vol. 3, 418.

65 See e.g., Walter Kaiser, *The Promise-Plan of God*, 219.

66 For more on this question see Herbert Wolf, "'The Desire Of All Nations' in Haggai 2:7: Messianic Or Not?" *JETS* 19 (1976), 97-102.

67 See below.

applied. Yet the person is told, "It is a fearful thing to fall into the hands of the living God" (Heb. 10:31). Here, as in Hebrews 6:5-6, there is no chance of repentance.[68]

To whom is this aimed? The two quotations from Deuteronomy 32:35 and 36 in Hebrews 10:30 aim it squarely at Jews. The quotation from Habakkuk 2:3 calls to mind the second advent (Heb. 10:37), whereas the Habakkuk 2:4 quotation exhorts the reader to keep going and not turn back into perdition (Heb. 10:38).

I will not tarry now to speak of Hebrews 11, only to say that the impression left on the reader is of the ongoing sojourn of the faithful and the carrying forward of Israel's story into the future.[69] The insertion of a short exposition of the faith of Abraham in Hebrews 11:17-19 is particularly poignant as the writer highlights the hermeneutical aspects of true faith.[70]

The eschatological note is struck again in Hebrews 12:25-28, where the reader is reminded that they are "receiving a kingdom" (Heb. 12:28). Indeed, in the final chapter we are encouraged to "go outside the camp" (Heb. 13:13) and view ourselves as having here "no continuing city," but seeking "the one to come" (Heb. 13:14). This world is not our home, but it will be.

The Hermeneutical Importance of Abraham's Faith

I want to turn back to chapter 11 to examine what I consider to be a crucial passage for biblical hermeneutics:

> By faith Abraham, when he was tested, offered up Isaac, and he who had received the promises offered up his only begotten *son*, of whom it was said, "In Isaac your seed shall be called," concluding that God *was* able to raise *him* up, even from the dead, from which he also received him in a figurative sense (Heb. 11:17-19).

I examined this text in Volume One,[71] but something needs to be said here as well. That Abraham exercised great faith in obeying God and taking his son Isaac up Mt. Moriah to sacrifice him is notable. But equally important is how Abraham *interpreted* God's words and *acted* upon them. The text explains the line of reasoning that the patriarch employed. He did not, even when under the most extreme temptations, spiritualize or reinterpret God's command to sacrifice his son Isaac (Gen. 22:1-18). Surely Yahweh didn't mean it literally? This was Abraham's long-awaited son, his beloved son, the son of the covenant! How can Yahweh want Abraham to do such a thing when He has made a solemn oath to maintain Abraham's posterity and the promises made to him? That doesn't sound like God!

I hope you can see that, as well as the emotional pressure upon Abraham as a doting father, there was the theological problem of the righteousness of God. How

68 See also the example of Esau, who "found no place for repentance, though he sought it diligently with tears" (Heb. 12:16-17).
69 Richard B. Hays, *Reading with the Grain of Scripture*, 314-315.
70 See "The Hermeneutical Importance of Abraham's Faith" below.
71 See *The Words of the Covenant*, Vol. 1, 138-140.

did this affect Abraham's hermeneutics? His faith? The author of Hebrews tells us: "concluding that God *was* able to raise *him* up, even from the dead" (Heb. 11:19). This is the epitome of faith! In the face of what could have seemed like the destruction of all his hopes, Abraham's faith directed his hermeneutics, and he reasoned that if he killed Isaac, then Yahweh would just *have* to raise him up again—or else prove false to His covenant! It was in the assurance that this was what was going to happen that Abraham raised the knife (Gen. 22:10). Faith guided his reason. Faith trusts God means what He says and recognizes that our job is to glorify God by taking Him at His word without falling back on typology or spiritualization.

Let me recall to you what was said about the incident of the boat in the storm in Mark 4:35-41 (cf. Matt. 8:23-27; Lk. 8:22-25). Jesus accused the disciples of lacking faith in His words in their panic (Mk. 4:40). If they had reasoned like Abraham, they would have concluded that they would be safe and would have let Jesus continue sleeping (Mk. 4:38). Hence, faith is hermeneutical.

But there is such a thing as figurative language. The Bible is filled with it, and the passage under discussion refers to it when it declares that Abraham "received him [i.e., Isaac] in a figurative sense" (Heb. 11:19). F. F. Bruce says that this "figure" (*parabole*) anticipated the raising of Jesus from the dead.[72]

In all of the examples in Hebrews 11, we see faith illustrated by works. This reminds us of what James says about the relationship between faith and works in James 2:20-24,[73] a letter that is addressed to "the twelve tribes... scattered abroad" (Jam. 1:1). For these writers, their faith will be tested to see of what sort it is. If it is rooted in the risen Messiah, then it will result in an outlook that does not correspond to the way most people look at things, and this will be seen in their way of life.

These "Hebrews" are to focus on "the world to come" (Heb. 2:5). As the sermon ends, they are reminded that here they "have no continuing city, but... seek the one to come" (Heb. 13:14). It is my opinion that the book does double duty. It reminds Christians in the Church that Christ is their High Priest and that they are party to the New covenant made in Him, and because of that, they have unobstructed access to the throne room of Almighty God in prayer. But it seems to me also to look beyond this into what Jeremiah called "the Time of Jacob's Trouble" and address, in particular, the Jews in the Tribulation who have heard that Jesus is indeed their Messiah and prepares them for His soon coming in fulfillment of the prophetic tradition.

God's Oath is an Anchor for the Soul

In the middle of Hebrews 6, there is an important section where God's covenant with Abraham is brought to the fore, and the concept of covenant, particularly the covenant oath, is brought out.

72 F. F. Bruce, *The Epistle to the Hebrews*, 312.

73 In calling attention to this, I am not saying that Jam. 2 contradicts Paul's theology. James is pointing out that simply claiming to have faith is an empty claim. True faith will discover itself by what it does.

> For when God made a promise to Abraham, because He could swear by no one greater, He swore by Himself... For men indeed swear by the greater, and an oath for confirmation *is* for them an end of all dispute. Thus God, determining to show more abundantly to the heirs of promise the immutability of His counsel, confirmed *it* by an oath, that by two immutable things, in which it *is* impossible for God to lie, we might have strong consolation, who have fled for refuge to lay hold of the hope set before *us* (Heb. 6:13, 16-18).

This passage uses the Abrahamic covenant as an example, but it is about the inalterability of God's oaths. The centerpiece of the passage is the declaration that "an oath for confirmation is...an end of all dispute" (Heb. 6:16). Without that, nothing else that is stated in the passage would be worth saying. This is precisely the point that I have been trying to make concerning the oath within the divine covenants. God's oaths are adamant. They cannot be changed in any way. To attempt to do so, one must use an undermining mechanism such as typology or generalization to redirect the precise surface meaning of the oaths.

The passage shows us God as He is—the *covenant* God. Taking as an analogy a human oath, where it was for "confirmation... for them an end of all dispute" (Heb. 6:16). *That* is why our gracious God made covenants! Let this statement settle down into your mind and heart. God's oaths are in Scripture to end all dispute! Of what could there be dispute? How about God's Creation Project? Here it is in brief:

1. This earth was preserved through the Flood, and its predictability was secured by the Noahic covenant (Gen. 9:11).

2. From one man (Abraham) God raised a promised son (Isaac) from whom would come the nation of Israel, who will be given a land with specified dimensions (Gen. 15).

3. God, through Moses, gave Israel the Ten Commandments (Exod. 20:1-17; Deut. 5:1-22), nine of which are universal covenantal moral truths.

4. The valiant deed of Phinehas in his zeal for Yahweh's name caused Him to make an everlasting "Priestly" covenant for his descendants, the Zadokites (Num. 25:6-13).

5. The kingdom of Israel had its king and dynasty chosen by God (2 Sam. 7:1-29; Psa. 89), and his throne (i.e., the reign of David's dynasty) would be everlasting (1 Chron. 17:12-14; Psa. 89:36; Isa. 9:6-7).

6. The remnant of Israel will be redeemed through the coming King who will be "a covenant for the people," a "New covenant," both for Jew and Gentile, ruling from Jerusalem over a regenerated earth (Isa. 11:1-10; 49:1-8; Dan. 7:13-14).

I have tried to show that the NT story fully complies with this covenant structure, especially once the New covenant is understood as being made with the "new man" (Eph. 2:15), the Church beginning at the first advent. But this same New covenant awaits its predicted OT fulfillments at Jesus' second coming. How can all this be known and known for certain? The answer is here: God has made covenant oaths which ought to drive away misunderstanding and "end all dispute." The "two immutable things" (Heb. 6:18) are the Word of God and the covenant oaths of God which confirm it.[74] Since God's covenants are made to end all dispute, it behooves the people of God to make them so. That is Biblical Covenantalism. Biblical Covenantalism, defined as the Bible's real covenantal teaching,[75] is "an anchor for the soul" (Heb. 6:19), which is secured by Jesus Christ Himself as our High Priest (Heb. 6:20).

No Continuing City: The Eschatology of Hebrews

The opening verses of the book of Hebrews include the line "at the end of these days" (Heb. 1:2). The phrase is translated by Lane and by Attridge as "in these final days."[76] Lane has a note claiming it is "a common Septuagintal idiom."[77] The phrase likely refers to the times after the ascension of Christ to the second advent.[78] I say "likely" because if Jesus detains His coming for another two thousand years or so, it would seem that the phrase will lose its coherence. It could be that the idea is of a more proleptic order. However one understands it, the phrase is a verbal springboard that focuses attention on the future.

Hebrews 1:2 also mentions that the Son is "appointed heir of all things" by God. We are not told precisely what "all things" are, but one is reminded of Jesus' own words to His disciples in Matthew 28:18: "All authority has been given to Me in heaven and on earth."[79] But even this saying does not tell us concretely what Christ's use of power will look like. He has an inheritance (Heb. 1:4), and the citation of Psalm 45:6 (Heb. 1:8) speaks of a throne and a scepter (cf. Gen. 49:10; Num. 24:17). There is an intimation then that the New covenant Kingdom is in view.

This inkling receives solid confirmation in Hebrews 2:5 and the author's declaration that he is speaking of "the world to come." The word rendered "world" is *oikoumene*, meaning "the inhabited earth." So, the reference is to the next age when the earth will be inhabited by those who qualify through their faith in Jesus. Attridge observes, "Hebrews mentions that world not only because an eschatological dimension

74 Harold W. Attridge, *The Epistle to the Hebrews*, Hermeneia (Philadelphia: Fortress, 1989), 181.

75 My attempt at following the Bible's covenantal teaching is not to be confused with the infallible doctrine of the Bible itself. I am simply trying my best to provide an accurate account. Hence, one should distinguish between the noun (my name for my approach), and the adjective (Scripture's revelation of the covenants). Hopefully, there is a close correspondence!

76 William L. Lane, *Hebrews 1–8*, 4-5, 10. Harold W. Attridge, *Hebrews*, 35.

77 William L. Lane, *Hebrews 1–8*, 5.

78 See also 2 Tim. 1:3; 1 Pet. 1:20; 2 Pet. 3:3; Jude 18.

79 See also Rom. 14:9.

is present in the texts cited and interpreted in the first two chapters but also in order to emphasize the reality of that new age."[80]

The future age is in the author's sights as he composes his letter. The Son's "house" (*oikos*) is to be equated with "the world to come" (Heb. 2:5) and with the "inheritance" (Heb. 1:4). This is why the reader is urged to "hold fast the confidence and the rejoicing of the hope firm to the end." Something similar is stated in Hebrews 6:11, "We desire that each one of you show the same diligence to the full assurance of hope until the end." The word "end" (*telos*) refers, then, to the onset of the "world to come," which the addressees are to strive for so that they may "inherit the promises" (Heb. 6:12). Hence, there is a case for seeing Christ's "house" in Hebrews 3:6 as His inheritance; an inheritance that His saints may enter (Heb. 1:14).[81]

The reference to Hebrews 1:14 brings up the author's use of the term "salvation," which in Hebrews speaks of completed salvation (Heb. 2:3, 10; 5:9; 6:9; 9:28). Hence, "He is also able to save to the uttermost those who come to God through Him" (Heb. 7:25).

Hebrews 4 is where the author explores the concept of "rest," although notice its introduction in Hebrews 3:11 is sandwiched between the warnings about the end in Hebrews 3:6 and 14. Certainly, in Hebrews 4:1, the "promise... entering His rest" is eschatological. This "rest" is connected with the seventh day sabbath in Hebrews 4:4, quoting Genesis 2:2.[82] Again, the eschatological focus is found in Hebrews 4:3: "For we who have believed do enter that rest." Is this rest the individual soul's journey to heaven after death? That is how many take it, but a good argument can be made for it being the coming aeon. The rest that Joshua led Israel to in Canaan had physical dimensions and topography, yet that was not permanent (Heb. 4:8). Therefore, we are told, "There remains therefore a rest for the people of God" (Heb. 4:9), and diligence is needed to enter into it (Heb. 4:11).

Eschatology resurfaces in Hebrews 9, where the theme of inheritance is again brought up (Heb. 9:15). Christ will be returning, and when He does, He will bring salvation with Him (Heb. 9:28). Because this will be Christ's second coming in glory, the salvation here is the completed redemption of both body and soul. Until that time, Christ is depicted as "waiting till His enemies are made His footstool" (Heb. 10:13; cf. Psa. 110:1). The saints are, therefore, to urge holiness and obedience upon one another in light of the approaching Day (Heb. 10:25; cf. 10:37). Endurance is required, that "you may receive the promise" (Heb. 10:36, 39).

As I commented above, the whole of Hebrews 11, with its great "cloud of witnesses" (Heb. 12:1), contains a noticeable forward thrust. At the end of a chapter that includes the record of Abraham looking for a city "whose Builder and Maker is God" (Heb. 11:10 cf. Heb. 11:16), we are told, "For all these, having obtained a good

80 Harold W. Attridge, *Hebrews*, 70.

81 "For we have become partakers of Christ if we hold the beginning of our confidence steadfast to the end" (Heb. 3:14). Notice the conditionality attached to the promises in Hebrews. Cf. Heb. 6:4, "partakers of the Holy Spirit."

82 See also Heb. 4:10.

testimony through faith, did not receive the promise, God having provided something better for us, that they should not be made perfect apart from us" (Heb. 11:39-40).

The reader is thus thrown into the narrative. "We" along with "them," will one day be "made perfect." In Hebrews the word "perfect" (*teleioun*) means bringing someone or something to completion in God's eyes. Hence, in Hebrews 2:10, Jesus becomes our High Priest[83] and "the captain of [our] salvation" (cf. Heb. 12:2) by being made perfect through suffering. In Hebrews 12:23 we read about "the general assembly and church of the firstborn who are registered in heaven, to God the Judge of all, to the spirits of just men made perfect."

Through the work of Christ, these saints have been perfected (cf. Heb. 10:14), and those in the assembly of the firstborn are those who have gone before and who now reside in a blissful state in heavenly Jerusalem (Heb. 12:22). Although many differ from me on this, I do not believe the "church of the firstborn" means the Church from Christ's ascension to his return. I may be wrong, but I believe this *ekklesia* is "the people of God" of Hebrews 4:9, who are Israelites. If it is the NT Church,[84] the picture above remains unchanged, although I question whether the translation "church" is warranted in the context.[85]

Hebrews 12 closes with a reference to "Him who speaks from heaven" (Heb. 12:25) and a quotation from Haggai 2:6 about the shaking of the created order (Heb. 12:26), no doubt meaning the second coming (cf. Matt. 24:29).[86] After this "shaking" of creation Hebrews 12:28 declares, "We are receiving a kingdom which cannot be shaken." This is only the second time the word "kingdom" has been used in the book. The other time was in Hebrews 1:8, a quotation from Psalm 45:8. Finally, in the middle of chapter 13, the author writes, "For here we have no continuing city, but we seek the one to come" (Heb. 13:14). The "one to come" will be in "the world to come" (Heb. 2:5). Whether he has in mind New Jerusalem (Rev. 3:12; 21:2) or not I cannot say. If he does, then he is looking beyond the Millennial Kingdom into the new heaven and new earth of 2 Peter 2:13 and Revelation 21:1.

83 See Heb. 2:17.

84 Homer A. Kent, *The Epistle to the Hebrews*, 272-273.

85 Lane believes it is all the saints from both Testaments (William L. Lane, *Hebrews 9–13*, 469), although he includes an interesting note: "Lecuyer has shown that the entire formulation in v. 23a is rooted in the description of Israel in the Pentateuch. The Israelites are designated the ἐκκλησία, "'congregation,' in Deut. 4:10; 9:10; 18:16 LXX (cf. Acts 7:38), while the occasion when God addressed the people at Sinai is called ἡμέρα [τῆς] ἐκκλησίας, 'the day of the gathering'" (Ibid., 468).

86 On this subject see e.g., George N. H. Peters, *The Theocratic Kingdom*, Vol. 2, 494-498.

18

THE REST OF THE GENERAL EPISTLES

But above all, my brethren, do not swear, either by heaven or by earth or with any other oath. But let your "Yes" be "Yes," and your "No," "No," lest you fall into judgment.
– James 5:12

I have felt it necessary to spend quite a lot of time on the book of Hebrews in order to show that it is a book of the New covenant Christ. As such, I believe it spans both the Church age and, if the pretribulation snatching out of the Church is true, the coming Tribulation. This is why the warning passages, taken at face value without skirting them, teach that a person who is within the New covenant and has been bought with the blood of Christ must "endure to the end" (cf. Matt. 24:13).

It has taken some effort to get here, but if one is going to go where the covenants of God point, there appears to be no alternative. God's *message* of salvation is not the same in every age. This truth is so plain and clear in the Bible itself, yet our theological tendencies rewrite biblical history. But Noah was not accounted righteous by believing that his descendants would be as many as the stars in number. Abraham, Isaac, Jacob, Moses, David, or Josiah, for that matter, were not justified by believing that Jesus of Nazareth was the Messiah and that He died on a Roman cross for their sins and rose again from the dead. Nowhere in the Gospels do John the Baptist, Jesus Himself, or His disciples openly preach anything like 1 Corinthians 15:1-4. Granted grace was the operative instrument of salvation, what then was to be believed prior to Pentecost? These are just the stubborn facts, like it or not. If they are not engaged head-on, we have no right to say we are dealing faithfully with the text of Scripture.

In making this claim, I am, of course, sensitive to the fact that hackles will be raised. I have attempted to assuage the protests somewhat with the "Appendix on Salvation in the Tribulation," and the "Appendix on Trying to Get the Rapture Right." Although it will be by grace through faith, as in every age, I believe there is enough evidence to show that the salvation promised is not exactly of the same type as that offered to those in the Church. It is closer to the salvation offered in the Gospels, where it comes with the message of repentance and good works in view of the coming King and kingdom. I have taken pains throughout this volume to demonstrate this thesis, knowing at the same time how much easier (though far less scripturally cogent) it would be to simply state that every believer in every age is incorporated into the Church and is promised a glorified body like Christ so that we all amount to one homogeneous entity—the one people of God.

Nice as that sounds, it does not line up with the covenantal teaching of the Bible, nor with plain and clear prophecy that depends on it. For example, in Revelation 21:1–22:6 we read about the New Jerusalem coming down from heaven to the new earth. It appears to be the dwelling place of the Church, the Bride of Christ. But we also read of different nations coming in and out of its gates (Rev. 21:23-26). Many nations populate the new earth. Among them is the nation of Israel, in fulfillment of its covenant promises. This is where it ends up, as we shall see in more detail later.

James

The Epistle of James begins with a sentence that again may rattle the cages: "James, a bondservant of God and of the Lord Jesus Christ, <u>to the twelve tribes</u> which are scattered abroad: Greetings" (Jam. 1:1).

The principal addressees of this epistle are Jews. To state the contrary is, in my opinion, to indulge in flagrant misinterpretation. Why would the leader of the Church in Jerusalem address Gentiles in such a way? This is especially true because, along with many other writers, I believe that the book of James, written by the Lord's brother,[1] is one of the earliest books of the NT,[2] written probably in the 40s A.D.[3] At such an early date, it is decidedly unlikely that the phrase "to the twelve tribes which are scattered abroad" would mean anything else but to the Jewish Diaspora.

Like the book of Hebrews, James has suffered somewhat from what Luke Timothy Johnson called "the Pauline fixation."[4] This is where Paul's categories are read into other inspired authors with the outcome that those non-Pauline writings are not understood first as discrete works. While it may be pointed out that Scripture does not contradict and so little harm is done, that is a little naïve, especially for dispensationalist interpreters. No intelligent reader would claim that the whole Bible is addressed directly to the NT Church. Further, no intelligent premillennialist would claim that everything in the Synoptic Gospels or the book of Revelation is directed at the Church in the way Paul's epistles are. These works must be read for what they are

1 See James D. G. Dunn, *Neither Jew Nor Greek: A Contested Identity* (Grand Rapids: Eerdmans, 2015), 514-515.

2 See Craig L. Blomberg, *A New Testament Theology*, 137. He thinks Jude is also early.

3 Despite its early date, it is notable for the quality of its Greek. See Herbert W. Bateman and William C. Varner, *James: An Exegetical Guide for Preaching and Teaching*, Big Greek Idea Series (Grand Rapids: Kregel, 2022), 44-48.

4 As cited by James D. G. Dunn, *Beginning From Jerusalem*, 1123 n. 89.

and then compared with Paul. This is precisely what ought to be done with Hebrews and the General Epistles.

While the emphases in Hebrews *may* be particularly important in helping Tribulation saints—consider its stress on vigilance, striving, practical faith, and waiting for the Kingdom—something similar might be said in the case of James, even though I do not see James as matching Hebrews' theological intent. I do believe that James' admonitions are relevant to both epochs, Church and Tribulation,[5] since it is largely concerned with practical living.

The structural relationship of James to the Sermon on the Mount[6] enhances its concern with doing the word, not just hearing it (Jam. 1:22-25). He wants to see works accompanying a profession of faith (Jam. 2:14-26). Christopher Morgan notices, "As examples of faith, works, and mercy, James points to Abraham and Rahab—a patriarch and a prostitute, a Jew and a Gentile. God's grace that leads to our initial faith also brings about our continued faith, which is tied to covenant faithfulness."[7]

As such, James is written to the saints, not to unbelievers. He inveighs against the wealthy several times (Jam. 1:10-11; 2:1-9; 5:1-6), warns about taming the tongue (Jan. 1:26; 3:1-12), and promotes true wisdom over against what is false (Jam. 3:13-18).[8] He pulls no punches. The strife in the world is mainly caused by pride (Jam. 4:1-6) and would be massively reduced if men would learn humility (Jam. 4:7-10, 13-16). He advocates for the great power of prayer (Jam. 5:13-18).

The most noteworthy passage, as far as this biblical theology is concerned, comes in James 5:

> Therefore be patient, brethren, until the coming of the Lord. See *how* the farmer waits for the precious fruit of the earth, waiting patiently for it until it receives the early and latter rain. You also be patient. Establish your hearts, for the coming of the Lord is at hand. Do not grumble against one another, brethren, lest you be condemned. Behold, the Judge is standing at the door! My brethren, take the prophets, who spoke in the name of the Lord, as an example of suffering and patience. Indeed we count them blessed who endure. You have heard of the perseverance of Job and seen the end *intended by* the Lord—that the Lord is very compassionate and merciful (Jam. 5:7-11).

---

5 This assumes, of course, that the pretribulation removal of the Church is correct. If it is not the point is moot.

6 See, for example, Virgil V. Porter Jr., "The Sermon on the Mount in the Book of James, Part 1," *BSAC* 162 (July 2005), 344-60; and Idem., "The Sermon on the Mount in the Book of James, Part 2," *BSAC* 162 (Oct. 2005), 470-82. Davids writes of the "high degree of intertextuality between James and the Matthean form of the teaching of Jesus, and in particular, the Sermon of the Mount" (Peter H. Davids, *A Theology of James, Peter, and Jude* [Grand Rapids: Zondervan, 2014], 43).

7 Christopher W. Morgan, "Integrated Spirituality," in *Biblical Spirituality*, ed. Christopher W. Morgan (Wheaton, IL: Crossway, 2019), 148.

8 The book of James is often included within the genre of Wisdom literature. See James D. G. Dunn, *Beginning From Jerusalem*, 1131.

James cannot close his letter without speaking about the second coming. He represents it as a patient wait between the first and second advents. Nevertheless, "the coming of the Lord is at hand" (Jam. 5:8), with "the Judge," Jesus Christ, "standing at the door" (Jam. 5:9).

Of course, we understand that the time gap between the first and second advent is very lengthy in human terms. It is, therefore, a little surprising that this kind of language crops up numerous times in the NT. Paul exclaims that God will soon crush Satan under the saints' feet (Rom. 16:20). John ends the book of Revelation by saying that the things he wrote about "must shortly take place" (Rev. 22:6; cf. 1:3). Someone reading these claims nearly two thousand years ago might well have thought that the Lord's coming would occur in their lifetime. I do not claim to know why there has been such a long wait for the second coming, other than to say that many of the things that John wrote about could not have been fulfilled even in the recent past. I believe we live in the days when literal fulfillment of these prophecies is a possibility. Peter, of course, helps with this somewhat by reminding us that with the Lord, "one day *is* as a thousand years, and a thousand years as one day" (1 Pet. 3:8). From His standpoint, it is nothing, even though two thousand years is a fair chunk of earth history.

But it is possible that James 5:8-9 is a veiled reference to the imminence of the rapture of the Church. Certainly, good arguments have been adduced in its favor.[9] What is clearer is that the admonition to persevere befits the lives of many of the Lord's people both now and in the coming Tribulation. And it is perhaps worth taking note that James says that Elijah sealed up heaven for "three years and six months" (Jam. 5:17). That number will be worth remembering when we look at Revelation 11.

Before moving on, there is one more verse that I need to call to your attention: "But above all, my brethren, do not swear, either by heaven or by earth or with any other oath. But let your "Yes" be "Yes," and *your* "No," "No," lest you fall into judgment" (Jam. 5:12). This verse recalls the words of Jesus in Matthew 5:37. It applies to normal day-to-day situations and not to judicial circumstances where an oath to tell the whole truth is appropriate. I bring it up just to point out that if anyone does not need to swear an oath, it would be the One who cannot lie (Tit. 1:2), whose word is truth (Jn. 17:17), and whose words establish the very laws of thought and integrity which we live by (Psa. 119:130). And yet God makes covenants! He swears oaths! He does this out of a gracious disposition toward us. He knows that "every man is a liar" (Rom. 3:4). And if this grace is not to be lost and forgotten, the question must be asked, "Why does God make covenants?" The reply must be that He does not make them about unimportant or tangential matters, but about the most important things. We, therefore, are duty-bound to pay heed to the oaths that God has sworn, for God is true (Rom. 3:4) and He will bring to pass the very things He has sworn to do.

9 Earl D. Radmacher, "The Imminent Return of the Lord," *CTSJ* 4 (July 1998), esp. 16. Also, John F. MacArthur, Jr., "Is Christ's Return Imminent?" *TMS* 11 (Spring 2000), 7-18.

1 Peter

The book of 1 Peter is also marked by a Jewish flavor. This comes across pointedly in 1 Peter 1:18,[10] which talks about "the tradition of your fathers." The book certainly possesses strong Jewish overtones.[11] Jim Sibley writes:

> The available textual data most often cited that bears on the nature of the recipients are found in 1:1, 14, 18; 2:10; and 4:3–5. Most commentators decide that the audience must have been Gentile on the basis of 1:14 and 18, and fit the remaining evidence into this schema. Primary attention then must be given to these verses.[12]

Sibley ably dismantles the weak inference for Gentile readership based upon 1 Peter 1:14 and 18 by simply showing that Paul, a Jew, referred to his past life in a similar fashion (e.g., Eph. 2:3; 1 Tim. 1:13).[13] And given that Peter ministered to the Jews (Gal. 2:8-9), is it any surprise to find him writing to Jewish believers? And if this is indeed the case, it would not be unusual to find a concentrated use of the Hebrew Scriptures in the letter. Again, Sibley is to the point: "There is a greater concentration of Old Testament quotations and allusions in 1 Peter than in any other New Testament book. This is not proof that the recipients were Jewish, but it is evidence that should be considered."[14]

Two of the most edifying opening chapters in the whole Bible are found in 1 and 2 Peter. They are the go-to places for Christian discipleship. But Peter clearly wants to fix the attention of these Jewish saints on their future rewards as an encouragement to persevere. Davids calls 1 Peter "a parenetic letter,"[15] by which he means an

---

10 Many point to the opening verse, 1 Pet. 1:1, with its reference to those "pilgrims" (NKJV) or "aliens" (NASB) in "the dispersion" (*diaspora*). As an example: "Some argue from the name, Strangers, that the Gentiles are here meant, which seems not to be; for proselyte Gentiles were indeed called strangers in Jerusalem, and by the Jews; but were not the Jews strangers in these places—Pontus, Galatia, Cappadocia, Asia, and Bithynia?—Not strangers dwelling together in a prosperous flourishing condition, as a well-planted colony, but strangers of the dispersion, scattered to and fro" (Robert Leighton, *Commentary on First Peter* [Grand Rapids: Kregel, 1981], 12). This opinion is echoed by Witherington who observes, "In light of the highly Jewish character of 1 Peter anyway, it seems logical to conclude that, since in all the above references it is Jews who are called resident aliens, we should surely conclude that this is likely in 1 Peter as well" (Ben Witherington III, *Letters and Homilies for Hellenized Christians: a Socio-Rhetorical Commentary on 1–2 Peter* [Downers Grove, IL: InterVarsity, 2007], 24).

11 "No New Testament letter is so consistently addressed, directly or indirectly, to 'Israel,' that is (on the face of it) to Jews" (J. Ramsey Michaels, 1 Peter, WBC [Waco, TX: Word, 1988], xlv), as cited by W. Edward Glenny, "The Israelite Imagery of 1 Peter 2," in *Dispensationalism, Israel and the Church*, eds. Craig A. Blaising and Darrell L. Bock (Grand Rapids: Zondervan, 1992), 156 n. 2. I am also indebted to Jim R. Sibley, "You Talkin' To Me? 1 Peter 2:4-10 and A Theology of Israel," *Southwestern Journal of Theology* 59 (Fall 2016), 59-75.

12 Jim R. Sibley, "You Talkin' To Me? 1 Peter 2:4-10 and A Theology of Israel," 6.

13 Keener gets around this by saying that Peter was just employing "language that Jews often used for such behaviors" (Craig S. Keener, *1 Peter: A Commentary* [Grand Rapids: Baker, 2021], 105-106).

14 Jim R. Sibley, "You Talkin' To Me? 1 Peter 2:4-10 and A Theology of Israel," 13.

15 Peter H. Davids, *A Theology of James, Peter, and Jude*, 130.

admonitory work.[16] Peter opens his first letter with a reference to "an inheritance incorruptible and undefiled and that does not fade away, reserved in heaven for you" (1 Pet. 1:4). The apostle could be construed as asserting that heaven is the final and eternal destination of believers. However, since Peter will himself refer to "a new heavens and earth" in 2 Peter 3, such an understanding is unlikely.

1 Peter 2:4-10 and the Specter of Supercessionism

Along with Matthew 21:43, 1 Peter 2:4-10 are ground-zero for those interpreters who teach that the Church is the "true" or "new Israel," which by definition means that "old Israel"—the people of the nation to whom Yahweh made covenants—has no more future as a nation. Sam Storms defines supercessionism, or replacement theology, this way: "Replacement theology would assert that God has uprooted and eternally cast aside the olive tree which is Israel and has planted, in its place, an entirely new one, the Church. All the promises given to the former have been transferred to the latter."[17]

As you can see, replacement theology teaches that there is no future Davidic Kingdom plan for Israel. Basically, the role of Israel and all of its promises have been transferred to the Church.[18] We are told this even though the covenants with Abraham (e.g., Gen. 15: 4-18; 22:16-17; 26:3-4; Isa. 62:1-7; Jer. 33:26), Phinehas (Num. 25:10; Psa. 106:28-31; Jer. 33:17-22; Mal. 3:1-4), and David (e.g., Psa. 89:14-29; 132:11-14; 1 Chron. 17:22; Isa. 9:7; Jer. 33:15-26) are unilateral and irrevocable (cf. Rom. 11:29), all the more so once the New covenant re-energizes them (cf. Jer. 31:31-36; Ezek. 36:22-30; Rom. 11:26-28). But this does not deter good men from asserting such things as this:

> One passage that highlights how the Church is the antitype of Israel through Jesus is 1 Peter 2:4-10. From the beginning of the epistle, Peter identifies his primarily Gentile audience with the language of exile and diaspora, imagery of OT Israel now applied to the eschatological people of God and foreseen in the prophets (1 Pet 1:10-12). In 1 Peter 2:4-10, the identity and function of the church are presented as the new Israel through Christ...Through union in Christ, God's new temple of believers <u>takes on Israel's identity and role</u> in a heightened eschatological sense.[19]

---

16 James D. G. Dunn, *Neither Jew Nor Greek: A Contested Identity*, 729. Dunn does not believe Peter wrote these epistles.

17 Sam Storms, *Kingdom Come: The Amillennial Alternative* (Fearn, Scotland: Mentor, 2013), 195.

18 These promises have also been transformed into more spiritual realities so that neither the content of the covenant oaths nor the original designees remain the same. It has been our insistence that this sort of alteration is impossible with God's covenants.

19 Brent E. Parker, "The Israel-Christ-Church Relationship," in *Progressive Covenantalism*, eds. Stephen J. Wellum and Brent E. Parker (Nashville: B&H, 2016), 64-65 (my emphasis).

Though worded differently, this quotation fits well with the definition of replacement theology given above. Parker bases his view that Gentiles are the target audience for the epistle by referencing 1 Peter 1:14, 18, 21, and 4:2-4.[20] But 1 Peter 1:14 is only effective if one believes that formerly unregenerate Jews could not be guilty of "lusts," "ignorance," or "aimless conduct," which is a stretch (Rom. 2:17-24). First Peter 1:21 proves nothing either way, and 1 Peter 4:2-4 really only carries any weight if one already assumes the letter is written to Gentiles. If, however, it is addressed to a mainly Jewish readership, such OT figures of speech as are scattered throughout 1 Peter 2:4-10 are to be expected. For example, 1 Peter 2:9 declares, "You are a chosen race, a royal priesthood, a holy nation, a people for God's own possession..."

Since the apostle is addressing the remnant (cf. Rom. 11:5), one can understand why he would employ this resonant terminology, especially to Jews who were experiencing trials and persecution (1 Pet. 3:16-17; 4:1-4, 12-16). The Church is not a "race" or a "nation," but Diaspora Jews could be addressed that way.[21]

A Covenant Christ

Seeing then that there is a very good case for a Jewish audience for 1 Peter, the book has a covenantal orientation if we take Peter's constant references to Jesus as the Christ into consideration. Daniel Block writes:

> Peter never mentions David or the Davidic covenant in his book. But without reference to the history of the messianic hope rooted in David, the role of Jesus as Messiah is incomprehensible. Even with the strong Davidic tradition in which the Jews would have been schooled, according to Peter, the history of the prophetic institution is a history into the manner in which the hope of salvation, grounded in the work of the Messiah, would be fulfilled.[22]

Put another way, for these Jews, Jesus' surname would not have been "Christ," but He would be Jesus *the* Christ, the inheritor of the Davidic throne (cf. Matt. 22:42).

2 Peter

Turning now to 2 Peter, I will assume that the author is the apostle who wrote 1 Peter. As with the first chapter of 1 Peter, 2 Peter 1 is a wonderful summary of Christian discipleship goals. This letter is shorter than 1 Peter, and the themes are different. They deal with false teachers and the dissolution of the present order in terms of judgment. This makes it much closer in content to Jude, which either influenced 2 Peter or was influenced by it.[23] At least that is the way it is often viewed.

20 Ibid., 64 n. 61.
21 W. Edward Glenny, "The Israelite Imagery of 1 Peter 2," 186-187.
22 Daniel I. Block, *Covenant*, 609.
23 Peter H. Davids, *A Theology of James, Peter, and Jude*, 203-208.

Testimony to the Transfiguration

As the first chapter closes, Peter inserts a memory he had of the Transfiguration of Jesus on the mount, to which he was an eyewitness (Mk. 9:2ff.).

> For we did not follow cunningly devised fables when we made known to you the power and coming of our Lord Jesus Christ, but were eyewitnesses of His majesty. For He received from God the Father honor and glory when such a voice came to Him from the Excellent Glory: "This is My beloved Son, in whom I am well pleased." And we heard this voice which came from heaven when we were with Him on the holy mountain (2 Pet. 1:16-18).

Peter directly relates the event to "the power and coming of our Lord Jesus Christ" (2 Pet. 1:16). By this, I think Gundry is right when he says Peter is "using the transfiguration as a preview that guarantees the second coming."[24] That is a good way to put it.[25] Just as the miracles of Jesus previewed His transformative presence when He comes as the Prince of Peace (Isa. 9:6), even so His great transfiguration, in which "as He prayed, the appearance of His face was altered, and His robe became white and glistening" (Lk. 9:29) preannounces His coming in glory (Matt. 25:31). He will come to bring in the long-awaited Kingdom (Matt. 6:10; Rev. 12:10). And this interpretation is supported in the immediate context: "For so an entrance will be supplied to you abundantly into the everlasting kingdom of our Lord and Savior Jesus Christ" (2 Pet. 1:11).

The words of the Father that Peter heard on the mount recall Psalm 2:7, which in context depicts the King in His Kingdom (Psa. 2:6-9), which buttresses the eschatological interpretation of the Transfiguration and 2 Peter 1:16-18.

Scoffers in the Last Days

Second Peter 3 turns the attention to "the last days" (2 Pet. 3:3) and "the promise of his coming" (2 Pet. 3:4). He bases what he will go on to say on the foundation of the prophets and the apostles (2 Pet. 3:2). Citing the scoffers who point out that essentially nothing has changed and there is no reason to believe Christ will return to cause change (2 Pet. 3:4), Peter then indulges in a little cosmology. I do not wish to get into that cosmology here, although I do believe that when everything is seen for what it is, the views of Peter in 2 Peter 3:5 (not to mention Moses in Genesis 1) will be shown to be accurate. God will have the last laugh.

---

24 Robert H. Gundry, *Commentary on the New Testament*, 958. See also D. Edmond Hiebert, *Second Peter and Jude: An Expositional Commentary* (Greenville, SC: Unusual Publications, 1989), 71-72.

25 Not everyone is so adamant about the second coming connection. Matthew S. Harmon, *The God Who Judges and Saves: A Theology of 2 Peter and Jude* (Wheaton, IL: Crossway, 2023), doesn't even mention it.

The destruction of the original earth in the worldwide Flood is used as a contrast to the coming judgment of the earth in fire. This produces the triad of: (1) this world before the Flood (Eden to the Ark), (2) this world from the Flood to the second coming, and (3) this world from the second coming to the dissolution.[26]

But is it a dissolution? Not everyone agrees. McClain notices that the word "new" (*kainos*) can mean new in character as well as new in substance.[27] But the problem does not lie with the word *kainos*, but in the description of the destruction of the heaven and earth which Peter supplies:

> But the day of the Lord will come as a thief in the night, in which the heavens will pass away with a great noise, and the elements will melt with fervent heat; both the earth and the works that are in it will be burned up. Therefore, since all these things will be dissolved, what manner of persons ought you to be in holy conduct and godliness, looking for and hastening the coming of the day of God, because of which the heavens will be dissolved, being on fire, and the elements will melt with fervent heat? (2 Pet. 3:10-12, my emphasis).

Notice that the obliteration of the present creation is termed by Peter "the Day of the Lord" (2 Pet. 3:10). He employs several verbs to describe the kind of destruction involved. It is true that none of these verbs ("pass away," "melt," "burned up,"[28] "dissolved") requires an utter dissolution or annihilation of the present creation. But when we look at what is being dissolved, we find it is the "elements," the *stoicheion* that are being referred to. The *stoicheion* are the basic constituents of reality, not just the structures and topography of the land. Hiebert writes, "The physical structure of the present world will disintegrate, not necessarily be annihilated."[29] I can go with that.[30]

Here we must bring in three passages from elsewhere in the NT, Matthew 24:35 and Revelation 20:11 and 21:1:

> Heaven and earth will pass away, but My words will by no means pass away (Matt. 24:35).

> Then I saw a great white throne and Him who sat on it, from whose face the earth and the heaven fled away. And there was found no place for them (Rev. 20:11).

26 Ibid., 965; Peter H. Davids, *A Theology of James, Peter, and Jude*, 240.

27 Alva J. McClain, *The Greatness of the Kingdom*, 510.

28 Vlach and others note that this word means "to lay bare" or "expose" and he is right (Michael J. Vlach. *He Will Reign Forever*, 512-513). But I do not think all this tips the balance in favor of a renovated earth rather than a completely replaced one when the other verbs and passages are brought alongside. Whichever way it turns out, I shall be more than satisfied with the results!

29 Also D. Edmond Hiebert, *Second Peter and Jude: An Expositional Commentary*, 160.

30 I fully realize that *stoicheia* can refer to evil spirits or even false teachings (and the spirits behind them). For a full analysis which favors the latter view, see J. Richard Middleton, *A New Heaven and a New Earth: Reclaiming Biblical Eschatology* (Grand Rapids: Baker, 2014), 189-200.

> Now I saw a new heaven and a new earth, for the first heaven and the first earth had passed away. Also there was no more sea (Rev. 21:1).

In Matthew 24:35, Jesus has just been describing the End Times, and He finishes off by comparing the destruction of the present order of things, both heaven and earth, with the endurance of His words. One may claim that this is mere hyperbole, but I am not so sure. There is little reason to state the destruction of the present creation in this way unless He is revealing a fact. And notice that the whole creation is in view, not just the earth. It is the same with the two Revelation passages. Both heaven and earth are affected, and the verb *pheugo* ("fled away") in Revelation 20:11 calls to mind the image of something vanishing out of sight.

Whether the present heavens and earth are to be renovated or replaced is neither here nor there in the scheme of things, but when a theological perspective is added in the shape of Revelation 22:3, "there shall be no more curse," I am inclined to state the total annihilation view. It seems to me that the curse on the ground that God pronounced in Genesis 3:17 goes deeper than what a renovation will produce.[31]

EXCURSUS: The Day of the Lord in the New Testament

In 2 Peter 3 the Day of the Lord refers to the utter destruction of the present created order, either by annihilation or renovation. Since Revelation 20 puts this destruction a thousand years after the setting up of Christ's earthly Kingdom,[32] it means that in 2 Peter 3:10-12, the Day of the Lord is confined to that final conflagration.

The NT does not employ the phrase "Day of the Lord" to refer to historical visitations of divine wrath like the OT sometimes does. Peter and Paul, who are the only NT writers who use the designation, always use it to refer to the eschaton. The main NT texts are Acts 2:20; 1 Corinthians 5:5; 2 Corinthians 1:14; 1 Thessalonians 5:2; and the 2 Peter 3 passage we have already considered.

> 1. Acts 2:20 is from Peter's quotation of Joel 2:28-32 at Pentecost. I have already expounded that text in my chapter on Acts. Acts 2:20 quotes Joel 2:31, which mentions the Day of the Lord in the context of the setting up of the Kingdom at the second coming.[33] So, the Day of the Lord in that passage refers to the very end of the Tribulation and the onset of the reign of Christ when the Spirit is manifested in the saints.
>
> 2. First Corinthians 5:5 concerns the practice of perverted sin in the Corinthian Church. Paul writes that he has judged the individual who committed the deed and has delivered him over to Satan "that his spirit may be saved in the day of the Lord Jesus." I believe this verse ought to be read in light of 1 Corinthians 1:7b-8, which speaks of Christians "eagerly waiting for the revelation of our Lord Jesus Christ, who will also confirm you to the end, that you may be

31 Job 15:15 also states that, "the heavens are not pure in His sight."

32 See below.

33 Alva J. McClain, *The Greatness of the Kingdom*, 400.

blameless in the day of our Lord Jesus Christ." That revelation or coming of the Lord is, I believe, the pretribulational rapture, although that identification is not infallible. It may refer to the second coming proper. In either case, the "judgment seat of Christ" is surely also in view (2 Cor. 5:10).

3. Second Corinthians 1:14 refers to when all the saints are together in "the end" (2 Cor. 1:13). That is to say, the apostle is thinking about the blessing it will be when they all are with the Lord, speaking about each other in the blissful Kingdom.

4. First Thessalonians 5:2 refers to the "sudden destruction" (1 Thess. 5:3) that will be visited upon the wicked in the Day of the Lord. This implies that the "Day" is the onset of the Tribulation.

In these four passages, plus 2 Peter 3:10-12, the "Day of the Lord" is an eschatological period involving the commencement of the Tribulation, the rapture and judgment seat of Christ, the second coming, the inauguration of the Kingdom of God upon earth, and the end of the Millennium when the present heavens and earth are "burned up." As in the OT,[34] it does not refer to just one event, but to a cluster of events surrounding the End Times.

Jude

The short Epistle of Jude contains a number of fascinating passages, concerned in the main with the importance of contending for the faith (Jude 3) against those false brethren who "turn the grace of our God into lewdness and deny the only Lord God and our Lord Jesus Christ" (Jude 4). These apostates are similar in kind to the unbelievers in the wilderness wanderings (Jude 5), the perverted men of Sodom and Gomorrah in Abraham's day (Jude 7), and even the angels who cohabited with human women in Genesis 6:1-4 (Jude 6). Hence, the theme of judgment for rebellion runs through the little book.[35]

Many are aware of the quotation in Jude 14-15 attributed by Jude to Enoch (Gen. 5:18-24). Although there are many popular Bible teachers who have jumped on the "Book of Enoch" bandwagon, it needs to be kept in mind that the manuscript evidence for that book is fragmentary, and its contents are a collection of related writings rather than one single work.[36] Jude 14-15 supposedly quotes from 1 Enoch 1:9, but we do not have any clear pre-Jude manuscript of the verse to be able to demonstrate the assertion. Besides, the book of Enoch claims Enoch was 500 years old in 1 Enoch 58:1, when we know he was 365 (Gen. 5:23). Although not strictly apocryphal, the book includes ridiculous assertions, like many of the Apocrypha, such as saying that there were giants some 450 feet tall (1 Enoch 7:12). Finally, and fatally for its claim to

34 See *The Words of the Covenant*, Vol. 1, 346-349.
35 Andreas J. Köstenberger and Gregory Goswell, *Biblical Theology*, 667.
36 See George W. E. Nickelsburg, "Enoch, First Book of," *The Anchor Bible Dictionary*, Vol. 2 (New York: Doubleday, 1992), 508-516.

be accurate (nevermind inspired), 1 Enoch 71:14 identifies Enoch as the messianic "son of man"!

If Jude did quote from 1 Enoch 1:9 (which I think is up for debate),[37] this must be treated similarly to the way Paul cites Epimenides (Tit. 1:12), Aratus (Acts 17:28), and Menander (1 Cor. 15:33). The inspired writer makes use of a well-known passage to drive home an important and accepted truth without having to endorse the author or his outlook (or indeed his "facts").

Jude does not include anything about God's covenants, but it would be remiss of me not to call attention to his beautiful doxology and the marvelous New covenant truth it contains: "Now to Him who is able to keep you from stumbling, and to present you faultless before the presence of His glory with exceeding joy..." (Jude 24). This is such an uplifting statement, and I think it summarizes the New covenant's efficacy so well that I cannot bypass it. Not only has God saved us from our sins, He keeps tabs on us throughout our pilgrimage in this life so as to keep us from stumbling (i.e., finally destroying ourselves). And His purpose is to present us before Himself. We are accustomed to think that our greatest joy will be to see Him (and it will be), but God's "exceeding joy" is to see us with Him once this hard life is past! Hallelujah!

Summary of Part Seven

Hebrews

- Hebrews claims to be addressed to a specific group, but this does not negate the fact that much of it applies directly to the Church.

- The reader must fully acknowledge that Hebrews was written by a highly sophisticated author who knew precisely how to say what he wanted to say.

- The book's imagery—which includes contrasts between the Canaanite Conquest and entering into "Rest," of earthly Sinai and heavenly Zion, of the old [Mosaic] covenant and the New covenant, of the two High Priestly sacrifices, etc.—is all deliberately drawn from Jewish history to appeal to Jews.

- The author tells us that he is writing about "the world to come" (Heb. 2:5). It is a mistake not to take this note seriously in our exposition of the book.

- The Warning Passages (e.g., in Heb. 3, 6, and 10) are worded to stir obedience and perseverance. They do not give the appearance of mere saber-rattling.

37 Peter H. Davids, in his various works on the General Epistles, believes Jude was influenced by the book, but I demur. For a full assessment of the matter see Peter J. Gentry and Andrew M. Fountain, "Reassessing Jude's Use of Enochic Traditions (With Notes on the Later Reception History)," *Tyndale Bulletin* 68 (2017), 261-286.

• If one allows the warnings to speak for themselves and resists the urge to allow (at least for the present) a Pauline theology of eternal security to influence one's reading of the text, it does appear that Hebrews warns about forfeiting one's entrance into the coming Kingdom. Where to fit this becomes a challenge.

• The strongly prophetic character of the book makes it fit well into a setting similar to Matthew 24/Mark 13.

• Pretribulationists are obliged to address the question of a revelation suited to Tribulation saints after the Church is removed. The doctrine of the saints cannot remain the same if the Church is no longer present.

• This is certainly not to say that Hebrews does not apply to the Church. However, its warnings, prophetic nature, and Hebraic character may indicate that it will do double duty as a Tribulation epistle.

• The themes of the High Priesthood of Christ and the New covenant He mediates dominate the book. If Hebrews possesses any application to the Church (which it certainly does), then Christ must be the High Priest of the Church, and He can only be that if Christians are parties to the New covenant He mediates. Hebrews is about the New covenant Christ.

The Rest of the General Epistles

• The Epistle of James again seems to be aimed at Jews. Hence, James, like Hebrews, may do double duty in the Church and again in the Tribulation. Many of its themes can be traced to the Sermon on the Mount and its Kingdom ethics.

• First Peter also exhibits a marked Jewish flavor. Here though, there is little evidence of it not being written for the Church entirely.

• What was said above about its Jewish tenor ought to guide our understanding of 1 Peter 2 and the readership to whom it was sent. The Jewish descriptions in 1 Peter 2:4-10 fit Israel's covenantal aspirations, even if the recipients were Christian.

• Second Peter interprets Jesus' Transfiguration as a portent of the second coming.

• Peter appears to teach the wholesale desolation of the present cosmos and its replacement with a completely new cosmos.

• The Day of the Lord in Peter describes an eschatological period covering the start of the Tribulation to the creation of the new heaven and new earth.

- Jude is an admonition to guard the truth, employing various OT tales that draw attention to some dark realities of the spirit realm.

- If Jude does cite the apocryphal (not lost) book of 1 Enoch, he does so not as an endorsement of all of its contents, but similarly to Paul's use of Greek poets, to illustrate a truth.

PART EIGHT:
COVENANT ECHOES IN REVELATION

19

CONVERGING THEMES IN THE APOCALYPSE

The angel whom I saw standing on the sea and on the land raised up his hand to heaven and swore by Him who lives forever and ever, who created heaven and the things that are in it, the earth and the things that are in it, and the sea and the things that are in it, that there should be delay no longer.
– Revelation 10:5-6

We arrive at the last book of the Bible. And wouldn't you know it, we run into a flurry of confusing approaches! There is a lot of controversy about how the book of Revelation is to be understood. *The Commentary of the New Testament Use of the Old*[1] tends toward an idealist-spiritual interpretation, wherein all of the numbers and visions are symbolic to such a degree that neither the OT allusions nor the Johannine "employment" of them bear any literal meanings. It is fair to say that the vast majority of scholars reject what I may call the "literal" interpretation of the book.[2]

From all that has preceded this chapter, it is obvious that my approach to the Revelation of John will attempt to follow the covenantal-plain sense that has been employed throughout *The Words of the Covenant*.[3] But this is not to dismiss the truth that Revelation has a lot of symbolism within it. Why exactly such symbolism is used is an important topic in itself. Many writers believe that because the Church was undergoing increased persecution under Emperor Domitian, John decided to couch his book in the shroud of symbols we read throughout the work: visions, parables,

1 D. A. Carson and G. K. Beale, eds., *The Commentary of the New Testament Use of the Old*.
2 By "literal," of course, I do not mean to deny figures of speech or other literary devices.
3 Readers who wish to know my views on "apocalyptic" interpretation may consult my Appendix 3 of Vol. 1, 395-409. I think the following snippet from a recent work says a great deal: "In an apocalyptic vision such as this, logic has no firm place" (Stephen S. Smalley, *The Revelation to John: A Commentary on the Greek Text of the Apocalypse* [Downers Grove, IL: InterVarsity, 2005], 212).

emblematic numbers, fabulous beasts, "Israel," the abyss, the Four Horsemen, the list goes on. The notion is that the Christian initiates could decipher John's meaning and derive comfort and strength for the churches to "disentangle themselves and their allegiances from the corrupting influence of the Roman imperial power, economics, and cult and strengthen their allegiance to God and the Lamb"[4] without the "world" knowing what was going on.[5] The message was concealed so as not to bring about persecution. Victory is ours in Jesus! That was the real message.[6]

As much as the flesh might want to throw in its lot with the majority of authorities, neither my method nor my conscience will allow me to do so. My reasons for this are multiform: the title of the book, the allusions (particularly to Daniel), the specificity of some of the descriptions, the prophetic note and its agreement with what has come before it, and then there is the simple but persuasive fact that the book makes a great deal of sense when taken at face value—even if a few matters of sequence may be up for some debate. Having said this, the varied approaches to the book will necessitate some sorting out of the viewpoints.

The Book of Revelation as the Capstone of Scripture

The book of Revelation is often called the capstone of the Bible,[7] but what exactly does that mean? If one is of amil- or postmil- persuasion, it comes down to saying that Christ and the Church win in the end.[8] Since that is precisely what Paul managed to say in far clearer and more concise terms in 1 Corinthians 15:54-57 and Ephesians 1:17-23, one wonders why John's oblique and wordy book was included in the Canon. But if the Apocalypse is treated as a prophecy of the final days of this age before the return of Christ and is understood to mainly deal with the details of Jeremiah's "time of Jacob's trouble" (Jer. 30:7), Daniel's seventieth week (Dan. 9:24-27; 12:1-7), and of the Kingdom program thereafter, its function is far easier to grasp. Being the capstone of the rest of the Scripture *in that way* makes it essential that the book's details be given a lot of attention. It also makes it relevant to history, no matter whether one lives in the first century or the twenty-first. The transition depicted is from "this present evil age" (Gal. 1:4) to a time when "The kingdoms of this world have become the

4 Joshua W. Jipp, *The Messianic Theology of the New Testament*, 284-285.

5 Presumably John did this for the sake of his readers. It is difficult to think of this "son of thunder" (Mk. 3:17) being concerned with disguising his message from the authorities because of persecution.

6 E.g., I. Howard Marshall, *New Testament Theology*, 549, 560-561; G. R. Beasley-Murray, "Revelation, Book of," in *Dictionary of the Later New Testament & Its Development*, eds. Ralph P. Martin and Peter H. Davids (Downers Grove, IL: InterVarsity, 1997), 1035.

7 E.g., Brian J. Tabb, *All Things New: Revelation as Canonical Capstone* (Downers Grove, IL: InterVarsity, 2019).

8 Tabb writes, "I argue that the Apocalypse presents itself as the climax of biblical prophecy that shows how various Old Testament prophecies and patterns find their consummation in the present and future reign of Jesus Christ, who decisively defeats his foes, saves his people and restores all things" (Brian J. Tabb, *All Things New*, 2). In calling Revelation a prophecy, Tabb explains, "The designation 'book of prophecy' refers primarily 'to divine disclosure demanding ethical response, in line with Old Testament "prophecy," which primarily addresses present situations and only secondarily foretells'" (Ibid., 6), citing Beale.

kingdoms of our Lord and of His Christ, and He shall reign forever and ever!" (Rev. 11:15).

My aim here is not to provide a commentary on the book, but rather focus my attention on its theological and covenantal teaching.[9] Because it is a tricky book to understand, I will also give more extended comments on certain texts to clue in the reader to my overall understanding of the work and how it fits the rest of the biblical picture. Amillennial scholars like G. K. Beale and Steve Moyise have done sterling work in analyzing the allusions to the OT, especially allusions to the prophets Isaiah, Ezekiel, Daniel, and Zechariah, as well as the Psalms. But it must be kept in mind that they spiritualize those OT books too, so it will come as no surprise that Revelation is given similar treatment.[10]

A Book of Blessing

Revelation 1:3 informs us of a blessing upon readers and hearers who "keep" the words of the *prophecy* of this book. This condition *requires that the words can be readily understood.* Likewise, Revelation 22:7 says, "Blessed is he who keeps the words of the prophecy of this book." Unless the book of Revelation is comprehensible, people will not know how to "keep" what is written in it, and these two bookends may as well not be there, for they would be out of sync with the rest of the book. Unless the book can be understood enough to be "kept," no blessing could ever be obtained.

And just here we collide with the fact that the Apocalypse suffers from multiple interpretations. What is more, modern commentaries often combine different approaches, resulting in an eclectic reading. The question is, did John intend that eclecticism? This is what makes Revelation 1:3 and 22:7 so crucial (along with the fact that John tells us it is a prophecy, and a prophecy couched in inscrutable terminology might mean anything).

A Way of Understanding the Book (With Which I Disagree)

Along these lines, I have here before me as I write a book titled *The Theology of the Book of Revelation.* It was written by Richard Bauckham, who is an outstanding NT scholar from whom I have learned much.[11] Bauckham is always worth reading, and seldom does one come away from him having not been benefitted by the experience. And the same is true with this book, although not in the way one might think. The author is helpful in telling us that the seven letters to the churches in chapters 2 and 3 are not really letters but "prophetic messages."[12] He says that "Revelation is a literary work composed with astonishing care and skill."[13] He says the book's theology "is

9 In my view, the three best commentaries on Revelation are by Robert L. Thomas, Tony Garland, and Buist Fanning.

10 How strange it is to find these scholars interpreting a book laden with OT allusions with the NT!

11 Richard Bauckham, *The Theology of the Book of Revelation* (Cambridge University Press, 2001).

12 Ibid., 2.

13 Ibid., 3.

highly theocentric,"[14] and that God's name is interpreted in its relation to the world.[15] Along with this God-centeredness is the book's high Christology[16] and note of victory.[17] This is all most useful.

However, as an accurate interpretation of the book of Revelation, I am afraid I must take issue with it. Among the many interpretations I must disagree with are that John "takes up and reinterprets" the OT prophets[18] and that John "has taken some of his contemporaries' worst experiences and worst fears of wars and natural disasters, and blown them up to apocalyptic proportions, and cast them in biblically allusive terms."[19]

Since Bauckham holds that John has not written the book to predict the future,[20] he looks for events *around John's time* to relate things to. He provides a specimen of this when he claims, "The sacking of Babylon by the beast and his allies alludes to the contemporary myth of the return of Nero to destroy Rome."[21] The beast, in any case, "represents the military and political power of the Roman Emperors."[22] The wounded head of the beast in Revelation 13:3 "is the emperor Nero, who committed suicide with a sword (cf. 13:14),"[23] while the false prophet (Rev. 13:11ff.) "probably represents the imperial priesthood in the cities of the province of Asia."[24] As far as the 144,000 in Revelation 7 are concerned, one is relieved to read that they remain Israelites, but one is not so happy to discover that they are an army brought together for "military violence" in the cause of a "holy war."[25] The two witnesses of Revelation 11:3-12 are, we are told, "the church in its faithful witness to the world."[26] Speaking of Revelation 11, the "holy city" that is trampled by the Gentiles in Revelation 11:2 is not Jerusalem but is, in fact, the Church. The author suggests that after John has done a little reinterpreting of Daniel (8:9-14; 11:21; 12:11) and the Gospels (Matt. 24:15; Mk. 13:14; Lk. 21:20-24), the "holy city" now refers "to the persecution of the church in the symbolic three-and-a-half-year period of the church's conflict with the Roman Empire."[27] John, it seems, has taken upon himself a thorough reimagining of the OT Prophets.[28]

14 Ibid., 23, 140.
15 Ibid., 30, 55.
16 Ibid., 63-65, 67, 104-105.
17 Ibid., 79, 90, 105, 107, 114.
18 Ibid., 4.
19 Ibid., 20.
20 Ibid.
21 Ibid., 21.
22 Ibid., 35.
23 Ibid., 37.
24 Ibid., 38.
25 Ibid., 77-78.
26 Ibid., 84-85.
27 Ibid., 127.
28 Ibid., 69.

A Selection of Other (Mis)Understandings

Bauckham is definitely not the only one who proposes such reinterpretations. Before we explore the Apocalypse of John using a covenant-based plain-sense reading, I want to take notice of interpretations from those authors who cannot bring themselves to read the book in the same sort of way. Therefore, I have chosen two highly esteemed scholars to sample: G. K. Beale and Tremper Longman.[29] I shall choose some of the prominent features in the book and see how they interpret them.[30] Let us begin with the identity of the 144,000 in Revelation 7.

After giving four or five views on the identity of the 144,000, Beale asserts that the number is figurative,[31] being "the square of twelve multiplied by one thousand, or the multiple of the squares of ten and twelve multiplied by ten."[32] This, we are told, highlights "completeness and perfection,"[33] although that is nowhere taught in the text. Going then to Revelation 21, Beale notices the names of the twelve tribes on the gates of New Jerusalem and the names of the twelve apostles on the foundation stones (Rev. 21:12, 14). He also calls attention to the fact that the wall of the city is one-hundred and forty-four cubits (Rev. 21:17), and since "This city represents the whole people of God (Rev. 21:9-10),"[34] it is natural to see a correlation between the New Jerusalem (which Beale believes is a "figurative structure"[35]) and the 144,000 Israelites in Revelation 7.[36] Beale tells us that the 144,000 are "redeemed Israelites who have been saved *out* of the twelve tribes as a remnant."[37] But as he continues, it becomes clear that not only is the number figurative, so are the Israelites! This is the Church that has been "portrayed in the Apocalypse under the OT guise of the true people of God, the true Israel."[38] Beale holds to the improbability that John had the literal twelve tribes in mind[39] since those tribes have been lost to history.[40] Beale claims that the way to make

29 Saying they are highly esteemed does not mean that I believe they are trustworthy interpreters of the Apocalypse, just that many people pay attention to them.

30 I shall throw in some citations from some other writers too.

31 G. K. Beale, *The Book of Revelation*, NIGNTC (Grand Rapids: Eerdmans, 1999), 416.

32 Ibid., 416-417.

33 Brian J. Tabb, *All Things New*, 102.

34 G. K. Beale, *The Book of Revelation*, 417. In actual fact, Rev. 21:9-10 do not say any such thing.

35 Ibid.

36 When these same 144,000 are seen in heaven in Rev. 14:3-4, and are described as male virgins, this is usually understood figuratively as "symbolic of the church's spiritual purity, in no way implying that only single, celibate male servants of God receive his seal of protection" (Dennis E. Johnson, *Triumph of the Lamb: A Commentary on Revelation* [Phillipsburg, NJ: 2001], 131). Presumably the 144,000 were *not* male virgins while on earth.

37 Ibid.

38 Ibid., 418.

39 "A few commentators interpret the 144,000 as a literal reference to the nation Israel...This interpretation seriously complicates the book of Revelation by bringing in racial distinctions which no longer exist within the NT purview. It disregards the historical fact that ten of the twelve tribes disappeared in Assyria and the remaining two lost their separate identity when Jerusalem fell in A.D. 70" (Robert H. Mounce, *The Book of Revelation* [Grand Rapids: Eerdmans, 1977], 168). I want to ask who is really disregarding what? Doesn't the apostle John bring in the "racial distinctions"?

40 Ibid., 419. "'Israel' itself cannot be taken in a literal sense, since the twelve tribes as such did not exist in the first century AD (despite Josephus *Ant.* 11.133-134)" (Stephen S. Smalley, *The*

sense of Revelation 7:1-8 is to place it prior to Revelation 6:1-8, and then put Revelation 7:9-17 after Revelation 6:12-17.[41]

Moving on to the innumerable multitude of Revelation 7:9ff., the claim is that they are exactly the same as the 144,000 Israelites just mentioned. Beale says, "The likelihood is that there is only one group, portrayed from different perspectives.[42] The first pictures the Church as the restored remnant of true Israel."[43] This is supersessionism on full display.[44]

When we turn to the half an hour silence in Revelation 8:1, we are told that it "carries the connotation of 'primeval silence.'"[45] The details of the temple and the holy city trampled by the Gentiles (Rev. 11:1-2) refer to the "Christian community," and the two witnesses in that chapter are figurative along with their plagues (Rev. 11:6).[46] The dead bodies of the two witnesses "probably does not indicate that the entire church will be exterminated so that it cannot bear witness any longer. Rather, it emphasizes by hyperbole that the true Church will seem defeated in its role as witness..."[47] One begins to wonder if John can state anything in a straightforward manner. Why, for example, would he describe the *seeming* destruction of the Church as *total* destruction?

Let us not stop to wonder about such things, as there is more to consider. Beale says that the three-and-a-half-year time of tribulation (cf. Dan. 7:25; 9:27, 12:7) "commences at Christ's ascension and continues until his return,"[48] and the "woman" in the chapter is the Church, not Israel, although this time he does begin to take seriously the clear reference to Genesis 37.[49] However, he soon brings the interpretation back to "another example of the church being equated with the twelve tribes of

Revelation to John, 185). It is no argument to claim that because this list is not identical to OT lists of the twelve tribes it has to be figurative. Even Longman shows that the OT lists themselves vary greatly, although, like Rev. 7, all the named tribes are actually Israelite tribes. See Tremper Longman III, *Revelation Through Old Testament Eyes* (Grand Rapids: Kregel, 2022), 120-121. Longman proceeds to spiritualize the tribes. He believes that the "great tribulation" of Rev. 7:14 is speaking about a first century persecution of Christians (Ibid., 124).

41 Beale, *The Book of Revelation*, 406.

42 Beale has been taken to task for this by Joel R. Willits, "The 144,000 in Revelation 7 and 14: Old Testament Intratextual Clues to Their Identity," in *From Creation to New Creation: Biblical Theology and Exegesis*, eds. Daniel M. Gurtner and Benjamin L. Gladd (Peabody, MA: Hendricksen, 2013).

43 Beale, *The Book of Revelation*, 424.

44 Examples of supersessionism occur throughout Beale's book *A New Testament Biblical Theology*, e.g., 161, 173, 182 n. 65, 211, 215, 307, 574, 671, 680, 770. I do not use "supersessionism" as a dirty word, but as a true description of what certain interpretations of the Bible produce.

45 Beale, *The Book of Revelation*, 449.

46 Ibid., 581-587.

47 Ibid., 590.

48 Ibid., 646. Poythress states that "it is related to the three and a half days mentioned in 11:9, 11" (Vern S. Poythress, *The Returning King: A Guide to the Book of Revelation* [Phillipsburg, NJ: P&R, 2000], 128). Longman believes the several ways John describes the three and a half years all symbolize God's ultimate control of history (Tremper Longman III, *Revelation Through Old Testament Eyes*, 166).

49 Ibid., 625-626.

Israel."[50] The beast of Revelation 13:1-3 is the satanic world system,[51] and of the fatal wound which one of the heads received (Rev. 13:3), he has this to say:

> The wound appeared to be fatal, and, indeed, it really was. Nevertheless, the devil's continued activity through his agents makes it appear to John as though he has overcome the mortal blow dealt him at Christ's death and resurrection. Despite defeat, the devil and his forces continue to exist.[52]

Of course, the six mentions of a "thousand years" in Revelation 20:2, 3, 4, 5, 6, 7 is "Inaugurated during the Church Age by God's Curtailment of Satan's Ability to Deceive the Nations and to Annihilate the Church."[53] Moreover, Satan's binding and incarceration (Rev. 20:2-3) isn't literal but is just another way of saying that Jesus now has authority over him.[54] Why then doesn't John just simply say it? Finally, "New Jerusalem" (Rev. 21:1–22:5) could not possibly be literal since its dimensions are impossible.[55] With many others,[56] Beale believes the idea of "New Jerusalem" (Rev. 21–22) is shaped by Ezekiel's temple vision: "That Ezekiel is in mind is clear because of the repeated reference to the Ezekiel 40–48 temple vision in the preceding and following context of 22:1."[57]

Any reader of Ezekiel 40–48 and Revelation 21–22 will find similarities between them (e.g., tree of life, streams of water, etc.), but, as usual, it is not the similarities that are decisive for interpretation but the differences—and there are big differences. For a start, Ezekiel's temple is in Israel on this earth (Ezek. 40:2; 45:8; cf. 47:18-20) where the new moon is recorded (Ezek. 46:1-3), and the "great sea" is sailed (Ezek. 47:10). When the New Jerusalem descends from heaven to the new earth there will be "no more sea" (Rev. 21:1-2). Neither will there be any more sun and moon (Rev. 21:23). The descriptions of the gates and walls of the two structures are totally different. And then there is the huge difference in size. Although massive,[58] Ezekiel's

50 Ibid., 626-627. Like Beale, Longman acknowledges that Genesis 37 refers to Israel but since he believes "Israel" equates to "the people of God" then the "woman" in Rev. 12 must be the Church (Tremper Longman III, *Revelation Through Old Testament Eyes*, 184).

51 G. K. Beale, *The Book of Revelation*, 686.

52 Ibid., 688. What this "deadly wound" actually means is that the devil lost his authority over the saints (689). Longman, *Revelation Through Old Testament Eyes*, 210, cites Metzger and DeSilva in linking the number 666 (or 616) with Nero.

53 Ibid., 984 (this is a heading).

54 Ibid., 985-987.

55 Ibid., 1073-1074.

56 An influential work in this vogue is William J. Dumbrell's thorough *The End of the Beginning: Revelation 21–22 and the Old Testament* (Eugene, Wipf & Stock, 2001). It becomes clear early on that Dumbrell sees New Jerusalem as a symbol and non-literal. See Ibid., 4.

57 G. K. Beale, *The Book of Revelation*, 1103.

58 Together with its environs, the temple of Ezekiel 40–48 would take up a good part of southern Israel (Judea), being approximately 52 miles by 22 miles, although the complex itself will take up about 1 square mile. See J. Randall Price, *The Temple and Bible Prophecy: A Definitive Look at Its Past, Present, and Future* (Eugene, OR: Harvest House, 2005); and John W. Schmitt & J. Carl Laney, *Messiah's Coming Temple: Ezekiel's Prophetic Vision of the Future Temple* (Grand Rapids: Kregel, 2014).

temple is on a mountain (Ezek. 40:2; cf. Isa. 2:2-3; Mic. 4:2; Zech. 8:3), while New Jerusalem is larger than any mountain, extending some 1,400 or 1,500 miles square! Unless one spiritualizes these structures completely so that they represent something else—which is precisely what Beale, Dumbrell, and others do—they very clearly are not close to being the same.

No Middle Ground Between the Eschatological Approaches

As I stated above, I do not hold to this interpretation of the book of Revelation. Nor do I believe this sort of "saying what you don't mean" is how God speaks. Although a respectful hearing is due to those who have come to very different conclusions than those I present below, the non-literal approach (if I may call it that) is, in my estimation, quite unbiblical. It essentially negates God's covenant oaths and shifts the ground of faith away from what God *says* onto man's reinterpretation of what God says. This applies not only to Revelation but also to vast areas of the Bible, including the prophetical writings of the Major and Minor Prophets, much of the Gospels, Romans 9–11, 2 Thessalonians 2, and Hebrews. Many godly men and women hold to amillennialism and postmillennialism, and I have benefitted greatly from many of their writings. But on these matters, I believe they are woefully wrong and have led many people astray.[59] One must choose which of these approaches is closest to God's intended meaning. The question boils down to this: What does God want me to put my faith in? The interpretations I advocate rely upon the simple yet profound premise that God means what He says. The covenants God has made still mean what they meant when He swore their oaths, and so can and should be taken at face value. Amillennialists and postmillennialists demur.[60] They have the liberty to do so, but we ought not to kid ourselves that the disagreement is superficial.

Confining ourselves to the book of Revelation before us, such esteemed authors give reasons for their conclusions, but to my way of thinking, they turn the apostle John into the greatest obfuscator in Scripture, which is not a positive attribute if you want your words to be understood and kept (Rev. 1:3; 22:9), never mind if you entitle your book "the book of *Revelation*" (or "revealing"). But under the influence of amillennialism, many of John's symbols evidently refer to the Church, so it might have been aptly called "the book of creative repetition."[61]

For the record, I intend to proceed as if the 144,000 Israelites are what the text in Revelation 7 says they are, and that they differ from the innumerable multitude from every nation described next, which is also exactly what the text says it is. John tells us in Revelation 14:4 that the 144,000 are redeemed from the earth as "the firstfruits." That they are referred to as such plainly entails that a great many of the redeemed will follow them. Hence, they *cannot* be equated with the whole company "of all nations, tribes, peoples, and tongues" in Revelation 7:9ff.

59 Naturally, they would say the same thing about me.

60 Historic premillennialists generally spiritualize much of Scripture too, thereby being guilty of morphing the covenant oaths of God.

61 Or even, "A hundred or more ways to say the same thing without ever coming to the point."

The silence of Revelation 8:1 really lasts for about half an hour. The "woman" of Revelation 12 is Israel, not the Church. The thousand years mentioned repeatedly in Revelation 20 means a thousand years, and Satan is incarcerated in the abyss for that period of time—he is not simply on a long chain.[62] Finally, New Jerusalem is (or will be) a real place, and its given dimensions are completely accurate.

As we read Revelation, we naturally need to distinguish between things that are clear symbols (e.g., the "woman," the "beasts") and the things they represent (i.e., Israel, the Antichrist, and the False Prophet), but we nowhere have permission to alter the plain sense by applying these symbols to the Church and spiritualizing the numbers and revealed identities provided by John. Call me naïve, but when the covenants are brought in as reading aids, the text does not require spiritualizing. Let us, therefore, interpret the book of Revelation in that light.

A Proposed Structure for the Book

We must continually remind ourselves that we are reading the book of Revelation and not the book of Obfuscation. The idea that it is a kind of underground coded document meant to evade scrutiny from a persecuting emperor (Domitian) is extremely implausible. There is definitely some back-and-forthing happening. But the question is where is it, and what does it mean? We must all admit that getting everything in its right place is not easy. With that in mind, here is my attempt at outlining the structure of John's Apocalypse:[63]

1. Prologue (1:1-8)
2. Vision of the Exalted Christ and the Letters to the Churches (1:9–3:22)
3. Prelude: The Throne in Heaven and the Lamb Who is Worthy (4:1–5:14)
4. The First Six Seals: Year 1 to Year 7 of the Tribulation (6:1-17)
5. Interlude: 144,000 from Israel and the Innumerable Multitude (7:1-17)
6. The Seventh Seal Introduces the First Six Trumpets (8:1–9:21)
7. Interlude: John and the Little Book (10:1-11)
8. Interlude: Jerusalem Overrun and the Two Witnesses (11:1-14)
9. The Seventh Trumpet (11:15-19)
10. Interlude: The Woman and the Dragon (12:1-18)
11. Interlude: The Two Beasts (13:1-18)

62 As a great example of the impossibility of rapprochement between futurist and non-futurist interpretations of prophecy generally, and Rev. 20 in particular, see Matthew Waymeyer, *Revelation 20 and the Millennial Debate* (The Woodlands, TX, Kress, 2004).

63 Interpreters offer many different outlines of the book because beyond the basic sections (Rev. 1–3; 4–5; 6–18; 19–22) a clear structure is hard to identify. Cf. Buist M. Fanning, *Revelation*, 58. Some have proposed a chiastic structure. E.g., James M. Hamilton, Jr., *God's Glory in Salvation Through Judgment: A Biblical Theology* (Wheaton, IL: Crossway, 2010), 544.

12. Interlude: Preview of the Lamb's Victory (14:1-20)
13. Prelude: The Seven Angels with Their Bowls of Judgment (15:1-8)
14. The Seven Bowls Poured Out Upon the Earth (16:1-21)
15. Vision Concerning Babylon (17:1–19:5)
16. The Lamb's Marriage, Christ's Return, and the Beast's Defeat (19:6-21)
17. The Millennium and Final Judgment (20:1-15)
18. Vision of the New Heavens and Earth and New Jerusalem (21:1–22:5)
19. Epilogue (22:6-21)

Establishing a Chronology

One's layout of the book will be a result of the hermeneutics employed. My understanding of the book's chronology is that the letters to the seven churches speak to congregations that existed in the first century but also address prophetic aspects. These churches do not set out the history of the Church, and it is a major hermeneutical error to read such a thing into the chapters. Contrary to many good dispensationalists, I hold that the sixth seal records the second coming of Christ. Revelation 6:12-17 (the sixth seal) must come after Revelation 8:12-13 (the fourth trumpet) because what happens in Revelation 6:12-17 is so climactic. The stars fall from heaven (Rev. 6:13; cf. Matt. 24:29). The sky is rolled up like a scroll (Rev. 6:14; cf. Isa. 34:4). The mighty men hide themselves in the rocks and caves (Rev. 6:15; cf. Isa. 2:21), crying out to the mountains to fall upon them (Rev. 6:16; cf. Lk. 23:29-30). Most, if not all, of these are second advent passages. Therefore, Revelation 6 provides a sweep through the seventieth week from beginning to end. This provides a frame into which one can try to fit the other parts of the book using the time markers John gives.

Major Chronological Markers

The apostle John has included enough detail in parts of his work to be able to pick out certain chronological markers. In my opinion, we are given a pass through the entire seven-year Tribulation in Revelation 6:1-17. The first clear time-marker is not encountered until Revelation 11:1-3 where Jerusalem is said to be trampled by the Gentiles for forty-two months (Rev. 11:2), which is three and a half years. The same period is also when the two witnesses (whom I believe are Moses and Elijah) are said to prophesy (Rev. 11:3-6). Does this happen in the first part of the seven-year period or the second?[64] It is hard to be dogmatic about it (so I won't be). It seems that the apostle was not concerned with the details of when exactly these things occur within the seventieth week. My guess is that these happen in the first half of the Tribulation.

The next clear marker comes in Revelation 12:6, where the woman (Israel) flees into the wilderness and is provided with food for "one thousand two hundred and

64 I exclude the possibility of the middle.

sixty days." This matches Matthew 24:15-22, which occurs right before Christ's return (it would seem senseless for them to have the protection withdrawn before this). Hence, Israel is persecuted by Satan (Rev. 12:9) for the last half of the Tribulation. The blaspheming "Beast" of Revelation 13:5-6 recalls the Little Horn of Daniel 7:25 and the "Man of Sin" of 2 Thessalonians 2:3-4. The Beast (Antichrist) is "given authority to continue for forty-two months" (Rev. 13:5). This is the time when the power of Israel will be "completely shattered" (Dan. 12:7; cf. Matt. 24:21-22/Mk. 13:19-20), which calls to mind "the time of Jacob's trouble" in Jeremiah 30:7. Hence, the focus of these time-markers is on the second half of the seventieth week.

The next clear time-marker is the second advent, as recorded in Revelation 19:11ff., with the thousand-year reign of Jesus upon this earth right after (Rev. 20:1-6). This present earth is replaced by the New Creation in Revelation 21 and 22.

Filling in Some Details

Can we now fit some more of the book's details into the framework above? Let us have a go. Starting off with the Prelude to the Seven Seals (Rev. 4:1–5:14), Revelation 4:1 states, "And the first voice which I heard was like a trumpet speaking with me, saying, 'Come up here, and I will show you things which must take place after this.'" Here we note that the voice tells John that he will be told of future things. Exactly when these future events will occur, we are not told, but after the Lamb opens the first six seals in Revelation 6 it becomes apparent that we are dealing with the last days. In fact, we are looking at the seven-year Tribulation predicted by Daniel (Dan. 9:24-27).

As indicated above, I take the breaking of the first six seals to start in Year 1 of the Tribulation and end in Year 7 (I believe the seventh seal, which introduces the trumpets, probably starts at around the mid-point).[65] Hence, the white horse rider of Revelation 6:1, who I think is the Antichrist, comes on the scene right at the start of the seventieth week.

Coming back to Revelation 11 and the first time-marker, we see the overrunning of the "holy city" (Jerusalem) by the Gentiles for forty-two months. If it happens at the start of the Tribulation, then it is hard to reconcile that with the "covenant" mentioned in Daniel 9:27a or with the building of the temple itself. Surely there would need to be some appreciable time between the cutting of the covenant and the building of the temple. That is, unless the temple is already built before the pact is signed. We don't have all the information, but I side with those who think the forty-two months refers to the first half of the Tribulation, even given the problem above. If that is the case, then the two witnesses prophesy also at that time (Rev. 11:1-12). Their ascension into heaven occurs just after the half-way point when the Beast rises from the dead after receiving a mortal blow (Rev. 13:3-4; cf. 2 Thess. 2:3-4).

65 The central portion of the book contains three sets of judgments: the seals, the trumpets, and the bowls. A crucial question is whether these represent the same incidents and chronology or whether the chronological fulfillment of the trumpets overlap the last of the seals, and the bowls overlap the last trumpets resulting in a staggered or telescopic unveiling. Although one ought not to be overly dogmatic about it, a decision needs to made about the chronological unfolding of the events of the three sets of judgments.

If this is correct, then I am persuaded it means that the Beast of Revelation 13:1-7 is one and the same as the figure who comes out of the abyss in Revelation 9:11 (cf. Rev. 17:8). Notice, "When they finish their testimony, the beast that ascends out of the bottomless pit will make war against them, overcome them, and kill them" (Rev. 11:7). Since no other figure has been identified as ascending out of the bottomless pit but the angel of Revelation 9:11, the reference in Revelation 13 and 17 must refer to the same being. Therefore, I believe the events of Revelation 9:1-11 happen at the mid-point of the seventieth week.

If this is right, it opens up the interesting possibility that whoever this "angel" is, he is connected to the Antichrist in some way after he is killed and revivified (Rev. 13:3). When he rises from the dead, "he [is] given authority to continue for forty-two months" (Rev. 13:5). His tyranny ends with the second coming of Jesus Christ (2 Thess. 2:8; Dan. 7:21-22).

If we go back a little to Revelation 7 and the sealing of the 144,000, it could be that this sealing happens at the onset of the seventieth week (in which case, the sealing of these Israelites jumps back to the first year of the Tribulation). If that is so, then they are sealed during the ministries of the two witnesses of Revelation 11. However, it could just as well be that the 144,000 are sealed for the second half of the seventieth week. I do not agree with the view that chapter 7 necessarily comes right after chapter 6 (e.g., Thomas,[66] Garland[67]), though I may be mistaken. That said, I cannot bring myself to believe that Revelation 6:12-17 occurs only at the mid-point of the chronology of events.

The dragon chasing the woman (Israel) into the wilderness is in the second part of this timeline and matches well the persecution of "the saints of the Most High" by the little horn in Daniel 7:21, 25 and the intensification of things after the risen "Beast" demands worship (Rev. 13:7ff.). Jesus' warning in Matthew 24:9-22 fits this scenario well (notice "those that are in Judea" in Matt. 24:16, and the mention of the sabbath in Matt. 24:20). It also matches Paul's description in 2 Thessalonians 2:3-7.

With that said, the career of the first "Beast" of Revelation 13 spans the whole seven years, which equates with the "one week" covenant in Daniel 9:27, a covenant that is breached "in the middle of the week," as elucidated by Revelation 13:3-7. After he is killed, this man-devil rises from the dead (Rev. 13:3-5) and demands worship from the inhabitants of the earth (Rev. 13:8, 15-18; cf. 2 Thess. 2:3-4), setting up an image of himself in the holy place of a rebuilt temple in Jerusalem (Rev. 13:14-15; Matt. 24:15ff./Mk. 13:14ff.).

In Revelation 14 we discover that the 144,000, who are all male virgins (Rev. 14:4), are all before the throne of God in heaven (Rev. 14:5). If we take the usual view that the sealing of these Jewish men taking place at the second part of the seventieth week, then they are "redeemed from the earth" (Rev. 14:3) just before the Tribulation

66 Robert L. Thomas, *Revelation: An Exegetical Commentary*, 2 Volumes (Chicago: Moody, 1992).

67 Tony Garland, *A Testimony of Jesus Christ: A Commentary on the Book of Revelation*, 2 Volumes (Camano Island, WA: SpiritAndTruth, 2004).

ends. Revelation 14:9-13 refers to the mark of the beast and his number 666 (Rev. 13:18), so it is a reference to the second half of the seven-year period.

Revelation 14 is also the first place in the book where the city of "Babylon" shows up (Rev. 14:8). This city (and everywhere it is referred to in Revelation) could very well be literal Babylon (which is my belief), or it could perhaps be another city renamed, coming to prominence in the Tribulation.

As for other markers in Revelation, it appears that the "marriage supper of the Lamb" takes place before the second coming (Rev. 19:6-16), which, if true, lends some additional support to the pretribulational view since the Church would have to be in heaven for it to occur. "Gog and Magog" appear at the end of the thousand years in Revelation 20:8. In the first volume, I argued that in Ezekiel 37 and 38 Gog and Magog represent "the forces which will be arrayed against Israel to attempt to wipe it off the face of the map." If that position is correct, then the Gog and Magog of Revelation 20 are a reprise of those foes spoken of by Ezekiel. I am, however, open to the possibility that Ezekiel 38–39 prophesies the battle of Revelation 20:7-10, although, on balance, I still think the chronology of Ezekiel 36 to 48 tilts the scales the other way. Thereafter, there is the Millennium of Revelation 20 and the New Creation after that (Rev. 21–22).

Internal Explanations

If one takes a good look at the symbols and numbers that John uses, for the most part they are decipherable within the context. The seven stars are angels, and the seven lampstands are churches (Rev. 1:20). Notice that the number seven is not reinterpreted. It means seven. The four horsemen of Revelation 6 bring with them specific and actual plagues.[68] In the same vein, chapter 7 opens with a scene of four angels standing "on the four corners of the earth" (Rev. 7:1). We don't need to pay a genius to figure out for us that this describes the four points of the compass. What these angels do is to prevent the wind from blowing. In other words, they have a plainly spelled-out function. Then we read about the sealing (on the foreheads) of "the servants of God" (Rev. 7:3). Who are these servants? That's easy. We are told in the most clear and straightforward way who they are. They are "one hundred and forty-four thousand of all the tribes of the children of Israel" (Rev. 7:4). But what does that mean?[69] Perhaps John is using code here to fool the Roman authorities? John reveals even that to us. They comprise 12,000 from each of the tribes of Israel: Judah, Reuben, Gad, Asher, Naphtali, Manasseh, Simeon, Levi, Issachar, Zebulun, Joseph, and Benjamin (Rev.

68 Apart from the first, whose resemblance to the Christ depicted in Rev. 19:11ff. may signify that he is a pseudo- or anti-christ. Although I think this is correct, the allusion is quite subtle. And for that reason, Rev. 6:1 is not a clear introduction of the Antichrist.

69 See the essay by Alan Kurschner, "Should the 144,000 in Revelation 7:3-8 Be Identified as the Great Multitude in 7:9-13? – A Response to Gregory K. Beale," in *The Future Restoration of Israel: A Response to Supercessionism*, eds. Stanley E. Porter and Alan E. Kurschner (Eugene, OR: Pickwick Publications, 2023), 143-159.

7:5-8). Easy! All twelve tribes are readily recognizable from their corresponding OT footprints.[70] Just do a search and up they pop!

After the listing of the twelve tribes, we read about a numberless mass of people who have been redeemed from the earth. They are described as "of all nations, tribes, peoples, and tongues" (Rev. 7:9), which, to this reader, has always differentiated them from the Israelites mentioned right above. This differentiation is only on the surface, according to most interpreters, since they tell us that the two groups are, in fact, one and the same. John, that most inscrutable of apostles, has just been describing the Church since he mentioned "the servants of God" back in Revelation 7:3! Supposedly, the description of the twelve tribes in great detail in Revelation 7:4-8 could have been dispensed with because what he really meant to say is found (at last!) in verse 9.[71] Presumably, John is back to saying what he really means in Revelation 7:13-17.

But I digress. As Revelation 8 gets underway, we are presented with a time period of "about half an hour" (Rev. 8:1). The lack of any further explanation of what this time period actually is prompts me to believe it means "about half an hour."[72] The seven trumpets blown by seven angels are also literal in meaning (Rev. 8:2ff.). If we look at the sixth angel in Revelation 9:13ff., we can see that when he blows his trumpet another four angels are released (Rev. 9:15). All this might be strange, but it can be followed.

When we turn to chapter 11, we can know the name of the city through "the temple of God" (Rev. 11:1) and its "court" (Rev. 11:2), which could only be situated in Jerusalem. Although it is given some unflattering nicknames in verse 8, this does not disguise the fact that it was Jerusalem, "where also our Lord was crucified."

Moving on to Revelation 12, the "woman" can be identified by the allusion to Genesis 37. She is Israel. There is enough information on the male child of Revelation 12:2, 4-6 to know that it refers to Jesus at His first coming. The question of when the woman flees from the dragon is best answered by noting that it is for a period of one thousand two hundred and sixty days (Rev. 12:6), which connects it with Daniel 7:25 and 12:7 and the Great Tribulation passages in Revelation 11:3 and 13:5 (cf. Rev. 12:14). This "fleeing" also resonates with Jesus' warning in Matthew 24:15-22/Mark 13:14-23. The jump from the first to the second advent of Christ in Revelation 12:5-6 just repeats the well-established pattern of fusing the two advents that one sees in Isaiah 9:6-7; 61:1-2; Micah 5:2; Zechariah 9:9-10; Malachi 3:1-3, etc. This makes perfect sense if the woman is the nation of Israel.

---

70 The omission of the tribe of Dan (see also 1 Chron. 4–7) is linked by some to the tradition that Antichrist would come from there. E.g., Bruce M. Metzger, *Breaking the Code: Understanding the Book of Revelation* (Nashville: Abingdon Press, 1993), 60 n. 1. Dan introduced idolatry into Israel (Judg. 18). This is not the position I take since it is never hinted at elsewhere in Scripture.

71 I sometimes imagine a messenger attuned to John's opaqueness standing over the aged apostle waiting for him to finish writing and wondering why he was writing out the names of the tribes so carefully only to have explained to him that what John really meant was that they all refer to the Church. Raised eyebrows all round. But that is my sense of humor I suppose.

72 Please forgive the irony. I am not aiming it at anyone in particular. But there are many examples in Revelation where the numbers used are clearly not symbolic.

The first beast of Revelation 13 is a "him" who is worshipped (Rev. 13:4), and whose number (666) is the number of a man (Rev. 13:18). Those who try to make the first beast (Antichrist) a system or institution are not taking these prompts seriously. Since he is a pseudo-Christ, it is to be expected that he has a prophetic forerunner in a similar vein to John the Baptist. Hence, we are told of the False Prophet (Rev. 13:11ff.; cf. 19:20; 20:10). Other explanations within the text could be shown (I shall examine Revelation 20 and the New Jerusalem below). But this ought to suffice to show that the premature spiritualization of the Apocalypse by many interpreters is unwarranted.

The Jewish Flavor of the Apocalypse

I think that one of the very first things we need to note about the book of Revelation is its decidedly Jewish tone.[73] The book speaks of David, the throne, Jerusalem, the Lion of the tribe of Judah, the twelve tribes of Israel, the two witnesses, the ark of the testimony, and the commandments of Moses. References to Israel and hints of its promises abound. If Revelation is a book for the Church about the Church, why this Jewish flavor?[74] Even the language of the book, though Greek, is salted with Hebraisms. Bullinger notes that "though the language is Greek, the idiom is Hebrew."[75] Fanning observes that "John wrote a Semitized form of Greek."[76] And everyone knows that Revelation alludes to more of the OT than any other NT book.

Some cogent explanation of this phenomenon has to be forthcoming. It is not enough to say that this way of writing just helped John make his connections to the Hebrew Bible. Without bringing up the covenantal links that exist throughout Revelation (see below), just a look at the contents of the book will underscore its decidedly Jewish appearance:

1. The "synagogue of Satan" is mentioned in Revelation 2:9 and 3:9. Many commentators believe that this ungodly group was composed of Jews (hence "synagogue"), and that their claim to be true Jews was false because they rejected/subverted Christ's truth. In my opinion, these people call themselves Jews but are not descended from the twelve tribes.

2. The Lion of the tribe of Judah, the Root of David (Rev. 5:5). This recalls Genesis 49:8-10 and Jacob's great messianic prophecy.

3. The 144,000 Jewish male virgins (Rev. 7:3-8; 14:1-5). Try as they might to turn these men (whom Bauckham and others believe to be an army in Rev. 7) into men and women of spiritual purity, the facts stand against it. These are men from the twelve tribes of Israel.

73 Granted, this can be overstated. See Eckhard J. Schnabel, *New Testament Theology*, 30.

74 Written at the close of the first century, it comes too late to be explained by the predominance of Jewish converts to Christianity.

75 E. W. Bullinger, *The Apocalypse, or "The Day of the Lord,"* (London: Samuel Bagster, 1972), 4-6.

76 Buist M. Fanning, *Revelation*, ZECNT (Grand Rapids: Zondervan, 2020), 53.

4. The temple of God in "the holy city" upon earth (Rev. 11:1-2). Outside the temple, we are told, is given to the Gentiles. Hence, a clear ethnic distinction is made.

5. The two witnesses who perform miracles associated with Moses and Elijah (Rev. 11:3-12). The OT tenor of these witnesses cannot be missed.

6. Earthly Jerusalem (Rev. 11:8), where Christ was crucified.

7. The woman clothed with the sun (Rev. 12:1-6). Despite valiant attempts to get around the obvious, the allusion to Israel is patent. Genesis 37:9-10 and Joseph's second dream concerning his family is recorded—Joseph being the twelfth star.

8. Believers are said to "sing the song of Moses, the servant of God, and the song of the Lamb" (Rev. 15:3). The song of Moses (Exod. 15:1-19) rejoices in the deliverance of Israel through the miracle of the Red Sea.

9. Gentiles are only mentioned once in the book, in Revelation 11:2.

10. The male child in Revelation 12:5 is obviously Jesus (Psa. 2; Rev. 19:15). Who gives birth to Christ? Israel.

11. It is telling that the Jewishness of Revelation starts to become clear only after the seven churches (which represent the whole Church) are dealt with, and the attention turns to what is *going* to happen. The Church and Israel are not spoken of in the same breath until Revelation 21. Hence, even though the seven churches of Asia Minor are prominent in the first three chapters, once the large central section launches, the mood is far more Jewish.

12. Finally, as Bullinger observes, "All the imagery—the Temple, the Tabernacle, the Ark of the Covenant, the Altar, the Incense, the heads of the twenty-four courses of Priests (the pattern of which David's was a copy, 1 Chron. xxviii. 19...), all this belongs peculiarly to Israel."[77] Even New Jerusalem is shaped like the Holy of Holies.[78]

Literal and Symbolic—A Quick Journey through Revelation

Trying to get one's head around the mixture of symbols in the book of Revelation is not an easy matter. The symbols create a visual picture in the mind of the reader. The

77 E. W. Bullinger, *The Apocalypse*, 5-6.

78 Mike Stallard has drawn attention to the similarities between the description of Jesus in Rev. 1:13-16 and the "Ancient of Days" in Dan. 7:9-10. There are elements which are shared between the two which point to the divine origin of Jesus, but the descriptions also differ notably. See Mike Stallard "Israel in the Book of Revelation," https://www.youtube.com/watch?v=szb7OaFZqvY&t=3167s.

question is, when are the symbols literal, and when are they not? Let us inquire further into this question.

When John beholds the glorified Jesus in chapter 1, he sees a real person, a Man who puts His hand on John (Rev. 1:17). Yet Christ's right hand is said to hold seven stars in it, and Christ has a sword coming out of His mouth (Rev. 1:16). This sword is later depicted as the instrument with which He smites the nations (Rev. 19:15). What does this mean? Here we see a symbolic artifact (the sword) combined with a literal sight of a man. The sash of gold that He wears shows Him to be noble (Rev. 1:13). His white hair and flaming eyes (Rev. 1:14), not to mention His glowing bronze feet (Rev. 1:15), may tempt us to infer that He is ancient, wise, and penetrating in knowledge. On the other hand, it may be that the glorified Jesus really looks like that since no explanation of His appearance is given! It is instructive that straight after He tells John to write down "the things which you have seen, and the things which are, and the things which will take place after this," He deciphers the meaning of the stars and the lampstands (Rev. 1:19-20). That appears to indicate the way the revealing will proceed: a vision of something strange followed by some explanatory remarks.

Of course, this is only partially true. When one reads the letters to the seven churches, a number of things that we would love to know more details about are simply mentioned in passing. These include the "Nicolaitans" in the letters to Ephesus (Rev. 2:6) and Pergamos (Rev. 2:15), "the synagogue of Satan" that is spoken of in the address to Smyrna (Rev. 2:9) and Philadelphia (Rev. 3:9), and the identity of "Jezebel" in Thyatira (Rev. 2:20). I would like more information on the Book of Life in Revelation 3:5,[79] and I would like to know for sure if "the hour of trial which shall come upon the whole world" (Rev. 3:10) refers to the whole Tribulation, a part of it, or to none of it.

Moving on from the letters to the seven churches, we cannot with certainty identify the twenty-four elders before God's throne (Rev. 4:4), although we can note how David organized twenty-four orders of priests in 1 Chronicles 24:4 and 25:9-31.[80] Are they the same as the "watchers" spoken of by Daniel (Dan. 4:17)? Possibly. Who knows for sure? As they feature quite prominently in the narrative (Rev. 4:4, 10; 5:8, 14; 11:16; 19:4), there is every reason to think that the number twenty-four is literal.

---

79 Being in this "Book of Life" gains one access to the New Jerusalem (Rev. 21:27), whereas not having your name in the Book of Life exposes one to wrath (Rev. 20:15). Yet there is a threat that some of the names written in the Book will be removed (Rev. 3:5; 22:19). When Paul refers to it in Phil. 4:13, he does not mention this threat, probably because it is not a threat to those in the Church (Rom. 8:28-39). This may be because Revelation speaks of those in the Tribulation after the removal of the Church, and that Tribulation saints must "endure" (e.g., by not receiving the mark of the beast). If they don't endure their names are blotted out of the Lamb's Book. (See here my remarks on "Hebrews as a Tribulation Letter" above). This way of presenting things might not be comfortable to think about, but I think it at least has the benefit of being textually honest. I am just trying to comprehend what the text says and make sense of it without resorting to twisting John's words.

80 "Most of the apocalyptic symbolism used by John in Revelation finds its root in the Old Testament, which often provides the interpretive key necessary to understand the imagery" (H. Hall Harris, "A Theology of John's Writings," in *A Biblical Theology of the New Testament*, eds. Roy B. Zuck and Darrell L. Bock [Chicago: Moody Bible Institute, 1994], 173 n. 11). I would word this sentence slightly differently, but the main point is well made.

The four horsemen of Revelation 6 were seen by John, but I doubt they will be seen by anyone else. The effect of their missions is the devastation of the earth, bringing disease, famine, natural calamities, and societal disarray. It is the effects of their work that will be seen by earth's unfortunate inhabitants. In Revelation 6:13 we are told that all the stars fell. In Revelation 8:12 there are still stars there, which means Revelation 6:13 comes after Revelation 8:12.

I have commented on the 144,000 of Revelation 7 above, but amillennial interpreters believe that the number and the description of them provided by the inspired author are non-literal. On the other hand, they believe that the multitude that no one could number of all peoples is literal. The 144,000 Israelites in Revelation 7 stem from twelve tribes upon the earth, which are clearly named (Rev. 7:1-8), and they are male virgins according to Revelation 14:4. Dispensational premillennialists rightly assert, therefore, that both groups ought to be understood literally, which means that they are not the same.[81]

The infernal horsemen of the sixth trumpet (Rev. 9:16-19) are numbered. Why point out their number if they are unreal? Didn't Elisha and his servant see supernatural horses of fire and chariots of fire on the hills around them (cf. 2 Ki. 6:17)? They were there! These actual sightings should not be swept aside by the magical term "apocalyptic."[82]

In chapter 12 we are told forthrightly that the seven-headed dragon is "the Devil and Satan" (Rev. 12:9). The dragon pursues a "woman clothed with the sun with a crown of twelve stars on her head and the moon under her feet" (Rev. 12:1). Who is this woman? Well, one more detail may help. She was pregnant (Rev. 12:4), and her child "was to rule all nations with a rod of iron" (Rev. 12:5; cf. Psa. 2:8-9; Rev. 19:15). The child can be none other than Christ, who is "the root of David" (Rev. 5:5; cf. 22:6)—an Israelite. The identity of the child is further corroborated when John tells us, "And her Child was caught up to God and His throne" (Rev. 12:5b).

This cannot be the Church, for the Church is not yet married to Christ (see Rev. 19:6, 9). Ergo, the Church cannot be pictured as a pregnant woman! Neither did the Church bring forth Christ. Christ brought forth the Church through His resurrection. As Revelation is chock-full of OT allusions, has John inserted one here related to the woman? The answer is yes.

> Then he dreamed still another dream and told it to his brothers, and said, "Look, I have dreamed another dream. And this time, the sun, the moon, and the eleven stars bowed down to me." So he told *it* to his father and his brothers; and his father rebuked him and said to him, "What *is* this dream that you have dreamed? Shall your mother and I and your brothers indeed come to bow down to the earth before you?" (Gen. 37:9-10, my emphasis).

81 Buist M. Fanning, *Revelation*, 265-267.

82 In my opinion, Christians in the West especially do not take the supernatural realm seriously enough.

Jacob's rebuke of Joseph shows that he understood the dream as a reference to him, possibly to Rachel (Joseph's mother, Gen. 35:24), although Leah is more likely, and Joseph's eleven brothers. It doesn't take a genius to add Joseph to the eleven stars to make the twelve tribes of Israel, with Jacob being portrayed as the sun and Leah/Rachel as the moon. The reason for the female imagery is because of the birth of the Man-Child (Rev. 12:4-5). Beale believes that the woman represents the entirety of the saints from before and after the first advent.[83] This is extraordinary for someone who has made his name searching out and identifying OT allusions in the NT. Beale's Covenant Theology prevents him from separating Israel from the Church. Revelation 12 is silent about the spirituality of the woman; that is simply not important. To my mind, at least, any interpretation of Revelation 12:1 that ends up making her other than Israel is a circumlocution.[84]

Coming back to the dragon, he gives his power to the beast in Revelation 13,[85] who is himself "a man" (Rev. 13:18). Likewise, the second beast of Revelation 13, who assists the first beast, is identified later in the book as "the false prophet" (Rev. 16:13; 19:20; 20:10).

Not all of our questions are answered, and sometimes those that are leave us with more questions for which definitive answers elude us, but Scripture is not written to satisfy our curiosity, only to inform us. In my opinion, the elusive aspect of the book will become far less so as the events themselves come to pass. I think a good example of this is the correlation between the angel of the bottomless pit (Rev. 9:11), whose name is Abaddon or Apollyon, and the beast who "will ascend out of the bottomless pit and go to perdition" (Rev. 17:8).

Fortunately, this is not so in many other cases. The lampstands are clearly identified by Jesus as churches (hence, we ought not to think that these lampstands are Jewish menorahs). The seven stars in Christ's hand represent seven angels, and the seven lampstands portray seven churches. The stars and the lampstands are symbols, but their enumeration is seven. The Two Witnesses of Revelation 11 are best identified by the miracles they perform, which (in a book so pervaded with OT allusions) leads us to Moses and Elijah.[86]

---

83 G. K. Beale, *Revelation* 625-627.

84 Some dispensational interpreters (e.g., Michael Svigel) believe the male child is the Church, which would make the catching up of the child a rapture. I cannot agree with this view. Some who support a prewrath position try to make the "offspring" of the woman in Rev. 12:17 the Church. But it is far more likely that the woman is the Jews in Israel and "the rest of her offspring" are Jews outside of Israel.

85 It is likely that this satanic power is given to the Beast at the time of his "resurrection."

86 Although even dispensational authors have posited Moses and Enoch, such identification ignores the clues given in the text by the inspired author. Moses and Elijah appear at the Mount of Transfiguration (Matt. 17), which itself is a preview to Christ's second coming (2 Pet. 1:16-18). Moses and Elijah are also (coincidently) the last two men mentioned in our OT. Enoch, on the other hand, is not given such attention. Even amillennialist Greg Beale, who turns the two witnesses into the Church, holds that Moses and Elijah are being alluded to in Rev. 11. See G. K. Beale, *Revelation*, 582-583. Cf. Tremper Longman III, *Revelation Through Old Testament Eyes*, 169-170. Longman straddles the fence between two actual prophets or the two witnesses representing the Church, but he does recognize the connections to Moses and Elijah.

What about those odd chapters which speak of Babylon (Rev. 17–18)? Is Babylon the ancient city of which the OT Prophets speak? The "Babel" of Genesis 10:10 and 11:9? Revelation 17:18 calls Babylon a "great" city, an adjective that is fastened to the name Babylon each time it appears in Revelation (Rev. 14:8; 16:19; 17:5; 18:2, 10, 21). Fanning believes the weight of the available evidence makes Rome the "Babylon" John has in mind.[87] Strong arguments in favor of the actual city on the Euphrates by Charles Dyer[88] and Andy Woods[89] have also been put forth. The "woman" who rides the beast is identified as "that great city which reigns over the kings of the earth" (Rev. 17:18). On the other hand, the beast, as we have seen, is a man. This indicates that the city (the woman) will have power over the beast for a period of time. The "kings" in the context would probably be those spoken of in the immediate context (Rev. 17:10).

Whatever interpretation is fixed to the name "Babylon," the fact remains it *is* depicted as an actual city, and no humdrum city either, but the major world city of the time (Rev. 17:18; 18:10, 16, 18, 19). In Revelation 17:5 we read, "Mystery, Babylon the great." Some believe that the word "mystery" qualifies the name "Babylon" in such a way that it points to something other than a literal city, perhaps a system. But how a system can be "utterly burned with fire" is hard to envisage (Rev. 18:8). From our present vantage point, it is impossible to be dogmatic about every detail. The descriptive title "the great" appended to the name "Babylon," and the identification of it as "the great city which reigns over the kings of the earth" (Rev. 17:18), together with it being described as a "dwelling place of demons" (Rev. 18:2) indicates that "the great city Babylon" is indeed meant. I see no good reason to strictly divide the city itself from its influence over the world.[90]

In Revelation 19:11ff., the white horse rider is Christ Jesus, "the Lord of Lords and King of Kings" (Rev. 19:16). He is not to be confused with the white horse rider of Revelation 6:1, even though the earlier rider is *like* the Lord.

Then we come to Revelation 20, and the dispute heats up. Amillennialists insist that the words "Then I saw" (*kai eidon*) prove that chapter 20 does not follow chronologically from chapter 19.[91] What is at stake in the decision is the whole interpretation of a chapter (Rev. 20) which gives every appearance of recording the imprisonment of Satan for a thousand years (Rev. 20:1-3), the reign of Christ upon this earth for a thousand years (Rev. 20:4-6), the loosing of Satan, His ignominious defeat (cf. Gen. 3:15c), and the Final Judgment (Rev. 20:7-15). If we follow the apparent meaning of the words employed by the apostle, we certainly get a very good segue into the last two chapters. As Revelation 20 ends, we are told that this present cursed earth is gone

87 Buist M. Fanning, *Revelation*, 440-446.

88 Charles H. Dyer, *The Rise of Babylon: Sign of the Times* (Chicago: Moody, 2003).

89 Andrew M. Woods, *Babylon: The Bookends of Prophetic History* (Taos, NM: Dispensational Publishing House: 2021).

90 If "Babylon the great" is actual Babylon, then it would appear that a good deal of rebuilding of the city as well as dredging the Euphrates River would still need to be done before it could be described in such terms as the book of Revelation describes it.

91 See G. K. Beale, *The Book of Revelation*, 974-983. "Does it [i.e., the "and" of 20:1] indicate continued historical sequence following on the heels of 19:21, or does it merely serve as a more general transition between visions?" (Ibid., 975).

(Rev. 20:11) and is replaced by a "new heaven and a new earth, for the first heaven and the first earth had passed away" (Rev. 21:1). This, to me, is decisive. Attempts to disengage Revelation 20 from 21 look like ingenious efforts to get around the obvious.

Once we arrive at Revelation 21 and 22 and the disclosure of the New Jerusalem coming down out of heaven to the new earth, we still have to contend with interpreters who wish to persuade us that the New Jerusalem is not literal—it is also just a symbol. Many of these same scholars want to tell us that the opening chapters of Genesis are figurative and cannot be taken literally. Forgive me, but it seems that among the thousands of inspired words in the Bible, it is mainly the ones that have to do with personal salvation that can be taken literally. How utterly different this is from the hermeneutics of Abraham in Genesis 22![92]

EXCURSUS: Babylon the Great City

There has always been a vibrant debate around whether the "Babylon" mentioned in the Apocalypse is the actual ancient city of Mesopotamia (modern Iraq), some other city, or indeed institution. On the face of it, if ancient Babylon is not intended, it is reasonable to ask why John called the city (and he calls it a city repeatedly) by that name. It first appears in Revelation 14:8, where no clue is given that it means something other than actual Babylon. As this is the first use of the name in this book, a clue to a separate identity would be expected. Every instance of "Babylon" in the OT, and with one possible exception in the NT, means actual Babylon. The "Babylon" in 1 Peter 5:13 may refer to Rome.[93] However, it could just as well be literal Babylon.[94] It is my opinion that literal Babylon is the city of Revelation 14, 16, 17, and 18. But this does not mean that I have no questions. I think Revelation 17:9 and 18:17-18 pose problems for this view: "Here is the mind which has wisdom: The seven heads are seven mountains on which the woman sits" (Rev. 17:9). This is the strongest verse against the identification of "Babylon" as the ancient Mesopotamian city. Babylon is on a plain (cf. Gen. 11:2), not built upon seven hills.

The other passage that argues against actual Babylon is this: "For in one hour such great riches came to nothing.' Every shipmaster, all who travel by ship, sailors, and as many as trade on the sea, stood at a distance and cried out when they saw the smoke of her burning, saying, 'What is like this great city?'" (Rev. 18:17-18). Babylon lies on the Euphrates River, which is not navigable to modern shipping. It would, therefore, take a considerable amount of work to open it up to ships. Moreover, although much work has been done to rebuild Babylon's walls, a great deal of construction would be needed to turn it into "that great city Babylon, that mighty city!" (Rev.

92 See "The Birth of Isaac and the Hermeneutical Test of Faith" in *The Words of the Covenant*, Vol. 1, 138-140.

93 Craig S. Keener, *1 Peter: A Commentary* (Grand Rapids: Baker, 2021), 403-406; Buist M. Fanning, *Revelation*, 393.

94 For 1 Pet. 5:13, see Tony Garland, *A Testimony of Jesus Christ*, Vol. 2, 200; John Calvin, *Commentaries on the Catholic Epistles*, trans. John Owen, Reprint ed. (Grand Rapids: Baker, 1981), 155.

18:10). That said, in the absence of any qualifications in the text,[95] it seems best to leave the "problems" above to God's providence and to hold to literal Babylon as the city referred to in Revelation 14 through 18. Its central location on a map of the world definitely suits a world capital.

Covenantal Allusions in the Apocalypse

As he begins his prophecy, John says that he is a fellow brother in the "tribulation and kingdom and patience of Jesus Christ" (Rev. 1:9). I think it is important to notice the word "kingdom" and ask whether it speaks of a kingdom that was present already in the first century A.D. or whether it refers to the future messianic Kingdom. It will not come as a surprise to learn that the answer depends upon the eschatological position adopted. As Christ is "He who has the key of David" (Rev. 3:7), "the Lion of the tribe of Judah, the Root of David" (Rev. 5:5), and "the Root and the Offspring of David, the Bright and Morning Star" (Rev. 22:16), I believe we are directed to an eschatological-covenantal fulfillment.

If, as I suspect, "the Lord's Day" is the Day of the Lord,[96] then that term has eschatological covenant connections. The Day of the Lord, in its eschatological manifestation, is the prelude to the New covenant Kingdom. It is the necessary preparation for the Kingdom to come. But even if "the Lord's Day" refers, as many scholars insist, to Sunday, then the covenant connection still would concern the New covenant, since the day of Christ's resurrection and the descent of the Holy Spirit on the day of Pentecost were on a Sunday—and those events are inextricably connected to the New covenant. So, either way, we have covenantal concerns as early as Revelation 1:10.

One writer has said it well: "A bedrock of the Apocalypse is that Jesus is the Davidic Messiah."[97] Jesus has a golden sash across His chest (Rev. 1:13), a symbol of royalty, and hence of His Davidic ancestry and privilege. His standing in the midst of the lampstands alludes to His New covenant priestly role.[98] This combination of Davidic and Melchizedekian elements is best understood as signifying Christ's present qualifications to be the great Priest-King of the next aeon. Jesus is the priest now as He mediates the New covenant to the Church (Heb. 12:24; cf. 1 Tim. 2:5). He will mediate the New covenant to Israel as a nation later (Jer. 31:31-34; Zech. 12:10). In either case, Christ must mediate between God and the sinner *before* they will accept His reign over them as their King. Therefore, we ought never to assume Christ is reigning

95 The name "Mystery, Babylon" in Rev. 17:5 refers to something *about* the city Babylon, not necessarily to the fact that some other city (or system) is given that name.
96 Although I will not press the point, seeing as the term "the Lord's Day" (Rev. 1:10) may not refer to the Day of the Lord. I still believe that this common view is examined, since the phrase is unique in the Bible.
97 Joshua W. Jipp, *The Messianic Theology of the New Testament*, 286.
98 G. K. Beale, *The Book of Revelation*, 208.

in His kingdom because He is functioning as High Priest. The covenants will come to fruition exactly as stipulated.[99]

Not only is Jesus dressed in royal regalia, He is said to hold "the key of David" (Rev. 3:7) and to be "the Root and the Offspring of David" (Rev. 22:16). Revelation 3:21 informs us that Jesus has a throne that is/will be His, and it is distinguished from the throne of His Father (cf. Matt. 19:28; 25:31). Even the most basic knowledge of the covenants will inform the reader that Christ's throne is the Davidic throne upon earth (Lk. 1:32-33).

When John despairs because there is no one in heaven or earth who is found worthy to break the seals in Revelation 5, he is answered, "But one of the elders said to me, 'Do not weep. Behold, the Lion of the tribe of Judah, the Root of David, has prevailed to open the scroll and to loose its seven seals'" (Rev. 5:5).

The Lamb, who is the crucified and risen Jesus, is the only one in God's whole realm who qualifies to open the seals.[100] This is doubtless because He represented heaven on the earth and wrought salvation for God's image-bearer, man (Jn. 17:1-26; Heb. 1:2-3), while securing the eventual "glorious liberty" of the earth itself (Rom. 8:21). Furthermore, Christ's selfless humiliation in His own world on behalf of His enemies is not approached by any other deed in heaven and earth. And since the judgments sealed inside the scroll are earth-judgments, the sole person who has wrought reconciliation between God and creation is the Lamb of God who took away the sin of the world (Jn. 1:29; Heb. 9:26).

I have made an argument in this book that *as* the Lamb of God, Jesus institutes the New covenant.[101] I, therefore, believe, on the basis of its proliferation in Revelation, that the covenant language in Revelation 21:3, "God Himself will be with them and be their God," and 21:7, "I will be his God and he shall be My son," relates to the New covenant.

As for the throne of David, if Satan has a throne upon the earth (Rev. 2:13), surely Jesus will have one? Indeed, He will: "Then the seventh angel sounded: And there were loud voices in heaven, saying, 'The kingdoms of this world have become *the kingdoms* of our Lord and of His Christ, and He shall reign forever and ever!'" (Rev. 11:15). The text declares that God the Father will rule *this* world and the one to come *through* His Son Jesus Christ.[102] The Son's throne will be in Jerusalem according to the OT (Jer. 3:17; Mic. 4:7-8; Ezek. 43:7).

---

99 It has always surprised me how this basic truth is missed by scholars. As one example, in the fine work by James M. Hamilton, Jr., *God's Glory in Salvation Through Judgment*, 550, he declares "When God makes covenants with his people, he promises that he will be true to his just and merciful character." But Hamilton's book fails to heed the oaths of those covenants or use them to guide the direction of his interpretations.

100 If the seven-sealed scroll cannot be opened, then the seven trumpets cannot be blown nor the seven bowls be poured out.

101 Israel is not under the New covenant until the second coming. It is conjecture on my part, but God wants His people to acknowledge the original covenant and the Messiah to whom it points (Deut. 18).

102 Christ's followers will have a hand in the rule of the coming kingdom. Rev. 2:27 cites (with a little alteration) Psa. 2:9. See also Rev. 12:5; 19:15.

Backtracking a bit, the presence of a sealed remnant of Israel in Revelation 7 connects us to the Abrahamic covenant, as does the "woman" in Revelation 12:1ff. Then, in Revelation 11:19, the ark of the covenant is seen, and it is impossible to miss an allusion to the old covenant. This is significant because, in Revelation 12:17, we read about those "who keep the commandments of God and have the testimony of Jesus Christ." It is, of course, the ark of the Mosaic covenant that was made on earth, and which pertains to the earth.[103]

God is only as good as His covenants. The book of Revelation describes the coming Tribulation and the defeat of the Antichrist. Then Christ, the coming Ruler, sets up His Kingdom rule "with a rod of iron," but in mercy and peace in exact correspondence to the Abrahamic, Priestly, and Davidic covenants. Yes, we must not forget the promise to Phinehas (Num. 25:10-13; Psa. 106:28-31). Ezekiel's temple will be built in Israel in the coming Millennium (Ezek. 40–48; cf. Isa. 2:2-3; Ezek. 37:26-28; Zech. 6:12-13). To quote from a psalm written in an era in which the promises seemed to be failing. God is clear: "My covenant I will not break, Nor alter the word that has gone out of My lips" (Psa. 89:34).

Major Interpretive Themes

Looking at Revelation as the prophetic capstone of the whole Bible, we can discern several key theological strains running through it. It is necessary to review these, as a wrong interpretation of the last book of the Bible can skew so many other things. The most prominent themes are nicely summarized in this quote: "The book of Revelation focuses particularly on the return of Jesus Christ to establish His kingdom on earth and His victory over the satanic forces which will arise to oppose Him at His return."[104] With this basic understanding, here are the major themes in the book.

Revelation as Prophecy

There is no doubt that the author of the book of Revelation thought he was writing a prophetic book. Look at what he says. Right off the bat he refers to "things which must shortly take place" (Rev. 1:1). He states that "the time *is* near" (Rev. 1:3)[105] and refers to "the things which will take place after this" (Rev. 1:19). In chapter 4, a voice from heaven tells John, "I will show you things which must take place after this" (Rev. 4:1). After he receives the strange little book, John is told, "You must prophesy again about many peoples, nations, tongues, and kings" (Rev. 10:11; cf. also Rev. 22:7, 10, 18-19). He is writing prophecy.

103 See also Rev. 12:17; 14:12; 15:3.

104 H. Hall Harris, "A Theology of John's Writings," 179-180.

105 These designations do not mean the events described in Rev. 6–19 take place immediately after John wrote in circa 95 A.D. Rather, "It is better to understand that these expressions reflect a 'soon' occurrence not in the sense of an exact chronology but in a prophetic time frame, describing what is certain to occur and could occur at any time without delay" (Buist M. Fanning, *Revelation*, 75). He supports this conclusion by noting how the phrase "what must happen soon" mirrors Dan. 2:28-29 in the LXX (Ibid., 74-75).

Contrariwise, nowhere does John tell his readers that he is writing an apocalyptic piece like the book of Enoch or the Testament of Levi.[106] His title, "The Revelation [*apokalypsis*] of Jesus Christ" (Rev. 1:1), is in no way identifying itself with a genre that would only be labeled as such after the fact.[107] I realize that in merely stating this, I look like I have my head in the ground, since prophets like Daniel, Ezekiel, and Zechariah contain many things that influence Revelation. But that influence is Scripture to Scripture, not extrabiblical. John is not conforming his book to non-inspired intertestamental works.[108] He is an inspired penman of Jesus Christ. Whatever likeness there is to "apocalypses" written prior to John is relatively superficial. If we insist on interpreting Revelation on the basis of the "apocalyptic," we ought to be aware that we are receiving no encouragement to do so from the author himself. As I said, the book of Revelation is a prophecy.

"Revelation" is simply the English equivalent of the Greek word "Apocalypse," an entirely appropriate name for the final book of Scripture.[109] That which it reveals is the future wrapping up of this present world system. It is folly to ignore this and to turn the distinction John makes into a literary genre that buries his stated intention beneath a mountain of rhetorical jargon.

If John himself designates his book as a "prophecy," isn't that enough? One might think so. But many non-premillennial interpreters resist this testimony. This has caused Garland to exclaim, "Perhaps the most puzzling statements encountered in the discussion of the purpose of the book of Revelation are those which assert that this most prophetic of New Testament books is not about predictive prophecy."[110]

Garland cites Beckwith as an example of this. But what is the meaning of the word "prophecy" in Revelation 1:3? Despite the plain and clear assertions by John, which indicate that he means "an inspired statement about the future" (see Rev. 1:1, 3, 19; 4:1; 10:11), G. K. Beale claims:

> A "blessing" will come on those who obey the divine imperatives...and a curse will come on those who do not (cf. 22:18-19). Therefore, *propheteia* ("prophecy") in v 3 is primarily a reference not to predictive revelation but to divine disclosure demanding an ethical response, in line with OT "prophecy," which primarily addresses present situations and only secondarily foretells.[111]

This, to me, is an extraordinary statement. It flies in the face of John's own declarations. John does not tell us he is writing an ethical treatise. He *does* tell us he is writing a prophecy. On top of this, Beale claims that the ethical aspect of prophecy was also

106 Apocalypses, as they later came to be known, are pseudonymous. But *the* Apocalypse is not.
107 See Appendix 3, "The Apocalyptic (Wrong) Turn," of *The Words of the Covenant*, Vol. 1, 395ff.
108 Although intertestamental books did fashion themselves after inspired books.
109 Richard Bauckham characterizes Revelation as "an apocalyptic prophecy in the form of a circular letter to seven churches in the Roman province of Asia" (*The Theology of the Book of Revelation*, 2).
110 Tony Garland, *A Testimony of Jesus Christ: A Commentary on the Book of Revelation*, Vol. 1, 36.
111 G. K. Beale, *The Book of Revelation*, 184-185.

what the OT Prophets wrote. I gave the lie to this in the first volume of this work.[112] In brief, OT prophets were Seers, both of short and long-term prophecy. Moreover, Yahweh's own way for people to distinguish a true prophet from a false one is whether what he predicts comes to pass (Deut. 18:22). The prophet Amos says this: "Surely the Lord GOD does nothing, unless He reveals His secret to His servants the prophets" (Amos 3:7).

This statement by Amos declares Yahweh to be the one who will not proceed with anything unless He tells His prophets *what He is going to do.* This is interesting in a number of ways. First, this concerns what God's intent is. Second, God employs human instruments to reveal what He is going to do. Third, Yahweh puts His great name on the line, as it were, through the mouths of His prophets. And fourth, this process has to eventuate in a recognizable fulfillment of God's words.

In Volume One, I went to the Cyrus prediction in Isaiah 44 to drive this home. Let us remind ourselves of the salient part of that passage. Speaking to Israel, He says:

> Thus says the LORD, your Redeemer, and He who formed you from the womb; I *am* the LORD, who makes all *things,*
> Who stretches out the heavens all alone,
> Who spreads abroad the earth by Myself...
> Who confirms the word of His servant, and performs the counsel of His messengers... (Isa. 44:24, 26a).

Here Yahweh uses the prophet Isaiah to speak to His people a message of salvation hope. Just as Yahweh the Creator will not give up on the world that He created, so He will not give up on the nation and people He created. But notice how God Himself calls our attention to His prophets. They are reliable because they prophesy God's words to the people. The context is not essentially ethical but predictive. In Isaiah, Yahweh not only predicts Jerusalem's future restoration and redemption (Isa. 44:24, 26, 28), He, through the prophet, also predicts the coming of Cyrus (Isa. 44:28-45:3). Yahweh "confirms" or "establishes" what His servants say, and He "performs" or "brings to completion" what His prophets say to Israel (Isa. 44:26). This is the way it was explained in the first volume:

> Since God has put His character on the line, He is not free to fulfill a prediction differently than His words through His prophets would lead people to expect. If a prophecy does not come about in line with what could have been reasonably expected, then Isaiah 44 tells us in so many words that it is not from God! If it were otherwise, it would be tantamount to God denying Himself (cf. 2 Tim. 2:13). This fixes prophecy, especially long-term prophecy, along with its interpretation, in stone.[113]

112 *The Words of the Covenant*, Vol. 1, 28-29, 223-228.
113 Ibid., 228.

This is why I do not accept Beale's understanding of OT prophecy, nor his description of what John means when he tells his readers he is writing a prophecy. Impressive as Beale's scholarship is, he does not give due attention to what the prophets themselves say they are doing.[114]

One more thing: we have to take care to read Revelation *as* a predictive prophecy. Garland writes:

> When interpreters overemphasize the immediate audience, it makes it difficult to see how God could reveal future events to those same readers without running foul of the limited scope of such interpreters. Indeed, this is the case in the book before us. When the application to the immediate audience dominates the purpose of the book, then interpreters tend to search the local history of the first readers in an attempt to find events which, in their mind, "match" the events described by God. Two such examples are the Roman practice of emperor worship and the myth that Nero would revive from the dead.[115]

The only reason an interpreter would wish to reorientate the reader towards a first century ethical reading of the book would be because he did not think he was reading *predictive* prophecy. But as Garland goes on to state simply, "Such interpretations do not match the plain meaning of the text."[116]

The Use of Numbers

Of course, numbers are given significant emphasis in the book. This emphasis causes the reader to wonder whether there is symbolic relevance to them and, if so, what that symbolism means. The truth is that the numbers are both actual numerical values and are, at the same time, often symbolic. As stated above, the stars and lampstands that John sees in Revelation 1 are symbols. They are not literal but signify literal things. But the number of them *is* literal. There really are seven stars and seven lampstands, and John really sees seven "spirits" before God's throne (Rev. 1:4). There are twenty-four elders,[117] seven Spirits, and four living creatures before the throne of God (Rev. 4–5). There really are seven seals on the scroll, seven trumpets are blown, and seven bowls poured out. Four horsemen go forth upon the loosing of the first four seals in chapter 6. None of these numbers are other than what they seem to be.

Continuing, there really are 144,000 Israelites, 12,000 from each of the designated tribes, who are sealed by God, and they are pictured as being upon earth (Rev. 7:3).

---

114 I am not, of course, insisting that the prophets were not concerned with the moral direction of the people. Of course, they were. But it does not take a prophet to inveigh against the times. Despite the insistence of some to the contrary, Scripture portrays the prophets as foreseers before they were forthtellers. That is to say, what made them prophets was their ability to predict the future.

115 Tony Garland, *A Testimony of Jesus Christ,* Vol. 1, 37.

116 Ibid.

117 How could a comparison be made with David's twenty-four priestly attendants in 1 Chron. 25 if it were otherwise?

These same are seen after they have been removed ("raptured"?) to heaven in Revelation 14. There we find out that they were all male virgins (Rev. 14:4). Hence, they cannot be the same as the innumerable multitude in heaven "of all nations, tribes, peoples, and tongues" (Rev. 7:9), who are pictured in heaven (Rev. 7:9), who were *not sealed* like the 144,000.

What about the vast army recounted in Revelation 9:13-19 (the sixth trumpet)? John expressly says that he "heard the number of them" (Rev. 9:16). That number was "two hundred million." If that is the number John was told, why would we think we were in any position to question it? John is not estimating it. He is informed of it. This army is on horseback, and "those who sat on them had breastplates of fiery red, hyacinth blue, and sulfur yellow; and the heads of the horses *were* like the heads of lions; and out of their mouths came fire, smoke, and brimstone" (Rev. 9:16-17). So be it! What does the number two hundred million signify, if not two hundred million? And what about the four angels at the Euphrates who released them (Rev. 9:14-15; cf. Rev. 7:1)? Are there not four of them? Seven thunders were heard in Revelation 10:3-4. After the two witnesses are killed by the "beast" in Revelation 11, their dead bodies literally lie in the streets of Jerusalem for "three and a half days" (Rev. 11:8-9). At some point in the future, it will be possible for those who are wise to reckon up the number 666 in reference to the coming Antichrist (Rev. 13:18).[118] Do we get full explanations of these things? The answer is no. But we are told how many of these varied phenomena John beheld and that he had the ability to count them. This indicates that the numbers are not to be spiritualized.

Is There Any Numerical Symbolism Involved?

With all this said, we must ask about the symbolism attached to the numbers. Undoubtedly, there are symbolic associations in many, if not most, circumstances. But the symbolism, whatever it is, is conveyed by the *actual* numbers 7, 12, 3 and a half, 144,000, etc. These numbers carry symbolic value but are not symbolic in themselves; they are literal numbers, not mere placeholders. And they are never interpreted as anything but real numbers by the author.

I think the most easily discernible numerical symbol in Revelation is the number 7. From its use in the opening chapters in the letters to the seven churches, it is clear that what is written is meant for a wide audience (e.g., "He who has an ear, let him hear what the Spirit says to the churches," Rev. 2:7, 11, 17, 29; 3:6, 13, 22).

Once we get to the hotly disputed territory that is Revelation 20, we need to understand that the battle rages here because it is a touchpoint for every eschatological

118 Several premillennialists are content with the identification of this figure with Nero (e.g., Buist M. Fanning, *Revelation*, 380; and Robert H. Gundry, *Commentary on the New Testament*, 1040), but I cannot agree that the apostle is telling Christians to calculate Nero's name nearly thirty years after he died. I much prefer the approach of Tony Garland in *A Testimony of Jesus Christ*, Vol. 1, 531-533. E. W. Bullinger finds a connection between this number and the ancient mysteries (which are being revived) and his comments are worthy of consideration (even if they may be a little obtuse). See *The Apocalypse*, 439-441. See also his book *Number in Scripture: Its Supernatural Design and Spiritual Significance* (Grand Rapids: Kregel, 1967), 284-286.

assertion that has gone before it. In this book, my eschatological assertions are embedded in the wording of God's covenants with man, especially in the oaths God took. Those oaths always had a telos in mind—a telos that was spelled out quite clearly in the covenantal development of Scripture. If that covenantal formation was not clearly delineated by the oaths, there would be no way to pinpoint fulfillment, which brings us back to Revelation 20. No less than six times in fifteen verses do we read of a stipulated thousand-year duration in which Satan is bound and imprisoned (Rev. 20:2-3) and that saints reign with Christ (Rev. 20:4, 6). To what could this millennial reign refer? Many say it refers to the present age between the cross and the return of Christ. If that were the case, one could see why such interpreters would put emphasis upon reading the numbers of Revelation as non-literal. The stress would be not upon what the text literally says but instead on what the numbers are supposed to imply. Others say that the thousand years in Revelation 20 is simply that, no more, no less. That is my position. I hold to it in the absence of any indication in the biblical text telling me that it does *not* mean a thousand years,[119] which is supported by its sixfold declaration.[120]

The Interpretation of Revelation 20

Since I have just mentioned the one thousand years in Revelation 20, let us stay with it. This is one of the chapters of Scripture that have become hermeneutical battlegrounds between premillennialists, a- and post-millennialists. Both amillennialists and postmillennialists view the chapter in an almost mystical way. This includes what, at first blush, appear to be strange interpretations of the imprisonment of Satan, the first resurrection, and the thousand years.

If one turns to the large Greek Text commentary by G. K. Beale, we can see that he believes the coming to life of the beheaded saints is a spiritual regeneration, that the thousand years is the entire Church age, and that Satan has been "bound" for the past two thousand years.[121] Beale gives seven lines of correspondence between Revelation 12 and 20.[122] He also connects passages in Ezekiel 38–39 to Revelation 19 and 20.[123] If one pursues a typological and spiritualized method of interpreting biblical prophecy, then this has to be the sort of conclusion that is arrived at, no matter how outrageously it contorts the sentences on the page. Let me confess to a peculiar kind of unbelief at this juncture—unbelief that the God who has set out so clearly what He intends to do in His covenants would close His Word to man by employing

119 "How could John have communicated to his audience a 1,000-year reign if it was in fact 1,000 literal years? He couldn't. There is no alternative" (Ian A. Hicks, personal communication).

120 Some hold that the main issue is whether Christ reigns on earth after His second coming and before the New Creation. E.g., Larry R. Helyer, *The Witness of Jesus, Paul and John,* 361. But if a fivefold repetition of 1,000 years may be symbolic, I think the argument for an intermediate reign is considerably weakened.

121 G. K. Beale, See *The Book of Revelation,* 984-1002. Many other scholars hold to these interpretations.

122 Ibid., 994.

123 Ibid., 976-980.

such obfuscatory verbiage and in a way that essentially renders His covenant oaths pointless.

When reading through the Apocalypse, it certainly looks as though what happens in chapter 20 is related chronologically and logically to the events in chapter 19. Historic premillennialist Craig Blomberg says it well:

> Revelation 20:1 may be one of the very worst choices in the Bible for a chapter break. John has just narrated the demise of two-thirds of the false trinity. The beast and false prophet have been thrown into the lake of fire. But, what of the third person, Satan himself? Is this the moment for his final and complete defeat? The answer comes immediately in 20:1-3: he is thrown into the Abyss to be locked up in chains for a thousand years.[124]

Besides all that, we need to remember all the passages that have led us to expect an intermediate Kingdom age between this present age and the new heavens and new earth. I am referring to places like Psalm 2; Isaiah 54; 65; Micah 4; Jeremiah 33; Ezekiel 36–48; and Zechariah 8 and 14. The mention of sinners, death, children, and old men makes it impossible to be the New Creation. But the child dying at a hundred years old and Jerusalem being known as "the City of Truth" makes it impossible to be the present age. Therefore, we are led to view the era in these OT prophecies as an intermediate kingdom era—the Millennium of Revelation 20.[125]

The Incarceration and Destruction of Satan

It is simply a fact that the believers in the first centuries of the Church were mostly premillennial,[126] whereas nowadays, most scholars tell us that we are in the Millennium and that Satan is bound as we speak. This leads me to say that if Satan is bound, then the angel who bound him should be fired as incompetent. First Peter 5:8-9 informs us that Satan is far from bound and imprisoned (even though many amillennialists fail to mention his incarceration). And why would Paul warn us to "Put on the whole armor of God, that you may be able to stand against the wiles of the devil" (Eph. 6:11), if Christians were impervious to them? If we are not impervious to these wiles, which surely include being deceived (cf. 2 Cor. 11:3), then what is the rationale for binding Satan?[127] What is the big deal?

---

124 Craig L. Blomberg, *A New Testament Theology*, 679. He continues, "This is why I cannot accept either amillennialism or postmillennialism. Both those eschatological systems have put a flashback in 20:1-3 to Jesus' first coming… But the seamless narration of the judgments of the three members of the unholy trinity is destroyed in so doing" (Ibid., 649-650).

125 On this, see Matt Waymeyer, *Amillennialism and the Age to Come,* and the pertinent chapters in George N. H. Peters, *The Theocratic Kingdom.*

126 Among many opinions that this is so, see Earle E. Cairns, "Eschatology and Church History, Part I," *BSAC* 115 (Apr 1958), 136-142. A wider study is Larry V. Crutchfield's six-part, "The Early Church Fathers and the Foundations of Dispensationalism," *Conservative Theological Journal* 2–3 (1998–1999).

127 The teaching that Rev. 20:3, "that he should deceive the nations no more," refers to Christians makes no sense to me. If Christians are not open to Satan's seductions, then such classics as Thomas Brooks' *Precious Remedies Against Satan's Devices* and William Gurnall's *The Christian in Complete Armour* would be much shorter than they are.

According to the text, Satan is bound with a chain—a spiritual chain is easier to make than a spiritual being—and then is cast into the same abyss that so efficiently held prisoner the demonic locusts of Revelation 9. He has no freedom to do anything! He is rendered inactive. This close confinement is for a thousand years for the express purpose of him not being able to deceive the nations (Rev. 20:1-3), something he does once he is released from his prison in Revelation 20:7.[128] It makes possible Christ's millennial reign over the world;[129] a world that includes both saved and glorified saints and those who have either made it through the "Sheep and Goats judgment" (Matt. 25:31-46) or are born in the Millennium. This rule of the Prince of Peace over the cursed but subdued earth "finds its roots in the covenants of promise in the Old Testament—the Abrahamic Covenant, the Davidic Covenant, and the New Covenant."[130]

At the end of Revelation 20, Satan is defeated in battle after his release from the pit and is then "cast into the lake of fire and brimstone where the beast and the false prophet are" (Rev. 20:10).[131] Since Revelation 19:20 records the casting of the first two members of the unholy trinity into the lake of fire prior to the thousand years, we are again given good reason to read Revelation 20 as succeeding Revelation 19. Moreover, this chronological movement continues as the present heavens and earth flee before the mighty presence of God in Revelation 20:11, and the new heavens and new earth are created in Revelation 21:1ff.

Stress on the "Great Tribulation"

If a person takes a spiritualizing approach to the book, they will see no need to have a prophetic work relating the final tragedy of Satan's rule over the earth (2 Cor. 4:4; 1 Jn. 5:19; cf. Eph. 6:12) and the glorious arrival of the long-promised King (Gen. 3:15; 49:10; Num. 24:14, 17; Isa. 11:1-10; Jer. 23:5-7; Dan. 7:13-14; Mal. 4:1-3). If, however, a person adopts what has been called the dispensational premillennial[132] understanding of Revelation, then the reason why Revelation completes the inspired Canon is readily apparent.

If the understanding of the seventieth week of Daniel 9 presented in Volume One is correct,[133] and it is seven years in duration, it appears that the last half of that period, the "time, times, and half a time" of Daniel and of John, is the most crucial time covered in this book.

128 The text stresses Satan's imprisonment, not his bonds.

129 Matthew Waymeyer, *Revelation 20 and the Millennial Debate* (The Woodlands, TX: Kress, 2004), 55.

130 Ibid., 56.

131 This final defeat of Satan also brings the cosmic drama full circle. The crushing of the serpent's skull (Gen. 3:15) happens at the end of the Millennium.

132 Although I call myself a Biblical Covenantalist, I am quite happy to be identified as a dispensational premillennialist as far as End Times are concerned. I am not, however, as satisfied with the moniker "dispensationalist" because I reject the conception of biblical theology based on an administrative (i.e., dispensations) rather than a covenantal structure.

133 See *The Words of the Covenant*, Vol. 1, 315-317.

The "Great Tribulation"

The interpretation of the last half of the Tribulation, which is often referred to as "the Great Tribulation" (cf. Matt. 24:21; Rev. 7:14), centers around the parallel phrases: "a time, times, and half a time" found in Revelation 12:14 (cf. Dan. 7:25; 12:7); "one thousand two hundred and sixty days" in Revelation 11:3 and 12:16; and "forty-two months" in Revelation 11:2 and 13:5. In Revelation 11:1-3 we read this:

> Then I was given a reed like a measuring rod. And the angel stood, saying, "Rise and measure the temple of God, the altar, and those who worship there. But leave out the court which is outside the temple, and do not measure it, for it has been given to the Gentiles. And they will tread the holy city underfoot *for* forty-two months. And I will give *power* to my two witnesses, and they will prophesy one thousand two hundred and sixty days, clothed in sackcloth."

From verse 2, we can see that the rebuilt temple and its court are in the hands of Gentiles (non-Jews) for "forty-two months," which is the same as the "one thousand two hundred and sixty days" of verse 3. Both come to three and a half years. It could be that the time known as the "Tribulation" or "Jacob's Trouble" is only this long in duration. I would have no strong objection to that thesis (but see below). Certainly, this time period is stressed a lot in Daniel and Revelation, as well as implied in Mark 13, Luke 21, and Matthew 24. However, enough trouble comes upon the earth in the first three and a half years to warrant including it within the Tribulation period.

The Hour of Temptation

There is another text that deserves consideration: "Because you have kept My command to persevere, I also will keep you from the hour of trial which shall come upon the whole world, to test those who dwell on the earth" (Rev. 3:10). This "hour of trial" will be worldwide. Moreover, the very designation leads us to distinguish the "hour of temptation" from the trials and difficulties that accompany this Christian life (e.g., 1 Pet. 1:6-7). No, this period is most likely the coming Tribulation.[134] This is the view of dispensationalist scholars, and I am fully in agreement with them.

A related question is how the Church will be "kept from the hour." This involves a decision about how to translate the verb and preposition combination, *tereso ek*. Do we render it as "kept through" or "kept from"? The most natural sense is the second option. This conclusion is bolstered by the fact that a specific time of trial is being indicated. As Tony Garland writes:

> The simple answer to the question at hand is found by reading the promise more carefully, for the promise is not to be kept from *the trial*, but

---

134 This has knock-on effects on how one interprets the letters to the seven churches.

> from *the hour of trial.* The church will not even experience the trial for it will be *kept from the hour* when the trial is visited upon the earth.[135]

If "kept from" is correct, then it does lend support for a pretribulation rapture. But it is a tangential support. It is not a slam dunk.[136] Still, while it is conceivable that God could protect His saints "through" the hour of trial, as He often has done in the past, this seems to clash with what we read in Revelation 6:9-11, where the souls of the saints are told that more of their brethren must suffer death as they suffered. However, it may find support from Revelation 7:9-17, where the multitude that no one could number are said to have come through "great tribulation" (Rev. 7:14). Although they endured tribulation, perhaps they survived somehow, and that is down to God "keeping" them? Perhaps, but this sounds like grasping at straws. It is far better to view the worldwide "hour of temptation" as synonymous with the Tribulation, or at least the "great tribulation" that has to be endured (Matt. 24:13).

In sum, a large chunk of the book of Revelation is taken up with the coming Tribulation. What does this mean? For one thing, it means that any interpreter of the book who does not teach the Tribulation has missed a key focus of the book. Another important thing to notice about this emphasis is that the future Tribulation is the denouement of this world's story. It presages the return and the great turnaround for creation. This is what the Apocalypse is mainly written for.

The Length of the Tribulation

Given that this designated three-and-a-half-year upheaval is the chief focus of Revelation 6–18, is there any indication that the Tribulation is longer? I think there is. In Matthew 24 the Lord Jesus refers to what He calls "the beginning of sorrows" (Matt. 24:8). As there is considerable overlap between Jesus' description and Revelation's middle section, it is reasonable to believe that this concerns a time right before the three and a half years (which Jesus calls a time of "great tribulation" in Matt. 24:21). Then Daniel 9:24-27 speaks of seventy weeks of years (490 years) of which a single "week" (7 years) remains.[137] This final "week" is divided into two by "the prince who shall come" (Antichrist), breaking his covenant (Dan. 9:27). It is reasonable to conclude that in the first half of the seventieth week, the covenant is in force.[138] The last half would be the "time, times, and half a time" referenced in Daniel 7:25; 12:7; and Revelation 12:14, which would be Jeremiah's "time of Jacob's trouble" (Jer. 30:7), and Jesus' "great tribulation" (Matt. 24:21; cf. Dan. 12:1).

From this evidence, I think we are on safe ground to believe that the Tribulation is seven years long. However, the main part of the Tribulation (the "Great Tribulation"),

---

135 Tony Garland, *A Testimony of Jesus Christ*, Vol. 1, 262.

136 For an exegetical defense of this reading, see Paul D. Feinberg's contribution to the book *Three Views on the Rapture: Pre- Mid- or Post-Tribulation*, ed. Richard R. Reiter (Grand Rapids: Zondervan, 1996).

137 See my treatment of this and related texts in Daniel in *The Words of the Covenant*, Vol. 1, 310-319.

138 It should be noted that even the Tribulation is covenantal, although the covenant is not a divine covenant.

the part that Scripture focuses on, is the final three-and-a-half-year period—the "time, times and half a time."

EXCURSUS: Apollyon, the Beast, and the False Prophet

The first mention of the title "the beast" in Revelation concerns the death of the two witnesses. Revelation 11:7 refers to "the beast that ascends out of the bottomless pit." The only available referent is to the "angel of the bottomless pit" in Revelation 9:11. Many premillennial interpreters resist the association between the Apollyon in Revelation 9:11 and the Beast of Revelation 11:7 (and 13:1-8), but the connection is there.[139] Allow me to explain further.

In chapter 11 we are told about the Two Witnesses (Rev. 11:3-6). Then we read of "the beast that ascends out of the abyss," just as though John takes for granted that the reader already knows who this "beast" is. Robert Thomas and Tony Garland identify this "beast" (*therion*) in Revelation 11 as Antichrist.[140] But if Revelation 9:11 and 11:7 are not connected, how does one explain John's apparent lack of concentration in introducing the beast so abruptly? If Revelation 9:11 is the sole verse that speaks about him, why would John bother naming him at all?

The "bottomless pit" is first referred to in Revelation 9, where verse 11 reveals its "king." Revelation 11:7 and 17:8, both of which speak of the beast who comes out of the bottomless pit, surely assume we recall the "angel" introduced earlier.[141]

If the beast of the abyss and the angel of the abyss are one and the same individual, then we have a logical explanation for the naming of the angel in Revelation 9:11, and the sudden mention of the beast in Revelation 11:7 is not so sudden. I fully realize that the commentators maintain a stony silence here, refusing to connect the two verses, but it certainly tidies up some loose ends.[142] This is why I link the angel of the bottomless pit (Rev. 9:11)[143] with the beast who ascends out of the bottomless pit (Rev. 11:7; 17:8). I understand this is controversial, but I want to tease it out a bit.

As stated already, the angel of the abyss is named in Hebrew and in Greek—Abaddon/Apollyon.[144] His names mean "destruction" or "destroyer." If Revelation 9:11 is irrelevant, the beast who ascends from the abyss and kills God's two witnesses in Revelation 11:7 does so with no introduction. He just arrives completely unannounced.

---

139 I do not expect to convince everyone of my equating Apollyon with the Beast. In the long run, I don't think it matters too much. At least from our present perspective.

140 Tony Garland, *A Testimony of Jesus Christ*, Vol. 1, 454-455.

141 Does the "beast" of the bottomless pit just appear out of nowhere? Back in chapter 9 we are not told that another being crawled out of the abyss. Surely John would have mentioned him emerging with the locust-scorpions once the lid had been removed in Rev. 9:1-2? Well, I think he did.

142 I.e., the otherwise strange double naming of the angel of the bottomless pit only to never bring him up again, the stylistically awkward introduction of the beast of the bottomless pit when accounting for the demise of the witnesses, and the failure of John to notice the ascent of the beast when commenting on the emergence of the infernal locusts along with their king.

143 An angel looks like a man (Gen. 18:2; Dan. 9:21; 12:6-7; Rev. 22:8-9; cf. Heb. 13:2).

144 I am open to the possible correspondence of "Apollyon" with Apollo. See G. K. Beale, *The Book of Revelation*, 503-504.

Additionally, this same "beast" goes into destruction (or perdition, *apoleia*) in Revelation 17:8. Here it is with the verse before it.

> But the angel said to me, "Why did you marvel? I will tell you the mystery of the woman and of the beast that carries her, which has the seven heads and the ten horns. The beast that you saw was, and is not, and will ascend out of the bottomless pit and go to perdition. And those who dwell on the earth will marvel, whose names are not written in the Book of Life from the foundation of the world, when they see the beast that was, and is not, and yet is" (Rev. 17:7-8).

"Why did you marvel?" As if there was nothing to marvel at! I've just landed at one of the trickiest passages in the Apocalypse. I included verse 7 because it harks back to the vision of the woman and the beast, which starts in verse 3. I'm not going to get technical about the details, but several things are said about the beast which pose problems for interpreters, among which are:

1. It has blasphemous names and has seven heads and ten horns (17:3).

2. The heads represent mountains, and the horns represent kings (17:9, 12).

3. Yet the beast is himself a king (17:11).

4. From John's time perspective, the beast appears to be past, present, and yet future. He/it "was, and is not, and yet is" (17:8).

5. Or, more likely, it could be that within the purview of the vision, the beast is past, present, and future. The references are about the career of the beast, with its death interruption (Rev. 13).

How can the beast be an individual, as he is in Revelation 17:11-13 (and Rev. 11:7), if he is depicted with heads equating to mountains and horns equaling other kings or kingdoms? I think if we focus more on the function of the image, things get a little clearer. As we have noted, the beast supports the harlot, but according to verses 12 and 13, the ten kings "receive authority" with the beast. They "are of one mind, and give their power and authority to the beast," therefore, they can be depicted in such a manner. This "key" helps us to see the continuity in the identity of the beast in Revelation.

As previously noted, in 2 Thessalonians 2:3 Paul calls Antichrist by the name "Son of Perdition" (*apoleia*).[145] The angel of the bottomless pit is Apollyon. Both words are derived from the verb *apollumi*. I believe this angel who comes from the abyss is the same as the beast who comes out of it. If Apollyon/the Beast comes from the abyss, does that mean that the "earth-dwellers" know where he came from? Do people even

145 Interestingly, Jesus referred to Judas Iscariot by the same name in Jn. 17:12 (He also called Judas a "*diabolos*" in Jn. 6:70). In Acts 1:25 Peter tantalizingly tells us that Judas at his death went "to his own place." The rabbit hole just seems to get deeper!

know about the "shaft of the abyss"? And if the Antichrist is *from* the abyss, is he fully human? My guess is that for the first half of the Tribulation, the Antichrist appears fully human. After his "resurrection," the spirit of the angel of the abyss enters him. Further details and/or corrections will be provided at that later time.

How certain am I of the connections I have made? I would say about 70% certain, so there is quite some room for error. I have posed some questions about the identity of the angel of the bottomless pit that I find intriguing. I have not attempted to give definitive answers. But I will leave you with this: I believe this personage is far stranger, frightening, and more beguiling than he is usually portrayed. The Tribulation will witness intensified supernatural activity, and the angel of the bottomless pit will take second place to no one in that tumultuous time.

When we turn to chapter 13, we see a strange beast emerging from the sea. The sea may refer to the nations, but I am skeptical. What is clear is that the beast in the vision looks like a leopard (Rev. 13:2).[146] Commentaries on the book of Daniel often demonstrate how the attributes of each of the beasts that appear in Daniel 7 help us to identify the corresponding empire being predicted.[147] Of course, these identifications could only be made with the benefit of hindsight. Similarly, the beasts featured in Revelation 13 have attributes that will aid in identifying them. One must take care here, though. The beasts of Daniel 7 represented empires or kingdoms as much as single rulers. John's beasts, however, refer distinctly to certain men (at least if one is thoroughly premillennial). In Revelation 13:18 we are specifically told that the "number of the beast" is "the number of a man." This blasphemer (Rev. 13:5-6/Dan. 7:25) is plainly the same as Daniel's "little horn" (Dan. 7:19-25). John even says of the beast that he makes "war with the saints" (Rev. 13:7/Dan. 7:21, 25) for a period of forty-two months, which, at three and a half years, is the same as "a time, times, and half a time" (Rev. 13:5 with Dan. 7:25).

What is more, Paul's description of "the man of sin"[148] who "opposes and exalts himself above all that is called God or that is worshiped" (2 Thess. 2:3-4) is brought to mind. Paul even calls this individual "the son of perdition," which calls to mind the names Abaddon and Apollyon in Revelation 9:11 and the destiny of the beast (Rev. 17:8, 11).

The "leopard" is a "him." This beast dies, but he lives again. The second beast is the false prophet (Rev. 13:11ff.). He is an infernal caricature of John the Baptist and more impressive than John, at least in his acts (Rev. 13:13-14). The image of the Antichrist that is made will be an extremely impressive thing, although it will be an abomination to heaven (Matt. 24:15). The False Prophet makes it come alive (Rev. 13:15).

The number of the beast has to be counted. It does not, therefore, seem to be a simple 666 (in spite of the misuse of it by Luciferians the world over). It is anyone's guess what will have to be counted, but since "it is the number of a man" (Rev. 13:18),

---

146 A leopard with the mouth of a lion and the feet of a bear, but a leopard, nonetheless.

147 See, for example, the works by Leon J. Wood, J. Paul Tanner, as well as Tony Garland's online commentary on Daniel (still in progress).

148 This has not prevented a- and post-millennialists from interpreting the "man of sin" to be a "system of sin"!

it could be that at that time, every person will have a number, but only his will add up to 666.[149] Who but God knows?

Major Theological Themes

God Almighty

Even the casual reader of the book of Revelation can see that God's rule and judgments are prominent.[150] John is taken in a vision to the very throne room of Yahweh where he beholds One sitting on a throne whose attendants call "Lord God Almighty" (Rev. 4:8). God in heaven receives the glory that is His due, but upon earth, of course, that is not so—at least not until the end of the book.

On several occasions, God's creatures are said to be before the throne. For instance, in chapter 4, we see the four living creatures (Rev. 4:6) and the twenty-four elders (Rev. 4:10). In Revelation 5:11 the throne is surrounded by millions of angels, while in Revelation 7:9ff., multitudes of the saved stand before the throne.[151] This is where the 144,000 end up in Revelation 14:3-5. Finally, it is from the throne that the word of power comes, "Behold, I make all things new" (Rev. 21:5).

Throughout the Apocalypse, these references present God as the eschatological God who meets us at the end of our sojourn. He is the Maker of heaven and earth (Psa. 115:15, NASB), the One who wraps up history and the Creation Project (Isa. 34:4; 2 Pet. 3:7; Rev. 20:11), and the Creator of the eternal realm (Isa. 65:17; 66:22; 2 Pet. 3:13; Rev. 21:1ff.).

The Person of Christ

When we first encounter Jesus Christ in Revelation 1:12-20, He is seen as the eternally "living one" who has been victorious over death and holds "the keys of death and of Hades" in His hand (Rev. 1:18). John has already announced Him by combining parts of Daniel 7:13 and Zechariah 12:10-12 (Rev. 1:7), whereby he signals to the reader that the revealing to come mainly concerns the time of the end. Revelation 2 and 3 demonstrate that He is Lord over the churches. Christ appears as a Lamb who has been sacrificed numerous times in the book (e.g., Rev. 5:6, 12-13, 6:1, 16; 7:14; 12:11; 13:8). Hence, Christ's work as a sacrifice for sinners is highlighted, especially in the first half of the book.

149 We must reject any symbolical view of this enigmatic number. For instance, "The repetitive '666', therefore, stands for those human and secular forces, including the Romes of any period, which are oppressive and unjust, and seek to dethrone the Creator and enthrone the creature. John is not referring here in the first place to individual and historical tyrants; he is speaking of varied types of authority which use power wrongly, so as to induce doctrinal error and ethical compromise" (Stephen S. Smalley, *The Revelation to John*, 352-353).

150 I. Howard Marshall, *New Testament Theology*, 561.

151 "In Revelation there is still another distinctive emphasis on God as 'the one who sits on the throne' in heaven, the all-powerful cosmic ruler (e.g., 1:4; 4:2, 9-10; 5:1, 7, 13; 6:16; 7:10, 15; 19:4; 21:5)" (Larry W. Hurtado, *God in New Testament Theology* [Nashville: Abingdon, 2010], 97).

Jesus, as the Lamb, is also "Lord of lords and King of kings" (Rev. 17:14), which seems counter-intuitive, but He has come for salvation and redemption, not just for humanity, but for the natural order as well. And when it comes to the new heavens and new earth, He is called the Lamb, who, along with his Father, illuminates the New Jerusalem in Revelation 21:23.

In Revelation 19:7-9 we are told about "the marriage supper of the Lamb." Here we are clearly on eschatological ground. The time has come for celebration—for Jesus to partake of the fruit of the vine with His redeemed ones in the Kingdom of God (cf. Mk. 14:25).

Revelation does not use the name "Jesus" as often as one would have thought. Thus, in chapter 22, when we get a first-person announcement—"I, Jesus, have sent My angel to testify to you these things in the churches. I am the Root and the Offspring of David, the Bright and Morning Star" (Rev. 22:16)—it arrests our attention.

The Completion of the Creation Project

Throughout this work I have referred to the grand program of the Creator God for the world by the term "The Creation Project." Unsurprisingly, the book of Revelation includes several key references to creation. It may seem innocuous to call attention to the promise of eating from "the tree of life" (Rev. 2:7), but this promise, which finds its match in Revelation 22:2 and 12 in the New Jerusalem, shows that humanity and creation are designed for each other. God, who "made every tree grow that is pleasant to the sight and good for food" (Gen. 2:9), will always surround His saints with the marvels of a created order. And even in the Millennial Kingdom, when aging and death will not be completely purged from the earth (Isa. 65:20), the Creator will make the world into such a place that:

> The mountains and the hills
> Shall break forth into singing before you,
> And all the trees of the field shall clap their hands (Isa. 55:12b).

And, "justice will dwell in the wilderness, and righteousness remain in the fruitful field" (Isa. 32:16). We are reminded by these promises that the creator God (Rev. 4:11) is now pleased for human beings to enjoy what He has made for them to the full.

The Hand of God Against Creation

Nevertheless, as one gets into the central section of the Apocalypse, it is impossible not to notice how the created realm is smitten by the Almighty. In Revelation 6 the Third Horseman brings a dearth of food (Rev. 6:5-6), and the opening of the sixth seal involves the shaking of the heavens and the earth (Rev. 6:12-16; cf. Heb. 12:26). The seventh chapter begins with the wind being restrained, and the angels whose job it will be to "harm the earth" are to wait until the 144,000 are sealed (Rev. 7:1-3). And, of course, the earth is distressed greatly under the trumpet and bowl judgments (Rev. 8:7-13; 16:1-21). Finally, Revelation 20:11 declares, "Then I saw a great white throne and Him who sat on it, from whose face the earth and the heaven fled away. And there was found no place for them."

This announcement is confirmed by the first verse of the next chapter: "Now I saw a new heaven and a new earth, for the first heaven and the first earth had passed away" (Rev. 21:1). This is then followed by Yahweh's voice proclaiming, "Behold, I make all things new" (Rev. 21:5).

It certainly looks as though this present earth is to be destroyed and replaced by a brand new world after the Millennium.[152] What I take away from this is that once Jesus has reigned in justice and peace for a thousand years and, at the close of that time, has dispatched Satan in no uncertain fashion (Rev. 20:7-10; cf. Gen. 3:15), the "Creation Project" will be completed. Having won everything back for the Father, Jesus presents this earth to Him as a gift (1 Cor. 15:24-28), just as the Father gave it to the Son (Col. 1:16). Jesus' reign has been in righteousness and equity (Isa. 11:4; 32:1). He has suppressed the groanings of the cursed earth, pacified the wild beasts, and beautified every corner of the world. It is a beautiful picture.

But Jesus also proves that the sinfulness of man, even under the most tranquil and just circumstances, and with Satan the deceiver imprisoned, will continue to resist God. It is the final justification of Yahweh's ways with willful man, the final proof that men's hearts are obdurate in the face of true goodness, and the vindication of the necessity to replace "the former things" (Rev. 21:4) with a new creation where sin will never enter. The creation of the new heavens and new earth (Rev. 21:1–22:5) will mean that there will be no more curse (Rev. 22:3), and the glories that will ensue will be glories fit not only for a thousand years but for eternity.

The Book of Life

Christ blots names out of the Lamb's Book of Life (Rev. 3:5; cf. 13:8; 21:27). According to Revelation 17:8, we read, "Those who dwell on the earth will marvel, whose names are not written in the Book of Life from the foundation of the world." Here we note that the names of many people (those designated "earth-dwellers") were never in the Book of Life. But in Revelation 3:5 Christ says that he will "not blot out his name from the Book of Life." This raises a paradox. If the Book of Life did not at any time contain the names of non-believers, and Revelation 3:5 suggests that Jesus may blot names out of the Book of Life, then how can this be reconciled? Let me be clear. There ought to be *no* names for Jesus to blot out of the Book in the first place. And why would names be written into a book only to be removed at a later date? My answer to this quandary relates back to my re-reading of the book of Hebrews. In brief,

152 This accords with Peter's words, "the elements will melt with fervent heat; both the earth and the works that are in it will be burned up" (2 Pet. 3:10; cf. 3:7, 12). However, I respect the opinions of those who disagree with me about this.

if one can relate Revelation 3:5 to the Tribulation, then we have people who believe in Jesus Christ but who may forfeit it![153]

The New Jerusalem (Real or Imaginary?)

From what is written about New Jerusalem (Rev. 21:2; cf. 3:12), it appears to be closely connected with the Church. The description only tells us that New Jerusalem descends out of heaven to earth, but it doesn't satisfy our curiosity as to whether it orbits the new earth or settles upon it. Still, there are some matters we may clear up with more warrant. Revelation 19:7-9 speaks of the Marriage of the Lamb:

> Let us rejoice and be glad and give the glory to Him, for the marriage of the Lamb has come and His bride has made herself ready." And it was given to her to clothe herself in fine linen, bright and clean; for the fine linen is the righteous acts of the saints. And he said to me, "Write, 'Blessed are those who are invited to the marriage supper of the Lamb.'" And he said to me, "These are true words of God."

Since the Church is espoused to Christ (Eph. 5:25, 32), I am confident that this text refers to the Church. Since the next mention of a bride in Revelation 21 is to New Jerusalem, I conclude that the bride of Revelation 19 is the bride of Revelation 21, the Church in its eternal home. All humanity is allowed into New Jerusalem, but not all will dwell there. It appears to be the dwelling of the Church (Rev. 21:9-10). We read:

> And I saw the holy city, new Jerusalem, coming down out of heaven from God, made ready as a bride adorned for her husband... And one of the seven angels who had the seven bowls full of the seven last plagues, came and spoke with me, saying, "Come here, I shall show you the bride, the wife of the Lamb." And he carried me away in the Spirit to a great and high mountain, and showed me the holy city, Jerusalem, coming down out of heaven from God, having the glory of God. Her brilliance was like a very costly stone, as a stone of crystal-clear jasper. It had a great and high wall, with twelve gates, and at the gates twelve angels; and names were written on them, which are those of the twelve tribes of the sons of Israel. There were three gates on the east and three gates on the north and three gates on the south and three gates on the west. And the wall of the city had twelve foundation stones, and on them were the twelve names of the twelve apostles of the Lamb (Rev. 21:2, 9-14).

153 I again want to state that this is a viable option, in my opinion. Others have tried to explain the problem of "conditional" texts in Revelation and Hebrews (see below) but I am not convinced that they are leaving Paul, an unconditionalist, and relating to these texts on their own merits. I would much rather eternal security was the doctrine across the board, but although I certainly see it in Paul, I don't see much of it in the OT, nor do I clearly spy it in the prophetic-Tribulational setting of parts of Hebrews and Revelation. My reader is of course free to differ.

There are many whose theology acts as a universal acid on this passage, reducing the city to a mere symbol[154] and, in utter disregard of the context, bundling together the Church with the nations that are said to be on the earth in the chapter (Rev. 21:24-26). But it is clear enough that there is a distinction made between the peoples in the city and the nations on earth. And although Israel is not named in the chapter, the fact that its land grant is "everlasting" (Gen. 17:8; Psa. 105:10-11; Ezek. 37:26) surely means that it has its own distinct position among the nations in eternity. For our present purposes, it is enough to say that the Church has a special relationship to the second Person of the Trinity in the same way that national Israel does to the first Person of the Trinity. Since "salvation is of the Jews," we should not be surprised to read of the gates of the city being named after the twelve tribes of Israel. But *all* the saved are redeemed and reconciled by Jesus Christ.

The Final Scenario—The Brief Report of the New Heavens and New Earth

We have come a long way from the original creation of the heavens and earth and the making of man in Genesis 1. That world was destroyed in the worldwide flood (Gen. 7–8), and the world as it now exists is governed by covenants. The Noahic covenant provides the uniformity principle for the outplay of history. The covenant with Abraham furnishes the nation Israel, who will be used to make His great name known among the nations[155] and produce the line from whom God's coming Ruler will spring (Gen. 22:18; 49:8-10). The same covenant guarantees a land for Israel (Gen. 12:7; 17:4-8; 35:1-12; Ezek. 34:13; Amos 9:15). The covenant with Phinehas and his descendants, the Zadokites, ensures that a temple cult will be present in Jerusalem in the Kingdom era (Num. 25:12-13; Ezek. 44). Then the Davidic covenant provides the dynasty that will rule over Israel (1 Sam. 16–Matt. 1) and the whole world through Messiah Jesus. Finally, the New covenant, which was brought into being at the cross, is the means by which all the elect in every age will enter eternity. It is this covenant in Christ's precious blood that secures the literal fulfillment of God's other covenants[156] in the Millennial Kingdom and the eternal Kingdom that follows.

The whole Story of the Bible builds to this crescendo. The role of the Apocalypse is to (1) set out the details of the impending Tribulation and the evil world ruler who will pursue the saints in that seven-year period. (2) To tell the saints that Jesus Christ will have the victory over Satan, the Antichrist, and the Christ-hating inhabitants of earth, and will set up a reign of peace and justice upon earth exactly as foretold by the

154 E.g., "It is much more likely that the figurative language of a 'new Jerusalem' should be understood in terms of a new relationship...The new Jerusalem is not the Church...but the new covenant" (Stephen S. Smalley, *The Revelation to John*, 536).

155 See Alan Hultberg, "The Future Restoration of Israel: Some Theological Considerations," in *The Future Restoration of Israel: A Response to Supercessionism*, eds. Stanley E. Porter and Alan E. Kurschner (Eugene, OR: Pickwick Publications, 2023), 166-169.

156 The Mosaic covenant is replaced with the New covenant, which incorporates within it aspects of the first covenant. This includes certain tokens of covenant identity for Israel as a nation among other nations.

Prophets. (3) Finally, it gives us a glimpse of how the Creation Project ends and how the New Heaven and New Earth come to be. The final two chapters of Revelation, the last two chapters of the Holy Bible, cap off the story, not of the Creation Project, since, in my understanding, the eternal Kingdom is another creation—the endless story—but of the purpose of the first creation and its blighted history.

The Creation Project comes together perfectly; and the new Creation Project, which is eternal, well, that requires another revelation. One thing that can be asserted without contradiction is that the New Creation will be covenantal. This is proved by the use of the covenant formulary: "And I heard a loud voice from heaven saying, 'Behold, the tabernacle of God is with men, and He will dwell with them, and they shall be His people. God Himself will be with them and be their God'" (Rev. 21:3). Although this is pronounced of New Jerusalem, the picture John paints is of a threefold humanity in blissful communion with each other and with their sovereign and benevolent Creator—the covenant God!

20

THE PEOPLE(S) OF GOD

The city had no need of the sun or of the moon to shine in it, for the glory of God illuminated it. The Lamb is its light. And the nations of those who are saved shall walk in its light, and the kings of the earth bring their glory and honor into it.
- Revelation 21:23-24

According to the prophetic witness of the OT, at the completion of the eschaton, one will find blessings upon Israel and blessings upon the Gentile nations. We hear nothing of the Church for the simple reason that the Church was not included by the Spirit in the revelations He granted to the writers of the Hebrew Bible. Once we come to the NT, where, of course, the Church receives the lion's share of the attention, the picture can get a little confused, especially if the interpreter thinks that the fulfillment of OT prophecy must be looked for almost entirely at the first advent of Christ.

In the book of Revelation, the Church and Israel are addressed. But they are not addressed at the same time. Because of the preponderance of the NT that concerns itself with the Church, it is not surprising that the OT prophetic picture is not spoken about, at least until we arrive at the final book. And even then, it is not until we reach the final chapters that the prophetic picture begins to take clear shape.

Christ and the Triadic People of God

Due to Christ's central role as the Redeemer, and owing to the fact that His redeeming blood is wholly "the blood of the new covenant" (Heb. 12:24), all who will ever be redeemed—whether they live before or after the cross—will be redeemed under the terms of the New covenant. As I have been at pains to emphasize, Christ is Himself the New covenant!

Saying that He is the New covenant does not mean that it is all Christ is. He is far more than that. But as it pertains to the salvation of sinners, I have stressed Jesus' unavoidable role. And unless someone can show that Christ's blood is only *partly* the blood of the New covenant (with part left over to apply elsewhere?), we must conclude that all redemption is, in the end, New covenant redemption.

However, this does not mean that all the redeemed are incorporated within the Christian Church (nor indeed within Israel). Such a teaching is alien to Scripture and is sustained only by inferring doctrine in spite of Scripture.

God made this world with humans in mind. He will restore it with us in mind. But the restoration will be gradual. First, He must die and be raised in glory (Lk. 24:26), having instituted the New covenant in His blood and made it with the Church (1 Cor. 11:23-26). At His second advent, He will make it with the nation of Israel (Jer. 31:31-34; Ezek. 36:22-28) and then with the nations. Through the New covenant, which is inseparable from the Person and Work of Jesus Himself, the covenant promises of God will finally find their literal fulfillment. In this, Jesus draws the two Testaments together.

I shall say more about this further on. But this brings us to the hope promised to "the Jew, the Gentile, and the Church of God" (1 Cor. 10:32). I want to show how Christ's role in history necessitates His interaction with humanity, though distinctly organized into three separate people groups in the consummation. *Thus, one humanity will be represented by three humanities—a triadic three-in-one that reflects the Creator eternally.* I shall explore this relationship one by one, beginning with Israel.

Jesus and Israel

God's promises to the people of Israel—the literal descendants of Abraham, Isaac, and Jacob—are as strong, clear, and unequivocal as anything that God has spoken to non-Israelites in the Church. But I may say in brief that God's covenant with the Patriarchs was confirmed and re-confirmed by covenant oaths by which God bound His Name to the future glory of Israel (e.g., Ezek. 36:22-24; Dan. 9:18-19). These covenant promises to Israel, in which the land is so conspicuous (e.g., Gen. 15; Psa. 105:6-11), cannot undergo transformation or eventuate in unexpected and equivocal fulfillment without God impugning His own character. There is no double-speak with God. He does not use false balances (Prov. 16:11; Mic. 6:11). He will not require others to stick to "the words of the covenant" (Jer. 34:18) while exempting Himself from the same obligation. That is why Israel has hope (Mal. 3:6).[1]

The promise God made to Abraham, Isaac, Jacob, and their descendants contained temporal conditions regarding the occupation of the land and eschatological blessing (e.g., Lev. 26), but the core ingredients of the promises were unilateral and binding upon God alone. This is why I have made so much of Jeremiah 33:14-26 in my writing. The Royal grant to Israel was never a grant to a "shadow" fulfillment resulting in the Church, but to Israel as a separate called-out entity, and God through

1 That is also why we Gentiles have hope (1 Thess. 5:24).

Messiah must fulfill it. As one non-evangelical scholar has put it, "Then covenant is initiated by the suzerain who is obligated, not the vassal. The covenant is initiated by the suzerain, and is unconditional in the sense that no demands are imposed upon Abraham."[2]

Therein lies another important teaching of Jesus in Mathew 22:32: "But concerning the resurrection of the dead, have you not read what was spoken to you by God, saying, 'I am the God of Abraham, and the God of Isaac, and the God of Jacob'? God is not the God of the dead, but of the living" (my emphasis).

The Patriarchs today are living witnesses to God's covenant promises to them now and in the future. In his time, Abraham saw Christ's day and rejoiced (Jn. 8:56). He knew the Redeemer would come, and He knew that this would someday mean full covenant blessing through Him. That blessing happens when "Shiloh," the one to whom it belongs, comes and claims the king's scepter (Gen. 49:10; cf. Num. 24:17; Psa. 2:6-10; Zech. 6:12-13; 8:3; 14:9). The apostle places this occurrence at the *second coming* of Christ when He makes the New covenant with the remnant of Israel (Jer. 31:31-34; Rom. 11:25-27[3]). Thus, the redemption of all peoples has been achieved at Calvary. This is, in all cases, a New covenant redemption, or it is not a redemption at all. The *application* of the merits of Christ's sacrifice to the nation of Israel is *a second coming event*, occurring after the "days of vengeance" (Isa. 61:2b), at which time the outstanding covenant promises of peace, safety, prosperity, and land inheritance built into the other covenants will come to fruition, which is why so many times in the OT Israel's salvation is seen in terms of ethnic and geographical/agricultural blessing as well as spiritual salvation (e.g. Deut. 4:29-31; 30:5-6; Isa. 11:1-10; Hos. 2:16-20).[4]

Jesus is not Replacement Israel

At this juncture, it is necessary to debunk a recent ploy by supercessionists to arrogate Israel's covenant blessings for the Church by altering the names of the designees. Foremost among those who have done this are Graeme Goldsworthy and Greg Beale, but it is also the path taken by advocates of Progressive Covenantalism like Peter Gentry and Stephen Wellum.[5] How is this switch achieved?

The basic idea is that since Jesus is a Jew and He, unlike His countrymen, was obedient in all things, He is the only representative of Israel to inherit the covenant promises. Ergo, He stands in Israel's place as Israel and all the promises are fulfilled in Him—at His first coming! The Church fares better than national Israel because of its union with Christ. This means we can foul up and still inherit the blessings through Him. If anyone points out that this is both very unfair and disingenuous based on

2 David Noel Freedman, *Divine Commitment and Human Obligation: Ancient Israelite History and Religion*, Vol. 1 (Grand Rapids: Eerdmans, 1968), 173.

3 Paul cites two Isaianic New covenant passages.

4 New covenant truths are found mixed with the other covenants, especially in the Prophets (like Isa. 51:3, 6; 52:1-2, 9, 13; Jer. 23:5-8; 30:9-10; 32:37-41; 33:14-16; Ezek. 37:11-14, 21-26, etc.).

5 See Peter J. Gentry and Stephen J. Wellum, *Kingdom through Covenant*, 228, 243, 247, 598, 688-689, 716, and the charts on 619-620.

what God has promised Israel, the favorite proof-text, Romans 9:20 ("who are you to reply against God?...."), is quoted to stop the complaint in its tracks.

What none of these people can do is locate a text in Scripture that says anything like what they would like it to say. The best passage is Isaiah 49:3, which says, "And He said to Me, 'You are My Servant, Israel, in Whom I will show My glory.'"

In this verse, it is possible (even probable) that Messiah is referred to as "Israel."[6] But the context of Isaiah 49 makes it clear that He is not the *nation*, but rather He ensures the salvation and restoration of the nation (Isa. 49:5-6). Hence, Messiah is not ethnic Israel but "the Redeemer of Israel" (Isa. 49:7). Isaiah 49:6 also asserts, "He says, 'It is too small a thing that You should be My Servant to raise up the tribes of Jacob, and to restore the preserved ones of Israel; I will also make You a light of the nations so that My salvation may reach to the end of the earth'" (Isa. 49:6).

Not only will the Servant (Messiah) "raise up the tribes of Jacob, and restore the preserved ones of Israel," He will also bring salvation to the nations. Verse 7 tells Israel that God will do this because He is faithful! Then we get this: "Thus says the LORD, 'In a favorable time I have answered You, and in a day of salvation I have helped You; and I will keep You and give You for a covenant of the people, to restore the land, to make them inherit the desolate heritages'" (Isa. 49:7).

I have commented on this previously when we used it to show that Jesus *is* the New covenant. By this, I mean to say that He becomes the New covenant because He is the One who is *the Sacrifice* (Eph. 5:2; Heb. 9:16-17), and He is the One who Mediates it (Heb. 9:15; 1 Tim. 2:5). To be connected to Christ's resurrected life is also to be connected to the New covenant. Notice also how the land promise to Israel is alive and well. Consider this in the context:

> But Zion said, "The LORD has forsaken me, And the Lord has forgotten me." Can a woman forget her nursing child, and have no compassion on the son of her womb? Even these may forget, but I will not forget you. Behold, I have inscribed you on the palms of My hands; Your walls are continually before Me (Isa. 49:16).

These words are spoken to national Israel[7]—in particular, to "the preserved ones" (the remnant) of verse 6. The upshot is that those who identify Christ as Israel yet fail to read how He is their Surety have misused a text for their own aims, and been willfully careless about reading in context. Jesus ensures the covenant survival of national Israel in their God-given land (cf. Matt. 19:28; Acts 26:6-7). No wonder, since, like it or not, Israel is still the apple of God's eye (Zech. 2:8). Hence, Israel is one eschatological people of God.

6 I am also inclined to think Jn. 15:1 with Jer. 2:21 and Psa. 80:8 corroborate this.

7 Note, "Your walls" (Isa. 49:16c).

The Church is a New Testament Institution

First of all, we must dismiss this view, held by many pious men throughout history, that the Church is in the OT. The New covenant was not made in the OT, and I have shown the Church to be a New covenant institution. The NT records the making of the New covenant in Jesus' blood (Lk. 22:20; 1 Cor. 11:25). This is why Jesus spoke of the Church as future in Matthew 16:18 (cf. Jn. 7:39). The Christian Church is the Body of Christ and is inescapably joined to the resurrection of Christ (Eph. 2:4-6; Col. 2:12; cf. 1 Cor. 12:13; Rom. 14:9). Thus, it was quite literally impossible for the Church to exist prior to the death and resurrection of Jesus. The Apostle Paul writes, "Therefore, my brethren, you also were made to die to the Law through the body of Christ, so <u>that you might be joined to another, to Him who was raised from the dead</u>, in order that we might bear fruit for God" (Rom. 7:4, my emphasis).

The Great Commission could not be given until "all power" was given to the risen Christ (Matt. 28:18ff.). The preaching in the book of Acts relies on the resurrection (Acts 2:14, 24; 4:2; 10:40; 13:22-23; 15:6-11; 17:18, etc.). Paul's admonitions to holiness in Romans 6 are predicated on our vital connection to the resurrection. Moreover, the Church is built upon Christ (1 Cor. 3:11; cf. Rom. 10:9) and "the apostles and [NT] prophets" (Eph. 2:20). If the Church is a New covenant community (as it is in 2 Cor. 3), it stands to reason that it could not be in existence before the New covenant was made.

All this means that those saved *before* the inauguration of the Church, both among the nations and in ancient Israel, are separate from the Church. Israel was (cf. Hos. 2:2; Jer. 3:8) and shall be (Hos. 2:19) married to Yahweh—whom we equate in most instances with God the Father. The Church shall be married to Christ (2 Cor. 11:2; Eph. 5:25, 32; Rev. 19:6-9). We cannot entertain a theology that has these OT saints in some suspended animation until Jesus has died and risen, only to then be joined surreptitiously to the NT Body of Christ. Though we insist that their salvation was firmly grounded in the foreseen merits of the cross, that is not the same thing as declaring them all within the sphere of the Church. There is no necessity forced upon us by Scripture to include the saints of all the ages within the Church.

By Intention the Church is Mainly Gentile

Another often overlooked point, but one that ought to be considered, is the frank truth that the Church, although it has its seeds in Jewish soil (Acts 1–7), is intentionally predominantly Gentile in its constitution. The Apostolic teaching is that the Church's design is to bring the Gentiles into relationship with God. This can be viewed along at least two related lines:

1. The Jews rejected Christ and are judicially blinded to this very day (Rom. 11:8-10, 25, 28).

2. We are awaiting "the fullness of the Gentiles" (Rom. 11:25). Once this period has concluded, God will once again turn to Israel—the natural branches (one of the worst exegetical foul-ups is to equate the Olive Tree with its branches!).

Although any Jew who today repents and receives Jesus as Savior is incorporated into the Church (Eph. 2:12-16),[8] Paul teaches that God will yet deal again with the nation of Israel, "the natural branches."

What the Church Is

The Church is, at its core, a called together population of redeemed peoples, Jew and Gentile, but mostly Gentile, permanently indwelt by the Spirit, and betrothed to the risen Christ. Because this conception is unknown within the pages of the OT, the Church as "the Body of Christ" is called "the mystery which has been hidden from ages and from generations, but now has been revealed to His saints" (Col. 1:26). It is not, contrary to some, that the concept of the Church was known by OT saints but not realized until the NT era. That blatantly contradicts Paul's statement in Colossians 1. Rather, the idea of the Church was "hidden in God" (Eph. 3:9); it was a secret (*musterion*) that no one but God knew about until God disclosed it.[9]

Everyone understands that the OT is filled with promises of salvation for the Gentile nations. It is the presence of these promises that smooths out the transition between the Testaments and explains the "lack of surprise" at the Church's existence in the apostolic writings. But this turning to the Gentiles because of the neglect of Messiah by Israel was no more foreseeable from an OT perspective than a huge time gap between the first and second advents was foreseeable.

The NT Church is a covenant entity. As we have seen, in Galatians 3 Paul explicitly relates the Church to the Abrahamic covenant. In Galatians 3:16 the apostle writes, "Now to Abraham and his Seed were the promises made. He does not say, 'And to seeds,' as of many, but as of one, 'And to your Seed,' who is Christ."

It is essential to carefully note the particular part of the Abrahamic covenant which the apostle assigns to the Church. Both in Galatians 3:8 and Romans 4:16-17 Paul assiduously picks out the promise of Genesis 12:3 and 22:18. He is not like those unconcerned exegetes who carelessly ascribe *all* the covenant promises contained within the Abrahamic covenant to the Church.

What might be called my main thesis is that Christ will perform all this restorative and promissory work by the New covenant, which, in Him (Isa. 49:8), provides

8 Contra N. T. Wright (*Paul and the Faithfulness of God*, 1443-1449), these verses in Eph. 2 are not to be understood as asserting that, in Christ, Jews are no longer Jews and Gentiles no longer Gentiles, only that Jew and Gentile are one in the Church. Hence, Jewish Christians are not bound to divest themselves of their OT covenantal traditions as long as those "markers" are not pushed on Gentile believers (which would be Galatianism).

9 See Jeremy M. Thomas, "The 'Mystery' of Progressive Dispensationalism," *Conservative Theological Journal* 9 (Dec 2005), 297ff.

the requisite cleansing unto righteousness that obligates God to fulfill His covenants. This Christ-centered approach is what I call "Biblical Covenantalism."

Distinguishing Israel and the Church

I have shown that there is a solid case—given the promises of God vouchsafed to the nation Israel (especially in the OT) and to the Church (exclusively in the NT), together with the separate "betrothals" of Israel to God the Father (e.g. Isa. 54:5), and the Church to the Lord Jesus (Eph. 5:31)—to distinguish between them in the eschaton. I see no reason to paper over these distinctions for the sake of some forced union in the coming aeon. The passages I have called attention to in this volume and its predecessor are as authoritative as anything else in the Word of God and must not be ignored simply because they make people uncomfortable. Attempting to force together biblical texts that point to a plurality of redeemed people-groups and make them refer to one group for the sake of perceived theological tidiness always results in the debasement of "uncooperative" texts, and also of those people. Think, for example, of what would happen to the Jews as Jews if they were all absorbed into the Gentile Church over the centuries—there would be none left, and God's covenant promises to them would be incapable of fulfillment. There is a difference between union and unity. I believe Christ brings covenantal unity but in plurality.

If the Bible, which is one Book, declares that God will save and restore Israel nationally (and it certainly does), after which time Israel will act as a magnet attracting the nations (cf. Isa. 2:2-4; Ezek. 37:20-28; Zech. 8:22-23; 14:16-19), and this turn of events is yet to occur, then that teaching must find a place within our theology. A man who will not make peace with the passages we have adduced, but who instead enters into a kind of skirmish with them, is not placing himself under their authority. I am not saying counterarguments cannot be brought forward. If they can be, then they should be. But when clear declarations of Scripture are passed over because they do not square with a certain theological preference, we cannot say that there is a true commitment to the whole counsel of God.

Before Israel

There was a lot of time that passed and a multitude of people who were saved before the call of Abraham. Prior to Abraham, Isaac, Jacob, and the twelve tribes, there was no "chosen people" whom God singled out for His own (Psa. 114:7; 1 Ki. 8:48, 53; Isa. 2:3; 43:1, 21). Sinners were saved, but they were not within Israel. This hardly requires any proof. Since these saints were not part of Israel (which was not yet in existence), which people-group will they be in at the close of history?

Job was probably contemporary with Isaac and Jacob, and he certainly entertained hope of a resurrected life (Job 19:25-27). Was he an Israelite without knowing it? Is it not more likely that he joins those like Noah and Melchizedek within another set of saved humanity? The saved of the nations?

Before the Church

I have shown that the Church was not in existence until after the resurrection of Jesus (e.g., Eph. 1:20-22; 4:7-12). We cannot, therefore, avail ourselves of the rather too convenient remedy of placing the saints of all ages into the Body of Christ. This answer can have absolutely no warrant unless someone can demonstrate how this can be. Nobody has yet proved it to my knowledge, although many unsatisfactory arguments have been used to try to accomplish it. If the Church is not in the OT, and there are people outside of Israel who were saved before or during the era of the Abrahamic and the Mosaic covenants, they can neither be in Israel nor in the Church.

After the Church

We realize that there is now no salvation outside the Body of Christ (Eph. 2:20-22), but we must also realize that the Body of Christ hasn't always been here. Nor will it be here after it has been removed once "the fulness of the Gentiles has come in" (Rom. 11:25). Paul's argument in Romans 11:11-30 is of great importance here. I'm not sure it's a great idea visually, but I divide the passage below with some notations. The biblical text is in italics:

> *I say then, they did not stumble* [cf. Rom. 9:32-33] *so as to fall, did they? May it never be! But by their transgression salvation has come to the Gentiles, to make them jealous. Now if their transgression be riches for the world and their failure be riches for the Gentiles*
>
> The world is "the Gentiles," who we have said are the main peoples who comprise the Church.
>
> *how much more will their fulfillment be!* [there is to be a future "fulfillment" for Israel] *But I am speaking to you who are Gentiles. Inasmuch then as I am an apostle of Gentiles, I magnify my ministry, if somehow I might move to jealousy my fellow countrymen and <u>save some of them</u>.*
>
> Paul is aware that only some Israelites will be saved now.
>
> *For if their rejection be the reconciliation of the world, what will their acceptance be but life from the dead?*
>
> Though Israel has been "rejected," they will be "accepted," which fits Hosea 2.
>
> *And if the first piece of dough be holy, the lump is also; and if the root be holy, the branches are too.*
>
> This begins the Olive Tree metaphor, which is so often misunderstood.
>
> *But if some of the branches were broken off, and you* [Gentiles], *being a wild olive, were grafted in among them and became partaker <u>with them of the rich</u>*

root of the olive tree, [since Israel is the branches broken off, the "root" cannot BE Israel] *do not be arrogant toward the branches; but if you are arrogant, remember that it is not you who supports the root, but the root supports you.*

Whatever the root is, it is firstly Israel's root.

You will say then, "Branches were broken off so that I might be grafted in." Quite right, they were broken off for their unbelief, but you stand by your faith. Do not be conceited, but fear; for if God did not spare the natural branches [Israel], *neither will He spare you. Behold then the kindness and severity of God; to those who fell, severity, but to you, God's kindness, if you continue in His kindness; otherwise you also will be cut off.*

Which may perhaps allude to the future apostasy in 2 Thessalonians 2:3.

And they also, if they do not continue in their unbelief, will be grafted in; for God is able to graft them in again. [how can Israel be grafted into Israel?] *For if you were cut off from what is by nature a wild olive tree,* [probably the world system] *and were grafted contrary to nature into a cultivated olive tree, how much more shall these who are the natural branches be grafted into their own olive tree?*

The question to be answered, then, is, "What is the olive tree?"

For I do not want you, brethren, to be uninformed of this mystery, lest you be wise in your own estimation, that a partial hardening has happened to Israel [the natural branches] *until the fulness of the Gentiles has come in;*

Israel must wait for this "until" the fulness of the Gentiles, which awaits the "fulness of the Gentiles."

and thus all Israel [the nation, see 11:1-3] *will be saved; just as it is written, "The Deliverer will come from Zion,*

Jerusalem; more precisely, the city of David (cf. 1 Kings 8:1).

He will remove ungodliness from Jacob." [again showing the nation is in view] *"And this is My covenant with them, When I take away their sins."*

This is the New covenant since that is the covenant which takes away sins.

From the standpoint of the gospel they are enemies for your sake, but from the standpoint of God's choice they are beloved for the sake of the fathers; [Abraham, Isaac, and Jacob] *for the gifts and the calling of God are irrevocable.*

When God gives gifts to a people and makes covenant promises, He will ensure the gifts get to those to whom they were given, and the covenants will be

> fulfilled in precisely the way He made them. It is these covenant promises that are the "trunk" of the Olive tree (Rom. 9:4-5; 11:26-27).[10]

Israel will receive its covenanted gifts through first receiving salvation via the New covenant in Christ (Rom. 11:26-27). These gifts to the remnant of Israel will come from God's oaths in the Abrahamic, Priestly, and Davidic covenants mediated through the New covenant. The Church will receive those covenant blessings meant for it (Gal. 3:29; Eph. 2:4-7; 1 Pet. 1:4), also through the New covenant. But is there a third people group?

The Nations Coming to Israel's Light

We have seen that Revelation 21 has those inhabiting New Jerusalem (whom I have equated with the Church), but it also mentions "the nations [that] shall walk by its light, and the kings of the earth shall bring their glory into it. And in the daytime (for there shall be no night there) its gates shall never be closed; and they shall bring the glory and the honor of the nations into it" (Rev. 21:24-26).

Clearly, unless one is prepared, under the guise of so-called "apocalyptic literature," to deny what this text affirms, there will be distinguishable nations in the new heavens and new earth. These nations comprise a third eschatological grouping. Israel will be *among* these nations on the new earth (and before that in the Millennial Kingdom), but they will also be a separate entity from them. This statement cannot be proved from Revelation 21, but it can be shown to be so from other biblical texts.

Isaiah 11:1-10, which occurs when "He will strike the earth with the rod of His mouth" (v. 4; cf. Rev. 12:5), that is, at His second coming and reign (Psa. 2:9; Rev. 2:27; 19:15), when creation is restored (Isa. 11:6-9; cf. Hos. 2:18; Acts 3:19-21; Rom. 8:18-23), indicates that at that time the nations will be gathered to the Lord. Zechariah 8:22 declares there will come a time when "many peoples and mighty nations will come to seek the LORD of hosts in Jerusalem and to entreat the favor of the LORD."

This is to occur precisely in connection with Gentiles wishing to follow redeemed Israel in worship of the true God (Zech. 8:23; cf. Mic. 4:1-2; Isa. 2:2-3). The timing is when "I will return to Zion and will dwell in the midst of Jerusalem. Then Jerusalem will be called the City of Truth" (Zech. 8:3).

The verses that close the book of Zechariah, which come after the Lord's return (14:4), tell the same story (Zech. 14:9, 16ff.). Zephaniah 3:9-20 relates it again. *What these passages have in common is that they are set within the context of Christ's second advent and Kingdom reign.* When the everlasting nature of Israel's covenants is considered (e.g., Psa. 105:10; Num. 25:13; Jer. 32:37-41; Ezek. 37:26) and placed in the context of the New Creation of Revelation 21, the resultant picture is inevitable: *there will be three peoples of God—Israel, the Church, and the Nations.* But as these passages also make clear, *there will be close fellowship among them, a triad of peoples reflecting the persons of the Trinity*—a real brotherhood of man. To quote a recent

10 A tree may be deprived of all its branches, but it is still a tree. Branches by themselves without a trunk are not a tree.

writer, "Human life is nationed life on a national homeland, and the Bible's soteriological project intends to bring God's light and life to all human social and national structures. Salvation intends to redeem human *theocratic* life."[11]

In the end there will be three peoples of God and one people of God. There will be nations of peoples in the New Creation. And no wonder, isn't human society made to image God as much as the individual human being?

A Summary of the Three Peoples in One Concept

A triad is a group of three. As used by theologians like John Frame, it refers to the three-in-oneness of an entity. In Appendix A of his *The Doctrine of God*,[12] Frame lists many examples, some of the most obvious being:

1. Length, width, height
2. Beginning, middle, end
3. I, you, he
4. Faith, hope, love
5. The world, the flesh and the devil
6. Thought, word, deed
7. Liquid, solid, gas
8. Past, present, future
9. Husband, wife, child
10. Melody, harmony, rhythm

Some of the more interesting ones have to do with Speech-Acts: locution, illocution, perlocution; Ethical perspectives: teleological deontological, existential; and divine disclosure: revelation, inspiration, illumination. Frame himself has become known for his triad of "Lordship Attributes": Control, authority, and presence, as well as his viewing of things from situational, normative, and existential perspectives.[13] These are all three-in-one and one-in-three. They reflect the world as it is in both its material and immaterial aspects. All I am calling attention to here is that it should not seem

11 Mark R. Saucy, "One Nation under God," in *The Future Restoration of Israel: A Response to Supercessionism*, eds. Stanley E. Porter and Alan E. Kurschner (Eugene, OR: Pickwick Publications, 2023), 131.

12 John M. Frame, *The Doctrine of God: A Theology of Lordship* (Phillipsburg, NJ: P&R, 2002), 743-750.

13 Ibid., 36-102.

surprising to anyone that those made in the image of the Triune God would compose a triad of peoples. Take a look out of the window; God loves variety (cf. Acts 17:26).[14]

I have explained that the Father's particular connection with Israel and the Son's particular relation to the Church is set forth quite plainly in the Bible. I can find no similar teaching concerning the relation of the nations to the Holy Spirit. But since in the age to come, "the earth will be full of the knowledge of the LORD As the waters cover the sea" (Isa. 11:9), it is feasible at least that a special Spirit-nations relationship will be revealed in the future Kingdom. If not, the silence cannot be used as an argument against the Father-Israel relation (Isa. 54:5) or the Christ-Church relation (Eph. 5:25, 29).

Saying all this does not mean that the Father does not bear a loving relationship with the Church, nor that the Son does not bear a loving communion with Israel. We are not forced by any of this to regard the divine affections as split between competing parties. The Trinity directs love to bless all God's elect. The unique relations that at least two of the divine Persons have toward Israel and the Church respectively should perhaps be seen as expressions of the unique attributes of each *hypostasis*: paternity, sonship, and procession in an extra-trinitarian movement.

The covenantal relation of both groups to Christ is a fundamental fact of salvation and hope. Christ is "set forth" by the Father and the Spirit to bring humanity to the Godhead, and I am suggesting that this will be done with Israel, the Church, and the gathered nations enjoying special (though not exclusive) relationships with Father, Son, and Holy Spirit respectively.

Be that as it may, let us not miss the main point. The Bible reveals that three people-groups from human history will be present in the eschaton. This is assured by the covenants that God has made and shall fulfill with these parties; covenants that He has placed Himself under obligation to fulfill. And God will certainly fulfill His own covenant word in accordance with His truthful and unchanging character. The means by which this three-in-one scheme will be achieved is through the Lord Jesus Christ, who is Israel's Messiah, the Church's Head, and the nations' Light (another triad!).

14 It ought to be noted that within the nations themselves there will be a great deal of variety.

21

THE CHRISTOCENTRISM OF THE BIBLE

The first man was of the earth, made of dust; the second Man is the Lord from heaven. - 1 Corinthians 15:47

God is Only as Good as His Word

Centuries passed before the time of the birth of Jesus. He was born in the small hamlet of Bethlehem Judah around the year 7–5 B.C.[1] Bethlehem was the town where David was born (1 Sam. 17:12), and also was the place where the Messiah would come from (Mic. 5:2). Yahweh had pinpointed Bethlehem so no other birthplace would be accepted for the Christ. Not Jerusalem, not Rome, but tiny Bethlehem. God means what He says. And the Messiah would be born precisely at the time Yahweh had chosen (Gal. 4:4).

Luke records the angel's proclamation: "He will be great, and will be called the Son of the Highest; and the Lord God will give Him the throne of His father David. And He will reign over the house of Jacob forever, and of His kingdom there will be no end" (Lk. 1:32-33).

What happened? After Jesus was born, He lived in obscurity until bursting onto the scene around the year A.D. 26,[2] heralded by the imposing figure of John the Baptist (Jn. 1:19-34). He uttered words of wisdom that no one had heard the like of before (Jn. 7:46), and performed incredible miracles beyond what even Elijah and Elisha managed (e.g., Matt. 12:15; 14:13-21; Mk. 1:21-29, 40-42; 2:10-12; 3:1-5, 11; Jn. 5:2-9; 9:1-7; 11:38-44).

1 This dating is approximate but is very plausible. See e.g., Ethelbert Stauffer, *Jesus and His Story* (NY: Alfred A. Knopf, 1967), 6-8.

2 See, e.g., Harold W. Hoehner, *Chronological Aspects of the Life of Christ* (Grand Rapids: Zondervan, 1977), 30-31.

But He was rejected and crucified (Mk. 8:31; Acts 4:11; 1 Pet. 2:4); this "King" who would supposedly reign forever (Mk. 15:25). He rose from the dead (Rom. 14:9) and ascended back into heaven (Lk. 24:50-51; Acts 1:11), where He has been at the right hand of the throne of God ever since (Eph. 1:20; Col. 3:1), and where He is interceding for the saints. But He is not reigning over them (Rom. 8:34; Heb. 8:1).[3] Although it is true that the spiritual powers have been made subject to Him (1 Pet. 3:22), there is yet no sign of the prophesied reign of *shalom* that was expected on the back of so many OT promises (e.g., Psa. 2:6-8; 110:2; Mic. 4:7; 5:2; Isa. 1:27; 2:4; 9:6-7; 11:1-10; 32:16; 42:1, 4; Jer. 23:5; 33:14-16; Dan. 2:44-45; 7:13-14; Zech. 2:10-12; 14:9).

The difference between what the covenant promises of the OT emphasized (and what was repeated by the angel Gabriel at Jesus' birth, Lk. 1:26-33) and what has happened since has caused many Christians to look for different interpretations of the prophecies to confirm their fulfillment in unexpected ways.

Well, if God is the kind of communicator who swears oaths to do specific things and then does them in unexpected ways, then He is the kind of communicator it is very hard to put faith in. Such a God did not do what He said He would do. We don't put faith in someone who has repeatedly shown that they don't mean what they say. We want them to be as good as their word. I realize that those who believe the "unexpected fulfillment" hypothesis think it makes God "better" than His word, but that is special pleading masquerading as piety.[4] Holding to this view logically entails us remaining noncommittal in the face of God's sworn testimony. We dare not believe what God says because we believe God's words might not mean what they appear to say. Hence, faith dies amid this uncertainty.

To fill in the void left by not believing that God's covenant words can be taken literally, many claim that Christ is to be seen in every text of Scripture. The *way* they see Him, however, is via typology—an interpretive practice that too often acts as a ruse. Not that some typological correspondences aren't real, but many times, they are read into the text rather than being suggested by it.

The Lord from Heaven

As the text at the head of this chapter declares,[5] Jesus Christ came to restore what Adam forfeited. Adam is "the first man" and, by implication, the head of the human race. Unfortunately, the human race has fallen in Adam (1 Cor. 15:22a) and must be disconnected from him if it is to be redeemed. Adam's doom was to return to the dust from whence he was made (Gen. 2:7; 3:19).

3 Many amillennialists hold that Christ is reigning over the saints in heaven. But this is an anticlimax judging by Lk. 1:32-33, not to mention the covenant prophecies in the OT (e.g., Psa. 2:6, 9; Isa. 11:1-10; Jer. 23:5-6; Zech. 14:16-19; cf. Matt. 19:28; Heb. 10:12-13).

4 In my opinion, the same thing is true of supersessionism. See e.g., Miguel G. Echevarria and Benjamin P. Laird, *40 Questions About the Apostle Paul* (Grand Rapids: Kregel, 2023), 302-305.

5 "The first man was of the earth, made of dust; the second Man is the Lord from heaven" (1 Cor. 15:47).

This is where "the second Man" enters in. Jesus is not from Adam's line but is the exalted "Lord from heaven." Heaven had to come to fallen earth in the form of the Creator and Ruler of heaven itself to put humanity right again. That the creation was fixed by the Creator is no great surprise on the face of it. But for sinful human beings to be fixed, the Creator involved Himself in the deepest expression of love's self-humiliation. Let us remind ourselves of the roles that the Son of God had to take on so that we could be rescued:

1. The Son of God agreed to take a place lower than the Father so that He could serve the Father's purpose.

2. This service meant that the Son would have to become a creature, being dependent for years on his parents.

3. He was the most exalted Being, yet chose obscurity and hardship in His own world.

4. When He did embark upon a brief ministry, He met spiritual and political resistance from the most influential people of His day. He also frequently encountered "followers" with wrong motives who did not care to think upon His words.

5. He went through life knowing He would be rejected. He was the rightful King whom heaven recognized, but earth refused.

6. He was betrayed by one of His closest associates.

7. He was wrongly accused and convicted, then brutally beaten.

8. He endured the worst death Rome could dream up while being baited and laughed at in His agony and humiliation.

9 Even now, He watches as the risen Messiah as His name is used as a cuss word, and His claims are ignored by His own people and by so many who need His help.

10. As the second Man, Jesus remains a Man for eternity. The God-Man, yes, but a Man all the same.

The salvation of sinners is the greatest undertaking in all history. It could only be achieved by the greatest Person showing the greatest love and humility.

The Creator Dies in His Own Creation

It bears repeating that the Christocentric[6] orientation of Scripture may be summed up in this sentence: The Creator of the world became one of His creatures, but was rejected and murdered by them, dying for them and conquering death for them, and will one day return to reign in justice and peace over the world He put right.

This characterization of Christ's centrality to the Creation Project of God will be expanded below, but I do want to stress that one cannot validly push Christ into every nook and cranny of Scripture via typology and spiritualization and then lay claim to representing Scripture's Christocentricity. The importance of Christ in the Bible comes about as a result of two things: (1) Messianic prophecy and fulfillment, and (2) Christ's status as the second Person of the Divine Trinity. The first of these is, broadly speaking, more exegetical, while the second is more theological. Christ's importance does not come about by piously reading Him into texts of the Bible where He is plainly absent.

Real Christocentricity

When I say Christ is the central Person of Scripture, what I mean is that He is the central Protagonist of God's Creation Project. God created all things through Jesus Christ (Eph. 3:9, Jn. 1:3), and all things created through Him were also created for Him (Col. 1:16). At this present hour the whole creation is upheld through Him (Col. 1:17; Heb. 1:3). He is the Lord of all (Acts 10:36) and is therefore the only one who has the wisdom and the power to overcome Satan (Matt. 4:1-11), which one day He will to the uttermost (Gen. 3:15).

That first inkling of His coming ("He shall bruise your head, and you shall bruise His heel," Gen. 3:15b) reveals Him as the one who will dislodge the interloper and knock him off his pedestal, reclaiming creation for God—for Himself. He would come from Israel, from the tribe of Judah, and would reign over the Kingdom (Gen. 49:8-10). He would be born in Bethlehem (Mic. 5:2), even though He was "from everlasting." This "encroachment" of the Creator into the Devil's realm came about because God is not about to give up on something He has made and gifted to His Son and let the Deceiver get away with it. Sin, Death, and Satan are no match for God. All three will be triumphed over through Christ (Jn. 1:29; 8:52; Rom. 5:21; 6:9; 16:20; 1 Cor. 15:21-26; Heb. 2:9, 14; 9:26; 1 Jn. 3:8).

Jesus is the Messiah, the Christ (Psa. 45:6-7; Heb. 1:8-9; Matt. 26:63-64; Lk. 3:22; 1 Jn. 5:6), the King of Israel (Zech 9:9; Matt. 2:1-6; Lk. 1:29-33), who will also rule over the entire world (Psa. 2:8; Isa. 11:1-10; Rev. 11:15; Zech 14:9).

Perhaps the greatest of all ironies is that "He was in the world, and the world was made through Him, and the world did not know Him" (Jn. 1:10) since "He made Himself of no reputation" (Phil. 2:7). He is the stone that the builders rejected (Psa.

---

6 It might help if I say something about the difference between "Christocentric" and "Christotelic" aspects of Scripture, especially in Reformed theology. Basically, a Christotelic reading of Scripture is that which holds that the OT authors anticipated or predicted (as in alluded to) Christ, even though they may not have been fully cognizant of the prediction. A Christocentric reading holds that the OT authors knew they were writing about Christ.

118:22; Matt. 21:42), who is the stone that will smash all of the kingdoms of man and set up God's Kingdom upon earth (Dan. 2:45).

The OT is a story about Israel (Exodus–2 Chronicles), and its main figure is the coming Messiah (e.g., Deut. 18:15-19; Psa. 2:8-10; 22:1-31; 110:1-4; Isa. 9:6-7; 11:1-10; 42:1-7; 49:3-13; 52:11-53:12; Jer. 23:5-6; 33:14-16; Dan. 7:13-14; 9:26; Mic. 5:2; Zech. 9:9-10; 12:10; 13:7; Mal. 3:1; 4:1-2). Reading these prophecies at face value should persuade anyone that Israel's hope is intertwined with their completed fulfillment in the first *and* second comings of Jesus Christ.

The NT is a story about Israel (e.g., The Synoptics, Hebrews, Revelation) and about the Church (e.g., John, Acts, Epistles of Paul, Hebrews), though often their fortunes are connected (e.g., Romans, Hebrews, James, Epistles of Peter, Revelation). This is not to say, for example, that the Synoptics are not for the Church, only that they mostly record Jesus' mission to Israel prior to the inception of the Church in Acts 2. Thus, the "gospel" preached in the Synoptics did not include Christ's death and resurrection like it would after His ascension (1 Cor. 15:1-4). In the Church, the love of God is found in Jesus Christ (Rom. 8:29), and through Him, access by the Spirit to the Father (Eph. 2:18). The Church is not a geopolitical entity like Israel. Therefore, it cannot be the recipient of geopolitical promises made to Israel. Differences must be observed even more than similarities.

The Covenants and The Messianic Hope

Once the messianic prophecies get going in the Hebrew Bible, it does not take long for them to become closely connected to the divine covenants. A moment's thought should hardly find this surprising as God is the Father of the Messiah, and His covenantal plan structures the Creation Project, which, in the end, is for Christ (Col. 1:16).

The story of the Christ begins before the covenants of God come to be. From before the foundation of the world (1 Pet. 1:20; Rev. 13:8), Jesus had a body prepared for Him (Heb. 10:5). This body enabled the Son of God, the divine Logos, to experience life as a weak human being. Looking at Him, there would be nothing to indicate that He was "the Lord of Glory" (1 Cor. 2:8; cf. Isa. 53:2).

The first covenant we read about in the Bible is the Noahic covenant found in Genesis 9:1-17 with the specific oath in Genesis 9:11.[7] That is, only after the great flood did Yahweh make a covenant with men. I only record this phenomenon; I do not have an explanation for it other than to surmise that covenants apply only in "the heavens and the earth which are now" (2 Pet. 3:7).

The second covenant we come across in the Bible is the covenant with Abraham, first referred to in Genesis 12:1-7 and initiated in Genesis 15. The oath of the covenant is three-pronged. God made an oath to give Abraham a son (Gen. 15:4) from whom a race of descendants would come (Gen. 15:5), and to whom a specified land

7 I go into my reasons for saying this, as well as for rejecting the ideas of a covenant of redemption, works, grace, creation, or even an Adamic and Edenic covenant in *The Words of the Covenant*, Vol. 1, 116-120.

would be given (Gen. 15:12-21). None of the Abrahamic texts tell us that the covenant includes salvation from sin. Immediately someone will want to point me to Genesis 22:18, "In your seed all the nations of the earth shall be blessed, because you have obeyed My voice." Paul's note in Galatians 3:16 that this text points to Christ tells us that Christ, as a descendant of Abraham (Matt. 1:1), does fulfill the hope of Genesis 12:3; 18:18; 22:18; 26:4; and 28:14 (cf. Gal. 3:8). However, while Christ's redemptive act secures blessing for the Gentiles (Acts 11:18), the Abrahamic covenant only supplies the Agent of salvation via genealogy, but not the salvation itself.[8] The terms of the

Abrahamic covenant, like the terms of the Noahic, Mosaic, Priestly, and Davidic covenants, do not include the promise of redemption and the forgiveness of sin.

As revelation continues, we encounter messianic prophecy coming into contact with covenant promise in Jacob's blessing of Judah in Genesis 49:8-10:

> Judah, you are he whom your brothers shall praise;
> Your hand shall be on the neck of your enemies;
> Your father's children shall bow down before you.
> Judah is a lion's whelp;
> From the prey, my son, you have gone up.
> He bows down, he lies down as a lion;
> And as a lion, who shall rouse him?
> The scepter shall not depart from Judah,
> Nor a lawgiver from between his feet,
> Until Shiloh comes;
> And to Him shall be the obedience of the people.

Verse 8 declares that Judah will prevail over all his enemies and will be the preeminent tribe. This is because of the one to come, the one who will lie down like a lion (Gen. 49:9)—a line which is repeated by Balaam in Numbers 24:9 alongside a strong allusion to the Abrahamic covenant in Genesis 12:3.[9] We see then that an individual is in view, and this impression is confirmed by the next verse. According to Genesis 49:10, a "Him" will yield the scepter of power over Israel.[10] Balaam again repeats this promise in Numbers 24:17:

> I see Him, but not now;
> I behold Him, but not near;
> A Star shall come out of Jacob;
> A Scepter shall rise out of Israel

8 Much the same could be said for the Davidic covenant.

9 Additionally, Num. 24:8a includes the line, "God brings him out of Egypt," which appears to stand behind Hos. 11:1. See John H. Sailhamer, "Hosea 11:1 And Matthew 2:15," *WTJ* 63 (Spring 2001), 94-95.

10 It is probable that the "king" and the "kingdom" predicted by Balaam in Num. 24:7 refers to Christ.

Moreover, the psalmist refers to this scepter in Psalm 45:6, which is then applied directly to Christ by the author of Hebrews (Heb. 1:8). With these references to Him being a King, the Messiah is being connected to the coming covenant with David (2 Sam. 7; 1 Chron. 17; Psa. 89; 132).

Once history brings us to the exodus and the wilderness journeys, Moses is given a prophecy about an individual like him who will speak God's words to the people (Deut. 28:15-19). This, of course, is in the context of the Mosaic covenant.

From the time of the Mosaic covenant to the crucifixion and resurrection of Jesus Christ, all subsequent covenants of God (namely, the Davidic and Priestly) come under the auspices of the Mosaic covenant, although they also transcend it. This is because the Davidic and Priestly covenants, along with the Abrahamic covenant, are "everlasting" covenants, whereas the Mosaic covenant is not.[11] What replaces the Mosaic covenant is the New covenant. With the New covenant, we get redemption through faith in a substitute supplied to wayward mankind. A change of mind through a "new heart" by the Spirit (Deut. 30:5-6; Ezek. 36:26-27; 2 Cor. 3:3). This is what is absolutely necessary if the Abrahamic, Priestly, and Davidic covenants are to be fulfilled to the letter.

If one tries to imagine Israel being placed in their covenanted land forever without receiving their Messiah, it is unthinkable. Therefore, the Abrahamic and Davidic covenants are unfulfillable without the work of the Spirit to change the heart (Ezek. 36:27; 37:14; Jer. 24:7; 31:34; cf. Jn. 3:3, 5). That is, they are unfulfillable without the New covenant. And the New covenant is all about Jesus Christ!

Let this statement settle down into your mind and heart. God's oaths are in Scripture to end all dispute (Heb. 6:16)! But what could be in dispute? How about God's Creation Project?[12]

I have tried to show that the NT story fully complies with this covenant structure, especially once the New covenant is understood as being made with the "new man" (Eph. 2:15), the Church beginning at the first advent. But this same New covenant awaits its predicted OT fulfillments at Jesus' second coming. How can all this be known and known for certain? The answer is here: God has made covenant oaths that ought to drive away misunderstanding and "end all dispute." The "two immutable things" (Heb. 6:18) are the Word of God and God's covenant oaths, which confirm it.[13] Since God's covenants are made to end all dispute, it behooves the people of God to make them so. That is Biblical Covenantalism. Biblical Covenantalism, defined as

11 Daniel Block says the same thing about the "Israelite" (Mosaic) covenant too, by referencing Lev. 24:8 and Exod. 31:16-17 (*Covenant*, 276, cf. 288). But Lev. 24:8 is about the bread offering on the Sabbath and Exod. 31:16-17 is about keeping the Sabbath. Neither reference is about the (Mosaic) covenant itself! As a matter of fact, the Bible *never* calls the Mosaic/Sinaitic covenant "everlasting." How could it, since it is superseded by the New covenant (Heb. 8:13; 9:15)?

12 For a brief summary of God's creation project, see page 432 earlier in this volume.

13 Harold W. Attridge, *The Epistle to the Hebrews*, Hermeneia (Philadelphia: Fortress, 1989), 181.

the Bible's real covenantal teaching,[14] is "an anchor for the soul" (Heb. 6:19), which is secured by Jesus Christ Himself as our High Priest (Heb. 6:20).

The Kingdom of Christ is the New covenant Kingdom. In that Kingdom, Israel will be given its Abrahamic land (Gen. 15:18), and the Son of David will sit upon the dynastic throne in Jerusalem (Isa. 9:7; Lk. 1:32-33; Matt. 19:28).

But what about the Priestly covenant with Phinehas and his heirs (Num. 25:10-13; Psa. 106:28-31)? I wrote about this in the first volume,[15] and as far as my lights take me, I believe that the absence of a High Priest in Ezekiel's Millennial Temple (Ezek. 40–48) is because Jesus, as the High Priest after the Order of Melchizedek, will preside over it. As He combines the high priesthood and the kingship in Himself (Zech. 6:13), Jesus will bring unity between the two. Thus, by Him, Yahweh will redeem and beautify His created order, and Jesus, the Son of God, will be the most glorious Being in the Creation Project, until eternity dawns and new experiences of life with God unfold.

In the End

In the end, everything is down to the coming King who was waited for under many names: the Seed of the woman (Gen. 3:15); Shiloh, "the One to whom it [the scepter] belongs" (Gen. 49:10); the Prophet (Deut. 18:15-19); the Commander of the Lord's host (Josh. 5:14-15); the Branch (Isa. 11:1; Jer. 23:5; Zech. 6:14); Immanuel (Isa. 7:14); the Prince of Peace (Isa. 9:6); the Servant of Yahweh (Isa. 42:1-8; 53:1-12); the Messenger of the Covenant (Mal. 3:1). He is "the Son of Man" (Dan. 7:13), the Messiah, the Prince (Dan. 9:25). Now He *has* come.

> He was in the world, and the world was made through Him, and the world did not know Him. He came to His own, and His own did not receive Him. But as many as received Him, to them He gave the right to become children of God, to those who believe in His name (Jn. 1:10-12).

His name is the Lord Jesus Christ, and He is coming back!

All praise be to Jesus Christ through the Spirit to the glory of the Father. The God of the covenants! Amen.

14 My attempt at following the Bible's covenantal teaching is not to be confused with the infallible doctrine of the Bible itself. I am simply trying my best to provide an accurate account. Hence, one should distinguish between the noun (my name for my approach), and the adjective (Scripture's revelation of the covenants). Hopefully, there is a close correspondence!

15 *The Words of the Covenant*, Vol. 1, 167-168.

Summary of Part Eight

The Apocalypse

• The book of Revelation is primarily a prophecy.

• Because Revelation is such a hermeneutical hornet's nest, it is necessary to set out the correct approach to its teaching, including its imagery, as dictated by the divine covenants.

• Revelation contains a blessing for those who "keep" its words. But its words cannot be kept unless they are plain enough to be understood. Ergo, the book must be interpreted with a "literal" as opposed to a "spiritual" hermeneutic.

• Eclectic-realist interpretations of Revelation, as practiced by many in Evangelical scholarship, turn the book into an obfuscation and not unveiling. Hence, there can be no middle ground between a dispensational premillennial approach and a non-literal "spiritual" approach.

• The book's narrative includes many allusions to the OT, in particular to the Prophets. These overlap with their characterization of the Last Days. Along with these allusions, one meets with many explanations (at least partial) of the meaning of John's images in the book.

• The Apocalypse has a very distinct Jewish look, especially after the first three chapters. Much of its vision matches depictions of the Great Tribulation in Daniel and the Olivet Discourse.

• There are a lot of covenant connections in Revelation, mostly to the Davidic covenant.

• The numbers in Revelation should be interpreted in a normative, plain-sense fashion and not spiritualized.

• Revelation 20 pointedly describes a one-thousand year reign of Christ on earth, where Satan is shut up in the abyss. Then Satan is released, but only to be defeated in accordance with the Bible's oldest prophecy (Gen. 3:15). Then comes the final judgment and the creation of the new heavens and earth.

• The Creation Project is completed at this time.

• The New Jerusalem is a literal cubed-shaped city of enormous size that descends from heaven to the new Earth. It appears to be the dwelling place of the Church, with the nations living around it.

The People(s) of God

• When the data of the rest of the NT is combined with Revelation 21 and 22, there is reason to think there will be a triad of peoples, a three-in-one humanity, in the New Creation.

• Jesus is the King and Messiah of the nation of Israel, and its covenants will be realized after His second coming.

• Hence, the Bible distinguishes Israel and the Church.

• A third people group will exist in eternity: the nations. These will comprise the saved throughout history, who are neither in the Church nor a part of restored Israel.

• This three-in-one character of the peoples of God will reflect the Trinity and will display another aspect of humanity's creation in God's image.

The Christocentrism of the Bible

• The Story of the Bible is only possible because of the Son of God, who is both co-Creator, Redeemer, and coming King of Creation. Biblical Covenantalism is deliberately Christocentric because the Person of Jesus Christ is at the heart of God's Creation Project.

• Real Christocentricity does not rely upon typology and spiritualization. Types exist, but they never drive the biblical narrative. The covenants of Yahweh drive the Bible's story, and they are fixed, not elastic, nor open to transformation.

• The Noahic, Abrahamic, Priestly, Davidic, and New covenants all have unconditional oaths which guarantee their literal fulfillment. That fulfillment is dependent upon the one work of the Lord Jesus Christ in His first and second advents, especially in His coming reign of peace, righteousness, and joy in the Kingdom of God.

APPENDICES

These appendices are provided to answer more fully some of the questions that may have arisen in the reader's mind while perusing the main text. Some of them are lengthy, and for that, I apologize, but I hope their length is justified. I wanted *The Words of the Covenant* to be self-contained, hence these essays. I've arranged them in some kind of a logical order.

APPENDIX A:

CONTRASTING DISPENSATIONALISM AND BIBLICAL COVENANTALISM

A Little Back-Story

As many of my readers will know, I have spent a lot of time and energy trying to place dispensational theology on what I believe is a more secure footing. Dispensationalism has not produced many top-line academic works, especially in the last half century, and with only one or two exceptions, it presents itself as static and unwilling to improve. In the meantime, it has been frozen out of mainstream evangelical scholarship, and its influence has dwindled. One example among many will suffice: the huge 8-volume IVP Dictionaries, which cover the entire Bible and are written by hundreds of top scholars across the broad sweep of evangelicalism, include scarcely any contribution by dispensational scholars. The *Dictionary of the Old Testament Prophets* has (as far as I can tell) only one entry by a dispensationalist: Robert Chisholm on "Retribution" (and I'm not sure Chisholm is much of a dispensationalist).[1]

In reflecting on the reasons for this, I eventually asked myself a rather obvious question: Does the Bible ground its biblical theology upon the dispensations or on something else? Re-reading the Bible with this question uppermost in my mind led me to the conclusion that the Bible does indeed base its theology on something other than changing administrations. It roots itself in the divine covenants! From this was born what I have called Biblical Covenantalism. It retains all that makes dispensationalism good,[2] but refocuses it on the covenants of God. The result is, I believe, a far more robust and intellectually promising system that is there to be developed.

1 Mark J. Boda and J. Gordon McConville, eds., *Dictionary of the Old Testament Prophets* (Downers Grove, IL: InterVarsity, 2012).

2 My approach retains and defends a normative plain-sense hermeneutic, a futurist premillennialism, a coming Tribulation and Antichrist figure, a distinction between Israel and the Church,

Anyway, here are what I think are the main contrasts between my approach (BC) and traditional dispensational theology (DT):

1. DT is led by its very name to define itself by an aspect of its approach which is really tangential to its overall genius. This definition circumscribes the outlook and understanding of its adherents and places blinkers (blinders) on their theological vision. Dispensations are just not that important; the biblical covenants are. Dispensationalism is limited because of what dispensations can do (i.e., describe one aspect).

BC defines itself by the covenants of God found within the pages of Scripture. Because these covenants, correctly understood, comprehend God's declared purposes for the creation (not just Israel, His chosen people), they expand one's theological vision. BC is expansive because of what the covenants of Scripture can do (i.e., describe a purpose and prescribe God's outlook).

2. DT derives its hermeneutics from "without" by asserting the normal or literal sense via grammatical-historical hermeneutics. There is little attempt to derive this hermeneutics from the Bible itself.

BC seeks to derive its hermeneutics (which corresponds to traditional grammatical-historical hermeneutics) from "within" the Bible itself, in deference to the Biblical Worldview. This acknowledges the comprehensive relationship between revelation and knowledge. There is a "God's words = God's actions" hermeneutical sequence in Scripture which is amplified by the covenants.

3. DT often struggles with the New covenant and its application. Some believe the New covenant is only for Israel; some believe that the Church somehow "participates" in the New covenant without being a party to it.

BC, because it pays special attention to the covenants and their inter-relationships, comprehends the Christocentric arrangement of the other covenants around the New covenant. Christ and the New covenant are identified with each other, allowing one to see how all beneficiaries of God's grace have a covenantal relation to Him in the end. Thus, the terms of the other covenants are released to be fulfilled once the parties to those covenants (whether national Israel or the Gentiles or both) have passed under the New covenant in Christ.

4. DT is not redemptively focused, meaning it does not concentrate on the teleological goals of God in Christ for the future of the whole created realm.

BC is redemptively focused in the sense given above.

---

a literal thousand-year intermediate Kingdom; and even a pretribulational rapture. In that sense, I am happy to be called a dispensational premillennialist. However, I cannot agree with Dispensationalism as a methodological system, since the divine covenants are far more prominent, sure, and prescriptive than the "dispensations" and how they are expounded in the major works.

5. DT tends, therefore, not to be as Christological as Covenant Theology.

BC is just as Christological as Covenant Theology, though not artificially reading Christ into foreign contexts. Stressing, as it does, the truth that this creation is made through and for Christ, is redeemed by Christ, and will be ruled over and restored by Christ.

6. DT tends to restrict its restrict its focus to the areas of ecclesiology and eschatology, which, in consequence, confines its thinking and productivity to those areas. It cannot be developed into a worldview system under these confines (hence, it is not prescriptive). This confinement is only exacerbated by the way dispensationalism defines itself.

BC is far more expansive, influencing every area of systematic theology and worldview through its reflection on the outcome and repercussions of the biblical covenants and the centrality of Christ.

7. DT emphasizes the end of the Bible and places little importance on the doctrine of Creation and its outworking in God's overall plan.

BC puts a lot of stress upon Creation and sees history in terms of the combined outworking of teleology and eschatology which was built into Creation from the beginning. The Bible is an eschatological (and also teleological) book from beginning to end.

8. DT uses dispensations as a category, which are not used by other theological viewpoints to describe their system. Hence, one ends up comparing apples with oranges.

BC, in contrast, stresses the covenants of God found within the Bible and can, therefore, engage in dialogue with those systems that employ theological covenants.

APPENDIX B:

FORTY REASONS FOR NOT REINTERPRETING THE OLD TESTAMENT WITH THE NEW TESTAMENT

Here are forty reasons (there could be more but it's a good number) why a student of the Bible should not adopt the common tactic of reading the NT back into the OT, with the resultant outcome that the clear statements of the OT passages are altered and mutated to mean something which, without universal prevenient prophetic inspiration, no OT saint (or NT saint who did not have access to the right apostolic books) could have known. If we come to the NT without the mental furniture provided by the OT, we will always be in danger of misrepresenting the teaching in *both* Testaments.[1]

I believe, of course, that the NT does throw much light upon the OT text. But it never imposes itself upon the OT in such a way as to essentially treat it as a sort of 'palimpsest' over which an improved NT message must be imposed.[2]

1. Neither Testament instructs us to reinterpret the OT by the NT. Hence, we venture into uncertain waters when we allow this.

2. It would mean no one could correctly interpret the OT until they had the NT. In many cases, this deficit would last for a good three centuries or more after the first coming of Jesus Christ.

---

1 The OT was, we must recall, the Bible of the first Christians.

2 By way of illustration, there are huge ramifications in making a dubious allusion in Jn. 7:38 to Zech. 14:8 a basis for a doctrine of the expansion of the spiritual temple over the face of the earth. Such a questionable doctrine essentially evaporates huge amounts of OT material from, e.g., Num. 25; Psa. 106; Isa. 2; 33; 49; Jer. 30–33; Ezek. 34; 36–37; 40–48; Amos 9; Mic. 4–5; Zeph. 3; Zech. 2; 6; 8; 12–14; and Mal. 3, as well as all those other passages which intersect with them. The cost is too high, as well as quite unnecessary.

3. It forces the NT into teaching things it never explicitly says (e.g., that the Church is "the New Israel" or the seventh day Sabbath is now the first day "Christian Sabbath").

4. It forces the OT into teaching things it really does not mean (e.g., that the Church is in the OT; that God has divorced Israel forever).

5. It would require the Lord Jesus to have used a brand-new set of hermeneutical rules (e.g., Lk. 24:44), rules not accessible until the completion and general availability of the entire NT. These would have to include rules for each "genre," which would not have been apparent to anyone interpreting the OT on its own terms.

6. If the OT cannot be interpreted without the NT, then what it says on its own account cannot be trusted, as it could well be a "type" or "shadow" needing to be reinterpreted by the NT.

7. Thus, it would mean the seemingly clear predictions about the coming One in the OT could not be relied upon to present a reliable, non-typological, non-symbolic picture needing to be deciphered by the NT. The most clearly expressed promises of God in the OT (e.g., Gen. 15; Jer. 33:15-26; Ezek. 40-48; Zech. 14:16-21) would be vulnerable to being eventually turned into types and shadows.

8. It would excuse anyone (e.g., the scribes in Jn. 5:35ff.) for *not* accepting Jesus' claims based on OT prophecies—since those prophecies would require the NT to reinterpret them, and they did not have the NT.

9. Any rejection of this, with a corresponding assertion that the OT prophecies about Christ did mean what they said, would create the strange hermeneutical paradox of finding clear, plain-sense testimony to Christ in the OT while claiming the OT cannot be interpreted without the NT.

10. The divining of these OT types and shadows is no easy task, especially as the NT does not provide any specific help on the matter.

11. Hence, this approach pulls a typological shroud over the OT, denying its Author the credit of meaning what He says and saying what He means (e.g., what does one make of the specificity of Jer. 33:14-26 or Zech. 8 or Zeph. 3?).

12. If the Author of the OT does not mean what He appears to say but is, in reality, speaking in types, shadows, and symbols, which He will apparently reveal later, what assurance is there that He is not *still* speaking in types, shadows and symbols in the NT? This problem is intensified because many places in the NT are still said to be types, shadows, and symbols (e.g., the temple in 2 Thess. 2 and most of Revelation).

13. It imposes a "unity" on the Bible which is symbolic and metaphorical *only*. Hence, taking the Bible in a normal, plain sense (the sense scholars advocating this view take for granted their readers will adopt with them) would destroy any unity between the Testaments. It would also make the Bible into an esoteric document indecipherable by outsiders.

14. However, a high degree of unity *can* be achieved by linking together the OT and NT literature in a plain sense, even though every question the interpreter may have will not be answered. Hence, the position that the NT must reinterpret the OT ignores or rejects the fact that, taken literally (in the sense defined above), the OT makes perfectly good sense. It just may not say what certain readers want it to say.

15. Claiming the types and shadows in the OT (which supposedly include the land given to national Israel, the throne in Jerusalem, the temple of Ezekiel, etc.) are given their proper concrete meanings by the NT implies that neither the believer nor the unbeliever can comprehend God's promises solely from the OT.

16. Thus, no unbeliever could be accused of unbelief so long as they only possessed the OT since the apparatus for belief (the NT) was not within their grasp.

17. This all makes mincemeat of any claim for the perspicuity of Scripture. At the very least, it makes clarity an attribute possessed only by parts of the NT.

18. Thus, the OT is deprived of its own hermeneutical integrity. This would render warnings such as that found in Proverbs 30:5-6 utterly pointless.

19. A corollary to this is that the authority of the OT to speak in its own voice is undermined.

20. In consequence of the above, the status of the OT as the "Word of God" would be logically inferior to the status of the NT. The result is that the NT (which refers to the OT as the "Word of God") is more inspired than the OT, producing the unwelcome outcome of two levels of inspiration.

21. It devalues the OT as its own witness to God and His plans. For example, if the promises given to ethnic Israel of land, throne, temple, etc. are somehow "fulfilled" in Jesus and the Church, what was the point of speaking about them so pointedly? Why would God swear an oath to perform them? Cramming everything into Christ not only destroys the clarity and unity of Scripture in the ways already mentioned, it also reduces the biblical covenants down to the debated promise of Genesis 3:15. The [true] expansion seen in the covenants (with all their categorical statements) is deflated into a single soundbite of "the Promised Seed-Redeemer has now come, and all is fulfilled in Him."

This casts aspersions on God as a communicator and as a covenant-Maker, since there was absolutely no need for God to say many of the things He said in the OT, let alone bind himself by oaths to fulfill them.

22. It forces one to adopt a promise-fulfillment scheme between the Testaments, ignoring the fact that the OT possesses no such promise scheme, but rather a more relational covenant-blessing scheme.

23. It effectively shoves aside the hermeneutical import of the inspired intertextual usage of an earlier OT text by later OT writers (e.g., earlier covenants cited in Psa. 89:33-37; 105:6-12; 106:30-31; 132:11-12; Jer. 33:17-18, 20-22, 25-26; Ezek. 37:14, 21-26). God is always taken at face value (e.g., 2 Ki. 1:3-4, 16-17; 5:10, 14; Dan. 9:2, 13). This sets up an expectation that covenant commitments will find "fulfillment" in expected ways, certainly not in completely unforeseeable ones.

24. It forces clear, descriptive language into an unnecessary semantic mold. A classic example is Ezekiel's Temple in Ezek. 40ff. According to this view, it is not a physical temple, even though a physical temple is clearly described.

25. It impels a simplistic and overly dependent reliance on the confused and confusing genre labeled "apocalyptic"—a genre about which there is no clear scholarly definitional consensus.

26. It would make the specific wording of the covenant oaths, which God took for man's benefit, misleading and hence unreliable as a witness to God's intentions. This sets a poor precedent for people making covenants and not sticking to what they actually promise to do (e.g., Jer. 34:18; cf. 33:15ff. and 35:13-16). This encourages theological nominalism, wherein God's oath can be altered just because He says it can.

27. Since interpreters in the OT (Psa. 105:6-12), NT (Acts 1:6), and even the intertestamental period (e.g., Tobit 14:4-7) took the covenant promises at face value (i.e., to correspond precisely to the people and things they explicitly refer to), this would mean God's testimony to Himself and His works in those promises, which God knew would be interpreted that way, was calculated to mislead the saints. Hence, a "pious transformation" of OT covenant terms through certain favored interpretations of NT texts makes God disingenuous.

28. The character of any being, be it man or angel, but God especially, is bound to the words agreed to in a covenant they may make (cf. Jer. 33:14, 24-26; 34:18). This being so, God could not make such covenants and then fulfill them in a way totally foreign to the plain wording of the oaths He took; at least not without it testifying against His own holy veracious character. Hence, not even God could "expand" His oaths in such a fashion that would literally mislead thousands of saints.

29. A God who would "transform" His promises in such an unanticipated way could never be trusted not to "transform" His promises to us in the Gospel. There might be a difference between the Gospel message, as we preach it (relying on the face value language of the NT), and God's real intentions when He eventually fulfills the promises in the Gospel. Since it is asserted that He did so in the past, it is conceivable that He might do so again in the future. Perhaps the promises to the Church will be "fulfilled" in totally unexpected ways with a people other than the Church?

30. Exegetically, it would entail taking passages in both Testaments literally and non-literally at the same time (e.g., Isa. 9:6-7; 49:6; Mic. 5:2; Zech. 9:9; Lk. 1:31-33; Rev. 7).

31. Exegetically, it would also impose structural discontinuities into prophetic books (e.g., God's glory departs a literal temple by the east gate in Ezekiel 10 but apparently returns to a spiritual temple through a spiritual east gate in Ezekiel 43!).

32. In addition, it makes the Creator of language the greatest rambler in all literature. Why did God not just tell the prophet, "When the Messiah comes, He will be the temple, and all those in Him will be called the temple"? That would have saved thousands of misleading words at the end of Ezekiel.

33. It ignores the life-setting of the disciples' question in Acts 1:6 in the context of their already having had forty days teaching about the very thing they asked about (the Kingdom, see Acts 1:3). This reflects badly on the clarity of the risen Lord's teaching about the Kingdom. But the tenacity with which these disciples still clung to literal fulfillments would also prove the validity of #'s 23, 26, 27, 28, and 32 above.

34. This resistance to the clear expectation of the disciples also ignores the question of the disciples, which was about the timing of the restoration of the Kingdom to Israel, not its nature.

35. It turns the admonition to "keep" the words of the prophecy in Revelation 1:3 into an absurdity, for how many people can "keep" something when they are uncertain of what is being "revealed"?

36. It makes the unwarranted assumption that there can only be one people of God. Since the OT speaks of Israel and the nations (e.g., Zech. 14:16ff.), Paul speaks of Israel and the Church (e.g., Rom. 11:25, 28; Gal. 6:16; 1 Cor. 10:32; cf. Acts 26:7), and the Book of Revelation speaks of Israel separated from the nations (Rev. 7), and those in New Jerusalem are distinguished from "the kings of the earth" (Rev. 21:9–22:5), it seems precarious to place every saved person from all ages into the Church.

37. In reality, what happens is the theological presuppositions of the interpreter are read into the NT text and then back into the OT. There is a corresponding breakdown between what the biblical text says and what it is assumed to mean. Thus, it is the interpretation of the reader and not the wording of the biblical text that is often the authority for what the Bible is allowed to teach.

38. This view also results in pitting NT authors against themselves. For example, if "spiritual resurrection" is read into John 5:25 on the rather flimsy basis of an allusion to Daniel 12:1-2, that interpretation can then be foisted on Revelation 20:4-6 to make John refer to a spiritual resurrection in that place too. Again, if Jesus is said to refer to His physical body as "this temple" in John 2:19, then He is not allowed to refer to a physical temple building in Revelation 11:1-2. This looks like what might be called "textual preferencing."

39. This view, which teaches a God who prevaricates in the promises and covenants He makes, also tempts its adherents to adopt equivocation themselves when they are asked to expound OT covenantal language in its original context. It often tempts them to avoid specific OT passages, where particulars are hard to interpret in light of their supposed fulfillment in the NT. It also makes one over-sensitive to words like "literal" and "replacement," even though these words are used freely when not discussing matters germane to this subject.

40. Finally, there is no critical awareness of many of the problems enumerated above because that awareness is provided by the OT texts and the specific wording of those texts, which, of course, are not allowed a voice on par with what the NT text is assumed to mean. Only verses that preserve the desired theological picture are allowed to mean what they say. Hence, a vicious circle is created when the NT reinterprets the Old. This is a hermeneutical circle which ought not to be presupposed.

I offer these forty reasons not because I care to defend "Dispensationalism." I couldn't really care less to defend a system. I offer them because they put forward real questions that require real answers from the student of Scripture, whichever side of the fence one eventually finds oneself.

APPENDIX C:

PLACING THE PROPER EMPHASIS UPON THE RABBINIC TRADITIONS

Whole ministries have been brought into being which rely heavily on the view that Jesus and the apostles operated within a Jewish milieu that can be described in detail and that has to be understood if we're going to gain fuller insight into the Scriptures. We hear a lot about the "Jewishness of Jesus" (or Yeshua).[1] We are told that we cannot understand the Gospels unless we see them through the lens of ancient Judaism. This, however, presupposes that it is possible to confidently reproduce the Judaism of pre-70 A.D. incontrovertibly. But as a matter of fact, that is not an easy thing to do.[2] Besides the differences between Rabbinic Judaism and the early Tannaitic Judaism before the siege of Jerusalem (70 A.D.), which even include how the term "rabbi" was employed,[3] it must be firmly understood how thoroughly counter-cultural Jesus and His message was. "He shows friendship to people marginalized by the respectable,

1 I do not have a problem with this designation when it is used in Jewish evangelism. In fact, it is entirely appropriate. But we must realize it doesn't add one whit to our piety. Actually, "Yeshua" is Hebrew, and Hebrew was rarely spoken in Israel in His day. According to the esteemed Jewish historian David Flusser, "Yeshu" would have, in all probability, been His name in Galilee (*The Sage From Galilee*, 6).

2 I am aware that there have been advances in our understanding of First Century Judaism in the last 30 or so years, but from my reading of the critical scholars (who include N. T. Wright, J. D. G. Dunn, E. P. Sanders, Sean Freyne, and Lester Grabbe), I remain convinced that the primary historical sources for understanding the life and times of Jesus are the Gospels. Even Grabbe admits that Josephus is "the only Jewish historian whose works are extant to any degree" (Lester L. Grabbe, *An Introduction to Second Temple Judaism: History and Religion of the Jews in the Time of Nehemiah, the Maccabees, Hillel, and Jesus* [London, T&T Clark, 2010], 31). Josephus wrote circa 80–100 A.D. The works of Jewish authors like Geza Vermes (e.g., *Jesus the Jew*, *Jesus in His Jewish Context*) are shot through with the mostly discredited critical scholarship of Bultmann and his ilk. Even critical scholars reject this approach today. See e.g., Sean Freyne, *Jesus, a Jewish Galilean: A New Reading of the Jesus Story* (London, T&T Clark, 2004), 4-5.

3 Even if it were the case, Matthew, for example, "does not portray Jesus as a Jewish rabbi" (Donald Guthrie, *A Shorter Life of Christ* [Grand Rapids: Zondervan, 1970], 59).

religious society of the time because of a way of life that was, or was regarded as, incompatible with God's laws."[4]

Moreover, the pervasive influence of Hellenism, even in Israel at the time of Jesus, closes the gap somewhat between the Jews and their pagan neighbors.[5] While we may not agree with those who see a large pervasive influx of Hellenistic ideas and values in Israel, we can at least say that acquaintance with those ideas was widespread.[6] As one critical scholar has put it, Greco-Roman Hellenism was:

The comprehensive cultural melting pot that one finds in the lands first conquered and held by Alexander the Great and his successors and then by the Romans. This mixture was sufficiently similar across times and places for the culture to count as a single, comprehensive entity.[7]

With that said, we must heed the warning of NT scholar Paul Barnett, when he writes:

> The rural and lakeside world of Galilee, the high country of Gaulanitis-Trachonitis and the temple city Jerusalem of Jesus' time are regions and places more recoverable through the eyes of Josephus and the Gospel writers than through the Mishnah, targummim [sic] and Talmudim. Arising as they do in the later centuries from the changed religious culture of rabbinic Judaism, their vision of Galilee and Judea prior to A.D. 70 is rather more remote.[8]

The fact of the matter is that Talmudic and even "Mishnaic" Judaism is *not* in large part the Judaism of the OT nor of the NT.[9] The sources need to be used wisely. As David Instone-Brewer, a modern authority, has warned, "It is too easy to come to false conclusions by forgetting to look at dating and context."[10] Instone-Brewer goes on to say that "the Judaism that was rescued and recorded by Yohanan and his followers was not the same as the Judaism of New Testament times."[11]

---

4 I. Howard Marshall, *New Testament Theology*, 63.

5 Again, I realize men like Vermes have argued against this (see Geza Vermes, *Jesus in His Jewish Context*, 24), but his reliance upon unbelieving form critics of the past hardly helps his portrait of Jesus. Neither does his relating Jesus to other Galilean '*hasidim*' like Honi and Hanina ben Dosa. Still authoritative is Martin Hengel, *Judaism and Hellenism: Studies in their Encounter in Palestine during the Early Hellenistic Period* (London, SCM Press, 1974).

6 See Sean Freyne, *The Jesus Movement and Its Expansion: Meaning and Mission* (Grand Rapids, Eerdmans, 2014), 13-48.

7 Troels Engberg Pedersen as quoted by Joseph D. Fantin, "Background Studies," in *Interpreting the New Testament Text*, eds. Darrell L. Bock and Buist M. Fanning (Wheaton, IL: Crossway, 2006), 171.

8 Paul Barnett, *Jesus and the Rise of Early Christianity*, 111. Also, idem., *Jesus and the Logic of History* (Grand Rapids: Eerdmans, 1997), 20-21.

9 In the context of remarks about ancient Jewish sectarianism, N. T. Wright says the Mishnah "sketches a way of being Jewish which many Jews of earlier generations would neither have recognised nor approved" (N. T. Wright, *Paul and the Faithfulness of God*, 809).

10 David Instone-Brewer, "Introduction to the English Translation," *A Commentary on the New Testament from the Talmud & Midrash*, eds. Hermann L. Strack and Paul Billerbeck, Vol. 1 (Bellingham, WA, Lexham, 2022), xxvi. Brewer's introduction is essential reading. He closes it with, "If we try to uncover the culture or even history of New Testament times using this rabbinic material, as Strack-Billerbeck tempts us to do, we have to tread carefully" (Ibid., xxxvi).

11 Ibid., xxxi.

It should also be noted that the strain of Judaism that survived A.D. 70 was mainly Hillelite, which creates an imbalance that needs to be kept in mind.[12] These facts and others should be comprehended before delving into the Jewish traditions.[13] What ancient Jewish sources can do when rightly filtered is to *illustrate* the background of NT times. It is a blessing to finally have "Strack-Billerbeck" in English, but its use is not to detail Jewish theology but to "aid the interpretation of New Testament phrases and ideas."[14] Added to this, we must also acknowledge that the authority lent to "the Oral Law" in Rabbinic teaching is at odds with the Bible.[15]

For these reasons, I would advise extreme care in interpreting the life of Jesus via Rabbinic sources. It is easy to get into the weeds of conjecture, to entice God's people to set aside in their minds the sufficiency of Scripture and lead them to believe they have "the inside line" because they have read some selections from Jewish literature written long after the Second Temple period. The Gospels are enough.

---

12 Ibid.

13 A famous warning was sounded about this very thing by Jewish scholar Samuel Sandmel in his address, "Parallelomania," *Journal of Biblical Literature* 81 (1962), 1-13. Sandmel warned, "Abstractly, Qumran might have influenced the NT, or abstractly, it might not have, or Talmud the NT, or the Midrash Philo, or Philo Paul. The issue for the student is not the abstraction but the specific. Detailed study is the criterion, and the detailed study ought to respect the context and not be limited to juxtaposing mere excerpts. Two passages may sound the same in splendid isolation from their context, but when seen in context reflect difference rather than similarity" (Ibid., 2).

14 Instone-Brewer, "Introduction to the English Translation," xxx.

15 See the work by Eitan Bar and Golan Broshi, *Rabbinic Judaism Debunked: Debunking the Myth of Rabbinic Oral Law* (Self-published, 2019). Their conclusion is worth quoting: "A specter has been haunting the Jewish world for over two millennia–the specter of rabbinic authority; a man-made religion which has developed its own particular system of laws, distinct and separate from the Bible–one which has placed its shackles of legalism on the Jewish people, at least since the destruction of the Second Temple" (98).

Annotated Bibliography

This bibliography includes brief comments on the books I reference in this volume. Again, allow me to clarify that I reference these works not because I agree with their views, but because my minority position is better supported when those who disagree with me arrive at the same conclusion, rather than solely citing dispensationalists. With that said, I hope you will be helped by it.

An asterisk (*) means I recommend it even if I may disagree. A hashtag (#) means I have reviewed the work at my blog, paulmhenebury.com.

A

Abasciano, Brian J. "Clearing Up Misconceptions About Corporate Election." *Ashland Theological Journal* 41 (2009), 59-90. A response to several misunderstandings, among which is the idea that corporate election is antithetical to individual election.*

Alexander, T. Desmond and David W. Baker, eds. *Dictionary of the Old Testament: Pentateuch.* Downers Grove, IL: InterVarsity, 2003. While critical in areas, this is a must buy.*

Alexander, T. Desmond and Brian S. Rosner, eds. *New Dictionary of Biblical Theology.* Downers Grove, IL: IVP, 2000. Grab it if you can. Many good articles.

Allen, David L. *Lukan Authorship of Hebrews.* Nashville, B&H, 2010. I'm not convinced by Lukan authorship, but this is an interesting book.

Allen, David L. and Steve W. Lemke, eds. *The Return of Christ: A Premillennial Perspective.* Nashville, B&H, 2011. A mixed bag. Good chapters by Blaising, Allen, Cooper, Vlach. Poor stuff from Vines, Caner, Cox and Stanton.#

Allison, Gregg R. and Stephen J. Wellum, eds. *Building on the Foundations of Evangelical Theology: Essays in Honor of John S. Feinberg.* Wheaton, IL: Crossway, 2015. A fine collection (esp. Saucy and Yandell), with a response from Feinberg.

Anderson, Sir Robert. *The Coming Prince or The Seventy Weeks of Daniel.* London: Hodder and Stoughton, 1865. Classic treatment of the 70th Week.*

Arnold, Clinton E., ed. *Zondervan Illustrated Bible Backgrounds Commentary, Volume 1, Matthew, Mark, Luke.* Grand Rapids: Zondervan, 2002. This is a well-illustrated and helpful set.

Attridge, Harold W. *Hebrews: A Commentary on the Epistle to the Hebrews.* Hermeneia. Philadelphia: Fortress, 1989. Standard treatment. Buy it if you can get a good price. I was surprised by the rather sagging treatment of Heb. 9:16-17.

Averbeck, Richard E., "Israel, the Jewish People and God's Covenants," in *Israel, the Church, and the Middle East: A Biblical Response to the Current Conflict*, edited by Darrell L. Bock and Mitch Glaser. Grand Rapids, Kregel, 2018. Fine overview.*

———. "Sacrifices and Offerings," in *Dictionary of the Old Testament: Pentateuch*, edited by T. Desmond Alexander and David W. Baker. Downers Grove, IL: InterVarsity, 2003. Excellent article that covers all the bases.*

B

Baker, David L. *Two Testaments, One Bible: The Theological Relationship Between the Old and New Testaments.* 3rd ed. Downers Grove, IL: IVP, 2010. Highly recommended for those studying the subject. Solid and cautious.*

Balz, Horst, and Gerhard Schneider, eds. *Exegetical Dictionary of the New Testament.* Grand Rapids: Eerdmans, 1999. Very useful short yet accurate definitions.

Bar, Eitan, and Golan Broshi. *Rabbinic Judaism Debunked: Debunking the Myth of Rabbinic Oral Law.* One for Israel, 2022. Polemical, but a needed short book on the divergence of the Oral Law and Jewish traditions from the Bible.

Barbieri, Louis. *Mark.* Chicago: Moody, 1995. A solid dispensational commentary.

Barnett, Paul. *Jesus and the Rise of Early Christianity.* Downers Grove, IL: IVP, 1999. Excellent introduction to NT times.*

———. *Jesus and the Logic of History.* Grand Rapids: Eerdmans, 1997. A top-notch brief defense of the Jesus of history.*

Barrett, C. K. *The First Epistle to the Corinthians.* Peabody, MA: Hendrickson, 1985. Used to be a top pick. A bit liberal but helpful. Obtuse in places.

Barrs, Jerram. *Delighting in the Law of the Lord: God's Alternative to Legalism and Moralism.* Wheaton, IL: Crossway, 2013. Written with pastoral concern and with an eye to evangelism, this book helps one see the relevance of God's Law for human living.

Bartholomew, Craig G., et al., eds. *Reading Luke: Interpretation, Reflection, Formation.* Grand Rapids: Zondervan, 2005. I didn't get a lot from this book, or from the others in the series overall. Many chapters borrowed from other publications.

Bateman, Herbert W., IV, ed. *Four Views on the Warning Passages in Hebrews.* Grand Rapids: Kregel, 2007. Very good to and fro discussions. You'll get a good grasp of Hebrews from this.*

Bateman, Herbert W., IV, and William C. Varner. *James: An Exegetical Guide for Preaching and Teaching.* Big Greek Idea Series. Grand Rapids: Kregel, 2022. If you can handle Greek, this is terrific.*#

Bateman, Herbert W., IV, Darrell L. Bock, and Gordon H. Johnston. *Jesus the Messiah: Tracing the Promises, Expectations, and Coming of Israel's King.* Grand Rapids: Kregel, 2012. A solid, glossy paged study. I found Bateman's section a tad below Johnston and Bock, but all the authors do well.

Bates, Matthew W. *Salvation By Allegiance Alone: Rethinking Faith, Works, and the Gospel of Jesus the King.* Grand Rapids: Baker, 2017. Provides food for thought but ultimately fails, in large part because his thesis about Christ now reigning is faulty. Many things flow from bad premises. I prefer to think of faith as dependence. Great writer though.

Bauckham, Richard. *Jesus and the Eyewitnesses: The Gospels as Eyewitness Testimony.* Grand Rapids: Eerdmans, 2006. Fascinating multifaceted study which cements the Gospel accounts in their milieu.

———. *The Theology of the Book of Revelation.* Cambridge: Cambridge University Press, 2001. Ignores the prophetic character of the book. See my chapter on The Apocalypse.

Bavinck, Herman. *Reformed Dogmatics: Volume 4, Holy Spirit, Church, and New Creation.* Grand Rapids: Baker, 2008. The best of Reformed Systematic Theology. Excellent translation. I liked the previous volumes more, but this is still very good.*

Beacham, Roy E. "The Church Has No Legal Relationship to or Participation in the New Covenant." In *Dispensational Understanding of the New Covenant,* edited by Mike Stallard. A sterling effort. I respectfully demur.*

Beale, G. K. *A New Testament Biblical Theology.* Grand Rapids: Baker Academic, 2011. A long and determined attempt to impose a "cosmic temple" motif over the Bible. Amillennial and speculative. Doesn't interact much with opposing views.#

———. *Handbook on the New Testament Use of the Old Testament: Exegesis and Interpretation.* Grand Rapids: Baker, 2012. I'm no fan of Beale's conclusions, but there is some good material in this.

———. *The Book of Revelation.* NIGNTC. Grand Rapids: Eerdmans, 1999. Good on the Greek and OT sources, poor on interpretation.

———. "An Exegetical and Theological Consideration of The Hardening of Pharaoh's Heart in Exodus 4–14 and Romans 9." *Trinity Journal* 5, no. 2 (1984). A solid Calvinistic argument.*

———. "The Eschatology of Paul." In *Studies in the Pauline Epistles: Essays in Honor of Douglas J. Moo,* edited by Matthew S. Harmon and Jay E. Smith. Grand Rapids: Zondervan, 2014. Beale represents the antithesis of my position. Good thoughts on the resurrection as an eschatological event though.

Beale, G. K., and D. A. Carson, eds. *Commentary on the New Testament Use of the Old Testament.* Grand Rapids: Baker, 2007. Although it is predominantly amillennial, this is a useful work.

Beasley-Murray, G. R. *Jesus and the Kingdom of God.* Grand Rapids: Eerdmans, 1986. Mostly a review of scholarship up to that point, with the author's views appended. Well respected but unpersuasive.

———. *John.* WBC. Waco, TX: Word, 1987. Some liberal taints but a very capable commentary.

———. "Dying and Rising with Christ." In *Dictionary of Paul and His Letters,* edited by Gerald F. Hawthorne, et al. A disappointing article.

———. "Revelation, Book of." In *Dictionary of the Later New Testament and Its Development,* edited by Ralph P. Martin and Peter H. Davids. Downers Grove, IL: InterVarsity, 1997. A fine introduction if you reject dispensational premillennialism.

Beilby, James K., and Paul R. Eddy, eds. *The Historical Jesus: Five Views.* Downers Grove, IL: IVP, 2009. Takes a little patience (esp. reading Price and Crossan), but good chapters by Johnson, Dunn, and Bock.

Beker, J. Christiaan. *The Triumph of God: The Essence of Paul's Thought.* Minneapolis: Fortress, 1990. Takes the notion of "apocalyptic" too far. Although liberal, this is definitely worth skimming because Beker stresses the occasional nature of Paul's letters.

Benware, Paul N. *Understanding End Times Prophecy: A Comprehensive Approach.* Chicago: Moody, 2006. A very helpful and reliable work.*

Bernard, Thomas Delaney. *The Progress of Doctrine in the New Testament.* Various editions. Classic study of the arrangement of the NT books. Although I cannot endorse all he says, this deserves to be read by every Bible student.*

Berkouwer, G. C. *The Return of Christ.* Studies in Dogmatics. Grand Rapids: Eerdmans, 1972. A standard treatment. Basically amillennial. One of Berkouwer's most straightforward studies.

Bird, Michael F. *Evangelical Theology: A Biblical and Systematic Introduction.* Grand Rapids: Zondervan, 2013. Tries to be readable and "fun." I liked that he places eschatology further forward, even if it doesn't quite work. A useful second-string work.

———. "Paul's Messianic Eschatology and Supercessionism." In *God's Israel and the Israel of God,* edited by Michael F. Bird and Scot McKnight. Argues that Israel's future is inclusion in Christ through the Church. This guarantees the future disappearance of covenant Israel.

Bird, Michael F., and Scot McKnight, eds. *God's Israel and the Israel of God: Paul and Supercessionism.* Bellingham, WA: Lexham, 2023. A failed attempt to address a serious subject.#

Blaising, Craig A., and Darrell L. Bock. *Progressive Dispensationalism.* Grand Rapids: Baker, 2000. An important book for understanding PD. Two chapters on the covenants spoiled by their "complementary" inclusive hermeneutic which rubberizes them. This affects the way they view the kingdom in the present. They also tie dispensations too closely to the covenants, a common error.

———, eds. *Dispensationalism, Israel and the Church: The Search for Definition.* Grand Rapids: Zondervan, 1992. A good presentation of Prog. Disp. with counterarguments. Some strong chapters. One pushback from a more traditional Dispy would have been nice.*

Blaising, Craig A. "Biblical Hermeneutics." In *The New Christian Zionism,* edited by Gerald R. McDermott. Very solid overall treatment.*

———. "A Theology of Israel and the Church." In *Israel, the Church, and the Middle East: A Biblical Response to the Current Conflict,* edited by Darrell L. Bock and Mitch Glaser. Grand Rapids: Kregel, 2018. Nearly any article by this author is worth reading.*

Block, Daniel I. *Covenant: The Framework of God's Grand Plan of Redemption.* Grand Rapids: Baker, 2021. Somewhat informative but hampered by the author's very confusing naming of the covenants.#

Blomberg, Craig L. *Matthew.* Nashville, TN: Broadman Press, 1992. Informative and concise.

———. *A New Testament Theology.* Waco, TX: Baylor University Press, 2018. Irritating on the Gospels owing to his belief in Q. Still, Blomberg is a good thinker.

———. *Preaching the Parables: From Responsible Interpretation to Powerful Proclamation.* Grand Rapids: Baker, 2004. A good guide overall.

Bock, Darrell L., and Buist M. Fanning, eds. *Interpreting the New Testament Text: Introduction to the Art and Science of Exegesis.* Wheaton, IL: Crossway, 2006. A strong group of essays. One of the best works of its kind.

———, and Robert L. Webb, eds. *Key Events in the Life of the Historical Jesus: A Collaborative Exploration of Context and Coherence.* Grand Rapids: Eerdmans, 2010. Webb's introduction is almost positivist in orientation, but that apart, this is a great book given its self-imposed limitations. A bit more critical than I would have liked.*

———, and Mitch Glaser, eds. *Israel, the Church, and the Middle East: A Biblical Response to the Current Conflict.* Grand Rapids: Kregel, 2018. A good book with fine contributions by Averbeck, Blaising, and Vlach, and a really good chapter by Rydelnik.*#

Bock, Darrell L. *Luke.* 2 vols. BECNT. Grand Rapids: Baker, 1994. Many people's top pick on Luke.*

———. *Acts.* BECNT. Grand Rapids: Baker, 2007. A contender for the best overall work on this Bible book.*

———. "The Reign of the Lord Christ." In *Dispensationalism, Israel and the Church: The Search for Definition,* edited by Craig A. Blaising and Darrell L. Bock. Grand Rapids: Zondervan, 1992. See my chapter on Acts.

Boda, Mark J., and J. Gordon McConville, eds. *Dictionary of the Old Testament Prophets.* Downers Grove, IL: InterVarsity, 2012. Lots of good things here. I think this dictionary is one of the best in the series.*

Boettner, Loraine. *The Reformed Doctrine of Predestination.* Phillipsburg, NJ: P&R, 1976. Standard presentation of TULIP, by one of the first promulgators of it. Too much inference for my liking.

Boice, James M. *Witness and Revelation in the Gospel of John.* Grand Rapids: Zondervan, 1970. An interesting study. Basically, Boice's dissertation. An Appendix refutes the supposed link between Logos and the Memra of the Targums.

Bray, Gerald. *God Is Love: A Biblical and Systematic Theology.* Wheaton, IL: Crossway, 2012. Gets better as one keeps reading. A fine companion to the author's excellent *Historical Theology.*

Brindle, Wayne. "Biblical Evidence for the Imminence of the Rapture." *Bibliotheca Sacra* 158 (April-June 2001). One of the best arguments for this view I have read.*

Brooks, Thomas. *Precious Remedies Against Satan's Devices.* Edinburgh: Banner of Truth, 2021. Terrific and unrivaled (unless one knows Gilpin). Brooks is heavy on Ramist outlining, but this work is brilliant.*

Brown, Colin, ed. *New International Dictionary of New Testament Theology.* Grand Rapids: Zondervan, 1975. Still an important work. Corrected many of the excesses of Kittel.

Brown, Michael G., and Zach Keele. *Sacred Bond: Covenant Theology Explored.* Grandville, MI: Reformed Fellowship Inc., 2012. Touted by many as the best intro to CT. Belcher is better, but this should be read.

Brown, Sherri. *Gift Upon Gift: Covenant through Word in the Gospel of John.* Eugene, OR: Pickwick, 2010. A unique study which shows how John uses covenant to underpin his thesis.

Bruce, F. F. *The Book of Acts.* NICNT. Grand Rapids: Eerdmans, 1977. Still a standard commentary.*

———. *Paul: Apostle of the Heart Set Free.* Grand Rapids: Eerdmans, 1989. Good, but not Bruce's best.

———. *The Epistle to the Galatians.* NIGNTC. Grand Rapids: Eerdmans, 1982. Outstanding.*

———. *The Epistle of Paul to the Romans.* Tyndale. Grand Rapids: Eerdmans, 1983. For its length, this is excellent, but why so brief?*

———. *The Epistle to the Hebrews.* Grand Rapids: Eerdmans, 1990. Definitely one of the best on this book.*

Bruno, Chris, Jared Compton, and Kevin McFadden. *Biblical Theology According to the Apostles: How the Earliest Christians Told the Story of Israel.* Downers Grove, IL: IVP, 2020. I liked this book more than I thought I would. The authors cover seven episodes for study. They are careful in their approach, which I respect even when I disagree, which is quite often.

Bullinger, E. W. *The Apocalypse, or "The Day of the Lord."* London: Samuel Bagster, 1972. Hyper-dispensational, but worth having because Bullinger thinks outside the box.

———. *Number in Scripture: Its Supernatural Design and Spiritual Significance.* Grand Rapids: Kregel, 1967. A standard work. There is always a danger of seeing what isn't there.

Bultema, Harry. *Commentary on Isaiah.* Grand Rapids: Kregel, 1981. Not in-depth, but a worthwhile purchase. Premillennial.

Bunyan, John. *The Pilgrim's Progress.* Various editions. Too celebrated for me to add anything. This ought to be read repeatedly by every Christian!*

Burge, Gary M. *Jesus and the Land: The New Testament Challenge to "Holy Land" Theology.* Grand Rapids: Baker, 2012. Replacement theology at its worst.

———. "Territorial Religion, Johannine Christology, and the Vineyard of John 15." In *Jesus of Nazareth: Lord and Christ: Essays on the Historical Jesus and New Testament Christology,* edited by Joel B. Green and Max Turner. Grand Rapids: Eerdmans, 1994. Inference above exegesis.

Burgraff, David L. "Augustine: From the 'Not Yet' to the 'Already.'" In *Forsaking Israel: How It Happened and Why It Matters,* 2nd ed., edited by Larry D. Pettegrew. Excellent presentation of Augustine's influence on eschatology. Misconstrues Pelagius a bit (see now Ali Bonner's work).*

Burns, J. Lanier. "The Future of Ethnic Israel in Romans." In *Dispensationalism, Israel and the Church: The Search for Definition,* edited by Craig A. Blaising and Darrell L. Bock. A long and well-referenced, if overly genteel examination of Romans 9–11.

C

Cairns, Earle E. "Eschatology and Church History, Part I." *Bibliotheca Sacra* 115, no. 458 (April 1958). Informative.

Calvin, John. *Commentary on the First Epistle of Peter.* Grand Rapids: Baker, 1981. Calvin was a great commentator. This is terrific.*

Campbell, Constantine R. *Paul and the Hope of Glory.* Grand Rapids: Zondervan, 2020. Thoughtful Amillennial study on Pauline eschatology with some interesting exegesis.

Campbell, Donald K. "Galatians." In *Bible Knowledge Commentary: New Testament,* edited by John F. Walvoord and Roy B. Zuck. Victor Books, 1983. Solid but basic.

Campbell, Douglas A. *The Deliverance of God: An Apocalyptic Rereading of Justification in Paul.* Grand Rapids: Eerdmans, 2013. A giant erudite work focused on overturning Luther on justification, which rejects individualism and contractual categories. He doesn't succeed, but his work is influential.

Campbell, William S. "'Through Isaac Shall Your Seed Be Named' (Romans 9:7b): Israel and the Purpose of God in Romans." In *The Future Restoration of Israel,* edited by Stanley E. Porter and Alan E. Kurschner. Thought-provoking defense of corporate election.*#

———. "Covenant and New Covenant." In *Dictionary of Paul and His Letters,* edited by Gerald F. Hawthorne and Ralph P. Martin. Downers Grove, IL: InterVarsity, 1993. Solid and informative.

Capes, David B. *The Divine Christ: Paul, the Lord Jesus, and the Scriptures of Israel.* Grand Rapids: Baker, 2018. A study of Paul's use of OT YHWH texts applied to Christ.

Capes, David B., Rodney Reeves, and E. Randolph Richards. *Rediscovering Paul: An Introduction to His World, Letters and Theology.* Downers Grove, IL: InterVarsity, 2007. One of the best introductions on Paul.*

Carson, D. A. "Matthew." In *The Expositor's Bible Commentary,* vol. 8, edited by Frank E. Gaebelein. Grand Rapids: Zondervan, 1984. Very competent work which analyzes various approaches to the text before giving his viewpoints.*

Carson, D. A., and Douglas J. Moo. *An Introduction to the New Testament.* 2nd ed. Grand Rapids: Zondervan, 2005. One of the best conservative works of its kind.

Carson, D. A., Peter T. O'Brien, and Mark A. Seifrid, eds. *Justification and Variegated Nomism,* vol. 2, *The Paradoxes of Paul.* Grand Rapids: Baker, 2004. Somewhat dated (cf. Campbell and Barclay), but still important.

Chafer, Lewis Sperry. *Systematic Theology,* 8 vols. Dallas: Dallas Seminary Press, 1978. I used to take seminary students through these volumes. Overall, an excellent work, with some great unique sections. Leaves the heavy lifting to others in long quotations. A little jumbled in places and not good on the New covenant or baptism, but a classic work of older Dispensationalism.*

Chase, Mitchell L. *40 Questions About Typology and Allegory.* Grand Rapids: Kregel, 2020. Overall, this is an informative work. I'm a little wary of typology, and this book didn't allay my fears.

Chennattu, Rekha. *Johannine Discipleship as a Covenant Relationship.* Grand Rapids: Baker, 2005. A thoughtful study of the Upper Room and John's reliance on covenantal background.

Chisholm, Robert B., Jr. "Divine Hardening in the Old Testament." *Bibliotheca Sacra* 153, no. 612 (October 1996). Thorough word studies and chronology which argues for Pharaoh being an obstinate man prior to God's hardening of him.

Chou, Abner. *The Hermeneutics of the Biblical Writers.* Grand Rapids: Kregel, 2018. A good series of studies that I wish was expanded. Needs an index.

Clark, R. Scott. "Covenant Theology Is Not Replacement Theology." *Heidelblog.* August 2013. https://heidelblog.net/2013/08/covenanttheology-is-not-replacement-theology/. Unpersuasive as it fails to include all the versions of supersessionism.

Clendenen, E. Ray. "'Messenger of the Covenant' In Malachi 3:1 Once Again." *Journal of the Evangelical Theological Society* 62, no. 1 (March 2019). Persuasive reasoning in support of the messianic view.*

Clouse, Robert G., ed. *The Meaning of the Millennium: Four Views.* Downers Grove, IL: InterVarsity, 1977. Perhaps the earliest four views book. Very good except for Boettner's defense of Postmil.*

Clowney, Edmund P. "The Final Temple." In *Prophecy in the Making,* edited by Carl F. H. Henry. Carol Stream, IL: Creation House, 1971. An excellent presentation of the amil perspective.*

Cole, Graham A. *He Who Gives Life: The Doctrine of the Holy Spirit.* Wheaton, IL: Crossway, 2007. A good book in a good series.*

Compton, R. Bruce. "Dispensationalism, the Church, and the New Covenant." *Detroit Baptist Seminary Journal* 8 (Fall 2003). Very thorough discussion. Comes down on a participationist view.*

Cone, Christopher, ed. *An Introduction to the New Covenant.* Hurst, TX: Tyndale Seminary Press, 2013. Essays arguing against any relation of the New Covenant on Christians. Important for that reason.*

———. "The New Covenant in Hebrews." In *An Introduction to the New Covenant,* edited by Christopher Cone. The best argument that could be made for this position.

Constable, Thomas L. "Notes on Hebrews" (2023 edition). *Plano Bible Chapel.* https://www.planobiblechapel.org/tcon/notes/html/nt/hebrews/hebrews.html. Reliable notes from a terrific free source.*

Copenhaver, Adam, and Jeffrey D. Arthurs. *Colossians and Philemon: A Commentary for Biblical Preaching and Teaching.* Kerux Commentary Series. Grand Rapids: Kregel, 2022. Copenhaver's work is worth the price of the book.#

Craigie, Peter C. *The Book of Deuteronomy.* Grand Rapids: Eerdmans, 1976. Still a standard text.

Cranfield, C. E. B. *The Gospel According to St. Mark.* Cambridge: Cambridge University Press, 1966. Short but excellent. Knowledge of Greek really helps, but Cranfield explains things well.*

Crutchfield, Larry V. "The Early Church Fathers and the Foundations of Dispensationalism." In six parts. *The Conservative Theological Journal,* 1998-1999. A unique study.

D

Davids, Peter H. *A Theology of James, Peter, and Jude.* Grand Rapids: Zondervan, 2014. As one would expect from Davids, this is very informative. A tad critical though.

Dean, Robert. "A Critique of O. Palmer Robertson's Interpretation of Romans 11." *Pre-Trib Research Center.* Available at https://www.pre-trib.org/articles/all-articles/message/a-critique-of-o-palmer-robertson-s-interpretation-of-romans-11/read. A well-written critique.

Decker, Rodney J. "The Law, the New Covenant, and the Christian: Studies in Hebrews 7–10." *Dispensational Council.* Available at https://dispensationalcouncil.org/wp-content/uploads/2019/03/09_Rod_Decker_TheLaw_The_New_Covenant_and_the_Christian_Studies-in-Hebrews-7-10.pdf. Anything by Decker is worth reading.*

———. "The Church's Relationship to the New Covenant, Parts 1 and 2." *Bibliotheca Sacra* 152, no. 607 (July 1995) and 152, no. 608 (October 1995). Argues for participation of the Church in the NC, although only Israel is a full party. Good refutation of opposing views.*

———. "The Intentional Structure of Hebrews." *Journal of Ministry and Theology* 04, no. 2 (Fall 2000). The best in a series by Decker on Hebrews.*

Denault, Pascal. *The Distinctiveness of Baptist Covenant Theology.* Birmingham, AL: Solid Ground, 2016. An excellent historical and theological treatment of Baptist CT with solid responses to paedo-baptists.*

Delitzsch, Franz. *Commentary on the Old Testament* by C. F. Keil and F. Delitzsch, vol. VII, *Isaiah.* Grand Rapids: Eerdmans, 1969. Delitzsch is always worth consulting.

DeRouchie, Jason S., Oren R. Martin, and Andrew David Naselli. *40 Questions about Biblical Theology.* Grand Rapids: Kregel, 2020. First coming hermeneutics meets typological interpretation. Israel is just an antitype for the real. The present work is diametrically opposed to this opinion.#

DeYoung, Kevin. *Taking God at His Word: Why the Bible Is Knowable, Necessary, and Enough, and What That Means for You and Me.* Wheaton, IL: Crossway, 2016. Makes some sound points, but the author scarcely believes his title when prophecy is concerned.#

Diprose, Ronald E. *Israel and the Church: The Origin and Effects of Replacement Theology.* Waynesboro, GA: Authentic Media, 2004. An important modern treatment.*

———. "A Theology of the New Covenant: The Foundations of New Testament Theology." *Emmaus Journal* 16 (Winter 2007). Part of a series on the NT.

Donaldson, Amy M., and Timothy B. Sailors, eds. *New Testament Greek and Exegesis: Essays in Honor of Gerald F. Hawthorne.* Grand Rapids: Eerdmans, 2003. Some good essays and some not so good ones.

Doriani, Daniel M. *Matthew,* 2 vols. Phillipsburg, NJ: P&R Publishing, 2008. A pretty basic exposition.

Douma, Jochen. *The Ten Commandments: Manual for the Christian Life.* Phillipsburg, PA: P&R, 1996. Profound, thoughtful, stirring. Even where I disagree, I greatly appreciate this book.

Dumbrell, William J. *The Search for Order: Biblical Eschatology in Focus.* Grand Rapids: Baker, 1994. Influential amil study. The best study from this perspective.*

———. *The End of the Beginning: Revelation 21–22 and the Old Testament.* Eugene, OR: Wipf and Stock, 2001. An attempt to use the last chapters of Revelation to bolster amil typology. Has a good section on the New covenant.

Duncan, Ligon. "Covenant in the Early Church." In *Covenant Theology: Biblical, Theological, and Historical Perspectives,* edited by Guy Prentiss Waters, et al. Wheaton, IL: Crossway, 2020. Useful for those of CT sympathies.

Dunn, James D. G. *Jesus Remembered.* Grand Rapids: Eerdmans, 2003. Argues for the strong oral evidence for Jesus which led to the Gospels. I do not lean that way, but the book also includes much very useful exegesis.*

———. *Beginning From Jerusalem.* Grand Rapids: Eerdmans, 2009. Outstanding because Dunn provokes so many questions. A great writer who is voluminously well read and is always stimulating.*

———. *Neither Jew nor Greek: A Contested Identity.* Grand Rapids: Eerdmans, 2015. The third installment of Dunn's impressive "Christianity in the Making" series. More concerned with the reception of the NT but still very helpful. I don't agree with him half the time, and his critical views show more here, but he is an excellent conversation partner.

———. *The Theology of the Apostle Paul.* Grand Rapids: Eerdmans, 1998. The heavyweight in the field. Yes, he's wrong on "the works of the Law," and he could be better on Christ's preexistence, but there is so much good material here. Does superbly in routing the Pauline corpus (well, those he identifies as by Paul) through the book of Romans. Dunn is balanced and fair, even if too critical.*

———. "Paul's Theology." In *The Face of New Testament Studies: A Survey of Recent Research,* edited by Scot McKnight and Grant R. Osborne. Grand Rapids: Baker, 2004. Although he is a proponent of the New Perspective*, Dunn's essay is well balanced and extremely informative.*

Dunham, Kyle C. "The Kingdom of Christ and of God: A Traditional Dispensationalist Argument for Inaugurated Eschatology." A good study of Christ's kingship.

Dyer, Charles H. *The Rise of Babylon: Sign of the Times.* Chicago: Moody, 2003. Terrible cover. Good book.

———. "The Biblical Meaning of 'Fulfillment.'" In *Issues in Dispensationalism,* edited by Wesley R. Willis and John R. Master. Chicago: Moody, 1994. First-rate study. Recommended.*

E

Echevarria, Miguel G., and Benjamin P. Laird. *40 Questions About the Apostle Paul.* Grand Rapids: Kregel, 2023. The authors do a good job, but the eschatology is typological.#

Eddy, Paul Rhodes, and Gregory L. Boyd. *The Jesus Legend: A Case for the Historical Reliability of the Jesus Tradition.* Grand Rapids: Baker, 2007. Though somewhat over-reliant on secular historiography, there is a lot of great material in this book.

Edgar, Thomas R. "An Exegesis of Rapture Passages." In *Issues in Dispensationalism,* edited by Wesley R. Willis and John R. Master. Chicago: Moody, 1994. A very useful discussion.

Edwards, James R. *The Gospel of Mark.* Grand Rapids: Eerdmans, 2002. The best on Mark for my money. Edwards is always good.*

English, E. Schuyler. *Rethinking the Rapture.* Neptune, NJ: Loizeaux Brothers, 1954. A gallant but unconvincing attempt to find the rapture in 2 Thess. 2:3.

Erickson, Millard J. *God in Three Persons: A Contemporary Interpretation of the Trinity.* Grand Rapids: Baker, 1995. A first-class theologian writes a standard book on the topic.*

Evans, Craig A., and Stanley E. Porter, eds. *Dictionary of New Testament Background.* Downers Grove, IL: InterVarsity, 2000. A very well put together dictionary.*

Evans, Craig A. "Judaism, Post-A.D. 70." In *Dictionary of the Later New Testament and Its Development,* edited by Ralph P. Martin and Peter H. Davids. Downers Grove, IL: InterVarsity, 1997. A leading authority on the subject.*

———. *Luke.* Peabody, MA: Hendrickson, 1990. A very readable, solid work.

F

Fairbairn, Patrick. *The Revelation of Law in Scripture.* Phillipsburg, NJ: P&R, 1996. One of the most innovative writers of the 19th century. There is nothing like it, even when I cannot agree.*

Fanning, Buist M. *Revelation.* ZECNT. Grand Rapids: Zondervan, 2020. Erudite but clearly written, this PD treatment is one of the best on Revelation.*

———. "A Theology of Hebrews." In *A Biblical Theology of the New Testament,* edited by Roy B. Zuck. Thorough and informative.

Fazio, James I. *Two Commissions: Two Missionary Mandates in Matthew's Gospel.* El Cajon: Southern Evangelical Seminary Press, 2015. [Un]common sense exposition of the commissions in Matt. 10 and 28, coming to reliable conclusions based on the clues in the Gospel.

Fee, Gordon D. *God's Empowering Presence: The Holy Spirit in the Letters of Paul.* Peabody, MA: Hendrickson, 1994. There is nothing quite like this work. Fee exegetes all Paul's "Spirit" passages.*

———. *Pauline Christology: An Exegetical-Theological Study.* Peabody, MA: Hendrickson, 2007. Similar to the above, but this time centering on Paul's Christology.*

———. *1 and 2 Timothy, Titus.* Peabody, MA: Hendrickson, 1988. A generally excellent introductory commentary. Weak on the issue of women preachers.

Feinberg, John S., ed. *Continuity and Discontinuity: Perspectives on the Relationship Between the Old and New Testaments.* Wheaton, IL: Crossway, 1988. Classic discussions between Covenant Theologians and Dispensationalists. Important.*

Fergusson, James. *The Epistles of Paul to the Galatians, Ephesians, Philippians, Colossians and Thessalonians,* and David Dickson. *The Epistle to the Hebrews.* Edinburgh: The Banner of Truth Trust, 1878 (1659-74). Reprint of two 17th-century works. They repay patient reading if you've got the time.

Flusser, David R. *The Sage from Galilee: Rediscovering Jesus' Genius.* Grand Rapids: Eerdmans, 2007. An orthodox Jewish perspective.

Frame, John M. *The Doctrine of the Christian Life.* A Theology of Lordship. Phillipsburg, PA: P&R, 2008. Frame is one of the top evangelical scholars writing today. This is a very thorough and mature presentation.*

———. *The Doctrine of God.* A Theology of Lordship. Phillipsburg, NJ: P&R, 2002. A great "multi-perspectival" study of God which tries to be determinedly scriptural. This is a must-read for serious theologians. I demur from Frame's equation of responsibility and accountability.*

———. *Systematic Theology: An Introduction to Christian Belief.* Phillipsburg, NJ: P&R, 2014. Criticized for not relying enough on the Confessions, this is a strength rather than a weakness. To my mind, this is in the top 5 Systematics.*

Freedman, David Noel, ed. *The Anchor Bible Dictionary,* 6 vols. New York: Doubleday, 1992. The standard, but liberal.

———. *Divine Commitment and Human Obligation,* vol. 1, *Ancient Israelite History and Religion.* Grand Rapids: Eerdmans, 1968. Enlightening studies. Simplifies the discussion about covenants.

Fredrickson, Dave. "Which Are the New Covenant Passages in the Old Testament?" In *Dispensational Understanding of the New Covenant,* edited by Mike Stallard. Schaumburg, IL: Regular Baptist Books, 2012. Although I would add more texts to the list, I think this is an excellent chapter.*

Freyne, Sean. *Jesus, a Jewish Galilean: A New Reading of the Jesus Story.* London: T&T Clark, 2004. A scholarly yet quite devotional book.

———. *The Jesus Movement and Its Expansion: Meaning and Mission.* Grand Rapids: Eerdmans, 2014. One of the best books on Second Temple Judaism for NT students. Critical in places.*

Fruchtenbaum, Arnold G. *Yeshua: The Life of Messiah from A Messianic Jewish Perspective,* vol. 1. San Antonio, TX: Ariel, 2020. Some folks like this kind of work. I am not so keen. Although it has good insights, there is not enough detail where there needs to be (e.g., Greco-Roman background; language). Makes far too bold claims for Memra (see e.g., Boice above). The exposition of the NT text is quite shallow, and there is too much importing of later Jewish ideas. Consult someone like Freyne (above) alongside this.

Furnish, Victor Paul. *II Corinthians: A New Translation with Introduction and Commentary.* Garden City, NY: Doubleday, 1984. A tad liberal, but this is a good commentary.

G

Gaffin, Jr., Richard B. "The Usefulness of the Cross." *Westminster Theological Journal* 41, no. 2 (Spring 1979). Gaffin's inaugural address at Westminster Seminary. Explores some productive paths.*

———. *In the Fullness of Time: An Introduction to the Biblical Theology of Acts and Paul.* Wheaton, IL: Crossway, 2022. Gaffin is not the easiest to read, but he is a profound and original thinker representing the best of Westminster Seminary (Machen, Van Til, Murray). This book is not heavily footnoted and so lacks some balance. I commend it as a conversation partner even for those like me who dispute his findings.*

Gamble, Richard C. *The Whole Counsel of God, Volume 1: God's Mighty Acts in the Old Testament.* Phillipsburg, NJ: P&R, 2009. Clearly presented and thorough CT perspective.

———. *The Whole Counsel of God, Volume 2: The Full Revelation of God.* Phillipsburg, NJ: P&R, 2018. Concentrates on the NT. Very large and multifaceted Reformed treatment. I disagree nearly as much as I agree.*

Garland, Tony. *A Testimony of Jesus Christ: A Commentary on the Book of Revelation,* 2 vols. Camano Island, WA: SpiritAndTruth, 2004. To my mind, this is in the top 3 commentaries on Revelation. Patient, thorough, carefully thought through. Includes many illuminating excurses.*

———. "Daniel and the Times of the Gentiles." *SpiritAndTruth.org.* Available at https://www.spiritandtruth.org/teaching/documents/articles/125/125.pdf. Solid thinking leading to solid conclusions.*

Geisler, Norman L. *Systematic Theology, Volume 4: Church/Last Things.* Minneapolis: Bethany House, 2005. I don't care for the other 3 volumes as they put Thomistic philosophy too much in the driving seat. This one is excellent.*

Gentry, Peter J., and Stephen J. Wellum. *Kingdom through Covenant: A Biblical-Theological Understanding of the Covenants.* Wheaton, IL: Crossway, 2012. A valiant effort to refocus on the covenants. Sadly, their typology ends up distorting the meaning of those covenants.#

Gentry, Peter J., and Andrew M. Fountain. "Reassessing Jude's Use of Enochic Traditions (With Notes on the Later Reception History)." *Tyndale Bulletin* 68, no. 2 (2017). A thorough review of the data which advocates for caution in ascribing to Jude any reliance upon the book of Enoch.*

Gerstner, John H. *Wrongly Dividing the Word of Truth: A Critique of Dispensationalism.* 2nd ed. Nicene Council, 2009. Polemical. Misrepresents and caricatures dispensationalism. Not recommended.

Gilley, Gary E. "Things That Differ: The Fundamentals of Dispensationalism." *TOTT Ministries.* Available at https://tottministries.org/things-that-differ-the-fundamentals-of-dispensationalism/. A brief but helpful review of Stam's book.*

Gladd, Benjamin L. *From the Manger to the Throne: A Theology of Luke.* Wheaton, IL: Crossway, 2022. A decent introduction that does not emphasize Luke's "postponement" eschatology.

———. "Mark." In *A Biblical-Theological Introduction to the New Testament: The Gospel Realized,* edited by Michael J. Kruger. Wheaton, IL: Crossway, 2016. An insightful Reformed treatment.

Glasscock, Ed. *Matthew.* Chicago: Moody, 1997. To my mind, the most accurate overall commentary on this Gospel.*

Glass, Ronald N. "The Parables of the Kingdom: A Paradigm for Consistent Dispensational Hermeneutics." *Master's Seminary Journal* 5 (Spring/Fall 1994). An interesting article arguing for a more consistent literal hermeneutic in opposition to PD.

Gleaves, G. Scott. *Did Jesus Speak Greek?: The Emerging Evidence of Greek Dominance in First-Century Palestine.* Eugene, OR: Pickwick, 2015. The first part deals well with the substance of the title. The last part has some useful studies (e.g., Luke was a Jew).

Glenny, W. Edward. "Typology: A Summary of the Present Evangelical Discussion." *Journal of the Evangelical Theological Society* 40, no. 4 (December 1997): 627-38. An older but still helpful survey.

———. "The Israelite Imagery of 1 Peter 2." In *Dispensationalism, Israel and the Church,* edited by Craig A. Blaising and Darrell L. Bock. A needed study.

Grabbe, Lester L. *An Introduction to Second Temple Judaism: History and Religion of the Jews in the Time of Nehemiah, the Maccabees, Hillel, and Jesus.* London: T&T Clark, 2010. A massive historical study. Liberal but full of information.

———. "Jewish Wars with Rome." In *Dictionary of New Testament Background,* edited by Craig A. Evans and Stanley E. Porter. Downers Grove, IL: InterVarsity, 2000. Very informative.*

Goeman, Peter. *The Baptism Debate: Understanding and Evaluating Reformed Infant Baptism.* Raleigh, NC: Sojourner Press, 2023. Very ably demonstrates the assumptions which produce paedobaptist interpretations.*

———. "The Role of the LXX in James' Use of Amos 9:11-12 in Acts 15:15-18." *Journal of Dispensational Theology* 18, no. 54 (Summer/Fall 2014): 107-25. Argues that James also used Isaiah 45:21 and Zechariah 8:22 in Acts 15.

Godet, F. *A Commentary on the Gospel of Luke,* trans. E. W. Shalders. Edinburgh: T&T Clark, 1887. A highly competent exegetical work. Conservative and pastoral.*

———. *Commentary on the Epistle to the Romans.* Grand Rapids: Zondervan, 1956. Another fine commentary. Godet was an independent thinker who at times drifted into debated areas.

Goldsworthy, Graeme. *According to Plan: The Unfolding Revelation of God in the Bible.* Downers Grove, IL: IVP, 2002. Influential reading of the storyline of Scripture from a Reformed and spiritualizing perspective. Includes a terrific "Van Tillian" exposition of the sufficiency of Scripture.

Gorman, Michael J. *Cruciformity: Paul's Narrative Spirituality of the Cross.* Grand Rapids: Eerdmans, 2001. An important work on the role of dying to self through going to the cross.*

———. *Participating in Christ: Explorations in Paul's Theology and Spirituality.* Grand Rapids: Baker, 2019. I like the emphasis on participation in this book. I don't accept theosis, but Gorman is on to something.*

———. *The Death of the Messiah and the Birth of the New Covenant: A (Not so) New Model of the Atonement.* Eugene, OR: Cascade, 2014. This thought-provoking study into the purpose of the atonement and its links to the New Covenant is a real contribution to NT studies. And yes, there is room to disagree.*

Green, Joel B. *The Gospel of Luke.* NICNT. Grand Rapids: Eerdmans, 1997. Detailed exegesis with liberal tendencies.

Green, Joel B., Scot McKnight, and I. Howard Marshall, eds. *Dictionary of Jesus and the Gospels.* Downers Grove, IL: IVP, 1992. Generally speaking, this is an exceptional resource, but watch for liberal tarnishes.*

Green, Joel B., and Max Turner, eds. *Jesus of Nazareth: Lord and Christ: Essays on the Historical Jesus and New Testament Christology.* Grand Rapids: Eerdmans, 1994. FS for I. H. Marshall. Outstanding set of essays (Burge apart).*

Grier, W. J. *The Momentous Event.* Edinburgh: Banner of Truth, 1976. Recommended at Seminaries in the UK. Hardly up to the job of a full critique of dispensationalism.

Grisanti, Michael. "A Critique of Gentry and Wellum's *Kingdom Through Covenant: An Old Testament Perspective.*" *Master's Seminary Journal* 26, no. 1 (Spring 2015). Excellent critique from an OT scholar.*

Gundry, Robert H. *The Use of the Old Testament in St. Matthew's Gospel.* Leiden: E. J. Brill, 1967. An oft-cited study.

———. *Commentary on the New Testament.* Peabody, MA: Hendrickson, 2010. A surprisingly good NT commentary which tries to faithfully and accurately expound the text. Has none of the author's more controversial tendencies.*#

Gundry, Stanley N., ed. *Five Views on Law and Gospel.* Grand Rapids: Zondervan, 1996. Five views are a bit much, but this is well done.

Gunn, David. "An Overview of New Covenant Passages, Ostensible and Actual." In *An Introduction to the New Covenant,* edited by Christopher Cone. A solid treatment of NC texts from the perspective of an Israel-only advocate. Too selective for me. Sometimes he takes away what he appears to give.

Gunn, George. "Second Corinthians 3:6 and the New Covenant." In *An Introduction to the New Covenant,* edited by Christopher Cone. Does not include the dispensational view that the Church is a full participant in the NC. With respect, a valiant attempt to interpret Paul's language against what it appears to say.

Gurnall, William. *The Christian in Complete Armour.* Peabody, MA: Hendrickson, 2010. Unparalleled in scope. A wonderful example of faithful Puritan pulpit ministry.*

Gurtner, Daniel M., and Benjamin L. Gladd, eds. *From Creation to New Creation: Biblical Theology and Exegesis.* Peabody, MA: Hendrickson, 2013. A good set of pro and con articles in honor of G. K. Beale. Especially good are the chapters that take issue with Beale's program (e.g., Block, Willits).

Guthrie, Donald. *New Testament Theology.* Downers Grove, IL: IVP, 1981. A sound canonical exposition of NT Theology.*

———. *A Shorter Life of Christ.* Grand Rapids: Zondervan, 1970. Reprinted from a dictionary article. Well done, but would have been better with some editorial adjustments.

Guthrie, George H. "Hebrews." In *Commentary on the New Testament Use of the Old Testament,* edited by G. K. Beale and D. A. Carson. Grand Rapids: Baker, 2007. An expert on Hebrews. First rate.*

H

Hafemann, Scott J. "The Covenant Relationship." In *Central Themes in Biblical Theology: Mapping Unity and Diversity,* edited by Scott J. Hafemann and Paul R. House. Grand Rapids: Baker, 2007. I didn't like this when I first read it, but I'm glad I gave it another chance. Minus the eschatology, this is a really good piece. He calls Paul "An Apostle of the New Covenant."*

———, and Paul R. House, eds. *Central Themes in Biblical Theology: Mapping Unity and Diversity.* Grand Rapids: Baker, 2007. A strong selection of chapters on themes like covenant, atonement, the Day of the Lord, etc.

Hagner, Donald A. *Matthew 1–13.* Dallas: Word Books, WBC, 1993. Liberal traces amid great exegesis. Get it for the latter.*

———. *Matthew 14–28.* Dallas: Word Books, 1995.*

Hahn, Scott W. "Kingdom and Church in Luke-Acts." In *Reading Luke,* edited by Craig G. Bartholomew et al. The most interesting essay in a disappointing book.

Hall, Joseph. *Contemplations on the Historical Passages of the Old and New Testaments.* London: T. Nelson and Sons, 1868. A great homiletical overview of Bible history. Why has no one reprinted Bishop Hall's works?*

Hamilton, Jr., James M. *Typology: Understanding the Bible's Promise-Shaped Patterns.* Grand Rapids: Zondervan, 2022. The author has thought deeply about the "perception-shaping promises" of the OT and how they raised certain typological expectations among Bible readers. He shows this by providing his own translation to highlight commonalities and by displaying repeated emphases. I remain unpersuaded.

———. *God's Glory in Salvation Through Judgment: A Biblical Theology.* Wheaton, IL: Crossway, 2010. A competent Biblical Theology, but lacks a treatment of the Covenants.

———. *God's Indwelling Presence: The Holy Spirit in the Old and New Testaments.* Nashville: B&H, 2006. An honest effort to resolve the matter of the Spirit's work in OT saints. Not fully convincing but commendable.*

———. "The Skull Crushing Seed of the Woman: Inner-Biblical Interpretation of Genesis 3:15." *Southern Baptist Journal of Theology* 10, no. 2 (Summer 2006). An interesting study.

Harmon, Matthew S. *The God Who Judges and Saves: A Theology of 2 Peter and Jude.* Wheaton, IL: Crossway, 2023. Reformed treatment of these books. Needs to take the supernatural "weirdness" of the books more seriously.

———. "Allegory, Typology, or Something Else? Revisiting Galatians 4:21–5:1." In *Studies in the Pauline Epistles: Essays in Honor of Douglas J. Moo,* edited by Matthew S. Harmon and Jay E. Smith. Grand Rapids: Zondervan, 2014. I'm not a big fan of some intertextuality studies because they tend to raise more questions than they answer. This one channels Gen. 16ff. through Isa. 54:1.

Harmon, Matthew S., and Jay E. Smith, eds. *Studies in the Pauline Epistles: Essays in Honor of Douglas J. Moo.* Grand Rapids: Zondervan, 2014. A very well-put-together group of essays with a stellar set of contributors. I couldn't disagree more with Caneday and Beale, but I am glad to have their essays, not to mention those of Dunn and Westerholm.*

Harris III, W. Hall, et al. *The NET Bible,* First edition. *Bible.org,* 2005. A great study tool.*

Harris, H. Hall. "A Theology of John's Writings." In *A Biblical Theology of the New Testament,* edited by Roy. B. Zuck. 1994. A worthwhile assessment of John's theology.*

Hart, John F. "Should Pretribulationists Reconsider the Rapture in Matthew 24:36–44?" Part 2. *Journal of the Grace Evangelical Society* 21, no. 40 (Spring 2008). Although I cannot agree with the conclusions, I applaud this author's attempt to take another look at this passage.

Hart, John F. "Should Pretribulationists Reconsider the Rapture in Matthew 24:36–44?" *Journal of the Grace Evangelical Society* 20, no. 39 (Autumn 2007): 47–70.

Hawthorne, Gerald F. *The Presence and The Power: The Significance of the Holy Spirit in the Life and Ministry of Jesus.* Eugene, OR: Wipf and Stock, 2003. A good study on an important subject.

Hawthorne, Gerald F., Ralph P. Martin, et al., eds. *Dictionary of Paul and His Letters.* Downers Grove, IL: IVP, 1993. A very important dictionary.*

Hays, Richard B., and Joel B. Green. "The Use of the Old Testament by New Testament Writers." In *Hearing the New Testament,* edited by Joel B. Green. Grand Rapids: Eerdmans, 1995. I was surprised at the careful way the subject was handled by these scholars.

Hays, Richard B. *Echoes of Scripture in the Gospels.* Waco, TX: Baylor University Press, 2016. Even if one doesn't accept all the "echoes" Hays finds (and I don't), one has to be mightily impressed with the subtlety of the author's thought. Hays is a superb exegete.*

———. *Echoes of Scripture in the Letters of Paul.* New Haven: Yale University Press, 1989. A smaller book than the above but marked by the same scrupulous touch. This is not to say I am okay with the conclusions, but Hays is certainly a top scholar.

———. *Reading with the Grain of Scripture.* Grand Rapids: Eerdmans, 2020. A group of penetrating essays on various subjects. Parts 3 and 4 on Paul and NT Theology respectively are especially good.*

———. *The Conversion of the Imagination: Paul as Interpreter of Israel's Scripture.* New Haven: Yale University Press, 1989. Mostly early essays on Paul with a response to the first "Echoes" book.

Helyer, Larry R. *The Witness of Jesus, Paul and John: An Exploration of Biblical Theology.* Downers Grove, IL: IVP, 2008. Helyer's books are always informative and strive to be fair. Laddian eschatology.*

———. *Exploring Jewish Literature of the Second Temple Period: A Guide for New Testament Students.* Downers Grove, IL: IVP, 2002. An impressive and readable introduction.*

Hendriksen, William. *A Commentary on the Gospel of John.* London: Banner of Truth, 1964. As long as one can navigate the dogmatic theology, this is a very good preacher's commentary.

Henebury, Paul Martin. *Method and Function in Dispensational Theology: A Theological Prolegomenon.* Dissertation presented to the Faculty of Tyndale Theological Seminary, 2006. This is the work that started me on my quest to find another motif (God's covenants) other than dispensations or theological covenants by which to read the Bible. I would change parts of it to reflect my understandings of covenant.

———. *The Words of the Covenant: Volume One, Old Testament Expectation.* Maitland, FL: Xulon, 2021. I find myself in complete agreement with this author. It's like our minds are one.

———. *Deciphering Covenant Theology.* Forthcoming, D.V. Hopefully, this will see the light of day since I believe it fills a gap.

———. "Jesus Christ, The Logos of God: An Inquiry into the Johannine Prologue and Its Significance." *Conservative Theological Journal* 8, no. 23 (March 2004). An attempt to provide a rounded introduction to John's Logos concept.

Hengel, Martin. *Judaism and Hellenism: Studies in their Encounter in Palestine during the Early Hellenistic Period.* London: SCM Press, 1974. Two volumes in one. Brilliant and quite readable. The second volume is the notes.*

Hengstenberg, E. W. *Christology of the Old Testament,* 2 vols. Edinburgh: T & T Clark, 1861. Written in the mid-19th century, there is still nothing comparable.*

Henry, Carl F. H. *God, Revelation and Authority,* vol. 3. Wheaton, IL: Crossway, 1999. Many people criticize Henry for being too rationalist. This isn't helped by his "verificationalist" prolegomena in Vol. 1. However, there is a great deal of very good conservative material in these volumes.*

———, ed. *Prophecy in the Making.* Carol Stream, IL: Creation House, 1971. An older set of essays from different perspectives.

Henry, Matthew. *Matthew Henry's Commentary,* in one volume, edited by Rev. Leslie F. Church. Grand Rapids: Zondervan, 1961. Henry is at once devotional and sagacious. A great work of the Puritan era.*

Hiebert, D. Edmond. *Second Peter and Jude: An Expositional Commentary.* Greenville, SC: Bob Jones University Press, 1989. Hiebert's works are always good.*

———. *The Gospel of Mark: An Expositional Commentary.* Greenville, SC: Bob Jones University Press, 1994. A top-running exposition of the text. The format is not the best, but the material is very good.*

Hill, David. *The Gospel of Matthew.* NCBC. Grand Rapids: Eerdmans, 1982. Nicely written. Used to be highly recommended. Critical in places.

Hoch, Jr., Carl B. *All Things New: The Significance of Newness for Biblical Theology.* Grand Rapids: Baker, 1995. A very fine series of studies from a PD point of view. Valuable appendix on the meaning of "Israel" in the NT.*

Hodges, Zane C. "Regeneration: A New Covenant Blessing." *Journal of the Grace Evangelical Society* 18, no. 35 (Autumn 2005). Short, interesting, but not compelling.

———. "Hebrews." In *The Bible Knowledge Commentary: New Testament,* edited by John F. Walvoord and Roy B. Zuck. Good commentary but unpersuasive on the Warning Passages.

Hoekema, Anthony A. *The Bible and the Future.* Grand Rapids: Eerdmans, 1994. Important because the author challenged the reigning "kingdom up in heaven" position of most amils.

Hoehner, Harold W. *Ephesians: An Exegetical Commentary.* Grand Rapids: Baker, 2003. The best on Ephesians. Excellent in every way. Why can't other dispensationalists write works like this?*

———. *Chronological Aspects of the Life of Christ.* Grand Rapids: Zondervan, 1978. An important reworking of Anderson's chronology.*

Hogg, C. F., and W. E. Vine. *The Epistles of Paul the Apostle to the Thessalonians.* London: Pickering and Inglis, 1929. An older exegetical commentary which is worth having.

Holwerda, David E. *Jesus and Israel: One Covenant or Two?* Grand Rapids: Eerdmans, 1995. Often cited as a definitive study of why the Church in Christ is the new Israel. Includes an unsatisfactory exegesis of Rom. 9–11.

Hooker, Morna D. *The Gospel According to Saint Mark.* Peabody, MA: Hendrickson, 1991. An oft-cited work that is full of insight. Not my first choice, though.

Horner, Barry E. *Future Israel.* Nashville: B&H, 2005. A very good study by a concerned premillennialist.*

Hughes, Philip Edgcumbe. *Paul's Second Epistle to the Corinthians.* London: Marshall, Morgan and Scott, 1962. An excellent older commentary on this great epistle.*

———. *A Commentary on the Epistle to the Hebrews.* Grand Rapids: Eerdmans, 1977. I like everything I've read by this author, even though I don't always agree with him.*

Hullinger, Jerry M. "A Reexamination of Pharaoh's Hard Heart with Regard to Egyptian Religion." *Journal of Dispensational Theology* 16, no. 47 (April 2012). A well-grounded full explanation.*

Hultberg, Alan. "The Future Restoration of Israel: Some Theological Considerations." In *The Future Restoration of Israel,* edited by Stanley E. Porter and Alan E. Kurschner. Lots of Scripture references and interaction with scholars. A first-rate study.*#

Hurtado, Larry W. *God in New Testament Theology.* Nashville: Abingdon, 2010. A very careful analysis. Typical Hurtado.*

———. *Lord Jesus Christ: Devotion to Jesus in Earliest Christianity.* Grand Rapids: Eerdmans, 2003. A superlative treatment of the first Christians' understanding and acknowledgement of Jesus.*

I

Instone-Brewer, David. "Introduction to the English Translation." In *A Commentary on the New Testament from the Talmud and Midrash,* vol. 1, by Hermann L. Strack and Paul Billerbeck. Bellingham, WA: Lexham, 2022. Instone-Brewer is an authority on the subject. His Introduction warning of the misuse of "Rabbinic parallels" is much needed. The S–B is beautifully presented.*

J

James, Steven L. *New Creation Eschatology and the Land: A Survey of Contemporary Approaches.* Eugene, OR: Wipf and Stock, 2017. A well-reasoned and informative exposition of the "landedness" of the New Creation. Recommended.*#

Jeremias, Joachim. *Rediscovering the Parables.* New York: SCM Press, 1966. A more popular presentation of Jeremias's findings.

Jipp, Joshua W. *Christ is King: Paul's Royal Ideology.* Minneapolis: Fortress, 2015. I cannot agree that Christ is reigning now, but this study provides good material on the meaning of the title.

———. *The Messianic Theology of the New Testament.* Grand Rapids: Eerdmans, 2020. I don't know where Jipp gets the idea that NT theologies are passe, but whatever his opinion on that, he has written a helpful methodical book on the Messiah theme in the NT. Amillennial.*

Jobes, Karen H. *John Through Old Testament Eyes.* Grand Rapids: Kregel, 2021. A useful commentary which doesn't really live up to its title.#

Jocz, Jakob. *The Covenant: A Theology of Human Destiny.* Grand Rapids: Eerdmans, 1968. Good as far as he places needed emphasis on the importance of God as a covenant God. Not so good in his handling of the actual covenants themselves.

Johnson, Dennis E. *Triumph of the Lamb: A Commentary on Revelation.* Phillipsburg, NJ: P&R, 2001. A typical amillennial treatment. More readable than most.#

———. *Him We Proclaim: Preaching Christ from All the Scriptures.* Phillipsburg, NJ: P&R, 2007. Adheres to Covenant Theology and reads the OT through the NT.

Johnson, D. H. "Logos." In *Dictionary of Jesus and the Gospels,* edited by Joel B. Green, Scot McKnight, and I. Howard Marshall. Downers Grove, IL: IVP, 1992. An informative article.

Johnson, Elliott. *A Dispensational Biblical Theology.* Allen, TX: Bold Grace Ministries, 2016. I was a bit disappointed with this book. Better in the NT than the OT, with some sound insights. Holds to the Gap Theory! I respect Johnson and just expected more.

———. "Prophetic Fulfillment: The Already and Not Yet." In *Issues in Dispensationalism,* edited by Wesley R. Willis and John R. Master. A very good interaction with the concept.*

Johnson, Jr., S. Lewis. "Paul and 'The Israel of God': An Exegetical and Eschatological Case-Study." In *Essays in Honor of J. Dwight Pentecost,* edited by Stanley D. Toussaint and Charles H. Dyer. Chicago: Moody, 1986. One of the best discussions of the subject in print.*

Josephus, Flavius. *Antiquities of the Jews,* many editions. Important for backgrounds.

K

Kaiser, Walter C. *The Promise-Plan of God: A Biblical Theology of the Old and New Testaments.* Grand Rapids: Zondervan, 2008. I cannot get on board with his "Promise Theology," but this is one of the best one-stop Biblical Theologies.*

———. "Kingdom Promises as Spiritual and National." In *Continuity and Discontinuity,* edited by John S. Feinberg. A good treatment.

Kaiser, Walter C., and Moises Silva. *Introduction to Biblical Hermeneutics: The Search for Meaning.* 2nd ed. Grand Rapids: Zondervan, 2007. It seems odd that two authors with such differing eschatological and hermeneutical assumptions should write this book, but it's actually very helpful.

Kane, Robert. *Through the Moral Maze: Searching for Absolute Values in a Pluralistic World.* Armonk, NY: North Castle Books, 1996. A penetrating discussion of moral mores which does not fall into the either/or fallacy. Needs to be supplemented, but still recommended.*

Keener, Craig S. *The Historical Jesus of the Gospels.* Grand Rapids: Eerdmans, 2009. Lavishly footnoted (Keener's footnotes are always worthwhile). An outstanding contribution to the field. It is elegantly written, and despite its length, there is no wastage of words. Throughout his argument, Keener is open about his own biases, even as he exposes the biases in the less conservative academics with whom he chooses to interact.*#

———. *1 Peter: A Commentary.* Grand Rapids: Baker, 2021. Lots of informative sidebars, but I wasn't sold on his viewpoints.

Kent, Jr., Homer A. *The Epistle to the Hebrews.* Grand Rapids: Baker, 1972. Brief reliable study. Takes the "saber-rattling" approach to the Warning Passages.

Kinzer, Mark S. "Zionism in Luke–Acts." In *The New Christian Zionism: Fresh Perspectives on Israel and the Land,* edited by Gerald R. McDermott. Downers Grove, IL: InterVarsity Press, 2016. Kinzer is an important Messianic Jewish voice. This was a good chapter.

Klooster, Fred H. "The Biblical Method of Salvation: Continuity." In *Continuity and Discontinuity: Perspectives on the Relationship Between the Old and New Testaments,* edited by John S. Feinberg. Wheaton, IL: Crossway, 1988. Inferential hermeneutics masquerading as progressive revelation. Supersessionist and postmillennial.

Köstenberger, Andreas J. *The Jesus of the Gospels: An Introduction.* Grand Rapids: Kregel, 2020. Informative studies on the Four Gospels, but a bit dull in places.

———, and Gregory Goswell. *Biblical Theology: A Canonical, Thematic and Ethical Approach.* Wheaton, IL: Crossway, 2023. A large, well-conceived volume, which can get a bit repetitive owing to its stringent method. Competent. The thing I liked most about this book is its prudent and helpful footnotes.

———, and Robert W. Yarbrough, eds. *Understanding the Times: New Testament Studies in the 21st Century.* Wheaton, IL: Crossway, 2011. FS for D. A. Carson. There are some good chapters here, but I was a bit underwhelmed.

Kreitzer, L. J. "Eschatology." In *Dictionary of Paul and His Letters,* edited by Gerald F. Hawthorne and Ralph P. Martin. Downers Grove, IL: InterVarsity, 1993. This is a very full article. Argues that the Kingdom of God is mainly future for Paul.*

Kurschner, Alan E. "Should the 144,000 in Revelation 7:3-8 Be Identified as the Great Multitude in 7:9-13? – A Response to Gregory K. Beale." In *The Future Restoration of Israel,* edited by Stanley E. Porter and Alan E. Kurschner. Counters Beale's unrealistic view.*

L

Ladd, George Eldon. *The Presence of the Future: The Eschatology of Biblical Realism.* Grand Rapids: Eerdmans, 1996. Classic study putting forth the concept of already/not yet eschatology. Very influential. I demur, but I liked some of the chapters.

———. *A Theology of the New Testament.* Grand Rapids: Eerdmans, 1983. Still a top NT Theology.*

———. *The Blessed Hope: A Biblical Study of the Second Advent and the Rapture.* Grand Rapids: Eerdmans, 1990. An argument for posttribulationism.

Lane, William L. *The Gospel of Mark.* NICNT. Grand Rapids: Eerdmans, 1974. Though critical, this is a good commentary.

———. *Hebrews,* 2 vols. WBC. Nashville: Thomas Nelson, 1991. Perhaps the best all-round work on Hebrews.*

———. "Theios Aner Christology and the Gospel of Mark." In *New Dimensions in New Testament Study,* edited by Richard N. Longenecker and Merrill C. Tenney. Grand Rapids: Zondervan, 1974. A good study against Th. Weedon's liberal history of religions view.

Laney, J. Carl. *John.* Chicago: Moody, 1992. A competent premillennial commentary.*

Lanier, Greg. *Old Made New: A Guide to the New Testament Use of the Old Testament.* Wheaton: Crossway, 2022. From a Covenant Theology perspective, this work contains much useful information.

LaRondelle, Hans K. *The Israel of God in Prophecy: Principles of Prophetic Interpretation.* Berrien Springs: Andrews University Press, 1993. An SDA work which is routinely utilized by supersessionists.

Leighton, Robert. *Commentary on First Peter.* Grand Rapids: Kregel, 1981. A great Churchman of the past wrote this commentary. Very devout and not to be missed, but exegetes will need to look elsewhere.

Le Peau, Andrew T. *Mark Through Old Testament Eyes.* Grand Rapids: Kregel, 2017. There is some good material in this commentary, but I think it fails to live up to its title.#

Letham, Robert. *The Holy Trinity: In Scripture, History, Theology, and Worship.* Phillipsburg, NJ: P&R, 2019. Vies with Erickson as the best treatment on the subject.*

———. *Systematic Theology.* Wheaton: Crossway, 2019. This one has not gotten the attention it deserves. Letham starts with the Trinity and attaches other doctrines to that hub. Reformed, erudite, readable. One of the top five systematics in my book.*

Liefeld, Walter L. "Luke." In *EBC,* vol. 8, edited by Frank E. Gaebelein. Grand Rapids: Zondervan, 1984. Competent work within the limits the author had to work in.

Lincoln, Andrew T. *The Gospel According to Saint John.* New York: Continuum, 2005. Underrated but full of insight. A great foil for other commentaries on John.*

———. *Truth on Trial: The Lawsuit Motif in the Fourth Gospel.* Eugene, OR: Wipf and Stock, 2019. Posits that John's use of witness terminology creates a lawsuit/counter lawsuit motif reaching back into Isaiah.

Lindars, Barnabas. *The Gospel of John.* NCBC. Grand Rapids: Eerdmans, 1982. A little idiosyncratic but scholarly.

Lindsey, F. Duane. "Isaiah's Songs of the Servant Part 1: The Call of the Servant in Isaiah 42:1-9." *Bibliotheca Sacra* 139, no. 553 (January 1982). I think he stops too short in his analysis of Isa. 42:6, but this is a helpful article.

Longenecker, Bruce W. "Moral Character and Divine Generosity: Acts 13:13-52 and the Narrative Dynamics of Luke-Acts." In *New Testament Greek and Exegesis: Essays in Honor of Gerald F. Hawthorne,* edited by Amy M. Donaldson and Timothy B. Sailors. Grand Rapids: Eerdmans, 2003. Excellent exegesis of Paul's first speech.*

Longenecker, R. N. *The Epistle to the Romans.* NIGNTC. Grand Rapids: Eerdmans, 2016. Detailed and balanced. Not stuck in a Reformed mold. One of the best Romans commentaries.*

———. "Acts," ad loc. In *EBC,* vol. 10, edited by Frank L. Gaebelein. A superb work for the format.*

Longenecker, Richard N., and Merrill C. Tenney, eds. *New Dimensions in New Testament Study.* Grand Rapids: Zondervan, 1974. Although quite old, there are some very good essays in this book.

Longman III, Tremper. *Revelation Through Old Testament Eyes.* Grand Rapids: Kregel, 2022. If you want a shorter exposition of the amillennial approach to Revelation, this is worth getting.

Lowery, David K. "2 Corinthians." In *BKCNT,* edited by John F. Walvoord and Roy B. Zuck. Victor Books, 1997. A fine exposition.

M

MacArthur, Jr., John F. "Is Christ's Return Imminent?" *TMS* 11, no. 1 (Spring 2000). A good argument for imminence.

MacMillan, J. Douglas. *Jesus, Power Without Measure: The Work of the Holy Spirit in the Life of Our Lord.* Darlington: Evangelical Press, 2015. A fine discussion of the subject matter.

Maier, Gerhard. *Biblical Hermeneutics.* Translated by Robert W. Yarbrough. Wheaton, IL: Crossway, 1994. Maier was a big name in German scholarship. I like this book for its respect of plain-sense and its care in not going to extremes.

Marshall, I. Howard. *New Testament Theology: Many Witnesses, One Gospel.* Downers Grove, IL: InterVarsity, 2004. I love reading Marshall for his style and balance. He was a great scholar. This is perhaps the top NT Theology available.*

———. *Commentary on Luke.* NIGTC. Grand Rapids: Eerdmans, 1989. I know many do not like the layout of this book. It could be me, but I have little trouble with it. The comments are really well worded so that this reads very well. The exegesis is terrific.*

———. *Jesus the Saviour: Studies in New Testament Theology.* Downers Grove, IL: IVP, 1990. A collection of Marshall's essays on Christ in NT Theology. I do not agree with him on many things (esp. covenant in the NT), but he is a good foil.

———. "Lamb of God." In *Dictionary of Jesus and the Gospels,* edited by Joel B. Green, et al. Helpful.

Martin, Ralph P. *New Testament Foundations: A Guide for Students,* 2 vols. Eugene: Wipf and Stock, 1999. Though he is too critical, Martin was a top NT scholar who wrote with great clarity. There is a great deal of good information in these volumes.

———, and Peter H. Davids, eds. *Dictionary of the Later New Testament and Its Development.* Downers Grove, IL: InterVarsity, 1997. Too liberal in places, but there are some very good contributions here.

Master, John R. "The New Covenant." In *Issues in Dispensationalism,* edited by John R. Master and Wesley R. Willis. Chicago: Moody, 1994. Believes Jer. 31 defines the New Covenant and that the NC does not come into being until the eschaton. He thinks this is the dispensational view. Unconvincing but worth interacting with.

———, and Wesley R. Willis, eds. *Issues in Dispensationalism.* Chicago: Moody, 1994. Some very good essays (e.g., Dyer, Fruchtenbaum, Johnson, Feinberg) and some lesser lights.

Mayhue, Richard L. "Jesus: A Preterist Or A Futurist?" *Masters Seminary Journal* 14, no. 1 (Spring 2003). A well-reasoned argument for futurism.

Mays, James Luther. *Amos.* Philadelphia: Westminster Press, 1969. Informative but liberal.

McClain, Alva J. *The Greatness of the Kingdom.* Grand Rapids: Zondervan, 1959. A seminal work on the Kingdom which every serious student of Scripture should study.*

———. *Romans: The Gospel of God's Grace.* Chicago: Moody, 1986. A basic running commentary.

McComiskey, Thomas Edward. *The Covenants of Promise: A Theology of the Old Testament Covenants.* Grand Rapids: Baker, 1985. Tries to streamline the biblical covenants. Covenant Theology but very thoughtful.*

McDermott, Gerald R., ed. *The New Christian Zionism: Fresh Perspectives on Israel and the Land.* Downers Grove, IL: InterVarsity, 2016. Several excellent and timely chapters reversing the modern trend towards amillennialism and supersessionism.*

McFadden, Kevin W. *Faith in the Son of God: The Place of Christ-Oriented Faith within Pauline Theology.* Wheaton: Crossway, 2021. A thorough, thoughtful restatement of the traditional doctrine and part response to writers like Matthew Bates. This is an impressive young scholar.*

McGrew, Lydia. *Hidden in Plain View: Undesigned Coincidences in the Gospels and Acts.* Chillicothe, OH: DeWard Publishing, 2017. A repristination of Blunt's classic study. Fascinating.*

McKelvey, Michael G. "The New Covenant as Promised in the Major Prophets." In *Covenant Theology: Biblical, Theological, and Historical Perspectives,* edited by Guy Prentiss Waters, et al. Wheaton: Crossway, 2020. Although written by a Covenant Theologian, this is a sound all-round survey. It's a shame the theological covenants overwhelm the biblical covenants.*

McKnight, Scot, and Grant R. Osborne, eds. *The Face of New Testament Studies: A Survey of Recent Research.* Grand Rapids: Baker, 2004. Lives up to its title extremely well.*

Mendenhall, George E., and Gary A. Herion. "Covenant." In *The Anchor Bible Dictionary,* vol. 1, edited by David Noel Freedman. New York: Doubleday, 1992. Certainly, this is written from a liberal-critical point of view, but it is informative.

Metzger, Bruce M. *Breaking the Code: Understanding the Book of Revelation.* Nashville: Abingdon Press, 1993. I don't believe the "code" has been correctly identified.

Meyer, Ryan E. "The Interpretation of Matthew 10:23b." *Detroit Baptist Seminary Journal* 24 (2019). A thorough exegetical and theological analysis of this important passage. Argues for imminency.*

Michaels, J. Ramsey. *1 Peter.* WBC. Waco, TX: Word, 1988. Good exegesis but critical.

Middleton, J. Richard. *A New Heaven and a New Earth: Reclaiming Biblical Eschatology.* Grand Rapids: Baker, 2014. An impressive presentation of amillennial eschatology influenced by N. T. Wright. He is no fan of dispensationalism.

Miller, Paul E. *A Loving Life: In a World of Broken Relationships.* Wheaton, IL: Crossway, 2014. A very stirring study of hesed love in *Ruth.**

———. *J-Curve: Dying and Rising with Jesus in Everyday Life.* Wheaton, IL: Crossway, 2019. First-class practical treatment of a vital but neglected doctrine. Miller is a good theologian.*

Moo, Douglas J. *The Epistle to the Romans.* NICNT. Grand Rapids: Eerdmans, 1996. Rated the best commentary on Romans by most authorities.*

———. *A Theology of Paul and His Letters: The Gift of the New Realm in Christ.* Grand Rapids: Zondervan, 2021. A very thorough evangelical treatment which provides good coverage of all the main facets of Paul's thought. Relies quite a lot on Dunn.*

———. "The Law of Moses or the Law of Christ." In *Continuity and Discontinuity,* edited by John S. Feinberg. One of the most even-handed treatments I've read.*

Morgan, Christopher W. "Integrated Spirituality." In *Biblical Spirituality,* edited by Christopher W. Morgan. Wheaton, IL: Crossway, 2019. Excellent study of spirituality in the book of James.*

Morgan, G. Campbell. *The Crises of the Christ,* various editions. Studies several crisis points in the life of Jesus.*

Morris, Leon. *The Gospel According to Matthew.* Grand Rapids: Eerdmans, 1992. No fireworks but a competent commentary. I like this work more than most seem to.

———. *The Gospel According to St. Luke.* TNTC. Grand Rapids: Eerdmans, 1975. Still a good basic commentary, except for the eschatology.

———. *The Gospel According to John.* Grand Rapids: Eerdmans, 1979. The best all-round commentary on this Gospel.*

———. *The First Epistle of Paul to the Corinthians: An Introduction and Commentary.* Grand Rapids: Eerdmans, 1975. Fully to the standard of this respected scholar.

———. *The Apostolic Preaching of the Cross.* London: Tyndale Press, 1983. A classic study of aspects of the atonement including "covenant" and "propitiation."*

Motyer, S. "Israel (Nation)." In *New Dictionary of Biblical Theology,* edited by T. Desmond Alexander, et al. A top scholar on the use of the OT in the NT writes about Israel. Supersessionist.

Mounce, Robert H. *Matthew.* Peabody, MA: Hendrickson, 1991. Packs a lot of good content into a short space. Somewhat critical.

———. *The Book of Revelation.* Grand Rapids: Eerdmans, 1977. Premillennial but also idealistic cum eclectic work.

Munck, Johannes. *Paul and the Salvation of Mankind.* Richmond, VA: John Knox Press, 1959. Liberal dogmatism at its worst, but one or two redeeming features.

Murray, John. *The Covenant of Grace.* Phillipsburg, NJ: P&R, 1953. Good evaluation of the subject from a leading Covenant Theologian.

———. *The Epistle to the Romans.* NICNT. Grand Rapids: Eerdmans, 1982. Very solid Reformed treatment.

N

Nash, Ronald H. *The Gospel and the Greeks: Did the New Testament Borrow from Pagan Thought?* Phillipsburg, NJ: P&R, 2003. Good informative chapters. I wasn't convinced with his Logos theory of Hebrews.

Neusner, Jacob. *Judaism When Christianity Began: A Survey of Belief and Practice.* Louisville: Westminster John Knox Press, 2002. A good basic introduction to Rabbinic Judaism(s) circa A.D. 200–500.

Newman, Carey C. "Covenant, New Covenant." In *Dictionary of the Later New Testament and Its Development,* edited by Ralph P. Martin and Peter H. Davids. Downers Grove, IL: InterVarsity, 1997. Relatively short but informative article which stresses the strong connection between the OT and the NT writers. I disagree with the author's view that the other covenants should be understood through the Mosaic covenant.*

Nichols, Greg. *Covenant Theology: A Reformed and Baptist Perspective on God's Covenants.* Solid Ground Books, 2014. A little idiosyncratic, but worthwhile because of the overviews of other theologians and his extensive treatment of the Abrahamic covenant from a Covenant Theology point of view.

Nickelsburg, George W. E. "Enoch, First Book of." In *The Anchor Bible Dictionary,* vol. 2, edited by David Noel Freedman. New York: Doubleday, 1992. Reliable guide to a book that should not be in the Bible, despite what some theorists say.

Niehaus, Jeffrey J. *Biblical Theology: The Special Grace Covenants,* vol. 3. Wooster, OH: Weaver Book Company, 2022. A good independent study which is still basically Covenant Theology.

Nolland, John. *The Gospel of Matthew.* NIGTC. Grand Rapids: Eerdmans, 2005. Beautifully written and nuanced exegesis. Critical in places.*

Novenson, Matthew. *Christ Among the Messiahs: Christ Language in Paul and Messiah Language in Ancient Judaism.* Oxford: Oxford University Press, 2012. Writes for the academy. This wickedly expensive book shows that *Christos* is used as an honorific, not as a name. I still think there is something to be said for "Christ" as a title.

———. *Paul, Then and Now.* Grand Rapids: Eerdmans, 2022. An intriguing collection of essays on various Pauline themes. Critical but instructive.

O

O'Brien, Peter T. *The Letter to the Hebrews.* Grand Rapids: Eerdmans, 2010. Yes, I caught some (unintended) plagiarism (e.g., of F. F. Bruce), but this is one of the best on this book.*

———. "God as the Speaking God." In *Understanding the Times: New Testament Studies in the 21st Century,* edited by Andreas J. Köstenberger and Robert W. Yarbrough. Wheaton, IL: Crossway, 2011. A nice exploration of the doctrine of God in Hebrews.

Olander, David E. "The Importance of the Davidic Covenant." *Journal of Dispensational Theology* 10, no. 31 (December 2006). An important reminder of the currency of the Davidic covenant.*

Oliver, Isaac. *Luke's Jewish Eschatology: The National Restoration of Israel in Luke-Acts.* Oxford: Oxford University Press, 2021. Concentrates on Acts 1:6-8 and argues for a more literal interpretation. Luke's eschatology has often had to suffer under the cosh of first coming hermeneutics.

Orr, James. *The Progress of Dogma.* New York: A. C. Armstrong and Son, 1907. This is a classic historical theology. It is quite condensed.*

———. *The Resurrection of Jesus.* London: Hodder and Stoughton, 1908. A stirring defense of the reality of Christ's resurrection against the critical ideas circulating in his day.*

Orr, Peter. *The Beginning of the Gospel: A Theology of Mark.* Wheaton, IL: Crossway, 2022. Competent mid-level introductory material. But if you already own a good commentary...?

Owen, John. *Exposition of the Epistle to the Hebrews,* vol. 3. Edinburgh: Banner of Truth, 1991. Enormous in every way. Owen the expositor is easier to read than Owen the theologian. John Owen is a deeply spiritual author.*

P

Paige, T. "Holy Spirit." In *Dictionary of Paul and His Letters,* edited by Gerald Hawthorne, et al. A solid article.

Parker, Brent E. "The Israel-Christ-Church Relationship." In *Progressive Covenantalism,* edited by Stephen J. Wellum and Brent Parker. Nashville: B&H, 2016. I'm sorry, but this is the diametric opposite of my position. That doesn't mean I despise it. Just that it is not the "Covenantalism" I find in the Bible.

Pember, G. H. *The Antichrist, Babylon, and the Coming of the Kingdom.* London: Hodder and Stoughton, 1888. Pember was a great writer. This is a rather odd mix of biblical and historical exposition. Holds to Rome as Babylon in Revelation 17.

Pentecost, J. Dwight. *Thy Kingdom Come: Tracing God's Kingdom Program and Covenant Promises Throughout History.* Grand Rapids: Kregel, 1995. Good use of dispensations and covenants. Notable is the use of Scripture alone.*

———. *Things to Come: A Study in Biblical Eschatology.* Grand Rapids: Zondervan, 1976. One of the finest texts on eschatology ever published. Good reliance on Peters. The style is "scholastic" and it needs updating.*

———. *The Divine Comforter: The Person and Work of the Holy Spirit.* Chicago: Moody Press, 1977. An excellent study of the Third Person.*

Perrin, Nicholas. *The Kingdom of God: A Biblical Theology.* Grand Rapids: Zondervan, 2019. An agile mind. Lots of information but rooted in first coming interpretation.

Peters, George N. H. *The Theocratic Kingdom,* 3 vols. Grand Rapids: Kregel, 1972. An extraordinary book. Notable for several reasons, not least because it is theocentric and so avoids treating eschatology in isolation. Not perfect (e.g. holds to a partial rapture), but the work on the subject. The person who masters Peters will be a formidable Bible teacher.*

Pettegrew, Larry D., ed. *Forsaking Israel: How It Happened and Why it Matters.* The Woodlands, TX, 2021. Mainly by Pettegrew with a few other essays thrown in. A worthy historical and biblical study of the title. A good book to give to anyone interested in biblical Israel.*

———. *The New Covenant Ministry of the Holy Spirit.* The Woodlands, TX: Kress, 2013. A key work in relating the New covenant with the work of the Spirit. Although I recommend it, I would have loved to have seen him go all out for the Church's full participation in the New covenant.*

———. "The New Covenant." *Masters Seminary Journal* 10 (Fall 1999). Excellent.*

Pickering, Ernest. "Distinctive Teachings of Ultra-Dispensationalism." *Central Conservative Baptist Theological Seminary Quarterly* 04, no. 4 (Winter 1961). A refutation of this position focusing on J. C. O'Hair and Cornelius Stam.

Piepgrass, C. E. "A Study of the New Testament References to the Old Testament Covenants." Th.D. diss., Dallas Theological Seminary, 1968. I haven't read this work. I need to!

Piper, John. *The Justification of God: An Exegetical and Theological Study of Romans 9:1-23.* Grand Rapids: Baker, 1993. Highly regarded Calvinist apologetic. Argues for individual election, which I think misses Paul's whole point.

Pitre, Brant, Michael P. Barber, and John A. Kincaid. *Paul, A New Covenant Jew: Rethinking Pauline Theology.* Grand Rapids: Eerdmans, 2019. A thought-provoking study which positions Paul and his New covenant teaching where it ought to be. This is not to say I hold to their view on justification.*#

Porter, Stanley E. *The Apostle Paul: His Life, Thought, and Letters.* Grand Rapids: Eerdmans, 2016. Thorough and informative without being overly long. Careful defense of the Pauline authorship of the Letters.

Porter, Jr., Virgil V. "The Sermon on the Mount in the Book of James, Part 1." *Bibliotheca Sacra* 162, no. 647 (July 2005).

———. "The Sermon on the Mount in the Book of James, Part 2." *Bibliotheca Sacra* 162, no. 648 (October 2005). This is a very helpful study.

Poythress, Vern S. *The Returning King: A Guide to the Book of Revelation.* Phillipsburg, NJ: P&R, 2000. Amillennial treatment.

———. *Theophany: A Biblical Theology of God's Appearing.* Phillipsburg, NJ: P&R, 2020. This author has a prodigious output. Stretches the idea a bit, but this is an excellent place to go to study Theophanies in Scripture.*

Pratt, Jr., Richard. "Reformed Theology is Covenant Theology." June 1, 2010. https://www.ligonier.org/learn/articles/reformed-theology-covenant-theology. Nice corrective which makes the case that Reformed Theology is more than the doctrines of grace.

Price, J. Randall. *The Temple and Bible Prophecy: A Definitive Look at Its Past, Present, and Future.* Harvest House, 2005. A very informative and full study.*

Provan, Charles D. *The Church is Israel Now: The Transfer of Conditional Privilege.* Ross House Books, 2004. Builds on the thesis that because certain designations are used of the Church as are used of OT Israel, that means, well, look at the title. Replacement theology.

———. "The Church is Israel Now." http://www.preteristarchive.com/PartialPreterism/provan-charles_dd_01.html. See above.

Pryor, John W. *John: Evangelist of the Covenant People.* Downers Grove, IL: InterVarsity, 1992. This is a good book to read alongside the commentaries on John.

Q

Quarles, Charles L. *Matthew.* EBTC. Bellingham, WA: Lexham, 2022. Lengthy yet accessible. Quarles knows how to write a commentary. Definitely one of the best recent efforts.*

R

Rackham, Richard Belward. *The Acts of the Apostles: An Exposition.* London: Methuen, 1922. A great classic from an earlier era.*

Radmacher, Earl D. "The Imminent Return of the Lord." *CTSJ* 4, no. 3 (July 1998). A worthy survey of the textual data.

Reiter, Richard R. *Three Views on the Rapture: Pre-, Mid-, or Post-Tribulation.* Grand Rapids: Zondervan, 1996. Three very able contributions. This has since been replaced by an edition that switches out Mid-trib with PreWrath.

Reymond, Robert L. *A New Systematic Theology of the Christian Faith,* 2nd ed. Nashville: Thomas Nelson Publishers, 2002. Very Reformed and not friendly to dispensationalism. Adopts an intriguing supralapsarian view of the fall. Terrific Prolegomena which is less Clarkian than I expected. Very competent.*#

Ridderbos, Herman. *The Coming of the Kingdom.* Phillipsburg, NJ: P&R, 1962. An important amillennial work.

———. *The Gospel of John: A Theological Commentary.* Grand Rapids: Eerdmans, 1992. There is nothing like this. One of my favorite John commentaries.*

———. *Paul: An Outline of His Theology.* Grand Rapids: Eerdmans, 1975. Academic in style but very thorough.*

Riddlebarger, Kim. *A Case for Amillennialism: Understanding the End Times.* Grand Rapids: Baker, 2003. Sets out amillennialism well.

———. *The Man of Sin: Uncovering the Truth About the Antichrist.* Grand Rapids: Baker, 2006. Amillennial work which dispensationalists can benefit from.

Robertson, A. T. *Word Pictures in the New Testament.* Nashville: Broadman Press, 1930. Although word studies have had their day, Robertson was perhaps the best at them.

Robertson, O. Palmer. *The Christ of the Covenants.* Phillipsburg, NJ: P&R, 1980. Standard Covenant Theology approach. Gives different names to the theological covenants, which can cause confusion. Has a chapter refuting dispensationalism. A go-to for anyone who wants to know Covenant Theology.*

———. *The Israel of God: Yesterday, Today, Tomorrow.* Phillipsburg, NJ: P&R, 2000. Supersessionist and wrong-headed. Better to pay attention to God's oaths!

Rogers, Jr., Cleon L. "The Davidic Covenant in the Gospels." *Bibliotheca Sacra* 150, no. 600 (October 1993). A very good article.*

Rudolph, David. "Zionism in Pauline Literature." In *The New Christian Zionism,* edited by Gerald R. McDermott. A full overview of "transference theology," especially as based upon a misinterpretation of Romans 4:13. Recommended.*

———. "A Messianic Jewish Response." In *God's Israel and the Israel of God: Paul and Supersessionism,* edited by Michael F. Bird and Scot McKnight. Bellingham, WA: Lexham, 2023. The best essay in a disappointing book, and the only one defending Israel's covenant rights.

Rydelnik, Michael, and James Spencer. "Isaiah." In *The Moody Bible Commentary,* edited by Michael Rydelnik and Michael Vanlaningham. Chicago: Moody, 2014. Really good use of the space.

———, and Michael Vanlaningham, eds. *The Moody Bible Commentary.* Chicago: Moody, 2014. A high-quality one-volume commentary.*

Ryrie, Charles C. *Dispensationalism.* Chicago: Moody, 1995. Essential reading. Ryrie was a great communicator. I can't fully get on board with his sine qua non, and I wish he had given more thought to the covenants, but this is highly recommended.*#

———. *Biblical Theology of the New Testament.* Dubuque, IA: ECS Ministries, 2005. Disappointing. Not Ryrie at his best.

S

Sailhamer, John H. *The Meaning of the Pentateuch: Revelation, Composition and Interpretation.* Downers Grove, IL: IVP, 2009. One of the books that has influenced me most. Needed an editor's touch, but the material is superb. And yes, I take issue here and there.*#

———. "Hosea 11:1 And Matthew 2:15." *Westminster Theological Journal* 63 (Spring 2001). Sailhamer is always interesting to read.*

Sandmel, Samuel. "Parallelomania." *Journal of Biblical Literature* 81 (1962). Influential address which is still important and needs to be heeded more than it is.*

Saucy, Mark R. "One Nation under God: Does the World Need an Israelite Theocracy?" In *The Future Restoration of Israel: A Response to Supersessionism,* edited by Stanley E. Porter and Alan E. Kurschner. Eugene, OR: Pickwick, 2023. One of the top 3 articles in a generally excellent work.*#

———. "The Kingdom-of-God Sayings in Matthew." *Bibliotheca Sacra* 151, no. 602 (April 1994). I wish Saucy would produce more.*

———. *The Kingdom of God in the Teaching of Jesus in 20th Century Theology.* Dallas: Word, 1997. Valuable historical surveys with some first-rate chapters presenting the author's position. PD but very useful.*

Saucy, Robert L. *The Case for Progressive Dispensationalism: The Interface Between Dispensational and Non-Dispensational Theology.* Grand Rapids: Zondervan, 1993. By now a classic PD work. Should be read by all because of its thoughtful consideration of many debated topics. I disagree with his understanding of "mystery."*

———. "Does the Apostle Paul Reverse the Prophetic Tradition of the Salvation of Israel and the Nations?" In *Building on the Foundations of Evangelical Theology: Essays in Honor of John S. Feinberg,* edited by Gregg R. Allison and Stephen J. Wellum. Wheaton, IL: Crossway, 2015. A very good corrective essay.*

Sauer, Erich. *From Eternity to Eternity: An Outline of the Divine Purposes.* Grand Rapids: Eerdmans, 1954. A concise yet full survey of Scripture which is premillennial but goes its own way.*

Schep, J. A. *The Nature of the Resurrection Body: A Study of the Biblical Data.* Grand Rapids: Eerdmans, 1964. Proves among other things that *anastasis* refers to physical resurrection in the NT.*

Schlatter, Adolf. *Do We Know Jesus?* Grand Rapids: Kregel, 2005. Readable, stirring devotional from one of the great NT scholars of the early 20th century.*

Schmitt, John W., and J. Carl Laney. *Messiah's Coming Temple: Ezekiel's Prophetic Vision of the Future Temple.* Grand Rapids: Kregel, 2014. Excellent detailed treatment.*

Schnabel, Eckhard J. *Early Christian Mission,* 2 vols. Downers Grove, IL: InterVarsity, 2004. Voluminous and remarkable. There's more here than simply a record of the Church's nascent mission efforts.*

———. *Jesus in Jerusalem: The Last Days.* Grand Rapids: Eerdmans, 2018. Perhaps the standard on the final days of Jesus. Opts for an A.D. 30 date for the crucifixion.*

———. *New Testament Theology.* Grand Rapids: Baker, 2024. Because it has just appeared I haven't read that much of this work. What I have read is outstanding.*

Schreiner, Patrick. *Matthew, Disciple and Scribe: The First Gospel and Its Portrait of Jesus.* Grand Rapids: Baker Academic, 2019. This author always picks interesting things to write about. Employs a first coming hermeneutic leading to typological interpretation.

Schreiner, Thomas R. *Covenant and God's Purpose for the World.* Wheaton, IL: Crossway, 2017. Schreiner is a top evangelical scholar. This little book is a mixture of good and not so good.

———. *Paul, Apostle of God's Glory in Christ: A Pauline Theology.* Downers Grove, IL: IVP, 2001. One of the best on Paul.*

———. *Romans.* BECNT. Grand Rapids: Baker, 1998. As above, this is one of the must-have Romans works.*

———. *The King in His Beauty: A Biblical Theology of the Old and New Testaments.* Grand Rapids: Baker, 2013. A really good Biblical Theology in many ways, although his inaugurated eschatology is a problem.

——— and Shaun D. Wright, eds. *Believer's Baptism: Sign of the New Covenant in Christ.* Nashville: B&H, 2007. A persuasive work when arguing against paedobaptism. Not so reliable on the covenants themselves.

——— and Ardel B. Caneday. *The Race Set Before Us: A Biblical Theology of Perseverance and Assurance.* Downers Grove, IL: InterVarsity, 2001. An influential argument for what I call the Divine saber-rattling hypothesis on the Warning Passages.

Schutz, John Howard. *Paul and the Anatomy of Apostolic Authority.* Louisville: John Knox Press, 2007. Although critical in places, this exploration of apostolic authority through the Gospel is an important contribution.*

Scobie, Charles H. H. *The Ways of Our God: An Approach to Biblical Theology.* Grand Rapids: Eerdmans, 2003. Encyclopedic. Organized more around doctrines. A tad critical but very good.*

Seccombe, David. *The King of God's Kingdom: A Solution to the Puzzle of Jesus.* Carlisle: Paternoster Press, 2002. Half apologetic, half a study of the Gospels. Devotional in tone. Good but too expensive.

Seebass, H. "*Miseo.*" In *New International Dictionary of New Testament Theology,* edited by Colin Brown. Grand Rapids: Zondervan, 1975. An excellent work in general.

Seifrid, Mark A. *Christ Our Righteousness: Paul's Theology of Justification.* Downers Grove, IL: InterVarsity, 2000. Tends to center Paul's theology around "righteousness." This can be a little obtuse in places. A good theological monograph.*

———. "Unrighteous by Faith: Apostolic Proclamation in Romans 1:18-3:20." In *Justification and Variegated Nomism,* vol. 2, *The Paradoxes of Paul,* edited by D. A. Carson, Peter T. O'Brien, and Mark A. Seifrid. Grand Rapids: Baker, 2004. A fine contribution to a fine volume.

———. "In Christ." In *Dictionary of Paul and His Letters,* edited by Gerald F. Hawthorne, Ralph P. Martin, et al. A very competent article.*

Showers, Renald E. *There Really Is A Difference: A Comparison of Covenant and Dispensational Theology.* Bellmawr, NJ: Friends of Israel, 1993. A good book, but not a balanced comparison of the two systems. More a defense of dispensationalism. If read on that premise, it is recommended.*

Sibley, Jim R. "You Talkin' To Me? 1 Peter 2:4-10 and A Theology of Israel." *Southwestern Journal of Theology* 59, no. 1 (Fall 2016). Full of Scripture. Well-argued and persuasive.*

Smalley, Stephen S. *The Revelation to John: A Commentary on the Greek Text of the Apocalypse.* Downers Grove, IL: InterVarsity, 2005. For any in the idealist camp, this may be the best commentary. Nicely written and not verbose (think Beale). There is a lot of good exegesis here. It's the conclusions I struggle with. Reads the book as a cosmic drama, which makes sense if you don't take it literally.

Smelley, Hutson. *Better with Jesus: A Mission 119 Guide Through Hebrews.* Self-published, 2015. A good set of studies.

Smith, Gary V. *Isaiah 40–66: An Exegetical and Theological Exposition of Holy Scripture.* NAC. Nashville: B&H Publishing Group, 2009. Smith is an expert on the Prophets. This is very informative.*

Soulen, R. Kendall. *The God of Israel and Christian Theology.* Minneapolis: Fortress, 1996. An influential study in supersessionism.*

Spencer, F. Scott. *Journeying through Acts: A Literary-Cultural Reading.* Grand Rapids: Baker, 2004. As an introduction to Acts, this has a lot going for it.

Spicq, Ceslas. *Theological Lexicon of the New Testament,* vol. 3, translated and edited by James D. Ernest. Peabody, MA: Hendrickson, 1996. Spicq doesn't cover every word in the NT, but those he does are given much thoughtful attention.*

Stallard, Mike, ed. *Dispensational Understanding of the New Covenant.* Schaumburg, IL: Regular Baptist Books, 2012. An important set of articles on the subject of the title. Very well done but lacks a clear representative of the "Church as full party" position.*

———. "Israel in the Book of Revelation." *Council of Dispensational Hermeneutics Paper,* 2021. Available at https://www.youtube.com/watch?v=szb7OaFZqvYandt=3167s. A good coverage in an online lecture.

———. "Hermeneutics and Matthew 13," Parts 1 and 2. *Conservative Theological Journal* 5, no. 15 (August 2001) and *CTJ* 5, no. 16 (December 2001). Part 1 argues for the necessity of literal interpretation, while Part 2 applies this approach to the parables in Matthew 13. Highly recommended.*

Stauffer, Ethelbert. *Jesus and His Story.* New York: Alfred Knopf, 1957. A short but deep study.

Stein, Robert H. "Jesus, The Destruction of Jerusalem, and the Coming of the Son of Man in Luke 21:5-38." *Southern Baptist Journal of Theology* 16, no. 3 (Fall 2012). Inaugurated eschatology.

———. "Last Supper." In *Dictionary of Jesus and the Gospels,* edited by Joel B. Green, et al. A solid, slightly critical article.

Storms, Sam. *Kingdom Come: The Amillennial Alternative.* Rosshire, Scotland: Mentor, 2013. Quite long-winded, but this covers the bases of Amillennial interpretation over against dispensationalism and Premillennialism. Proves that we read prophetic Scripture very differently.

Stott, John R. W. *The Epistles of John.* Leicester: InterVarsity, 1990. Stott was a great communicator. This is fully up to par with his other works.

Strack, Hermann L. and Paul Billerbeck. *A Commentary on the New Testament from the Talmud and Midrash,* vol. 1. Bellingham, WA: Lexham, 2022. Massive and beautifully presented. Instone-Brewer's warning in his Introduction must be heeded.*

Strickland, Wayne G. "The Inauguration of the Law of Christ with the Gospel of Christ: A Dispensational View." In *Five Views on Law and Gospel,* edited by Stanley N. Gundry. Grand Rapids: Zondervan, 1996. A reasonable presentation, but I preferred Moo's approach.

Stuhlmacher, Peter. *Biblical Theology of the New Testament,* translated and edited by Daniel P. Bailey. Grand Rapids: Eerdmans, 2018. Large and detailed (e.g., different sized type for in-depth discussions). Places a welcome emphasis on the proclamation of Jesus. I found myself reading large chunks of this at a single sitting.*

Svigel, Michael J. "The Apocalypse of John and the Rapture of the Church: A Reevaluation." *Trinity Journal* 22 (2001): 53-67. An intriguing but unconvincing argument for Revelation 12:5 as a rapture proof.

T

Tabb, Brian J. *After Emmaus: How the Church Fulfills the Mission of Christ.* Wheaton, IL: Crossway, 2021. Tabb is an intelligent writer and there are good biblical theological things in this book, even when strapped with first coming hermeneutics.

———. *All Things New: Revelation as Canonical Capstone.* Downers Grove, IL: InterVarsity, 2019. A study of the themes of Revelation from a realized eschatology perspective. Very well done even though I disagree.*

Tanner, J. Paul. *Daniel.* EEC. Bellingham, WA: Lexham Press, 2020. I believe the combination of exegesis, background, and theology in this book put it on top of the pile. This thorough analysis must now be the go-to work on Daniel.*

Thielman, Frank. *Theology of the New Testament: A Canonical and Thematic Approach.* Grand Rapids: Zondervan, 2005. Well-organized Reformed treatment.

Thiselton, Anthony C. *The Living Paul: An Introduction to the Apostle's Life and Thought.* Downers Grove, IL: IVP, 2009. Thiselton is an important Christian thinker. This book is informative as an introductory text.

Thomas, Jeremy M. "The 'Mystery' of Progressive Dispensationalism." *Conservative Theological Journal* 9, no. 28 (December 2005). A thoughtful rebuttal.

Thomas, Robert L. *Evangelical Hermeneutics: The New Versus the Old.* Grand Rapids: Kregel, 2003. A much-needed corrective, written mostly by Thomas, which shows that all forms of "grammatical-historical hermeneutics" are not created equal.*

———. *Revelation: An Exegetical Commentary,* 2 vols. Chicago: Moody, 1992. All-round the best commentary on Revelation.*

Thompson, Alan J. *The Acts of the Risen Lord Jesus: Luke's Account of God's Unfolding Plan.* Downers Grove, IL: IVP, 2011. A rather one-sided interpretation of Acts guided by the idea that the kingdom has been set up in the new Israel, which is the Church.

Toussaint, Stanley D. *Behold the King: A Study of Matthew.* Grand Rapids: Kregel, 1980. Not a full commentary, but a very competent thematic study of the first Gospel.*

———. "The Church and Israel." *Conservative Theological Journal* 2 (December 1998). Solid basic treatment.

———. "Acts." In *The Bible Knowledge Commentary: New Testament,* edited by John F. Walvoord and Roy B. Zuck. This is the best treatment of Acts that one could hope for in a single volume Bible Commentary.*

Toussaint, Stanley D., and Charles H. Dyer, eds. *Essays in Honor of J. Dwight Pentecost.* Chicago: Moody, 1986. Many Festschrifts are not all that interesting. This one includes some great articles.*

Treat, Jeremy R. *The Crucified King: Atonement and Kingdom in Systematic and Biblical Theology.* Grand Rapids: Zondervan, 2014. Ties the cross, from where he thinks Christ reigns (!), to the kingdom. Misunderstands the Kingdom because he doesn't listen to the covenants.

Trobisch, David. *On the Origin of Christian Scripture: The Evolution of the New Testament Canon in the Second Century.* Minneapolis: Fortress, 2023. An acknowledged expert on the subject, Trobisch is an independent thinker. I do not follow the author's reconstruction of a full second century NT canon, but Trobisch is good at showing that the first Christians did not have a full NT by which to interpret the OT.

Turretin, Francis. *Institutes of Elenctic Theology,* 3 vols., trans. G. M. Giger, ed. J. T. Dennison, 1997. Phillipsburg, NJ: PandR, 1997. The best of scholastic Reformed theology. "Elenctic" refers to the method of asking and answering questions. Deep, erudite, exhaustive.*

Twelftree, G. H. "Temptation of Jesus." In *Dictionary of Jesus and the Gospels,* edited by Joel B. Green, et al. A very good article.

U

Unger, Merrill F. *Unger's Commentary on the Old Testament: Malachi.* Chicago: Moody, 1981. Unger's notes on the text. Good but to my mind (ironically) he jumps too quickly to prophetic interpretation.

V

Vaillancourt, Ian J. *The Dawning of Redemption: The Story of the Pentateuch and the Hope of the Gospel.* Wheaton, IL: Crossway, 2022. A very accessible introduction to the Pentateuch.

VanGemeren, Willem. *The Progress of Redemption.* Carlisle, UK: Paternoster, 1995. VanGemeren was very prolific in the 80's and 90's. This is one of the best Reformed Biblical Theologies. Divides redemptive history into 12 epochs.*

Vanhoye, Albert. *A Structured Translation of the Epistle to the Hebrews,* trans. James Swetnam. Rome: Pontifical Biblical Institute, 1964. Two studies by the author. The first on genre, the second a literal translation highlighting the structure of Hebrews.

———. *Structure and Message of the Epistle to the Hebrews.* Subsidia Biblica 12. Rome: Gregorian and Biblical Press, 1989. An influential synthetic approach.

———. *The Letter to the Hebrews: A New Commentary.* Mahwah, NJ: Paulist Press, 2015. A relatively brief yet scholarly Roman Catholic commentary.

VanLaningham, Michael G. "A Response to the Progressive Covenantalists' (and Others') View of the Land Promises for Israel." In *The Future Restoration of Israel: A Response to Supersessionism,* edited by Stanley E. Porter and Alan E. Kurschner. Eugene, OR: Pickwick, 2023. A very good and needed critique honing in on Gentry and Wellum's *Kingdom through Covenant.**

———. "Romans." In *The Moody Bible Commentary,* edited by Michael Rydelnik and Michael VanLaningham. A solid treatment.

Van Oosterzee, J. J. *The Gospel According to Luke,* Lange's Commentary, Vol. 8. Grand Rapids: Zondervan, 1980. Although he took the kenotic position this is a really good older commentary.*

Venema, Cornelis P. *Christ and Covenant Theology: Essays on Election, Republication, and the Covenants.* Phillipsburg, NJ: PandR, 2017. Written for the gallery. The first two parts are the best in my opinion.

Vermes, Geza. *Jesus the Jew.* Minneapolis: Fortress, 1981. Does strive to bring Jesus back into His milieu. Bultmannian.

———. *Jesus in His Jewish Context.* Minneapolis: Fortress, 2003. See above. A bit of psychologizing thrown in.

Vlach, Michael J. *He Will Reign Forever: A Biblical Theology of the Kingdom of God.* Silverton, OR: Lampion, 2017. The first Biblical Theology I would place into someone's hands. I hope one day Vlach will expand this book.* #

———. *The New Creation Model: A Paradigm for Discovering God's Restoration Purposes from Creation to New Creation.* Cary, NC: Theological Studies Press, 2023. A great argument for God's future refurbishment of this world in the Kingdom of God. An important step forward for dispensational theology, especially in terms of prolegomena.*

———. *The Old in the New: Understanding How the New Testament Authors Quoted the Old Testament.* The Woodlands: Kress, 2021. A good look at the OT in the NT from a dispensational point of view. Needs a fuller coverage of some passages.*

———. *The New Covenant Lawgiver: Jesus and Law in Matthew 5:17-48,* published independently, 2022. Vlach focuses on the latter part of Matthew 5 to show that Christ issues New Covenant Law.

———. *Has the Church Replaced Israel?: A Theological Evaluation.* Nashville: B&H, 2010. A first-rate work on supersessionism.*

———. "Six Views on New Covenant Fulfillment," https://mikevlach.blogspot.com/2019/07/six-views-on-new-covenant-fulfillment.html. A capable delineation of the subject matter.*

———. "The Eschatology of the Pauline Epistles." In *The Return of Christ: A Premillennial Perspective,* edited by David L. Allen and Steve W. Lemke. Nashville: B&H, 2011. I wish this chapter were longer, but what we've got is great. Believes (correctly) we are living in a New Covenant era.* #

Vos, Geerhardus. *The Pauline Eschatology.* Phillipsburg, NJ: PandR, 1979. Still one of the best expositions of amillennial eschatology. Not easy reading.

———. "Hebrews, the Epistle of the Diatheke." In *The Princeton Theological Review,* Vol. 13, No. 4 [1915]. A classic essay.

———. *Reformed Dogmatics: Ecclesiology, The Means of Grace, Eschatology,* Vol. 5. Bellingham, WA: Lexham Press, 2016. Written in typical question and answer format, this is a bit of a bore unless one is into these kinds of things. Noteworthy though are the deeply reflective brief answers Vos gives, even as a young man.

W

Wallace, Daniel B. *Greek Grammar Beyond the Basics: An Exegetical Syntax of the New Testament.* Grand Rapids: Zondervan, 1996. The standard text.*

Walter, N. "ἔθνος" in *Exegetical Dictionary of the New Testament,* edited by Horst Balz and Gerhard Schneider, Vol. 1. Grand Rapids: Eerdmans, 1999. Quite comprehensive considering space requirements.

Waltke, Bruce. "Kingdom Promises as Spiritual," in *Continuity and Discontinuity: Perspectives on the Relationship Between the Testaments,* edited by John S. Feinberg. A former dispensationalist writes in favor of reinterpretation and spiritualizing.

Walton, John H. *Covenant: God's Plan, God's Purpose.* Grand Rapids: Zondervan, 1994. Walton is his own man, and this makes him both creatively good but also questionable. Too reductive for my taste.

Walvoord, John F. *The Millennial Kingdom.* Grand Rapids: Zondervan, 1981. Not an academic work per se, this book sets out and critiques the various views on the Millennium and defends dispensational premillennialism.*

———. *The Revelation of Jesus Christ.* London: Marshall, Morgan and Scott, 1966. A competent dispensational work.

———. *The Blessed Hope and The Tribulation: A Historical and Biblical Study of Posttribulationism.* Grand Rapids: Zondervan, 1976. A reply to Ladd. One of Walvoord's best.*

Walvoord, John F. and Roy B. Zuck, eds. *Bible Knowledge Commentary: New Testament.* Victor Books, 1983. The best all-round basic Bible commentary.*

Ware, Bruce A. "The New Covenant and the People(s) of God," in *Dispensationalism, Israel and the Church,* edited by Craig A. Blaising and Darrell L. Bock. Everyone ought to read this study by Ware. To my way of thinking, this is the best one-stop piece of writing on the New Covenant. This does not make me a PD; it just means I think Ware does a great job.*

Ware, James P. *Paul's Theology in Context: Creation, Incarnation, Covenant and Kingdom.* Grand Rapids: Eerdmans, 2019. An excellent piece of work written with deference to better-known scholars, but which makes a solid contribution. Focuses on the themes of Creation, Incarnation, Covenant, and Kingdom. To my mind, this is the top textbook on Paul.*

Warfield, B. B. *The Inspiration and Authority of Scripture.* Phillipsburg, NJ: 1948. A series of brilliant articles gathered into one volume.*

Waters, Guy Prentice. "Covenant in Paul," in *Covenant Theology: Biblical, Theological, and Historical Perspectives,* edited by Guy Prentice Waters, et al. Wheaton, IL: Crossway, 2020.

Typical CT thinking on the biblical covenants, interpreting them in terms of CT. My book is an answer to just such an approach.

Waters, Guy Prentiss, J. Nicholas Reid, and John R. Muether, eds. *Covenant Theology: Biblical, Theological, and Historical Perspectives,* Wheaton, IL: Crossway, 2020. Outstanding overall survey of CT with many authors. Have a Bible on hand! Poor chapter on dispensationalism.*

Watson, Thomas. *Heaven Taken By Storm: Showing the Holy Violence A Christian is to Put Forth in the Pursuit After Glory.* Ligonier, PA: Soli Deo Gloria, 1992. Short but powerful admonishments to pursue the Christian life. For some reason that says more about me than anything, Watson is not one of my favorite Puritans, but this is gold.*

Watts, Rikki E. *Isaiah's New Exodus in Mark.* Grand Rapids: Baker, 2001. Everybody cites this work. It epitomizes so much current NT scholarship. But I think much of the application/interpretation is wrong-headed. The Servant Songs (esp. Isa. 42 and 49) go beyond the first century to the eschaton.

Waymeyer, Matt. *A Biblical Critique of Infant Baptism.* The Woodlands, TX: 2008. A strong critique.

———. *Revelation 20 and the Millennial Debate.* The Woodlands, TX: Kress, 2004. Easy to read syllabus format. This little book repays study.*

———. *Amillennialism and the Age to Come: A Premillennial Critique of the Two-Age Model.* The Woodlands, TX: Kress, 2016. Waymeyer is one of dispensationalism's best scholars. This is excellent in its examination of texts and the claims of amillennialists.*

Webb, Robert L. "Jesus' Baptism by John: Its Historicity and Significance," in *Key Events in the Life of the Historical Jesus: A Collaborative Exploration of Context and Coherence,* edited by Darrell L. Bock and Robert L. Webb. Grand Rapids: Eerdmans, 2010. Webb is an authority on John the Baptist. This is a helpful study and far better than the same author's Introduction to the volume.

Wenham, John W. *Redating Matthew, Mark and Luke: A Fresh Assault on the Synoptic Problem.* Leicester: IVP, 1992. A really superb challenge to the consensus. Argues for Matthean priority and early dates.*

Wessel, Walter W. "Mark," in *EBC,* Vol. 8, edited by Frank E. Gaebelein. Grand Rapids: Zondervan, 1984. A good use of the limited space afforded him.

Westerholm, Stephen. *Understanding Paul: The Early Christian Worldview of the Letter to the Romans.* Grand Rapids: Baker, 2004. I did not enjoy this as much as I thought I would. Still, this is a good book.

Wilkins, Michael J. "Matthew," in *Zondervan Illustrated Bible Backgrounds Commentary,* Vol. 1, Matthew, Mark, Luke, edited by Clinton E. Arnold. Grand Rapids: Zondervan, 2002. Wilkins is a go-to scholar on Matthew.*

———. "Peter's Declaration concerning Jesus' Identity in Caesarea Philippi," in *Key Events in the Life of the Historical Jesus,* edited by Darrell L. Bock and Robert L. Webb. A fascinating essay. One of the highlights of the book.*

Williamson, Paul R. *Sealed with an Oath: Covenant in God's Unfolding Purpose,* New Studies in Biblical Theology. Downers Grove, IL: InterVarsity, 2007. Although he leans Reformed, this is a superb study. Williamson highlights the oath of a covenant as its sine qua non. Also features compelling arguments for the consistent translation of diatheke as "covenant" in the NT. This is the first port of call for students of the covenants.*

Willis, Wesley R. and John R. Master, eds. *Issues in Dispensationalism.* Chicago: Moody, 1994. Some chapters are better than others, the good chapters are worth the price of the book.

Willits, Joel. "Zionism in the Gospel of Matthew," in *The New Christian Zionism,* edited by Gerald R. McDermott. Argues convincingly for Matthew's interest in the "landedness" of Israel. Willits is an authority on this Gospel.*

———. "The 144,000 in Revelation 7 and 14: Old Testament Intratextual Clues to Their Identity," in *From Creation to New Creation: Biblical Theology and Exegesis,* edited by Daniel M. Gurtner and Benjamin L. Gladd. Peabody, MA: 2013. A strong rebuttal of G. K. Beale's idealist view by a former student.*

Witherington III, Ben. *Grace in Galatia: A Commentary on Paul's Letter to the Galatians.* Grand Rapids: Eerdmans, 1998. One of the best commentaries on Galatians.*

———. *Jesus, Paul, and the End of the World: A Comparative Study in New Testament Eschatology.* Downers Grove, IL: InterVarsity, 1992. I cannot agree with the author, but this is a well-written study.

——— with Darlene Hyatt. *Paul's Letter to the Romans: A Socio-Rhetorical Commentary.* Grand Rapids: Eerdmans, 2004. A thoughtful treatment with interesting exegesis.

———. *Letters and Homilies for Hellenized Christians,* Vol. 2, A Socio-Rhetorical Commentary on 1–2 Peter. Downers Grove, IL: InterVarsity, 2007. A very helpful commentary for pastors because of the author's concern for social context. Some good excurses.*

———. "Paul, Galatians, and Supercessionism," in *God's Israel and the Israel of God: Paul and Supersessionism,* edited by Michael F. Bird and Scot McKnight. Bellingham, WA: Lexham, 2023. The best of the three chapters that open this volume.

———. "The Influence of Galatians on Hebrews," *New Testament Studies,* Vol. 37, No. 1 (Jan. 1991). An intriguing argument for Pauline influence.

Witsius, Herman. *The Economy of the Covenant Between God and Man: Comprehending A Complete System of Divinity,* 2 Vols. Escondido, CA: den Dulk Christian Foundation, 1990. A classic presentation of CT. Includes the "covenant of redemption" within the "covenant of grace." Rich, devout, but not persuasive.*

Wolf, Herbert. "'The Desire of All Nations' in Haggai 2:7: Messianic or Not?" *JETS* 19:2 (1976): 97-102. A helpful exegetical evaluation of Haggai 2:7 with reference to Heb. 12:26ff., which shows sympathy for a double meaning (wealth plus messianic) of the passage.

Woodall, David. "2 Corinthians," in *The Moody Bible Commentary,* edited by Michael Rydelnik and Michael Vanlaningham. Chicago: Moody, 2014. A competent use of allotted space.

Woods, Andrew M. *The Coming Kingdom: What Is the Kingdom and How Is Kingdom Now Theology Changing the Focus of the Church?* Duluth, MN: 2016. Clear and well-structured. Does not break new ground, but a timely study.*

———. *Babylon: The Bookends of Prophetic History.* Dispensational Publishing House, 2021. A good place to go for a short yet reliable rebuttal of spiritualized interpretations of Babylon.

———. *The Falling Away: Spiritual Departure or Physical Rapture?: A Second Look at 2 Thessalonians 2:3.* Taos, NM: Dispensational Publishing House, 2018. A revising of E. S. English's arguments. Interesting yet I remain unpersuaded.

Wright, N. T. *The Climax of the Covenant: Christ and the Law in Pauline Theology.* Minneapolis: Fortress, 1993. An academic work which put Wright on the map. One does not have to agree with Wright's exegesis or conclusion in order to appreciate him. Argues that Christ fulfils Israel's call. Good chapter on 2 Cor. 3.

———. *The New Testament and the People of God.* Minneapolis: Fortress Press, 1992. Wright's argument for a critical realist worldview (see also A. McGrath), while interesting, will not transfix many readers. Perceptive introduction to background matters. An early rolling out of his "exile" theology.

———. *Jesus and the Victory of God.* Minneapolis: Fortress Press, 1996. An impressive work in more than one sense. Great surveys of scholarship. Wright's supersessionism bleeds through and he stands unnecessarily aloof from Christ's claim to divinity.

———. *The Resurrection of the Son of God.* Minneapolis: Fortress, 2003. The best of the series in my opinion. This is a brilliant sequential study of the resurrection from the background of ancient cultures up.*

———. *Paul and the Faithfulness of God,* 2 Vols. Minneapolis: Fortress, 2013. Considered Wright's magnum opus, this is certainly an impressive (as well as massive) work on Paul. I really don't like his "exile" theology, which is given a lot of pages in this work, but no student of Paul can be without this.*

———. *Paul: In Fresh Perspective.* Minneapolis: Fortress, 2006. Wright is at his best here. He does like the word "fresh."*

——— and Michael F. Bird. *The New Testament in Its World: An Introduction to the History, Literature, and Theology of the First Christians.* Grand Rapids: Zondervan, 2019. Beautifully produced volume with glossy pages and good photographs. Eminently readable. As well as summarizing the previous volumes in *Christian Origins and the Question of God,* this gives us a glimpse into what is to come.*

Y

Youngblood, Ronald F. "Day of the Lord," in *Nelson's New Illustrated Bible Dictionary.* Nashville: Thomas Nelson, 1995. A solid article in a very good one-volume dictionary.

Z

Zahl, Paul F. M. *Grace in Practice: A Theology of Everyday Life.* Grand Rapids: Eerdmans, 2007. Defines grace as "one-way love" (although all love is really one-way). Good in places but bases his work around assertions which are not always valid (e.g., that all marriages begin with fervent grace). I don't care for his view on prisons either. A shame, because I like this author.

Zuber, Kevin D. "1 Thessalonians," in *The Moody Bible Commentary,* edited by Michael Rydelnik and Michael VanLaningham. Chicago: Moody, 2014. A very competent piece of work. Good theological reflection.*

Zuck, Roy B., ed. *A Biblical Theology of the New Testament.* Chicago: Moody, 1994. Full of information. I don't like the format much, but this is a good work.

INDEX OF SCRIPTURE

Haggai

Zechariah

Malachi

Matthew

Mark

Luke

Acts

Romans

1 Corinthians

2 Corinthians

Galatians

Ephesians

INDEX OF AUTHORS

D

E

F

G

H

I

J

K

L

M

Made in the USA
Monee, IL
25 November 2024